Photo Reconnaissance

Photo Reconnaissance

ANDREW J. BROOKES

LONDON

IAN ALLAN LTD

First published 1975

ISBN 0 7110 0570 2

Published by Ian Allan Ltd, Shepperton, Surrey.
Photoset, printed and bound in Great Britain by
REDWOOD BURN LIMITED
Trowbridge & Esher.

Contents

The Reconnaissance Pilots

After the bombing, when the men are home
(All who are coming) when reports are in,
And every cock has shaken his red comb
Calling upon the morning to begin,
Then these adventure with the morning sun
To see the wounds and judge the damage done.

Sometimes below them, somewhere in the smoke,
Their fallen comrades see them with sad hearts
For homes they will not see this weary while;
Then flying iron whangs in jagged parts
And super courage blends with super guile
To keep the picture with the lens unbroke.

John Masefield
'A Generation Risen'

Foreword

by the Rt Hon ANTHONY BARBER

Andrew Brookes has written a most fascinating history of photographic reconnaissance. So often in such accounts the detailed treatment which results from close research produces a narrative which is obscure and tedious to read. Here there is just the right amount of detail to hold the attention of the reader.

It was in 1940 that I was seconded from the Army to the RAF, and the following year I joined PRU at Benson. Mr Brookes has captured perfectly the feelings of those of us who flew those superb pale blue long-range Spitfires, without either armament or radio – the sense of loneliness; the intense cold, flying at 30,000 feet without heating; the primitive navigation aids consisting mainly of a simple map of Europe; the trust which we put in those meticulous and devoted mechanics who maintained our single engine aircraft and, dare I say it, the pride which we felt in having been hand-picked by the Commanding Officer, Geoffrey Tuttle.

Sometimes today, when our country is being run down by all and sundry, I think of those times. And, now that I have retired from active politics, I realise that if those of us in successive post-war Governments have not succeeded in what we set out to achieve, the fault has been our inability to foster a spirit of national pride which I believe is still there to be tapped.

Here is a book for all who enjoy a true story of dedication and endeavour.

A. B.

Acknowledgements

Many people have helped to convert this book from a daydream into a literary fact, not least of whom were Sqn Ldr F. H. W. 'Red' Harrington, who first 'volunteered' my services to write a squadron history that became a book, and Alfred Price who gave me the impetus to carry on when I felt like consigning the whole project into the waste-paper basket. I would also like to thank the staffs of the Air Historical Branch and of the Joint School of Photography, Cosford, for their invaluable help and assistance, and all members of the RAF, both past and present, who have given up so much of their time to write to me and to put up with my incessant questioning. It is they who ultimately made this book possible by giving me something exciting to write about, and this history is dedicated to everyone everywhere who helped to lift the camera into the sky.

I gratefully acknowledge permission given to reproduce Crown Copyright photographs and material, and photographs from many sources. Thanks are especially due to Mr E. Hine of the Imperial War Museum for his kind assistance. I am also grateful for the help and information I have received from the following books, from which I have taken quotations:

A Generation Risen, John Masefield and E. Seager, Collins
Airpower in Korea, Col J. T. Stewart, Van Nostrand
Airpower: Key to Survival, Alexander P. de Seversky, Herbert Jenkins
Aviator Extraordinary, F. S. Cotton and Ralph Barker, Chatto and Windus
Briefed to Attack, H. Pughe-Lloyd,
Evidence in Camera, Constance Babington-Smith, Chatto and Windus
(Reproduced by permission of A. D. Peters and Company)
Flight to Arras, Antoine de St Exupéry, Heinemann
History of the Second World War, Capt B. H. Liddell-Hart, Cassell
In Full Flight, Capt A. Spooner, Macdonald
Instruments of Darkness, Alfred Price, Kimber
La Photographie en Ballon, Gaston Tissandiér,
Manual of Photographic Interpretation, American Society of Photogrammetry
Overview, George Goddard and De Witt S. Copp, Doubleday

Photo Reconnaissance

Sagitarius Rising, Cecil Lewis, Peter Davies
Secret and Personal, F. W. Winterbotham, Kimber
The Arms of Krupp, William Manchester, Michael Joseph
The Center, Stewart Alsop, Harper and Row
The Mare's Nest, David Irving, Kimber
The Strategic Air Offensive Against Germany, Sir Charles Webster and Noble Frankland, HMSO
To Lose a Battle: France 1940, Alistair Horne, Macmillan
Transactions of the Optical Society, March 1919
V 2, General Dornberger
War at Sea, Capt S. W. Roskill, HMSO
War in the Air, Sir Walter Raleigh and N. A. Jones, Clarendon Press
Years of Combat, Lord Douglas of Kirtleside, Collins

Finally I must thank my wife who not only edited my efforts, corrected my spelling and proved conclusively that my grammar is appalling, but who also accepted my nightly communion with tomes, paper and ink without once ever sueing for divorce.

CHAPTER ONE

In the Beginning . . .

Reconnaissance, or observation, can never be superseded; knowledge comes before power; and the air is first of all a place to see from. Sir Walter Raleigh.

Reconnaissance is as old as war itself. Five centuries before the birth of Christ the Chinese strategist Sun Tzu instructed his captains to "know your enemy and know yourself and you can fight a hundred battles without disaster". Three hundred years later Polybius the Greek wrote that a good general must "apply himself to learn the inclinations and character of his enemy", while the Duke of Wellington ascribed much of his success to his care in studying what was happening "upon the other side of the hill". The best military commanders have always been those who realised that the more they knew of their opponent's positions, the greater was their opportunity for engaging him at a time and place most calculated to ensure his defeat.

Until the nineteenth century however, reconnaissance was restricted to that which could be seen from the top of a hill or from the back of a horse. This not only led to scouts and spies seeing a limited part of the overall picture but also to misinterpreting what they saw. The French under Tilly were defeated by the Swedes at Breitenfeld in 1631, not because the French general lacked battlefield intelligence, but because the information he had was false. Von Clausewitz summed up the state of the art when he wrote "a great part of the information obtained in war is contradictory, a still greater part is false, and by far the greatest part is of doubtful character . . . In a few words, most reports are false, and the timidity of men acts as a multiplier of lies and untruths."

Two advances changed all this – the development of the flying machine and the invention of the camera. The first manned flight was made in 1783 by Pilâtre de Rozier and the Marquis d'Arlandes in a Montgolfier hot-air balloon, and observation balloons were used for the first time in anger by the French at the Battle of Fleurus in 1794. Man now had a far clearer picture of what was going on around him, and the aerial observer, by virtue of the fact that he could now see over hills, behind trees, and into ditches, could have a far greater appreciation of the overall progress of a campaign.

The distinction of taking the world's first photograph fell to Joseph Nicéphore Niepce in 1826, but it was many years before camera and flying machine were used together. A French colonel of engineers, Aimé Laussedat, suggested in 1845 that aerial photography might be useful for map-making, but although he was known to have experimented with a kite-borne camera in the 1850s, there is no record of his achievements.[1]

In 1851 a wood engraving entitled "A Balloon View of London Taken by the Daguerreotype Process" was offered for sale to visitors to the Great Exhibition in London. It is unlikely that this view was copied from a daguerreotype because this process necessitated exposures of at least a few seconds and a balloon, as it gyrated and turned, would have made a poor photographic platform. Aerial photography only became practicable once shorter exposure times than those of the daguerreotype were feasible, which meant after Frederick Scott Archer invented the collodion, or wet plate process, in 1851.

Credit for the first aerial exposure must go to Gaspard Felix Tournachon, better known in the fashionable circles of Paris as Nadar. A very competent photographer, he decided in 1858 to experiment with balloons as a means of taking photographs from the air with the object of undertaking nothing less than a gigantic aerial survey of France. Nadar believed that a good camera fitted to a captive balloon was a far simpler and more reliable means of surveying the land than the laborious conventional method necessitating "a mass of trigonometrical formulae, unreliable instruments, plane tables, compasses, alidades and graphometers, besides the gangs of convicts employed to cross valleys, difficult country, vineyards and swamps."

Putting the cart before the horse, Nadar took out patents on October 23rd, 1858 for "an entirely new system of photography, whereby photographic birds-eye views of portions of the earth's surface may be taken", and then set about trying to put his ideas into practice. With the collodion process the plates had to be coated, exposed and developed on the spot, so Nadar had to turn the basket of his balloon into a darkroom by covering it with a tent of orange material lined with black. His initial experiments proved fruitless until one evening he landed near the village of Petit-Bicetre, two or three leagues from Paris, where he stayed overnight. The next day he found that the gas had contracted during the night so he ascended in the morning with the valve closed; to his delight a faint but exact image appeared on his photographic plate at a height of 80 metres. The cause of his previous failures was now obvious – hydrogen sulphide escaping through the open balloon valve had clouded his collodion plates. "My idea had been justified!" he recorded triumphantly; "aerial photography was possible."

The French Minister for War tried to prevail upon Nadar to take photographs from his balloon for the army of Napoleon III, but without success. It is often said that Nadar, a man of many talents – photographer, journalist, caricaturist, and friend of Impressionists like Renoir – refused because of his devout pacifism. This may well have been in the back of his mind, but Nadar declined for the much more practical reason that he did not feel sufficiently sure of his process to undertake field operations. It took him a further ten years of trial and effort before he managed to expose a clear picture of the centre of Paris from a balloon moored at the Hippodrome. Nadar photo-

[1] However he was awarded a prize for his work in this field by the Madrid Academy of Science in 1863.

graphed the capital on several occasions after that from up to 1,500 feet, but his results were often blurred because he could not compensate for the rotary motion of his balloon.

The first American aerial photograph was taken by William H. Helme and James W. Black over Providence, Rhode Island in August 1860. William Helme, a dentist by profession, wrote of his experiences five days after the event in the 'Providence Journal': "The idea that it was possible to get photographic pictures of the appearance of the earth grew into a conviction when I thought of the wonderful success of the art in taking street scenes of moving objects in bright sunlight, by the instantaneous opening and closing of the light upon the sensitive plate of the camera. The application seeming to offer chances of success when tried in a balloon, kept as nearly at rest as possible, I was induced to undertake the experiment. . . .

Mr James W. Black, of the firm of Black and Batchelder, eminent photographic artists of Boston, was consulted, and he immediately expressed himself anxious to try the experiment; . . . Messrs. King and Allen, the well known and successful aeronauts of this city, furnished their finest balloon, "The Queen of the Air", on the most liberal terms."

They ascended on the afternoon of Thursday, August 16th. "It had been our intention to test the apparatus and chemicals while the balloon was confined by a cable to an elevation of twelve hundred feet . . . and afterwards to ascend high and clear above." However, "these preliminary experiments proved the want of sunlight to be an impediment, so after two trials it was deemed best to abandon the attempt for the day.

Of these two trial pictures, one was of a view westward, and enclosed a portion of Federal Hill. . . . All the buildings included are sharply defined and well-marked though wanting in light. The second picture was to the southward and along the western shore of the bay. One of the particular misfortunes which sometimes, though rarely, happens, the cracking of the collodion films when drying, spoiled this plate, and the print from it looks as if an earthquake was plunging the whole region round about into chaos, but enough is preserved to show what the picture might have been.

These trial photographs . . . furnish abundant evidence that photography can be applied, under favourable circumstances, to the production of bird's eye views of towns and cities; for mapping out with accuracy the coasts and harbours on the borders of countries and for delineating the roads, lakes and watercourses of the inland. Of course it must be kept in remembrance that these pictures were from a low elevation of twelve hundred feet; from an elevation of twelve or fifteen *thousand* feet, a much wider extent of country could be brought in the field of the camera."

The first British ascent with a camera was made on June 3rd, 1863 by Henry Coxwell and James Glaisher, but although they ascended to "about four miles and a quarter" in 52 minutes they could not photograph because of "thick atmosphere and a large amount of vapour". Coxwell made a more successful attempt later in 1863 with Henry Negretti, a London scientific instrument maker.

The problem of carrying cumbersome darkrooms aloft was finally solved by the development of gelatine-bromide dry plates by Richard Leach Maddox, a London physician, in 1871. Maddox disliked the fumes released by collodion and so he proposed gelatine as a less noxious medium for suspending the light-sensitive silver salts. This new process was not only more sensitive it also meant that plates could be developed when the emulsion was dry, so photographers could wait until their balloons had landed. Only the camera now need go aloft.

The first photographic experiments with dry plates in a free balloon took place in France on June 8th, 1879. A museum was being opened at Arcueil-Cachan, and to celebrate the occasion M. Triboulet, a member of the Society of Balloon Meteorologists, ascended with his photographic apparatus in a balloon piloted by M. Jovis. The balloon rose above a great crowd of spectators and drifted towards Paris. At 1,500 feet over the Paris Observatory, M. Triboulet succeeded in photographing the panorama spread out below. Then a rain storm began and the balloon, heavy with water, descended at speed. It grazed the towers of Notre-Dame and finally came to rest in the Seine. Balloon and crew were towed ashore by some boatmen.

The episode had a sad ending. Customs officers, realising that the balloon had entered Paris without passing through the city walls, insisted on searching it in case contraband was aboard. Such was their zeal that an official opened the camera to see what was inside and shone a light on to the glass plate which M. Triboulet had so carefully exposed above Paris.

A British Army officer, Major H. Elsdale of the Grenadier Guards, conducted a series of trials with cameras attached to small free balloons, each with a clockwork device designed to expose plates at regular intervals and then rip the fabric to bring the apparatus back to earth. He exposed his first plates over Nova Scotia in 1883.

Although Elsdale commanded a balloon detachment in Bechuanaland in 1884, the first official balloon section was not incorporated into the British Army until 1890. All sorts of experiments were tried by the Royal Engineers over the next few years and by the end of the century some British balloons carried as many as eight cameras, spaced equidistantly around the basket, to photograph the whole of the terrain below.

However, the expense of renting balloons and employing aeronauts was usually prohibitive and poorer photographic pioneers had to make do with aerial devices like kites. Perhaps the most imaginative form of aerial platform was that of a German doctor, Julius Neubronner, who in 1903 patented a pigeon camera weighing only 2½ ozs which could automatically expose a 1½ in square negative every 30 seconds. The 'Scientific American' noted: "As a carrier pigeon, after starting, at first describes a spiral line, it is quite easy to take a number of views of a given position of the ground from different points of view. After once determining the position of its cote (which it recognises from a distance upwards of 20 miles) the pigeon flies towards its goal in a straight line and at the uniform speed of an express train, so that the route to be recorded photographically can be determined in advance."

The first exposure from a heavier than air machine was made by L. P. Bonvillain, a Pathé cameraman, who flew as a passenger in one of Wilbur Wright's demonstration flights from the Camp d'Auvours, near Le Mans, in 1908. The following year, Wilbur Wright permitted an anonymous photographer to accompany him on a flight from Centocelle near Rome. The photographer took his 'bioscope' with him and, as the aircraft flew precariously over the Italian countryside, this unknown worthy took the first aerial motion pictures in history.

The first British photographs from an aeroplane were taken by a photographer from the 'Nottingham Guardian', Charles F. Shaw, from a Farman biplane in 1910. "There is the wonderful exhileration of rushing through the air at a terrific speed," he wrote, "with the wind whipping the tears like raindrops down your cheeks. . . . One must experience to realise the difficulty of holding a camera and changing plates whilst tearing through the air at an altitude of 400 feet. More than once the picture machine was all but blown away, and it was rather more than inconvenient to place the lens between the network of wires and bamboo poles in order to view the scene one wished to reproduce."

While others were doing the experimenting and researching the Italians were using heavier than air craft in war. In September 1911 Italy went to war with Turkey over the control of Libya. On October 23rd, Captain Carlo Piazza took off to reconnoitre Turkish emplacements in his Blériot and he was soon convinced of the importance of recording the findings from such reconnaissance flights. On November 11th, in his capacity as commander of the air flotilla in Libya, he sent a request to HQ for a 'Bébé Zeiss' camera for use while airborne. He never received it despite repeated pleas, so finally on February 23rd, 1912 Capt Piazza applied to the Photo Section of the Engineer Corps at Tripoli for the loan of one of their cameras. This instrument was fixed below his aircraft so that the lens pointed vertically downwards – however in this position Captain Piazza stood no chance of reaching the camera to change the plates so he was limited to one exposure per sortie.

The results were so impressive that another pilot, Captain Ricardo Moizo, also borrowed a camera and fitted it to his aeroplane. The sum total of these officers' efforts during the campaign did not amount to much in terms of numbers of prints but they did point the way to the future. Inaccuracies on maps were highlighted by reference to their photographs, and they were able to do some survey work from the air in addition to accurate troop and battery spotting. The Italian-Turkish war was a limited beginning but it showed, to those who were willing to look, that aerial photography had a great potential.

One place where these results were not generally appreciated was in Britain. No aerial photographs were used for map making in the United Kingdom before the Great War – in fact the Army Survey personnel who went to France in 1914 had never considered the matter at all.[1] It was the French who

[1] The first official British maps from aerial prints were made of Neuve Chapelle in 1915.

led the way, under conditions of great secrecy, in photographic expertise before the War. Photographs taken during French manoeuvres in 1911 were very impressive though the British end was kept up by Major P. A. Charrier of the Royal Munster Fusiliers who, as British military observer at the exercises, took some very creditable plates from a Maurice Farman Longhorn.

Military aviation only started to become respectable in Britain on April 13th, 1912 with the creation of the Royal Flying Corps. The operational formations were divided into a Naval and a Military Wing, and an experimental unit was set up within the latter in March 1913 to deal with 'novel' theories like aerial photography. Government funds were scanty however, and whatever practical results there were came from the efforts of a few enthusiastic amateurs. Luckily there were several of these on 3 Squadron. The officers had to buy their own cameras, and with no skilled photographer in their midst they had to learn the lessons and discover the pitfalls for themselves. Nevertheless they did produce some lasting results. 3 Sqn devised a Pan-Ross type camera with a 6 in lens that was to become the standard RFC camera until 1915. The crews developed their own negatives in the air and they would land with the negatives ready to print. On one day the Squadron managed to take a complete set of photographs of the Solent and Isle of Wight defences from 5,000 feet.

But all this effort made only a limited impression upon the military commanders of the day. For a start there were many in high office who regarded the aeroplane as little more than a toy and of no practical value in a major war. The cavalry was still the great forager of information and in pre-war exercises the aeroplane was given little chance to convince the cynics that it would ever replace the man on the horse. Then there were the limitations of the machines themselves. In 1914, aircraft were little more than wood and fabric held precariously together by wire and string. It seemed a miracle that they could fly long enough to defy gravity let alone carry cumbersome photographic equipment over any distances. Even supporters of manned flight had reservations about carrying cameras; crews had enough to do staying airborne without bothering about changing plates and developing negatives. It was only as aircraft became more reliable and stable that the army officers who flew in them turned their thoughts to photography from the air. They were soon won over; it was much easier to study a print at leisure on the ground than to cruise around in an icy gale noting troop and gun positions with a stub of pencil on a map.

In addition there were those who thought that photography was best suited to the airship. For a long time suitable accommodation was not asked for, nor provided, in aircraft specifications. As a result, aircraft at the start of hostilities suddenly found their surfaces cluttered up with fitments, cameras, and instruments; machines sporting such ironmongery became known as 'Christmas Trees' and the modifications did nothing for their speed and manoeuvrability.

Suffice it to say, therefore, that for a variety of reasons the RFC sailed for France at the outbreak of war with only six cameras to their name. It needed a war to convince the sceptics that a man in the air had anything to offer the army in battle; they were soon to find that a man with a camera could provide twice as much.

CHAPTER TWO

The First World War

The consensus of expert opinion, as expressed at the various inter-Allied conferences on aerial photography, is that at least two-thirds of all military information is either obtained or verified by aerial photography. Lieut Edward Steichen – OC Photo Section of the American Expeditionary Force.

We have beaten the Germans in nearly every invention or development of engines of war. But it is in the realm of aviation photography that our supremacy has been most conspicuous. Spencer Leigh Hughes MP, 1919.

At the outbreak of war in 1914 the four squadrons of the RFC moved into France alongside the British Army to act as airborne eyes for the soldiers on the ground. "The single use in war for which the machines of the Military Wing of the Royal Flying Corps were designed and the men trained was . . . reconnaissance," wrote Sir Walter Raleigh in 'War in the Air'. As yet there were no specialisations like bombing or ground attack – just airborne cavalry who were expected to fly along, perhaps for hours on end, laboriously recording troop and gun positions on military maps. These were the tasks given to Capt P. B. Joubert de la Ferté of 3 Sqn, and Lieut G. W. Mapplebeck of 4 Sqn, when they set out on the first RFC missions of the war on August 19th, 1914.

In the beginning though there was little that the RFC could do to influence the battle on the ground. Airframes were in pitifully short supply and the army was sceptical of any information they managed to bring back. The situation only changed after the retreat from Mons when the front stabilised, the armies dug in, and the RFC found its feet and wings. As more squadrons arrived in France the RFC was divided into Corps and Army Wings which became responsible for tactical and strategic reconnaissance respectively. Tactical reconnaissance centred around the immediate confrontation area to keep field commanders informed of local German dispositions so that they could alter their own accordingly. This meant patrolling the lines, spotting for the artillery, locating enemy batteries, sketching the trenches, and in time foiling the enemy's attempts to carry out similar duties. Strategic reconnaissance started where tactical left off – in 1914 this meant all work beyond five miles of the front – to help the army commander to understand his opponent's mind so that he could try to predict any future plans of campaign. These definitions have remained constant up to the present day; only the scale has changed. In 1914 Capt Joubert de la Ferté had only to cover 40 miles to be deep inside enemy territory; today the strategic reconnaissance pilot has to cover several thousands of miles to discover what his potential opponent has taken very great pains to keep hidden from him.

Even in the early days of the war it was becoming increasingly evident that the human eye had its limitations. Observers could only absorb, or concentrate on, a limited amount of data at 70 mph in the standard reconnaissance aircraft of the time, the BE 2a. Even if an observer thought he saw what he was looking for among the wealth of information that was visible beneath him, he might be mistaken – the most skilled eye could confuse stretches of tar on a road for troops on the move, or shadows cast by gravestones as a bivouac site. It was also impossible for the human brain to absorb everything of interest on a two hour flight – a man looking for troop movements might miss fresh excavations or aircraft concentrations. The problem was compounded by the lack of trained observers to man the growing number of reconnaissance aircraft reaching the front. The number of sorties was increasing at a time when the wastage of war was taking its toll of experienced crews, and there was not time to train an adequate number of replacements.

The camera was the best solution to all these problems. "The camera," wrote the authors of 'War in the Air', "pictures only what is there, omits nothing, provides a record which can be easily duplicated, and supplies a means for recording . . . the multitudinous changes that take place within the restless area of an army at war." Not only could the camera record everything on the ground below the lens, but it was infinitely more sensitive than the unaided human eye. "Photographic instruments operate efficiently in circumstances where the human eye fails: where light is too bright or too dim . . . where objects are too small or too far away; and where movements are too slow, too fast or too confused."[1] The resulting prints could be examined at leisure on the ground by specialists in the fields of artillery, aircraft, or communications, who would extract far more value from them than from a human report. "It is not sufficient," wrote Major Gamble in 1919, "to know that there are certain trenches in a particular portion of a sector; it is necessary to know the form of the trench, its relation to other defences, the state of the ground, and what obstacles would be encountered were an attack to be made."[2] It was asking too much of a human being to appreciate all this as he peered with tired and streaming eyes into a freezing airstream, and once it was recognised that it was easier to train a non-commissioned photographer rather than a skilled visual observer to accompany the pilot, cameras began to appear in larger numbers at the front.

Visual reconnaissances would far outnumber photographic missions for some time, especially while cameras were so fragile and inefficient, in short supply, or when time was too limited to take and develop photographs. However, as sorties became longer, involving deeper penetrations into enemy airspace at increasingly higher altitudes, and as cameras became more dependable, far greater reliance was placed upon photographic evidence to reveal the enemy's plans and preparations.

[1] 'Manual of Photographic Interpretation' – American Society of Photogrammetry.

[2] 'Transactions of the Optical Society' – March 1919.

In the winter of 1914, 3 Sqn continued to lead the way in photographic expertise. When the Squadron moved to France the crews took their private cameras with them even though there was no official requirement for photography from the RFC. The honour of exposing the first operational plates of the war fell to Lieut G. F. Petyman of 3 Sqn – on September 15th he brought back five exposures taken over German trenches.

The Squadron continued its experiments during the Battle of the Aisne but the results were indistinct and the army was not impressed. Perseverence brought improvements by the end of the year, but the prints were in no way comparable to those achieved by the French. The CO of the Military Wing, Lieut Col Sykes, finally sent for the CO of 3 Sqn, Major W. G. H. Salmond, and showed him a map of German trenches produced from excellent French aerial photographs. Sykes wanted his squadrons to go and do likewise, and he instructed Salmond to visit a French Corps HQ and pick as many brains as possible.

Major Salmond soon discovered a fundamental difference between the two Allied approaches to aerial photography; whereas the French had set up highly centralised and specialised units, lavishly supplied with brains and equipment, the RFC was largely dependent for its photo-intelligence on a few scattered sections that were little more than one-man bands. Lieut Charles Curtis Darley of 3 Sqn was a case in point. Darley, a gunnery officer who had represented the army as a middle-weight boxer before the war, took his own exposures and then processed them himself, with chemicals he had bought out of his own pocket in Béthune, in a dark-room he had personally fitted out in the stables of the château where the squadron was billeted. After all this he had to visit the Corps HQ to interpret the prints personally because there was no-one among the staff officers there who was qualified to do it. By the end of January 1915, Darley had collected together enough prints to produce a map of the British and German trench system along the whole front covered by 3 Sqn. Major Salmond took this map to the Corps HQ where he created a minor sensation by pointing out the value of the information on the prints to all concerned.

Another young observer by the name of Sholto Douglas had a similar introduction to aerial photography. Not long after he joined 2 Sqn it came to the ears of those in command that he had been interested in photography as a school boy, whereupon, "I promptly found myself appointed the squadron specialist." There was no laid down procedure for the work, so he cut a hole in the cockpit floor of his BE 2a, and when the target nearly filled the opening he pushed the camera through and exposed a plate. "This procedure was not too easy in the cramped space available," he later recalled, "especially as the weather was cold and bulky flying kit a necessity. Each plate had to be changed by hand and I spoilt many plates by clumsy handling with frozen fingers." He wrote to his father at the time saying that, "My slight knowledge of photography has proved of immense use. Today I got several snapshots of German trenches on our front from a height of five thousand feet." Sholto Douglas later wrote that his use of the word "snapshots" might seem a little wry in years to come when photo-reconnaissance had become a specialised art, but it did at least show to what extent the men of the RFC in early 1915 were beginners in the business.

Major Salmond recommended that British aerial photography should be "regularised" by concentrating all photographic personnel into sections with one section for each flying Wing. More men and materials should be made available to relieve the burden imposed on enthusiastic amateurs, and he recommended that an experimental section be set up to standardise and develop procedures and equipment for the whole Flying Corps. Sir David Henderson approved these proposals and the experimental section was handed over to two young lieutenants, J.T.C. Moore-Brabazon and C.D.M. Campbell. Moore-Brabazon, a pilot recently posted to 9 Sqn, was selected for his zeal and organising ability, while Campbell was chosen for his photographic expertise. Flt Sgt V.C. Laws and 2nd Air Mechanic W.O. Corse completed the team.

The first priority was a new camera. The apparatus designed by 3 Sqn, made from an ordinary light-weight press-photographer's camera, with a bellows and fragile fabric focal-plane shutter, was totally incapable of withstanding the effects of wind and vibration at 70 mph for any length of time. A much more robust instrument was needed, and Moore-Brabazon and Campbell were sent back to England with a free hand to produce what was wanted.

So it came to pass, on a cold Friday afternoon in February 1915, that Mr Richard Hesketh, secretary of the Thornton-Pickard Photographic Manufacturing Company of Altrincham, was summoned to the town house of Lieut Moore-Brabazon in Queens Gate. After an hour and twenty minutes over a piece of foolscap paper they produced a rectangular tapering box-type design that was shortly to become the 'A type' camera. The A type was basically a brass-bound conical box built of polished mahogany to withstand rough usage. The 8in lens, focused on infinity, was recessed into the front to protect the fabric focal-plane shutter from the effects of the airstream. The 5in × 4in plates were carried in Mackenzie Wishart envelopes and inserted one after another by hand into an adapter of the same make – by drawing out the slide of this adapter the plate was automatically uncovered for exposure, and re-covered afterwards by closing the slide.

The new camera was used for the first time over the village of Fauquissant on March 2nd,1915. There were still a few drawbacks. Being a hand-held camera, the observer had to grip the A type through leather straps or by a brass handle and lean over the side of the cockpit to take his plates. Many observers nearly fell out when they leant overboard for the first time clutching this weighty contraption whilst wearing gauntlets – as the old hands said, you didn't bounce if you fell out of an aeroplane holding an A type at 8,000 feet.

But even if the observer kept his safety belt on and his feet braced, his problems weren't over. By fumbling about in thick gloves or with frozen fingers he had to make eleven separate operations before he could expose the first plate, followed by ten more for each plate after that. Still, it was better than drawing laborious and grubby sketch-maps over the trenches.

The experimental section soon found that it was impossible to produce mosaics and overlapping strips from a camera being waved about by nervous or freezing hands. Good map-making demanded a camera fixed in the vertical position, and the operators' problems were greatly reduced once the camera was fitted to the side of the aircraft. Thus in the summer of 1915 the 'C type' camera was introduced.

The C type utilised the body of the A type but in place of the Mackenzie-Wishart slide there was a semi-automatic plate-changing device. Two magazines were placed on top of the camera; a full one containing 18 plates and an empty one underneath it. To make an exposure the operator pushed the camera handle until the word 'set' appeared in the indicator, then he returned it to normal and pulled the release cord. After each exposure the bottom plate would drop to one side into the empty magazine and a new one would fall into place by gravity. An operator could continue in this fashion until he had exposed all 18 plates and then replace the now empty magazine with another full one if he wanted to continue.

The introduction of a magazine meant that exposures could now be made in rapid succession. If approximately 60% of overlap was allowed between successive prints, the pair could be viewed through a stereoscope to produce a three-dimensional effect. Stereoscopy is based on the fact that the eye is a computer rather than a camera and that we use both eyes at the same time to measure distance and appreciate form. The 'base' of the human range finder is governed by the interpupillary distance of 2½ in, and as this 'base' is very small, normal vision has 'stereoscopic' or range finding power only up to 300 yards. The same stereoscopic effect (extending over much greater distances) can be achieved by placing two photographs of the same object, taken from slightly different points of view, underneath a stereoscope. A camera with an 8 in lens flying at 60 mph at 10,000 feet would photograph an area 6,250 feet × 5,000 feet with its 5 in × 4 in plate; if the time exposure between each print was 14.5 seconds, the aircraft would cover 1,250 feet between the two prints, producing a 'stereoscopic pair' showing the same country from a different point of view. When placed under a stereoscope, this overlap would be seen in the form of a three-dimensional model, combining the respective advantages of vertical and oblique photography and making accurate interpretation very much easier.

The principal weakness of the C type was the fragility of the cord which operated the focal plane shutter. It was easily broken, especially during the winter months when any moisture on it froze at high altitudes. There was also the drag problem of having a bulky instrument protruding into the airstream. To overcome this it was decided to fit the camera inside the aeroplane, but as there was no room for it in the cockpit, the apparatus had to be redesigned to be operated from a distance. This brought the RFC to the 'E type'.

With the exception of the magazines, the E type was constructed entirely of metal. It was the first RFC camera with an adjustable lens mount and the C type cord was replaced by a ratchet gear activated from afar by an endless cord. However, at a time when pilots and observers had their hands full flying accurately and fending off the enemy, the E type was still too demanding in time and attention. It was back to the drawing board to design an apparatus that needed the minimum assistance from its operator.

The result – the Williamson L type – should have been a great improvement on its predecessors when it came into service in 1916. Capable of use either inside or outside the fuselage it could be operated mechanically or automatically at will. When set to automatic use, the only call on the operator was to depress the release lever to actually take the photograph. The mechanical drive came from a small propeller intruded into the airstream; this drove a flexible shaft which in turn was attached to a large mutilated driving pinion. One complete revolution of this pinion changed the plate and reset the shutter before reaching a portion of the wheel from which the teeth had been removed. The propeller was then free to rotate without actuating the mechanism, but once the release lever had been operated to take a photograph, the mutilated wheel would be engaged once more to make another revolution ready for the next exposure. However this system worked better in theory than in practice. The L type, complete with its cassette of 18 plates, weighed 35 lbs and the cumbersome mechanism often jammed. Rather than risk an abortive sortie, crews invariably disconnected the windmill drive and changed the plates manually via a Bowden cable.

There were hundreds of L types in service by the end of the war, but the ultimate development was the LB camera. Although similar in operation to the L type, the LB had the advantage of interchangeable lens mounts which could accommodate lenses between 4 in and 20 in focal length. With panchromatic plates the LB could be used up to 20,000 feet and its clarity with long lenses was demonstrated when a print exposed over Ostend at 17,000 feet clearly showed the black crosses on a seaplane's wings.

One particularly enthusiastic supporter of aerial photography at this time, and a driving force in securing its acceptance by the army, was Lieut Col Trenchard. Not only did he whole-heartedly endorse Salmond's recommendations but he also took a great delight in correcting those army officers who regarded aviation as little more than an easy way out of the trenches. Some conservative elements even went so far as to say that the reconnaissance aircraft was an unethical intrusion into the gentlemanly pursuit of war – it was not quite cricket to spy into an enemy's backyard and photograph him with his trousers down. Trenchard often carried photographs of enemy trenches around with him, and it appealed to his dry sense of humour to push them under the noses of the army staffs, who would view them with only mild and polite interest despite the fact that they were planning attacks in the very same areas as were covered by the prints.

The great man also encouraged the acceptance and improvement of aerial photography within the RFC. His biographer records that it was part of Trenchard's practice "to whip up emulation by setting the camera enthusiasts at odds with each other", especially between Sholto Douglas on 2 Sqn and Darley down the front on 3 Sqn. "Whenever Trenchard visited our squadron," wrote Sholto Douglas, "he would pull out of his pocket a bunch of

Darley's photographs which he would show to me with encominiums, apparently believing that he was inciting me to better efforts. But as Darley and I discovered in talking with each other that Trenchard used to do the same thing the other way around on his visits to No 3 Squadron, showing Darley my best efforts, we soon agreed that the old boy was wasting his time."

While Trenchard was educating the army by subtlety, Moore-Brabazon was more open about it. When the young Lieutenant saw how inept the army was at interpreting prints, he produced six copies of a book on aerial photography which he sent to the Intelligence Staffs at various Corps' HQ. He was hauled before Trenchard and admonished for trying to instruct Intelligence Officers in their job. Downcast he left the office only to be called back in again and told by a now smiling Trenchard that the reprimand came from higher authority and that he personally was delighted with what Moore-Brabazon was trying to do.

The first breach in the wall of army conservatism was made in February 1915. The Germans had dug in around some brick-stacks to the south of the La Bassée Canal and they had become such a nuisance that it was decided to launch an Anglo-French infantry attack to drive them out. Darley was sent off with his observer, Lieut V. H. N. Wadham, to reconnoitre the area and they brought back the best set of prints taken so far in the war. Both prints and Darley were taken by Trenchard to a conference of British and French generals where the photographs were handed around for scrutiny. They showed that the German engineers had built a long sap[1] underneath the Allied front, a fact hitherto unappreciated by the French under whose positions it ran, and as a result the plan of attack was modified. The prints were also so clear that it was possible to choose beforehand the precise meeting point for the junction of the two armies during the assault.

The moral was obvious to those who were willing to see it. With photographic intelligence one could cut down the chances of failure drastically. Up to then generals had had to rely on aged and inaccurate maps that bore no relation to the actual terrain now resplendent with obstacles and trenches. As armies grew bigger and bigger, and as engagements became increasingly obscured by distance, smoke, and mud, a military leader could ill afford to send his men blindly into the unknown. The chances of success would be greatly increased by the provision of accurate maps and these could only be kept up to date from day to day by the aerial camera.

Here lay the great value of Darley's prints of La Bassée; there on the table was the latest evidence, less than a few hours old, on which any officer could accurately base his campaign. Warfare need no longer be a hit and miss affair, a fact readily appreciable to General Joffre who asked for copies of Darley's photographs. Once the top men were won over, their subordinates soon followed.

By the end of February, 2 and 3 Sqns had built up a mosaic of the whole German trench system in front of the First Army back to a depth of 700–1500

[1] A tunnel driven under the opponents' lines into which mines could be placed and exploded.

yards. All features of interest were transferred on to a 1:8000 map to give Haig a clear idea of the terrain he had to cover during his proposed spring offensive at Neuve Chapelle. Some 1,500 copies of this map were distributed to commanders before the attack and, "for the first time in its history, the British army went into action with a picture of the hidden intricacies of the enemy defences." The lesson was repeated again at Loos and Aubers Ridge; to Trenchard and the RFC it was all very encouraging.

But aerial reconnaissance was not only concerned with British offensives; as more aircraft reached the front so more and more sorties were dispatched behind enemy lines to try to pre-empt any German schemes for attack. By the autumn of 1915 the Army Wings were flying daily to photograph the German supply routes and storage dumps to see if any undue activity was taking place. Regular cover here was essential; it was no use having a set of 'one-off' prints of an isolated part of the front because there was nothing with which to compare it. A photograph of an airfield full of aeroplanes was of little value without a print of the same airfield taken recently, to show whether the aircraft were there as part of a new offensive build-up or if they were based there all the time. It was only when the RFC had enough aircraft to look at everything worth looking at time and time again that it was safe to make any predictions about a new German offensive.

The French air service had shown at Verdun that decentralisation was vital if aerial intelligence was to be disseminated quickly. They had set up processing sections at each Corps HQ, where the pilots handed over their prints to be developed at great speed for distribution to companies and batteries. As many as 5,000 prints a day could be processed at these forward sections and corps commanders could have prints in their hands within an hour of their exposure over enemy lines. General Mangin relied heavily upon such rapid intelligence when he attacked Fort Douaumont on May 22nd, 1916.

The British on the other hand still depended on Wing photo sections which had become very overburdened by 1916. The Battle of the Somme was in the offing and decentralisation and expansion were essential if prints were to be distributed in time to be of value. In the middle of April therefore the RFC was reorganised into brigades, with one brigade for each army in the field. Every brigade was subdivided into a Corps and an Army Wing, the former being responsible primarily for artillery observation, contact patrols, and photography within five miles of the front, and the latter having the job of reconnoitring, bomb dropping, and photography beyond this. Each squadron within a Corps Wing was given its own small photo section to process the exposures made over local trench systems, barbed wire, trench mortars, and hostile battery positions. In an Army Wing, only one squadron was equipped with a photo section to provide the prints demanded by the Army commander on such topics as hostile aerodromes, dumps, and lines of communication behind the front.

For day after day, both before, during, and after the Battle of the Somme, the reconnaissance machines photographed the whole front. For a start they aimed to provide accurate information on the latest enemy positions and to locate places where the advance might be delayed. Then they took photographs to assist the pre-assault artillery bombardment. After a feature had been subjected to constant fire for a few hours, an aircraft would go over to photograph the results. If the fire was shown to be successful then the guns would range on to another target; if not, then the prints would show the degree of inaccuracy of the shell-fire and the gunners could adjust their sights accordingly.

When the German trenches had been softened up, the aerial camera would monitor the infantry advance. Each evening the reconnaissance aircraft would return, their fabrics and struts often in tatters from the attentions of the troops below. The plates would then be processed, reproduced, and distributed as quickly as hands and motor-bikes could carry them to battery company, corps, and army commanders. At all levels the prints were eagerly awaited. Battery commanders looked for the results of their fire; corps commanders peered through magnifying glasses to see how well their men were doing; the generals looked to see how much progress their armies had made, where they were being held up, and where the Germans were pouring in reinforcements to try to stem the tide. Plans would be modified accordingly, orders issued, and the muddy hell would continue.

All this valuable reconnaissance was undertaken in the face of mounting German fighter opposition. The Germans not unnaturally felt aggrieved at the invasion of this privacy because the main element of any good attack was surprise, and you could never surprise anyone if he knew your every move well in advance. General von Below underlined this concern when he sent the following order to his 6th Army squadrons:

"The main object of fighting in the air is to enable our photographic registrations and photographic reconnaissances to be carried out and at the same time to prevent that of the enemy. All other tasks . . . must be secondary to this main objective."

Similarly the Allies were not happy when their plans were exposed to the German viewfinders, so each side sent up armed interceptors to pluck out the 'eyes' of the opposition, which in turn were guarded by armed machines to protect them from attack. The age of the aerial dog-fight had begun.

RFC losses had increased dramatically following the introduction of the Fokker monoplane in appreciable numbers after October 1915. The Fokker, complete with forward-firing machine-gun, arrived at the Western front at the same time as an order from the German High Command that Allied reconnaissance aircraft must be prevented from discovering that large troop transfers had taken place from the Eastern to the Western fronts in preparation for a new offensive. By the winter of 1915 the RFC was taking a bit of a hiding.

Losses in the last quarter of the year were such that Trenchard was forced to issue the following instruction to all squadrons on January 14th, 1916:

"Until the Royal Flying Corps is in possession of a machine as good as or better than the German Fokker, it seems that a change in the tactics employed becomes necessary. . . . It must be laid down as a hard and fast rule that a machine proceeding on reconnaissance must be escorted by at least three other fighting machines. . . . Aeroplanes proceeding on photographic duty east of the line should be similarly escorted."

At the same time as they were being forced to fly in defensive formations, the RFC was also having to fly higher and higher to escape from the attentions of the German anti-aircraft batteries. In 1914 even low altitudes were sufficient to give adequate protection from ground fire – the average British sortie was flown at 4000 feet whereas the Germans believed that if they flew at the "limited tactical height" of 2,500 feet their aircraft would be protected from all hostile fire as if by some mysterious agency. This supposed immunity was rudely shattered by 'Archie'.[1] Although a height of 4,000 feet had been sufficient in 1914 to escape from any erratic and disorganised ground fire that might come from below, by 1916 an aircraft flying at four times that height would not have been immune from anti-aircraft emplacements. As the range and accuracy of anti-aircraft guns improved so the aerodynamics experts had to improve and redesign their airframes and engines to operate between 15,000 and 20,000 feet.

Against the combined threat of the 'Fokker scourge' and Archie, the main photographic aircraft of the time the BE 2c, had had its day. As a photographic platform it was marvellous – its aerodynamic stability made it perfect for the job. But this inherent stability proved its undoing – too stable to dodge the Fokker and too slow to outrun it, the BE 2c was an easy prey over the trenches in 1916. Young men like Cecil Lewis, a newly arrived pilot on 9 Sqn, had to put up with a machine that was totally unsuited to the task in hand.

"After ten hours (of practice flying) came my first real job – to photograph the enemy second-line trenches. The lines, from the air, had none of the significance they had from the ground, mainly because all the contours were non-existent. The local undulations, valleys, ravines, ditches, hillsides, which gave advantage to one side or the other, were flattened out. All you saw was two more or less parallel trenches, clearer in some places than in others according to the colour of the earth thrown up in making them. They faced each other across the barren strip of No-Man's-Land, and behind them started a complicated network of communication trenches, second-line trenches, more communication trenches, and then the third-line trenches.

"The surveying of the German line was very difficult from the ground. You couldn't very well walk about with a theodolite and a chain in full view of the enemy, so the making of maps was largely a matter of aerial photography. In the Spring of 1916, with the big offensive on the Somme preparing, the accuracy of these maps was of the greatest importance. So our job that day was to go over the front line at 7,500 feet and fly all along the enemy second-line trenches from Montauban, round the Fricourt salient and up to Boiselle, photographing as we went.

[1] The colloquial name for anti-aircraft fire.

"If there was ever an aeroplane unsuited for active service, it was the BE 2c. The pilot sat slightly aft of the main planes and had a fair view above and below, except where the lower main plane obscured the ground forward; but the observer, who sat in front of him, could see practically nothing, for he was wedged under the small centre section, with a plane above, another below, and bracing wires all around. He carried a gun for defence purposes; but he could not fire it forward because of the propeller. Backwards, the centre-section struts, wires, and the tail plane cramped his style.

"The observer could not operate the camera from his seat because of the plane directly below him, so it was clamped on outside the fuselage, beside the pilot; a big, square, shiny mahogany box with a handle on top to change the plates. To make an exposure you pulled a ring on the end of a cord. To sight it, you leaned over the side and looked through a ball and cross-wire finder. The pilot, then, had to fly the machine with his left hand, get over the spot on the ground he wanted to photograph – not so easy as you might think – put his arm out into the seventy-mile-an-hour wind, and push the camera handle back and forward to change the plates, pulling the string between each operation. Photography in 1916 was somewhat amateurish."

On new machines like the FE 2b, introduced to fly higher and give a better account of themselves, the camera came into its own. The human eye becomes increasingly inefficient the higher it goes; from 2,000 feet it can pick out men and machines, from 5,000 feet it can discern encampments and buildings, but from three miles up it can only see large features like towns and rivers. The brain also has difficulty plotting features accurately to within several hundred yards from great heights.

A good photograph can overcome these problems. The human eye with a focal length of 0.5 in, viewing a 10 feet object from a height of 5,000 feet, will produce a retina image of 0.001 in or a scale of 1:120,000. A camera with a 12 in lens would record the same object in a fraction of a second at a scale of 1:5,000, which could always be examined through a magnifying glass to provide more detailed information. Features can be plotted precisely if the interpreter knows the scale of the print and uses accurate measuring equipment. Photographic interpretation had become much more of a science by 1916; an intelligence officer no longer just looked for a building – he examined the shadow and used this to assess the height, size, or depth of the construction. Ammunition dumps, invisible from the air, could be identified by the tracks leading up to them; headquarters could be recognised by the distinctive cable trench pattern laid around them during construction. All this detective work was passed to artillery commanders who could then bring devastating fire to bear on vital points rather than expend their shells indiscriminately.

Despite all the hard work that had been devoted to the improvement of aerial photography by 1916, in the shape of good cameras, well-trained crews, and efficient processing sections, the problem of aircraft vulnerability still remained. At first this was masked by sheer weight of numbers: "July and August 1916 were the blackest days in the history of German military aviation," wrote Oswald Boelcke's biographer. "Large formations of enemy aircraft disported themselves unhindered behind our lines. The enemy had gained complete command of the air." It was not unusual for fifteen fighting machines to escort three camera aircraft over the German lines, a fact that underlined the inefficient and wasteful process that was photographic reconnaissance. No one ever really appreciated that aerial photography was a special case. Photographic work involved flying to a target such as a stretch of railway line and cruising up and down it for perhaps half-an-hour while the camera turned. Such a profile was unalterable as long as a stable platform was necessary for accurate prints, but it was equally obvious that such a mission, with the minds of the crew otherwise engaged, would be a sitting-duck. Of the 80 machines shot down by von Richtofen, 47 were of the reconnaissance variety; it would be interesting to know how many of these were engaged in photography at the time.

There were various ways around the problem for the Corps Squadrons. Although the British tactical aircraft worked incessantly over enemy lines, their German counterparts photographed obliquely from positions low over their own territory where they could be defended by ground fire and where the RFC attacked from the air at their peril. But there was no such sanctuary for the long-range crews. For them there were only two solutions; they either had to be heavily defended or possess a performance superior to anything that the enemy could pit against them. The RFC made the worst choice. The sitting-duck had to be protected, so cameras were fitted to fighting machines, which were in turn escorted by more fighting machines. The second solution would have been much better. There was no reason why the camera aircraft should have been a sitting-duck at all. The British built several aeroplanes over the years that were equal to the challenge of the opposition, but they were never employed because the RFC failed to accord the same priority to securing photography as the Germans did to preventing it. Time and again cumbersome two-seaters were sent up, resplendent with guns and cameras, with little chance of outmatching the best in the German air service. There was no need for this; a high performance aircraft, when stripped of all surplus weight like armament and an observer to operate it, would always fly that little bit higher and faster than its armed counterpart. This would have been the way to escape destruction in the First World War – to fix a camera on to the best machines on the inventory and to outfly the Germans rather than outfight them. The RAF did it with a cleaned-up Spitfire in 1939; the RFC could have done it with a Sopwith Tabloid in 1914. At a time when the BE 2a had a top speed of 70 mph, Howard Pixton was soundly beating the best in Europe by winning the Schneider Trophy in a Tabloid capable of 92 mph. Ironically this excellent little Sopwith aircraft was never produced in large numbers because it lacked provision for defensive armament.

Later on in the war, the RFC persevered with another mass-produced inadequacy, the RE 8; capable of only 103 mph at 5,000 feet it had little to recommend it apart from its great stability. Even while Trenchard was bemoaning the fact that his Corps squadrons were lacking in aircraft "of a suitable type to do all the work required by the artillery, such as photography at a distance behind the lines", Frank Barnwell's Bristol Monoplane was delighting its pilots with an excellent all round field of vision, a rate of climb of 10,000 feet in ten minutes, and a top speed of 128 mph at 5,400 feet.

In the absence of a specialised photographic aircraft, the RFC had to make do and devise tactics accordingly. In March 1917, at the same time as the planning started for the ritual spring offensive, this time at Arras, the General Staff laid down the exact escort procedure to be used. The manual "Fighting in the Air" decreed that fighter-reconnaissance machines were to keep close formation in two rows of three, the aircraft with the camera being in the middle of the front row. The flanks were to fly slightly higher and the second row slightly higher again. The escorts were ordered not to seek engagements but were to fight if necessary to allow the photographic aeroplane to finish its work and get away.

But a protective formation of only five escorts was usually insufficient, especially over sensitive German areas. An example of this, and the dramatic consequences of too few protective guns, was provided by one particular task during the Battle of Arras. On April 13th, 1917, six RE 8s of 59 Sqn took off at 0815 hrs to try to photograph the Drocourt-Quéant switch line. Two of the aircraft had cameras and the rest were to act as escorts. As the sortie involved flying close to Douai airfield, a base which housed a large part of the German fighter force, photography was planned to take place during the offensive patrols of 9 and 13 Wings. Luck was not with 59 Sqn as it turned out; the offensive patrols failed to materialise and all six RE 8s were isolated and shot down by six German single seaters led by von Richtofen. Only two of the aircrew survived.

The following day the same task was given to 11 Sqn and this time ten aircraft, six FE 2bs from 11 Sqn and four Nieuport single-seaters from 29 Sqn, took off. The photography was timed to coincide with the routine patrols of 19 and 60 Sqns. Despite this show of strength the formation was attacked by Halberstadt and Albatross fighters. The Germans were so successful that the FE 2b with the camera had to break off without exposing any plates.

Two days later, six FE 2bs and four Nieuports took to the air again, this time to be escorted by an even stronger offensive patrol comprising 48, 60, and 1 (Naval) Sqns. During the twenty-five minutes of photography, the Bristol fighters of 48 Sqn and the Sopwith Triplanes of 1 (Naval) Sqn flew up and down over Douai but the challenge went unaccepted.

This one particular task highlighted the drawbacks inherent in the tactics employed in photo-reconnaissance during the First World War. A task that should have been completed in one day by one high speed, high flying aircraft had in fact taken four days, ten lives and the resources of five squadrons. The scale of the endeavour to secure the prints showed how important aerial photography had become but it also revealed how wasteful the process was. It was not until the RFC received new aircraft such as the SE 5, Bristol Fighter, DH 4, and Sopwith Pup in any numbers that these tactics stood any chance of working well. Until then, the reconnaissance crews had to put up with 'Bloody April'.

There were other misfortunes to plague the photographers. Layers of cloud between lens and ground could make photography a waste of time, and there are not many cloud-free days in Western Europe. Then there were the maddening technical failures – an observer's diary recorded the frustrations:

"March 24, 1917 . . . on photography of Hindenburg line. . . . Started taking photos but string to shutter broke after 4 exposures . . ."

"March 25, 1917 . . . on photography . . . string broke again after six exposures . . ."

"April 3, 1917 . . . on photography . . . Wynne and Mackenzie shot down . . . got over lines and shutter string broke as usual. Hun dived on us but we drove him off . . . Engine conked out through air lock in tank . . ."

As we look back today it is virtually impossible to appreciate the physical and psychological strains imposed on men during these flights. "Flying is pleasurable enough, in short doses," wrote Cecil Lewis, "and was even in those days reasonably safe . . . But to fly on a straight line, taking photos of the enemy trenches, an easy Archie target, within range of the ground machine guns, bumped by the eddies of passing shells and pestered by enemy scouts, that required nerve. And it would have to be done twice a day, day after day, until you were hit or went home. Small wonder if, under this strain, pilots lived a wild life and wined and womanised to excess." Photography needed a cool head and a calm hand, and yet there they sat, without parachutes, in fragile machines, exposed to freezing cold and biting winds, at the mercy of the weather and a single primitive engine. With adrenalin flowing they had to operate deep into enemy airspace, often several times a day, the pilot concentrating on flying accurately and the observer's mind on the ground below. Yet both, in the backs of their minds, were ever waiting for the first burst of enemy gunfire to rip through their spars and fabric. It did the nerves no good at all if then the shutter-string broke. Even after it was all over they had to get the prints home; unless the evidence could be brought back for analysis, the whole sortie would have been a waste of time. That clear and accurate photographs could be exposed day after day under pressures like these was wonderful; that more aircrews did not crack-up under the strain was miraculous.

The story of the development of photo-reconnaissance in other theatres followed the same pattern of the inspired few leading the rest. Service cameras were in very short supply and it was a case of having to make do with whatever was available. In the Spring of 1915 Flt Lt C. H. Butler of 3 Sqn took some crude but useful photographs of the Dardanelles landing beaches with a small folding Goertz-Anschutz camera. He borrowed a better French instrument in May which he fixed beside his seat alongside the aircraft nacelle. Between April 4th and the end of June 1915, Flt Lt Butler exposed some 700 plates which he made into photographic maps of each important area for use by the army HQ. He was badly wounded at the end of June and it was not until the end of August that the work was started up again by a newly inaugurated photographic section. However, despite much useful cover of Turkish emplacements aerial photography played only a small part in the reconnaissance effort expended by the RFC.

There were other isolated advances in Africa. On April 25th, 1915 the German light cruiser *Königsberg* was located after a long search and photographed by a Goertz-Anschutz camera strapped to a Short seaplane up the Kikjunga Channel in German East Africa. The aerial camera was also used during the search for the German army in East Africa. In December 1915, Lieut Cherry Kearton, famous before the war for his wild life photography, was transferred to East Africa to supervise the development and printing of plates exposed by RNAS Caudrons. Conditions were pretty primitive – Kearton had to construct a darkroom from Caudron packing cases – but he was soon passing to the army staffs regular supplies of prints exposed by the Naval air detachment over German positions.

A bit nearer home, the Royal Navy had also found a need for aerial photography on the Belgian coast. During a bombardment of Ostend on September 7th, 1915, an attacking force had discovered to their cost the existence of a new German coastal battery. This was the Tirpitz Battery, a complex of 28 cm guns with an effective range of 35,000 yards, and as far as the Admiralty were concerned they had to go. Periodically French guns were trained on the Battery and aircraft from the Dunkirk squadrons would go in after each onslaught to photograph the results. At first they operated from low altitudes, but as the German anti-aircraft fire became more accurate the reconnaissance aircraft had to fly higher if they wanted to photograph in safety. Minor improvements in service cameras were negated by the greater heights from which they had to operate, and in the end standard lenses were just not up to providing the accurate shell damage assessments required by the Navy. The problem was solved in uniquely British fashion – Admiral Bacon, the officer commanding the Dover Patrol, gave the officer in charge of his photo-section a blank cheque on his personal account to go to London and buy the best lens available. The officer returned with two excellent lenses which were first employed in a suitable apparatus over the Tirpitz Battery on the morning of July 9th, 1916. Unfortunately, although the clarity was excellent, the area covered by each frame was so small that the actual guns were omitted. A gunsight view-finder was hastily added and the camera suspended from the aircraft so that it could command a greater radius of vision under the machine. The results were everything that could have been desired – a print taken from 14,000 feet on July 29th showed the guns and shell-damage at double the size of any previous cover.

Ever since he assumed command of the Dover Patrol, Admiral Bacon had dreamt of landing Allied troops on the Belgian coast to coincide with a thrust on the main front. 1917 promised to be the right year, and a proposal was put forward to coordinate an invasion of the Belgian ports at the same time as the main advance inland.

Although the Admiral was 28 years ahead of the Normandy landings, he was just as thorough in his planning. The beaches chosen for the assault lay between Nieuport and Middlekerke, and the Admiral believed that if the operation was to come to grief it would be on these beaches, where uneven slopes or hidden obstacles could prevent pontoons from ever reaching the shore. The beaches had to be surveyed first.

As this part of the coast lay in enemy hands it could not be surveyed from the ground, so the Admiral used the same method of inspection that would be used before D-Day – photography from the air. If one watches the tide fall on a calm day, the waters' edge forms in effect a series of contours along the beach. The Admiral reasoned that if photographs were taken from an aeroplane at regular intervals, for example every time the tide fell one foot, then it should be possible to map the whole beach gradient by plotting these contour lines. Obviously it was not possible to fly over the beaches every time the tide dropped exactly one foot, but as long as the time of each exposure was carefully noted, the intermediate positions of the beach gradient could be extrapolated.

For this task Admiral Bacon called once more on the cameras of the Dunkirk air squadrons. Over the past year they had photographed the whole German defence system from Nieuport to the Dutch frontier, bringing back a wealth of detailed information on coastal batteries, topography, beaches, and heights of sea-walls for the ships of the Dover Patrol. Now, on July 2nd, 1917, crews from 2 (Naval) Sqn were sent to photograph the invasion beaches at twenty minute intervals between 11.25 and 17.36 hrs, while other aircraft operated to the east of Ostend so that German suspicions would not be unduly aroused. From the beach prints, the naval staffs were able to compile detailed charts and cross-sections of the whole stretch of coastline to be invaded. To check the accuracy of the calculations, a similar experiment was attempted near Dunkirk, only this time the beach was surveyed conventionally from the ground as well. The results coincided almost exactly. As Admiral Bacon said, "It was a good performance to deduce the slope of a beach to within an accuracy of six inches from photographs taken 14,000 feet up in the air."[1] Unfortunately the labours came to nothing; as the Battle of Ypres failed to achieve the required breakthrough in Flanders, the Belgian invasion was postponed indefinitely.

In the skies over the Battle of Ypres the aerial camera reached new literal and metaphorical heights. Corps squadrons were now responsible for reconnaissance to a depth of 5000 yards behind the German front line. Army squadrons flew everything beyond this, and by now they were following the bombers as they attacked the German rear. Between 24th and 25th September alone, 2,500 prints were produced of German airfields and railway junctions that had been bombed from the air. During the whole of September the RFC exposed a record number of 14,678 plates and distributed a total of 346,999 prints.

[1] 2 (Naval) Sqn also did sterling photographic work before the blockade of Zebrugge in 1918.

By 1918 a great photographic map of the whole Western front had been built up for use by the army planners. Every day it was amended as new prints arrived, and, by watching the changes that took place, interpreters could see the growing preparations for Ludendorff's last great offensive in the Spring of 1918. All the activity was concentrated in front of General Gough's Fifth Army; new supply and ammunition dumps, hospital camps, and airfields were appearing, and every day the network of light railways behind the German lines was seen to be expanding. One especially interesting exposure over Bullecourt showed an overnight appearance of small white objects; when a 9.2 in howitzer was ranged on them, the resulting explosions showed them to have been boxes of ammunition.

Photo-reconnaissance in the German Army Air Service developed in the same way as in the RFC – as an aerial servant of the army with separate Flieger Abteilungen[1] attached to Corps and Army HQs for tactical and strategic duties respectively. Only the scale of their involvement differed; shortly after the war started the Germans had the capability to photograph the entire Western Front every two weeks. They encouraged aerial photography to such an extent that a certain Leut Fricke was awarded the Pour le Mérite for organising this branch of the Service. The British never set up pure photographic units, preferring to strap cameras onto any aircraft of any reconnaissance squadron; the Germans followed suit with their Corps Abteilungen, but by 1916 each Army HQ usually had its own Reihenbildzug[2] of three specially equipped camera aircraft.

As befitted the finest lens makers in the world, the Germans produced some excellent cameras. Standard types included the Flieger Kammer FK II with a 50cm lens, the Flieger Kammer FK III with a 70cm lens, the Flieger Kammer Stab for large area cover, and a hand-held Pistolen Kammer. The interesting thing was that only the Flieger Kammer Stab used glass plates; all the rest employed films. Roll-film cameras had been pioneered in the German Air Service by Oberleutnant Oskar Messter, a motion picture cameraman, who designed a semi-automatic film camera which was to be the prototype of all modern aerial cameras. Later on in the war he designed a fully automatic film camera, powered by a mechanical drive connected to a small propeller in the airstream which exposed the film at regular intervals and turned the magazines. This was the Reihenbildner – literally translated as 'series pictures' – which was primarily intended for mapping; from 8,200 feet, an area 37.3 x 3.1 miles could be covered by 250 overlapping prints.

Cameras like this were carried by Lichtbild (Lb) – 'lantern-slide' – aeroplanes. The Germans gave a lot more thought to the needs of aerial photography, as shown by the design of the two-seater LFG Roland C II. For a start it was far sleeker and more streamlined than its opposite numbers leaving the Royal Aircraft Factory. The pilot sat well forward, while his observer, in charge of the camera, sat immediately behind with a commanding view all

[1] Aviation Units.

[2] Detachment of Photographic Aircraft.

round. Downward vision was enhanced by cut-outs at the wing roots and by transparent panels in the fuselage sides.

It was with aircraft and cameras like these that the German Army Air Service managed to expose around 4,000 negatives a day as Ludendorff prepared for his last great offensive in 1918. The German C-in-C had long been convinced that complete photographic cover of the intended battlefield was essential for success. He wrote on January 1st, 1918:

" . . . complete *photographic reconnaissance* (his italics) with no gaps must be ensured. This is of decisive importance." In his Manual on "The Attack on Position Warfare" Ludendorff stated that the needs of aerial photography were to be paramount when new aircraft reached the front – he placed fighters at the bottom of the list.

The British GHQ also demanded 'complete' cover in January 1918, and this not only meant prints of all sections of the front but also "photographs of the enemy's possible concentration areas . . . at such frequent intervals as will ensure that the progress of any preparations may be followed." These requirements would seem to be obvious, but it is true to say that they were forgotten during the inter-war years and had to be re-learnt at some cost in the Second World War.

* * * *

Outside Europe the aerial camera was proving most useful against the Turks. There were few accurate maps of the deserts of the Middle East available to the British forces in 1916; visual reconnaissance was therefore of little value because the aerial observer had no means of positioning his discoveries in the featureless desert. The problem was solved by Sir Archibald Murray, commander of the Mediterranean Expeditionary Force in Egypt. He wanted to launch an attack on a group of important Turkish desert posts, but first he needed accurate maps. Plates were exposed over the whole assault area, and, based on certain features already fixed by triangulation, the information on prints was transferred to a 1:20,000 squared map. Copies were distributed to air observers who were then able to give accurate positions of their sightings.

The most impressive application of photography in the Middle East was carried out by Lieut Hugh Hamshaw-Thomas. When he was appointed photo officer to 5 Wing at the beginning of 1917 there were no detailed maps whatsoever of southern Palestine, and yet this was to be the main area of future British operations against the Turks. So with two small photographic sections Hamshaw-Thomas attempted to map the whole area from the information revealed by the aerial camera.

Obstacles were as daunting as the working conditions were primitive. Darkrooms had to be constructed from old aircraft packing cases or tents, both of which were insufferably hot under the desert sun. Water and chemicals were in very short supply, as were cameras to take the pictures in the first place. Cut off from Europe, the photosections could expect little help or guidance from the experts, which meant that they had to improvise and solve most problems for themselves. Yet despite all these drawbacks, Lieut Hamshaw-Thomas and his men not only briefed the crews, loaded the cameras, and processed the results, but also succeeded in plotting 500 square miles of the Sinai-Palestine front and compiling twenty different maps of 1:20,000 scale for the army in nine months. The sections became so efficient that, during operations in the Beersheba area, photographs taken at midday were interpreted, drawn on maps, the updated maps photographed once more, and the resulting prints delivered to the forward HQs by 1700 hrs the same day. Under the circumstances it was a remarkable achievement.

The development of photographic reconnaissance during the First World War largely kept pace with that of the aeroplane. While aircraft remained close to the ground the intrepid aviator could make a close visual study of the ground below; as machines were driven higher and faster to escape from the attentions of the enemy, so photography developed as an adjunct to, and eventually as a substitute for, the naked eye. Prints and plates were no longer numbered in dozens as in 1914; before the Allied counter-offensive of 1918 alone, some 88,000 photographs were taken behind German lines. "It would have been impossible by any other means to have obtained the information that so materially assisted the rapidity and effectiveness of our victorious advance," recorded an army officer. By the Armistice there were approximately 9,000 RAF cameras in existence, and over the four years of war they were responsible for over half-a-million exposures.

Thus by November 11th, 1918, virtually every major application of photographic reconnaissance that was to be employed over the next 50 years had been tried and tested. Cameras were even preceeding and following the Independent Air Force raids into Germany itself. The introduction of the DH 9 with its range of 300 miles meant that strategically important factories and railway centres beyond the Rhine could be covered before and after each attack. The briefs given to bomber crews based on these prints were just as detailed, if not as elaborate, as those given to Bomber Command in 1942.

The great difference between the two World Wars lay in the contrasting uses of air power. Between 1914 and 1918 the RFC never really advanced beyond being a tool of the army on the ground; Sir John Slessor wrote that the First World War was "from the air point of view, above all, an Army Cooperation War", and even in 1918 cooperation flights outnumbered all other types of sortie by nineteen to one. During the inter-war years the RAF would still assist the other services, but its own strategy would develop as it learned to fight independently in its own environment. In the Second World War the RAF would come to grips with the enemy over his own territory in complete isolation from the army and navy; the Air Staff would then need the timely intelligence that photographic-reconnaissance could provide to be masters of their own destiny.

CHAPTER THREE

The Locust Years

The military organisation that has the best photographic intelligence will win the next war. Generaloberst Werner Freiherr von Fritsch – 1938.

Winston Churchill described the inter-war period as the "locust years" – the era that pacifism and retrenchment had eaten away. It was a time when men tried to forget the miseries of the Great War and succeeded only in forgetting the lessons they had learned from it. Drastic pruning was particularly evident in the RAF, and by the mid-twenties the Service had declined in stature from a massive and experienced fighting force into one of the more cost-effective weapons in the hands of colonial administrators.

In his Memorandum of 1919, Trenchard recognised the importance of aerial photography, which he classed alongside navigation, meteorology, and wireless as one of the "primary necessities" for which training was of "extreme importance". However, because Trenchard disliked specialists the RAF continued to believe that any squadron could carry and operate cameras, with the result that no one became particularly proficient in the art or bothered much about its application, and that everyone regarded aerial photography as a minor adjunct to their other duties.

What research impetus there was emanated from the RAF School of Photography at Farnborough. The School had been formed in 1912 as a section of No. 1 Airship Sqn, RFC, but it was mainly concerned with the improvement of cameras and the techniques of processing. In 1925 for example, Farnborough introduced the first standard film camera, the F 24[1], into service, thereby rendering plates obsolete.

The employment of these cameras tended to be confined to photographing the Empire. Aerial photography greatly assisted ground forces in their search for dissident native positions in Somaliland and the North-West Frontier, and also helped in surveying badly mapped regions. Between 1920 and 1922, the DH 9s of 47 Sqn and the F 2bs of 208 Sqn photographed the Nile between high and low tides on behalf of the Irrigation Department of the Public Works Ministry of the Egyptian Government.

Commendable as all this effort was, it reflected a decline in the application of aerial photography. Staff officers forgot that cover of troop concentrations or ports should be made at regular intervals so that the progress of prepara-

[1] It was decided during the First War to rename all plate cameras with the prefix 'P', signifying 'Plate'; the LB type for example became the P 7. All film cameras therefore were prefixed by the letter 'F' meaning 'Film'.

tions could be noted, or that plans for combined operations such as Zebrugge could be made from maps and models based on aerial prints, or that beach gradients could be measured from the air. By 1925 the aerial camera was once more a minor tool for use by the Army, on a par with binoculars and the theodolite.

The War Manual of 1928 reflected this retrogression by defining the division of responsibility very clearly. The RAF was tasked with taking and developing the photographs but the Army was responsible for their interpretation and distribution. The Army remained responsible for photo-interpretation until 1938, underlining the belief that photographic reconnaissance was for their benefit.

But because aerial photography was really an air specialisation, the Army tended to ignore it. No one was trained to look for shipping, or to plot bombing targets, or to look for new types of aircraft, yet it was in these fields that photo-intelligence was to play such an important part after 1939. There was only one fully trained photo-interpreter to meet the needs of all three Services in 1935, and that overworked and under-appreciated officer was Captain Tom Churchill at the School of Photography.

Thus, by failing to keep up with advances in aviation technology in the Thirties, and in neglecting the lessons of the First World War, the RAF had the worst of both worlds. All the defects became evident once the emaciated Royal Air Force took stock after the Abyssinian War.

The European political situation had deteriorated to such an extent by 1934 that the Chiefs of Staff, with not inconsiderable foresight, instructed the Joint Planners to prepare for a war with Germany in five years time. Such planning necessitated accurate and detailed intelligence, not only about military preparedness, but also on the whole framework of the German economy. A report by the Deputy Chiefs of Staff on 1st January 1936 recognised that the scale of any future war would be greatly extended. Advances in aviation had brought civilian and industrial targets within range of the manned bomber, and the scope of an intelligence network had to be immeasurably extended if a nation was to prepare adequately for war.

The age of total war had come about, and total war demanded total intelligence. Experience in the Mediterranean, however, raised serious doubts as to whether the RAF had the capability to secure even partial intelligence. The Mediterranean and the Red Sea were of crucial importance to Britain as lifelines to the Indian sub-continent, and by 1937 Mussolini was making preparations that threatened to close these trade routes in time of war. Reports began to trickle in that the Italians were constructing an underground air base on Pantellaria, a rocky island strategically placed athwart the narrows that separated the eastern and western bases of the Mediterranean. On April 15th 1937, the AOC Malta was requested to obtain "distant air photographs . . . to determine so far as possible the present state of aerodrome construction in Pantellaria." Three months later the island was covered by a flying boat of

202 Sqn[1] which brought back prints to show that an airfield was under construction to the east of Mount Gelkhamar.

Fears about Italian designs on the Red Sea were underlined by the British ambassador in Cairo, who reported "regarding an exodus of labour from the Yemen due, it is alleged, to the construction of forts and an aerodrome on the islands opposite Perim." Large-calibre guns were also reportedly being installed on the island of Dumeirah. On July 3rd, the Air Ministry signalled British Forces, Aden, and asked for photographs of the mainland and islands within a five mile radius of Dumeirah. It was emphasised that the flights had to take place inconspicuously outside the six-mile limit – British agents had even been withdrawn from Italian territories so that no action could be construed by the Italians as provocative and thereby drive them into even closer alliance with Germany. As long as British aircraft spied obliquely while on routine flights outside Italian airspace, no suspicions would be aroused.

The Dumeirah cover was taken by a Vincent of 8 Sqn on July 7th, 1937, but the dearth of processing facilities was made evident when the prints had to be sent back to Farnborough for interpretation by Capt Churchill because there was no one else who could do it.

With Mussolini's withdrawal from the League of Nations and his acceptance of the Anti-Comintern Pact, more and more centres of Italian influence came under scrutiny from the aerial camera. On November 17th, 1937, the Director of Naval Intelligence requested photographic cover of Tobruk "with the object of gaining information on the coast defences and general layout of the port." The RAF Middle East was pitifully unprepared for this task; they had fewer photographic resources at their disposal than at any time since 1915. The AOC Middle East found that he had no suitable aircraft for the job and no lens large enough – 20 in focal length was required – in his entire Command. In the event, the AOC had to commandeer an aircraft sent out from Britain to carry the Inspector-General to Alexandria. On January 3rd, 1938, Tobruk, Bardia, El Adem, Derna, and several off-shore islands were covered on the return journey to Malta. However the Navy had to wait another four months for the interpretation report because Capt Churchill was busy elsewhere. The fact that the Navy depended on the RAF for its photographs, and that the RAF depended on the goodwill of the Army to extract any information from them, showed the inadequacy of the system in 1938. These failings did not go unnoticed. In October 1936 Air Chief Marshal Sir John Steel wrote to the Secretary of State for Air expressing dissatisfaction with the existing "organisation for the control of photographic policy". He stressed the need for more training with aerial cameras which had "to a large extent been crowded out of the general syllabus of service training." The Deputy Chief of Air Staff (DCAS) also stated in January 1937 that "we must regard the development of long range photography as highly important and accord it a high degree of priority in research, development and training."

In 1936 the RAF set up an organisation to obtain as much information as

[1] 202 Sqn was formed from the 2 RNAS Sqn that undertook photography before the raid on Zebrugge in 1918.

possible about German industrial targets; a Squadron Leader travelled incognito throughout the Reich collecting maps and photographs while a Captain liaised with the French Deuxième Bureau de l'Armée de l'Air. It was they who provided the RAF with its first up to date prints of Hitler's Germany. The French had discontinued aerial surveillance of Germany in 1929 but they resumed their secret flights in the summer of 1936, concentrating on areas that bordered on their beloved Maginot Line, especially the vulnerable zone between the Moselle and the Rhine. There was so much potential in these clandestine flights that the British Secret Intelligence Service (SIS), motivated by the deteriorating international situation which tended to restrict the scope for conventional intelligence, decided to enlist the help of the aerial camera themselves.

The original impetus for collaboration came from Wg Cdr F. W. 'Fred' Winterbotham, Chief of Air Intelligence in the SIS, who was especially interested in the Luftwaffe air defence network guarding the German border. In their quest for the right 'agent' for the job, the Deuxième Bureau approached Mr Alfred J. Miranda of the American Armament Corporation, to see if he could recommend anyone. He had the very man in mind – an expatriate Australian by the name of F. S. Cotton.

Sidney Cotton was a remarkable man. A Queenslander by birth, he had learned his flying with the RNAS in the First War, where he invented the Sidcot flying-suit and went solo the first time he stepped into an aircraft cockpit. During the Twenties he pioneered an air mail service and aerial survey work in Newfoundland, undertook a two-month search for two missing Atlantic fliers, and organised an expedition to rescue Augustine Courtauld who was stranded on the Greenland ice-cap. By 1938 he was down on his luck following the collapse of his colour film business, but Cotton was always ready to bounce back if some new venture took his fancy, and in the autumn of 1938 he accepted Miranda's suggestion that he meet Winterbotham to discuss "certain work".

"It emerged," recollected Cotton,[1] "that the venture was to be a combined Anglo-French one, the French having put up most of the cash. They had already done some aerial photography in short-range aircraft over the Rhineland and the Siegfried Line, but they now wanted to operate a faster and more modern aircraft on longer trips into Germany and Italy. . . . I was to use the aircraft fairly frequently myself to substantiate the story of a privately owned British plane."

A private company, known as the Aeronautical Research and Sales Corporation, was formed to provide a legitimate cover for the operations at Heston aerodrome just outside London. The French had made do with a very old aircraft complete with an enormous and ancient wooden camera operated by a splendid old character with a flowing beard who was normally a portrait photographer in Paris. Such a system was too open to detection on longer flights. The SIS needed an airliner that could operate unobtrusively over

[1] "Aviator Extraordinary".

Europe; not so large that it would excite comment if it flew aimlessly about, and not so unusual that it would attract undue attention. Cotton chose the Lockheed 12A, a modern aircraft by European standards, which provided heated cabin space for five or six people. The Chief of Air Staff agreed to purchase one with surprisingly little persuasion, and it arrived in England towards the end of January 1939.

Cotton then asked for a good engineer co-pilot to look after the aircraft and to share the flying. Winterbotham suggested a young Canadian, Fg Off R. H. Niven, who had joined the RAF on a short-term commission in 1935 and who was due to transfer to the Reserve on February 1st, 1939. Bob Niven, a tall, zestful, and enthusiastic ex-bus driver from Calgary, made several flights with Cotton to Aero Club meetings in France. "Winterbotham agreed that I should warn him discreetly of what we were planning to do, to give him a chance to pull out, but Bob of course was keener than ever. We were ready to fly our first mission towards the end of February 1939."

On March 25th, Cotton and Niven flew over to France to pick up a Deuxième Bureau photographer named Bois. Operations began from a little-known airfield fifteen miles south-west of Paris called Toussous-le-Noble, and the first flight was detailed for March 30th to secure information over Krefeld, Hamm, Munster, and the Dutch frontier for any future attack on road and rail communications in Western Germany. The French idea was to cut a hole in the floor of the Lockheed, into which the camera lens could be inserted, and through which the camera could be jettisoned if they were forced down. The plan seemed reasonable, but Cotton was not very impressed with the mentality of the Deuxième Bureau which was still firmly rooted in the cloak and false beard era.

The first flight lasted for four hours and five minutes and was without incident. Two more sorties followed on 1st and 7th April over the Black Forest and Wurttemberg as this was an area where the Germans might concentrate troops prior to an assault on France through the Belfort Gap.

The last SIS flight of the series was planned for April 9th, and Bois came along as usual to give the briefing. Part of the mission was to substantiate reports of new airfields and armaments factories around Mannheim; take-off was therefore timed to allow for a preliminary run over Karlsruhe and thence to Mannheim to arrive at the same time as the morning passenger train from Strasbourg. This, Bois hoped, might help them to avoid detection.

The flight followed the normal air lane from Paris to Strasbourg, by which time the Lockheed was at 15,000 feet. After photographing the outskirts of Karlsruhe they headed north up the railway line to Heidelberg and then along the Neckar to Mannheim. By then they were at 20,000 feet, but even from this height Cotton could clearly see the vast concrete emplacements of the Siegfried Line. Beyond Mannheim they looped back to Ludwigshafen and Heidelberg, up the Neckar to Eberach, then north-west to the Rhine and Mannheim again. As there was no inter-com between the back and the front of the Lockheed, Bois, who was operating the camera, passed instructions to the cockpit by means of long pieces of string attached to Cotton's elbows.

When he wanted a change of direction, Bois would pull the appropriate string and Cotton would turn accordingly. They were just finishing their second run over Mannheim when Bois burst into the cockpit to say that he had just seen a small fighter aircraft climbing towards them. Cotton beat a hasty retreat into French airspace via Neustadt and Pirmasens and the interceptor was not seen again.

Cotton found liaison with the French to be a frustrating business. Not only were they too melodramatic but they were also very inefficient. The need for secrecy was paramount, which meant that even Cotton was not allowed to see the prints that he had taken, with the result that he had no means of judging how well he was doing his job. (When he was eventually shown the Mannheim photographs, Cotton could see that he had missed many of the most important targets even though he thought they had covered the area thoroughly.) Bois also dictated some rather erratic courses, which were designed to prevent detection but which, in Cotton's view, were likely to have the opposite effect.

Nevertheless the SIS was not in charge, and on April 17th Cotton and Niven set off to work under French direction over Italian bases in Tripolitania. The pantomime began again as soon as they reached Paris. Cotton was to act the part of a rich English milord, "a close friend of the King, passionately interested in ruins, flying down to Tunis for a holiday." For a task that needed anonymity and subterfuge, such a disguise seemed very inappropriate as it would excite comment everywhere they went.

They took-off from Toussous the next day at 06.10 hrs, breakfasted at Orange, and arrived at Bastia just before noon. Two days later the Lockheed crossed to Tunis. For five days an erudite English nobleman pottered around the local Roman ruins waiting for the Deuxième Bureau to declare the weather favourable. On April 25th everyone was ready for work to begin. Cotton wanted to take-off just behind an Italian air liner bound for Tripoli and follow it straight across the Bay of Tunis before turning south towards a new airfield at Castel Benito, but this was too simple for the French. They insisted that he fly south down the Tunisian coast to Ben Gardene, then east along the coast to a point some miles short of Tripoli, then south to Castel Benito. Although this route allowed several changes of course it was doubtful if anyone would be fooled by it; at 20,000 feet in the clear blue Mediterranean sky, the Lockheed could be seen coming miles away.

There was much to be photographed and the camera was left running for most of the seven hour flight. They returned to Tunis with 282 excellent overlapping photographs of approximately 1:20,000 scale, covering the ports of Tripoli and Zuara, five airfields including Castel Benito, and a number of roads, railways, and gun emplacements. But there were no laurel leaves for Cotton. His dissatisfaction with the Deuxième Bureau came to a head in Tunis and he was recalled under a cloud. Cotton had lost whatever confidence he ever had in French methods and competency; "if worthwhile results are to be obtained," he wrote, "I must have my own aircraft and operate in my own way."

He got his chance when two more Lockheeds arrived at Southampton in May. One was given to the French, to make a pair with the one they had retained after Tunis, and the other was flown up to Heston on May 11th where it was prepared for a new series of more ambitious sorties over Italian territory. Two 70-gallon fuel tanks were fitted into the fuselage to boost the still-air range from 700 to 1,600 miles. Holes were also cut in the entrance door and fuselage floor to accommodate Cotton's improved camera installation. The French had relied on a clumsy apparatus 5 feet tall by 15 in square; as the proposed flights would involve landing at Italian airfields, such an edifice might very easily be detected. Also one camera only covered a limited area; to gain the maximum value from the clandestine flights more photographic coverage was necessary.

Cotton experimented at first with three Leica cameras, one standing vertically upright and the others at an angle on either side. This fan of three was held in place by a specially constructed frame. However the Leicas were found to be too small. They had been designed for detailed surveillance of birds or the growth of plants, and although they produced very clear prints, the amount of detail recorded was very limited from 20,000 feet. So Cotton turned to the standard RAF camera – the F 24. A pair of these were fitted into a frame, and, allowing for a slight overlap, they were capable of photographing a strip approximately 11½ miles wide from 21,000 feet.

The F 24 also had the advantage of being much smaller than its French predecessor, being only 10 in high by 6 in square. The F 24s were light enough to be dismantled after landing and carried out of the Lockheed in elderly suitcases covered with old travel labels past the eyes of any customs officials. The camera port-holes in the door and cabin floor were covered by little flush-fitting panels that were almost impossible to detect.

All this took time, so it was not until June 14th that Cotton and Niven were finally ready to set off for the Mediterranean. Malta was the first stop for the supposedly wealthy English aristocrat who had visited Tunis some months previously. Once more he was off to explore the ruins of past civilisations, but this time his travels were to take him to the Red Sea. It was only supposed to be coincidental that his quest for the relics of antiquity took him over some of the most recently constructed military structures in the Italian Empire.

Cotton had tried to get approval to take a photographer along with him, but his request had been turned down on the grounds of cost. In Malta however, he was introduced to "a young man with a slide-rule mind who was keenly interested in aerial photography" known, because he was only 5 feet 4 in tall, as 'Shorty' Longbottom. Fg Off Maurice Longbottom was a pilot on 202 Sqn and Cotton was so impressed with his enthusiasm that he asked the AOC Malta if he could 'borrow' Shorty for two weeks to act as his photographer. The AOC declined; he was a little hurt at not being informed beforehand that the clandestine mission was passing through, and he was sure that his own 202 Sqn could do the job just as well. He was also a realist; the political repercussions if a serving officer was shot down over Italian territory did not bear thinking about. However, the AOC was willing to allow Longbottom 24 hours leave to accompany Cotton on a flight over Sicily the next day, when they photographed Comiso, Augusta, Catania, and Syracuse. "We got some excellent photographs, and I hoped they might soften the AOC's heart, but he still wouldn't release Shorty. Bob Niven and I took off at daybreak next day, June 16th, for the long flight to Cairo via Leros and Rhodes."

The cameras turned over the fortifications of Leros and above the airfields and anchorages of Cos and Rhodes. From Cairo they flew to Aden via Massawa and the new Caproni aircraft factory at Asmara. The next day was spent over the coast of Italian Somaliland which was dotted with submarine pens, and then up to the Haifan peninsula, where they saw what appeared to be an underwater pipeline which confirmed Royal Naval suspicions that Mussolini was planning to refuel his submarines outside the Red Sea.

The return journey encompassed Italian North Africa where a large supply dump was discovered, reputedly holding enough ammunition to keep the Italian army in business for two years. Bardia, El Adem, Tobruk, Derna, and Benghazi all came under scrutiny by the aerial camera before Cotton and Niven returned to England on June 25th, ostensibly from an air rally in Hungary.

During eleven days overseas, the Lockheed had spent 76 hours in the air and had returned with a wealth of information without arousing Italian suspicions. "I don't think there was any Italian aerodrome, barracks, naval base or other object of military interest in Southern Italy, the Eastern Mediterranean and North Africa which was not faithfully recorded in greatest detail by these splendid cameras," wrote Wg Cdr Winterbotham.

1938 had seen an improvement not only in Anglo-Italian relations because of Mussolini's pique at not being forewarned of Hitler's annexation of Austria, but also in the intelligence gathering capability of RAF aircraft in the Mediterranean. Both British and Italian governments promised to inform each other of any intention to build new naval or air bases to the east of 19° East, and this lull was put to good use by 202 Sqn who photographed most of the Italian North African coast from a safe distance.

The détente did not last for long, and on February 17th 1939, at the behest of the Admiralty, the Air Ministry sent the following signal to the AOC, Middle East:

"Admiralty require as soon as possible photographs of anchorages at Tobruk and Bomba for purpose of locating certain submarines. Arrange flight immediately . . ."

It was indicative of changes that had taken place during the previous year that it was possible to dispatch a flying boat immediately to complete the task while en-route for Alexandria. The following day a signal was sent to the Air Ministry:

"Photographic reconnaissance completed. Nothing observed at Bomba. Eight definitely at Tobruk anchorage . . ."

The Tobruk sightings were confirmed on the return flight to Malta and the prints were sent to London on February 22nd in the care of a naval officer

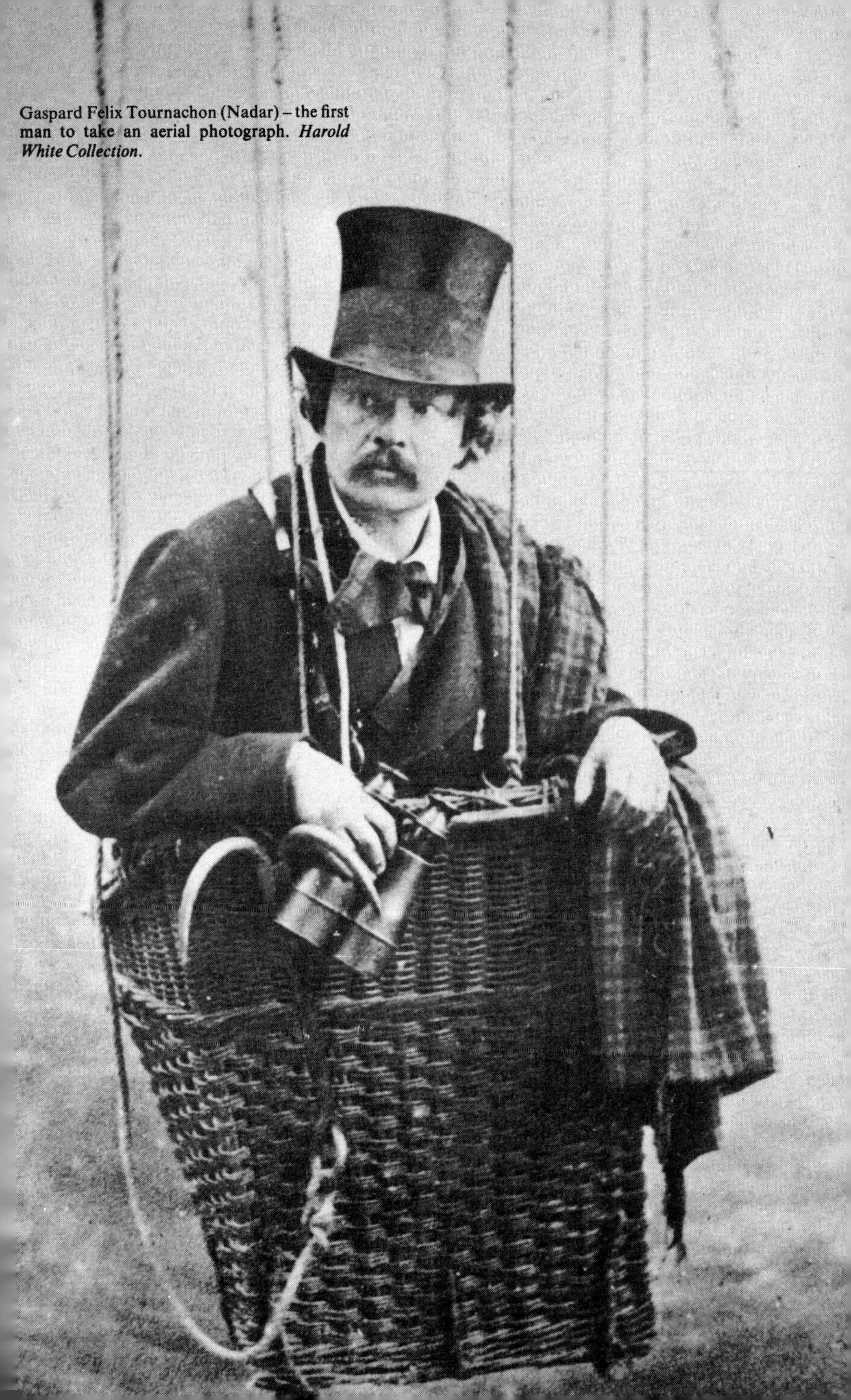

Gaspard Felix Tournachon (Nadar) – the first man to take an aerial photograph. *Harold White Collection*.

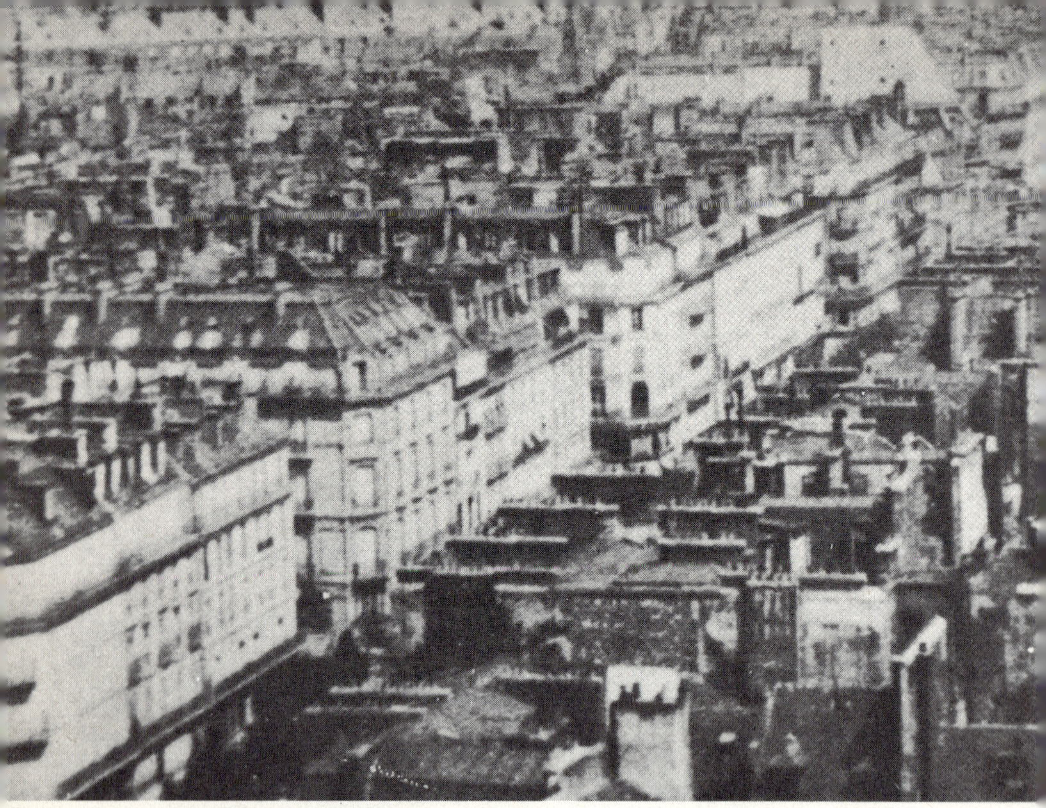

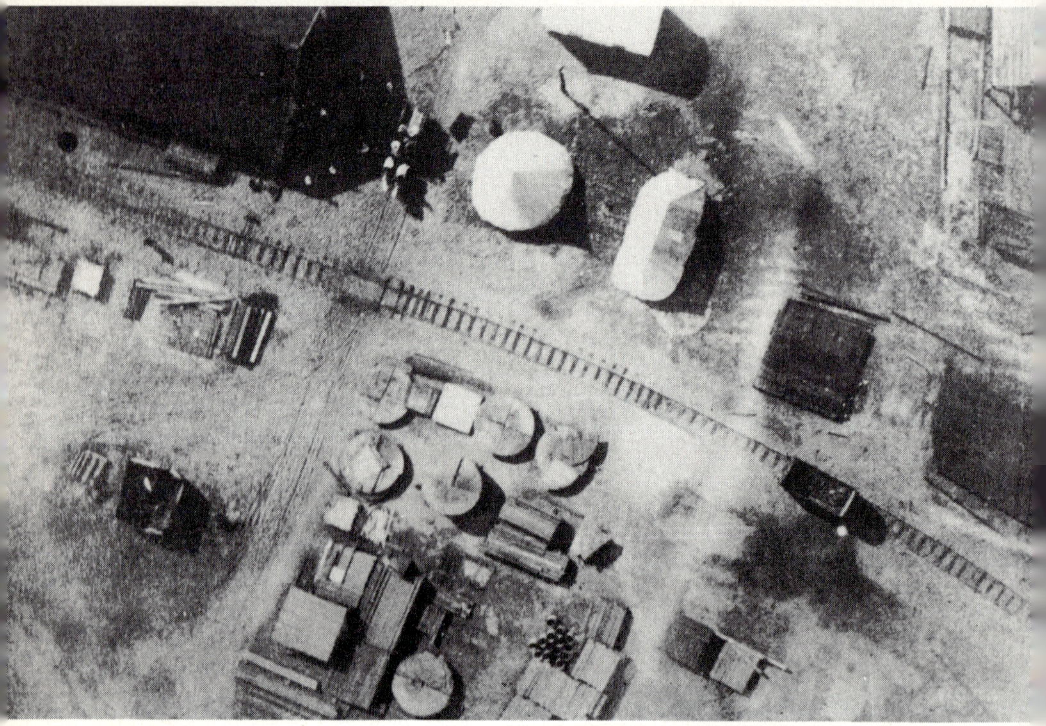

Top: A view of Paris taken by Nadar from a captive balloon at the Hippodrome, circa 1868. *Above:* Royal Engineers camp at Lydd, Kent exposed automatically in 1886 from a small free balloon launched by Maj H. Elsdale.

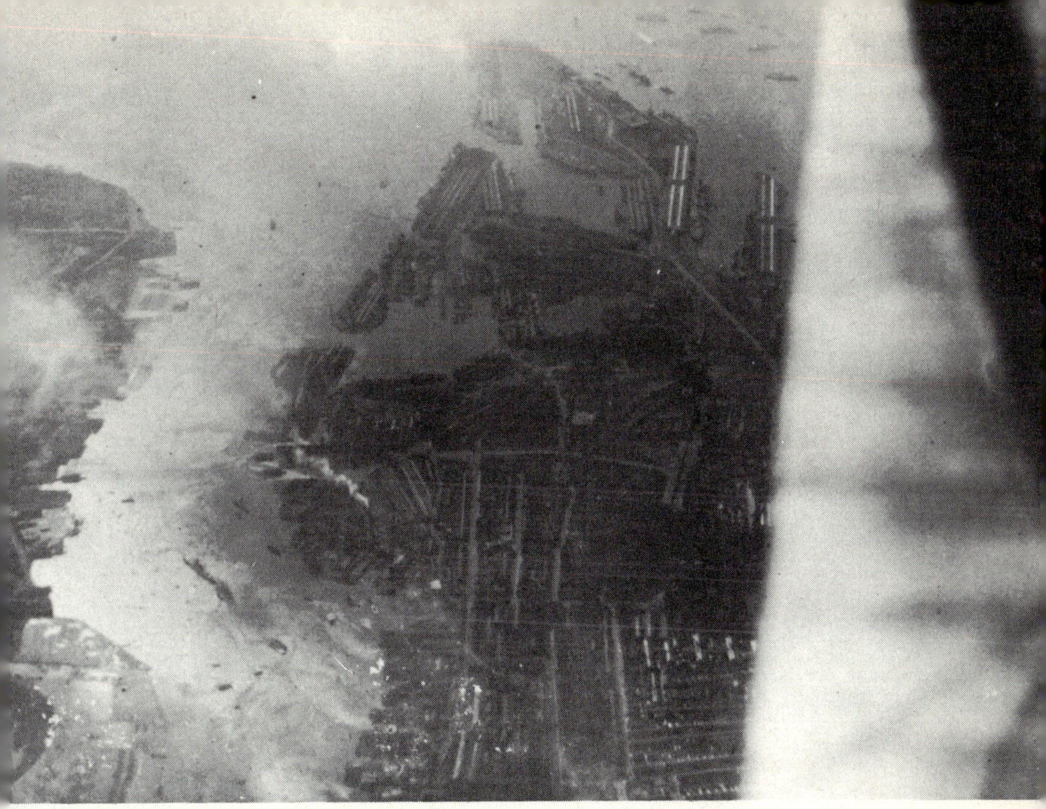

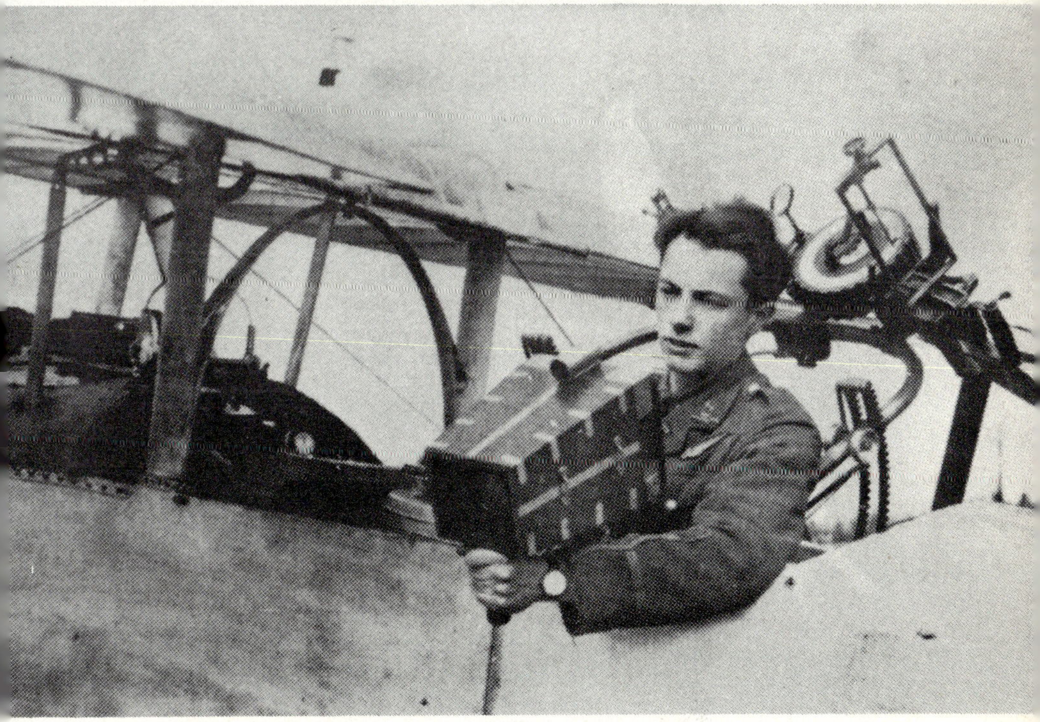

Top: Southampton Water as seen in 1913 from 5,000 ft by a camera attached to a BE2 of No 3 Sqn. *Above:* Lieut Tinne of 46 Sqn with an A-type camera in a Nieuport 12.

Below: A C-type camera on a BE 2c. *Bottom:* A BE 2c of 2 Sqn engaged on photography over France on December 27th, 1916. The camera is to the right of the pilot.

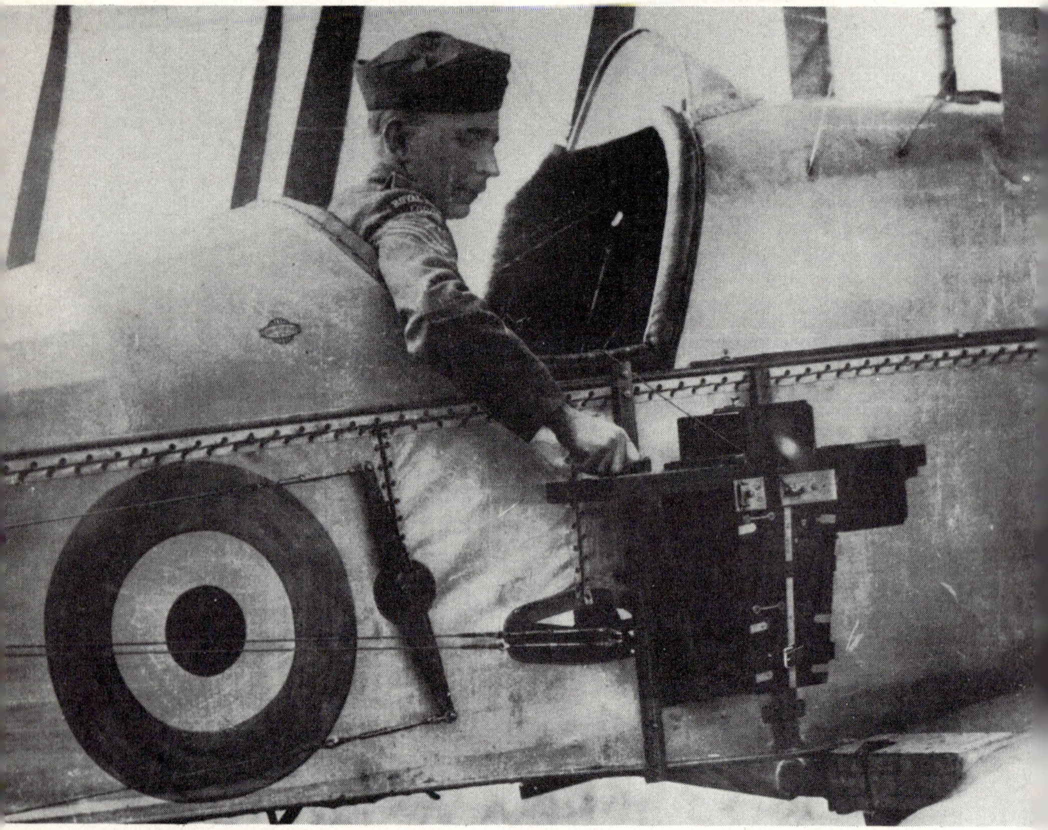

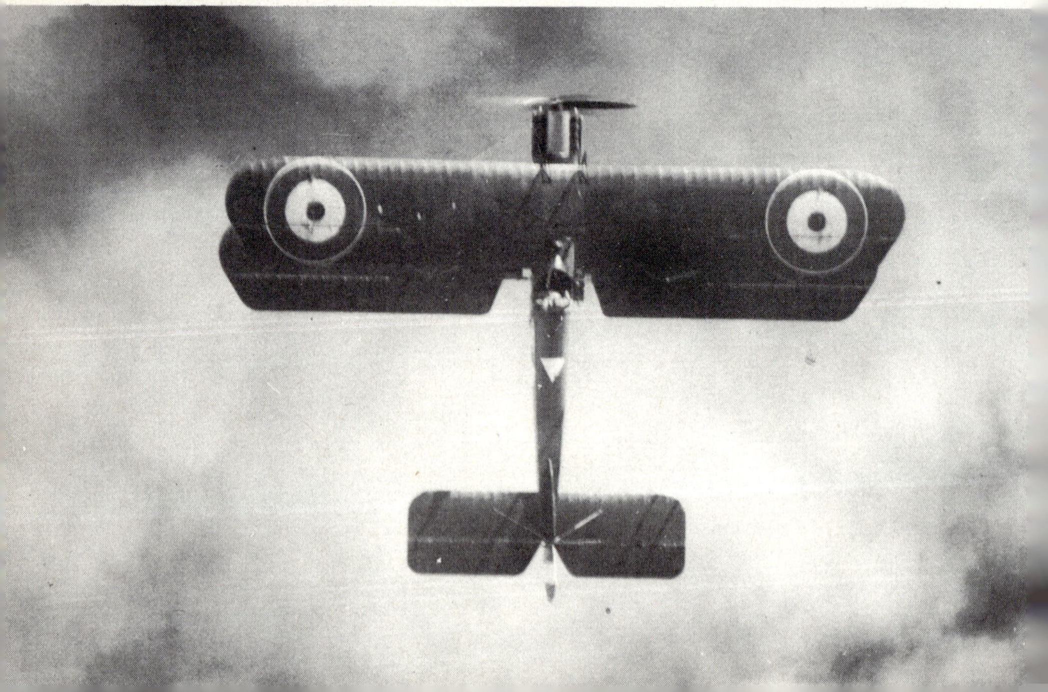

Below: An Avro 504 with its fuselage canvas rolled up to show a Williamson L type camera. Notice the windmill drive above the undercarriage. *Bottom:* The King of Montenegro inspecting an aerial camera at Fienvillers in 1916.

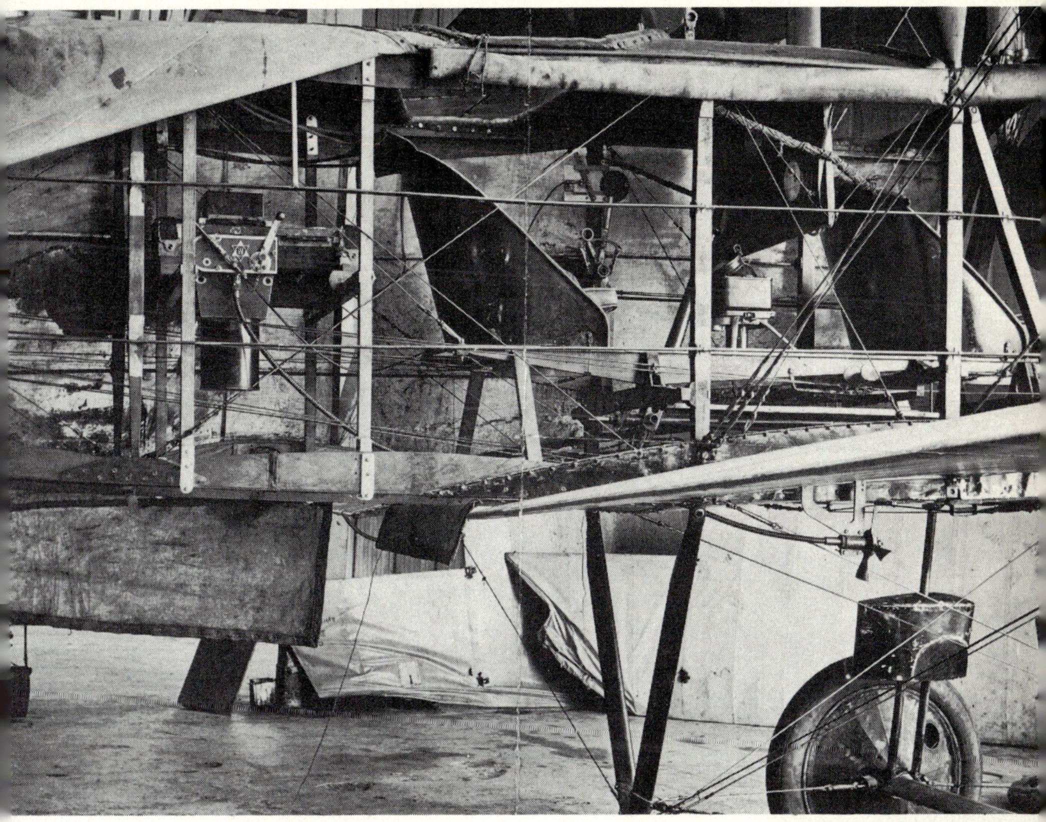

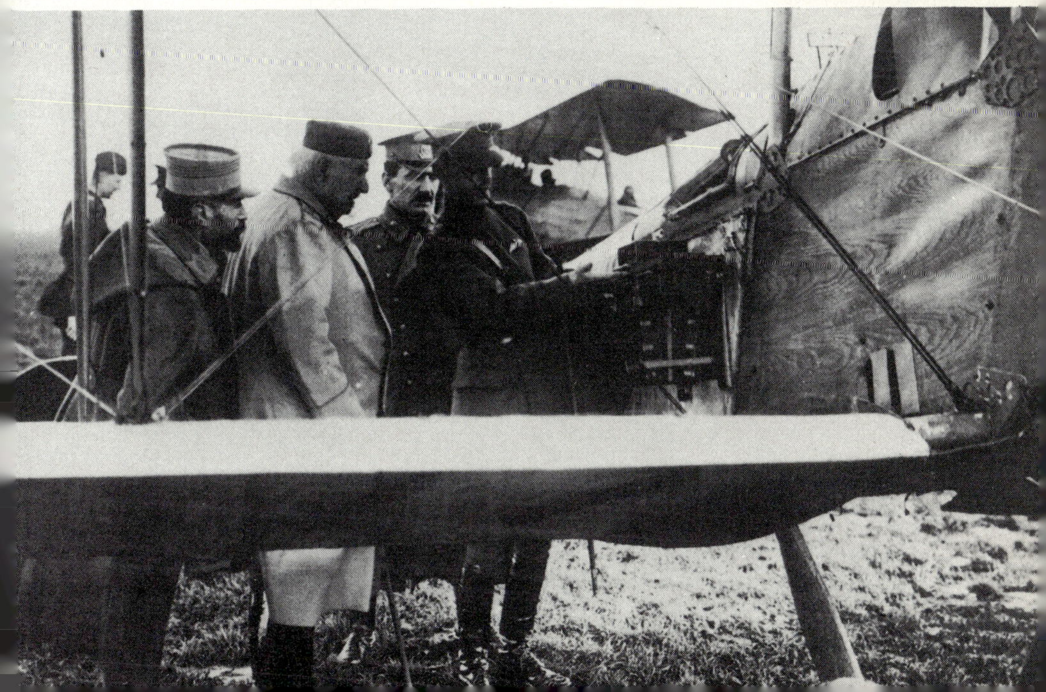

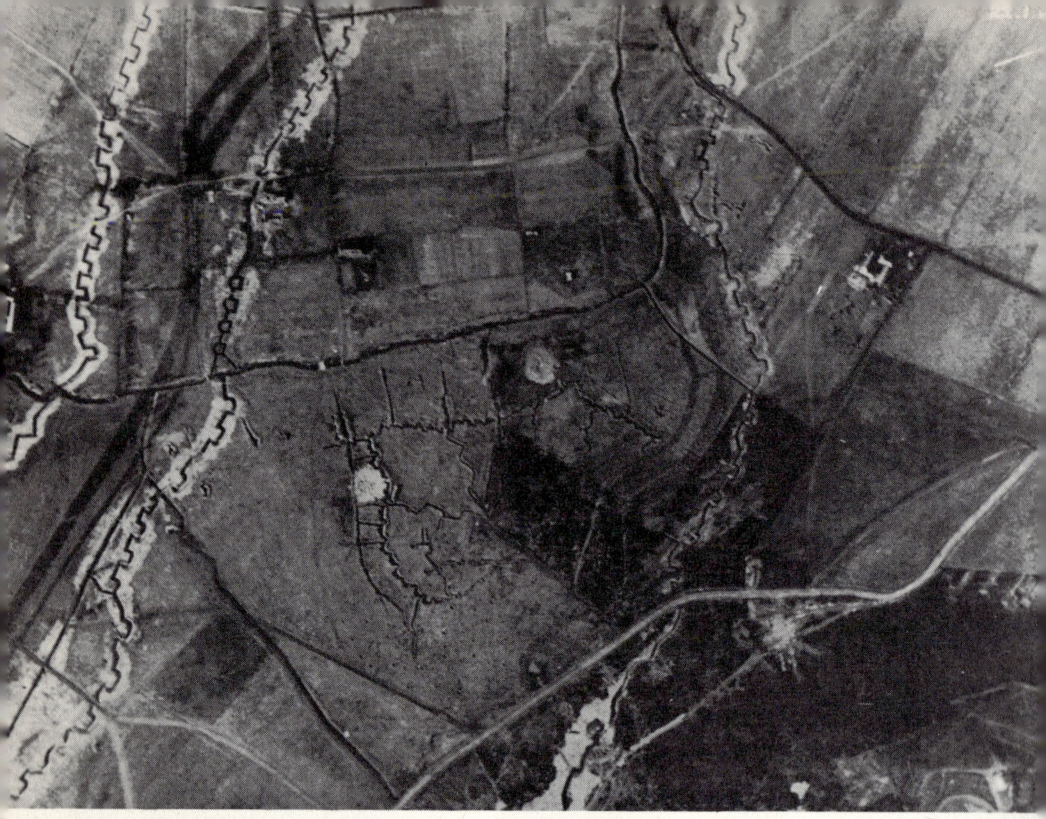

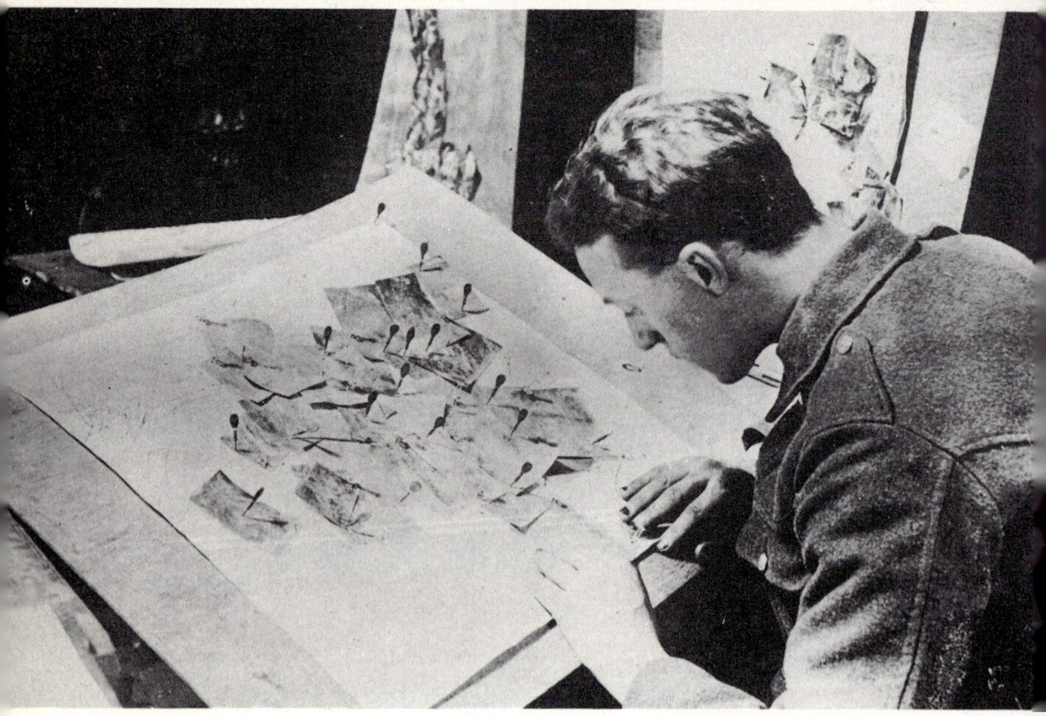

Top: A photograph of German trenches in January 1918. *Above:* Preparing a mosaic of air photographs taken over the Western Front. *IWM*

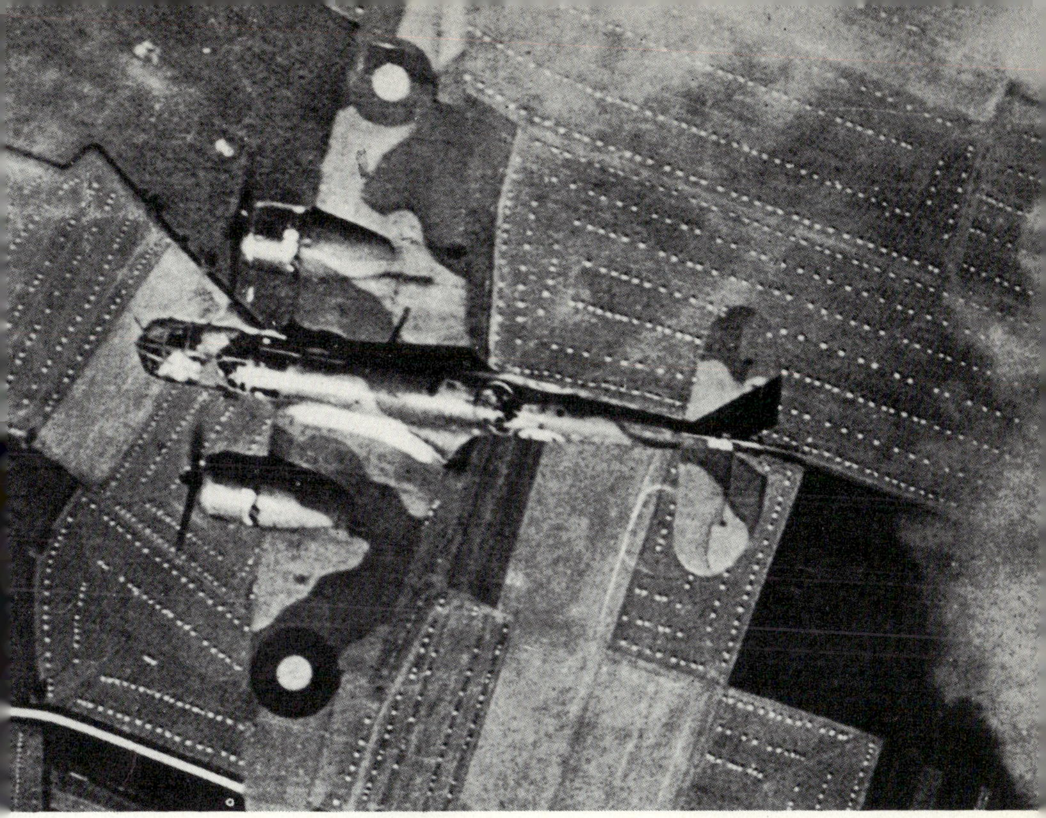

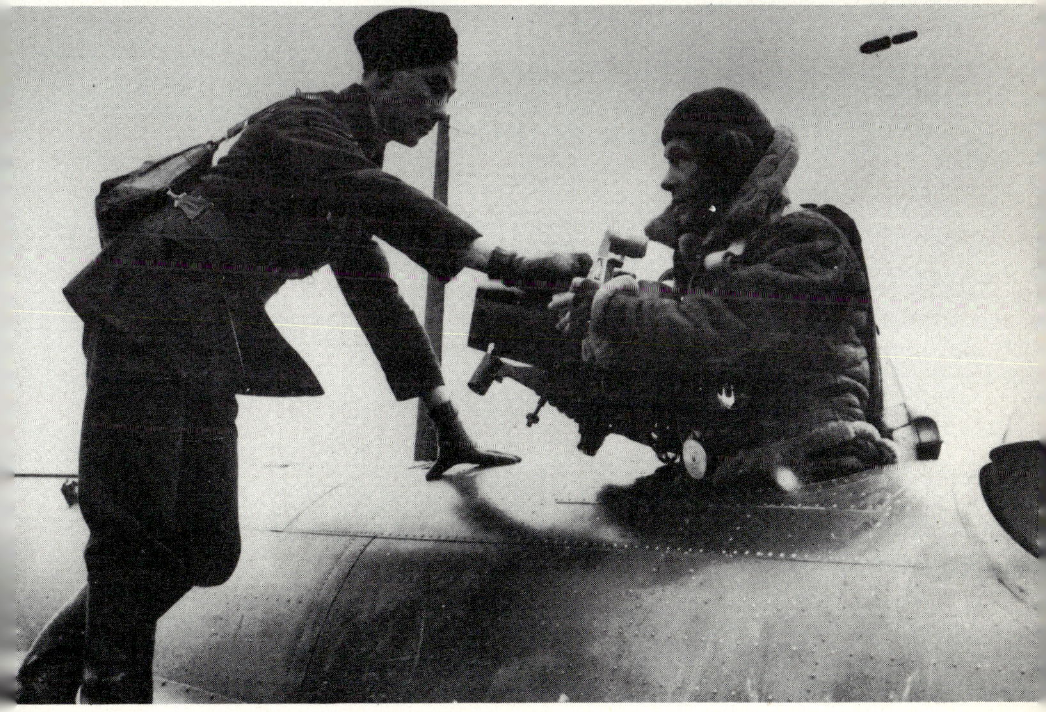

Top: Blenheim IV of 2 Gp merging with the fields below where haymaking is in progress.

Above: An F 24 camera being handed to a Blenheim observer.

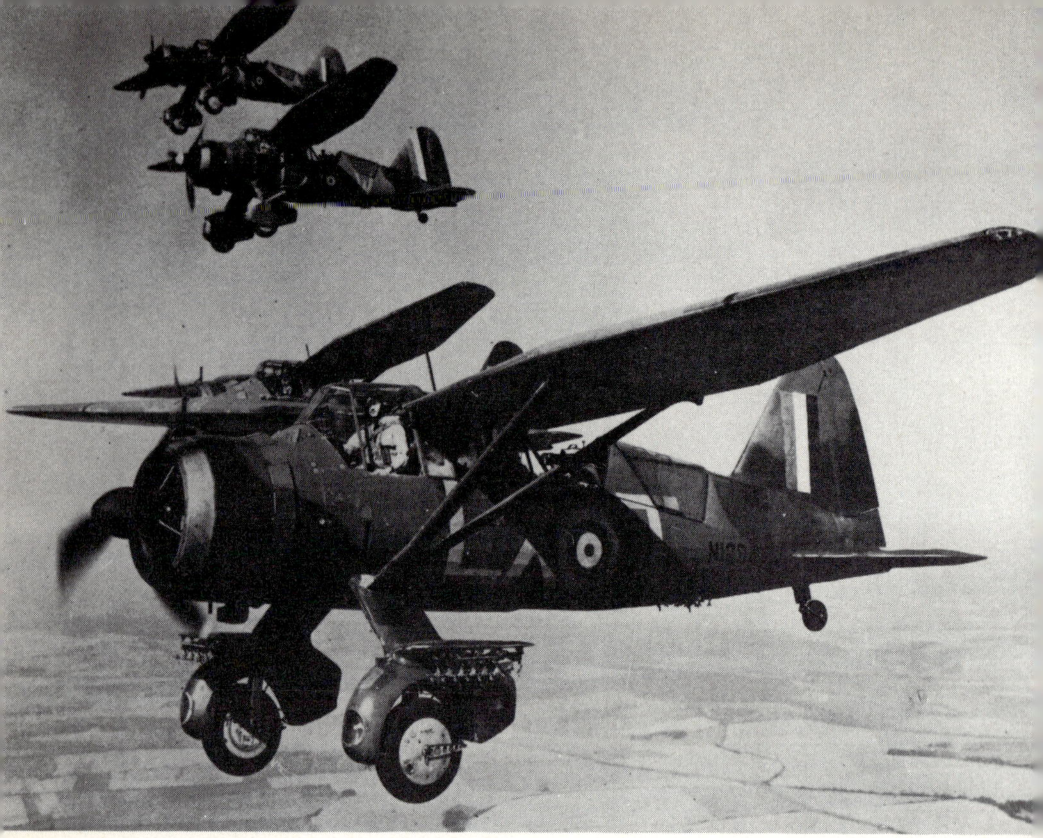

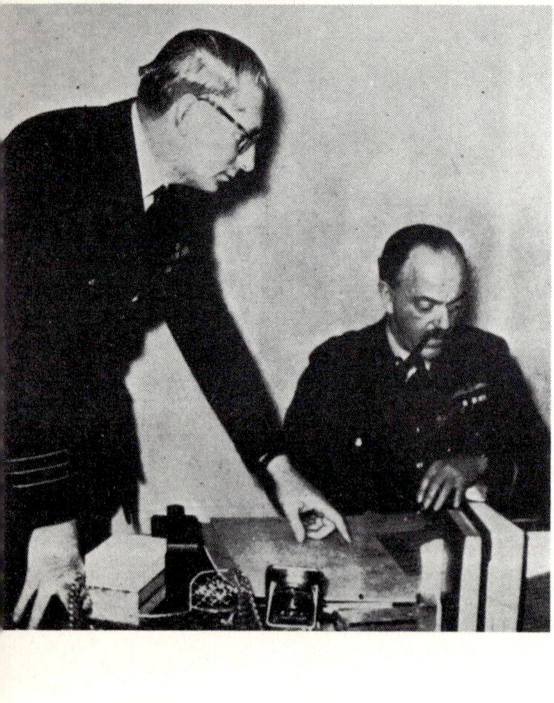

Above: Lysander army co-operation aircraft in echelon. Lysanders were tasked with tactical PR at the start of the Second World War in support of the British Army in France. *Left:* Sidney Cotton discussing a sortie with Air Marshal Sir Arthur Barratt. *Crown Copyright*

returning home on leave. Thus, within a few hours of sending the tasking, the Admiralty had the information it required, and the prints for confirmation a few days later. Cover of the islands, anchorages, ports, and seaplane bases of the Dodecanese, taken by 202 Sqn between March 30th and April 6th, was also back in Air Ministry hands eight days later. Such feats of efficiency would have been unthinkable eighteen months previously.

Nevertheless, it would be misguided to assume that all was well with aerial photography in the RAF by 1939. A time delay of one week between tasking and delivery of prints was a great improvement over 1937 standards, but it would still be seven days too long in the blitzkreig scenario just around the corner. Then again, although the SIS and 202 Sqn covered the same key areas in their travels, Cotton brought back far more intelligence data by flying vertically over targets than 202 Sqn did by photographing obliquely from outside the six-mile limit. With the best will in the world, cruising in a flying boat along the periphery of Mussolini's far-flung and not very well defended Empire was a world away from bringing information back from Germany against the might of the Luftwaffe.

One man who appreciated this more than most was the C-in-C Bomber Command, Air Chief Marshal Sir Edgar Ludlow-Hewitt. He realised that his Command would be very dependent on aerial intelligence in wartime to plan attacks and to assess their effectiveness. As visual reconnaissance would be of little value from the operational heights of 1939, he believed that the aerial camera had three important roles to play. First to enable the targets to be recognised, then to assess the damage done to them, and finally to find out, by prints taken at the actual moment of bomb release, which crews had successfully found their targets.

As early as 1937, Ludlow-Hewitt had advocated the development of a "special long range reconnaissance aircraft" to provide the photo-intelligence he needed. However his views were not widely supported. The financial restrictions of the inter-war years had created an Air Force that was too small to allow practical specialisation in both men and machines. For this reason, and because everyone else seemed to have more pressing claims for aircraft allocation, Ludlow-Hewitt decided to forego his long range reconnaissance aeroplane and make do with "special bomber aircraft" to bring back his prints.

In practice this meant the long-nosed Blenheim IVs of 2 Group – ie 107 Sqn at Wattisham, 21 Sqn and 82 Sqn at Watton, and 114 Sqn and 139 Sqn at Wyton.[1] But these were not specialist photographic squadrons; they were primarily bomber units tasked with the secondary role of carrying cameras as and when required. No one was willing to concede that aerial photography was a specialised art; cameras were still appendages that could be fitted to almost any aircraft, and operated by any observer, because they had all been taught the rudiments of photography while under training. Although the 2 Gp Blenheims were primarily responsible for photo-reconnaissance within

[1] When the RAF Air Component moved into France, two Blenheim Squadrons – 18 and 57 – went with them to form 70 Wg to provide strategic reconnaissance for the British Expeditionary Force (BEF).

Bomber Command, Battles, Whitleys, and Hampdens were all deemed capable of bringing back their share of prints when necessary. There were to be some rude awakenings just around the corner.

However the C-in-C Bomber Command was able to remedy some of the processing and interpretation problems highlighted in 1937. After promptings from Bomber Command, the Air Ministry established a department of air intelligence in January 1938 to coordinate photographic reconnaissance in the RAF. This new department – AI 1 (h) headed by Sqn Ldr Wheeler – was supplemented in May 1939 by the creation of an air intelligence cell at HQ Bomber Command, High Wycombe, and by the provision of Intelligence Officers (IOs) at station level, who were responsible for preliminary examination, plotting, and annotation of squadron prints. By September 1939 the ground organisation had been greatly improved since the days of Capt Churchill, but the matter of how the photographs were to be brought back was never really considered.

As tension mounted in the summer of 1939, conventional intelligence sources began to dry up or disappear altogether. Unfortunately this was a time when information on German war preparations was desperately needed. The Blenheims of 2 Gp were primed and ready to go, but as long as the uneasy peace continued they had to sit in East Anglia and wait. So the SIS was called in again. There were two main areas of concern – Winterbotham was particularly interested in the Luftwaffe defences of Western Germany, while the Navy needed to know the latest dispositions of the German Fleet. Cotton was briefed to use whatever subterfuge was necessary, but to photograph as much as he could while there was still time.

The disguise of the rich English aristocrat would fool no one in Germany, so Cotton resurrected his old colour film business and set out with his assistant, Niven, to sell colour film to the Reich. The usual 'luggage' of cameras was too risky – the German secret police were a far more thorough and suspicious breed than the colonial civil-servants of the Italian Empire – so an F 24 camera was boxed in beneath the Lockheed's cabin floor and camouflaged to look like a spare fuel tank. On the first trip to Berlin on July 26th, the 'fuel tank' remained empty in case the Germans stripped the aircraft, but no search was made. In fact Cotton's hosts were very friendly, and they were so impressed with the 'Kolossal Lockheed' that he was invited back to the Frankfurt Air Show to be held two days later.

The Air Show was a godsend to Cotton. Among the reception committee at Frankfurt was the Commandant of Templehof airfield, who asked if he could be taken up for a ride in the Lockheed. The opportunity for some unrestricted flying over Germany was too good to miss, and Cotton asked to be allowed to visit "the beautiful Rhine at Mannheim" which a mythical aunt had told him so much about. Not only was this an important area for Luftwaffe concentrations, but Cotton also remembered that he had only partially photographed the region four months earlier. Permission was readily granted for a pleasure flight the following day.

July 29th was a lovely day for cruising along over the Rhine. From 2000 feet one could see clearly the great waterway with its towns and landmarks, not to mention the new airfields and military constructions dotted about on either side. Cotton was shrewd enough to hand over control to his German passenger, not only to ensure that he would keep them airborne as long as possible while he was enjoying himself at the controls, but also because it would distract attention from any suspicious movements Cotton might make, such as pressing the camera button underneath his seat every time he wanted to take a photograph. The only drawback was a green light on the instrument panel which clicked on and off before and after an exposure, but the Commandant accepted Cotton's cool explanation that it was a device to indicate fuel flow to the engines. "I blessed my non-existent favourite aunt. On passing over a particularly conspicuous military-looking installation I blushingly hid my face in my hands. 'I'm sure I'm not supposed to see that,' I said. The Commandant laughed heartily at my joke."

Once he had been accepted in Germany as a business man, Cotton felt safe to start photography in earnest. On August 13th the 'sales-team' took-off for Berlin, and, by flying for endurance, covered the port of Wilhelmshaven and airfields under construction at Rustringham en-route. When they landed at Templehof the control officer asked why they had flown so far to the north to reach Berlin; Cotton, ever calm in a crisis, replied that he always flew on a great-circle route, and his piece of cool bluff was accepted without question. On the return journey they covered all the East Fresian islands from Wangeroog to Borkum in an attempt to discover how many German ships were anchored around Heligoland.

Two more trips were made to Berlin before the end of August. While returning home after one of these, Cotton 'lost his way' and was 'forced' to fly over the Siegfried Line for some time. By the end of the month, naval targets had become the main priority. The German Navy posed the greatest threat to British security in the short term, and it was essential to locate all their capital ships in case any had made a dash for the open sea to lie in wait for a declaration of war. Naval Intelligence therefore asked Cotton to photograph Wilhelmshaven again to see if any vessels had left port since it was last covered on August 13th. A small Beechcraft had been added to the SIS inventory in April and Cotton decided to use this as it would be less conspicuous than the Lockheed. Niven was detailed to fly it because he was several stones lighter than Cotton and this would give him an extra thousand feet of height to play with. The flight, on August 28th, was without incident. In the back of the Beechcraft was a camera operated by an amateur photographer who supplied the SIS with photographs for passports, genuine or otherwise, when required.

The following day Niven and Cotton went over Wilhelmshaven again in the Lockheed to take further prints. These confirmatory photographs showed that the naval force in the Jade comprised one Scharnhorst class battlecruiser, one armoured ship (possibly the 'Admiral Scheer'), the cruiser 'Emden', two destroyers, and Hitler's yacht 'Grille'. The 'Graf

Spee' had in fact made a dash for the Atlantic and it was too late to do anything about it. The next few months were to prove that the RAF's photographic reconnaissance organisation had missed the boat in more ways than one.

CHAPTER FOUR

Cotton's Circus

Photographic evidence is positive and undeniable and it therefore enables positive counter action to be taken – in fact demands it; but this is dangerous when you can only see part of the whole picture, because it almost inevitably causes the wrong emphasis in counter measures. The answer, of course, is to have enough reconnaissance aircraft and interpreters, and a properly geared organisation to provide a total picture. Wg Cdr Douglas Kendall.[1]

At the beginning of the Second World War, there were two British units theoretically capable of carrying out aerial reconnaissance over Germany. The first was 2 Gp of Bomber Command, well supplied with men and equipment, but which, in the opinion of its C-in-C, was unfitted to discharge its photographic reconnaissance role under wartime conditions. There was also a group of civilians at Heston who relied on subterfuge rather than sheer weight of numbers to get through, but once the war started they were expected to stand aside to let the professionals take over.

The most important target for Bomber Command in 1939 was the German Navy. They alone could strangle the British war effort by harassing the sea-lanes, and for many days before the outbreak of war a force of Blenheims had been standing by to bomb the naval base of Wilhelmshaven. At 1145 hrs on September 3rd, Fg Off A. McPherson of 139 Sqn took off from Wyton for the Schillig Roads on the first operational sortie of the war. His naval observer visually plotted the vessels at anchor, but the intense cold at 24,000 feet froze both the camera, half way through a magazine, and the radio so that the observer was unable to report the dispositions back to the waiting strike force. By the time the Blenheim landed back at Wyton the weather had deteriorated to such an extent that the bombing raid was thwarted by thunder-storms and darkness.

McPherson was sent on the same mission again the next day but low cloud forced him down to 300 feet over Brunsbuttel and Wilhelmshaven. Once again the wireless failed and the bomber crews had to wait for McPherson's return to be briefed. An attack was finally made from 500 feet, but because the bombs had been primed with delayed fuses for a medium level attack their destructive effect from 500 feet was minimal. The port defences were strong too; out of 19 aircraft that reached the target, 7 failed to return.

In his autobiography, Cotton was very scathing about the whole episode. He contended that the RAF was in possession of the SIS prints of

[1] 'Evidence in Camera.'

Wilhelmshaven and that the raid should have been planned on the basis of this intelligence. If the Blenheims had taken off at midday on September 3rd, while the weather was still fine, the RAF might well have achieved a military and psychological victory on the scale of Pearl Harbour.

Cotton's criticism had some validity. The RAF did appear to be more than a little prejudiced against the SIS and they may well have been suspicious of any prints not brought back by a regular unit. However there was a gap of four days between the last Lockheed flight over Wilhelmshaven and the outbreak of war, and a whole fleet could weigh anchor in 96 hours. It would have been pointless to send an attacking force against a target that was no longer there.

Having said this, the two reconnaissance flights from Wyton were not an auspicious beginning. McPherson's observer managed to take only 75 photographs before his camera froze, and time and again over the next few months thwarted Blenheim crews would return with stories of frozen mechanisms and ice-coated lenses. The F 24, with its standard fit of either 5 in or 8 in lenses, was just not designed for use in an unheated compartment around 20,000 feet. On November 25th, a typically frustrating day, four Blenheims took off from Wattisham for the North German coast. Each aircraft carried one camera with a 125 exposure magazine, yet they only managed to bring back three vertical prints of Heligoland and twelve of Cuxhaven. The sum total of their endeavours to plot German shipping was one vertical print of two trawlers.

The icing question was overshadowed by the growing realisation that the Blenheim IV stood little chance against the Luftwaffe. The first 48 Blenheim reconnaissance sorties of the war saw eight aircraft shot down in flames. This might have been barely acceptable if the remaining 40 missions had been successful, but eight of these were either driven back before they reached the target or failed to bring back any pictures because of icing. On December 29th, Air Marshal Joubert de la Ferté wrote that photographic reconnaissance of the German Fleet was "causing us losses out of all proportion to the results achieved."

The main reason for failure was the lack of a suitable reconnaissance aircraft to surmount the challenge presented by the Luftwaffe. There was no optimum weather situation for the Blenheim IV: if the conditions were bad, the cameras iced over or the ground remained obscured; if the skies were clear, the Blenheims provided a conspicuous target for the German fighters and anti-aircraft batteries. The failings of Bomber Command's reconnaissance force, evident to Ludlow-Hewitt as early as 1937, were summarised by Air Marshal Sir Richard Peck, the Director General of Operations, in 1940;

"Our pre-war policy was to organise for the taking of photographs by a large number of kinds of squadrons and to process them at the station with a small photographic section. We provided a programme for the production of a large number of cameras. We found, however, that for the most part, *the squadrons which we had organised to take photographs were tactically unable to penetrate to their targets.*" It was a tribute to the bravery of the crews of 2 Gp that, at a time when one in every six photographic aircraft failed to return, they brought back as many prints as they did.

The unproductive losses had to stop. This involved a return to first principles which in fact meant going back to Sidney Cotton, whose SIS Flight had been kept in existence to operate over politically sensitive areas. On September 12th, Cotton and Niven began operations over the West coast of Ireland to see if the German Navy was using any remote cove as a U-boat refuelling base. The Lockheed took off from Speke and brought back exposures from 10,000 feet, but this was too high for the C-in-C Plymouth who wanted cover from 2,000 feet so that any oil drums, pipelines, or fuel tanks would be clearly visible. Cotton obliged on September 26th and again on October 4th, but nothing suspicious was noted along the entire Irish Atlantic coastline. The co-operative Irish coastal batteries remained dormant throughout.

The RAF first turned to Cotton for assistance on September 15th. Not one 2 Gp reconnaissance mission had been completed successfully in the first two weeks of the war, and yet the Air Ministry was under daily pressure from the Admiralty for prints of the Dutch coast between Flushing and Ymuiden where a German force was reported to be concentrating. Cotton was summoned to a meeting of experts, chaired by Sir Richard Peck, which was to discuss the camera icing problem. "Every time we try to photograph an important target," said Peck, "which we have to do from high level to avoid enemy defences, the cameras freeze." Cotton replied that it was not the cameras that froze but the condensation on the lenses – there was nothing in the camera mechanism to freeze because the RAF used lubricants designed to withstand low temperatures. He had cured the condensation problem in the Lockheed by cutting holes in the floor that were slightly larger than the camera lenses to be pushed through them. This gap was sufficient to allow warm cabin air to be sucked out into the airstream and over the lenses, thereby preventing condensation. As no warm air came anywhere near the Blenheim cameras, which were installed on rails in the back of an unheated fuselage, they soon frosted over.

The discussion meandered on for some time around the problems of aerial photography until Peck finally brought up the question of the abortive sorties to the Dutch coast. The First Sea Lord was impatient for results and Peck asked Cotton if he could suggest any way of obtaining the material. "Lend me a Blenheim," he replied, "and I'll get the pictures right away." This was not the answer the meeting wanted to hear – they could not have a civilian shot down in an RAF aeroplane. The RAF had its own crews and they merely wanted Cotton's suggestions on improving operational efficiency. The meeting was adjourned until the next day when camera experts from Farnborough would be present to listen to Cotton's views on icing prevention. He left Whitehall a disappointed man.

"I went back to my office high above St James's Square and stared dejectedly out of the window, over the hills to the twin towers of the old Crystal

Palace and beyond. . . . Then I looked again at the blue sky and the clouds. It was one of those days when anyone who loves flying longs to get airborne. Why not? Why not take the Lockheed and go and get the pictures now?"

Within an hour of leaving Peck's office, Cotton was crossing the Kent coast at Ramsgate bound for the mouth of the Scheldt. The cameras turned over both Flushing and Ymuiden, and then it was back across the North Sea to Farnborough. The School of Photography worked all night developing and printing so that Cotton could be in Peck's office at 1000 hrs the next morning with an album of enlargements in his brief case.

"Peck opened the meeting and the talk proceeded much as it had done the day before. After half an hour I produced the album. 'Is this the sort of thing you want?' I asked.

Peck examined each print critically and was full of praise for the photography. The places were clearly marked with the respective place-names, but it was taken for granted that they were of pre-war origin . . .

'These are first class,' said Peck, handing the album round, 'but we wouldn't expect this sort of quality in wartime.' I fixed my eye on the middle distance and said nothing. Then someone asked when the prints were taken, and I pulled the pin.

'At three-fifteen yesterday.'"

The room erupted. The air was full of righteous indignation and Cotton was nearly drowned in a sea of injured pride. He left the meeting before he lost his temper.

News of the audacious incident soon spread, and the next day Cotton received an invitation from the Chief of Air Staff (CAS), Air Chief Marshal Sir Cyril Newall, to lunch with him at the United Services Club. Cotton had proved his point to the Air Staff, and so that the Service could benefit from his knowledge the CAS asked him to take charge of photographic reconnaissance in the RAF. Cotton was flattered but hesitant – not only was there a great deal to reorganise but his intrusion would be resented by many regular officers. The existing reconnaissance structure was too hide-bound by the past and had been moving in the wrong direction for far too long for Cotton to change it in 1939; it would be easier to start again with a small organisation staffed by unprejudiced minds, but Cotton only agreed to run it if he was given carte blanche in the choice of men, machines, and equipment. Sir Cyril agreed, and to give the new unit as much freedom as possible he decreed that Cotton should be responsible directly to him through Peck. "All this was too good to be true, and since I had spoken plainly and won my point I felt it was now time to soft-pedal a bit. So I said that I would do my best to keep within the red tape and general organisation of the Air Force. 'For God's sake don't do that, Cotton!' said Newall. 'Your value to me lies in your continuing to do things in your own unorthodox way. I want results.'"

At a meeting under Peck's chairmanship on September 22nd, "it was decided to form an experimental unit for the purpose of testing, and if found to be successful, developing certain novel methods of making photographic reconnaissances over enemy territory. The basis of the scheme was to be high speed and invisibility. In order to make the new unit productive from its inception, machines from other units were to be treated, to produce improved performance and camouflage."

The new unit formed around the SIS nucleus at Heston in the hope that no-one would suspect that secret work was being carried out on a civilian airfield. To make the dubious arrangement acceptable to higher authority, Cotton received the King's Commission as a Squadron Leader with the acting rank of Wing Commander. Bob Niven and Shorty Longbottom were posted in at Cotton's request; Niven had been recalled to active duty on September 2nd and Longbottom arrived from Malta at the end of the month. The establishment was made up to 8 officers, 30 airmen, a staff car, and a 15 cwt lorry, to operate from a small hangar and a wing of the Heston Club. Winterbotham formally handed over control of his SIS Flight to the Air Ministry, and on September 24th a rather surprised C-in-C Fighter Command found that a mysterious 'Heston Flight' had been added to the resources of 11 Group.

Aircraft were the first priority. Cotton, Niven, and Longbottom had discussed the requirements of a good photographic reconnaissance aircraft in Malta before the war, and Longbottom had recorded their conclusions in a Memorandum entitled "Photographic Reconnaissance of Enemy Territory in War", which he had submitted to the Air Ministry in August 1939. It divided reconnaissance into two categories – tactical work in the immediate vicinity of the front line, and strategic reconnaissance of enemy territory behind the area of conflict. As the former was being adequately carried out by the Lysanders of Army Cooperation Command, the Memorandum centred around strategic operations.

Reconnaissance deep into enemy territory, reasoned Longbottom, ran the same risks as a bomber raid; there was no way of silencing the anti-aircraft batteries by bombardment as at the front line, and important targets were likely to be protected by elaborate defences. So far he agreed with Bomber Command who had used the same type of aircraft on both bombing and reconnaissance missions. But Longbottom went further and said that aerial photography was more dangerous than bombing. Bombers could fly in formation and carry defensive armament and did not have to linger over their targets, whereas the reconnaissance aircraft had to stay certainly long enough for the defensive fighter organisation to be brought into operation. Once the bombs had dropped, the strike operation was finished, whereas the photographic pilot still had to get his information back to base. Wireless transmissions would increase the chances of detection.

"Clearly, therefore," wrote Longbottom, "this type of reconnaissance must be done in such a manner as to avoid the enemy fighters and AA defences as completely as possible. The best method of doing this appears to be the use of a single small machine, relying solely on its speed, climb, and ceiling to avoid detection." Such an aircraft would not try to outfight the enemy, as every reconnaissance machine had tried to do since 1914, but would avoid barrage balloons and anti-aircraft fire by altitude and enemy interceptors by speed. If the small single-seater was stripped of radio and armament, it could carry more fuel to extend its range. "As most fighters have a very good take off performance, due to their great reserve of engine power, they could be considerably overloaded with further fuel, giving even greater range."

In clear weather this aeroplane would fly high enough not to be seen or heard by a human observer; its small size would be camouflaged to make it as inconspicuous as possible. In cloudy weather it would operate in or above cloud, just descending for long enough to take photographs and then back up to height again.

The Luftwaffe claimed that their 8.8cm anti-aircraft gun was effective up to 25,000 feet, so Longbottom asked for a machine that could operate around 30,000 feet with a top speed well in excess of 300mph to evade the best German fighter, the Me 109. On the basis of these criteria, the Blenheim IV was a non-starter with its top speed of 266mph at 11,800 feet and an operational ceiling of 22,000 feet. Longbottom wanted the fastest fighter in service, and he concluded that "as speed is one of the most important characteristics it will be assumed that the Spitfire will be used."

With the Memorandum in mind, Cotton went to see the Director General of Research and Development, Air Cdr Tedder, to try to acquire two Spitfires. Tedder spent an hour telling Cotton that Spitfires were like gold, and although they were the aircraft Heston wanted, they were the one type they could not have. Two technical experts with long-suffering faces spent the rest of the day saying that it was technically impossible to fit cameras into a Spitfire, that the Blenheim was the answer to the problem, and finally that the Blenheim was all that Cotton could have. Despite the ample evidence that they were unsuitable, two Blenheim IVs arrived at Heston three days later.

To stand any chance of survival over Germany, the Blenheim needed more speed. In an effort to streamline the whole airframe the Heston workshops filled in all superfluous holes and smoothed or streamlined all projections. A spinner was fitted to each propeller to improve engine cooling so that the gills need not be opened and produce drag, and all the thick manufacturer's dope was stripped off and replaced with a hard, semi-gloss dope which gave a very smooth surface. The result was a performance increase of 18mph, which, although impressive, was nothing like sufficient to escape from the attentions of an Me 109.

The Heston Flight examined every possible British and American aircraft in an attempt to find an alternative to the Spitfire. Cotton's approach infuriated the higher echelons at times. One day he was given a Wellington at Bassingbourne to see if it was suitable for photographic work. For days he experimented with it, cutting holes in the floor and fitting cameras in every available position, until he finally decided it was no use and left it in pieces. Weeks later the RAF asked for the return of its Wellington, only to be told that it had been abandoned at some obscure airfield. "You can have it back now," said Cotton.

Great hopes were pinned on the Westland Whirlwind, but although its twin Peregrine engines were capable of 360mph, its service ceiling was found to be only 28,000 feet. All avenues of investigation turned out to be dead-ends or led back to the Spitfire. Failing Tedder, Cotton decided to make use of the fact that his unit was in Fighter Command to try to talk a Spitfire out of the main operating agency.

Once again the answer was a firm refusal. The C-in-C, ACM Sir Hugh Dowding, had written – "Earnestly request that my Spitfire resources may not be trenched upon for any purpose whatever than home defence fighting." It would take a remarkable man to talk Dowding out of one of his precious Spitfires; Cotton was more than remarkable, he got two.

The two men first met in October 1939. Dowding had been very impressed by Cotton's success in improving Blenheim performance and he visited Heston to see the results for himself. Cotton was invited to tea at Stanmore Park where arrangements were made to 'Cottonize' eight Blenheims a week in a requisitioned British Airways hangar at Heston. As a mark of gratitude Dowding asked if there was anything he could do for the Heston Flight. "'There is one thing, sir,' I said, fully realizing what I was asking and fully expecting a shocked refusal. 'Could you lend me a couple of Spitfires?'

Dowding's face remained for the moment inscrutable. 'What for?'

I expounded my views on the requirements of photographic reconnaissance, and Dowding listened politely enough – even perhaps attentively, I could not tell which. There was a pause when I had finished, and then Dowding spoke.

'When would you like them?'

'Yesterday!'

'Would nine o'clock tomorrow do?'"

At 0900 the following day, two Spitfires landed at Heston.

The first task was to make the sleek fighter even faster. Although the Spitfire I had a top speed of 362mph and was perfectly capable of holding its own against the Me 109, latest intelligence suggested that the Germans were developing a superior fighter, the Me 112U. So the two Spitfires were 'cleaned up' in the Heston workshops; all armament and surplus weight was removed, the gun holes were filled by metal plates and all cracks blocked with plaster of Paris, and all external surfaces were polished into a hard, sleek gloss. The Heston Spitfires were to escape destruction by sheer turn of speed instead of fire-power and their top speed was raised to 396mph.

Then there was the question of range. The Blenheim had a range of 1,950 miles but the basic Spitfire I was only capable of approximately 400 miles. This had to be doubled if Heston was to operate over German territory, but in the long term Cotton wanted an aircraft that could reach Berlin.

Longbottom converted Cotton's ideas into technical practicalities. In his Memorandum he postulated that such ranges were feasible in the Spitfire. Taking the Spitfire I, with a Merlin II engine and VP propeller, the all-up-weight was as follows:

Tare weight	4598 lbs
Service load	658 lbs
84 galls fuel	630 lbs

Oil	49 lbs
TOTAL	5935 lbs

He calculated that they could dispense with up to 450 lbs of Service load, in the form of guns and ammunition, and that the all-up-weight could be safely increased to accommodate more fuel as follows:

Tare weight (including extra tanks)	4650 lbs
Service load (pilot, cameras etc.)	268 lbs
Oil	60 lbs
240 galls. fuel	1880 lbs
TOTAL	6858 lbs

This represented an increase of 15% in all-up-weight, and allowing for 20 galls during taxying and take-off, would increase the range to 1500 miles at 300mph or 1800 miles at 250mph. Starting with 6858 lbs, Longbottom estimated that the service ceiling would be around 30,000 feet, the aircraft having cruise-climbed to height in friendly airspace. After two hours, 800 lbs of fuel would have been used, and the ceiling would have risen to 34,000 feet. During the later stages of the sortie, 35,000 feet would be possible as weight was further reduced – more than enough to cope with the projected altitude of the mysterious Me 112U, which in fact never materialised to worry Heston.

Unfortunately, the Royal Aircraft Establishment (RAE) at Farnborough disagreed violently with Longbottom's calculations. They believed that this extra tankage, together with a fuselage camera, would push the centre of gravity back beyond acceptable limits. Further research was necessary into the range question, but they were willing to allow Heston to install an F 24 camera with a 5 in lens in each wing of one Spitfire. The result was the Spitfire PR IA.[1]

Finally there was the camouflage. The most effective way to escape destruction was to avoid detection in the first place. Back in May 1939, Cotton had been standing at Heston when the Maharajah of Jodhpur departed in his private aeroplane. He soon lost sight of it even though the visibility was very good, because the aircraft had been painted a pale duck-egg green and it had merged into the background. Cotton, ever an astute business man, placed an immediate order with the Titanine Dope Company for a similar paint, registered it as 'Camotint', and used it on the Lockheed before the Red Sea sortie in June. Both Beechcraft and Blenheims were similarly treated, and when the Camotint had dried on the first PR Spitfire, he was ready to put his theories into practice.

As the maximum endurance of the PR IA was less than two hours, Cotton wanted to wait for clearance from the RAE to fit extra fuel tanks so that he could operate over Germany from southern England, but when permission was not forthcoming he decided to begin operations from France. On November 5th, a Special Survey Flight, comprising one Spitfire, its groundcrew, and a doctor to monitor the effects of high altitude flying, was detached

[1] As PR had now become an acceptable abbreviation for photographic reconnaissance, I shall continue to use it throughout this history.

from Heston[1] to Seclin, an airfield 10 miles from the Belgian border near Lille.

On November 18th Shorty Longbottom took off from Seclin on the first operational sortie by a PR Spitfire. He was bound for Aachen but bad weather forced him to return empty-handed. Two days later the Special Survey Flight moved further east to Coulommiers and on November 22nd Longbottom tried again. After refuelling at the forward airfield of Bar le Duc, he managed in the space of 100 minutes to photograph the Eupen-Elsenborn-Spa region of Belgium from 33,000 feet. Three more trial flights over Belgium were planned but they were all thwarted by cloud. However success in Belgian airspace would convince few sceptics – Germany was the real test, and on December 5th the Special Survey Flight moved over to Nancy on the Franco-German border.

Bad weather continued to plague the detachment and it was not until December 29th that Longbottom was able to fly a successful sortie over the Aachen-Cologne area. Niven 'covered' Kaiserlautern on New Year's Day and on January 3rd he photographed Wiesbaden and Mainz while Longbottom flew over part of the Ruhr valley. Low cloud again curtailed operations until January 10th when Longbottom made the final flight of the series over Rötgen-Diekirch.

Broadly speaking, the information brought back from the French flights fell into two categories. First there was the Siegfried Line and its northward extension. The Deuxième Bureau had been concerned about the German defences from Aachen to Bitburg since 1936; the Special Survey Flight provided them with the latest intelligence on the whole fortified line from Cleves to Saarbrucken. The second category was targets for Bomber Command. The Special Flight obtained cover of the Urf-See with its dam, and a mosaic of the Aachen–Cologne–Dusseldorf triangle. In addition the Advanced Air Striking Force was provided with target material in the Moselle and Nahe valleys and around Wiesbaden, Mainz, Kaiserlautern, and Saarbrucken.

Although the solitary Spitfire made only 15 flights, it provided an illuminating contrast to the achievements of the Blenheim IVs. The statistics spoke for themselves. (See Table on p. 56)

During two months and fifteen sorties, one solitary high level Spitfire achieved twice as much in half the time as seven Blenheim squadrons. Four of the abortive Spitfire sorties were due to bad weather; on only one occasion did the pilot have to break off because of interference from a German fighter, and then he left it far behind by opening up to full power.

Cotton had proved that his theories worked. By flying above 30,000 feet in a cleaned-up fighter he had overcome the interception problem; by fitting the wing cameras close to the engines for warmth, and then by ducting a stream of air over the lenses, he had overcome freezing condensation; by bringing back information time and again from one of the most heavily defended areas of the Reich, he achieved respectability for his ideas.

[1] The Heston Flight was re-named No 2 Camouflage Unit on November 1st, 1939 to disguise its true identity.

Photographic Sorties

Formation		*Sorties*	*Sorties when some photos achieved*	*Sorties when no photos achieved*	*Losses*	*% of losses*	*Total area covered*
Blenheim IV (3 Sept. 1939– 31 Dec. 1939)	2 Gp	47	31	16	8	17%	
	70 Wg[1]	42	14	28	8	19%	
	TOTAL	89	45	44	16	18%	2500 sq. mls
Spitfire PR IA (N 3071)	No. 2 Camouflage Unit	15	10	5	0	0%	5000 sq. mls

The work and trials at Heston were vindicated by a meeting held on January 3rd, 1940 to discuss the Requirements for Air Photography. For the first time the RAF accepted that reconnaissance was best carried out by a single machine evading the enemy defences rather than by a formation of armed aircraft trying to fight their way through the opposition. The experience of the Special Survey Flight encouraged further developments, and the conference not only agreed to increase the number of Heston Spitfires but it also ruled that development of PR aircraft should always be kept ahead of contemporary fighter performances. As a measure of its official acceptability, No 2 Camouflage Unit was renamed the Photographic Development Unit (PDU) on January 17th, 1940, with a brief to translate its ideas into operational reality so that high level PR units could eventually replace the Blenheim squadrons of 2 Group and 70 Wing.

The conference also authorised the development of improved aerial cameras. The F 24 with its 5 in lens was totally unsuited to high altitude work; it had been designed for use between 16,000 and 20,000 feet, not up to 36,000 feet where its scale of 1:74,500 was so minute as to be useless for detailed interpretation. Better cameras with longer focal length lenses were the long term answer; in the meantime 8 in lenses would be fitted to the F 24 whenever possible, giving 1:46,500 scale prints.

Cotton was also ensuring that the RAF got the best out of his prints. The two Photo-Interpreters (PIs) at Heston had been able to extract little detailed information from the first Spitfire photographs because they lacked both experience and modern equipment, so Cotton turned to an old friend, Major 'Lemnos' Hemming, who had looked after his aerial survey department in Newfoundland nearly twenty years earlier and who in December 1939 was running an aerial survey business in Wembley known as the Aircraft Operating Company. Hemming's firm enjoyed several advantages over the Interpretation Section at Heston in that it employed several skilled PIs and had the latest sophisticated equipment, a huge Swiss Wild[2] photogrammetric

[1] 18 and 57 Sqns in France.

[2] Pronounced 'Vilt'. Photogrammetry is the science of obtaining reliable measurements of objects from their photographic images.

machine. This instrument magnified prints by a factor of nine and also acted as a stereoscope to allow viewing through three dimensions. From 34,000 feet the 5 in square prints from an F 24 camera barely revealed a battleship; under the Wild machine a PI could tell it was the 'Tirpitz'.

Business had declined for the Aircraft Operating Company with the outbreak of war, and, as Wembley was only fifteen miles from Heston, Cotton suggested to Peck that they employ Hemming's facilities. Peck was sceptical so Cotton decided to use Wembley unofficially. It was a gross violation of the Official Secrets Act but Cotton felt perfectly justified because "there was a war on".

At the beginning of 1940 the Admiralty was particularly interested in photographs of the Jade estuary in preparation for a surprise motor torpedo boat attack on shipping in Wilhelmshaven in February. But before Cotton could accept the task he had first to overcome the range problem. Farnborough had relented slightly on the question of fuel and they were willing to allow the installation of a 29 gallon tank behind the pilot but no more. This variant, with a pair of F 24 wing cameras, was known as the PR IB, and the first one was collected from Farnborough by Longbottom on January 16th.

The PR IB had a safe range of 750 miles, and by using forward airfields in East Anglia such as Debden, Stradishall, Bircham Newton, and Horsham St Faith, the aircraft could reach the ports of NW Germany. No time was lost in trying to cover the Jade, and at 1255 hrs on January 18th, Longbottom took off from Bircham Newton for Wilhelmshaven. About 50 miles out from the Norfolk coast he ran into cloud and had to return empty-handed. Two days later he was again baulked by 10/10 cloud over the German coast.

Longbottom had to wait until February 10th to try again. By now the priorities had changed because Naval Intelligence had received a report that the new battleship 'Tirpitz' had left its graving dock at Wilhelmshaven. The Blenheims could neither confirm nor deny the report, so the Admiralty had to remain in suspense until February 10th to see if the massive vessel had put to sea. Longbottom left Debden at 1205 hrs and it was a relief to see the ground below as he crossed the German coast just south of Emden at 33,000 feet. He switched on the cameras over Emden and, after a run over the port, turned for Wilhelmshaven. While over the Schillig Roads he spotted a formation of twin-engined aircraft 20,000 feet below, but as they were heading away from him he continued northwards to Wangerooge before doubling back to Emden and home. The sortie had lasted for 3 hours and 20 minutes and had brought back the first photographs of enemy territory taken by a Spitfire from a British base. By virtue of the Wild machine, a young PI named Michael Spender was able to say that the Tirpitz was still in its graving dock; as a bonus, he also used the prints to produce some superb maps of the ports of Emden and Wilhelmshaven.

The Wilhelmshaven cover was shown to the First Sea Lord, Winston Churchill, and on February 13th he wrote to the Secretary of State for Air, Kingsley Wood, saying that the Navy was so impressed by the Wembley interpretation that if the RAF did not take over the Aircraft Operating Company, they most certainly would. Six weeks later Major Hemming received a letter saying that the Air Ministry wished to requisition his organisation.

Another result of the Emden-Wilhelmshaven prints was a desire for more. On February 15th, the PDU was instructed to reconnoitre Heligoland, Brunsbuttel, Cuxhaven, and Bremerhaven at the earliest possible opportunity, "with the object of locating units, flotilla craft and submarines of the German Navy." By February 19th the Air Ministry had accorded Heligoland first priority, but it made little difference – bad weather prevented PR anywhere over the German coast for ten days.

The PR Spitfire was not equipped to cope with very bad weather. A solitary pilot, devoid of all but the simplest navigational instruments, had great difficulty finding a distant pin-point covered by cloud. He also lacked the fuel reserves to wander around Europe 'unsure of his position'. The PDU pilots of 1940 were very much restricted to photographing what they could see.

As meteorological information on Germany was not very forthcoming, and as there was not time to wait for a clear blue sky, many aircraft took off in the hope that there would be breaks in the cloud where it mattered. More often than not these missions were fruitless in winter – out of the nineteen operational Spitfire sorties flown by the PDU during the first quarter of 1940, only six were successful and most of the remaining thirteen were thwarted by weather. A failure rate of 68% was unacceptable, especially as the Navy wanted photographs 'yesterday', so Cotton devised the 'H' plan. He had ordered three Lockheed Hudsons the previous November, and the first arrived in February to be converted to the PR role. The idea was to send a Hudson, with its crew of three including a navigator, to the target area if the weather was poor. It would follow the same route as the Spitfire and if the crew found that the weather was clear over Germany they would radio back to Heston and a Spitfire would get airborne. If the weather was bad, the Hudson would descend through cloud to the target area, drop below the cloud base just long enough to take the necessary photographs, and climb back into the safety of the clouds again.

At the beginning of February a young Flying Officer named Denis Slocum arrived at Heston to captain the Hudson. 'Slogger' Slocum had been posted to Scotland when he left his job as an airline pilot to join the RAF, but he flew at Heston while on leave and liked the atmosphere so much that he talked his CO into letting him transfer to the PDU.

The 'H' plan soon proved its worth. Slocum's crew flew eight missions between February 21st and March 2nd, and on all eight occasions the W/T operator had to report that the weather was too bad for a Spitfire and that they were going in themselves. Their most successful trip was on February 29th. Slocum broke cloud at 300 feet over Brunsbuttel, swept past the concentrated AA batteries, and up into the clouds again. There was no chance of a second run; the gunners might be caught unprepared the first time but they would be waiting for the second fly-past. Slocum brought back some excellent obliques of the Elbe estuary showing, among other things, an old battleship of the Schlesian class and details of the estuary defences.

After evading both Luftwaffe and weather on eight missions, Slocum was to lose his life in the most tragic circumstances. On March 2nd the PDU turned its attentions to the Ruhr, and as the skies were clear enough for a Spitfire sortie, the Hudson was sent to photograph Gravesend airfield. At 7,000 feet over the Kent countryside the unusual pale-green Hudson was intercepted by a Hurricane of Fighter Command and shot down in flames. The crew signalled their identification in vain. "They say our rear turret opened fire," recorded Cotton's diary. "We have no turret." Only Sgt J. A. M. Reid, the co-pilot, survived – he had been shot down by his own side once before over the Firth of Forth and he wryly told Cotton that he might do better if he changed sides. The PDU had suffered its first casualties of the war and from now on all Hudsons would be fitted with IFF.[1]

It was in February that Cotton first met Ludlow-Hewitt. Like the Navy, Bomber Command was not getting the intelligence material it required, and the C-in-C asked Cotton to lay on a mission to provide target mosaics of the industrial centres in the Ruhr.

There were three Spitfires available at Heston by the end of February – the original PR IA for training, and two PR IBs – and it was in one of the latter that Bob Niven took off on March 2nd for the Ruhr. By the time he crossed the Rhine he was at 30,000 feet and ready to switch on his cameras over Duisberg. Niven flew eastwards down the Ruhr valley, first to Essen, then Bochum, and on to Dortmund before turning round to parallel his outbound track back to the Rhine. The F 24s photographed the whole industrial area and were only switched off at the German frontier, whereupon Niven headed south round the edge of Holland and Belgium for home. The Luftwaffe put in an appearance as Niven approached the Luxembourg border, but by opening up to full throttle he left three Me 109s behind as though they were standing still.

The following day Cotton sent a second sortie to the Ruhr. This time the pilot was a newcomer to the PDU, Flt Lt Eric le Mesurier, who photographed the region immediately to the north-west of the Ruhr valley, including the strategically important towns of Emmerich, Duisberg, Kempen, and Geldern. The results of Niven's and Le Mesurier's efforts were processed, plotted, interpreted, and then re-photographed into a single annotated mosaic of the Ruhr complex. Cotton, ever the showman, took a copy of the mosaic to Ludlow-Hewitt and unrolled the large photograph before the C-in-C as though he was pulling a rabbit out of a hat. Ludlow-Hewitt's eyes, growing ever wider with amazement and delight, were his great reward.[2]

[1] Identification Friend or Foe. IFF equipment transmits a signal which is superimposed on the blip produced by the aircraft on a ground radar screen to show the Fighter Controllers that it is not an enemy intruder.

[2] Other accolades were forthcoming as well. On March 21st, Niven and Longbottom were awarded the DFC.

If the PDU went some way towards compensating for the deficiencies of 2 Group in the United Kingdom, no such assistance was forthcoming to 70 Wing in France. Yet if anything their problems were greater. They were tasked with providing strategic reconnaissance in a zone bounded by a curving line drawn from 51° on the Dutch border, through Munchen-Gladbach, Dusseldorf, Paderborn, and Hildesheim, and northwards to Lubeck, with the aim of investigating any extension of the Siegfried Line and detecting any preparations to invade the Low Countries. Up to the end of 1939, the two squadrons of 70 Wing lost eight aircraft and their crews, excluding non-operational losses, in an effort to secure 1,450 prints, of which 255 were wholly or partially spoilt. "Despite the persistent efforts that were made," said a report on the War Employment of the Air Component, "and the comparatively high price that was paid in crews and aircraft lost, the reconnaissance may be said to have failed in its object, in as much as nothing of a decisive nature was discovered right up to the last moment."

In January 1940 the CAS approved the creation of a special strategic reconnaissance unit in France, and the Commander of the British Air Forces in France, Air Marshal Sir Arthur Barratt, was officially informed that the new squadron would be under his operational control while remaining "from the photographic aspect, under the technical control and technical administration of the Officer Commanding the Photographic Development Unit at Heston". This arrangement was open to criticism. A divided chain of responsibility creates problems in a military service for ideally every man should have only one master, but not for the last time it was decided that PR was a special case. Barratt accepted the restrictions on his power because he realised that the PDU needed flexibility if it was to operate successfully in the fluid environment of France.

The arrival of the special strategic PR unit in France allowed Barratt to release 70 Wg to concentrate on their primary bombing role. The new squadron should have been called 'PDU (Overseas Section)', for so it was, but it was christened 212 Sqn in deference to Cotton's objections. Cotton believed that it was just as important for the PDU to remain unnoticed on the ground as it was for it to be inconspicuous in the air. Once the Germans discovered their true role in France, the unit would become a prime target for Luftwaffe raids. Anonymity and secrecy were essential; hence the misleading squadron title and the separate hangar at Lille/Seclin airfield into which a returning Spitfire would taxi, shut down, and be left under lock and key while the pilots and groundcrew returned to a local hotel, where they were billeted away from other personnel with orders to keep themselves to themselves.

The initial establishment for 212 Sqn comprised a headquarters staff, based at Tigeaux close to Barratt's HQ at Coulommiers, and three flights totalling, by June, 12 officers, 51 other ranks, and 8 Spitfires. In practice though, 212 Sqn was just a detachment of the PDU with personnel and aircraft interchanging between Heston and France at regular intervals.

On January 18th, 1940, barely a week after the return of the Special Survey Flight from Nancy, Niven flew the first 212 Sqn Spitfire out to Seclin. Cotton had been out to Coulommiers a few days earlier to discuss priorities with 'Ugly' Barratt. It transpired that Barratt was under pressure from the Commander of the British Expeditionary Force (BEF), General Lord Gort, for cover of the Belgian plain between Namur and Antwerp. Gort feared that the Germans would try to outflank the Maginot Line by dashing across the Low Countries to the Channel ports as in 1914 before turning south to occupy Paris. The Allied response would be to move from their positions on the Franco-Belgian border and to swing northwards to join up with the Dutch and Belgian armies in an attempt to stem the advance. To plan for this eventuality, Gort needed modern maps, but the Dutch and Belgians refused to cooperate in providing information for fear of antagonising Hitler. On December 19th, 1939, Gort had written to the War Office:

"The existing British maps of Belgium have been prepared from material which is in considerable need of revision, being based on a survey dating back to before 1914. The only way of meeting our deficiency is to obtain suitable air photographs, and then revise our maps. Otherwise, the British Expeditionary Force will be faced with fighting with obsolete maps of the operational area."

70 Wing could not help, as a conspicuous Blenheim over neutral Belgium would cause a diplomatic incident. A PDU Spitfire was the answer, but even then the operation had to be authorised unofficially because the Air Ministry would have to veto the proposal for political reasons if it came to their attention. Barratt was fortunate in dealing with a man who was totally unconcerned with regulations and 'official channels', and Cotton agreed to photograph Belgium. The story was put about that the Seclin Spitfires were part of an advanced training course for reconnaissance pilots – being so close to the border there was always a chance that the trainees might get 'lost' and find themselves over Belgian territory.

On January 19th, Niven started what were to be esoterically termed the X Series sorties. Between the middle of January and March 29th, a solitary Spitfire surveyed Belgium in a series of strips running north to south in the east, and then sloping obliquely in the west. The Belgians remained officially oblivious of what was going on – the only opposition was the weather. Nevertheless 212 Sqn virtually completed the task, ending only when the lone Spitfire was written off. On March 29th a pilot got lost, and by the time he discovered his true position he was forced to land at Laval airfield through lack of fuel. At the end of the landing run the Spitfire struck a patch of soft ground and went up on its nose. Cotton was furious. To his mind the worst crime of all was to fail to get back to base with the prints; he dismissed the pilot from his unit on the spot.

After each X sortie the films were flown back to Heston in the Lockheed for processing and interpretation. Although the prints were very small in scale – 1:46,500 with an 8 in lens, or 1:74,500 with a 5 in lens – Wembley managed to produce plans of 30 Belgian airfields to a scale of 1:10,000 by use of the Wild machine.

During the latter half of March, Seclin extended its scope of operations to encompass the Rhine between the Dutch frontier and Dusseldorf. The French C-in-C, General Georges, feared that the Germans might be massing pontoons and bridge-building equipment on their side of the Rhine, and as the HQ of the French Chief of Air Staff was near Tigeaux, they asked 212 Sqn for help. Between March 18th and 29th, the Spitfire IB took off seven times from Seclin, but each mission ended in failure because of the weather.

The first months of 1940 were a time of considerable expansion in the PDU – the Hudsons alone necessitated an extra six pilots, four observers and four photographers. By April 12th the establishment had grown to 28 officers and 278 other ranks, whose duties could be divided into three main categories. First there were the administrators – the operations officers, the equippers, and the photographic and intelligence staffs. They were the hub of the PDU and Cotton chose his staff officers as carefully as he selected his pilots. Because the CAS had given him carte blanche in recruitment, Cotton picked the best brains available, both inside and outside the Service. He turned to his contacts in the City of London – men of wealth, education, and experience of responsibility, who did not relish the thought of wasting their talents as conscripts. To these men Cotton offered a chance to use their flair and initiative in an organisation not bound by restrictions and bureaucracy. The whole business was highly irregular – Cotton thought nothing of commissioning a good businessman as a Squadron Leader on the spot. But it was invaluable in providing the PDU with an administrative corps d'élite – men who were not afraid to wield authority, make decisions, and if equipment was not readily available, provide it out of their large private fortunes. They were to build the PR organisation that was to stand the RAF in good stead throughout the war.

Then there were the pilots. At first the call went out for volunteers with Spitfire experience to join a 'hush-hush' outfit, but Cotton soon discovered that the average 'fighter-type' was no use to him. PR was a specialised art that needed special qualities. It took a cool head and steady nerves to fly alone for hours deep into enemy airspace, without a navigator or a radio for company and assistance, in the freezing cold above 30,000 feet. The sortie did not end once the aircraft had reached the target; a bomber pilot had justified his existence once he had dropped his bombs but a PR pilot still had to get his films home. Most fighter pilots were mentally unsuited to this work. They had been conditioned to fly for short periods of time, protected by guns and defensive formations, and encouraged by a constant radio background of directions, chatter, and volatile utterances. It was anathema to them to run away from trouble. They were marvellous in the hectic skies of the Battle of Britain but out of their depth in the rarefied and lonely environment of the PDU. There were no reassuring ·303 machine guns in the PR Spitfires.

Peck wrote to the Director of Postings in April to clarify the PDU requirements. "The fighter-pilot is not ordinarily suitable. Long distance reconnaissance in a single seater requires a skilful air pilotage and a temperament or aptitude different from that primarily required of a fighter-pilot. The knowledge which strategical reconnaissance bomber or army cooperation pilots possess is most valuable and suitable. As the Spitfire is unarmed it is most desirable that the pilot should have had experience of the war conditions which will confront him in the air, otherwise he runs a grave risk of being surprised. In view of the great height which has to be maintained for long periods by the Spitfire pilots, special physical endurance and resistance to the effects of altitude are necessary."

To find such men, Cotton turned to the Fairey Battle squadrons with the Advanced Air Striking Force (AASF) in France. Battle pilots were used to long reconnaissance sorties and self navigation, because the Battle navigator sat down in the aircraft well, away from the pilot and out of sight of the ground except for a hatch that looked vertically downwards. As the navigator could not see where the aircraft was going, the pilot often had to navigate for him.

There was no shortage of volunteers from the AASF to fly "something very fast". Many pilots were tired of the Phoney War in the Spring of 1940 and wanted to do something more positive to help the war effort. The first Battle pilots to be posted in to Heston to join Longbottom and Niven were Eric le Mesurier, Fg Off Alistair Taylor, Fg Off Spencer Ring, and Fg Off Wheatley. One of those not selected at first was Fg Off S. G. 'Billy' Wise on 105 Sqn at Rheims. His CO turned down his application to go to Heston and sent Wheatley instead. Wise was so fed up with kicking his heels in France that he went off to beat up the airfield in disgust.

Conversion and training at Heston were very rudimentary. None of the Battle pilots had any experience of high-speed single-seater fighters, and most had never flown much above 10,000 feet before. There were no such sophisticated aids as Pilots' Notes either – Cotton just showed them a Spitfire, pointed out the essential controls, and off they went to convert themselves on to type. No-one complained; the Battle flew like a lorry in comparison with the Spitfire.

Then came the 'do-it-yourself' course in aerial photography. Accuracy was not too difficult – the short-lensed F 24 photographed a very large area with each exposure. The standard operating procedure for uncomplicated high level photography was to navigate to a pre-arranged ground feature, trim the aircraft straight and level, switch on the cameras and hold a steady course until the run was completed. For a vertical exposure the pilot raised a wing, looked down to confirm he was tracking straight over the target, levelled the wings, and pressed the button on top of the control column. To take obliques he tracked parallel to the target. The only variable was the time interval between each exposure. The PIs needed a 60% fore and aft, and a 30% sideways, overlap on each print, and each pilot carried a card giving the time interval (TI) required depending on the height, ground-speed, and camera focal length.[1] After a few trial runs over southern England, a new pilot was sent off to photograph a relatively easy target like Flushing or Calais. It took approximately ten hours to convert a Battle pilot on to type and role; when Bill Wise

[1] The longer the focal length, the less the area covered by each photograph, and therefore the greater the number of exposures required for a given area.

was posted in to replace Wheatley, he arrived at Heston on April 8th and was operational at Seclin seventeen days later. There were no special clothing, no decompression tests, no pressurisation or cabin heating; PDU flying was simply a matter of wrapping up in the warmest clothing one had, ascending to the highest altitudes known to man, and of practising techniques one had never even heard of a month earlier, deep inside the airspace of the greatest military power on earth.

The third category at Heston comprised the workshops and servicing personnel. There was a full-time commitment to 'Cottonize' Blenheims for Fighter and Bomber Commands, as well as the operational and training flights to maintain. Engineering work increased four-fold between November 1939 and January 1940, and the number of missions doubled between February and April 1940 as the PDU changed from an experimental into an operational unit.

Most crucial of all was the development work on the PR Spitfire. As Supermarines had no spare capacity to devote to such a specialist requirement, basic fighter types were delivered to Heston where all research and development, trials and modifications were carried out. Cotton had to make improvements in easy stages, primarily to placate the RAE who would only approve one modification at a time, and also because the workshops were unable to cope with too many structural alterations at once.

Only three Spitfire PR IBs were built, and on March 18th, 1940 the first PR IC was rolled out of the workshops. This was the first PR Spitfire to have a fuselage camera; it had taken six months to convince Farnborough that an F 24 fuselage camera would not drastically displace the aircraft's centre of gravity. The canopy also sported a Perspex blister to enable the pilot to see straight downwards; designed by Cotton, these blisters greatly improved all-round vision from the cockpit, and they became a standard feature on all subsequent PR variants, as well as on many other RAF aircraft. In addition to the standard 85 gallons fighter fuel load and the 29 gallon tank of the PR IB, the IC incorporated a 30 gallon bulge tank in the starboard wing, balanced by a pair of F 24s under the port wing. The IC had a safe range of 900 miles, which brought Kiel into range, but it was only an intermediate stage in the campaign Cotton was pursuing to try to develop the really long-range, high performance aircraft envisaged in the Longbottom Memorandum.

As the PDU expanded Cotton decided that he needed an assistant to deal with the staff-work while he dashed back and forth across the Channel in the Lockheed to cajole and encourage his pilots. The obvious choice was Cotton's deputy at the time, Sqn Ldr Hugh MacPhail, a Great War pilot of considerable experience, who left his secure position with a Peruvian airline to rejoin the RAF in 1939 and fly at Heston. But MacPhail was also a flying man with neither the time nor the inclination to get involved in paperwork. The PDU needed a regular serving officer who could organise and administrate, deal with higher authority in a tactful manner, and who knew enough about the Service machine to work within it rather than against it.

Such a man was Sqn Ldr G. W. Tuttle, DFC. Geoffrey Tuttle was an ex-fighter pilot and AI flying instructor who became an engineer in order to get a permanent commission and then spent the rest of his RAF career trying to keep away from engineering. He was attached to the AASF in France in 1940 and Barratt was so impressed with his abilities as an administrator that he recommended Tuttle to Cotton as the very man for the PDU. On February 9th, after considerable pressure on the Air Ministry from Cotton, Geoffrey Tuttle was posted in to Heston as second in command.

Up to the German invasion of the Low Countries the Heston Flight, designated N Flight to differentiate it from 212 Sqn, was primarily involved in work for the Admiralty. As most of the Spitfires had moved over to France, N Flight was usually restricted to one aircraft and a couple of pilots to cover the ports of NW Germany. With the loss of the solitary Hudson, the H plan had to be put into abeyance until replacements arrived.

On March 22nd, the PDU lost its first Spitfire in action. Fg Off Wheatley took off from Stradishall in the original PR IB at 11 15 hrs and was never seen again. He was reportedly shot down at noon near Arnhem on the Dutch border, and it was assumed that he descended to stop making a condensation trail and was surprised by an enemy fighter. It was an important lesson for the PDU. Contrails were the main drawback to high level PR; a ground observer might not be able to see or hear a Spitfire above 30,000 feet, but he could clearly distinguish the long contrail streaming out behind it. Shorty Longbottom, the technical mentor of the PDU, had written a paper on 'Condensation Trails at High Altitude' in December 1939. "It has been found," he wrote, "that at high altitude over about 8,000 metres (27,000 feet), under certain conditions, aircraft in flight leave behind them a dense white trail of condensation . . .[1] The accuracy of AA fire possible under these circumstances may be judged from the fact that, on December 21st, 1939, whilst the Spitfire from this Unit was in the vicinity of Waxweiler (to the NNW of Trier) at a height of about 9,700 metres (32,000 feet), and was leaving a very pronounced condensation trail, out of some 20 or 30 shots fired at it, the average error was about $\frac{1}{4}$ to $\frac{1}{2}$ mile in direction, and about 200 feet in height, but some shots were much nearer, one being almost exact for height, and about 50 yards ahead of the machine."

To avoid the contrail layer, which usually manifests itself between 27,000 feet and 40,000 feet over southern England, a pilot had either to increase height to fly within the stratosphere, or descend to where the air is warmer so that condensation does not take place. In 1940, the first solution was out of the question so, to stop trailing, a pilot had to descend below 27,000 feet. But this meant exchanging one dilemma for another. "In the case of the aircraft of

[1] One of the combustion products of aviation fuels is water; this is ejected through the exhaust and tends to raise the relative humidity of the air behind the engines. At the same time, the heat generated by the engines tends to lower the relative humidity by raising the air temperature in the engine wake. The net result in certain conditions is to increase the humidity to saturation point so that a condensation trail is formed behind the aircraft. This phenomenum is usually confined to a critical air temperature band, averaging 10–20,000 feet in thickness, known as the contrail layer.

this Unit," wrote Longbottom, "it is highly undesirable to make a descent to that height over enemy territory, owing to the chances of encountering enemy fighters. These could almost certainly be outdistanced if seen in time, but in a small single-seater one might not always see an enemy making a cunning approach to attack at a height where his performance has not been badly impaired by the falling off of power, climb, speed etc."

Wheatley found himself on the horns of this dilemma. It was likely that he was trailing and so he descended to make himself less conspicuous, only to be 'bounced' by an interceptor who was probably climbing up to investigate the contrail. Many ideas were propounded to minimise the risks – rear view mirrors were fitted to PR aircraft, not as is popularly believed to see if fighters were sneaking up behind, but to see if the aircraft was trailing. But no real solution could be found until engines were developed to take reconnaissance aircraft above the critical temperature layer. Then contrails became an ally – many a PR pilot owed his survival to the early sighting of an enemy interceptor climbing up towards him, invisible save for the tell-tale trail. Until then there was no alternative but extended eye-balls for the duration of a sortie.

Eric le Mesurier flew the IC type on its first mission on March 22nd. He tried to photograph the island of Sylt after a Bomber Command raid but was forced back by cloud. Four times between March 22nd and April 6th, le Mesurier and Longbottom, the duty pilots at Heston while everyone else was in France, tried to confirm Longbottom's calculations that the PR IC could reach Kiel. This port was particularly important at the time. The Admiralty had originally requested cover of the dockyards at Bremen, Bremerhaven, Hamburg, and the submarine pens at Neustadt, but when a formation of returning Whitleys reported that every ship in the German Navy appeared to be moving towards Lübeck and Kiel, these ports moved to the top of the priority list. At the fifth attempt on April 7th, Longbottom finally overcame the weather, airframe icing, and engine troubles which had baulked previous sorties, and got through to Kiel. Two cameras broke down as he approached the Holtenau end of the Kiel canal, and after the port had been photographed the third stopped working over Brunsbuttel. At 33,000 feet between Brunsbuttel and Cuxhaven he saw a German fighter 1,000 feet below, but he shook it off without difficulty.

The prints showed that the port of Kiel was crammed with shipping and that the Holtenau airfield was bursting at the seams with line after line of Ju 52 transports. Two days later the whole lot was thrown into the invasion of Norway and Denmark.

The lessons of the First World War were being re-learned. One set of prints in isolation told little – and the PIs in Britain had no yardstick with which to compare the activity at Kiel. Had the IC type been available a few months earlier, it would have photographed a much emptier port in February, and everyone would have been sure on April 7th that something was being planned. As it was, no-one could tell with any certainty that the activity at Kiel was anything out of the ordinary.

With only one Spitfire at Heston, N Flight could only concentrate on one priority at a time, and for the rest of April this was the anchorages of Heligoland. On May 1st, at the fifth time of trying, le Mesurier overcame the weather and brought back vertical photographs of Heligoland as well as pictures of "ships heading NE between Borkum and Heligoland". The Air Ministry emphasised the value to the Navy of any visual sightings of shipping which the PDU might make, and pilots were encouraged to switch on their cameras over any vessels of interest.

On his return from Heligoland, le Mesurier's oil pressure gauge fell to zero, and as if to demonstrate the close ties between Heston and 212 Sqn he diverted into Seclin. Two days later both he and Longbottom were back in France to take their turn with 212 Sqn, while 'Spen' Ring and Bill Wise took their place at Heston.

212 Sqn by now was divided into two Flights, both concentrating on watching for signs of a pending German invasion of France or the Low Countries. 'A' Flight was concerned with photography over the Rhine from Cologne to Mainz, operating from Seclin until April 11th and then from Meaux /Villenoy. Meaux was the main centre of French photo-interpretation and this expertise was placed at Cotton's disposal so that, with the two photographic processing trailers delivered to the squadron on March 21st, Barratt's staff did not have to wait on Heston for the delivery of their prints. While A Flight was responsible for the region immediately behind the Dutch frontier, B Flight at Nancy watched the area to the south of Koblenz. They were much more productive than A Flight; there was seldom more than one Spitfire at Meaux, and between April 11th and May 10th flying was possible on only nine days. Out of thirteen sorties, six failed because of low cloud, three had to be abandoned because of contrails, and out of the remaining four, only three pilots found their targets and two of these were frustrated by the breakdown of the port camera.

B Flight also started off with one aircraft, entrusted to Flt Lt Clark and Fg Off Taylor. Their work started where A Flight left off and involved a watch on the Rhine from Koblenz to Mannheim for signs of new bridge construction.

On April 16th, Fg Off C. D. Milne ferried another Spitfire over from Seclin. He also brought fine weather with him and the next few days saw a burst of reconnaissance activity. The French had asked for several special tasks from Nancy – cover of the Danube petroleum refineries between Bratislava and Regensburg, the locks along the Ludwig canal from the Danube to the Main, the Main from Bamberg to Mainz, the Neckar from Plochingen to Mannheim, and the Brenner Pass for good measure. Four sorties on April 19th and 20th covered the Rhine down to Basle, and on April 21st Milne tried to photograph the Brenner Pass, but he had to be content with the north shores of Lake Constance because of cloud. He went up again that day to try to finish the surveillance of the Ludwig canal started that morning by Taylor, but Milne never came back. He was shot down in the IA-type over Bavaria.

During the next two days the remaining Spitfire completed photography over the Brenner and its surrounding countryside from 33,000 feet before the weather clamped down once more. By the time the clouds lifted Germany had invaded the Low Countries and there were more important targets to cover.

On May 7th, three days before the Germans launched their assault, Cotton went to see Barratt with a negative exposed the previous day. The pilot had been filling in certain gaps remaining from the X series task and he had left his cameras running as he crossed the Luxembourg-Germany border. Below stretched the wooded countryside of the Ardennes, a forested area hitherto regarded as a natural barrier against armoured vehicles. The Ardennes played a great part in Allied strategic thinking, for their defensive plan, should the Germans attack, had been based on three considerations. First, that the Maginot Line, stretching from the Swiss frontier to Longwy, was impregnable; second, that the wooded Ardennes between Longwy and Namur would prohibit the movement of large forces, especially armoured ones; and finally, that because of these two considerations the Germans would resurrect the Schlieffen Plan of 1914 and drive across the Belgian plain. For this reason, British reconnaissance efforts had concentrated on the Belgian-German border, yet when the Spitfire magazines were unloaded on May 6th, a young PI, Plt Off Douglas Kendall, identified a number of tanks beneath the Ardennes foliage.

Barratt ordered an immediate low-level PR sortie to confirm the sighting, and when the Spitfire returned Kendall estimated that some 400 tanks were massed in the 'impassable' area. Barratt immediately informed the Air Ministry but they gave his report little credence, so on May 9th, Cotton was dispatched with copies of the prints to Bomber Command. "Barratt's idea was that a strong force from Bomber Command should be briefed to shower incendiaries on the forest area beyond the Luxembourg border, starting forest fires which might develop into major conflagrations. Our photographs showed that these areas were thick with tanks, ammunition dumps, armoured vehicles, and petrol and oil supplies, which would certainly add to the blaze."

Unfortunately for Cotton, Ludlow-Hewitt had been replaced at High Wycombe by Sir Charles Portal, and the interview was not a success. It was hardly surprising that the C-in-C, faced by an unknown Wing Commander brandishing numerous photographs and pleading that Bomber Command suspend all operations to concentrate on the forests of Luxembourg, should remain unconvinced. Bomber Command received its taskings from the War Cabinet, and as no one in London was willing to accept the evidence of the 212 Sqn prints, either because their implication was unpalatable or because they suspected a ruse, there was nothing that Portal could do. "Unless we can convince them and get them to take appropriate action at once," Barratt had told Cotton, "it might be disastrous." They did not and it was; the next day the panzers crossed the Moselle.

Hitler, having realised that the Allies would expect a repeat performance of the Schlieffen Plan, had decided that his armoured divisions "should be concentrated in the direction of Sedan, where the enemy does not expect our main thrust." Against the advice of his senior military advisers, Hitler accepted an audacious scheme proposed by one of his junior commanders, von Manstein, code-named 'Sichelschnitt' – the cut of the sickle. Army Group B was to be launched against southern Holland and northern Belgium, to act as a 'matador's cloak' to the Allies who were expecting the main thrust to come in this area. However the actual offensive would come further south, between Aachen and Luxembourg, where von Kleist's panzer Group would spearhead the attack by Army Group A, designed to enter France between Namur and Sedan, drive at full speed for Amiens, and cut off the Allied armies that had rushed to the north of the Somme to counter the feint by Army Group B.

It is interesting, though academic, to speculate on what might have been. If only Cotton's photographs had been accepted in London (and there were other reports, such as that from the French attaché in Berne, to suggest that the main German effort was to be made at Sedan), and if Bomber Command had dropped everything to drop everything on the Ardennes, where seven out of the ten panzer divisions in the German army were concentrated, the history of the Second World War might well have been different.

The lessons were obvious, as lessons usually are with hindsight. No military man, unless he is a fool, will attack where or when his opponent expects him, and conversely, a defender is asking a great deal if he prepares for an attack in his own time and on his strongest positions. The Ardennes, Pearl Harbour, and Singapore bear witness to the value of audacious and unconventional planning, and provide a mocking epitaph to outdated and complacent thinking. "These generals are too correct," lamented Hitler; "no tricks ever occur to them." There is a great temptation in war to believe that what is beyond the technical or intellectual capacity of one's own side is also beyond that of one's opponent. The aerial camera should never be regarded as an infallible oracle, but neither should its findings be accepted only when they substantiate accepted shibboleths and ignored when they reveal unpalatable truths.

When the Germans attacked, Barratt recalled the 212 Sqn detachments to Meaux to be near his HQ at Coulommiers. The squadron, now commanded by Flt Lt Douglas Wilson, an ex-Blenheim pilot from 40 Sqn, was Barratt's only strategic reconnaissance force – 70 Wing had been released for bombing duties and the only other purely reconnaissance aircraft in France were the army cooperation Lysanders. Every morning Wilson received a telegram from Coulommiers via the French signals section listing the targets for the day in order of precedence. He would choose which ones they were to go for, depending on the weather, and allocate tasks to particular pilots.

On May 10th there was still no indication that the Germans were planning anything other than a sweep through the Low Countries. The Armée de l'Air was responsible for the Ardennes, and Barratt detailed 212 Sqn to photograph parts of Belgium on behalf of Lord Gort. The Squadron was not really involved with the Ardennes breakthrough until May 14th. The crux of von Manstein's plan was to secure a bridgehead across the Meuse before the French could bring up reinforcements, and it was therefore imperative that the fortifications at Sedan were taken before the Allies realised what was happening. In this the Germans were not hindered by the inefficient reconnaissance formations of the French air force.

The failure by the Armée de l'Air to discover the German build-up in the Ardennes, or to appreciate the importance of the thrust when it started, provided an illuminating contrast to 212 Sqn. "After the loss of several planes," wrote Alistair Horne,[1] "at the end of September 1939 the Bloch 131s were withdrawn from daylight operations and put on night work only, the Bréguet and Potez reconnaissance planes were instructed to operate only 'behind battery positions', and the Moreaux were permitted to 'approach between one and two kilometres from the lines, on condition that they operated in patrols of two'. General Ruby wrote that the French reconnaissance aircraft 'could not pass over our lines except under fear of death'. Less charitably, Air Marshal Barratt, who from the very first had been appalled at the apathy and defeatism that he found in the French Air Force, declared that their reconnaissance teams simply 'would not leave the floor, often they gave the *excuse* that the weather was too bad.'"

The French were demoralised before they started. Unlike 212 Sqn, they lacked faith in their cause, their leaders, and their aircraft; bad weather was a welcome excuse rather than a frustration. Antoine de St Exupéry, poet and reconnaissance pilot with Group 2-33, committed the innermost thoughts of his contemporaries to paper:[2]

"In all seriousness the Staffs issue orders that never reach anybody. They ask us for intelligence impossible to provide. But the air arm cannot undertake to explain war to the Staffs. Reconnaissance pilots might be able to test or verify the Staffs' hypotheses. But there are no longer any hypotheses. Fifty reconnaissance crews are asked to sketch the face of a war that has no face. The Staffs appeal to us as if we were a tribe of fortune-tellers."

This could never have been written by a PDU pilot. To him, no intelligence was impossible to provide even though 212 Sqn had nothing approaching the 50 reconnaissance crews available to Meaux. The French lacked men like Cotton to inspire and fill the aircrews with self-assurance. Even when France fell, Cotton told Barratt that it was pitiful to see the expressions on the faces of his men when told to evacuate because "abandoning the job was the last thing they wanted to do."

For months beforehand, and for the first four days of the German advance, Allied reconnaissance over the Ardennes had been dependent on men who were afraid of the Luftwaffe and who were convinced that their efforts were as futile as dashing 'glassfuls of water into a forest fire'. "The fact is," concluded Alistair Horne, "that during the crucial month of April, only four French aircraft were lost through enemy action, hardly an excessively high price to have paid when one considers the mortal danger then confronting France." As a result the Germans were across the Meuse before the Allied High Command fully realised where the main German thrust lay. Four precious days had been wasted before 212 Sqn were called in, and four days was too long in modern warfare to be without accurate intelligence. It also proved that no amount of

[1] "To Lose a Battle".

[2] "Flight to Arras".

equipment and organisation can compensate for a lack of motivation on the part of the men who use them.

By May 14th, Rommel had entered Houx and Guderian was in Sedan. Barratt decided to concentrate on Sedan and Fg Off Christie was sent to reconnoitre the Meuse between Mézières and Mouzon, and the Paliseuil-Sedan road. Barratt flung everything at the microcosms on the films that were bridges and pontoons swarming with troops and armour, but it was the blackest day in RAF history as 40 out of 71 bombers failed to come back.

On the evening of 14th, a dozen Blenheims attacked Rommel's bridgehead at Dinant. The Germans had to be halted, if only briefly, to allow French reinforcements to be brought up, and the best way to do this was to isolate Rommel from his columns moving up to cross the river. At 0745 hrs the following morning, a PR Spitfire took off to see if the raid on the bridges had been a success. The pilot followed the standard climb out from Meaux, heading north-east to reach 30,000 feet by Mézières. He then followed the Meuse from Poix-Terron to Namur and returned to base via Florennes and Marienbourg, landing at 1100 hrs. Every moment was precious in such a rapidly changing military situation, and as soon as the Spitfire landed the films were rushed to the photographic trailer. There was no time to make prints so Kendall had to interpret from the wet negatives. They told a sorry story. With a magnifying glass, Kendall could just distinguish a bridge on a negative exposed at 30,000 feet, and those at Dinant and Anhée were cruelly intact. Long streams of mechanised ants were crossing the Meuse; Rommel was strengthening his bridgehead every hour and Barratt had virtually nothing left to send against him.

In response to the German invasion, Bomber Command struck at the Ruhr. On May 13th, High Wycombe asked for prints of the Rhine to see if buoyancy mines deposited in the river had claimed any victims. Ironically, the only damage photographed involved a partially destroyed anti-mine barrage to the west of Karlsruhe. Two nights later, Bomber Command visited the Ruhr for the first time. Militarily the operation was of little value; it was essentially a reflex response to the razing of Rotterdam and little damage was caused. 212 Sqn could neither confirm nor deny this; although they flew two sorties on May 16th to assess the damage, the scale of the prints was too small to be of value.

Bad weather frustrated PR attempts over France during the next two days, by which time the panzers had passed the Sambre/Oise and Upper Escaut Lines and were wheeling towards the Channel coast.

After May 18th, the Front had moved sufficiently westward to be covered from Heston, and part of the Squadron was sent back to England. The weather was so bad that the French-based Spitfires could only be employed over German positions in central Belgium. On May 21st, the cloud lifted to allow photography over the Sambre bridges between Chauney and Landrecies following a series of raids by Hampdens and Whitleys, but then the weather 'clamped' down again for the next two days.

With the failure of the Weygand Plan, designed to re-establish contact between the Allied 1st Army Group in the north and French reserves to the south of the Somme, France was lost. The last fling had been flung and the RAF now concentrated on providing support for the retreat to Dunkirk. 212 Sqn continued over the next few days to watch for columns and dumps that could be bombed to try to relieve the pressure on the retreating armies. On May 25th they plotted German positions between Namur and Montherne and two days later they were over the Montreuil-Etaples area to look for two panzer divisions that were reportedly wheeling towards Boulogne. But there was little that could be done with this information. The AASF had been reduced to thirty aircraft by May 20th and Barratt discovered that knowledge without power can be a heart-breaking experience.

For six days the panzers rested and reformed ready to move south across the Somme. Dunkirk fell on June 4th, the most active day of the campaign for the PDU. While Heston watched over the armada of ships, five sorties were flown from Meaux, three by the same aircraft. The first detail took off at 0630 hrs bound for the airfields and roads around Sedan, the second flew over the Meuse between Charleville and Fumay, the third failed through engine trouble, and the fourth covered the Mézières-Fumay-Avesnes-Guise quadrilateral between the Meuse and the Somme. At 2005 hrs the fifth detail landed after photographing the Rhine between Bingen and Speyer in connection with the "Royal Marine Plan" to mine the river.

On the morning of June 5th, the Germans launched their offensive against the last major French line of resistance, the Weygand Line. Barratt's AASF had been increased to 100 aircraft but the Line lacked strength in depth to contain the panzers long enough for air power to be used effectively against them. Within two days the Germans had broken through.

The cameras concentrated once more on the German supply lines, and on June 7th, General Tetu asked Barratt for photographs of one of the main reinforcement arteries, the railway line from Maastricht to Aulnoye. The western part of the line up to Liège was covered around midday, and in the afternoon the same pilot took off to finish the job. His failure to do so illustrated some of the problems inherent in high altitude flying. He set course for Liège after climbing out to Mézières, but as he turned north his map slipped. He grabbed for it and in doing so dislodged his oxygen mask. By the time he regained consciousness the Spitfire was at 8,000 feet. Having discovered a glycol leak he force-landed between the obstacles on the abandoned Champagne airfield at Rheims. Repeated attempts at salvage failed, and four days later the French were asked to set fire to the machine.

As the Germans advanced on the Seine, 212 Sqn was evacuated to Orleans /Bricy on June 9th. For the next five days the PR Spitfires concentrated on the Seine bridges to determine which remained intact after bombardment. Cover of the river between Rouen and Mantes on June 10th produced prints obscured by smoking fuel dumps left by the retreating French, but still clear enough to show that eight out of twenty-six bridges were still intact. The Seine to the south of Vernon was photographed the next day and, although the main bridges were destroyed, the pilot could see that the Germans were constructing pontoons on both sides of the river. To record every detail he descended to 5,500 feet and brought back a wonderful set of pictures showing everything down to the last lorry and trailer. It was to be the last successful sortie by 212 Sqn in France.

Over the next few days the squadron retreated to Poitiers, then to Fontenay-le-Comte, and finally to the Channel port of La Rochelle. Only two Spitfires remained at Orleans, and these were ferried back to Heston on June 14th, managing a last photographic look at the Seine between Vernon and Elbeuf on the way home. Clark and Christie flew the two squadron Tiger Moths back via Brittany and Jersey with the front seats full of petrol cans, while Wilson returned, with the aid of a Michelin road map borrowed from a café wall, in a Fairey Battle he found abandoned at Orleans. The ground crews were progressively evacuated in either the Lockheed or a Hudson which flew out from Heston on a daily shuttle service. The final Hudson run on June 21st must have been one of the last RAF flights to leave France – the last of the groundcrew had to make their way back to England in a collier from Bordeaux.

Despite their limited resources, 212 Sqn achieved a great deal during the Battle of France. In the 36 days up to the departure from Orleans, operations were possible on all but 7 days, and one of these was occupied with the transfer from Meaux. Cotton did not lose a single man during the campaign, whereas the French Group 2-33 lost 17 out of 23 crews in three weeks. Most photography was achieved within 24 hours of it being tasked, and the unit was able to provide the Allied Staffs with a great deal of valuable information at a time when the situation on the ground was changing from hour to hour. Whether this information was put to any good use is debatable. However it is probably true to say that if Cotton had been allocated more aircraft for use in France, and if 212 Sqn had been employed over a much wider area during the 'Phoney War', the Allies would have suffered far fewer rude surprises in the Battle for France.

* * * *

Throughout May, N Flight at Heston had divided its time between the NW German ports and the land battle on the continent. However the scale of the effort was dependent on the number of PR Spitfires available in England at any one time – from May 10th to 15th the solitary Spitfire at Heston concentrated almost entirely on the Friesian Islands.

By May 19th the Heston strength had risen to four Spitfires following the partial withdrawal of 212 Sqn from France. Dunkirk and any dispositions that might interfere with the evacuation were the main objectives up to June 5th, but the most interesting missions took place outside Northern Europe. While most Allied eyes had been focused on Hitler in May, the Air Ministry had not forgotten his ally in Rome. Fearing a 'stab in the back' from Mussolini, plans were formulated to bomb strategic targets in northern Italy if necessary. These fell into three groups – the heavy industries of Turin, Milan, Genoa, and Venice; the airframe and aircraft component factories of Turin,

Milan, Genoa, and Vergiate; and the oil refineries of Genoa, Leghorn, Trieste, Brescia, and Naples.

The strike element was to be provided by aircraft from the carrier 'Argus' and a detachment of 4 Group, Bomber Command, based at Hyères in southern France. Pre-strike reconnaissance was essential, but as the force was to be dispatched as soon as Italy declared war, any PR had to be done in peacetime without offending Mussolini.

So, on May 11th, Longbottom flew from Heston to Meaux, exchanged aircraft, and carried on to Le Luc, an airfield some 30 miles from Marseilles. There he was joined by Eric le Mesurier, and in the next three days they photographed the main ports in the Gulf of Genoa, Milan, the harbour of Bari, and two of the main Italian approaches to France. But the situation deteriorated so rapidly in France that the detachment was recalled on May 14th, and the Spitfire handed back to 212 Sqn.

Work was resumed at Le Luc on May 28th. They finished all the tasks in northern Italy in eight days and were ready to reconnoitre further south by June 6th. Le Luc remained their main base – it was close to Hyères where the films were processed by the British Naval Detachment – but a forward refuelling point was necessary for the more distant flights. Bastia in Corsica was chosen initially, but when a pilot tried to land there en-route for Sardinia he found the airfield blocked by the French. Ajaccio was selected as an alternative, and on June 8th the first mission was sent to Naples. It was an opportune flight; the pilot reported that between four and five large, and five or six medium warships were at anchor, with another five large vessels actually entering port at the time of photography. The Allies therefore had a clear appreciation of the disposition of a substantial proportion of the Italian Fleet barely two days before Mussolini entered the war on June 10th.

From then on the Le Luc detachment, designated 'D Flight', concentrated on the likeliest and most accessible targets for attack, namely the ports of Genoa and La Spezia, and the industries of Milan and Turin. One pilot, setting course for Genoa at first light on June 14th, suddenly came across a fleet of seventeen warships with fighter umbrella steaming SW off Impera towards Nice. Believing it to be the Italian Fleet he turned for Hyères, where missions now landed to unload their films to save time, only to discover that he had seen the French Fleet returning from the bombardment of Naples. June 13th was an auspicious day for it saw the first 'kill' by the PDU. "While over Genoa," recorded Fg Off Christie, "a Fiat biplane fighter carried out a quarter attack on my right. So I descended into clouds. While returning to base I observed a twin bomber approaching the coast about 30 miles E of Cannes. It had Italian markings, a rear top turret and front turret. I could not see if it had a dustbin underneath. I carried out three attacks almost out of range from the beam, then as the turrets appeared to be unable to turn through more than 45 degrees I carried out full beam attacks passing over the top very low. After two attacks he descended and forced landed on the water. The crew of 5 climbed on to the wing and swam towards the shore. They had no lifebelts or dinghy. The machine sank in about 3 minutes nose first."

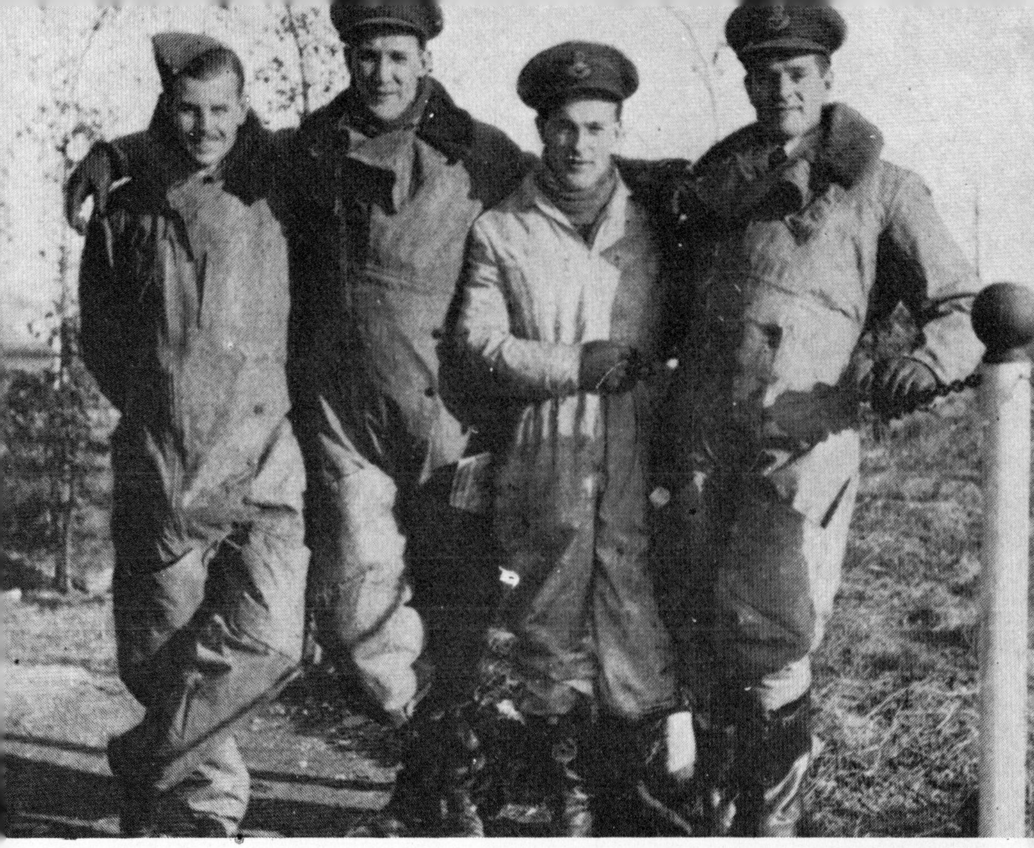

Above: A group of PDU pilots in France wearing Sidcot flying suits: Bob Niven is centre left and Shorty Longbottom centre right. *CC*
Right: Wg Cdr Geoffrey Tuttle, DFC in 1940. *Ball*

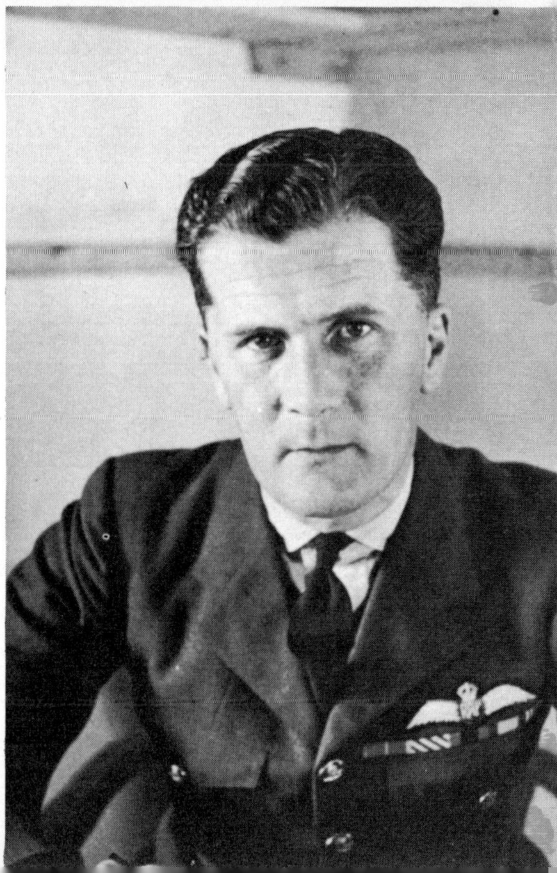

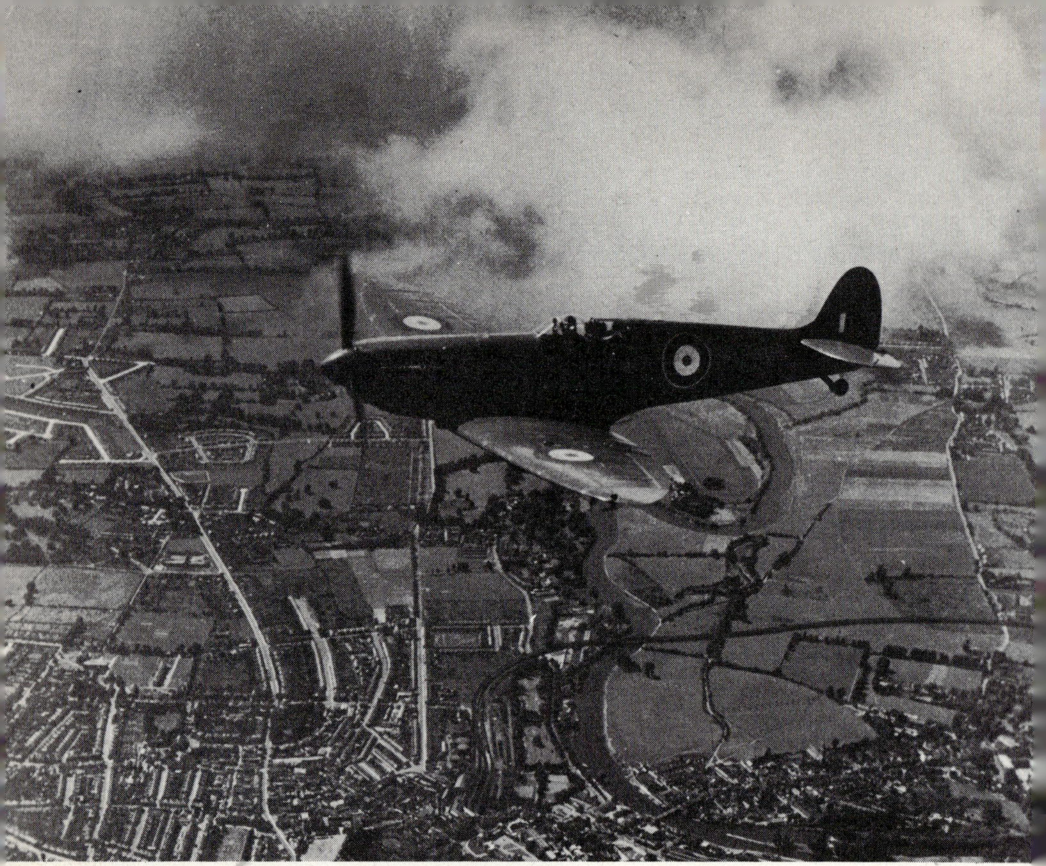

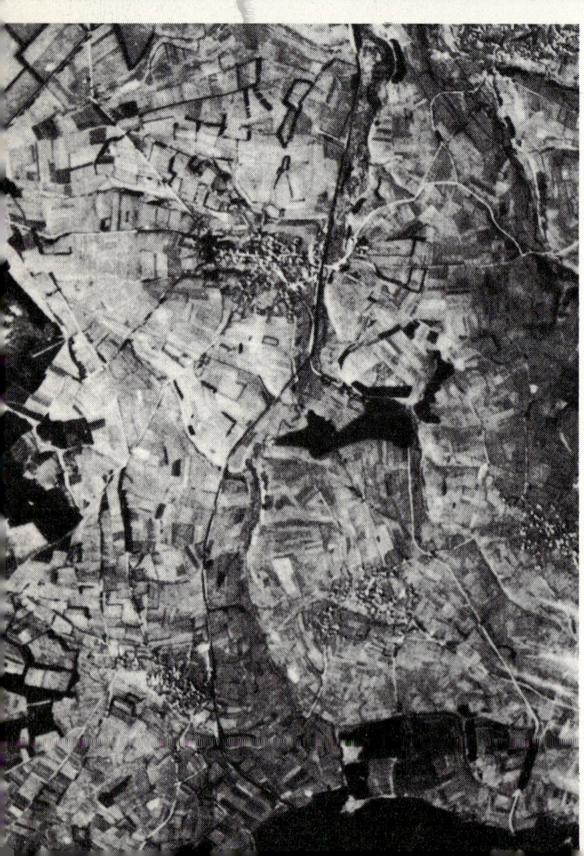

Above: A Spitfire PR IC, flown by Fg Off S. G. Wise, approaching Heston. *Wise. Left:* The Belgian village of Bullingen photographed by Shorty Longbottom on the first successful PR Spitfire sortie ever flown (November 22nd, 1939). Unfortunately it was taken with an F 24 camera with a 5in lens from 33,000 feet and the resulting small scale of 1:79,200 shows very little detail. Compare this with the photograph (*Top right*), which was exposed by an F 52 camera with a 36in lens over the same village in April 1944. Although this print was also taken from 34,000 feet, the scale of 1: 11,300 provides much more detail for the photo-interpreters and illustrates the advances made in aerial lenses over the war years. CC. *Bottom right:* "There I was . . ." (L to R) Fg Off Timothy Craxton, Fg Off Alistair Taylor and Flt Lt Douglas Wilson outside a 212 Sqn Mobile Field Photographic Section trailer in France. *Wilson*

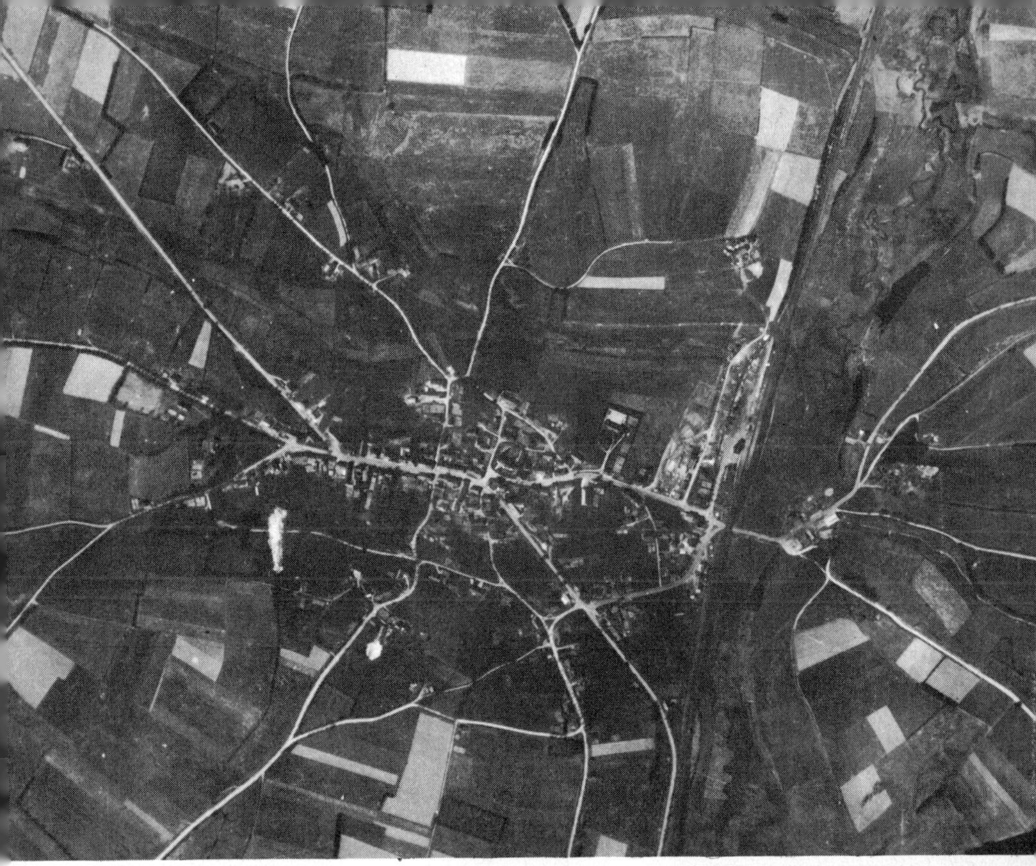

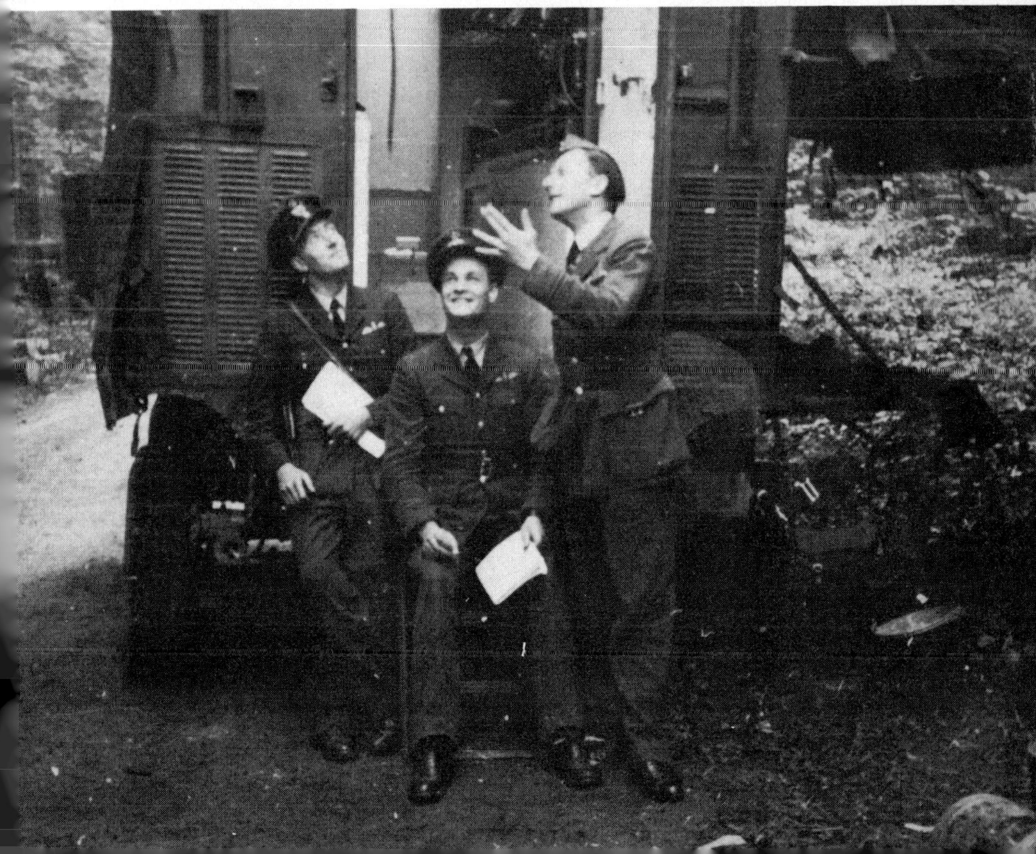

Below: A Spitfire PR IC at Wick with a Hudson in the background. *Wilson. Bottom:* German invasion barges assembled at Dunkirk in September 1940. Bomber Command has left its mark on the port – buildings around the upper of the two docks have been damaged together with cranes and haulage gear, while two big warehouses facing the other dock have been demolished. Damaged barges lie near the entrance to the upper dock. *IWM*

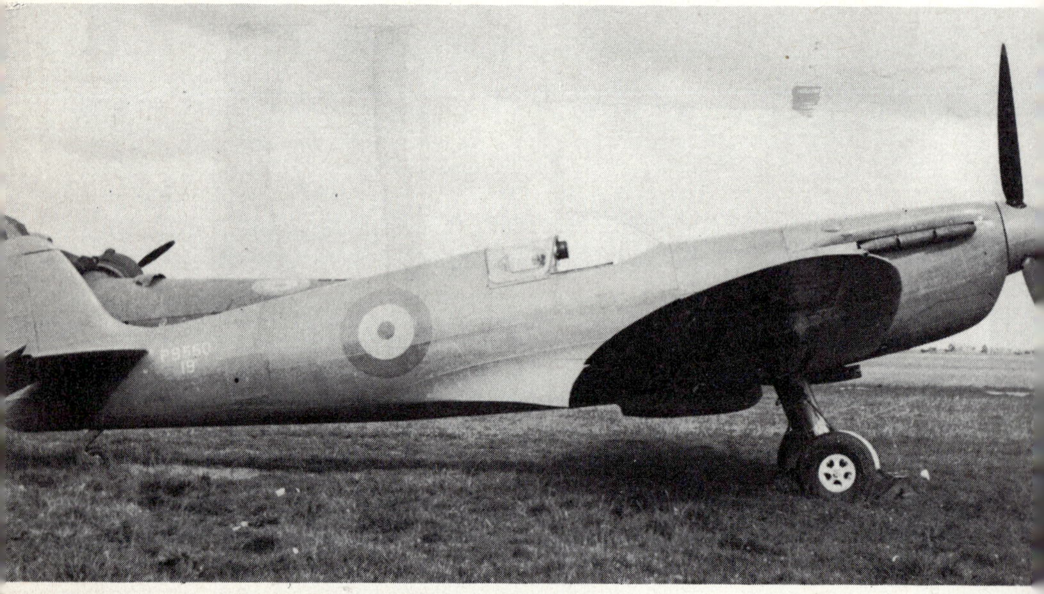

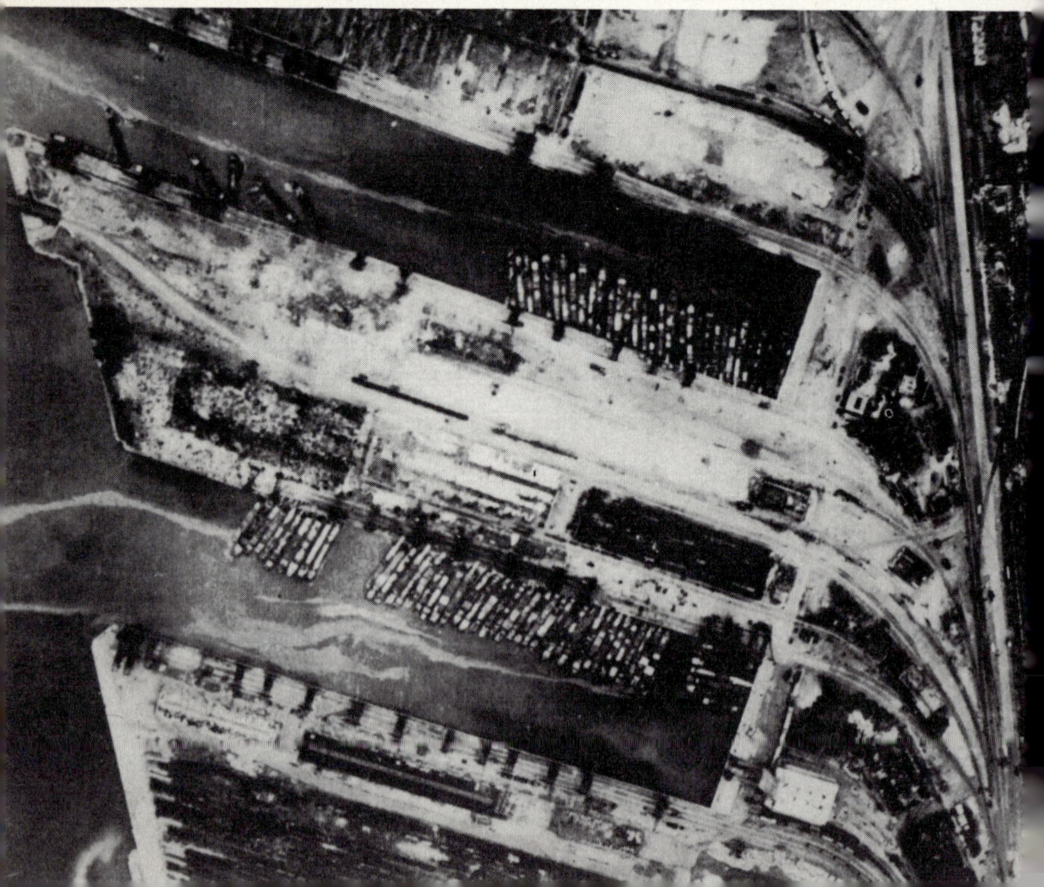

The funny part of the story was that the PR Spitfire was unarmed. Cotton was not too amused though – there was no place in his PDU for unnecessary dog-fights.

On June 15th, D Flight was ordered to evacuate from France. The projected bombing raids on Italy came to nothing – they were thwarted by the antagonism of the inhabitants of southern France who feared reprisals by the Italian air force. The groundcrews returned to England via Casablanca and Gibraltar while the Spitfires returned to Heston by way of Poitiers. It was indicative of the mobility of the Spitfire that the aircraft which was photographing La Spezia, Pisa, and Genoa on June 15th was on a mission over Amsterdam three days later.

As the PDU was being driven out of France, another conflict was taking place within the Air Ministry over who was to control the Unit. No one was happy with the existing arrangement. Heston was administered by Northolt as part of Fighter Command, but it came directly under the Air Ministry for all operational purposes. However, this arrangement was complicated by Cotton who acted as a law unto himself. In the beginning this tripartite system worked satisfactorily – every sortie was by nature an experiment with no one outside Heston in a position to advise or interfere. Cotton was allowed a great deal of latitude in deciding which targets should be covered and what resources he needed – as late as the end of February 1940, even though all taskings had theoretically to go through Peck's deputy, the Director of Military Cooperation, HQ BAFF was told that "all requests for special photographic reconnaissance will be referred, for the time being, straight to the PDU, Heston."

But attitudes hardened as the PDU changed from an experimental into an operational unit. Every other operational squadron in the United Kingdom was allocated to a functional Command, and pressures mounted to 'regularise' the PDU. The Air Staff agreed, but there was then the problem of to which Command it should belong. Much wrangling took place – "there was a great deal of prestige attached to it as the principal supplier of hot news," wrote Air Chief Marshal Sir Philip Joubert de la Ferté. The keenest bidder was Bomber Command. Ludlow-Hewitt had been pressing for such an organisation since 1937, and Niven's mosaic of the Ruhr on March 2nd had convinced him that the PDU should be placed under his command. The C-in-C set forth his case in a letter on March 10th:

"In the absence of special bombers capable of doing reconnaissance and photographic work over Germany, the Photographic Development Unit is a vital necessity to this Headquarters. . . . The needs of the Command in respect of Intelligence and 'eyes' can only be really efficiently met by the inclusion within the Command of a unit capable of carrying out reconnaissances and photographic flights whenever and wherever required . . . Conditions are often such that Blenheims cannot operate, and I have no alternative means of doing the work. Consequently, days pass when urgent information is required which I am unable to get and although Blenheims are sent out, again and again they only come back reporting that the weather on the other side is too fine and clear for them to obtain the information and return safely to base."

In addition, Ludlow-Hewitt complained of duplication between 2 Gp and the PDU, and of delays in the receipt of prints at High Wycombe. He therefore concluded by requesting that the PDU be incorporated into his Command so that he could have "the advantage of the advice and assistance of Wg Cdr Cotton, of whose experience, initiative and enterprise I have the highest opinion."

Bomber Command believed it should control the PDU because it was one of its biggest customers, but the Air Ministry saw this as one of the main drawbacks to Ludlow-Hewitt's request. Gp Capt Fraser, the Director of Military Cooperation, had defined the function of the PDU as "to provide intelligence information to satisfy the needs of the Admiralty, the Air Ministry, and Bomber Command respectively". If Bomber Command gained control, it might reverse these priorities to employ the Unit primarily for its own purposes and to the detriment of other agencies.

A compromise was accepted at a conference on 'The Future of Photographic Reconnaissance' held on June 10th. The meeting delineated the primary reconnaissance targets for the immediate future as the main ports and airfields of SW Norway, Jutland, NW Germany, the Low Countries, and that part of France under German control. All Cotton's efforts over the past year were vindicated by a statement that "high level photographic reconnaissance was by far the best method" of achieving this information.

The question of operational control was settled by giving all responsibility for reconnaissance of enemy ports to Coastal Command; broadly speaking, visual reconnaissance was to be carried out by the GR squadrons and photography by the PDU. It was hoped that Coastal Command, with less axes to grind, would employ the Unit to the benefit of all three Services.

Cotton, as usual, had suggested the best solution of all through the medium of a paper by Gp Capt Fraser:

"One solution might be the formation of a Photographic Reconnaissance Group, to include the whole of the organisation both at home and in France. This would ensure that not only Bomber Command, but also all the other 'users' . . . received consideration, according to the degree of priority laid down by the Air Ministry . . ." But few people agreed with Cotton that PR was such a specialised function that it merited an individual Group, and the proposal was rejected as impracticable. On June 18th, the PDU was handed over to Coastal Command.

Having decided who was to control the PDU, the next question was who should command it. Although Ludlow-Hewitt had the "highest opinion" of Cotton, there were very few senior officers who shared his admiration. Cotton was anathema to the orthodox staff officer because he showed contempt for Service rules of procedure. "There was the way I had got my first Spitfire, the use of Hemming's company before it was requisitioned, the continual war I had waged on apathy and delay, and so on – all these marked me down, from the Air Staff's point of view, as a nuisance." Many important people disliked the fact that the PDU had become known as "Cotton's Circus", reflecting the fact that it owed allegiance to Cotton and not to the Air Ministry.

Cotton in turn disliked Whitehall because he saw only the faceless facade of apparently jealous obstructionists. For all Cotton's drive, enthusiasm, and leadership, he was politically naïve. Having faced some opposition from the Air Ministry at the start, he despised the official machine, and consequently never took the trouble to understand it. Being inherently a dynamic individual, Cotton lacked the finesse to see that the Air Ministry could be manipulated to his own ends. "It's rusty and cumbersome," confided Barratt, "but in your case that works in your favour. Go ahead and make your own decisions and act on them, and they'll take ages to catch up with you."

Cotton never knew when to draw the line. At first his bloody-minded unorthodoxy was essential to secure Spitfires, push through modifications, and convince the sceptics that his ideas were worth supporting, but once his opponents had been converted and the men and machines arrived at Heston, he did not mellow. He continued to cut corners and by-pass seemingly irrelevant bureaucracy because time was so pressing in 1940, but he never stopped to consider the demands of other RAF units, or the implications for a fighting force if every commander adopted the same attitude as he did. Peck wrote almost despairingly of "the difficulties we have constantly to smooth out. The ideas have been good but to get the benefit of them we have suffered great inconvenience." Cotton refused to adapt to the Service conventions – Bill Wise never once saw him in uniform. Cotton always saw the Air Ministry as a brick wall because he lacked the military experience and the patience to understand it; instead of prising holes in the wall, he simply jumped over it.

Once the PDU became operational, even friends like Peck began to tire of smoothing ruffled feathers left in Cotton's wake. "The first and fundamental question," he wrote to the Deputy Chief of Air Staff in April, "is whether we go on with Cotton, enduring much tribulation for the value of whatever further ideas there may be – and I think there will be good ideas – or whether we regularise everything and dispense with Cotton".

Geoffrey Tuttle was summoned to the Air Ministry and asked if the PDU could now do without Cotton. Despite his great loyalty to Cotton, Tuttle had to admit that as the PDU was on its feet it could function like any other operational squadron, but he also told the VCAS that the Unit would never have been in such a strong position had it not been for its CO.

Once the decision had been taken to regularise the PDU by giving it to Coastal Command, Cotton had to go. He would always want to be his own master and would never calmly accept the transference of most of the control he now held to the C-in-C Coastal Command. Cotton was not dismissed because he offended too many people in high places, but because the Air Ministry realised that he could never accept the role of a conventional Wing Commander, and when it came to the question of who was to control the PDU – Wg Cdr Cotton or Air Chief Marshal Sir Frederick Bowhill – there could be only one answer.

On the same day that the PDU went into Coastal Command, Cotton was handed a letter as he stepped out of his Lockheed after a flight to France.

S. 58864/S.6 SECRET 16 June 1940

Sir,
I am commanded by the Air Council to inform you that they have recently had under review the question of the future status and organisation of the Photographic Development Unit and that, after careful consideration, they have reached the conclusion that this Unit which you have done so much to foster, should now be regarded as having passed beyond the stage of experimentation and should take its place as part of the ordinary organisation of the Royal Air Force.

2 It has accordingly been decided that it should be constituted as a unit of the Royal Air Force under the orders of the Commander-in-Chief, Coastal Command, and should be commanded by a regular serving officer. Wing Commander G. W. Tuttle, has been appointed.

3 I am to add that the Council wish to record how much they are indebted to you for the work you have done and for the great gifts of imagination and inventive thought which you have brought to bear on the development of the technique of photography in the Royal Air Force.

I am Sir,
Your obedient Servant,
Arthur Street

For all his faults Cotton deserved better than this. In less than twelve months he had revolutionised the art of photographic reconnaissance in the RAF. He had destroyed forever the myth that information had to be fought for, and he had established photographic reconnaissance as an individual and vitally important form of aerial intelligence. Cotton was not only a pioneer but also a great leader of men. He won his point because his men proved it for him. He fought for the best machines, equipment, and facilities that the RAF had to offer, and in return his crews flew and worked to the limits of their endurance because they accepted his theories and believed in his ideal.

Frederick Sidney Cotton would have achieved little in a peace-time air force, but he was a God-send during the transitional period of 1939. He cut red-tape, bullied the highest in the land, and created an organisation that would have taken anyone else years to achieve, if they had not given up in frustration long before. The hour cometh and so did the man. To his subordinates he gave all and demanded everything; to aviation he bequeathed a new concept of strategic reconnaissance that was to endure for over 30 years. In return, a grateful Service dismissed him with a terse letter and an OBE.

CHAPTER FIVE

The Photographic Reconnaissance Unit

Many shall run to and fro, and knowledge shall be increased. Daniel xii. 4.

The change in command made very little difference to the PDU. Coastal Command left Wg Cdr Tuttle to his own devices and, as he had virtually run the Unit on behalf of Cotton, few noticed the changeover. Many of the newer pilots had regarded Tuttle as their CO for several months, partly because he was the senior officer in uniform and partly because Cotton was rarely in evidence at Heston as he spent a great deal of time in France. The only thing that changed was the name of the Unit – on July 8th the PDU became the Photographic Reconnaissance Unit (PRU) at the same time as Wembley was rechristened the Photographic Intelligence Unit (PIU). Both were administratively controlled by HQ 16 Gp but received their operational taskings from Coastal Command.

The function of the PRU was defined at its inception as "photographic reconnaissance requiring deep penetration into enemy occupied territory and photographic reconnaissance of heavily defended areas which could not be carried out by ordinary reconnaissance aircraft." These roles were to become even more important with the fall of France.

At a time when Germany controlled the European coastline from Trondheim to the Pyrenees, and might launch an invasion of Britain from anywhere along it, British Intelligence was woefully short of information. Most conventional agents had either been captured or silenced after the occupation of France, and the few remaining, together with activities like the monitoring of German wireless frequencies, were unlikely to provide much reliable data. A Joint Intelligence Sub-Committee of the Committee of Imperial Defence (JIC) reviewed the situation and came to the depressing conclusion that the threat of a seaborne invasion was a problem which "our intelligence system has not been designed to handle". They concluded that the only reliable way to predict the size and embarkation point of any invasion was by "regular and systematic air reconnaissance, over all areas in which the seaborne expedition might be prepared, and from which it might sail".

However "all areas" encompassed 2,000 miles of coastline, and Tuttle's resources for such a mammoth surveillance task totalled eleven operational Spitfires – less than the complement of an average operational squadron. These were divided into eight PR IBs and three PR ICs, and, as the latter could only just reach Kiel from East Anglia, detachments to the north and west of the British Isles were essential to cover Norway and the Bay of Biscay.

Tuttle divided the Unit into four Flights. The Cornish airfield of St Eval was soon chosen as a home for B Flight under Flt Lt Clark, but the northern base was more of a problem. On June 25th Douglas Wilson was sent in a Blenheim to investigate the suitability of Montrose, Dyce, Lossiemouth, Wick, and Sumburgh. Sumburgh was the nearest to Norway, but being in the Shetlands it was rejected because Tuttle felt that a Spitfire pilot with no navigational or radio aids might have difficulty returning to a small group of islands. In the end Wick was chosen as a base for A Flight with Wilson in command. It was intended that each detachment would eventually have four Spitfires and a low-level Hudson, together with a Tiger Moth for communications. The PRU was now in position to watch the coast of Europe from Bergen to the Gironde.

Two flights remained at Heston – an operational flight responsible for NW Germany, the Low Countries, and northern France, and an experimental flight. The latter had a fascinating array of equipment. There were two Spitfires for trials with all manner of experimental fuel tankage, two more with guns for low level research, another with oblique cameras, two Wellingtons for night trials, two training Spitfires, and the original SIS aircraft. Cotton would have smiled to see it all; for months he had fought for resources like this and they only arrived once the Germans were just across the Channel. For nearly a year he had pleaded to be allowed to fit extra fuel tanks – now that range was essential, modifications were accepted with alacrity.

Towards the end of July 1940, two PR IF types were ready for use. This variant carried an extra 89 gallons of fuel – 29 gallons behind the pilot and a 30 gallon tank in each wing. Two F 24 14 in cameras were installed as a split-pair[1] in the fuselage and the result was an aircraft capable of 1,300 miles safe range. Even so this was not good enough. The Baltic was still out of range and many experts feared that the Germans might be building up an invasion force in Stettin. A really long range aircraft was needed, along the lines proposed by the Longbottom Memorandum a year earlier. Even the CAS encouraged the development of such a machine. He admitted to the JIC in July that "Stettin is beyond the range of our reconnaissance aircraft" but he added that the fitting of a special aircraft was being actively examined and that he would do everything possible to obtain the information required. The answer was the Spitfire PR ID type. First mooted by Cotton to Supermarines in October 1939, the ID type had been delayed by design complications. Whereas the PR IA, B, C, and F variants had been locally modified versions of the standard fighter, the D type needed specially constructed wings. 30 gallon tanks under the wings or behind the pilot were no problem to Heston, but the fitment of internal wing tanks capable of holding 115 gallons was beyond their limited resources. Supermarines were unable to produce special wings with leading-edge tanks

[1] Aerial cameras can be mounted with a tilt of up to 10° from the vertical without causing any apparent distortion in vertical photographs. If two cameras are fitted together and tilted slightly on either side of the vertical, the result is a 'split pair' capable of photographing a greater area for each exposure. The simultaneous prints are synchronised to allow for a small amount of lateral overlap.

because they conflicted with Fighter Command's requirement for cannon wings, and so Cotton's proposal floundered for lack of priority.

The CAS changed all that. The PR ID type was elevated to equal status with its fighter cousin, and within three months the first one arrived at the PRU Experimental Flight for trials. Two ID types were in fact produced, each with a split-pair of fuselage cameras, a 29 gallon fuselage tank, and provision for 57½ gallons in each wing leading-edge. The long range variant was so heavy with fuel that it was nicknamed 'the bowser', and with a range of 1,750 miles it brought Stettin, Trondheim, and Marseilles within range of the British Isles.

The first D type sortie was flown by Fg Off S. J. Millen on October 29th 1940. The 'bowser's' centre of gravity was down by the tail and the aircraft was very unstable for the first 30 minutes until fuel had been burnt off. Nevertheless Millen covered Stettin successfully on the longest PRU sortie to date – 5 hrs 20 mins – and earned a DFC as well as photographs of Stettin, Rostock, and North Germany.

There was one exception to the unarmed breed of PR Spitfires and that was the PR IG type. It resulted from an Air Staff requirement for a PR Spitfire to go in at low level over the invasion coast when detailed information was needed, with an armed capability to attack marauding German E Boats if the opportunity arose.

Within three days of the request, Heston produced the G type and evolved the technique of 'dicing'. The Hudsons had been introduced to photograph below cloud, but because of their lumbering speed and conspicuous profile they were unsuitable for very low level work over heavily defended areas. The much faster and sleeker G type was intended to hug the waves across the Channel to avoid detection, home onto a conspicuous coastal feature, and sweep past the dormant anti-aircraft batteries and over the target. An anonymous joker called it 'dicing with death' and the term 'dicing' was born.

Planning was the key to dicing success. The various landmarks and their ETAs had to be memorised beforehand because there was little time for map-reading at 50 feet with the throttle open. Tuttle briefed his pilots accordingly:

"You must spot your landmarks the second you see the coast. And switch on your cameras in good time before you whistle past your target. You've got to be right first time, because there isn't going to *be* a second time."[1]

Alistair Taylor was the best dicer at Heston because he knew the position and range of every flak battery, every airfield and the performance of its aircraft, and any other obstacles he was likely to meet en-route.

The golden rule of dicing was not to dice the same target in rapid succession because the element of surprise, so vital to success, might be lost if the enemy was prepared. Dicing, as its name implied, was a gamble, but pilots like Taylor who planned their sorties meticulously beforehand greatly lengthened the odds against themselves.

But the G type enjoyed only limited success as a photographic platform.

[1] *Evidence in Camera*, Constance Babington-Smith.

Wing tankage could not be added because of the cannons, so the extra fuel capacity was limited to the fuselage tank behind the pilot. As a result the G type was restricted in its employment to the Channel littoral between the Low Countries and the Cherbourg Peninsula. Retention of the armament was not a good idea either. Low level work was dangerous enough without encouraging pilots to stay and fight it out with the opposition instead of bringing their photographs back to England. Out of the nine losses sustained during 650 PRU missions between July and the end of October, four resulted from the relatively small proportion of low level sorties. A flight by Bill Wise on October 4th illustrated the temptations:

"I took off from Heston and set course for Dungeness where I crossed the coast under 4/10 cloud at 1000 feet. The cloud increased to about 8/10 towards Cap Gris Nez. About six miles north of the Cape was a Heinkel 59 alighting on the water. I was then about 850 feet above and I decided it would be a magnificent target to fire away at. About 500 yards away from the seaplane was a small rubber boat with two men inside paddling like the devil (ie at a rapid speed). As I was manoeuvring into position to finish off the Heinkel, bullets rushed past me at a frightening speed. I looked round and saw two yellow-nosed Me 109s on my tail, a most unpleasant and hostile sight. I took what cover I could in the clouds making a dash back for the English coast with the Me 109s on my tail firing occasional bursts. Owing to remarkable skill and magnificent flying I dodged the hail of bullets fired at me except for two that penetrated the fuselage of my aircraft and one through the starboard flap. At the end of the performance I decided that it would be unwise to go back to the French coast to photograph Calais and Boulogne with the enemy fighters somewhere in the Dover Straits. I landed at Heston with a sigh of relief at 1445 hrs." Only in exceptional circumstances were cannons compatible with cameras.

By the end of July, after a fifth flight had been added to photograph German-occupied airfields, Tuttle commanded 752 personnel spread over three RAF stations. Every morning, each detachment received by signal a list of taskings in order of priority; the flight-commanders would examine the weather forecast and decide which areas were best for photography that day. Tuttle delegated a great deal of operational responsibility to his flight-commanders but there was never any doubt who was in charge. Tasks were then allocated to individual pilots depending on the priority of the mission, the element of risk involved, weather, and experience of the aircrew concerned. Pre-flight planning was then left to the respective pilots. There was no standard operating procedure for PR – weather, defences, size of target, and range made every sortie different from the last one. A pilot might have to select a novel approach to a regular target because the AA batteries would be expecting the daily PRU 'milk-run'; he might choose to go in at low level if the cloud was bad or high level if the defences were heavy. Every pilot had his own preferences on the best techniques to employ, and any profile was acceptable as long as it brought results.

After landing, the exposures were rushed to Wembley, either by dispatch-rider from Heston, or express-train from Cornwall and Scotland. Films from Wick were flown down in the Tiger Moth to Inverness to catch the King's Cross express, or, when vitally important, flown directly to Heston in a requisitioned Spartan Executive that had been built for the King of Iraq but never delivered.

The PIU had also seen a considerable number of changes since the informal days of Cotton and Hemming. Sqn Ldr Peter Riddell had been posted in to Wembley from Bomber Command on June 26th with the same brief as Tuttle – to reorganise a highly efficient but not very Service-orientated concern so that it could cope with the growing number of prints from the PRU. After about a month, Riddell introduced the pattern of interpretation that was to last until the present day.

He divided interpretation into three successive stages, or 'Phases', which were defined by a WRAF PI, Constance Babbington-Smith, in her book 'Evidence in Camera'. "'First Phase' meant immediate reporting of important new items: the movements of ships and aircraft, of rail traffic and canal traffic; the extent of bomb damage and the position of ammunition dumps. In cases of special urgency this information was to be available three hours after the aircraft landed. 'Second Phase' reports were to be out within twenty-four hours, and they were to give not only quite a lot of detail on general activity but also, by dealing with a day's accumulation of cover, a coordinated view of what was going on. The 'Third Phase' reports, to be issued later, were to be very detailed statements for specialist recipients, on such things as airfields, factories and military installations."

Circumstances led to concentration on specific phases; during the invasion scare, everyone wanted the latest information so First Phase came into prominence. To save time, First Phase sections were established at St Eval in December and at Wick in February 1941, but the prints were then sent to the PIU for Second and Third Phase interpretation.

The period from June 18th to the end of August 1940 was one of uncertainty. Everyone expected an invasion but British Intelligence had no idea from which part of the Continental coast it might be launched. First suspicions centred on Scandinavia when the Military Attaché in Stockholm reported on June 10th that the Germans were reinforcing Norway at the rate of three troopships per day. Following a Coastal Command sighting of a large naval force off Trondheim, the JIC, now empowered to collate all invasion data and to warn the Cabinet when it seemed imminent, decided that PR of southern Norway was an urgent priority.

On the morning of June 30th a PRU Hudson took off from Leuchars and headed north-east across the North Sea. As it descended through the summer haze over Norway the oblique cameras were switched on to cover Bergen, then Haugesund and Stavanger, but none of them showed signs of any undue activity. Trondheim was out of range, but throughout the next month the

Spitfires of Wick watched the southern coast round to Oslo. No significant naval concentrations were noted; in fact there was a decline in traffic at Stavanger and Haugesund. The only scare occurred on August 1st when a conglomeration of small boats was apparently sighted in Christiansand. They turned out to be rafts of floating timber, but even this integral feature of the Norwegian economy could not be ignored in case the wood was intended for invasion barges.

Such was the scarcity of sinister activity that the JIC was moved to report on July 18th that "undue importance may be given to the preparations in Norway due to the increased volume of reports coming from this area." As the Norwegian scare subsided, attention was switched to shores nearer the British Isles. A report dated June 21st referred to a growth in barge traffic between Rotterdam and Maasluis, and coasters were said to be concentrating at the mouth of the Scheldt. Once again the PRU found little. An interpretation report after a sortie by Fg Off Christie on July 12th recorded that "barges in the Dutch and Belgian canals have been under constan air observation and have been bombed, as secondary targets, when opportunity offered," but it concluded that there was "no evidence that barges are being prepared for invasion." Christie's cover of the Scheldt revealed "negligible" barge and shipping movements, and another sortie that day showed the same degree of negative activity between Sluis and Calais.

Unfortunately, the limited number of Spitfires and Hudsons available to the PRU could not hope to cover every mile of the intricate waterway system of NW Europe. The JIC noted on July 14th that "the picture of barge movements presented by periodical air reconnaissance of portions of the enormous area covered by the canals is not complete enough in itself to indicate the purposes for which the barges are being used." Because this fragmented intelligence coincided with a period of acute tension, bogey armadas were suspected around every corner, of which the most plausible was purported to be at Kiel. It was suspected that an invasion force might concentrate in the safe waters of the Baltic, and particular attention was paid to shipping in the Kiel canal. When Longbottom had covered the port for the first time on April 7th, little notice had been taken of a group of small timber craft visible off Stickenhorn. However they caused considerable comment when the prints were re-examined in June, and when Kiel was photographed for the second time by Alistair Taylor on July 15th, the interpreters discovered that the craft had disappeared. The "Stickenhorn Units" were immediately elevated to the status of mechanically propelled pontoons which had been dispersed to join an invasion force massing elsewhere. Despite a period of frantic searching they were never found again. The "Stickenhorn Units" provided a good example of the limitations of PR; a totally irrelevant conglomeration of woodwork achieved an unjustified notoriety because it coincided with what the intelligence staffs were looking for in the place where they expected it. Similarly Stettin was accorded much greater importance than it deserved because it remained a mystery until brought within range by a PR ID in October. Aerial cameras will often provide the wrong picture if they do not take the whole picture.

By the beginning of September, the PRU had divided the coast of Europe into three categories so that their limited resources could be used to the maximum advantage where it mattered, and only infrequently where an invasion force was unlikely to congregate. The stretch from Den Helder to Cherbourg, and the Skaggerak, were photographed daily if weather permitted; the coast from Cherbourg to Bordeaux, the NW German ports from Emden to Kiel, and the Norwegian coastline south of Bergen were covered periodically; Denmark, Oslo, and north Norway were watched only infrequently.

The first signs of any real invasion preparations were noted by Bill Wise on September 1st. Although he photographed only the southernmost four miles of the South Beveland canal, as many as 71 barges could be seen, as well as 80 barges in the harbour of Hansweert. Across the Scheldt, along a 14 mile stretch of the Terneuzen-Ghent canal, the PIs counted an increase of approximately 200 barges since the middle of August, of which 50 were moving, all in a southerly direction. The following day, no fewer than 245 barges were visible in the South Beveland canal and Hansweert.

Slowly but surely the internal waterways of Holland and Belgium emptied of barge traffic. Between September 2nd and 6th, numbers in the South Beveland canal declined from 245 to 29, and in the Terneuzen-Ghent canal from 165 to 23. PR further south revealed that the barges were being towed in groups of three to six to the Channel ports. The build-up at Ostend was particularly notable; on August 28th there was not a single barge on prints of the port, but by the morning sortie of September 7th there were 270 in the harbour. When Plt Off Tony Hill covered the port again in the afternoon (for one sortie a day was no longer adequate to monitor the rapidly changing situation), the total had risen to 298 as more and more barges moved like lemmings down the Bruges-Ostend canal.

The story was the same in other Channel ports. A sortie on September 4th revealed that approximately 100 barges had arrived in Flushing over five days, and on the same day Fg Off Dakeyne photographed 50 self-propelled barges off Gris Nez. Two days later "processions of barges and large motor boats of E-boat type" were visible "moving south-west in trains of small groups travelling in line astern, to some extent accompanied by large shipping." Over two days 34 barges arrived at Dunkirk, at the same time as 53 barges, mainly between 120 feet and 180 feet in length, appeared in Calais.

The JIC, ever appreciative that their conclusions depended "so greatly upon air reconnaissance", reported on September 7th that "the movement of large numbers of self-propelled barges and small ships to the westward into Ostend, Dunkirk, Calais, Boulogne and Le Havre" suggested "a very early date for invasion, since these barges would not be moved unnecessarily early to positions so exposed to our bombing attack." Tension mounted in Whitehall; the Luftwaffe had transferred its attentions from fighter airfields to London two days earlier and this seemed to indicate, together with the barge concentrations, that an invasion was imminent. The PRU was ordered to provide round-the-clock daylight reconnaissance, and sometimes the Prime

Minister telephoned direct to the First Phase Section for the latest assessment of the situation.

On September 9th, "a procession of about 35 assorted tugs, trawlers and small coasters" was detected "eastward bound from Dunkirk to Ostend", apparently to tow more barges to the Channel ports. The convoys continued until September 18th when 1,044 barges were recorded on film in the five major ports between Flushing and Boulogne.

As a consequence, ports away from the Channel showed a corresponding decline in shipping. Merchant traffic in Bremen decreased from 63 to 17 vessels in the course of a week, and Hamburg showed a similar decline. These merchantmen were seen moving down the coast escorted by E-boats, apparently to support the invasion barges. The number of merchant ships in Le Havre increased from 2 to 52 in seven days, while at Antwerp 28 merchantmen arrived between August 31st and September 12th to reinforce the 625 barges that were to be seen crammed in the harbour six days later.

It would not be fair to give all the credit for this information to the PRU. Other RAF squadrons filled the gaps that were beyond Tuttle's limited resources, especially the long-range GR squadrons of Coastal Command which could reach as far north as Namsos. Photographs taken by Blenheims of 82 Sqn during a raid on Dunkirk on September 19th were of a sufficiently large scale (1:7,000) to reveal that the barges were being fitted with landing ramps. However, 85% of the PIU imput came from the PRU and, largely on the basis of this evidence, the JIC was able to report pessimistically on September 19th that some 240 merchant vessels with a potential capacity of 400,000 tons, and a barge fleet of 1629 capable of carrying 500,000 tons, were concentrated between Delfzijl and Brest.

But they never sailed for Britain. Luftwaffe losses in the Battle of Britain and a change in the weather caused Hitler to postpone 'Operation Sealion', and the barges and escorts were slowly dispersed, first out of range of Bomber Command and then back into the waterways of Europe. The redeployment became apparent to the PIU on September 23rd, and by the end of October there were only 448 barges remaining between Flushing and Boulogne.

On October 29th, Millen took off in the first Spitfire PR ID for the Baltic. The only naval vessels of any importance were the target battleship *Zahringen* and three minesweepers; the amount of merchant shipping present indicated only "fairly lively economic activity" and there was nothing at Stettin, Swinemünde, or Warnemünde "to suggest preparation for an overseas expedition". The enemy coast was clear from Stettin to Bordeaux.

As the invasion threat receded, Wembley had time to build up its Second and Third Phase sections. It was very wasteful to use a Kiel sortie just to plot ships in the harbour; a run of several dozen prints could reveal a wealth of information about harbour defences, flak and balloon positions, factories, communications, adjacent airfields and their aircraft, and many other points of military and economic interest. PIs became specialists in particular fields and, after an interesting sortie, the prints were passed from expert to expert to extract every item that might be of value. Millen's flight to the Baltic was a good case in point. In addition to shipping counts at Stettin, Swinemünde, Rostock, Warnemünde, Brunsbuttel, Cuxhaven, Wilhelmshaven, Emden, and Delfzijl, the PIs examined four airfields, three seaplane bases, six flak batteries, two W/T stations, two fuel stores, and two sets of barrage ballons. Such information might have had little value in 1940, but it marked the start of a long and detailed process of intelligence compilation that was to prove very useful when Britain was in a position to take the war back into continental Europe.

All this reconnaissance activity did not go unnoticed in Berlin. Cotton had sought anonymity for the PDU, not for melodramatic reasons, but because he realised that his unit would be singled out as a priority target if the Germans discovered its real role. St Eval was bombed on August 21st, 22nd, and 23rd resulting in a damaged Hudson propeller and wing. Heston received its first light bombs on August 26th but the Luftwaffe only concentrated on the 'eyes' of British Intelligence at the height of the invasion threat. A stick of bombs fell on the airfield on September 17th, followed by between 50 and 100 incendiaries the following day, and a parachute mine on September 19th demolished a hangar and damaged seventeen aircraft. Five Spitfires were put out of action when they were most needed, and although the majority were repaired within a few days, the episode proved that London was no place for such a vitally important unit. On October 2nd, Coastal Command was invited to consider an alternative base away from the bombs, winter fogs, and restrictive confines of west London. Benson airfield in Oxfordshire was selected, and on December 27th, 1940 the PRU moved to the relative safety of the upper reaches of the Thames.

* * * * *

Now that the PRU and PIU had become firmly established, it is interesting to compare them with their Luftwaffe counterparts. Unlike the British, the Germans put a lot of money and effort into creating a large and efficient PR organisation before the war, because the Luftwaffe High Command had a much greater appreciation of the importance of aerial reconnaissance, and especially photography, in a modern war. Support came right from the top; Goering was reputedly adept with, and impressed by, the aerial camera when he was an observer in 1915[1], and the Commander in Chief of the Army in 1938, Generaloberst Freiherr von Fritsch, wrote that "the military organisation that has the best photographic intelligence will win the next war."

Interest in aerial photography was kept alive in Germany during the Twenties and early Thirties by a small band of dedicated civilians. Although denied aircraft by the Treaty of Versailles, they acted as 'air representatives' on the staffs of each army division to advise on the application of air reconnaissance. These small divisional photo sections were incorporated into the Luftwaffe on its formation in 1935.

[1] As in many other respects, Goering thought he knew more than he did. During the Battle of Britain he would make impetuous interpretations of photographs, declaring authoritatively that some aircraft were dummies, and that certain airfields could confidently be erased from the enemy's order of battle.

Photo Reconnaissance

Reconnaissance squadrons in the Luftwaffe were divided into short-range Nahaufklärungsstaffeln[1] for tactical work in support of the army, and long-range Fernaufklärungsstaffeln[2] for strategic work. The first unit to stretch its wings was Aufklärungsstaffel A/88, formed in November 1936 to act as the land reconnaissance element of the Condor Legion in Spain. Staffeln were combined into Aufklärungsgruppen based at one airfield, and the expansion programme of 1937 called for six tactical reconnaissance Gruppen – Aufkl. Gr. (H)/111, 112, 113, 114, 115, and 212 – and six strategic Gruppen – Aufkl. Gr. (F)/121 at Neuhausen, 122 at Prenzlau, 123 at Grossenhain, 124 at Kassel, 125 at Würzburg, and 127 at Goslar.

Each Luftflotte had at least one composite Fernaufklärungsgruppe (FAG) to coordinate strategic reconnaissance activities within the Air Fleet's sphere of influence. In fact, one outstanding feature of the Luftflotten was the proportion of reconnaissance aircraft within the balanced force, comprising one-fifth of the total force of operational aircraft. By September 1939, there were some 80 Aufklärungsstaffeln available to support the war strategy of the coming months.

Standard tactical reconnaissance aircraft in 1939 were the He 46 and the Hs 126. The He 46 started life as a bi-plane in 1931 but dispensed with its lower wing over the years to give the observer a clearer view of the ground below. There were only 65 left in service in 1939, the main Nahaufklärungsflugzeug being the more modern Hs 126. The Luftwaffe had 275 of these high-winged monoplanes, similar in appearance and performance to the Lysander, and with a fully automatic camera in the fuselage bay.

The main Fernaufklärungsflugzeug of the day was the Do 17. There were still some 14 He 45s left in service – the long-range version of the He 46 that was equally long in the tooth – but the main brunt of strategic reconnaissance work was borne by Dornier's 'flying pencil'. In its heyday the Do 17 could out-pace any single-engined fighter in existence. A Do 17 V8 left everything behind in the 'Circuit of the Alps' in July 1937, and at a time when the Gloster Gauntlet, with a top speed of 230 mph, was entering RAF service, the graceful shoulder-winged Do 17 could reach 243 mph. The Luftwaffe had 257 at their disposal when Hitler invaded Poland.

The automatic Reihenbildner was still the main Luftwaffe camera, albeit improved and now fitted with Zeiss lenses of either 20, 50, or 75 cm focal length. As the Luftwaffe operated mainly at medium altitudes, the types most in evidence were the RB 20/30 and RB 50/30[3]. Hand-held cameras, with 20, 32, and 50 cm lenses, producing 18 cm square prints, were still in service with the He 45 Staffeln.

There were far more trained PIs in Germany than in Britain in 1939. The Luftwaffe photo-intelligence headquarters was located at Zossen, 13 miles

[1] Or Aufklärungsstaffeln (Heeres) – Army Cooperation Reconnaissance Squadron. Abbreviated to Aufkl. (H).

[2] Or Aufklärungsstaffeln (Fern) – Long-range Reconnaissance Squadron. Abbreviated to Aufkl. (F).

[3] The first figure refers to the focal length, the second to the print size, both in centimetres.

south of Berlin; known as the Stabsbildabteilung-Generalstab (Stabia-Gens) it was staffed by personnel from all three services. Five training schools – Hildesheim, Quedlinberg, Bad Voeslau, Munich, and Berlin/Schoenwalde – produced PIs for the Stabias at each Fleigerkorps HQ, and for the small Staffelbildgruppen of approximately 20 processers and interpreters attached to each Aufklärungsstaffeln. By September 1939, the Luftwaffe had 5200 ground processing and interpretation personnel at its disposal.

Massive decentralisation of resources differentiated the Luftwaffe from the RAF, due to the fact that each air force was geared to fighting a different type of war. British PR taskings came from a central agency such as Coastal Command, and the results were processed by centralised interpretation units at Wembley and High Wycombe, because the British were fighting a long-term, defensive war over a relatively small area. German military thinking, and hence that of the Luftwaffe, was based on a completely different philosophy. The Germans were on the offensive over a large geographical area, and their strategy was based on rapid blitzkrieg warfare. As the needs of the Army took priority, the Aufklärungsstaffeln were geared to the requirements of soldiers who wanted rapid and up to date information on an ever fluid military situation. Decentralisation was therefore essential; field commanders liaised with local Fliegerkorps HQs to request particular cover along their front, and because the information was needed in a hurry, it was processed and interpreted at the Stabia rather than at some rear organisation that was out of touch with the local situation. Speed was paramount in the blitzkrieg and the Luftwaffe distributed its PR organisation accordingly.

Initial interpretation after each sortie was carried out by the local Staffelbildgruppe, either from prints or directly from the negatives, and any information of tactical value had to be passed by telephone within 1½ hours. A written report and the films were passed up to the Stabia within 8 hours, where second stage interpretation was undertaken before the films were sent for further examination and filing at the Stabia-Gens. Consequently, the Stabia-Gens had a much more minor role to play than the PIU because the Germans were not as concerned with strategic considerations like the position of every Royal Naval vessel; instead they needed to know how many bridges were still intact over the Meuse, or the dispositions on a particular French airfield, and such intelligence could never have been provided with any speed if every film exposed over France had had to be interpreted at a single headquarters.

Whereas British PIs became experts in long-term subjects such as shipping and airfields, those in the Luftwaffe concentrated on battlefield terrain and fortifications. Just before the Battle of France, Luftwaffe prints revealed what appeared to be a large fortified bridgehead covering the proposed line of advance to the Meuse at Sedan. The success of 'Sichelschnitt' depended on von Rundstedt's tanks crossing the Meuse before the French realised what was happening, and many senior officers thought that the Ardennes plan should be cancelled because of the risk of delay in trying to breach the Sedan bridgehead.

Early in May 1940 the prints were given to an experienced Austrian PI who discovered what no-one else had noticed – that the fortifications were only under construction and not complete. Final doubts were dispelled; the German Army was ordered to "march like the devil" for the Channel, and the Meuse was crossed before the French had time to bring up their reserves to stem the advance.

German PIs were, however, generally much less flexible than their PIU counterparts. Although both air forces recruited from the better educated sections of society, over 60% of Luftwaffe PIs were NCOs, reflecting the German view that photo-interpretation was largely a mechanical process. In the Luftwaffe PIs were taught to 'read' rather than interpret prints. 'Photo-reading' involved the up-dating of maps from aerial photographs taken over the area of immediate operations; the photo-reader, when faced by an industrial complex, would only be able to declare that "it is an industrial complex". The photo-interpreter on the other hand would break the industrial complex down into its component parts.

The PIs of the Luftwaffe have often been berated because they did not use stereoscopes in their day to day work, and this has been cited as an example of their inferiority compared with the RAF. This criticism is unfair because circumstances alter cases. Speed was of the essence in a blitzkrieg environment and the Luftwaffe Photo Readers usually worked directly from negatives placed on a viewing screen. The Germans did possess some very fine stereoscopes, but their PIs rarely used them because any evaluation of the information they extracted from their prints was left to the Bildoffizier in charge of the Staffelbildgruppe. However, as the latter did little photo-interpretation, being more of an intelligence officer, he never built up the background of knowledge accumulated by the Third Phase PIs at Wembley. This did not really matter during the blitzkrieg phase – a trained monkey could tell whether a bridge was blown up or not – but it left the Germans at a severe disadvantage when they tried to employ PR for strategic purposes as the war progressed.

There were several Luftwaffe officers who played a large part in the initial development of PR in Germany: men like Generalmajor Fischer who supervised the training of PIs and who wrote a number of interpretation training manuals, or General Richard Schimpf who championed the technical development of aerial photography and photoorammetry before the war. But if there was a Luftwaffe equivalent of Sidney Cotton, it was Oberstleutnant Theodore Rowehl. The Kommando Rowehl[1] was established in 1937, directly under the control of Goering, with much the same brief as the SIS at Heston. Based at Staaken airfield, Berlin, the Kommando was equipped with a couple of He 111c passenger transports for clandestine photography over Britain, France, and Russia while ostensibly engaged on route-proving flights.

[1] Detachment Rowehl, or z.b.V. Staffeln beim RLM.

On the outbreak of war, the Kommando was expanded into the Aufklärungsgruppe Rowehl,[1] to act as the High Command's very own, and very secret, reconnaissance wing. Goering loved such cloak and dagger organisations, but as every other agency and most of the Luftwaffe was excluded from the secret, and thereby unable to use it for their own purposes, the potential of the unit was never fully exploited. However Rowehl, unlike Cotton, never lacked encouragement or support for his ideas from the top.

Rowehl too believed that high altitude was the best means of escaping detection and destruction, and throughout 1939 he experimented with all manner of prototypes to find the best machine. By the summer of 1940 his unit had grown into three Staffeln using Ju 86s and Do 217s over France and Britain. 2/Staffel operated Ju 86 P-ls and 2s, which were pressurised variants of the medium bomber stripped of all defensive armament and fitted with three automatic cameras. At a time when the Spitfire PR I could climb to 32,000 feet, the Ju 86 P-2 could make 39,370 feet, and on one sortie to Britain a reconnaissance pilot coaxed his aircraft up to 41,000 feet. Needless to say these PR forays remained unchallenged, and there are some marvellously comprehensive green books in existence which show the results of Rowehl's work. Several of these contained annotated aerial photographs of every RAF airfield of importance, whereas others described the location of everything of possible military interest in most British cities. While the British were taking down signposts to confuse a possible German invasion force, the PIs of the Luftwaffe were marking everything of interest in, for example, Leeds on enlarged photographs with Indian ink.

1/ and 3/Staffeln were equipped with Do 217 A-0s, long-range machines with their forward fuselages extended aft to accommodate two vertical cameras. By the end of 1940 they were operating over the Soviet Union in preparation for Barbarossa.

A fourth Staffel was added in January 1941 – 4/Aufkl. Gr. Ob.d.L. This was also known as the Test Centre for High Altitude Flight,[2] and it was here that Rowehl tested machines like the Hs 128. Henschel had designed this low-wing cantilever monoplane as a high-altitude research vehicle to test pressure cabins and DVL turbo superchargers, but Rowehl was so impressed with its potential that Henschel was instructed to modify the basic design into a reconnaissance variant to be known as the Hs 130A.

Initial engine teething troubles and a reduction in anticipated performance at altitude prevented the Hs 130A from becoming operational, so the first five prototypes were delivered to Echterdingen for development in 1941. By late November 1943, an Hs 130A-0/U6 with two DB 605B engines and superchargers, the GM boost system, a crew of two and a pair of cameras could reach 50,850 feet, but by then other aircraft had greater priority.

4/Staffel operated over the Soviet Union from Bucharest and Cracow with

[1] Aufklärungsgruppe Ob.d.L or Commander in Chief's Reconnaissance Gruppe.

[2] Versuchsstelle für Hohenfluge.

Ju 86Ps early in 1941, but when Hitler finally launched Barbarossa, the first three Staffeln of Rowehl's Gruppe moved to the Eastern front, leaving 4/Staffel in the west to continue its high level activities.

However the similarities between Rowehl's Gruppe and Cotton's PDU can be over-emphasised. The Luftwaffe was not on the defensive and the Do 17, and later the Ju 88, Me 110, and He 111, were perfectly adequate for PR in an environment where the Luftwaffe enjoyed massive air superiority.

The Luftwaffe had the aircraft to emulate the operational techniques devised at Heston but they saw no need to use them. In 1937 for instance, the Günter brothers had produced the revolutionary He 119 at Rostock. They designed it as an unarmed reconnaissance aircraft or bomber capable of eluding interception by virtue of its extremely high performance, and Siegfried and Walter Günter allowed no projections to spoil the aerodynamic cleanliness of their creation. Even the engine was buried in the fuselage, coupled to a single propeller by means of a long extension shaft passing through the cockpit. The entire nose section was covered with curved glass panels to allow a superlative field of vision for reconnaissance. At a time when the RAF firmly believed that it possessed the fastest bomber in the world, in the shape of the Blenheim with its top speed of 285 mph, the He 119 was capable of 354 mph, a ceiling of 26,250 feet and a range of 1,510 miles. These performance figures could have been improved with research, but a delegation from the Technischen Amt of the RLM[1] refused to accept the feasibility of an *unarmed* reconnaissance aircraft even though they were visibly impressed by its performance. They insisted on a conventional dorsal and ventral defensive armament fit, which cut its top speed by 15%. Consequently the He 119 never saw service to fulfil its designers' hopes, and it was soon relegated to the role of a flying engine test-bed.

We can only start to appreciate Cotton's contribution to the RAF and the drastic changes he wrought on British aerial thinking when we see the fate of the He 119 and realise that the Luftwaffe in 1940 was still sending out heavily defended reconnaissance aircraft to battle for much of its intelligence. Britain was fighting for her life but there were no such pressures on men like Rowehl, and therefore no need for a drastic reappraisal of priorities along the lines of the Longbottom Memorandum.

In 1941 de Havilland's vindicated the Günter brothers by bringing out their own version of the He 119, the PR Mosquito. By then the Germans had been forced on to the defensive and into a long drawn-out campaign, and the inadequacies of their policy of relying on quantity rather than quality, together with the lack of a man of Cotton's stature, soon became apparent.

With the indefinite postponement of Operation Sealion, the Royal Navy turned its full attention to the task of keeping open Britain's maritime trade routes. The *Graf Spee* had sneaked out of Wilhelmshaven on August 23rd, 1939 to cause havoc in the southern Atlantic, and she made the point that it

[1] Technical Office of the Ministry of Aviation.

was far easier to stop a German warship while still in the North Sea than to try to find her in the great oceans of the world. But to do this the Admiralty needed to know immediately that a ship had sailed, which necessitated regular photographic cover of every major western European port.

PRU areas of responsibility remained the same. Wick concentrated on the harbours and airfields of Scandanavia while St Eval watched the Bay of Biscay and Brittany. The flights rotated every three months or so, as in October 1940 when C Flight moved up to Wick and A Flight returned to Heston, so that everybody had his fair share of the bleak extremities of Britain as well as of the hotspots of London.

As it happened, the main German warships lay within range of Heston. The *Tirpitz* was fitting out in Wilhelmshaven, and between September 18th and 28th she was seen to have moved from the Bauhaufen to the Scheerhafen floating dock, and back to her original berth by October 10th. The *Bismarck*, nearing completion, moved from the Blohm und Voss shipyard at Hamburg to Kiel between September 11th and 23rd, and five days later the prints showed she had sailed again, this time beyond camera range to the Baltic for trials. The Wild machine could also tell from the small prints that the battle-cruisers *Scharnhorst* and *Gneisenau* were still in Kiel, together with the pocket-battleship *Lützow* and the embryo aircraft carrier *Graf Zeppelin*.

However all these discoveries created a false sense of security. It was easy for the PR pilot, six miles up in the troposphere, to become detached from reality. At 33,000 feet, unchained from "the surly bonds of earth", even the largest floating creation of steel could seem unreal, and 45,000 tons of destructive firepower came out on film like a fly on fly-paper. After a time complacency set in; if a vessel had stayed in the same berth for some time, surrounded by the normal paraphernalia of ship-yards, it was all too easy to assume that it was not going anywhere. Even a battleship could sail in an afternoon, and yet most ports were only covered once a week depending on weather and aircraft serviceability.

The Germans were shrewd enough to use this fact to their advantage. Although they could not stop a PR Spitfire, they could tell when it was there, and know with some certainty after it had gone that the PRU would not return for several days unless the PIs noticed anything suspicious. So the German Navy ensured that no suspicions could be aroused. Just before a warship was ready to sail, construction gangs would surround the ship and the dockyard would exude normality. A Spitfire would come and go and the PIs would reassure the Admiralty that at least one vessel showed no signs of moving for some time. A few hours later the warship would raise steam, slip anchor and set sail in the sure knowledge that no-one would miss it for several days. On November 29th, Flt Lt Arnold photographed the *Admiral Hipper* in her normal position in Brunsbuttel; the next day she was en route for the Atlantic.

The saga of the *Scharnhorst* and *Gneisenau* was another case in point. This pair of battlecruisers was visited by the PRU throughout the autumn at intervals varying from a week to a month depending on the number of targets with higher priority, the state of the weather at Kiel, or the virility of 'gremlins' at the time. According to the prints the ships did not move from September to December 21st, apart from an excursion by the *Scharnhorst* on September 23rd from the South Floating Dock to the Dockyard Wharf and back. They were photographed for the last time on December 21st, and by the time a PR Spitfire went over again on January 9th the berths were empty. In fact the battlecruisers left Kiel on December 27th and they were through the Great Belts and into the Atlantic before the Royal Navy could stop them.

It was not until March 28th 1941 and 115,000 tons of sunken Allied shipping later that the *Scharnhorst* and *Gneisenau* appeared on a PRU print again. An aircraft from *Ark Royal* sighted them 550 miles NNW of Cape Finisterre on March 20th, and the following day they were plotted by a Coastal Command flying boat, making for France. From March 22nd onwards aircraft from St Eval photographed every anchorage from Brest to Pauillac, but bad weather prevented confirmation of the battlecruisers' arrival in Brest until Plt Off Green flew over the port on March 28th.

The lessons of the *Scharnhorst* and *Gneisenau*, as well as the *Hipper* which managed to sneak out again undetected on February 1st, were readily appreciated. Continuous cover alone was valuable – it was no use trying to photograph everything once a fortnight; priority targets had to be determined and watched as often as possible. The Prime Minister insisted that the RAF concentrate on objectives connected with the Battle of the Atlantic and this meant ensuring that the battlecruisers never sailed again. 22 Sqn with their Beaufort torpedo bombers moved down to St Eval and Bomber Command sent some 200 aircraft to attack the ships in the first fortnight after their arrival. Between March 28th and April 30th 1941 over one-third of the total number of PRU sorties were directed against Brest, and on only one day in this period was no attempt made to photograph the harbour.

The value of such intensive PR soon became apparent. Despite the lack of success by Bomber Command in its attacks on the battlecruisers, one bomb did fall near the ships even though it failed to explode. Because of its proximity to this unexploded bomb, *Gneisenau* had to be moved out of dry dock, but as there was no room for her at the north quay where *Scharnhorst* was protected by a torpedo boom, it was decided to move *Gneisenau* into the harbour where she could be moored to a buoy for a few hours while the bomb was defused.

Thus, when a PR Spitfire returned to St Eval on 5th April, the PIs were able to report that the *Gneisenau* had left the sanctuary of dry dock and was now lying exposed in the inner harbour. The Beauforts were sent in and Fg Off K. Campbell of 22 Sqn earned a posthumous VC by placing a torpedo into *Gneisenau* seconds before he and his crew were shot down. Had it been at sea the battlecruiser would have surely sunk, but by placing every vessel in the harbour alongside her and pumping out the water the Germans managed to ease *Gneisenau* back into dry dock. Eight months later she was still undergoing repairs, and, as *Scharnhorst* needed a major engine refit, the German Navy was denied the chance of sending both vessels out into the Atlantic with *Bismarck* and *Prinz Eugen*.

Prints of German ports were useful to the PIU in other ways. Doenitz's submarines were causing great concern to British Naval Intelligence in 1941 because, unlike their surface counterparts which were built in relatively small numbers and usually launched in a blaze of publicity, there was little information available on U-boat numbers, dimensions, or characteristics. If the Admiralty was to counter the underwater challenge it needed to know the scale of the threat it was facing.

One of the most outstanding successes achieved by photo-reconnaissance during the Second World War was the accurate forecasting and assessment of German U-boat construction. But before the PIU could make any reliable estimate of numbers two requirements had to be fulfilled – regular and frequent cover of German ports, and better cameras. A battlecruiser might take four years to build but no-one knew how long the Germans needed to construct a U-boat; if sixteen similar and diminutive shapes were on the stocks in January, and sixteen were there in March, who could tell if they were the same sixteen, or a second batch if the Germans could assemble a submarine in a month. Only when the PRU concentrated on the German Fleet was the necessary frequency of cover obtained.

The small scale prints of the F 24 camera were also useless for such detailed interpretation work. A 500 ton U-boat was just over 60 metres long, and although it was possible to distinguish one on a 1:48,000 scale print, where 1 mm represented 53 metres, there was little chance of detecting much detail. To improve its cameras the RAF had to go backwards rather than forwards. The only suitable alternative to the F 24 was the F 8, a survey camera first introduced in 1926 but which had drifted out of service because of high costs and limited production. A few were discovered in India at the end of 1939 and they were shipped back to Farnborough for reconditioning and to be fitted with 14 in and 20 in lenses. They were re-introduced into RAF service in the spring of 1941, and an F 8 produced the large-scale prints of Kiel brought back by Plt Off Suckling and Flt Lt Clark on March 12th and 13th respectively, which made definite interpretation of minutiae like submarine construction possible for the first time.

The first step in the detection sequence was to discover which yards built U-boats. This was not as easy as it seemed because of the construction techniques employed by the German marine engineers. Keel plates were laid first, resembling those of an M-class mine-sweeper, and then a cradle was erected over the hull. This cradle grew with the submarine until it covered the vessel from stem to stern, thereby screening the U-boat frame and making detection very difficult on a poor quality print. After launching the vessel was no easier to find – another cradle surrounded the hull at a lower level so that only the conning tower protruded, and it was virtually impossible to see a conning tower against a grey background on a print exposed at 33,000 feet.

Once the PIU had found and followed a submarine through its various stages of construction, the PIs could then look at other yards and, depending on the length or type of cradles, assess the interval before the partially completed hulls would be ready to sail. The cradles, probably intended as a form of camouflage, now became a clear and unmistakable pointer. Thus, at the end of March 1941, the PIU felt confident to issue its first report on German submarines. They had counted 144 under construction to the west of Stettin, and they were able to point, by referring back to past prints, to the "vast drive in submarine construction which began in the latter half of 1940".

By September 1941 the PIU was not only able to record that the total number of keels had risen to 211, but they were also able to divide them into types. When Longbottom covered Kiel for the first time in April 1940, the U-boats in the Deutsche Werke were training vessels of 250 tons. Two months later, Bill Wise brought back the first pictures of a 500 ton operational type on the stocks. This variant accounted for 75% of all U-boat production up to September 1941, and it was the type that Michael Suckling photographed in such detail on March 12th. As the year progressed, larger boats of 740/750 tons appeared, and in September, 12 submarines of 1,000/1,200 tons were in evidence at the Deschimag Yard, Bremen.

Thus, by painstaking research and scrutinisation of thousands of prints at regular intervals, the Naval Section of the PIU was able to assess German U-boat capabilities and predict their numbers with considerable accuracy up to seven months in advance. This remarkable achievement meant that the Admiralty was not rudely surprised when Doenitz launched his Battle of the Atlantic.

Still the Royal Navy asked for more. Now that Italy had entered the war and the French had retired from it, the sea lanes of the Mediterranean became as exposed as those of the Atlantic. On November 2nd, 1940, four days after Millen's flight to Stettin, Flt Lt P. Corbishley took 'the bowser' down to Marseilles and Toulon in case the Royal Navy had to mount a pre-emptive raid on the Vichy Fleet. He brought back photographs that disclosed 103 vessels over 200 feet long in Marseilles, including twenty over 400 feet, and an equally clear plot of the shipping in Toulon. The Admiralty was also provided with reports on the boom defences, AA batteries, seaplane bases, and oil refineries in these coastal areas, and Corbishley was awarded an immediate DFC for his magnificent prints.

However the Spitfire PR ID could reach the south of France but no further, and to cover part of the Mediterranean the Air Staff decided to form a second PRU in Egypt. 2 PRU[1] was eventually to be equipped with Spitfires to watch the eastern Mediterranean, while a flight of Glenn Martin Marylands was to be sent to Malta to monitor southern Italy and the central narrows. By way of a bonus, the Admiralty also asked for regular PR of Murmansk to check on the Russian Navy, but a target 1,200 miles from the Shetlands was beyond the resources of even the ubiquitous PRU in 1941.

[1] Benson was numbered 1 PRU.

No 2 PRU was formed at Heliopolis, close by the HQ Middle East at Cairo, in March 1941, but there had been a PR component in Egypt for some time before this. Twelve months previously, during the 'Phoney War', the Allied staffs had considered ways of crippling Hitler's war machine before it could roll against France and the Low Countries. One of the more imaginative schemes came from General Weygand, the French military commander in Syria. He believed that the Germans were very dependent on the Russian oil-fields along the Caspian and the Black Sea, and that if the refineries of Baku, Grosni, and Batum were bombed by Allied aircraft from Syria, Hitler would be forced to postpone any plan of attack.

Any pre-strike reconnaissance from the Middle East would involve overflying neutral Turkey or Persia, so the task was given to Heston. Because of the long distances involved and the need to maintain diplomatic tranquility, a specially modified Lockheed 10A Electra and support party was dispatched to the Middle East, under the command of Sqn Ldr Hugh MacPhail. The detachment left Heston on March 23rd, 1940, arriving three days later at Heliopolis by way of Bordeaux, Marseilles, and Malta. On March 27th they followed the desert pipeline to Habbaniya in Iraq, where the landing had been timed to coincide with lunch so that the Electra would not attract much attention. However the crew had great difficulty restraining the amateur photographers as the aircraft was hidden away in a 5 Sqn hangar.

The next two days were taken up with cleaning the Lockheed and removing the RAF roundels, and at 0730 hrs on March 30th, MacPhail, Fg Off Burton, and two LAC photographers took off into the cloudless Mediterranean sky for the first sortie of the series. The Electra headed ENE across the flat valley of the Tigris and the Euphrates and then over the steadily rising snow-covered mountains of Persia to coast out at Alan on the Caspian Sea. They turned north and flew at 20,000 feet towards the Baku peninsula, reaching the refineries at 1145 hrs to begin the first of six uninterrupted photographic runs that were to last an hour. To complement the fixed vertical camera, LAC Dick took oblique photographs with a 14 in hand-held camera pushed through the emergency panel. He eventually collapsed with the effort of peering into the airstream without an oxygen mask at 20,000 feet in an outside air temperature of -20°C.

MacPhail landed back at Habbaniya at 1645 hrs with approximately 45 minutes fuel remaining. Nine and a quarter hours flying had produced two vertical and one oblique films which were processed during the evening and flown to Cairo for interpretation. During plotting a small gap was discovered between two runs owing to an increase in wind speed for which MacPhail had not allowed enough drift.

On Tuesday, April 2nd, the C-in-C Middle East, Air Chief Marshal Sir Arthur Longmore, decided that the Lockheed lacked the range to make Grosni from Habbaniya so this target was discounted. Three days later, the crew took off for the third and final sortie to Batum on the Black Sea. From Mosul northward the ground was covered by cloud until 30 miles from the Black Sea. The Electra crossed the coast just south of the Russo-Turkish border at 16,000 feet and turned towards Batum. On the second run over the refineries, MacPhail noticed four bursts of AA fire 4,000 feet below, followed by three more at 3,000 feet, and two only 2,000 feet away. The gunners were getting too accurate for MacPhail's liking, and as they had taken a fairly good line overlap with the oblique camera, he turned back to Iraq. By April 16th, they were all back at Heston.

Their prints were never used in anger because of the fall of France. The idea was rather impractical anyway – the deployment of an Anglo-French bomber force to Syria, a raid into Russia, and the assumption that such a limited operation would hinder the German war effort, were merely dreams in 1940. MacPhail's prints only served to feed Goebbels' propaganda machine. Copies of the films were given to the Deuxième Bureau in April 1940, and they were discovered by the Germans, together with a detailed plan of the proposed operation against the Caucasian oilfields, in a railway truck at La Charité station on June 9th. Hitler cited the project as an example of Allied duplicity in a speech to the Reichstag on July 20th, and it provided Molotov with a good excuse to put pressure on the governments of Turkey and Persia. "It must be observed," he stated, "that the repeated dispatch of these foreign reconnaissance aircraft could not aim at anything other but a complication of our relations with our neighbours."

The story had a humourous ending. When Germany invaded Russia in 1941, the Luftwaffe used the Heston prints to plan operations of their own. When these files were captured by the British in 1945, MacPhail's prints were displayed as examples of early German photographic reconnaissance.

At the beginning of June 1940, MacPhail returned to Egypt with Flt Lt R. G. M. Walker to photograph the Dodecanese from the Electra in case Italy entered the war. Air Chief Marshal Longmore was so impressed with their efforts that he kept the detachment in the Middle East to supplement his own limited reconnaissance resources. He created an Intelligence Photo Flight (IPF) to work directly under the control of the Senior Intelligence Staff Officer at AHQ ME, with the task of providing any intelligence and mapping information that was beyond the scope of Longmore's ordinary squadrons.

Until more aircraft became available at the beginning of 1941, all IPF work over the Mediterranean and Italian possessions had to be undertaken by the Electra. The blue Lockheed was christened 'Cloudy Joe', and its one fixed vertical F 24 camera and hand-held oblique camera turned over ports from Eritrea to the Dodecanese, and above the sands of Tripolitania to watch for any preparations to invade Egypt.

As there were no PR Spitfires to spare for the Middle East, it was originally intended that MacPhail should command a flight of Hurricanes in Egypt and a peripatetic flight of Marylands for army survey work or communications flying. This was then changed to two flights of Marylands, but when the whole consignment was sunk in transit in January 1941, three Hurricanes were given to the IPF as a temporary measure. The Hurricanes were modified locally – all armament was removed, extra fuel tanks fitted into the wings, and cameras installed in the rear fuselage.[1] The finished articles were coated in a matt royal blue dope to prevent detection in the clear blue desert sky. It was around this nucleus that 2 PRU came into existence on March 17th, 1941.

Then there was Malta. At the conference in the autumn of 1940 which authorised the creation of 2 PRU, it was recognised that there was a reconnaissance vacuum in the central Mediterranean. 1 PRU could reach as far south as Marseilles and 2 PRU could operate up to Benghazi, but the crucial anchorages of southern Italy lay in the void in between. Malta, placed strategically athwart the central Mediterranean narrows which separated Italy from her North African possessions, was an ideal reconnaissance base. As there were not enough fighters available to create another PRU, the island was allocated a share of the 150 Marylands ordered by France from the USA, but which the RAF had taken over once the Armée de l'Air had no further use for them.

Before the war the only aircraft with a PR capability on Malta was a Swordfish at Hal Far. It was part of the HQ Flight, and occasionally an F 24 camera would be installed and the Swordfish would go off to photograph the island's camouflage.

After the fall of France, a Latiquare seaplane arrived out of the blue, and for some time its crew of two operated out of Kalafrana and brought back the first pictures of enemy territory taken by a Malta-based aircraft. One day the seaplane failed to return, whereupon its reconnaissance role was taken over by a converted Hudson, until this too went missing leaving the island with only a few flying boats and an assortment of short-range aircraft to meet its commitments. Flying boats lacked both the speed and the armament to take on the massed defences around the naval bases of southern Italy, and as there were only nine flying boats available for the whole Mediterranean, the Italian Fleet was left alone while it stayed in port. Until the Marylands could be dispatched the Air Ministry promised to send out some extra fuel tanks to increase the range of the Lysanders, but no-one was particularly keen to overfly the heavily defended ports of Taranto or Brindisi in a 'long-range' Lysander.

The first three Marylands arrived on Malta in August 1940. Resembling 'flying pencils' like the Dornier Do 17, the Marylands were offered to the French as fighter-bombers with ground-attack and reconnaissance capabilities, and the few that saw service enjoyed the lowest casualty rate of any Armée de l'Air aircraft in the Battle of France. The RAF consignment was fitted with Pratt and Witney Twin Wasp engines instead of the original Wright Cyclones, resulting in a top speed of 304 mph and a ceiling of 30,000 feet. With a rate of climb in excess of that of the contemporary Gruman F-4 fighter, the Glenn Martin Maryland was equal to the task of taking on the Italian air force over the Mediterranean.

To find the men to service the Marylands, the AOC Malta, Air Vice Marshal Maynard, had to disband his Anti-Aircraft Cooperation Unit. Three

[1] Two had two F 24 8 in cameras each, and the third carried three F 24 14 in cameras – one vertical and two obliques.

crews were sent out from England, together with three more Marylands to be 'cannibalised' for spares, and 431 Long Range Reconnaissance Flight came into existence.

431 Flight was basically a general reconnaissance (GR), i.e. maritime, unit with a brief to patrol the Central Mediterranean looking for enemy vessels and attacking them whenever possible. PR was only a minor part of their work and they only used cameras when photographic confirmation of visual sightings was necessary. The Unit only came into prominence as a PR force with the raid on Taranto, and through the exploits of a young Pilot Officer named Warburton.

By the autumn of 1940 Admiral Cunningham, the C-in-C Mediterranean, had tired of waiting for the Italian Fleet to venture out of its safe anchorages to do battle with the Royal Navy. He therefore decided to take the Royal Navy to them in the form of a Fleet Air Arm attack on the naval base of Taranto. It was a daring and audacious plan, but it relied for its success on detailed information on the position of every Italian ship at anchor and the siting of all harbour defences. Cameras instead of bombs became the regular load of 431 Flight at the beginning of November, as the Marylands photographed the Taranto approaches and berths daily so that the PIs in Cairo could record arrivals, departures, anti-torpedo nets, and anti-aircraft defences. It was only through these prints that the Fleet Air Arm discovered that barrage-balloons had been erected around the southern half and part of the northern portion of the semicircular harbour, a fact that could have played havoc with the raid if it had gone unnoticed.

Adrian Warburton was one of the pilots on 431 Flight. A bank clerk before the war, he volunteered for the RAF in 1939 and was granted a short service commission as a pilot. He was a mousy individual whose prowess on a Botha squadron was so mediocre that his CO 'volunteered' him for a vacancy in Malta even though it was for an observer. Having passed the GR course, Warburton managed to navigate a Maryland to Malta via Gibraltar.

"From the moment when this mercurial officer arrived in Malta," wrote Captain A Spooner DSO, DFC,[1] "a strange affinity between place and person was born." Warburton was navigating a Maryland on an operational sortie within a few days of arriving, and a week later he was promoted to the pilot's seat. After a fortnight he was captain of a crew of three and all set to become one of the greatest PR pilots of the Second World War.

The air was very still and the sea very calm on November 10th when this young man of twenty-two was tasked with the final pre-strike reconnaissance of Taranto. The cloud was so low that even the birds were walking, but 'Warby' was unperturbed; the insignificant introvert had changed completely in the Mediterranean sunshine and he was now a man who could not recognise danger and therefore ignored it. With his navigator, Sgt Johnny Spires, and his gunner, Sgt Paddy Moran, Warby took off from Luqa and headed towards Calabria at zero feet under the cloud. As they clipped the waves

[1] "In Full Flight."

across the Gulf of Taranto, Warburton briefed his crew in all seriousness that he would stay inside the harbour until Spires had plotted every vessel on paper, and that he would fly low enough for Moran to read the name on the side of every ship. Warby had probably never heard of the term 'dicing', but that was what he intended to do.

Against the background noise of two hefty engines, the Maryland sped at full throttle towards Taranto. The Italians were totally unprepared for a visit in such poor weather – the barrage balloons were down – and Warburton flew twice around the outer harbour before anyone took any notice of him. On both circuits he operated the camera while Spires scribbled furiously on his map, but when the first AA battery acknowledged their existence at the end of the second run, the Maryland beat a hasty retreat out of range.

But Warburton was not satisfied that they had plotted the position of every ship in the harbour so he threw common sense to the wind and headed back into the wall of AA fire. The Maryland survived and, despite a 20-minute running battle with a Cr 42 on the way back, the crew returned with the news that 5 battleships, 14 cruisers, and 27 destroyers were berthed in the harbour. A magnificent set of prints were on board *Illustrious* the next day ready for the Fleet Air Arm attack that evening.

On the next morning, the CO of 431 Flt, Sqn Ldr E. A. Whiteley, photographed Taranto once more. Four runs were made over the wreckage and burning oil and from 6,000 feet Whiteley's crew brought back a wonderful photographic story of success. The battleship *Cavour* was beached and abandoned never to sail again; the battleships *Littorio* and *Duilio* were seriously damaged and remained out of action for half a year. In the inner harbour, two cruisers were listing to starboard surrounded by oil and two auxiliaries were half-submerged off the commercial basin. Half the Italian battlefleet had been immobilised for the loss of eleven torpedoes and two Swordfish torpedo bombers.

That evening, every Italian vessel that could raise steam weighed anchor for safer waters further north. The aerial camera had provided the intelligence for a pre-emptive strike that was not to be equalled in strategic importance in the Middle East until the destruction of the Egyptian air force while it sat on the ground in the 1967 Arab-Israeli war. Eleven torpedoes immobilised half a fleet because the Fleet Air Arm knew where to place them for maximum effect: they knew that because of the fearlessness of a failed Botha pilot named Warburton.

If the Royal Navy was satisfied with all this photographic effort on their behalf from Norway to the Middle East, Bomber Command most certainly was not. High Wycombe remained convinced that only they could win the war. The Army had been ejected from Europe and would be in no position to re-enter the continent for many years to come; the Royal Navy could prevent Britain from losing the war by protecting her supply-lines, but could never win it. Only the strategic bomber force so belovedly cultivated by Trenchard seemed capable of taking the war to Germany and, by striking at centres of population and industry, cripple Hitler's war effort and demoralise his people. For this reason Bomber Command believed that the PRU should involve itself less with the defensive struggle being waged by the Navy and should give priority instead to the offensive campaign mooted at High Wycombe.

Unfortunately there was little evidence in the first year of the war that Bomber Command could achieve such dramatic results. Early raids in 1939 had shown that the Wellingtons, Whitleys, and Hampdens were no match for the Luftwaffe in daylight, and at the beginning of 1940 Bomber Command had decided to seek sanctuary in darkness. However the transition from a day to a night force was not easily accomplished. Although the AOC 4 Group felt confident enough to state in February 1940 that "the accuracy of night bombing will differ little from daylight bombing", there were to be many unforeseen problems that were only to be forced into prominence by the PRU.

On the night of March 16th, 1940 the Luftwaffe bombed Scapa Flow. In retaliation, Bomber Command decided to attack the Hörnum seaplane base on the coastal island of Sylt. Hörnum was one of the main bases for German mine-laying operations in the North Sea, and it was politically acceptable because of its isolated position away from civilian homes. On March 19th, under cover of darkness, 50 Wellingtons, Hampdens, and Whitleys took off from Hemswell and Waddington for the German coast.[1]

The elated crews landed back in Lincolnshire with tales of success and destruction. Forty-one crews claimed to have identified and bombed Hörnum, leaving the airfield destroyed and the night sky ablaze with exploding fuel tanks and burning hangars. The fact that the German press denied that any damage had been caused and that the RAF had in fact bombed neutral Denmark was dismissed as propaganda. The aerial camera would prove to the world that Bomber Command was an accurate and destructive force.

The standard PR aircraft of the time, the Spitfire PR IB, lacked the range to make Sylt and back, so a Blenheim of 82 Sqn was dispatched to photograph the island. The prints it brought back were not very clear, but they were revealing enough. The seaplane base was uncomfortably intact – no amount of peering through magnifying glasses and stereoscopes could alter the fact that there was no apparent damage to the hangars, slipways, and oil tanks. The only signs of the raid were "a row of what appear to be bomb craters to the West of the quarters", and a house that was only a shell. It was impossible to determine the positions of the "many direct hits" claimed by the bomber crews – wherever they were, they were not at Hörnum.[2]

However it took more than this raid to convince Bomber Command that their aircraft were in no position to undertake accurate precision attacks at night. Bombing inaccuracies to date had been blamed on inexperience and the

[1] One of the Intelligence Officers who took part in the briefing at Hemswell was Flt Lt Hamshaw-Thomas, the photographic pioneer of Palestine in 1917, who had abandoned his botanical work at Cambridge to rejoin the RAF in 1939.

[2] It was later discovered that the force had bombed a Danish island to the north.

infant state of the art; with no experience of strategic bombing to refer to, Bomber Command maintained that proficiency could only be reached by trial and error. Conventional intelligence was too slow and imprecise to be of much value in assessing the error, and the bombing crews made unreliable witnesses because they only saw a limited part of the total picture, and much of that was obscured by smoke and darkness. They could also be deceived by appearances – a small quantity of burning oil could look like a very impressive fire. Only the aerial camera, operating in daylight when the dust had settled, seemed capable of providing a permanent and exact assessment.

At first the PRU only brought back a limited number of damage assessment photographs so the tendency was to blame the cameras, or the lack or poor quality of their prints, rather than the bomb-aimer if no damage could be detected on the photographs. In the end the C-in-C Bomber Command, Air Marshal Portal, became increasingly frustrated at having to take second place to the Admiralty for photographs, and he demanded a PRU of his own. The Air Staff agreed, and on November 16th, 1940, 3 PRU came into being under the control of HQ 3 Group.

Bomber Command's PRU was based at Oakington in the Cambridgeshire fens. Its first and only CO was a young Scotsman, Sqn Ldr P.B.B. Ogilvie, who had been plucked from the photo staff at High Wycombe and sent to organise the pilots and Spitfire PR ICs donated by Heston. The primary function of 3 PRU was "to obtain photographs of bombing targets at a scale suitable for damage assessment", but for such detailed work Ogilvie needed a camera with a longer focal length lens. The best scale obtainable from an F 24 was 1:24,000 at 30,000 feet – i.e. the whole of Liverpool could be recorded on one print 5 in square – and this was much too small for detailed interpretation. A 24 inch lens was the minimum length for good damage assessment photography – it could give a scale of 1:15,000 at 30,000′ or 1 mm to 15 metres – and Ogilvie hoped to use the American Fairchild camera with a 24 in lens as soon as it came into service. Until then, the standard 3 PRU fit was a split pair of F 24 8 inch cameras in the wing and an F 8 20 inch camera in the fuselage; the F 24s covered a large area in small scale for orientation purposes, while the F 8 took a number of large-scale photographs of everything within that area.

Ironically, the best camera at Oakington was of German construction. A Luftwaffe high level reconnaissance aircraft had been shot down over England in August and a Zeiss Ikon 75cm (approximately 30 in) telephoto lens was salvaged from the wreckage. This valuable instrument was 'acquired' by Ogilvie, and, when fitted to an F 8 camera, provided the most detailed photographs as yet obtained by the RAF.

Pat Ogilvie flew the unit's first operational sortie on November 29th to Cologne, where he made four runs over the city from 30,500 feet to photograph repair work since Bomber Command's last visit. Target files were soon opened on all major German cities and industrial centres within range, lavishly filled with annotated prints of likely future targets photographed from Oakington. This 'Bombers' Baedekar' was to be the most lasting legacy of 3 PRU.

Ogilvie also claimed the distinction of being the first PR pilot to photograph Berlin in wartime. A sortie to the German capital involved a round trip of 1,´50 miles, a distance only attainable by the Spitfire PR ID and IF types. As Benson possessed the only two 'bowsers' in existence, Oakington had to await delivery of its first IF type at the beginning of 1941. On March 14th, Pat Ogilvie took off at 0945 hrs and, after refuelling at Horsham St Faith, set course for Berlin. He crossed the Dutch coast at 1120 hrs and reached Hannover exactly on ETA. He then turned starboard, and flying just below the contrail layer at 27,000 feet, arrived over Berlin at 1225 hrs with just enough fuel left for ten minutes photography. He exposed 95 frames and turned for home. By the time he coasted in over Yarmouth he was down to 35 gallons and the Spitfire landed twenty minutes later with only 20 gallons remaining in the tanks. The mission had provided the first indications of the damage caused by Bomber Command's raid on the German capital the previous August, and two weeks later Patrick Bruce Bine Ogilvie was awarded the DSO.

It was damage assessment work such as this that was to prove more illuminating to Bomber Command than the provision of target material. There was a need for such 'evidence in camera'; the AOC 4 Gp, Air Vice Marshal Coningham, admitted that he had very little idea of the results achieved by his Whitleys, and his problem was illustrated by a raid on Essen on November 7th, 1940. Wellingtons went in first and 20 crews claimed to have heavily attacked the target, leaving flames and explosions that were visible 60 miles away. Yet at the same time as the last crews of 115 Sqn were leaving the long line of fire, 24 Hampdens of 5 Gp arrived at a completely blacked-out Essen. Only one crew saw a large fire on arrival, and when the rear force of Blenheims reached the city two hours later only "four flashes" were visible.

Bomber Command was therefore faced with conflicting reports from three different Groups, all claiming to have reached and bombed Essen and implying that the other formations had been elsewhere. The new C-in-C, Air Marshal Sir Richard Peirse, had no means of telling who was correct, and thereby remedying the errors that were evident, before 3 PRU became operational.

On the night of 16th December, 134 aircraft set course for the centre of Mannheim. In the van was a force of fire-raising Wellingtons, flown by the most experienced crews available, who were to mark the aiming point with incendiaries to guide the successive waves of Whitleys, Hampdens, and Blenheims. A total of 102 crews claimed to have bombed Mannheim on a perfect moonlight night. The town centre was reputedly in flames, and Peirse immediately sent a congratulatory signal to all formations. Five days later the weather was clear enough for a daylight reconnaissance by Fg Off J.H.L. Blount from Oakington. His photographic mosaic had a sobering effect. Despite 'considerable damage' the prints showed 'a wide dispersal of the attack' and Peirse was forced to conclude that the operation had "failed in its primary object".

The Mannheim prints provided, in the words of the AOC 5 Gp, "the first of any real evidence we have had as to the general standard of bombing accuracy which characterises our present night operations." Air Marshal Peirse believed that the fault lay in rigid adherence to his orders to bomb the incendiary fires, and that the bomb aimers had dropped their bombs into the flames instead of onto the target. He wrote that in future he expected the great majority of bombs to fall within a half-mile radius of the aiming point.

But he was being optimistic. On Christmas Eve, Fg Off D.S. Hood photographed the results of a raid on two oil refineries at Gelsenkirchen in the Ruhr. Although most of the 196 crews involved claimed to have hit the plants, there were no signs of recent repairs and very few bomb craters on the excellent photographs, whereas there should have been about 1,000. The PIs concluded that 260 tons of bombs had been dropped with little effect and that most of the bomb-aimers had missed their targets by an "immeasurable distance".

The same poor results were recorded by 3 PRU following raids on Dusseldorf, Hannover, Bremen, Cologne, and Hamburg over the next few months. At first it was suggested that hasty repairs had obscured the real damage and that less important craters were allowed to remain to deceive the RAF. But gradually the photographic evidence was accepted in preference to the crews' reports, especially as the standard and clarity of prints improved. An interpretation report on the Hamburg raid of March 13th showed how much detail could be extracted even from hazy prints – "direct hit on workmens' dining room at Howaldt Werke, Vulcan shipyards", "probable damage to a building which is believed to be the Post Office in Claus Groth St". The Germans were not above a bit of cunning subterfuge at times. A set of Hannover prints showed that the roof of the main railway station had been painted to look like a major road junction, and a large lake to the south of the city, which could be used as a good ground reference point for navigators, had been covered with rafts and camouflaged to blend in with the surrounding countryside. However the Germans could never have obscured the amount of damage that was reported as having taken place.

The bomber crews' reports were not fabrications – it was simply that most of the crews were not finding the targets they were supposed to bomb. High Wycombe was being very optimistic to expect otherwise with the primitive navigational aids available at the time. A Whitley or Hampden observer, aiming for a precision target such as an oil refinery 400 miles from base in the dead of night, with the odd dog-leg thrown in to evade the defences, was expected to be no more than 300 yards off target with little more to help him than dead-reckoning. If the forecast wind was wrong, or if cloud obscured a few crucial ground features, an aircraft could be up to 100 miles off course after several hours. If everything went well, the crew would assume they were over the target on ETA, especially if there were lights or fires below them. Decoys added to the confusion, attracting bombers like moths to a flame – a Third Phase Section was soon set up just to look for decoys. Crews were also deluded by the belief that any bomb dropped on Germany was a contribution to the war effort, with the result that after a long and arduous flight most observers were willing to declare that they were over the target even though they were often over cloud and had no means of confirming their position.

As a first step in analysing navigation errors, Bomber Command decided to fit night cameras into their aircraft to record the true position of the bomb-drops. Daylight cover could only tell where the bombers had not been; only the night camera could show where the bombs had fallen so that remedial measures could be taken. Consequently, 3 PRU was tasked "to undertake all night photography required by the RAF and to carry out development on this subject".

The RAF had first experimented with night cameras in 1917 over the experimental station at Orfordness. An FE 2b was used for the trials – flash bombs produced by the Woolwich Arsenal were dropped from 2000 feet over the marshes. Battlefield trials however were not a success – the flares illuminated British as well as German lines, much to the chagrin of the Army, and night photography was abandoned.

Night flares continued to be employed as target illuminators but night camera trials were not resumed until 1940. Two Wellingtons were allocated to Heston in the summer of 1940 for night PR trials in case a 24-hour watch had to be kept on the invasion beaches, but, as Bomber Command refused to surrender any of its precious flares, little progress was made. The Wellingtons were transferred to Oakington in November. They were IC variants with Pegasus XVIII engines, each fitted with two cameras in the mid-underturret aperture and equipped to carry 4.5 in flashes. Synchronisation of the cameras and flares with the bomb drop was the main problem. The cameras were operated automatically by the bomb release mechanism, but the timing of the ignition of the highly combustible flares presented difficulties – if they exploded too late, the camera shutter would have closed; if too early, the bomber might become a blazing inferno.

By February 1941, Oakington had solved these problems and was ready for its first night operational sortie. At 1805 hrs on February 5th, Flt Lt R. P. Elliott took off in a Wellington from Newmarket to bomb the *Hipper* in Brest. At 1958 hrs he was over the port only to discover that the heavy cruiser had sailed, but he dropped 2,000 lbs of bombs and made three photographic runs over the dockyard fires 11,000 feet below.

The next step was to fit night cameras into operational aircraft. Needless to say, they were not popular with the bomber crews. Not only did they have to spend valuable time over the target wrestling with highly inflammable canisters, but the only result was a set of prints that told everyone from the C-in-C downwards that the aircraft had been miles off target and that all the arduous effort had been a waste of time. The night camera was soon branded as an official spy.

Nevertheless, by June 1941 about one in ten aircraft of Bomber Command had been fitted with night cameras. These aircraft were usually positioned at the rear of a bombing force so that the flares would not distract the bomb-aimers. Between June 2nd and July 25th, 1941, 650 photographs were exposed on 100 separate raids spaced over 48 nights, and these, together with the interpretation reports, were analysed by a Ministry official, Mr. Butt, on August 18th. He found that only one-fifth of the total number of dispatched bombers could be said to have reached the target area, but this figure was misleading because it included sorties against relatively easy targets like the French ports. Over Germany as a whole, only one in four aircraft reached the target, while over the Ruhr, habitually covered by industrial haze and heavily defended, the proportion of aircraft bombing within five miles of the target was one in ten.

"The air photographs showed how little damage was being done," wrote Winston Churchill. "It also appeared that the crews knew this, and were discouraged by the poor results of so much hazard. Unless we could improve on this there did not seem much use in continuing night bombing."

The Butt Report marked the occasion when Bomber Command, in the words of the authors of the 'Strategic Air Offensive Against Germany', "virtually abandoned the aim of selective industrial attack and embraced that of general area bombing directed towards the reduction of German production and morale." The results of day and night photography proclaimed that changes would have to be made. As a first step, targets had to be selected that could be found at night with some degree of accuracy, i.e. large urban areas rather than specific pin-points. Over the long-term, maximum priority had to be accorded to the development of effective navigation and target location aids. "All these matters had been brought to the point of recognition by the reconnaissance photographs taken by Spitfires of the Photographic Reconnaissance Unit."

All photographic reconnaissance on behalf of the Admiralty and Bomber Command by 1 and 3 PRUs had been achieved at the expense of the JIC. The threat of invasion was still very real, but in February 1941 the JIC complained that it was not receiving enough cover of western Europe due to the "many conflicting demands and other claims on our aircraft". There was a feeling at the JIC, shared by such others as the War Office and the Ministry of Supply who were supposed to have access to 1 PRU, that UK reconnaissance resources had been pre-empted by two powerful pressure groups and that tasks from other agencies, no matter what their importance, were rarely accorded high priority.

On February 14th 1941, the JIC invited the Air Ministry "to consider the amalgamation and centralised control of the various photographic reconnaissance units". The proposal was received sympathetically because the Air Ministry was also dissatisfied with the existing arrangement. There were too many demands for reconnaissance to allow Bomber Command to monopolise a quarter of the PR Spitfires available to the RAF, and the lack of liaison between the PRUs was very wasteful. A Benson Spitfire might cover Wilhelmshaven in the morning to plot the ships in port, and an aircraft from Oakington would fly over in the afternoon to provide target material for a forthcoming raid. Tuttle became very angry one day when one of his aircraft ran into a hail of AA fire because the batteries had been alerted by one of Ogilvie's men ten minutes earlier. Surprise was as vital to PR as duplication was inefficient.

The Air Staff, recognising that 'Cotton's Circus' had only been replaced by two PR 'empires' in Coastal and Bomber Commands, decided to amalgamate both these PRUs and task them directly from the Air Ministry. The interpretation units at Wembley and High Wycombe were also to be combined into a Central Interpretation Unit (CIU) at Medmenham to reduce duplication. A proposal that a PR Group be created to provide "for the first time in Royal Air Force history a form of direction and supervision of all photographic activities" was rejected as it smacked of 'empire building'.

The only opposition to these proposals came from Bomber Command. Air Marshal Sir Richard Peirse objected to the loss of his interpretation sections and PRU on the grounds that 3 PRU was "a special unit trained and equipped for bomb damage assessment and almost exclusively concerned with the requirements of Bomber Command . . . Indeed it is practically the only means at my disposal of discovering the effect of my bombing attacks. Under the scheme now promulgated I shall have to deal with it through another Command and I am quite sure that the introduction of this uneconomical piece of mechanism can only retard an organisation essentially designed for speed, and cause needless friction." As a compromise, the Air Staff agreed that Bomber Command could have direct access to the CO of the PRU in connection with requests for damage assessment photography, but Peirse was still not satisfied. Nevertheless the merger was authorised and all photographic requirements for the three Services and RAF Commands in the UK were henceforth coordinated by ACAS(I)[1] at the Air Ministry. 3 PRU was disbanded and its resources combined with those at Benson to form the new 1 PRU on June 16th, 1941. The amalgamated Unit stayed under the operational control of Coastal Command, but the Air Ministry conceded that if Bomber Command found, after a prolonged trial, that the new arrangement was not a success, the question of control could be raised again.

"This takes us full circle," wrote Air Vice Marshal Sir Arthur Harris, then DCAS. "Originally PRU was the 'Cotton Club' – and a law unto itself. This was unsatisfactory, so it went to Coastal Command – and was a law unto Coastal Command. Then Bomber Command naturally demanded a better share and got a second PRU of its own. Now the proposal is to concentrate it again. A laborious way to rid ourselves of Cotton. But very probably the only way!"

[1] Assistant Chief of Air Staff (Intelligence).

CHAPTER SIX

A Sea of Pictures

Wide eyes that weary never
And wings that search the sea

Swinburne: 'To a Seamew'

As it turned out, Arthur Harris was wrong; Cotton had gone but no-one could exorcise his ghost. Try as they might, the Air Ministry would never 'regularise' the PRU until they conceded that PR was a specialised function necessitating its own controlling authority. The office of ACAS(I) was perfectly happy as long as its taskings in order of priority were fulfilled, and so it left the organisation at Benson to Coastal Command, which in turn tended to leave Tuttle to his own devices. Although the Command staffs at Northwood were sympathetic towards 1 PRU[1] they regarded PR as an adjunct to the real work of the Command. Coastal Command afforded priority to the war at sea, and as nobody at Northwood had much experience of high level PR operations, they tended to opt out of the day-to-day organisation at Benson, leaving the PRU to continue to make its own rules, follow its own procedures, and owe allegiance to no one but Tuttle.

Supply of equipment was a case in point. Nominally the PRU depended on the Maintenance Unit at Detling for its logistic support, but as Coastal Command was a poor relation within the RAF and as Benson had little priority within the Command, equipment was not readily forthcoming. It did not help when Benson requested non-standard or specialist items, or when the Maintenance Unit replied that they had never heard of the PRU, so Tuttle fell back on his unlimited local purchase account, another of Cotton's legacies, which meant that he could afford to act as a law unto himself.

Unlike Cotton, Tuttle cultivated senior officers and acted as a buffer against paper-work and trivia so that his pilots could concentrate on flying. He allowed his pilots a great deal of initiative because of the tremendous pressures facing them. There was the strain of scanning the skies for five hours, the concentration required to fly, navigate, and photograph accurately with fingers like ice, and most of all the intense loneliness. It was the same the next day and the next with no public acclaim and admiration, such as that accorded to fighter pilots, to fall back on. It was not surprising that the many frozen and exhausted pilots who eased themselves out of their cockpits every evening thought that there must be easier ways of fighting a war.

To the purist, the PRU was very disorganised. Flight Lieutenants, not

[1] Although officially 1 PRU, it continued to be known as 'the PRU'.

Group Captains, chose the missions from the daily requirement depending on the weather and aircraft serviceability; Pilot Officers and SNCOs, not Squadron Leaders, decided how they would tackle the task and whether or not to go for a secondary target if they saw that the primary one was unattainable. Every man was allowed to think for himself on the ground because he had to act for himself in the air. PR was a very personal business and this was reflected not only in the flexibility of action that Tuttle allowed his men, but also in the fact that all PRU pilots felt personally involved when one of their number was off on his lone mission. Everyone would accompany the pilot out to his aircraft and they would leave the crew-room to greet him on his return.

Niven and le Mesurier had moved on, to be replaced by equally professional successors such as Gordon Hughes. Fg Off Hughes was the finest test pilot Tuttle ever had, for he would bring back the most marvellously comprehensive notes from every air test. Born into a Quaker family, Gordon Hughes joined the PRU because of his aversion to armament and, lacking cannons, he became the great exponent of subtlety instead of fire-power to evade destruction. He was once asked if he ever regretted not having armament in his Spitfire:

"Oh no! Never! Don't you understand? That's the whole thing about PR. It's the only sort of front-line job in this war where you aren't asked to kill. You have weapons of a different sort, which aren't guns – they're your planning and your flying and your . . . perseverence. I mean, the will to keep on when things go wrong and you're frozen to death. And don't you see, it's much more effective too. If someone who wants to pinch your flowers breaks down your gate, smashes the fence, and tramples down half your garden, you certainly don't let him get away with it. But if someone slips into your garden before you know it, picks some flowers and slips away quietly and quickly, you may feel annoyed, but you probably let him go."[1]

Hughes was a meticulous perfectionist. He got up at 0500 hrs every morning and spent an hour in the Met office discussing the intricacies of the European weather forecast while everyone else slept on. His philosophy for survival was to make life as difficult as possible for the Luftwaffe. If he flew as high as he could and endured as much cold as possible, a German fighter pilot climbing up towards him, perhaps suffering from a hangover or with his mind on more interesting pursuits, might not be as keen to suffer discomfort as the PRU pilot whose life depended on it. To this end Hughes gave up alcohol and late nights and became a fitness fanatic so that he might have that bit more stamina than his opponent to endure long periods at high altitude. He believed that the PRU owed much of its success to this attitude of putting the pressure back on to the Luftwaffe.

There were others in the same coolly efficient mould. Tony Hill was the scion of a rich brewing family and a typical British gentleman, but beneath the quiet exterior was a very brave man who epitomised the 'press-on' spirit of the

[1] 'Evidence in Camera'.

PRU, F.A. Robinson, 'Freddie' Ball, and Donald Steventon were the three Cranwell men who were soon to make their mark as Flight Commanders. Donald Steventon, a native of Edgbaston, suffered intermittently from sinus trouble and the pain was so intense one day at altitude that he lost control and spun out of the sky. Nothing daunted he recovered and climbed back up to height again, only this time he opened the cockpit canopy slightly to allow a stream of bitterly cold air to freeze the painful side of his face so that he could carry on.

There were to be many others of equal courage and dedication in the PRU before the war ended, men who were never treated as heroes because their role was not a glamorous one. They were often quiet and unassuming men, more mature than the popular conception of an RAF pilot, who preferred to spend their time playing chess, discussing new ways of sneaking up on Brest, or picking the brains of PIs. To the rest of the RAF, PRU stood for 'Pilots' Rest Unit', but 'Rockfist' Rogan and all the other fictional heroes of aerial bravado would have found the life of a PR pilot too demanding for them.

That did not mean that there were no humorous incidents or 'line-shoots'. One Polish pilot flew a circuit at Benson with a petrified airman clinging to his tail, and when he landed complained that the aircraft was unstable. Another pilot brought back a very clear set of coastal prints, ostensibly taken over France, but which could only be plotted after hours of detective work at Medmenham when one PI recognised Brighton pier. The pilot had flown over cloud until he estimated he was over France and let down to photograph what he thought was the right coastal area, only to find later that he had been thwarted by a particularly strong headwind.

But one man rarely laughed and he was one of the best of them all. Alistair Taylor was educated at Kings School, Worcester, and joined the RAF in 1936. He served on Fairey Battles at Harwell before the war and, like many others, transferred to the PDU from France. Tall and very good looking, his only interest outside flying was cricket. He could not land an aircraft smoothly to save his life and he damaged several PR Spitfires in his time, but he was a natural PR pilot. After each sortie pilots went along to the First Phase Section with a rough sketch map of where they had flown so that the PIs would know where the prints were taken. Some pilots were miles out in their estimation of where they had been, especially if they had flown for hours above cloud. Not so with Taylor – his sketches were always spot on. He was good and he knew it. Contemptuous of lesser mortals, Alistair Taylor was so magnificently aloof and supremely self-confident that he was known as 'God' Taylor, or 'Ice' Taylor because of his cold, pale-blue eyes. Always meticulous in his planning and in his approach to PR, he was beholden to no one for advice or counsel and remained a lone-wolf in the crew-room. If Tuttle ever wanted to make sure of getting some prints, especially at low-level, he sent Taylor. Ever the great individualist, supreme in his own profession and oblivious to the world around him, Alistair Taylor was the first PRU pilot to complete a hundred missions and the first man to receive three DFCs in the Second World War.

Wg Cdr Geoffrey Tuttle was the amalgam that held this conglomerate of individuals together. Although a first-class aviator he never flew on a PR mission himself – his pilots ascribed his operational reticence to the fact that their CO always got lost. Tuttle's relationship with his men was one of trust, and he trusted them because he chose them himself. He was the only squadron commander in the RAF who was allowed to select any pilot he wanted and get him. Bringing back the prints was all that mattered – Tuttle told his pilots that he wanted them to come home safely, not because he liked their faces, but because the whole sortie would have been a waste of time if they did not. But he cared about his men as well; a pilot landing on one wheel would find Tuttle in his staff car at the wing tip to be first there to pull him out of the wreckage if anything went wrong.

On March 27th, 1941, the first two Spitfire PR IVs were delivered to Benson. The PR IV was the production derivative of the 'bowser', having special wings grafted on to the standard Mk V fighter airframe and a Merlin 45 engine. The fuselage tank had been omitted to provide camera space, but each leading-edge tank had been expanded to hold 66½ gallons, providing a total capacity of 218 gallons (ie 85 gallons of the standard fighter and 133 gallons in the wings). To supplement the F 24 camera under each wing there were three fuselage camera combinations – the W fit comprising two F 8s with 20 in lenses, the X fit of one F 24 with a 14 in lens, and after January 1942, the Y fit of one F 52 camera with a 36 in lens. The PR IV had a maximum permissible all-up-weight of 7,200 lbs, and a range of 1,800 miles, or enough to reach Danzig and allow ten minutes photography before coming back. Other modifications included a radio and 1½ gallons of drinking water, but the greatest improvement, as far as the pilots were concerned, was the installation of a cabin heater. Warm air was ducted from the engine through the cockpit and into the fuselage camera bay. The system had been devised at Heston and tried on a 'bowser', but it needed a Merlin 45 engine to work effectively; once cabin heating had been introduced it had a greater effect on morale than any other improvement to date.

The Benson Experimental Flight also put a great deal of thought into the outside as well as the inside of the PR IV. They experimented with various different forms of camouflage when duck-egg green was found to be of limited value at low level. Newspaper proved to be effective, but no one could stop it peeling off the aircraft at high speed. Pale pink was found to be best because it blended with the sun's rays diffused against the clouds. Alistair Taylor proved its worth on a 'dice' to Cherbourg on May 4th. He was at 3,500 feet when two Me 109s climbed through the clouds towards him. Although they passed within 50 yards, neither saw the pale pink Spitfire.

Pale duck-egg green was also found to be unsatisfactory at high level. 'Camotint' had been introduced by Cotton for SIS work around 20,000 feet and it lost much of its effect above 30,000 feet. Every shade of green was tried, then white, and finally blue. Sky blue was too light to blend into the darker skies of the sub-stratosphere, and after many expended tins of paint Benson created its own shade of blue – a dull sort of Prussian or cerulean blue – to be used and known in all theatres of war as 'PR blue'. Only red and blue type B roundels were used, and then only on the fuselage and upper wing surfaces. Serials and code-letters were not common in case they spoiled the camouflage effect, and they were only 4 in high white figures when applied. Personal embellishments were equally rare – Gordon Hughes was an exception when he painted a small 'e' on the nose of his aircraft because he signed himself 'Gordon e Hughes'.

In all, some 229 PR IVs were produced, every one of which was a tribute to the perseverence of Cotton and Tuttle and to the accuracy of Longbottom's theoretical assumptions in his Memorandum. The new Spitfire was to be the backbone of the RAF's PR organisation during the mid-war years.

The first time a PR IV was flown operationally was on April 5th, 1941 to northern Holland. Sergeant W. Morgan flew a more ambitious sortie three days later to Stettin and Swinemünde, and on April 10th Tony Hill photographed Copenhagen and Malmö for the first time. It was over Genoa though that the new aircraft was to demonstrate its paces. This Italian port had been a priority target for four months, ever since British naval Intelligence had received reports that the battleships *Littorio* and *Guilio Cesare* had moved there after Taranto. Genoa was beyond range of Malta's Marylands, but PR was necessary because Admiral Somerville planned to mount another naval air strike against the remnants of the Italian Navy. So on January 19th, 1941, Flt Lt P. Corbishley DFC had set off from England to try to stretch a 'bowser' down to the Gulf of Genoa. However he was blown off track, and finding himself over Corsica he decided to land at Malta and try again from there. Admiral Somerville then cancelled his proposed attack on Genoa, but Corbishley was nevertheless dispatched on February 2nd to confirm the number of warships in the harbour. He never found out – his Spitfire was hit by AA fire and he was forced to bale out. The 'bowser' crashed into a river near Via Reggia and its remains washed down to the sea; Corbishley became a prisoner of war.

It was left to Sgt Morgan and a Spitfire PR IV finally to photograph the Gulf of Genoa. On April 14th he left Benson and set course for northern Italy; 7 hours 10 minutes later he saw the south coast of England welcoming him back, and with only two gallons of fuel remaining he coaxed the Spitfire over the cliffs and into a field near Hawkinge. Sgt Morgan had covered Genoa and La Spezia in the longest flight to date by a Spitfire, and two days later he was awarded the DFM.

With the advent of flights of this duration, thought had to be given to the mundane but crucial problem of relieving the bladder while airborne. A P-tube was designed to be strapped to the pilot's leg, but the contents froze at height and no one relished the prospect of flying for hours with a bag of ice inside their trouser leg. Relieving oneself in the rarified atmosphere of the cockpit only resulted in a frozen film over the canopy, and no adequate answer to the problem was found, other than crossed-legs, until cabin pressurisation was introduced.

Besides the five Flights of 1 PRU, divided between Benson, Wick, and St Eval, there was one other PR unit in the UK in 1941. The JIC had finally despaired of ever getting enough cover of the European coastline from the PRU and so, in March 1941, 1416 Flight was formed at Hendon to watch for any signs of a German invasion on behalf of the JIC and the GOC Home Forces. The invasion threat practically disappeared once Hitler invaded Russia, but the Hendon Flight was given more Spitfire PR IGs, rechristened 140 Sqn, and given most of the low level work previously undertaken from Benson over the French coast on behalf of the Army so that 1 PRU could concentrate on its primary role, "namely long-range strategic photographic reconnaissance".

In the main, this still meant watching the movements of the German Navy. Every major vessel at Grand Admiral Raeder's disposal was watched as frequently as Tuttle's limited resources would allow, with St Eval particularly interested in the *Scharnhorst* and *Gneisenau* in Brest. Such diligence was not unwarranted; on February 6th, 1941, Hitler directed that German striking power was to be concentrated on the supply lines of the British Empire.

On May 18th, Admiral Lütjens took the *Bismarck* and *Prinz Eugen* out of Gdynia. For two days the force sailed through the Baltic unknown to the Admiralty, as Naval Intelligence heard nothing until May 20th when they received a report of a naval force passing through the Kattegat. Wick received a priority tasking the following day by telephone to search for "German ships" off the Norwegian coast. Two Spitfires took off immediately, one flown by Fg Off C. A. S. Greenhill DFC and the other by Plt Off M. F. Suckling. Greenhill, as the more experienced of the two, was given the most likely area if Lütjens' force maintained its speed, but because the German Admiral had decided to put into Grimstad Fiord, just south of Bergen, to refuel, it fell to the young Pilot Officer from Nottingham to find the squadron.

"I took off from Wick and flew to Sumburgh where I landed to refuel," wrote 'Babe' Suckling, so-called because of his young face, fair hair, and blue eyes. "Took off and set course for Bergen, climbing through two layers of cloud, 1,500 feet and 3,700 feet thick. Made a landfall south of Sogne Fiord and photographed shipping in Hjelte Fiord, Herlo aerodrome, and Flatoen seaplane base. Then I saw and photographed 1 *Hipper* class cruiser, 1 destroyer, and 4 MVs anchored 10 miles west of Bergen. I then did a run over Bergen and while doing so, saw what I took to be another *Hipper* class cruiser and 4 MVs anchored at eastern end of Fiord, 5 miles south of Bergen. Photographed these and returned immediately to Wick. Photographs showed the second cruiser to be a *Bismarck* class battleship."

A flight lasting just under three hours made Michael Frank Suckling into a hero overnight. The *Bismarck* and Lütjens' secret were out and the Royal Navy began to move in for the eventual kill. For Suckling though it was a short-lived triumph. In the middle of July his Flight moved down to Benson, and on July 21st, the same day that 1 and 3 PRUs amalgamated, he took off from Oxfordshire for the French coast. He had been briefed to photograph La Pallice, St Nazaire, and Lorient, but his sortie coincided with the only excursion of the *Scharnhorst* from Brest during her eleven month confinement. The Germans, anticipating a visit to every Biscay port from the PRU once the escape had been detected, had put their AA batteries on full alert. Over La Pallice an unsuspecting Fg Off Suckling DFC was blown out of the sky.

As it happened the PRU did not discover the absence of the battleship until July 22nd. The *Scharnhorst* was spotted by a PR Spitfire, whereupon she was attacked by Halifaxes on July 24th and driven into La Pallice. She limped back to Brest two days later with 3,000 tons of water in her engine-room.

With the demise of the *Bismarck*, the German Navy became a more manageable reconnaissance quantity. When Gordon Hughes discovered on June 4th that the *Prinz Eugen* had joined the *Scharnhorst* and *Gneisenau*, only the *Tirpitz, Lutzow, Hipper*, and *Scheer* remained outside Brest. This quartet was in the Baltic at the beginning of June 1941, but on June 13th Greenhill discovered the *Lutzow* passing through the Denmark Strait in the company of five destroyers. The flotilla was attacked by torpedo bombers and the *Lutzow* was forced into Kiel for repairs.

The *Lutzow* incident and the sinking of the *Bismarck* showed that the Admiralty was much better informed in 1941 than it had been a year earlier. It appeared that the Germans could no longer launch a force into the open seas without being detected. "Many factors contributed to this important result," wrote Captain S. W. Roskill in the *'War at Sea'*. "The Admiralty's Intelligence Centre, fed by the Photographic Reconnaissance Unit and the visual patrols of Coastal Command, by study of the enemy's wireless traffic and by reports from other sources, was now working with a speed and accuracy far removed from the uncertainties and failures of 1940."

The *Tirpitz* was watched like a new-born baby during the first nine months of 1941 while she was in Danzig being fitted-out. September 23rd was just like any other day to Flt Lt D. Salwey as he climbed into his Spitfire for another long, cold, routine trip to Danzig to reassure the Admiralty. But 7 hours and 50 minutes later he landed with the news that Tirpitz had sailed for the first time and was in the Baltic on gunnery trials. She might try to break out at any time.

The PRU watch on the German Fleet did have its limitations. On September 4th, Sgt Blythe discovered that the pocket-battleship *Scheer* had left Kiel. She was reported passing northwards through the Great Belt and later at the entrance of the Oslo Fiord, but by September 15th she had disappeared and a search of all likely ports could not locate her. Three days later, Flt Lt Watts found her back in her original berth at Swinemünde. Admiralty anxieties were again raised the following month when the *Scheer* moved to Hamburg, but no one knew she was there because bad weather prevented any effective reconnaissance until November 28th when she was photographed back in Swinemünde. "The stresses caused by these, actually insignificant, movements," concluded Capt Roskill, "show that, although regular photographic reconnaissance of the enemy's bases conferred inestimable advantages, it was liable to lead to exaggeration of the importance of any movement by a major warship. Photographic reconnaissance cannot therefore eliminate the need for intelligence about the enemy's intentions derived from other sources."

The Royal Navy could be caught off guard even when regular and effective PR was forthcoming, as the Channel Dash from Brest was to prove. Naval Intelligence insisted on twice daily cover of Brest to ensure that the *Scharnhorst, Gneisenau,* and *Prinz Eugen* remained in port. In fact the detachment at St Eval existed only to watch the great Finisterre seaport. Some 729 PRU missions were flown over Brest in 321 days and each one was expected to bring back prints of the ships; visual reports were not acceptable as pilots might be confused by decoys, so the Navy, caught so often unawares in the past, insisted on photographic proof. Even the barrier of weather had to be overcome where possible; five Spitfires were sent to find a break in the cloud without success on April 27th, 1941 before St Eval was allowed to concede defeat for the day by a nervous Admiralty.

The problems facing St Eval therefore were immense. Every German in Brest soon realised that a solitary blue Spitfire would visit them twice a day, and consequentlythe element of surprise, so vital to the PRU, was lost. Pilots could only try to redress the balance by varying their method of approach – if the sky were cloudy they could either cross the Channel at high-level and then power-dive through the clouds at the last moment, or sneak in over the waves. Even if the sky were clear, the Germans were often prepared for a high level mission. The Luftwaffe kept a standing patrol over Ushant, and on June 19th Sgt Brown was bounced by a pair of fighters at 30,000 feet over the harbour and he was forced to dive at full boost for the safety of some clouds 29,000 feet below. In the descent he reached such a speed that the pitot-head was blown off, but the Spitfire escaped.

Whatever the direction of approach or height employed, Brest sorties were really a sophisticated form of Russian roulette with luck playing a major part in success. Bill Wise recalls that once he was set up, with the cameras on, for an oblique low-level run, there was nothing more to do except fly through the hail of AA fire with his eyes closed and pray.

Flt Lt Wise, at the time in command of a flight, came through his spell at St Eval unscathed, but others were not so fortunate. Nine Spitfires failed to return from Brest in eleven months, four of which were lost in December 1941. Yet in spite of all this effort to make sure that the trio in Brest never sailed undetected again, that in fact was what they did. On January 25th, 1942, Fg Off Ball photographed the *Scharnhorst, Gneisenau,* and *Prinz Eugen* as usual in their regular berths. At the beginning of February they had been joined by a flotilla of torpedo boats, minesweepers, and destroyers and the Germans were seen to be minesweeping in the Channel. Despite an expenditure of 908 tons of bombs by Bomber Command over Brest in January, the two battlecruisers and the *Prinz Eugen* were apparently preparing for an imminent operation.

On February 3rd, Coastal Command started planned night air reconnaissance patrols with radar-carrying Hudsons; PRU patrols were increased but no photography was possible between February 4th and 7th because of bad weather. The next day Plt Off Cowan reported that all was well in Brest and that the *Gneisenau* had in fact moved into dry-dock. She was photographed back in the harbour on February 9th but bad weather thwarted operations again the following day. At 1615 hrs on February 11th, Freddie Ball found the triumvirate with smoking funnels surrounded by six destroyers and numerous minesweepers and torpedo boats, but a Bomber Command raid that evening returned with the news that the ships were still in port. This was reassuring because the Royal Navy believed that the Germans would only attempt a dash through the Channel under cover of darkness, which meant leaving Brest in daylight. Raeder, on the other hand, believed that surprise was vital and that he would never surprise the Royal Navy unless the ships left Brest at night. So at 2300 hrs, while the Admiralty was being reassured that all was well in Brest for another day, Admiral Ciliax ordered his flotilla to weigh anchor and set sail.

The Channel Dash was an unhappy ending to a story that had cost the PRU nine losses and 729 sorties. The Unit could not have done more to detect the break-out without having a Spitfire positioned over Brest for 24 hours a day. Suffice to say that the possibility of such a venture had been likely for eleven months and the PRU prints had been providing warning signals for over a week; it was a pity that this time had not been put to better use to devise a more effective British response to the challenge when it came.

PRU flights, like detective work, were 99% routine and only 1% excitement. PR was not a role that regularly brought back information that changed the whole face of the war – rather Benson, Wick and St Eval were involved in a steady process of bringing back fragments of intelligence from all over Europe that the CIU could build up, over a period of years, into a complete picture. When Gordon Hughes photographed 80 French airfields in a sortie, or when Fg Off Watts discovered that the Luftwaffe had moved a detachment of long-range maritime reconnaissance Fw 200 Condors up to Bordeaux, their prints would never cause a sensation like Suckling's cover of *Bismarck*, but over the years such routine PR would play a greater part in helping to win the war.

The task of interpreting and analysing all these pieces of photographic information fell to the CIU at Medmenham. The restricted and vulnerable confines of Wembley had been exchanged for the seclusion of a large mock-Tudor mansion called Danesfield on the banks of the Thames between Marlow and Henley. From Danesfield, or RAF Medmenham as it was officially titled, the Central Interpretation Unit looked after the processing and interpretation of all photographic reconnaissance by 1 PRU and 140 Sqn. In addition to controlling the First Phase detachments at the airfields and the Second and Third Phase staffs at Medmenham, the CIU also maintained a library of all aerial prints taken from the UK and built scale-models from them when required by Commands and Ministries.

When a PR pilot landed he reported immediately to the Intelligence Officer who wrote down such details as objectives, heights flown, weather en-route, and number of enemy interceptions on the 'Form Orange' which was signalled to the CIU as a warning that films would be arriving in a few hours time. While the pilot was drawing a trace of his route with the position of any targets he had photographed, the magazines would have been taken off the cameras and rushed to the developing room where the negatives would be passed through machines capable of developing, fixing, washing, and drying at a rate of four feet of film per minute. Negatives were then graded for light intensity, passed for printing, and then sent to the First Phase PIs who would examine them for any important information like troop movements or new shipping traffic. A completed First Phase report, known as the 'Form White', was then transmitted by teleprinter, or telephone if urgent, to any operational Commands or other services who might want to take immediate action.

First Phase processing and interpretation was no small task. On June 17th, for example, there were thirteen successful sorties from Benson alone. The first magazine arrived in the Photo Section at 1230 hrs and the last prints were completed at 2210 hrs. During the space of nine hours and forty minutes, some 37 films were processed and 6,800 prints issued; the temperature in the processing room remained at 95°F throughout.

When the Form White was completed, the films and two sets of prints were sent by express train or dispatch rider to the CIU, where Second Phase interpretation provided a more detailed account of any important activity. Third Phase interpretation was divided between specialised sections and it is worth looking at some of the achievements recorded by the naval Third Phase experts. Specialisation meant that PIs became so familiar with ships and dockyards that, even from a blurred print, they could extract everything of value, determine every pattern of activity, and eventually sense when something was wrong or different even if they could not put a finger on what it was.

By accurately measuring prints, naval PIs were able to provide the Admiralty with their first appreciation of the *Tirpitz*'s armament, and they were also able to say that the battleship, hitherto said to displace about 35,000 tons, was in fact over 40,000 tons. On a smaller scale, the Naval Section differentiated the various sub-classes of the *Narvik* type destroyers and discovered a later derivative known as the *Seetier* class from an aerial photograph. When the Baltic port of Elbing was covered for the first time in August 1942, the prints revealed an entirely new class of smaller German destroyer, henceforward known as the *Elbing* class.

One of the most dramatic pieces of long-term detective work by the naval experts at Medmenham concerned the search for Axis blockade runners. On September 3rd, 1939 there were 222 German merchant vessels spread around the world, some of which were pressed into service to run the maritime blockade of the Reich imposed by the Royal Navy. These blockade runners were carefully chosen: averaging 5–6,000 tons and varied in construction to avoid recognition as a class, they had a good turn of speed but were not so modern as to be conspicuous. Their role was to carry rare and valuable cargoes such as rubber from the Far East to ports in the Bay of Biscay, from whence their loads would be carried overland to the industries of Germany.

The first runner to get through was the *Ermland* in April 1941. A regular traffic followed, and by December twelve vessels out of sixteen had reached France and German propaganda became very boastful about their exploits. Random Royal Naval patrols were very wasteful and inefficient, and Naval Intelligence decided that much more detailed information about the runners and their routine was necessary if the blockade was to be enforced effectively. The first step was to identify the runners. As aerial cameras improved in clarity, so the Naval Section could begin to pick out individual Axis merchantmen, and over a time discern a pattern in their movements. Teutonic love of regular and standard procedure soon enabled Medmenham to discover the routine followed by any blockade runner about to set sail from Bordeaux. The vessel would first enter the dockyard for an overhaul, followed by bottom-cleaning in dry dock, and then go back to the dockyard for adjustments. After this she would move to the Bassens North for loading, and thence to the Customs House Quay to await a dark night to sneak into the Bay of Biscay. It was soon noticed that the Germans tried to synchronise these departures with arrivals from the Far East.

An example of this pattern was provided by the *MV Himalaya* in November 1942. She was first photographed in the Bordeaux dockyard on November 15th, and eight days later she was in the great floating dock at Pauillac. By March 18th, 1943 she was loaded up at Bassens North ready to sail; Coastal Command was alerted and the *Himalaya* was attacked by aircraft from Mountbatten as she left harbour and was driven back to the safety of the Gironde.

In future, adherence to this routine would brand a vessel as a blockade runner. Early in 1943 a modern fruiter, the *Alsterufur*, lay at anchor in Nantes. She was only a small vessel of 2,729 tons, and when she moved into a dockyard berth in February it was assumed that she was to be converted into a *Sperrbrecher*[1] like others of her type and size. Almost immediately, however, she moved to the loading quay at Bordeaux. Suspicions were confirmed when she broke out under cover of bad weather at the end of March, and although she reached the Far East, the PIs were ready for her return. She was sighted in the Atlantic the following December and sunk by aircraft of 311 Sqn.

1943 saw the demise of the blockade runners. The year opened with the sinking of the *Rhakotis* with her cargo of vegetable oils, fats, quinine bark, tin, tea, wolfram, and enough rubber to keep four armoured divisions in tyres for a year. On February 26th, the tanker *Herborg* was sunk by HMS *Sussex*, and by the end of April five more blockade runners had been destroyed. The last of these clandestine merchantmen, the *Himalaya*, never bothered to set sail – she was scuttled in Bordeaux in August 1944. The Royal Navy had closed the

[1] Armed merchant escort.

gaps in its blockade, but it needed the PRU and the Third Phase Section at Medmenham to show them how to do it.

Although the Air Ministry appreciated the contribution that PR could make in the overseas theatres, it was only after the immediate threat to Britain receded in the summer of 1941 that Whitehall felt they could spare more aircraft and equipment for use abroad. Sqn Ldr Peter Riddell was then sent out to the Middle East and India to assess reconnaissance requirements and report back. He found 2 PRU operating in Egypt in very much the same manner as the SIS in Britain at the start of the war. 2 PRU had been made responsible for all secret and clandestine reconnaissance throughout the Middle East, arriving unannounced at some airfield or other in either 'Cloudy Joe' or a blue Hurricane, operating from a closely guarded hangar for a time, and then off again as unspectacularly as before. Syria and the Lebanon were obvious targets – the Vichy French might enter the Middle Eastern campaign at any time on the Axis side – and Aleppo, Homs, and Ryak were photographed during June 1941 from Lydda. A Hurricane came back to Lydda on June 23rd to cover Beirut on behalf of the Army; after landing, MacPhail flew the films back to Heliopolis in 'Cloudy Joe' for processing, arriving back at Lydda again that evening in time to hand the prints to the local army commander at 2000 hours. The Vichy French were never over-enthusiastic about having their pictures taken, but their Moranes never attempted to intercept.

Following the revolt in Iraq, 2 PRU flew over the oil-fields in case they were occupied by unfriendly forces. The Unit also moved up to Habbaniya on July 30th to see whether the Soviet Union was preparing to invade Persia; a PR Hurricane detachment later moved up to Shaibah in southern Iraq to reconnoitre Persia prior to a British occupation of that vulnerable country.

Sqn Ldr Riddell was particularly impressed by the way in which 2 PRU, and the other overseas reconnaissance squadrons, had adapted whatever aircraft were available locally into the PR role. MacPhail was given a Beaufighter in August to supplement his three Hurricanes, and he had the guns removed and three F 24 cameras fitted. When his Unit returned from Habbaniya on August 16th, MacPhail divided his diminutive force into two flights to cater for the increasing number of special tasks. T Flight moved up to Fuka to watch Crete and Cyrenaica, while S Flight remained at Heliopolis to cover Cyprus and the Dodecanese. It all sounded very impressive on paper until one realised that T Flight had only one Beaufighter and 'Cloudy Joe' to its name.

2 PRU therefore had aircraft neither in sufficient numbers nor with adequate range and performance to monopolise strategic photographic reconnaissance throughout the Middle East as 1 PRU could do at home. MacPhail had to concentrate his limited resources on work of a clandestine or 'one-off' nature, leaving routine PR work over North Africa to be divided between the tactical army cooperation squadrons and 39 'long-range strategic reconnaissance' Sqn.

39 Sqn had been on the North-West Frontier during the Thirties, moving its Blenheim Is down to Singapore in 1939. It was essentially a GR squadron tasked with visual reconnaissance duties, but the crews did practise with aerial cameras over Singapore before moving back into India to Lahore. When Italy entered the war, the Squadron moved up to Aden and thence to Egypt in December 1940. Here they re-equipped with Marylands that had been shipped across the Atlantic to Takoradi in the Gold Coast and flown by Squadron crews across the African ferry route to their rear base at Wadi Natrum.

Most of 39 Sqn's operational work however was flown from the forward landing-ground of Maaten Bagush where the AOC 204 Gp, Air Cdre Collishaw, had his underground HQ. 39 Sqn was Collishaw's eyes, recording the changes in the strategic land and sea positions within his area of command, and using aerial cameras whenever confirmation of visual sightings was necessary. Taskings came directly from the 204 Gp planning cell under the desert, and pre-flight briefings were done the night before on maps laid out on the sand while the crews were eating their evening meal. The Sqn CO, Wg Cdr A. Bowman DSO, DFC and bar, would place a piece of bread on one target, a piece of corned beef on another, and so on until the map looked like a tablecloth. He would then allot the targets to specific crews.

The standard 39 Sqn 'milk-run' through Italian Cyrenaica went from Maaten Bagush up to the barbed wire boundary to look for gaps, then across the desert navigating by way of wadis and burnt out tanks to El Agheila, round the coast photographing shipping and airfields in Benghazi and Derna, and back to base. Sometimes they flew south to the oases of Suiva and Tarubub to make sure that the Arabs were still friendly, or north to make a search of the Eastern Mediterranean for shipping. The Squadron did record dramatic events at times, like the day a crew found a concentration of Ju 52 transports at Benina airfield, Benghazi; 39 Sqn only discovered their purpose when one of their Marylands brought back the first pictures of the invasion of Crete.

Crews could see for miles in the clear blue sky – it was just as well, for their only navigation aid was a radio compass and the only station they could tune it into was Radio Cairo, which transmitted on such a broad band as to be virtually useless.

The main opposition came from the flak batteries at Benghazi and Derna. Squadron crews had orders not to engage the enemy if they could help it and the Italians were very cooperative in this respect. It was not unusual for a Maryland on its way out to pass an Italian reconnaissance aircraft going in the opposite direction. The crews sometimes waved to each other – both sides had their own reconnaissance commitments to fulfil and they left one another to get on with them.

When crews landed back at Maaten Bagush they reported to Air Cdre Collishaw personally in his underground shelter. As soon as they entered the 'hole' the AOC would shout "Freddie" and a Group Captain would bring in cans of Australian beer. Surrounded by maps and the photographs, which had been developed in the MFPS[1] trailer outside, the crews would discuss with Collishaw any changes they had noted – a new set of tracks here, a new landing ground there. The AOC listened attentively – 39 Sqn was the only source of up to date strategic air intelligence he had.

Nevertheless 39 Sqn was not a specialist PR squadron on the lines of a PRU. Observers relied on their knowledge of the F 24 camera imparted during basic training, and it was a big day if a crew came back with more than 50 prints. It was only after the implementation of Peter Riddell's recommendation that a Middle East CIU[2] be set up and that 2 PRU be expanded with modern aircraft, that the aerial camera increased in importance in the Middle East and PR became a detailed and organised science as in Britain.

In spite of the arrival of further Marylands and the expansion of 431 Flt into 69 Sqn, Malta had only a maximum of seven aircraft at its disposal by March 1941 to cover the harbours of southern Italy and North Africa, and the sea-lanes in between. Two Hurricanes were modified locally in April to carry cameras, but with a range of 350 miles they could only be employed on short-range duties. The Marylands also lacked the range to reach the northern Italian ports of Genoa and Trieste so these were left to periodic cover by aircraft in transit from Benson.

Air Vice Marshal Hugh Pughe-Lloyd wrote in his autobiography 'Briefed to Attack' that when he took over the position of AOC Malta in May 1941 the key to the contest in the Mediterranean was the battle of supply. "Our task was to sink ships as often and as fast as we could: no supplies – no Rommel: no Rommel – no campaign in Africa." In order to sink ships, Pughe-Lloyd's aircraft had first to find them, and from the moment he arrived on the island the AOC used 69 Sqn like a true PRU man. "I've got to know *when* the ships are loading, what they are loading, and when they are going to sail," he told Malta's two PIs, Fg Off Howard Colvin and Fg Off Ray Herschel. Like Tuttle, Pughe-Lloyd did not care how his pilots operated as long as the prints were brought back and interpreted properly.

The regular watch on the ports of southern Italy and Italian North Africa soon paid dividends. The port authorities in Naples followed a regular routine in preparing a convoy. Four to six merchantmen would assemble before moving alongside the 'African Quay' for loading, and after the last hatches had been closed there would be a delay while the stevedores loaded an immense quantity of deck cargo. A Maryland would watch Naples regularly until the convoy sailed, when an attacking force of Blenheims and Beauforts would be sent in.

The PIs were soon able to compile a record of every Axis merchant ship plying between Italy and North Africa from the wealth of prints they received. Each vessel was given a history sheet listing its size, shape, speed,

[1] Mobile Field Photographic Section.

[2] The CIU was at Cairo with First Phase detachments in Egypt, the Western Desert and Malta.

Below: The camouflaged battlecruisers *Scharnhorst* and *Gneisenau* (Top left) in Brest on December 18th 1941. *CC. Bottom:* The battleship *Tirpitz* in the Aas Fiord, Norway, on February 15th, 1942. This oblique photograph shows floating camouflage units around the bow and stern, and netting draped between vessel and shore, to break the outline of the ship when viewed from above. *CC*

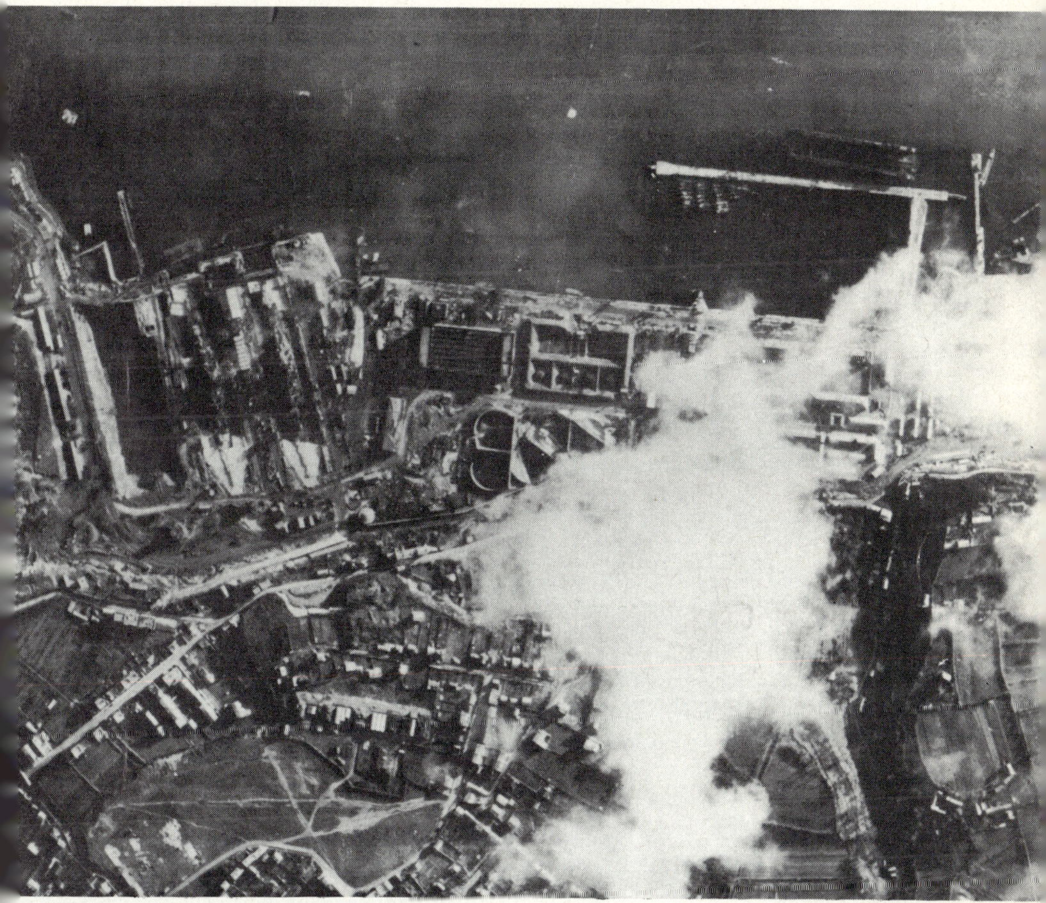

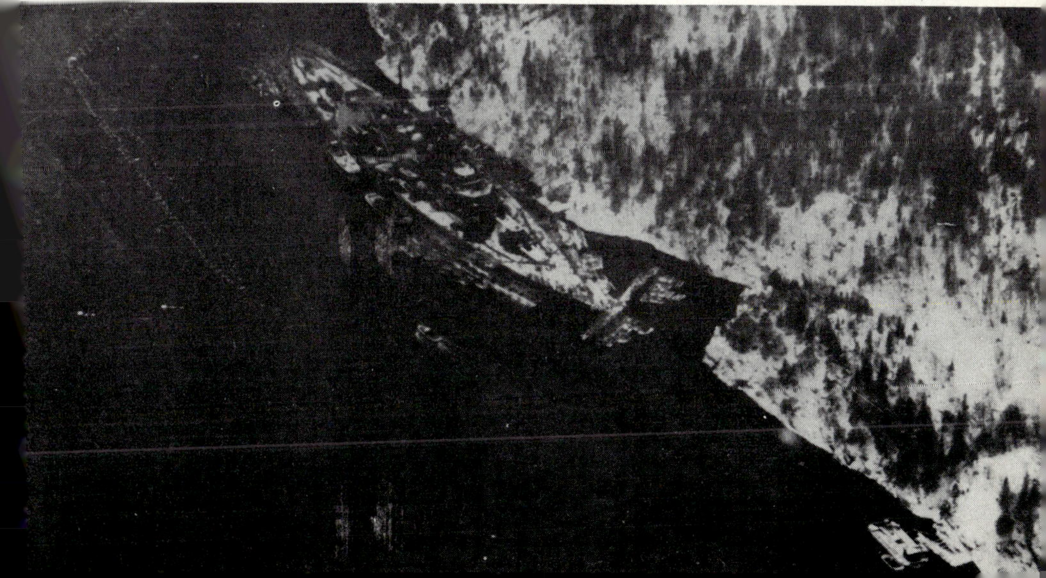

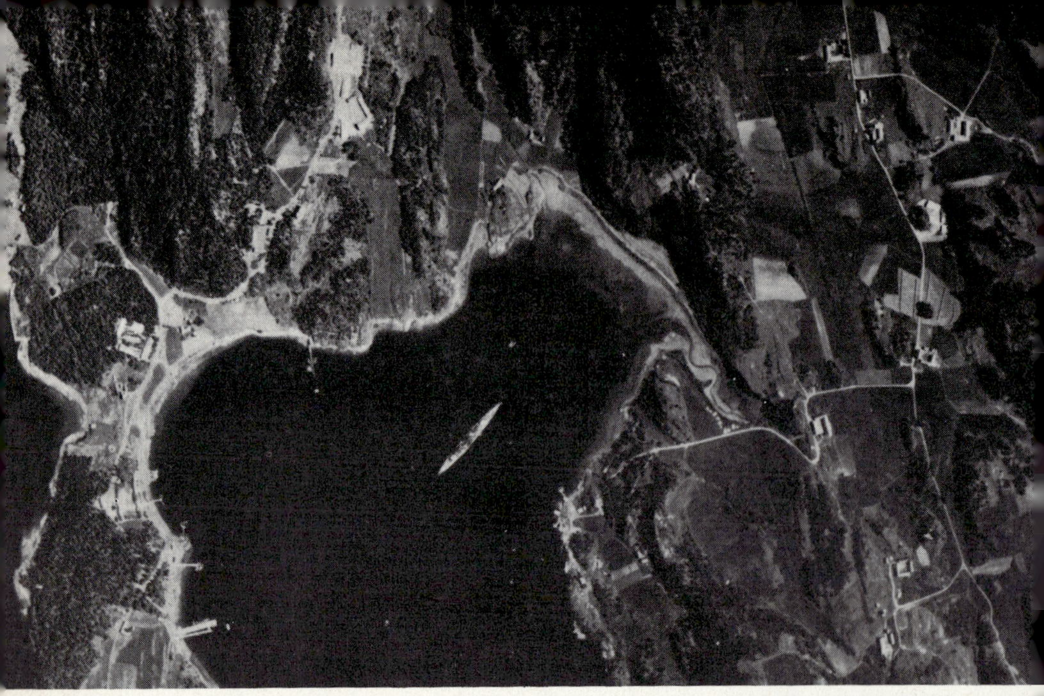

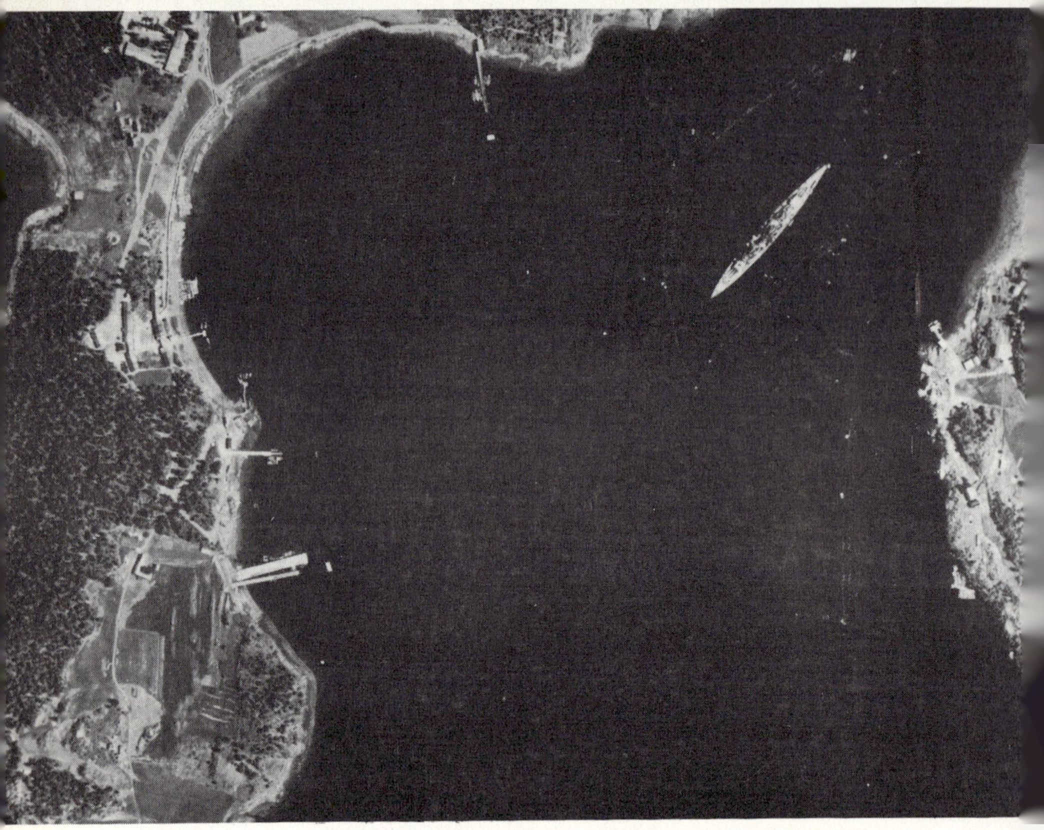

Top: The value of different lenses. The photograph was taken by a 14in lens and it shows the overall position of the *Tirpitz* in a Norwegian fiord. *Above:* The print was taken from the same aircraft with a 36in telephoto lens and it spotlights the battleship and its protective booms in detail. *CC*

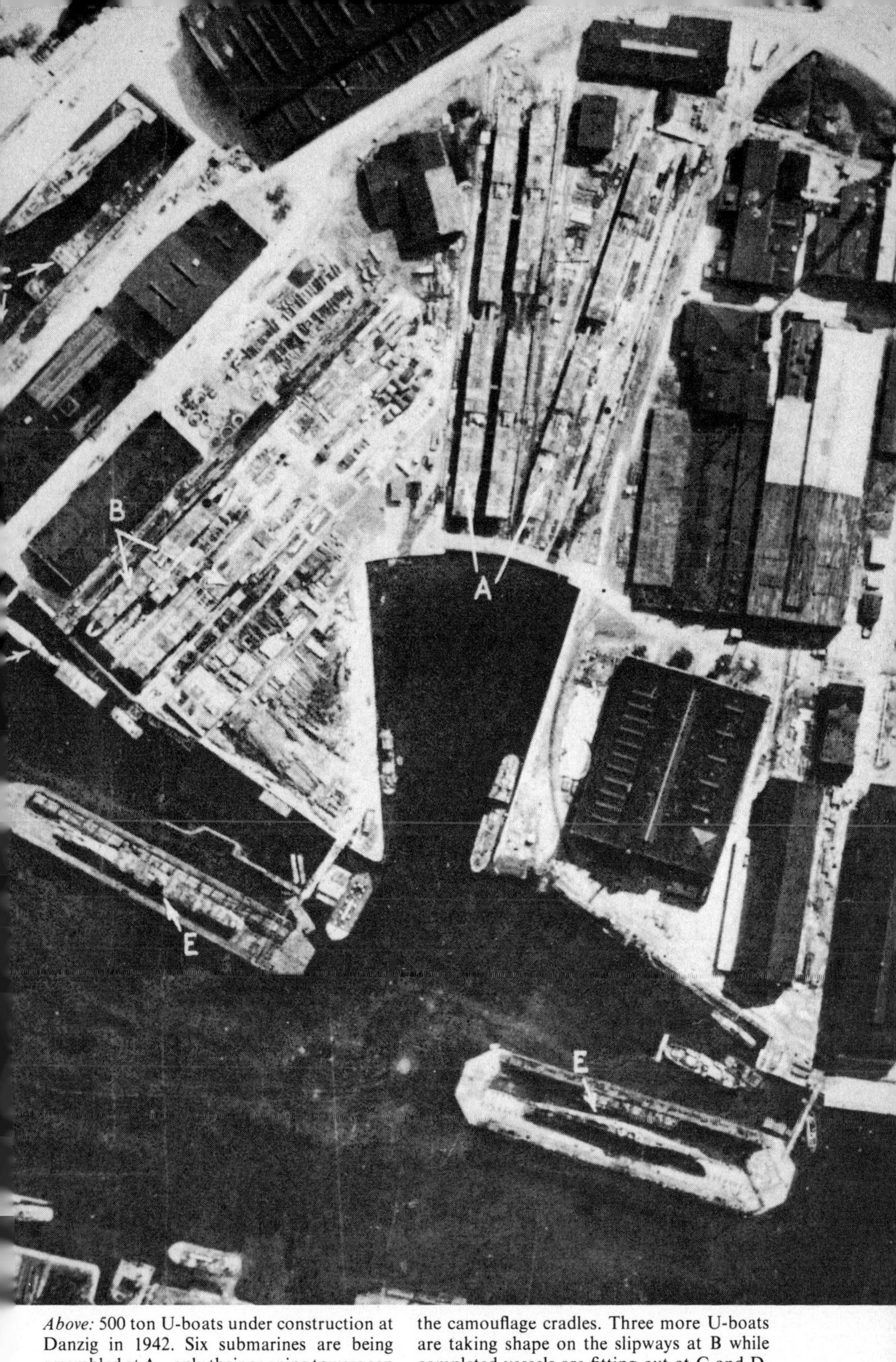

Above: 500 ton U-boats under construction at Danzig in 1942. Six submarines are being assembled at A – only their conning towers can be seen as the hulls are completely covered by the camouflage cradles. Three more U-boats are taking shape on the slipways at B while completed vessels are fitting out at C and D. Two submarines are in dry dock at E. *CC*

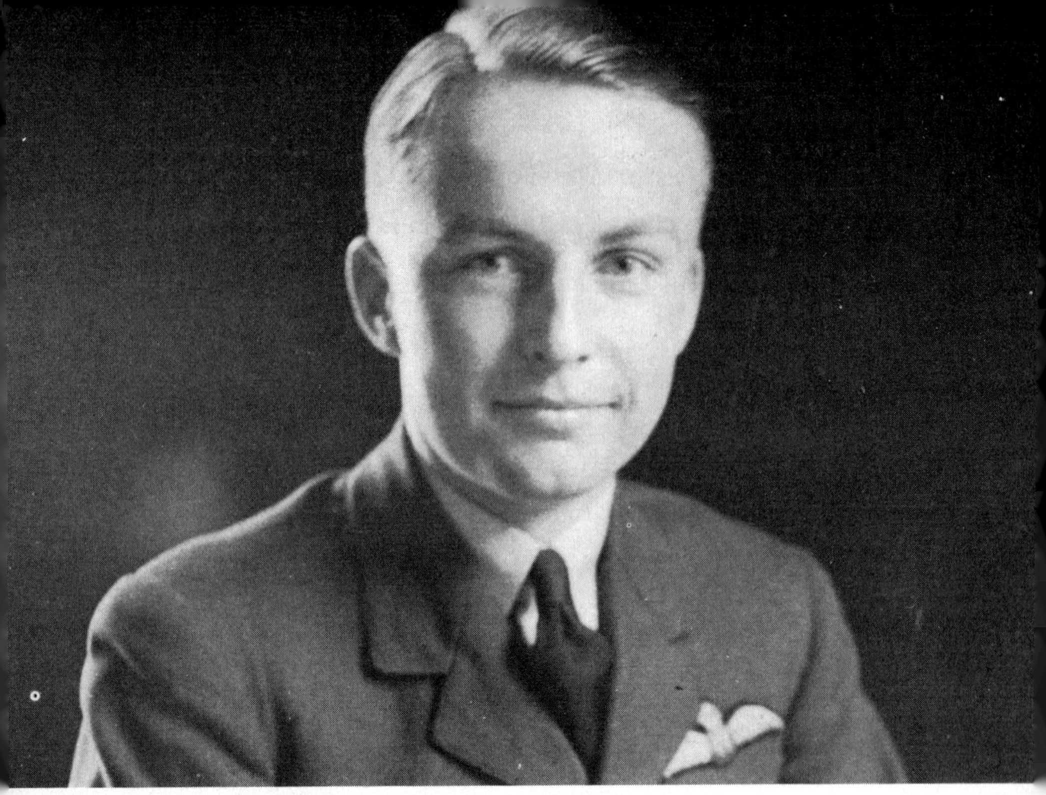

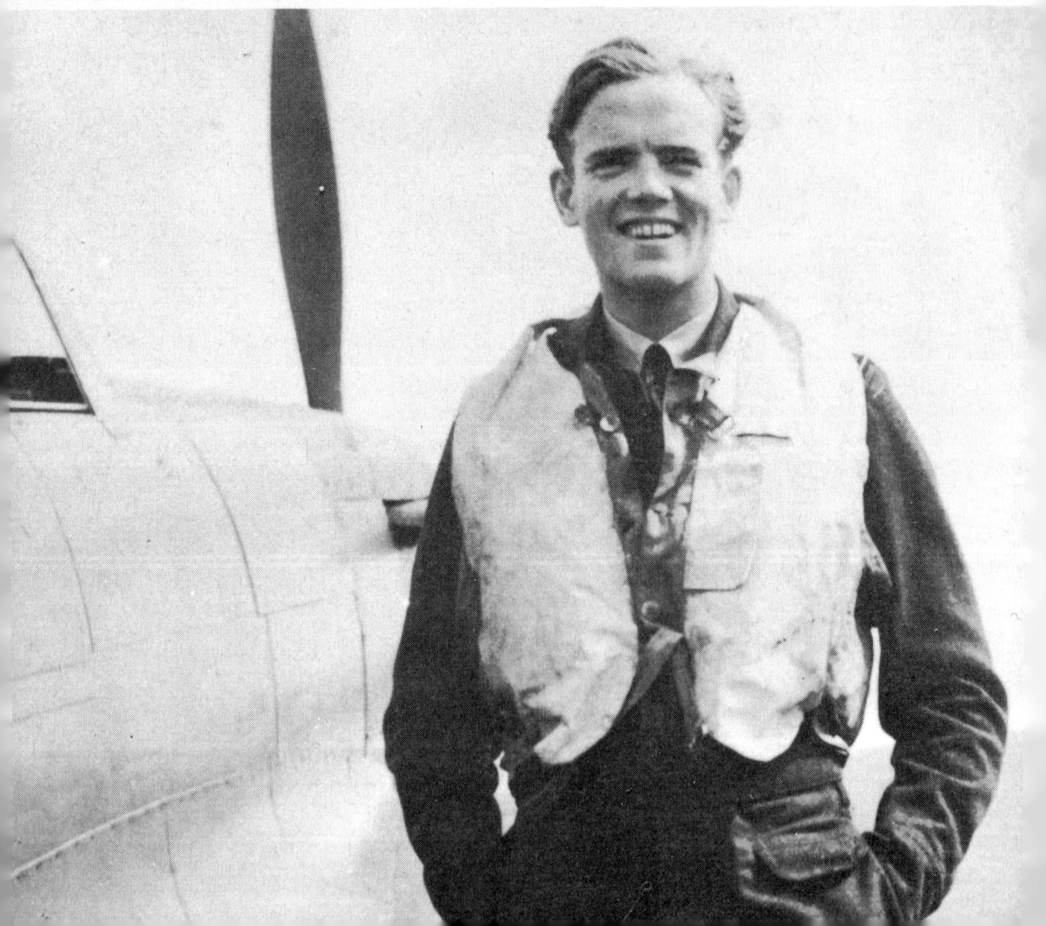

Top left: FG Off Michael 'Babe' Suckling, who discovered the *Bismarck* as she broke out into the North Sea on her first and last mission. Just a few of the many PRU pilots who distinguished themselves in the Second World War. *Bottom left:* Donald Steventon, *Below:* 'Bill' Wise, *Bottom:* The first man in the Second World War to be awarded three DFCs – Alistair Taylor. *Ball*

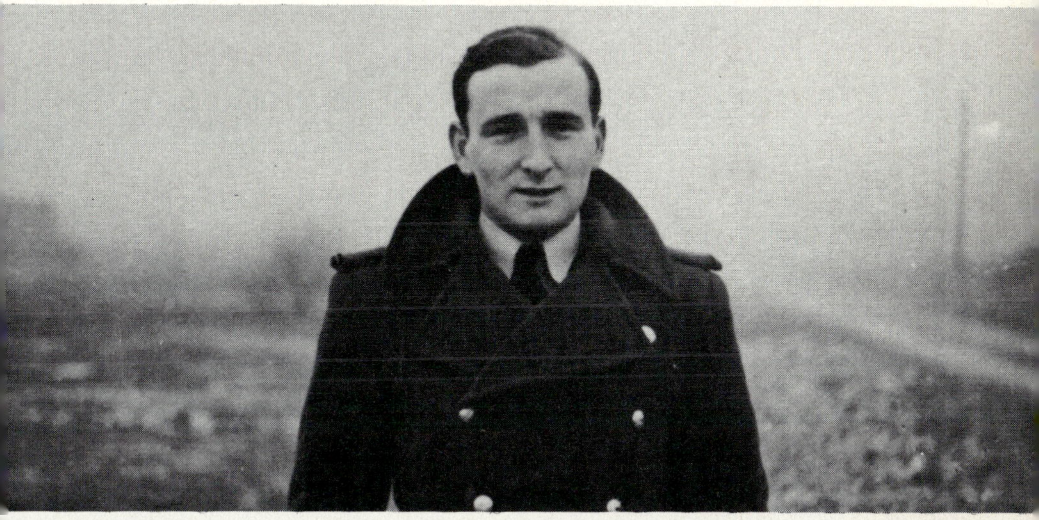

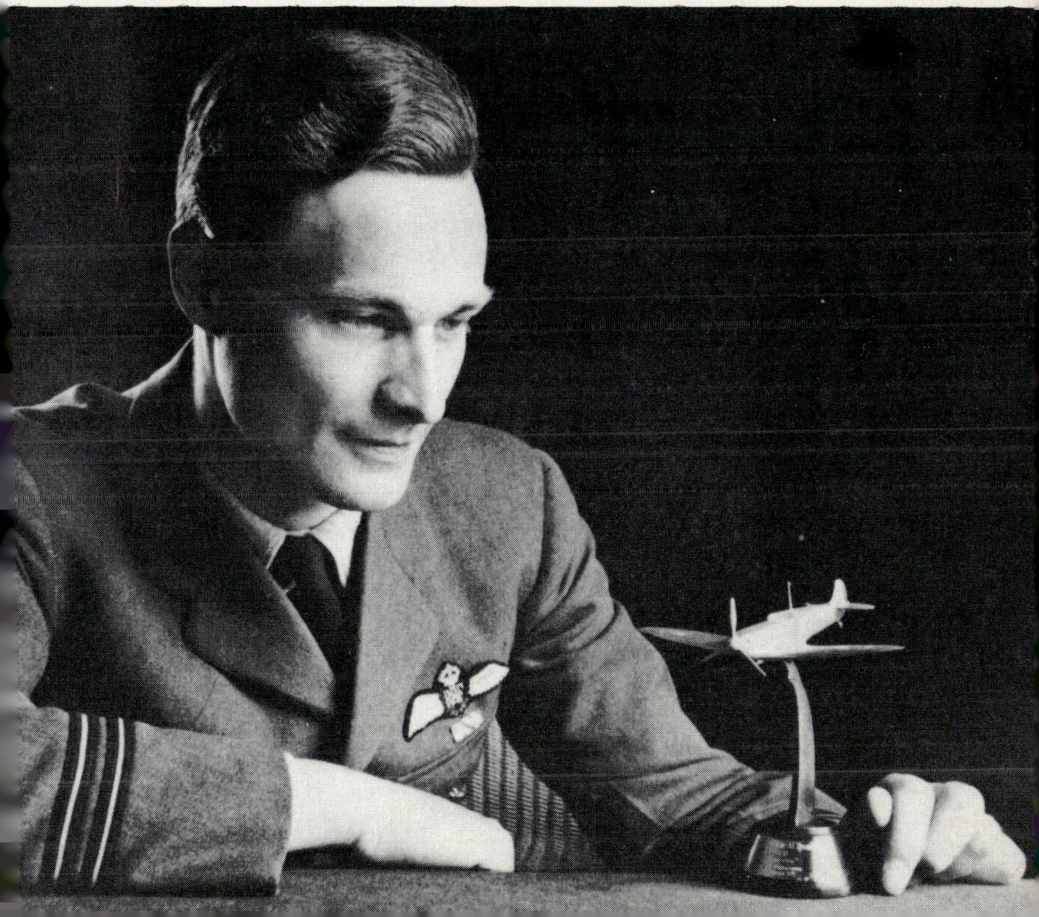

Below: The FREYA aerials at Auderville taken by Plt Off Manifould on February 22nd, 1941.

Bottom: Tony Hill.

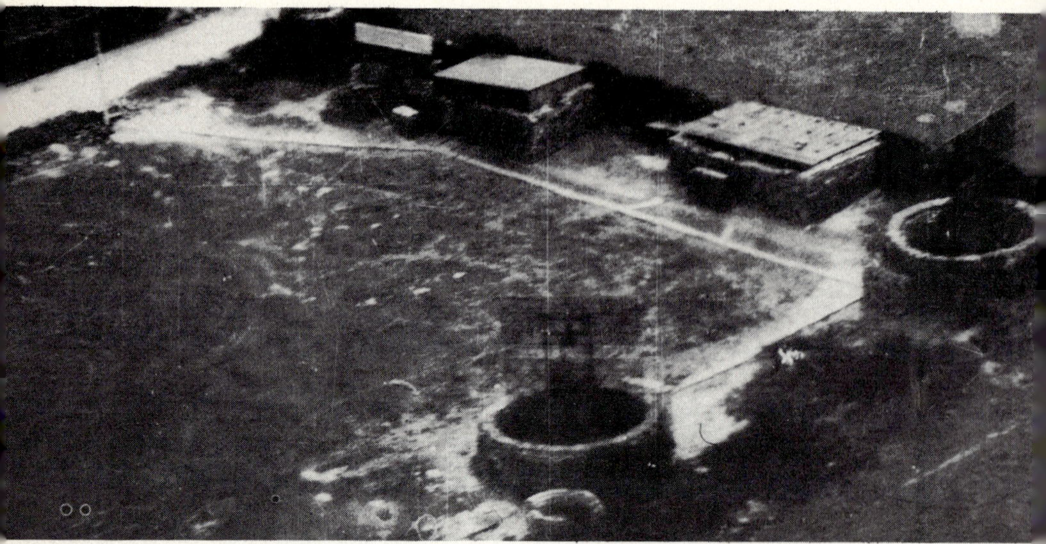

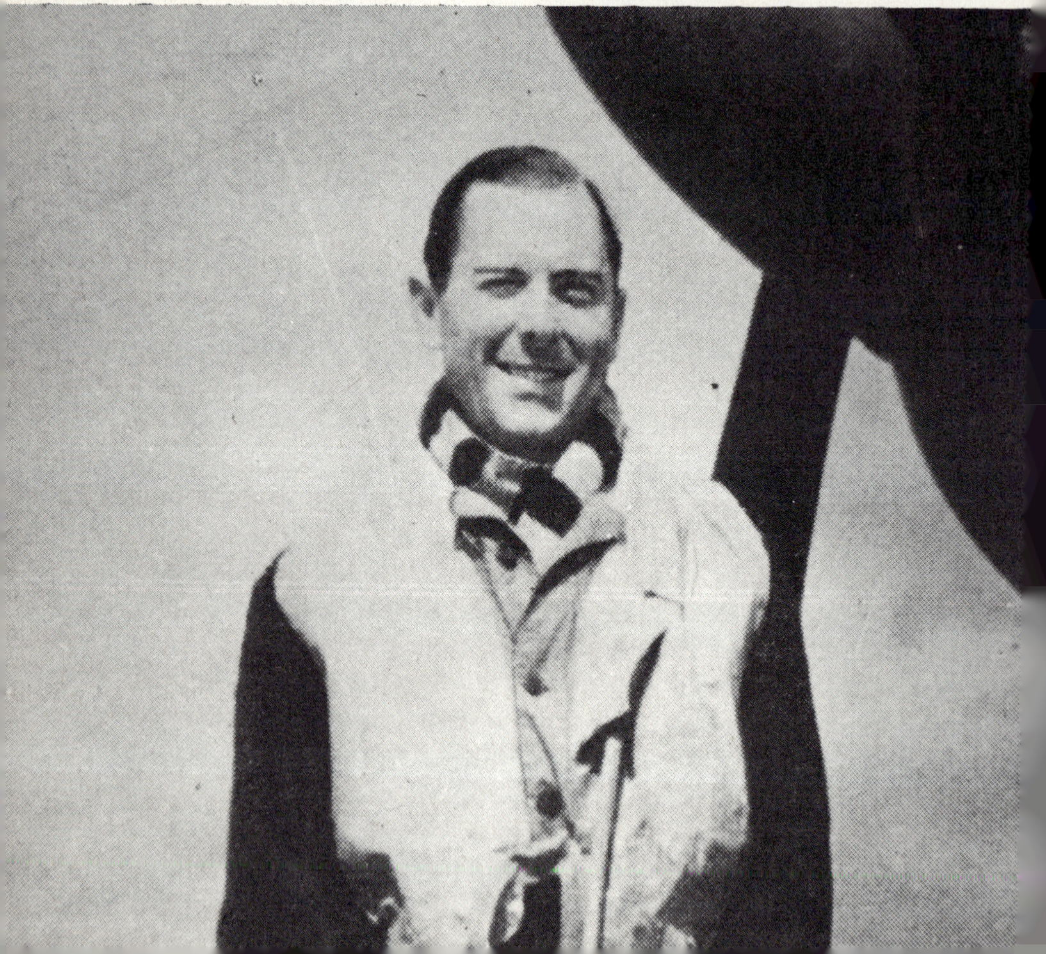

Below: Tony Hill's 'diced' photograph of the Bruneval *Wurzburg* radar with the sanatorium in the background. *Bottom:* An oblique photograph of a girder-type *Chimney* radar station, an early warning device designed to plot the range of intruder aircraft. This print was taken over Bergen-Aan-Zee by an F 52 camera with a 14in lens in the nose of a Mosquito PR XVI on August 21st, 1944. *CC*

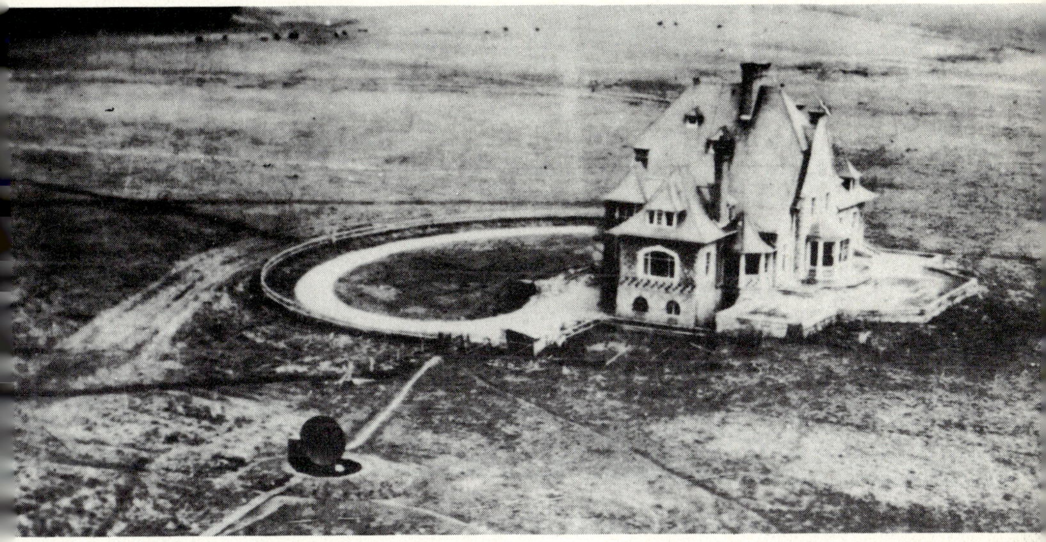

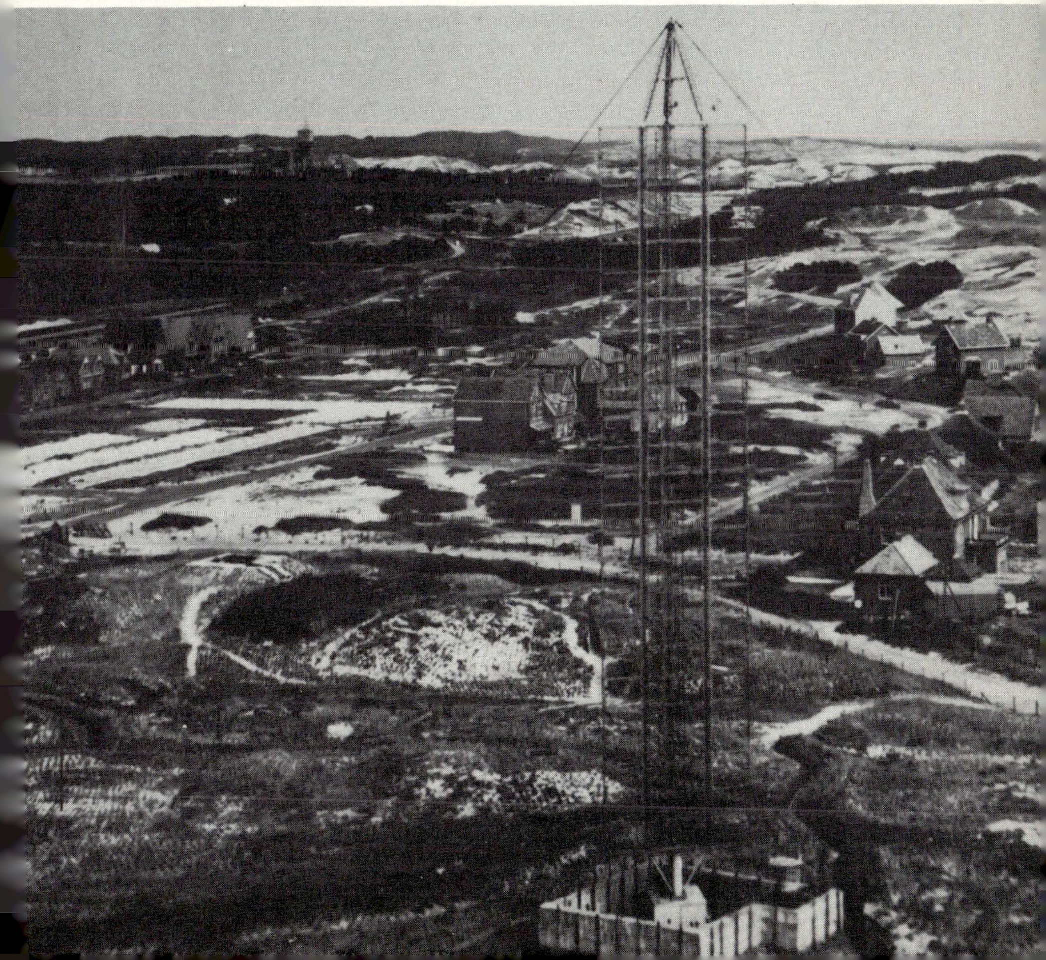

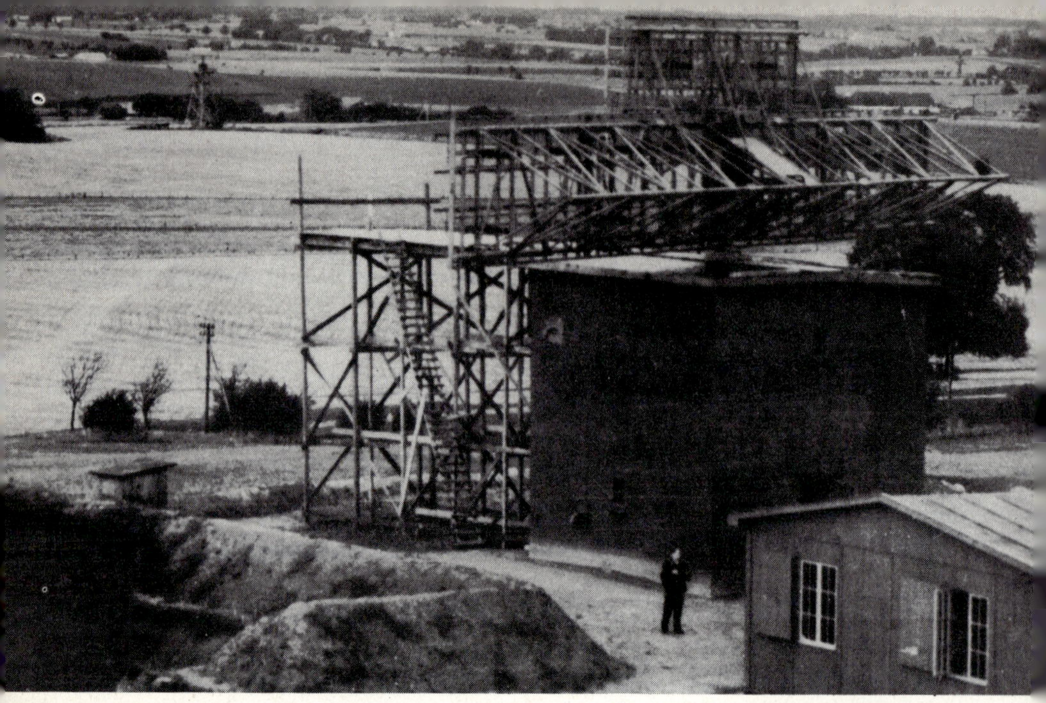

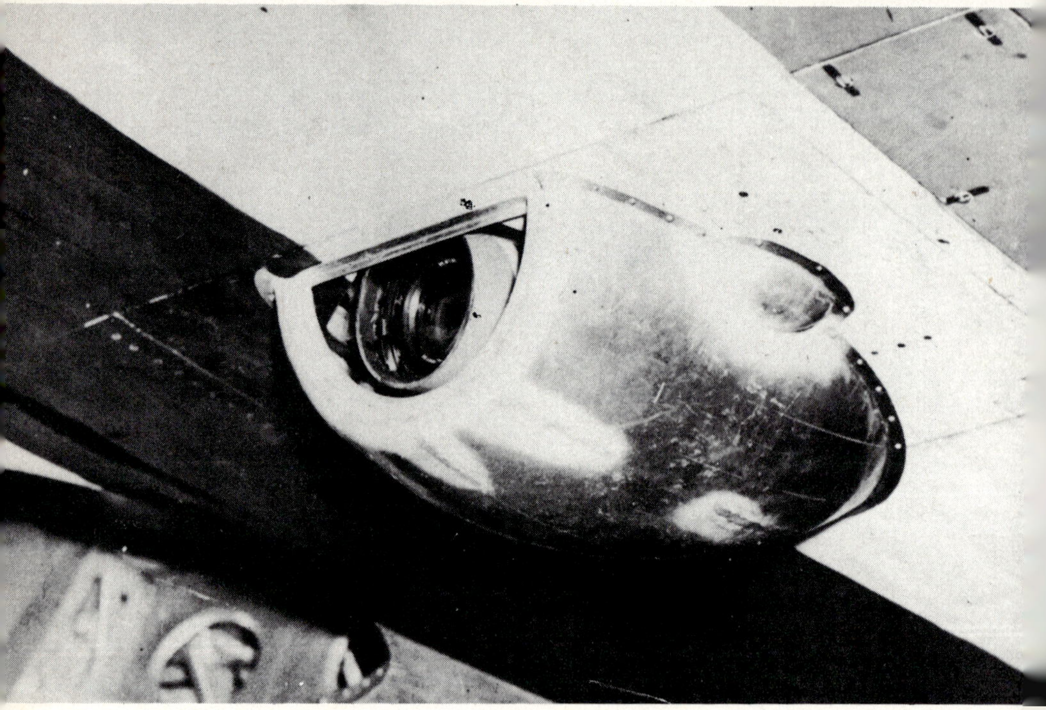

Top: Low level oblique of a Jagschloss height-finding radar at Ringsted/Tybjaerg. This station was still under construction when the photograph was taken on September 24th, 1944 because the wooden scaffolding surrounding the aerial has not yet been removed. *CC. Right:* Diagram of a standard PR Spitfire camera fit. *Above:* One of a pair of F 24 forward facing oblique cameras under the wings of a PR Spitfire. *IWM*

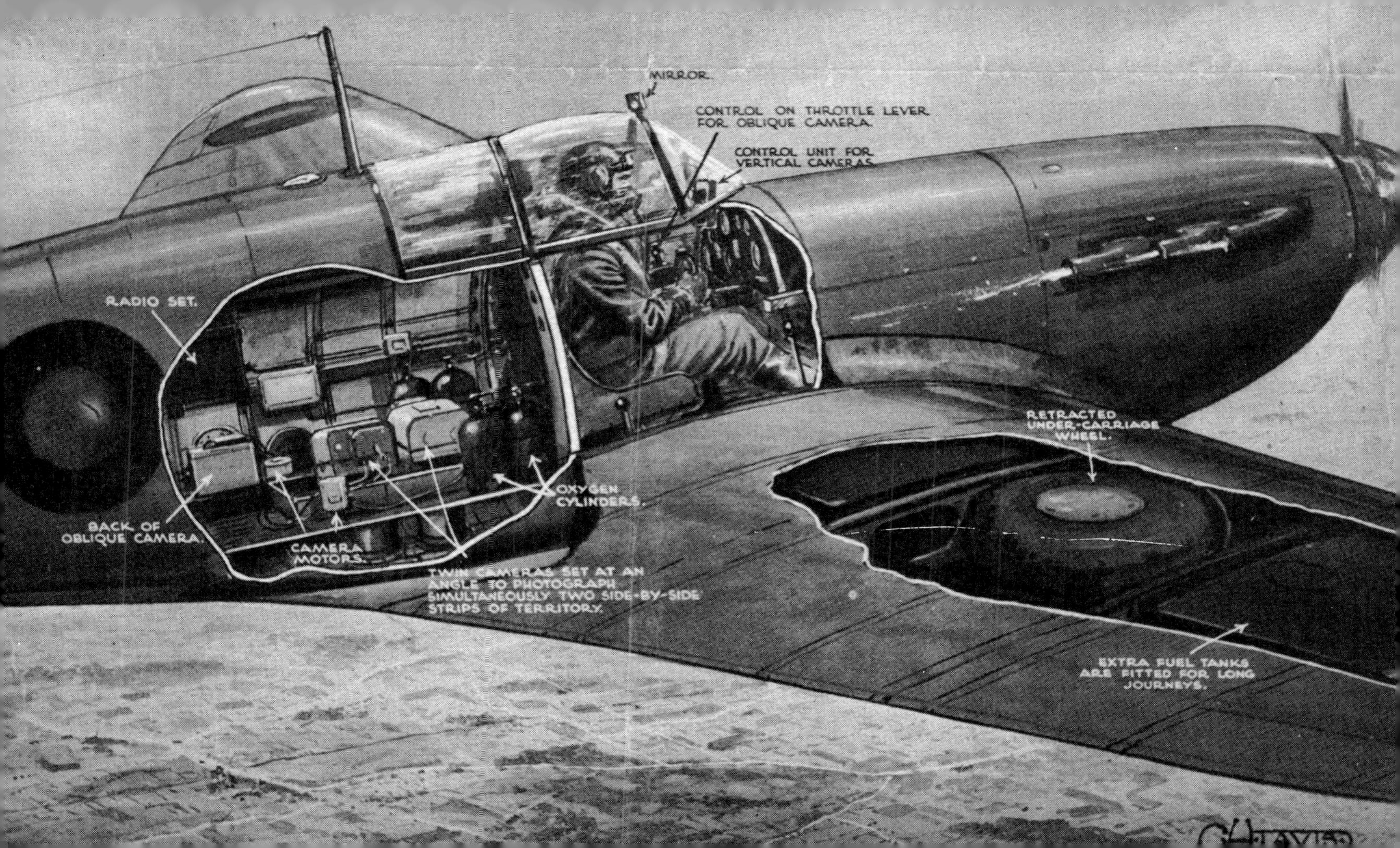
MIRROR.
CONTROL ON THROTTLE LEVER FOR OBLIQUE CAMERA.
CONTROL UNIT FOR VERTICAL CAMERAS.
RADIO SET.
BACK OF OBLIQUE CAMERA.
CAMERA MOTORS.
OXYGEN CYLINDERS.
TWIN CAMERAS SET AT AN ANGLE TO PHOTOGRAPH SIMULTANEOUSLY TWO SIDE-BY-SIDE STRIPS OF TERRITORY.
RETRACTED UNDER-CARRIAGE WHEEL.
EXTRA FUEL TANKS ARE FITTED FOR LONG JOURNEYS.

Below: Camera controls in the cockpit of a PR Spitfire. Cameras were switched on individually at the distribution box (bottom left) and the time-interval set via the Type 35 control box on top of the instrument panel. Exposures could be made manually by pressing the button on top of the control column or automatically by the control box. An orange light would illuminate when the camera was ready to take a picture, followed by a green light while the exposure was being made. After an exposure both lights would go out until the film was wound on, when the orange light would illuminate again. The frequency of the orange light depended on the TI set by the pilot. *CC*

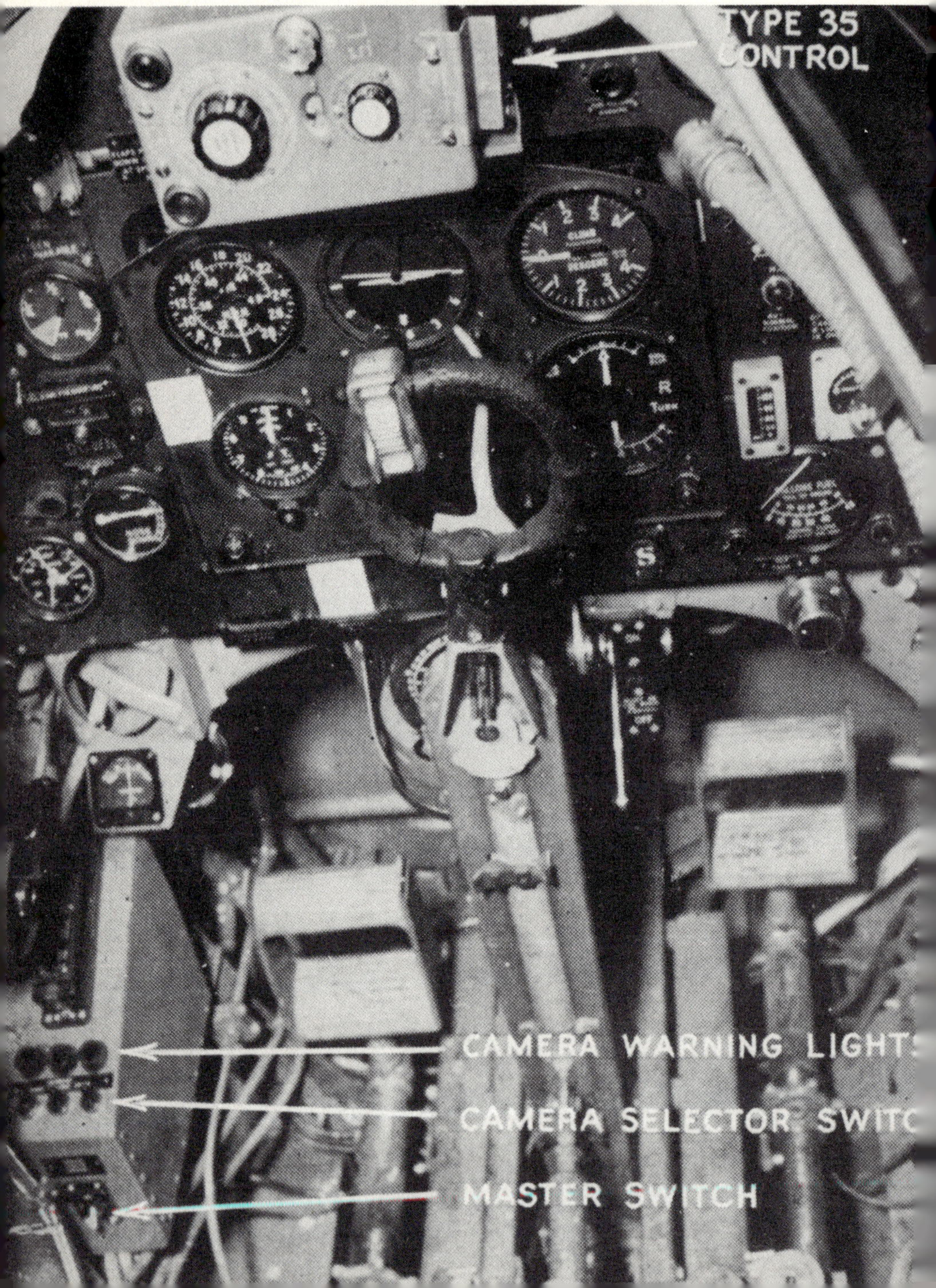

Below: Installing F 52 cameras into a PR Mosquito. *CC. Bottom:* Diagram of a standard PR Mosquito camera fit.

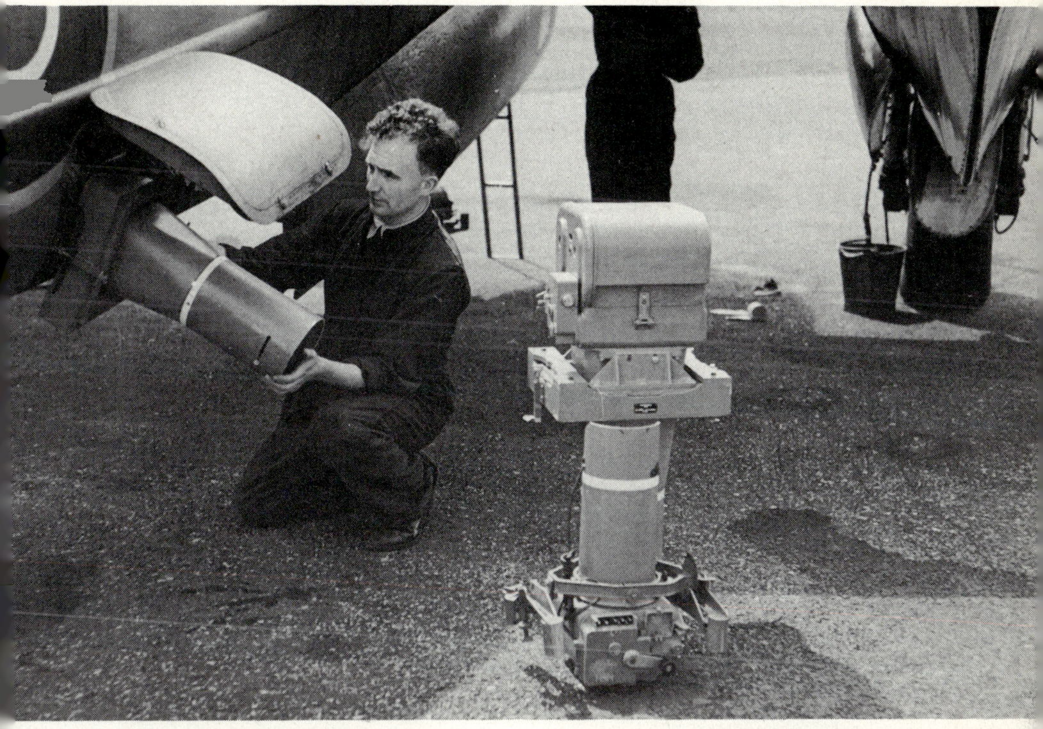

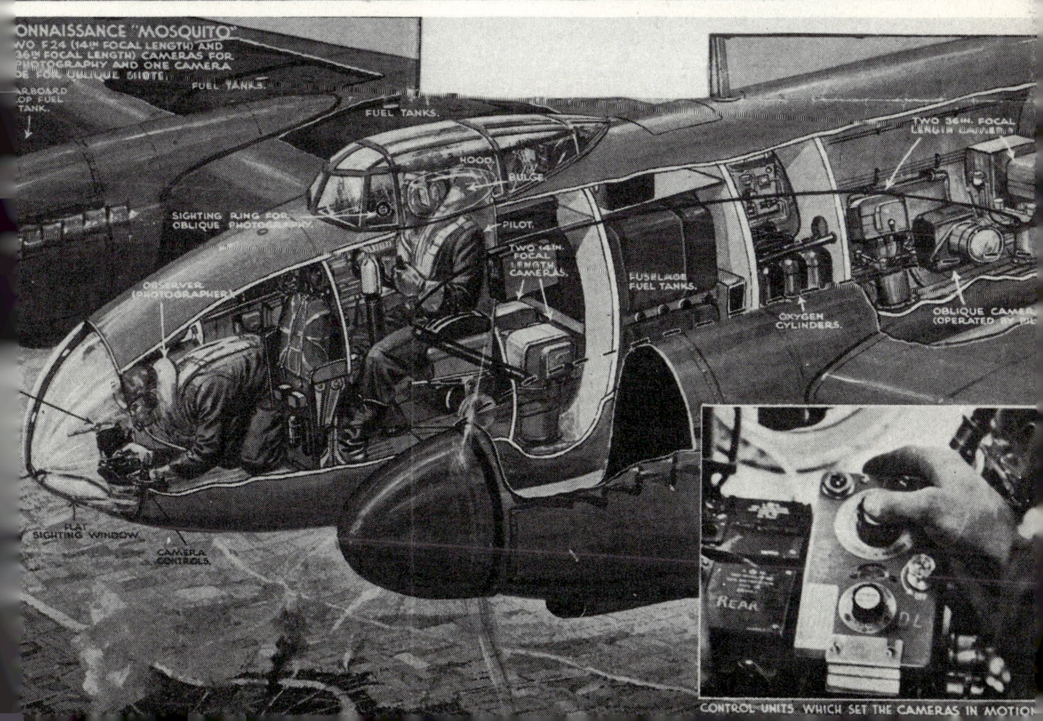

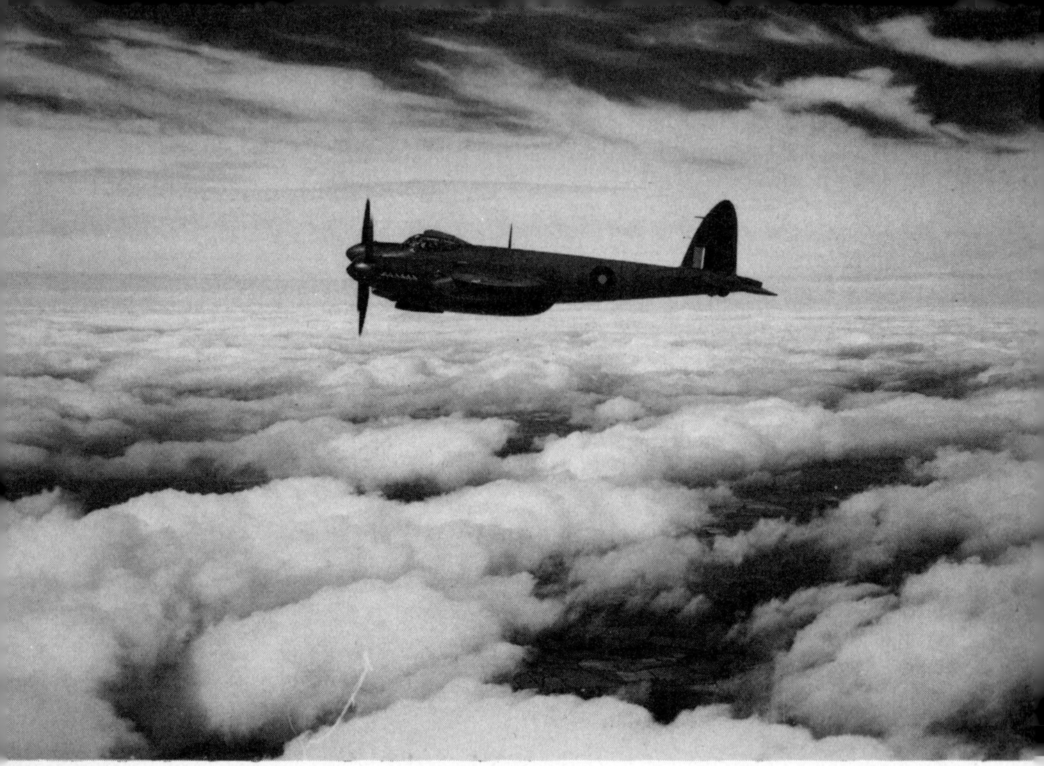

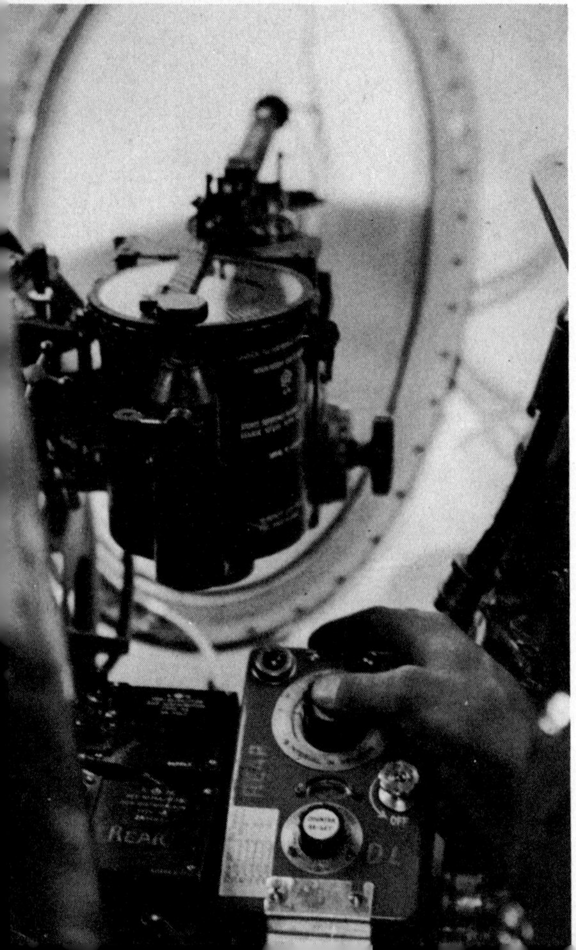

Above: A Mosquito PR IX on its way to Germany. *Left:* Having lined up the target, the Mosquito observer in the nose of the aircraft prepares to take a photograph. *Top right:* One of the world's first night aerial photographs – a railway line by a field in France taken by Capt F. A. Harper RFC in 1918. *Bottom right:* A night photograph taken by a Bomber Command aircraft during a raid on Nürnberg at the end of August 1942. The camera made its exposure just as the incendiaries started to fall and prints like this proved that the new navigational aids then entering service were helping Bomber Command to drop their bombs in the right place at last. *IWM*

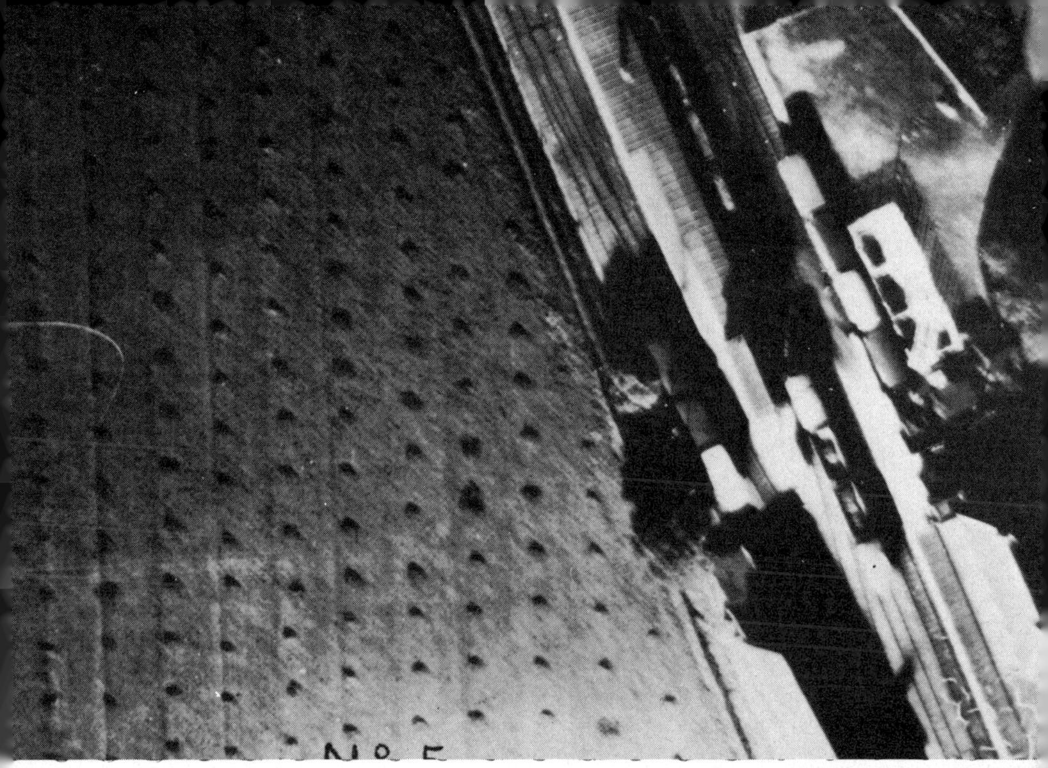

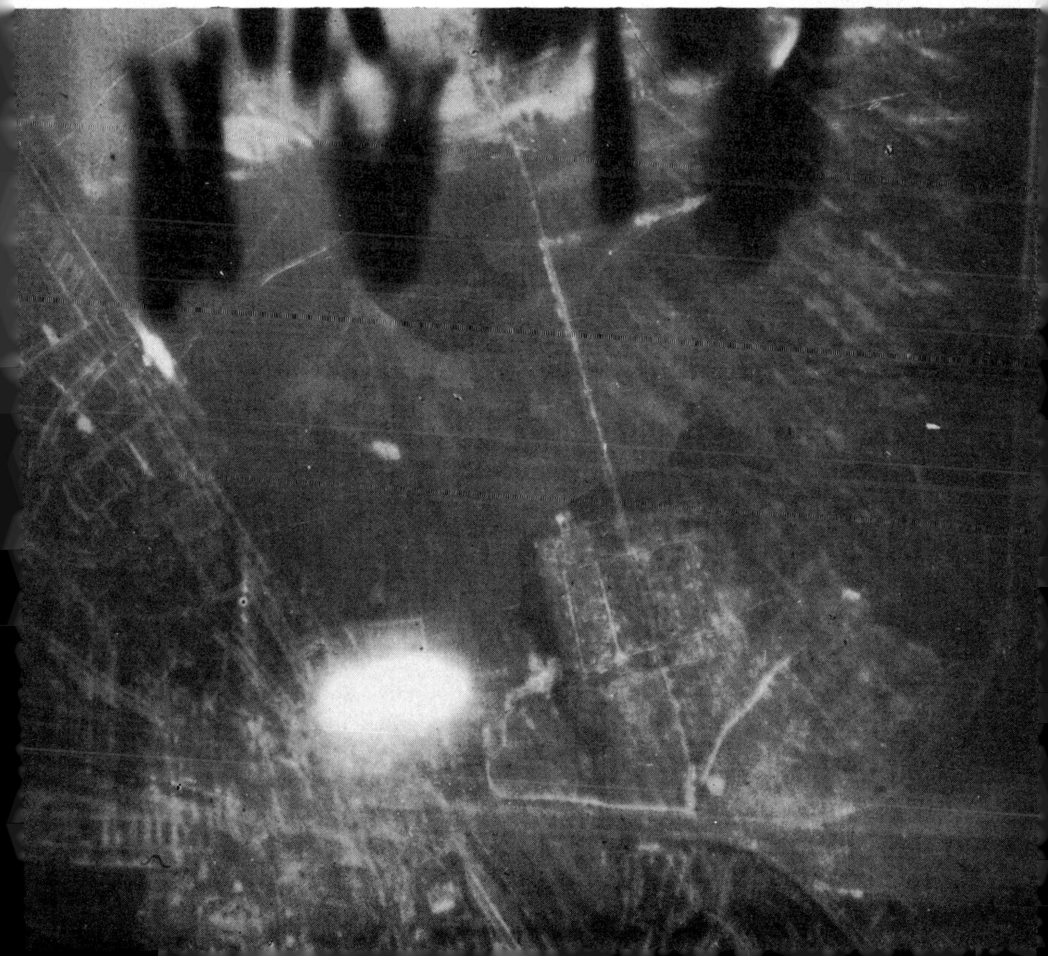

Below: A PR Mosquito prepares to take-off on a night mission. *Bottom:* Putting the aerial photographs to good use – Air Chief Marshal Sir Arthur Harris (centre) and his staff study maps and prints before planning an attack. *IWM*

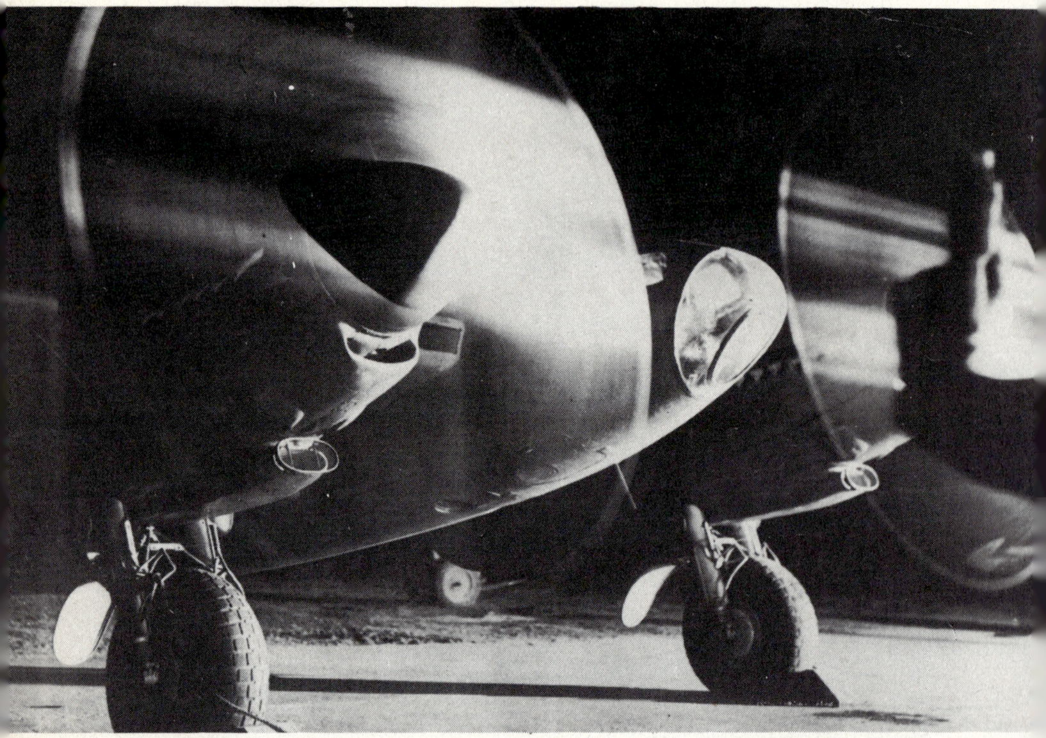

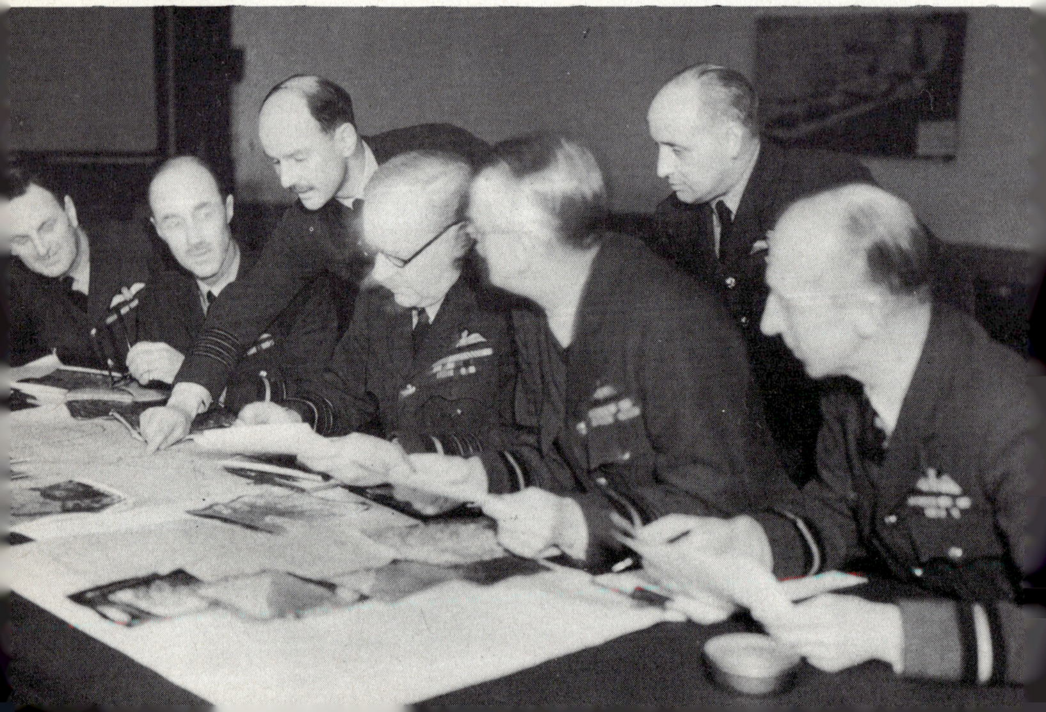

Daylight pre-strike and damage assessment photography was of inestimable value to Bomber Command in evaluating the results of their destructive efforts. *Below:* Shows an intact Luftschiffbau Zeppelin Works at Friedrichshafen producing light metal castings for radar equipment, aircraft and tank parts. The plant was bombed on several occasions during the next 18 months, culminating in the destruction of the giant airship hangar by the US 15th Air Force. *Bottom:* This was taken after this raid and it shows that the massive doors at either end have collapsed inwards. *CC*

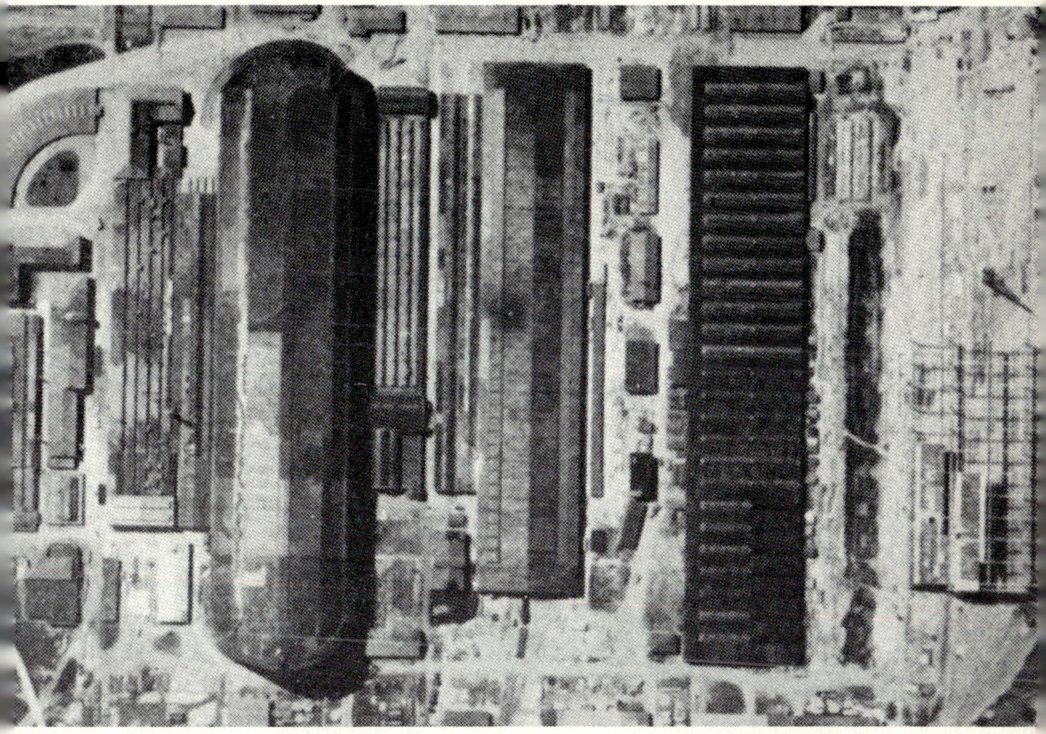

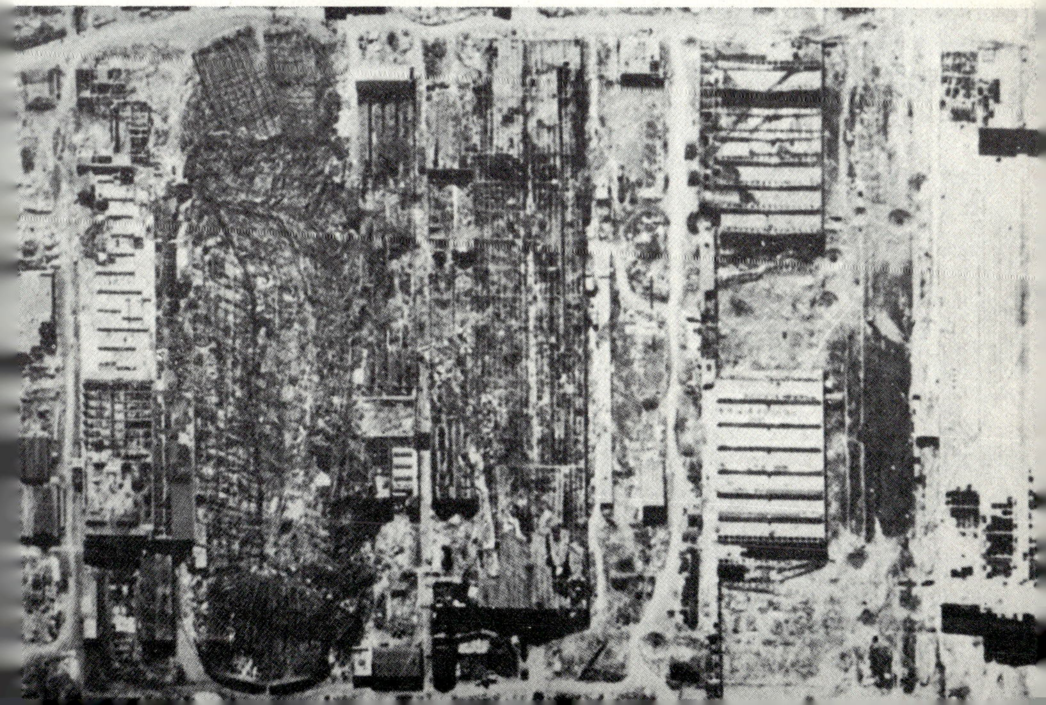

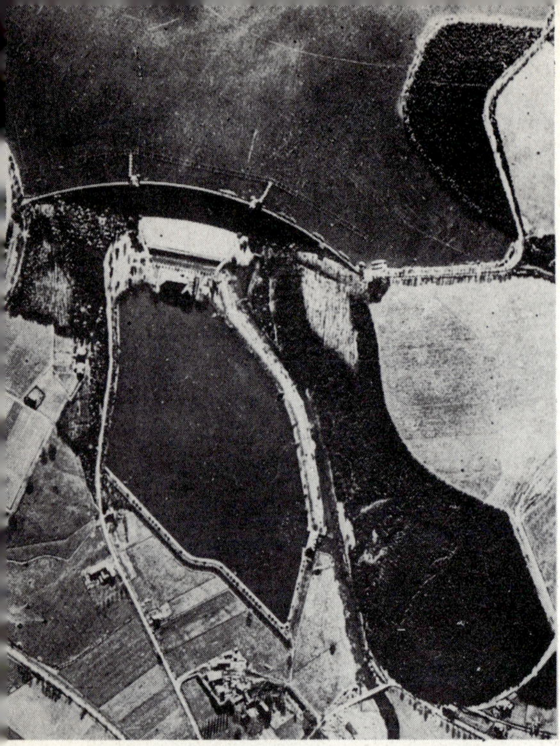

Left and Below: Before and after the raid on the Moehne Dam. The breach in the dam is 200 ft wide. *IWM*

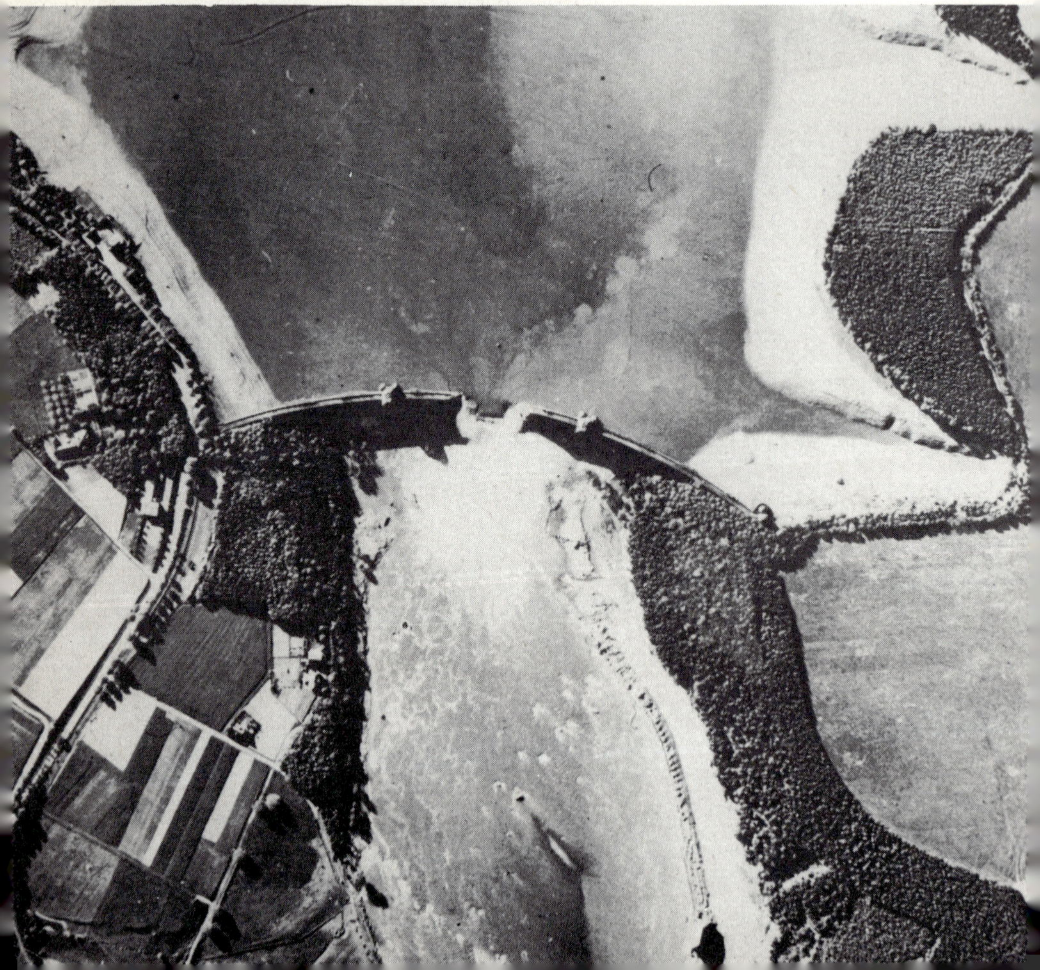

role, history since entering the record, which port it was at, how long it had been there, its position in the harbour, and whether it was loading or unloading. "We had our favourites of course," wrote 'Hugh-Pughe'. "One ship must have made four southbound voyages in the six months before we sank her in December 1941. There were three bottles of gin on the head of another but she bore a charmed life."

By September 25th the Italian Foreign Minister, Ciano, was writing in his diary that the Italian Navy was seriously considering recommending that Cyrenaica and Tripolitania be abandoned voluntarily rather than waiting until Italy was forced to do so through lack of shipping. Rommel had lost over 50% of his valuable stores while in transit across the central Mediterranean, and in the four months up to September, 351,000 tons of shipping had been destroyed and 186,800 tons severely damaged. While the Beauforts, Blenheims and the Royal Navy struck at the shipping-lanes, Wellingtons of 148 Sqn were pounding the docks at Tripoli. Photographs of Tripoli taken in September showed that the ships were having to use their own derricks to unload because the dockyard cranes had been destroyed. Unloading took three and a half times as long as it had done the previous June; by October there was so much wreckage at the quays that ships were having to unload in open water, and for eleven days no vessel could enter the choked port.

The number of convoys leaving Naples decreased sharply in October, and those that did sail hugged the Balkan coast round to Navarino before making the dash to Tripoli or Benghazi. 69 Squadron had to operate very warily now – if the Italians suspected that they were being watched they might never sail at all. Throughout November the Marylands watched a new convoy assembling in Naples. When it finally sailed for the Straits of Messina, Wg Cdr Dowland, the CO of 69 Sqn, had to keep his shadowing aircraft well out of sight or else the convoy would have made straight back for the safety of Naples. As soon as the ships had passed through the Straits, Dowland flew at full speed to Luqa, and within an hour a flotilla of cruisers was leaving the Grand Harbour.

In December 1941, the Italian Fleet moved south again to Taranto, only this time it was cocooned in booms, barrage-balloons, and AA batteries. Following a raid by Wellingtons, a Maryland flew over Taranto to photograph the damage and found that the protective booms had been moved away. A few days later, Warburton found a convoy of four merchant ships escorted, not by the usual handful of destroyers, but by two battleships, two cruisers, fifteen destroyers, and a host of Ju 88s. Bad weather prevented the Blenheims from taking off and this heavily defended convoy got through, but the Italians were obviously having to resort to desperate measures in a desperate situation. One particular convoy photographed leaving Naples fully laden was found a couple of days later in Palermo, having refused to go on without a stronger naval escort. It did not do them much good – Pughe-Lloyd remembers the great joy in the eyes of the Wellington crews as they examined the prints of so many bulging ships in Palermo. On February 2nd, 148 Sqn sank four out of the six vessels in the convoy and holed the harbour entrance for good measure.

The pilots on 69 Sqn – Dowland, Tennant, Potter, Drew, Bloxham, and Devine – thrived on their work, but the man who blossomed most under Hugh Pughe-Lloyd was Adrian Warburton. This great individualist was vividly described by Captain Spooner:

"He (Warburton) refused to park his aircraft in the dispersal areas. Instead he parked it as near to the Ops. room as he could. He navigated himself unerringly all over the Mediterranean – without adequate meteorological or navigational equipment. He went when they expected him and when they did not. He always came home undamaged, often followed by an armada of enemy fighters. . . . He chose to fly with AC2 Haddon and LAC Shirley, their role on board being to change the camera spools and count aloud the enemy fighters following him. He liked to take his coat off and to assist in servicing his own engines – a task for which he was not qualified. He would fly in almost any clothes provided they were *not* the official ones. A thigh-length pair of sheepskin leggings which he had acquired in Crete were characteristic. Above this he would wear Army battledress with air-force stripes (he was now an acting Flight Lieutenant). He preferred an Ascot cravat to a tie. He was proud of his ash-blonde hair, so let it grow to near shoulder-length. He had a notoriously grease-stained cap which he used to wear at times – on top of his flying helmet even. Against orders he smoked as he flew: he would take little part in mess life at Luqa, but instead could be found on occasions playing cards with the airmen at the dispersal site in one of the home-made huts there. Yet on one occasion, at a time when most of us had run out of buttons, polish and smart uniforms, he turned up in the mess immaculately dressed in order to meet the new Group Captain. He was like that – utterly unpredictable."

During the autumn of 1941, when the Italians seemed near capitulation in North Africa, even the Marylands captured the offensive spirit. They still retained their guns and carried a few bombs in case a 'target of opportunity' presented itself, but 69 Sqn crews were not supposed to seek engagements with Italian aircraft. However, in the last six months of 1941, 69 Sqn shot down fourteen Italian fighters, of which Drew got three and Warburton six. At one time, 'Warby' had more kills to his name than any fighter pilot on the island.

He was flying away from one conflict when one of his crew noticed that their pilot was in some difficulty.

"What are you doing, sir?" he asked.

"I'm extracting a bullet from my heart."

"Did you say your heart, sir?"

"Yes."

"Aren't you supposed to be dead, sir?"

"I suppose so," said Warburton, but he had more important things on his mind – his canopy had been shot away and one engine was on fire.

On another occasion, Warburton finished up at Catania after photographing eight Sicilian airfields. He was flying so low that Catania airfield gave him a 'Green' to land, so Warburton lowered his undercarriage. He carried out a final approach as if for landing, but at 50 feet he whipped his wheels up and, with all guns blazing, straffed everything on the tarmac, leaving two Ju 52s and two Italian torpedo-bombers in flames.

Warburton was supreme, but he owed much to the benevolence of Hugh Pughe-Lloyd. "There was something about his fair-haired good looks that reminded you of Lawrence of Arabia," recounted the AOC. "And like Lawrence he was absolutely unorthodox and a complete individualist. You had to let him do things in his own way . . ." Lloyd allowed Warburton a completely free rein and he responded by doing the impossible time and time again. He bore a charmed life and there was no Italian possession over which he could not photograph at will. "On and on he went: tireless, controversial, cynical, aloof. But in value absolutely beyond price." The ex-bank clerk found himself in Malta and, as a result, the RAF found one of its greatest war-time pilots.

In his less hectic moments, Pughe-Lloyd reflected on the ridiculousness of a situation in which seven Marylands could photograph every Italian port within range at will, whereas the massed strength of the Italian air force could never return the compliment. Their lack of success could be directly attributed to their adherence to the out-dated philosophy that air forces had to fight for their reconnaissance information because any information that could be obtained easily must not be worth having. Instead of sending one PR aircraft to sneak in and out of Luqa harbour before anyone noticed, the Axis made a field day of it by dispatching a reconnaissance aircraft surrounded by fighter escorts. They could be seen coming miles away. "If we had had to make all those preparations for all those escorts before getting our photographs we would have been out of business," commented Pughe-Lloyd. His way was Cotton's way and it paid dividends.

"We were obviously scoring heavily over the Axis in the contest of finding out what the other was doing," wrote Pughe-Lloyd. "I am at a loss to explain why the Axis don't come out and murder us for these activities." Hitler agreed, and, despairing of the Regio Aeronautica, he transferred Kesselring to Rome and moved the Fliegerkorps II to Sicily. On December 22nd, 1941 the Luftwaffe launched its blitz on the airfields of Luqa, Hal Far, and Takali, and by March 1942 all Pughe-Lloyd's bombers apart from a few Wellingtons had been withdrawn. The Italians recovered their Mare Nostrum by courtesy of the Luftwaffe and they could now reinforce Rommel at Gazala. Only one ship was sunk during February, and for a while the Axis convoys sailed unhindered.

Although the Italian Fleet posed the primary threat to the Royal Navy in the Mediterranean, the Admiralty was equally concerned about the future intentions of the French Navy. A relatively large proportion of the French Fleet had refused to sail for British ports after the defeat of France, moving instead to anchorages in French North Africa. In June 1940, the battleships *Jean Bart* and *Richelieu* were at Casablanca and Dakar respectively, while two more battleships, two battlecruisers, a seaplane carrier, and six large destroyers were berthed at Mers-el-Kebir. Nearby at Oran, there were seven more destroyers and four submarines, not to mention the six cruisers further along the coast at Algiers. If this powerful force threw its weight behind the Axis cause the British Mediterranean supply-lines would be severely threatened, so at the end of June 1940 the British Government authorised the Admiralty to take steps to watch French warships stationed abroad and to prevent them from falling under enemy control.

Gibraltar was the nearest base for aerial reconnaissance operations, but the British Government had given an undertaking to Spain in November 1939 that the Rock would only be used by Fleet Air Arm and training aircraft. A conflict of interests arose in 1940 between the Foreign Office, who wished to maintain the diplomatic peace, and the Admiralty, who wanted to use Gibraltar to watch the French Fleet, so a compromise was reached. French Marylands often landed at Gibraltar en route for North Africa, and two Marylands were handed over to 1 PRU in May 1941 for use in Gibraltar in the hope that the Spaniards would not notice any difference. A small First Phase Section was also set up on the Rock, and at 1835 hrs on June 24th Fg Off Peters landed at Gibraltar ready to start PR operations.

Peters' first mission on June 25th was to cover the Moroccan coast from the Algerian border to Ceuta. He also brought back oblique shots of the Spanish coast from Huelva round to Motril because British Naval Intelligence believed that U-boats were using the many inlets along the Spanish coast as refuelling and repair points. During the next twelve months, PRU Marylands covered all the North African coast from Bizerte to Dakar at regular intervals, returning to Benson after each detachment for periodic maintenance and to avoid any embarrassing Spanish questions. While Marylands peered into coves, the occasional high flying Spitfire would come down from Benson for a bit of inconspicuous photography over the larger Spanish ports. Sgt Blythe made the first PRU trip to the Spanish border in a Spitfire PR IV on August 14th, 1941, but he failed to bring back any prints from a flight lasting just over four hours. Flt Lt Steventon photographed Spain for the first time on August 28th, and from then on 1 PRU covered all the major ports of northern Spain round to Vigo whenever the need arose.[1]

The main drawback to the Spitfire PR IV was its limited range. Any target in the northern fiords of Norway, or in East Prussia, Bavaria, or Czechoslovakia remained an unknown quantity, yet these were increasingly the sort of targets that needed to be covered as the aerial offensive moved away from the Atlantic coastline and towards the interior of the Reich.

Try as they might, Supermarines could not fit any more fuel tankage into the PR Spitfire without reducing performance or displacing some cameras. Neither was a single-seater the right type of aircraft for really long-range missions. The demands imposed on one pilot became too much as the PR Spitfire

[1] One pilot who was shot down while returning from Spain on January 25th, 1942 was Fg Off A. Barber, later to become the Rt. Hon. Anthony Barber MP, and Chancellor of the Exchequer.

stayed airborne for longer – "beautiful day but went to sleep or something and overshot Nurnberg," wrote a pilot on September 22nd. Such distances could tax even a qualified observer, let alone a pilot who also had to fly his aircraft, operate the cameras accurately, and keep an ever open eye out for the enemy at the same time.

The Wick detachment had special problems in this respect. To reach their targets they had to fly over the wide and inhospitable North Sea with no towns or natural features to act as navigational reference points. I myself have often flown on PR sorties to the far northern latitudes with two navigators to guide me, and it has never ceased to amaze me how a solitary pilot, devoid of any of the sophisticated aids carried by aircraft today, could operate with such accuracy time and time again over such a forbidding and friendless expanse of water. At least they could be reasonably sure of finding Norway – the same could not be said of northern Scotland on the return journey. It was approximately 322 miles from Wick to Bergen, but this distance increased as the PR IV went up to Trondheim, and therefore many pilots decided to save 100 miles by landing back at Sumburgh in the Shetlands. The Shetlands presented a very small target from 30,000 feet, and were even harder to find beneath a layer of cloud with only a compass for guidance.

One of the problems attendant on flying higher than anyone had before, was that phenomena were encountered that no-one had realised existed. One of these was the jet stream, a belt of exceptionally fast air resulting from the large temperature gradients that can occur in horizontal bands in the mid-latitudes. At a time when meteorologists were forecasting conventional wind strengths for high altitude flights, jet streams were capable of providing an upper wind velocity of up to 200 knots. An unsuspecting pilot coming home from Trondheim might be expecting a tail-wind of 30 knots, only to get into a jet stream and experience a tail-wind component of five times that amount. It does not take much imagination to realise what would happen to a pilot who flew on and on looking for Sumburgh with declining fuel reserves, when in fact he would be many miles further West over the Atlantic.

Douglas Wilson was one of the first to feel the effects of the jet-stream in 1940. He was heading 240° on his return from Norway when he suddenly saw a group of islands below. He estimated that he was only half-way to the Shetlands so he dismissed the sighting as shadows from the clouds. Then he saw the glinting again, descended to have a look, and found himself over the west coast of the Shetlands. Another pilot aiming for Wick was blown so far south that he coasted in at Lindisfarne in Northumberland. Although a PRU pilot might never publicly admit it, he needed an observer to help him.

Cotton had written a Paper in September 1939 on the "Future Requirements for Photographic Aircraft". He foresaw an aeroplane, possibly a two-seater, having good downwards visibility and room for at least two cameras, with a top speed of 450mph, a service ceiling of at least 34,000 feet, and a range of 1500 miles at 300mph including half an hour at full throttle. "In principle, the machine should always be slightly faster than the fastest fighters in use," wrote Cotton. "This should always be possible, as the machine may always be a simplified and cleaned up form of fighter." Tuttle adhered to these criteria, and after testing every alternative – there were nineteen different types undergoing trials at Benson at one time – he pressed for the latest and most advanced two seater of the time, the de Havilland Mosquito.

Some indication of the importance attached to 1 PRU in 1941 may be derived from the fact that the first production Mosquito off the Hatfield assembly line was allocated to Benson. In their specification of December 1940, the Air Ministry ordered that twenty out of the first fifty aircraft for the RAF were to be PR versions, and on July 13th, 1941, eight months after the first prototype had flown, Geoffrey de Havilland flew the first PR Mosquito into Benson from Boscombe Down.

The next few months were spent installing cameras, changing the steel mountings for wooden ones to damp out vibration, and fitting camera heating. Two more Mosquitos arrived in August, and it was one of these that was wheeled out on September 17th for the first operational flight. At 1130 hrs, Sqn Ldr Rupert Clerke, a 25 year old ex-Etonian and stepson of Sir Edgar Ludlow-Hewitt, and his navigator, Sgt Sowerbutts, set course for the Franco-Spanish border. Over the Bay of Biscay the generator packed up, and with no power to drive the cameras Clerke was forced to return empty-handed. Two days later it was Alistair Taylor's turn and he managed to photograph Bordeaux successfully. The following day he covered Heligoland and Sylt in a Mosquito – even a new aircraft dare not go u/s with 'God' Taylor on board.

The Mosquito PR I soon sold itself to the PRU. Pilots forgave its tail shimmy, the yaw on take off, the leaking cockpit, and the smouldering engine cowlings, in exchange for improved design and performance. The twin Merlin 21s pushed out a top speed of 382mph, and one engine could bring the aircraft safely home. The Mosquito was capable of reaching 35,000 feet, travelling 2,180 miles, and carrying one oblique and three vertical cameras in its bomb-bay. All this plus VHF radio and extra navigation aids, not least of which was the navigator, made the Mosquito into a very potent and effective PR platform. "In my experience," wrote Major Hereward de Havilland, in charge of liaison between the manufacturers and the RAF, "it is the only aircraft which has initially not been branded by pilots as a death-trap in one way or other."

The first PR Mosquitos to arrive at Benson were formed into a Flight under Alistair Taylor, now a Sqn Ldr, and dispatched to Wick. Taylor named each of his aircraft after a drink – first there were 'Whisky', 'Benedictine', and 'Vodka', soon to be joined by 'Drambuie', 'Cointreau', and 'Crême de Menthe'! The Mosquito Flight flew sixteen successful sorties during October covering the Norwegian coast around Oslo, Kristiansand, Stavanger, Bergen, and Trondheim. Air Chief Marshal Joubert de la Ferté, then C-in-C Coastal Command, was soon to remark that one Mosquito could do the work of two Spitfires.

Wick's days as a permanent PRU base were numbered with the introduction of the Mosquito. Range was no longer so crucial, and, to cut down the time delay involved in getting prints down to Medmenham and Mosquito spares up to the far north of Scotland, the detachment moved down to Leuchars in Fife at the end of December. Wick and Sumburgh continued to be used as forward refuelling airfields whenever an extra long-range mission was necessary.

On December 4th, Alistair Taylor was down at Leuchars to check on its suitability as a Mosquito base. He was tasked that day with a routine sortie to Bergen and Trondheim, and together with his navigator, Sgt Horsfall, he climbed 'Benedictine' out through the murky weather and over the North Sea. Neither aircraft nor crew were ever to see the Firth of Tay again – the supremely confident and brilliantly efficient Alistair Taylor was shot down by anti-aircraft fire later that day. The circumstances of his death remain a mystery. No ordinary PRU pilot would have hung about once the AA batteries started up, but Taylor was extraordinary. Taylor knew no fear – he once took a set of obliques of a Gestapo headquarters from such a low altitude that he had to raise his wing to take a photograph. The prints were so magnificent that the PIs could see inside the windows. He had cheated death so often that perhaps he stayed in the danger area until he had completed his run, or until a shell hit him.

We do know that the Germans had recently introduced a new high-level AA gun in Norway and that they used it for the first time on December 4th. Geoffrey Tuttle believed that Taylor was caught by a lucky first burst, giving him no chance to appreciate the danger and turn away. Another theory was that Taylor sacrificed his life to guide the crippled Mosquito into the sea to save the new and highly secret aircraft from the Germans. Whatever happened, Alistair Taylor's luck ran out. Confident of his own ability and contemptuous of anyone who did not measure up to his meticulous standards, often disliked but always envied by his compatriots, Alistair Taylor was magnificent in his art. Douglas Wilson prophesied in 1940 that Taylor would either get a VC or kill himself – on December 4th, 1941 the gods took him back as one of their own.

The end of the year also saw the promotion of Geoffrey Tuttle and his replacement shortly afterwards by Spencer Ring. From now on life for the PRU increased in difficulty as its aircraft began to leave the comparatively safe coastal areas of Europe and operate further into the heart of hostile Axis airspace.

CHAPTER SEVEN

The Field of Vision Extends

Air power in general has . . . two supreme qualities: the capacity to range over the whole extent of enemy territory and its surrounding seas, and the flexibility to strike at will at the most vulnerable points in the opposing war machine. But to combine these qualities effectively the Air Staff must be fully informed, not only about fixed targets, but even more, about enemy activities and intentions. If we don't know the exact details of the enemy's anatomy, our air power may rain punches all over his bloated body without ever hitting the vital spots. Air Ministry Pamphlet No 328A.

The advocates of strategic bombing have been with us for half a century now . . . To them their solution was the only route to victory. It sounds so simple: destroy a nation's capacity to make war and it must sue for peace. This dogma has, moreover, a subtle advantage over direct confrontation. Your own men are relatively safe. If they do die, death is clean. Most important, you never see the real results of their work until the enemy has surrendered. A reconnaissance photograph is impersonal, dehumanised; the scale is too small to show, say, a dismembered child. 'The Arms of Krupp', William Manchester.

The Second World War was the first "boffins'" war. Total war meant total involvement for everyone and science was requisitioned to come to the aid of the military. Learned men of all disciplines left their colleges and laboratories to follow new research programmes, from physicists working on atomic weapons to geographers delineating the most combustible sectors of ancient German cities. This war was not to be won by the nations with the biggest battalions but by the side with the greatest scientific and technical superiority over the other.

To keep ahead of, and at times to catch up with, German research and development, scientific brains were also drafted into British Intelligence. In the spring of 1940, the Air Staff approved the addition of a scientific and technical section to its Directorate of Intelligence, and Sir Henry Tizard was invited to suggest a candidate to run it. He recommended Dr R. V. Jones, a tall solemn physicist who had worked with Lindemann at the Clarendon Laboratory, and Tizard later observed that he never had any reason to regret his choice.

Jones' section was tasked with sifting all intelligence information, including aerial photographs, to see if there were any interesting developments worth following up. One of the first things that attracted attention was German radar technology. In November 1939, the British Naval Attaché in

Oslo had received a report from an anonymous German scientist containing details of certain German technological research projects. Among the wealth of information in the Oslo Report was the revelation that the Germans possessed an aircraft detection system using coastal radio transmitters with a range of 75 miles, and a second type of early warning system using parabolic reflectors.

This information was received with scepticism in certain quarters, especially because it implied that German research in this field was ahead of British. Such a situation had serious implications for organisations like Medmenham; any PI could pick out a battleship even if it was a revolutionary battleship, but it was much harder to find a radar site if the experts could not agree on what it might look like, assuming that it existed at all.

Jones kept an open mind about the Oslo Report and looked for more information. On July 5th, 1940 one of his sources reported that German fighters had been able to intercept a British reconnaissance aircraft because of information from an early-warning radar system called '*Freya*'. The informant also revealed that there was a '*Freya*' site at Lannion in Brittany, and nine days later Jones heard of another one at Cap de la Hague on the north-west tip of the Cherbourg peninsula. He decided to follow up the reports on the radar sites in two ways – by monitoring any signals that might come from them, and by asking for PR cover of the particular areas.

Two 'special tasks' of Lannion and Cap de la Hague were flown by the PRU but with no success. An F 24 print could just record an array of '*Knickebein*' aerials – the largest system of Luftwaffe radio navigation installations with masts up to 100 feet high on turntables 300 feet in diameter – but nothing smaller. All that could be deduced from the special prints was that if '*Freya*' was there, it must be smaller than that.

When it received its first F 8 cameras with 20 in lenses, the PRU could have another try. On 22nd November, Plt Off W. K. Manifould photographed, amongst other things, the little village of Auderville on Cap de la Hague. This time there was no mistaking two small unexplained circles to the west of the village measuring some 20 feet across and looking like a pair of opera glasses laid lenses down. As yet the CIU had no specialised knowledge of such things – up to now their reports on radio stations had been confined to such statements as "there is a wireless at pinpoint x" – so the prints were enlarged and handed over to Dr Charles Frank, a physicist on Jones' staff. The time interval between the two prints of the 'opera glasses' was nine seconds, and as he looked at them through a stereoscope Dr Frank noticed that they were not identical. A thin white object on top of one of the 'circles' had moved through 90° and its shadow had grown from 0.1 mm on the first print to 2 mm on the second. "The difference was hardly greater than the resolving power of the photographs," wrote Alfred Price in 'Instruments of Darkness', "but it proved that whatever it was was rotating."

Previous cover of Auderville was examined, but there was no sign of the 'opera-glasses' on October 5th. They were not unlike flak batteries, but this theory was discounted because the 'circles' were too close to each other and there was no sign of the usual track activity associated with AA sites. Jones considered the discovery to be of sufficient importance to request a special low-level sortie to have a closer oblique look at the 'opera-glasses'.

On February 16th, 1941, Sgt Parrott flew a G type to Auderville, but the pre-set TI was so long that the circular objects were missed between two successive frames. However he was fired at by an adjacent flak battery as he swept by and Sgt Parrott thought the 'circles' looked like gun positions. Six days later Manifould went over at low level, and his magnificent obliques showed that each circle was surmounted by a rotating aerial array. After a year of patient searching, Reginald Jones had found a *'Freya'* at last.[1]

Freya provided early warning of an intruder up to 100 miles away, but this apparatus formed only part of the German aerial radar system. In 1940, protection of the Reich from night attacks had been entrusted to Major-General Josef Kammhuber, the 'General of Night Fighters', and he authorised the construction of a string of '*Himmelbett*' early warning zones. Each *Himmelbett* controlling station received its long range warning from a '*Freya*' site, which in turn was complemented by two '*Würzburg*' radars which measured the bearing and elevation of the intruder up to 25 miles.

Jones first heard of *Würzburg* in the winter of 1940. Two types were apparently in existence – a *'Giant Würzburg'* capable of ranging up to 45 miles with its 45 foot reflector, and a smaller mobile *Würzburg* existing in larger numbers. An agent sent a picture of a *Giant Würzburg* erected on a tower in Berlin Zoo, but of its smaller relation Jones knew nothing.

Throughout 1941, the PRU discovered more and more *Freya* sites, and on August 2nd Flt Lt Watts was detailed to cover a stretch of French coast from Etretat to Le Havre because another one had been reported under construction near the small village of Bruneval on the Cap d'Antifer. A Third Phase section of wireless specialists – G Section – was now in being at Medmenham under Sqn Ldr Claude Wavell, and they soon found a *Freya* aerial array from Watts' prints. But they also noticed that a track had been trodden along the cliff edge from the *Freya* site towards a large sanatorium which appeared to be an HQ building. The track continued to a point 750 yards past the sanatorium where it stopped by a small parabolic object. Nothing more definite could be extracted from the medium level vertical prints, so Jones decided to ask for another low level mission. Before he could do so, however, Tony Hill came to his assistance.

On December 3rd, Hill visited the CIU with Gordon Hughes. Hughes often covered the fifteen miles between Benson and Medmenham in his car to chat about photography with the interpreters. Sometimes a PI would suspect that something important was happening in a particular area but he lacked enough evidence to justify an official task; Hughes or one of the other pilots would then try to photograph it the next time they were in the area. Many important discoveries were made on this 'old boy' net and some not so important – an Air Marshal once asked Gordon Hughes to dice a creek near St

[1] Manifould returned the nearby AA fire this time and damaged part of the radar installation – it was shortly removed from Auderville.

Nazaire to see if his yacht, which he had abandoned at the start of the war, was still there.[1]

On this occasion Tony Hill had gone along with Hughes for the ride, and as he was interested in radio and electronics they dropped in to see Claude Wavell in G Section. During the conversation Wavell mentioned the Bruneval find and the need for more detailed photography. "You pilots annoy me," he joked. "You go over this place time and time again and never turn on your cameras soon enough!" "I'll get you the answer tomorrow," replied Hill.

His sortie the next day broke all the rules and was completely unofficial. Bruneval, like all *Freya* sites, was defended by flak batteries, and any low level mission against a protected target had to be specially authorised by the Air Ministry. Hill did not care; fired by the importance of the search, he set off to dice Bruneval. Unfortunately his camera did not share his enthusiasm and it broke down as he swept in over the cliffs of Cap d'Antifer. "It looks like an electric bowl-fire and it's about 10 feet across," he told Wavell that evening.

Hill tried again on December 5th, but this time he was not only breaking Air Ministry regulations but offending against the unwritten law of dicing. The German AA batteries had been caught unawares the day before – now they would be alert and ready. But there was no stopping Tony Hill once his mind was made up. As he taxied out he found himself behind three other PRU aircraft whose pilots had been officially briefed to operate over the same part of France. He stopped alongside them and told the three pilots that if he found any of them within twenty miles of Bruneval he would shoot them down. He got his photographs unmolested.

Hill's two prints of the site revealed a parabolic reflector similar to the one described in the Oslo Report. G Section measured the bowl and estimated its diameter as 2.79 metres,[2] coinciding with the hitherto unexplained 53 cm transmissions being picked up from that part of the coast by electronic monitoring aircraft. The only way to confirm that this was a small *Würzburg* was to examine it, and on February 27th a landing party from the Airborne Division stole into Bruneval and made off with the essential parts of the apparatus. Their success owed much to the 1:3000 scale model of the area produced from Hill's pictures by the CIU Model Section. "These excellent photographs," waxed a special minute to ACAS (I), "are a very valuable contribution to our study of the enemy's night defences, for they have provided us with positive knowledge which can be obtained in no other way." More eulogistically, Dr Jones placed them "among the classics of the war".

After the Bruneval raid the Germans surrounded their *Würzburg* sites with barbed wire, but this only served to spotlight such installations on future photographs. Five more 'bowl-fires' were discovered by February, and an extensive CIU search revealed that small *Würzburgs* were being erected for AA gun-laying in Greece, Crete, and North Africa as well. Those in northern Europe were originally positioned on the coast, but in March 1942 Dr Jones

[1] The Air Ministy took a dim view of all this unofficial photography and, despite its value, they soon banned all unofficial visits by the PRU to Medmenham.

[2] Actually 3 metres.

received a report of an inland radar station at Nieuwekerken in Belgium, close to the night-fighter base of St Trond. High level PR revealed a typical *Freya* station with a *Würzburg* parabolic dish neatly surrounded by a group of searchlights. Shortly afterwards another agent reported a night-fighter control centre at Domberg on the Dutch island of Walcheren, and, after aerial photography had shown another *Freya* and two parabolic dishes, Tony Hill was sent over at low-level on May 2nd. He started his run in from the north, and just as he switched on his oblique camera a Luftwaffe operator started to climb the ladder leading to the cabin at the rear of the second dish. As he stood there, riveted to the spot with his hand on the fifth rung, the astonished German could have had no idea that he would be used as a human yardstick by the grateful CIU.

The parabolic reflectors at Domberg were similar to the 'bowl-fires' at Bruneval, but the dish itself was made of wire-mesh stretched over a framework like a basket. From then on, for want of a better name, this reflector type was known as the *'Basket'*. In fact it was a *Giant Würzburg*, similar to that on Berlin Zoo, and Domberg and Nieuwekerken were night-fighter control stations.

More nerve centres were soon found at Zonhoven and Jodoigne – in fact there was one every twenty miles in a line protecting the Ruhr. This was the Kammhuber Line, with *Freyas* and *Würzburgs* providing the night eyes that controlled the searchlights and flak batteries, and which directed the night fighters to such good effect against Bomber Command.

Now that Jones had discovered one of Germany's most important and best kept secrets, he could use the PRU to fill in the additional pieces to complete the picture. At the beginning of 1942 they had found only nine radar stations on the Continent, but by the end of the year they had photographed over seventy. New ones periodically appeared. In early May 1942, Jones heard of an unusual tower on the dunes of the Hook of Holland, and another dice by Tony Hill revealed a new coast-watching *Freya*. Every additional variant was given an evocative name, depending on its shape and size – after the '*Bowl*' and the '*Basket*' came the '*Hoarding*' and the '*Chimney*'.

The PRU also located over 700 radio stations in 1942, ranging from a 900 foot giant at Le Croix d'Huis near Bordeaux to a minute aerial at Roanne. The Germans even went as far as constructing dummy installations – there were a couple of imitation Knickebein aerials at St Jean au Doigt and Gué de la Lande – but they did not fool the Third Phase experts at Medmenham. During the first three years of its life, G Section discovered and plotted 3,300 fixed radio and radar stations in the European theatre alone. The aerial camera had discovered the Germans' electronic eyes; Bomber Command was soon to put them out.

The Model Section at Medmenham had been formed with the invasion of Europe in mind. The landings at Gallipoli in 1915 had floundered through lack of adequate preparation and intelligence, and army planners in 1941 realised that the success of any similar operation would depend on the provision of up to date information on the proposed area of operations and the dissemination of this data to the assault forces in an easily understandable form. Conventional maps and charts had severe limitations in these respects. Most maps of France, for instance, were of pre-war vintage, lacking any information about the defence works or troop emplacements erected by the Germans since 1940. It also took an exceptional soldier to look at a map and know exactly what the terrain would hold for him at night.

Both these drawbacks could be overcome by the aerial camera. First the PIs could extract all the latest intelligence information from the prints, and then the model makers of V Section could translate this into three-dimensional models, one perhaps showing, by subtle use of lighting, the coastline as it would appear at night, or another revealing the ground as a commander would see it from the beach. After examining the excellent models of the Vemork heavy water factory at Rjukan in Norway prior to their raid on February 27th 1943, the commando team involved asserted that they knew the terrain "better than their own back garden".

In March 1942, the thorny question of PRU priorities was raised again. Between December 10th 1941 and January 20th 1942, no less than 37% of the total effort expended by Bomber Command had been harnessed to the unrewarding task of bombing three warships in Brest. Once the 'Brest Question' had been settled by the Channel Dash on February 12th Bomber Command was at long last directed to use its strength in the way it wanted, i.e. against "the morale of the enemy civil population, and in particular, of the industrial workers" by attacking factories and industrial plants in the Ruhr that lay within range of the first of the new navigational aids, 'Gee'.

The new C-in-C Bomber Command, Air Chief Marshal Sir Arthur Harris, found however that High Wycombe still lacked priority when it came to the provision of target and damage assessment material. Naval Intelligence continued to demand daily cover of the damaged *Scharnhorst* and *Gneisenau* in Kiel, and Harris wrote bitterly that he "obtained daily photographs of the *Scharnhorst* and the *Gneisenau* and other targets of a naval nature, whilst for two and a half months he had failed to obtain a single photograph of Hüls, to confirm his impression that the blitz there was a particularly successful one".

Arthur Harris had a genuine grievance, and from March 1942 onwards the PRU followed more and more of the bombing raids. The latest bombing directive laid down that French factories working for Germany were acceptable targets, and on the night of March 3rd, 235 aircraft of Bomber Command set out for the Renault motor and armaments factory at Billancourt on the outskirts of Paris. To forestall any public criticism of an attack on a French factory situated in a built-up area, and to counter German attempts to camouflage the damage, it was imperative to publish photographs of the results as soon as possible after the raid. Billancourt was also the first target to be attacked using the 'Shaker' or 'flare' technique. With the introduction of 'Gee', the standard bombing force was now to be divided into three sections –

the illuminators, the target markers, and the followers. The illuminators were to carry Gee, (though on this raid they did not do so as the scientists were only concerned with trying out the flare technique), with which they would navigate the force to the bombing zone and drop triple flares up wind of the target at ten second intervals. This produced a flare path six miles long, into which the target markers, following behind, would drop their incendiary bombs at a rate of two per minute. It was hoped that the followers, not equipped with Gee, would then deposit their high explosive loads into this belt of flames, resulting in a far greater degree of accuracy than any strategic bombing had been able to achieve before.

There were therefore quite a few reputations at stake and even more fingers crossed when Flt Lt Victor Ricketts and his observer, Sgt Boris Lukhmanoff, took off from Benson in their Mosquito at 1115 hrs on the morning after the raid. It was a miserable day with the rain pouring down and visibility severely restricted. Nevertheless they managed to find a hole in the cloud near Rouen and followed the Seine at 900 feet until they reached the Renault factory. By weaving in and out of cloud at around 500 feet they managed three runs over the holed factory roof before returning to land at the only airfield they could find in cloud-covered southern England. Ricketts and Lukhmanoff gave a brief report to the local intelligence-officer on their visual sightings, their films were developed and printed by hand, and both reports and prints were dispatched to Bomber Command by 2010 hrs that evening. In spite of the appalling weather, Sgt Lukhmanoff had managed to expose five obliques to show that "very great devastation of the target" had been achieved. 31 out of 35 buildings were seen to have been hit by high explosives or incendiaries, and experts estimated that 40% of the Renault machine-tools had been destroyed.

On March 28th, Bomber Command moved north to the Baltic. 234 aircraft were dispatched in three waves to Lübeck, an old Hanseatic port that was beyond Gee range but which was easy to find on the coast, and a target that lent itself to the Shaker aiming technique because the old town centre was largely built of wood. Flt Lt Robinson brought back prints on April 12th that showed "large areas of total destruction amounting to probably 45-50% of the whole city". The main railway station and central electricity generating station were damaged, along with numerous warehouses and workshops, and it was estimated that 200 acres of Lübeck had been devastated by high explosives and incendiaries, including some 2,000 houses and a dozen factories. The cathedral, Reichsbank, and Market Hall had been razed to the ground.

A fortnight later, Plt Off Crakenthorp followed a raid on Rostock, another Hanseatic port that was easy to find, lightly defended, and built to burn. Among its southern suburbs was the Heinkel factory of Marienehe, and this had been chosen as the main aiming point for part of the force. Thirteen returning bombers brought back night pictures of the factory itself and every single one of the 52 night prints taken were exposed over the target area. When Crakenthorp went over in daylight he had difficulty photographing the damage because of the pall of smoke hanging over the debris. His prints were a great morale booster for Bomber Command; they showed that 70% of the old city had been destroyed and Rostock was deemed to be incapable of functioning effectively for some time.

Such predicions however were of limited credence. Although the extent of bomb damage could be accurately measured from aerial photographs in 1942, the consequences of such damage tended to be overestimated. Factories with lost roofs could often restart production immediately, and, even if a building was destroyed, the machinery inside might remain intact to be transferred to another building. On April 26th many experts believed that much of Rostock had ceased to exist, but because of the drive and resourcefulness of the Mecklenburg Gauleiter the principal war factories were nearly back to 100% production by April 29th.

On May 30th, Air Chief Marshal Harris threw his first thousand bomber raid against an unsuspecting Cologne. At 0500 hrs on the next morning, Fg Off E. D. L. Lee looked down on Cologne from his blue Spitfire at 23,500 feet. Fires were everywhere, from the city centre to the suburbs, and over it all was a great cumulo-nimbus type of smoke cloud rising to 15,000 feet. As it cleared in the dawn, Lee photographed the "heavy and widespread" damage that was "on a much larger scale than anything previously inflicted on a German city". 600 acres of Cologne, half of which were in the city centre, appeared to have been completely destroyed. The prints showed that no "considerable" part of Cologne was free from damage.

The effectiveness of the Shaker technique had still to be tried against the concentrated defences of the Ruhr, and two days after the holocaust of Cologne the indefatigable Harris sent 956 bombers against Essen. Apart from the size of the raid, there were few parallels with Cologne. Several bomb aimers admitted aiming at fires sighted on ETA, while others bombed blindly from Gee fixes. Stories filtered through of fires scattered throughout the Ruhr and night photographs confirmed that the bombing had been dispersed. Out of 73 prints showing ground detail, none showed the Krupps complex and only eight could be plotted within five miles of it. Several were exposed miles to the west around Duisburg and Hamborn. The PRU went over on June 2nd, 3rd, 5th, and 6th and they produced evidence showing little damage in Essen and none to the Krupps works. Approximately forty homes were found to have been damaged in the suburbs and a few railway coaches to the west of the station were burnt out. However Oberhausen had been severely damaged and it became clear that the brunt of the raid had fallen on Mülheim and Duisburg.

The final raid in 'Operation Millenium' was launched on June 25th against the city of Bremen, in particular its docks, Deschimag submarine yards, and Focke-Wulfe aircraft factory. The weather forecast at 2100 hrs predicted a relatively clear night, but very few of the illuminators could see the ground when they got there and 117 aircraft in the advanced force had to bomb blindly on Gee. The main force aimed at the resulting glow while the rear wave relied on Gee bombing. Only two night photographs showed any ground detail through the clouds and these could not be plotted.

PR by Fg Off McMaster the next day showed that the attack had not been a complete failure. The damage had been limited but "useful", a large block of the Focke-Wulfe factory having been burnt out and a considerable part of the city destroyed. The docks on the other hand appeared to have escaped injury.

The Essen and Bremen operations dispelled some of the euphoria generated by the results at Billancourt, Lübeck, Rostock, and Cologne. On these four initial raids the usefulness of Gee and Shaker had been exaggerated because the skies had been clear and the crews could identify and bomb their targets visually. The moon on each occasion had been over 90% full and great damage had been caused at Lübeck and Rostock because the towns had, in Harris' words, been "built like a fire-lighter rather than a human habitation", and not because of any exceptional navigational ability on the part of the crews involved. Neither were Billancourt, Lübeck, or Rostock heavily defended, and, despite the hope that a thousand bomber raid would swamp the defences, one bomber was brought down every seven minutes over Cologne.

Once the weather clamped down and Bomber Command took on industrial haze and concentrated AA fire, the proportion of bombs dropped outside the target area increased considerably. At Essen, 109 out of the 131 night prints plotted were exposed between 5 and 100 miles away from the aiming point. The excellent photographs taken after the 'Thousand Bomber' raids did show that Bomber Command had destroyed an estimated 3,000 houses and rendered 50,000 people homeless, but Gee and sheer weight of numbers were still not enough – more accurate navigation and bomb-aiming aids were necessary if Bomber Command was to become a rapier instead of a cudgel.

One consequence of the smoke clouds billowing up from Rostock and Cologne was that PR pilots could no longer watch the conflagration below and remain detached from it. The dividing line between the men who fought and killed, and those who watched the killing, had become irrevocably blurred. As Bomber Command increased its destructive capability by learning lessons from the aerial camera, so the PRU pilot who took the prints on which a raid was planned, or from which the damage was assessed to see if another attack was necessary, became just as much a contributor to that destruction and desolation as the man who dropped the bombs.

Despite this shift of emphasis towards Bomber Command, the First Sea Lord insisted that responsibility for all reconnaissance north of latitude 54°N should remain with the Admiralty. The *Scharnhorst* and *Gneisenau* would pose no threat for some time; a sortie by Fg Off Bayley on March 2nd showed that both were undergoing repairs after the Channel Dash, the *Gneisenau* being in dry-dock in Kiel and the *Scharnhorst* alongside her in the centre dockyard basin. In fact the German ports provided little of naval interest during 1942, Admiralty and PRU interest being centred further north in Norway. The *Tirpitz* had left the Baltic in January for Trondheim because Hitler feared an Allied invasion of Norway, and she was joined in the Aas Fiord by the *Hipper* two months later. Churchill and the Admiralty did not realise that they were there to act as floating shore-batteries, and, fearing a

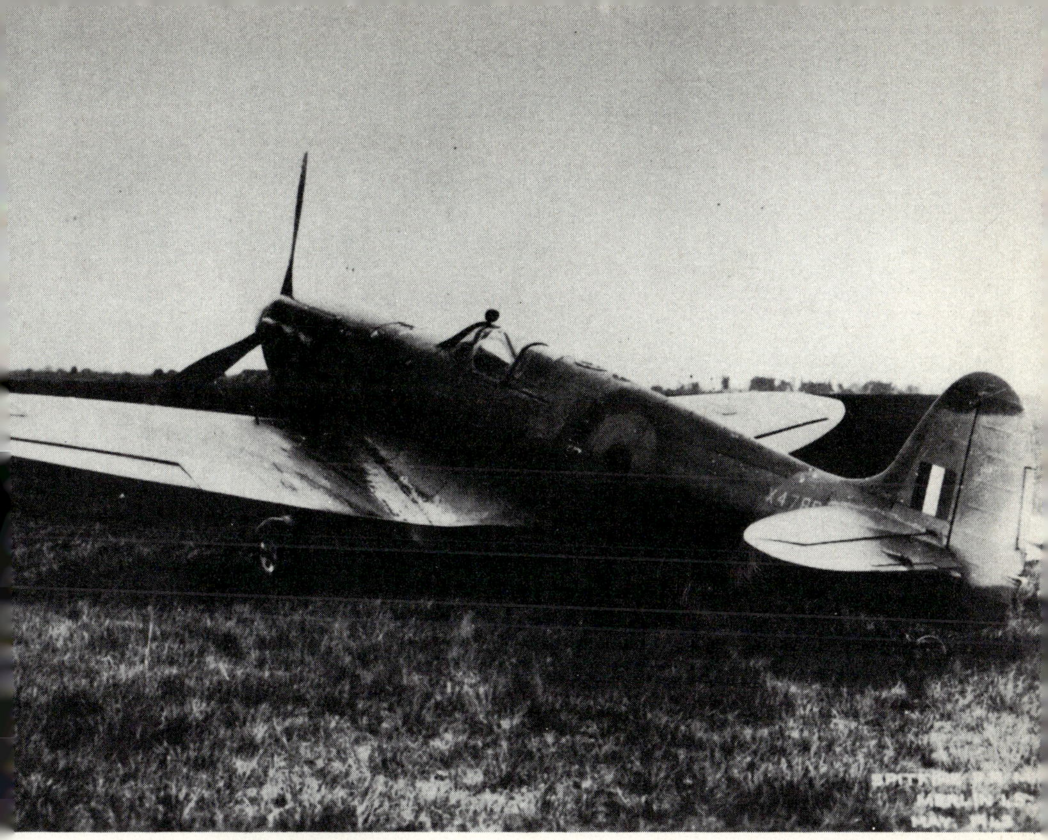

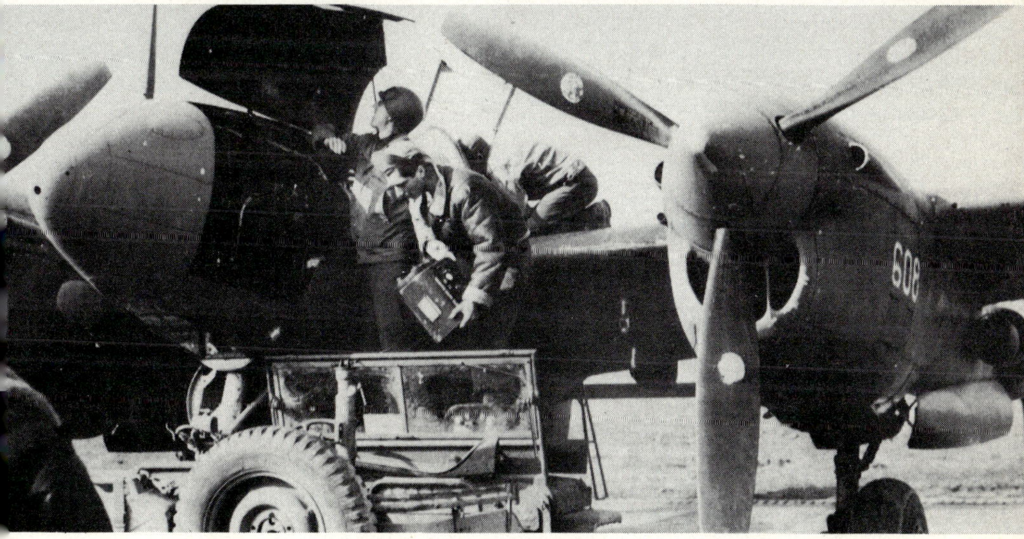

Top: One of the armed breed of PR Spitfires used on low-level missions over the Low Countries and France – the Spitfire PR VII. This was basically a Mk V fighter with 8 × .303in Browning guns and a bullet-proof windscreen in addition to one vertical F 24 5in and one vertical and one oblique F 24 14in cameras. *Vickers Ltd. Above:* Part of the American contribution to the photographic watch over the Axis – Cpl R. C. Aldridge and Sgt F. A. Shortino remove exposed film capsules from a Lightning F5 of the 9th AAF after a mission on October 29th 1944. *IWM*

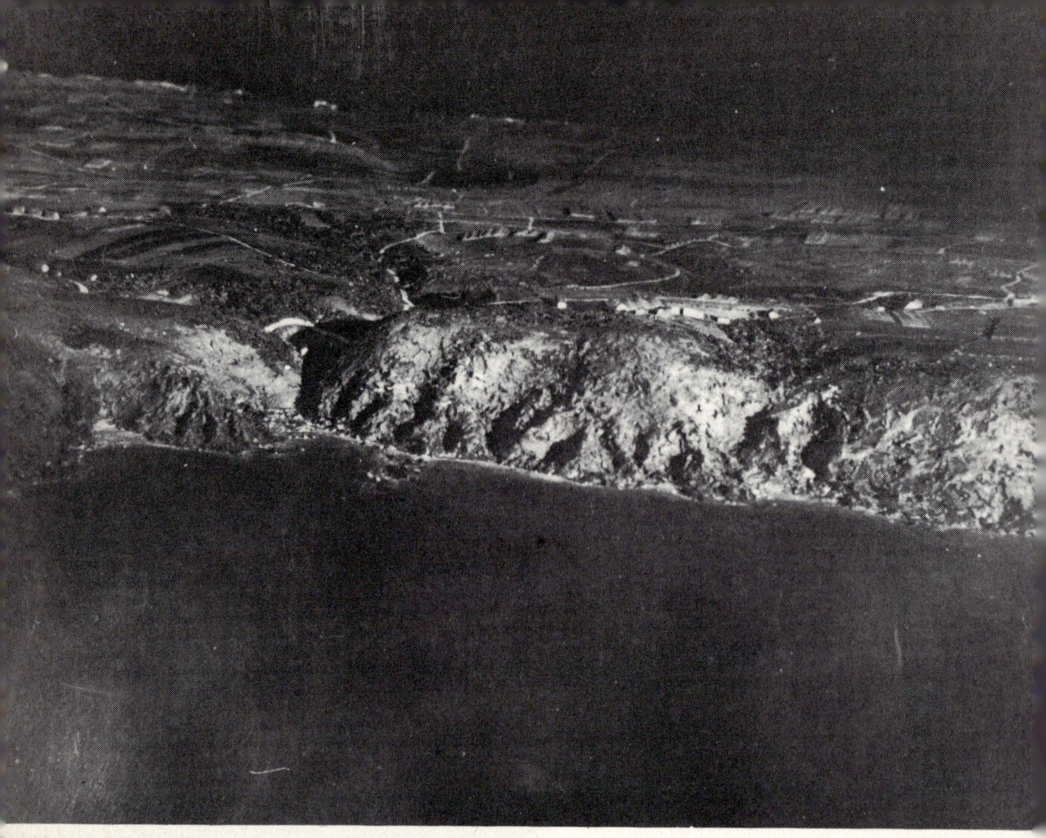

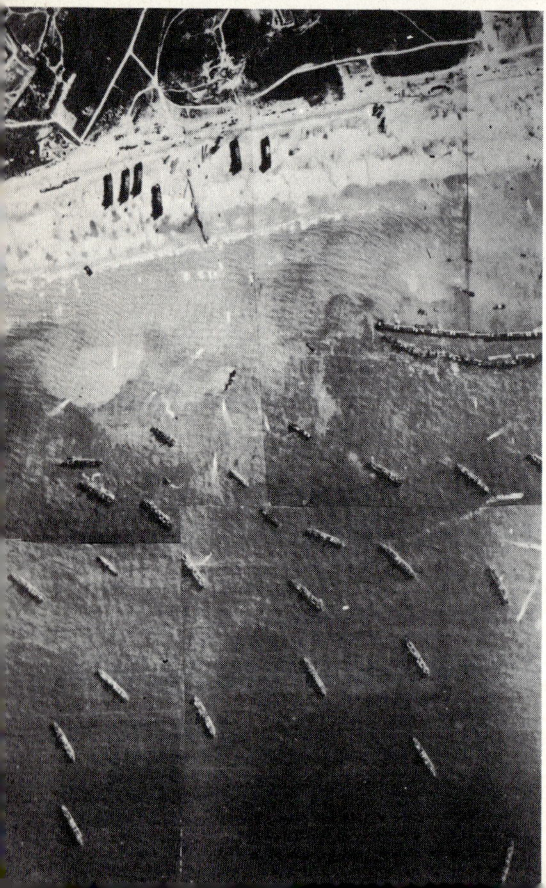

Above: Photograph of a model made from aerial photographs in preparation for a moonlight parachute drop. *Left:* Photographic mosaic made up of prints taken over a stretch of D-Day beach. An artificial harbour has been formed by shipping at the top right of the picture – notice the calm water behind it compared with that outside the 'breakwater'. *IWM*. *Top right:* Gordon e Hughes making a post-flight report to Intelligence Officer Edward Hornby. *Hughes*. *Bottom right:* Sqn Ldr John Merifield (left) with Wg Cdr the Lord Malcolm Douglas-Hamilton.

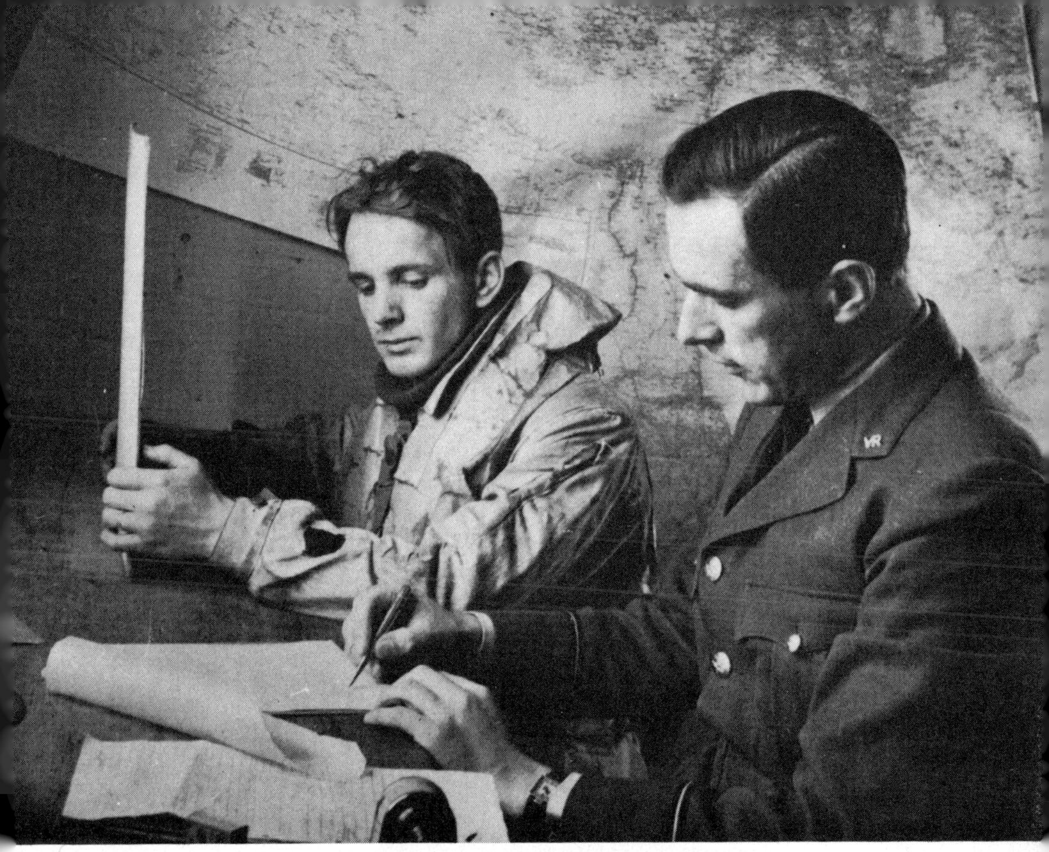
VR

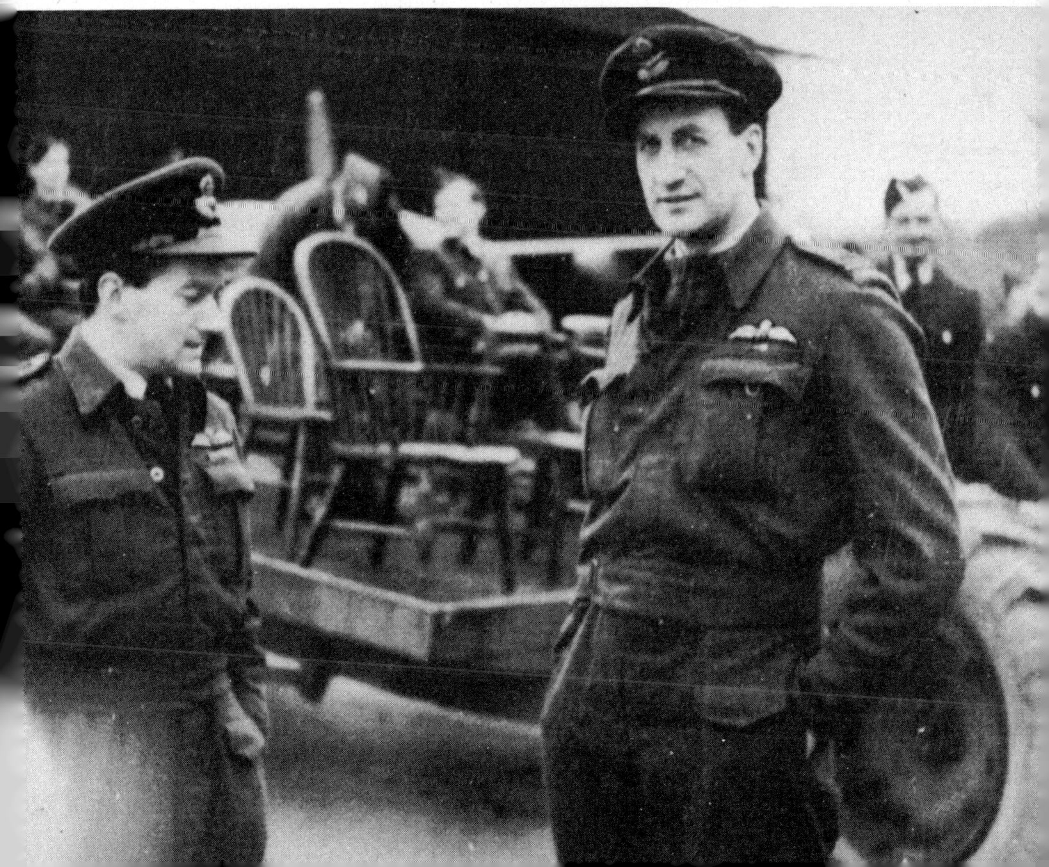

Below: The northern tip of Peenemünde peninsula showing the elliptical Test Stand VII. Two flying-bomb launching ramps are visible on the reclaimed foreshore at top right. *CC* *Bottom:* A low-level oblique of the Normandy landing beaches on D-day plus 6, photographed by John Merifield. *Craig.* *Right:* The Test Stand after a bomber raid in September 1944. *CC*

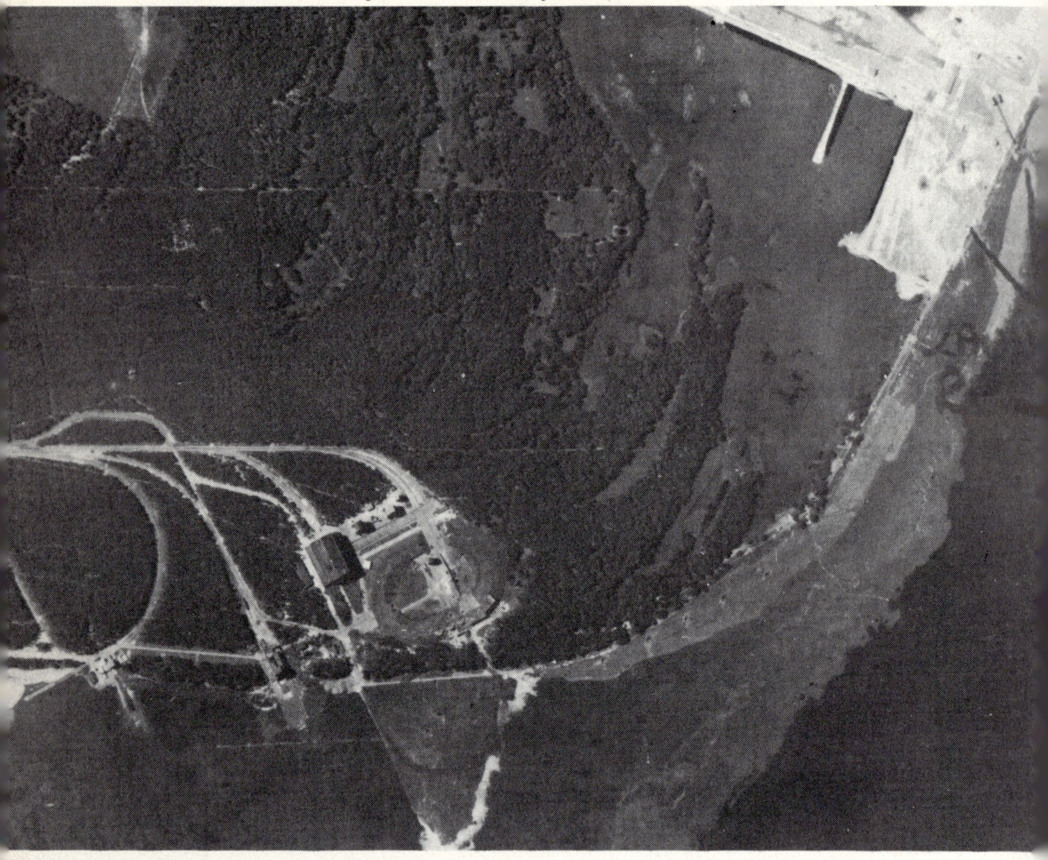

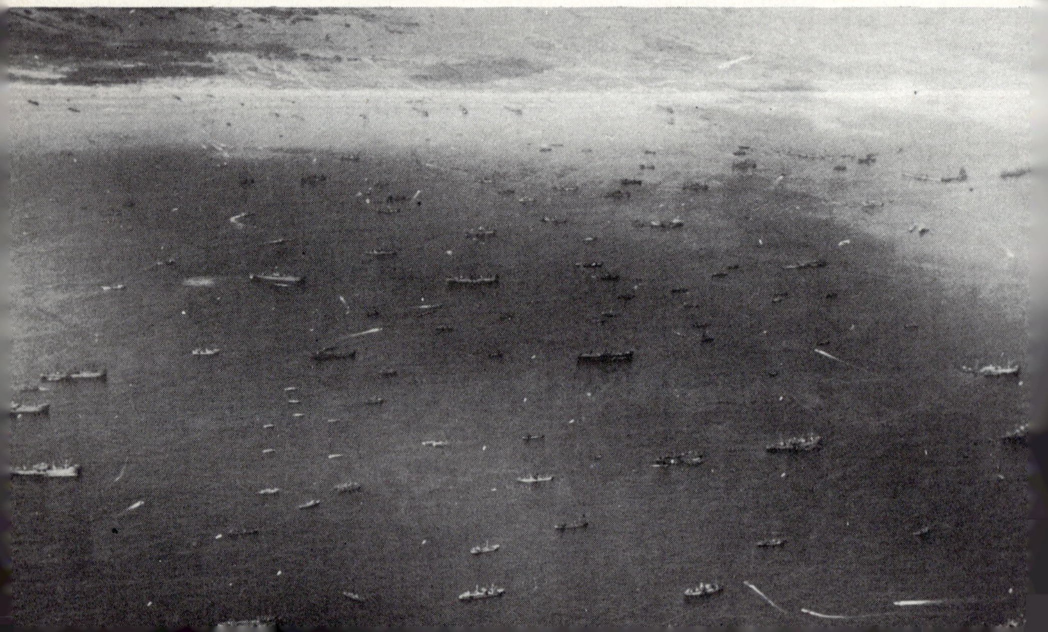

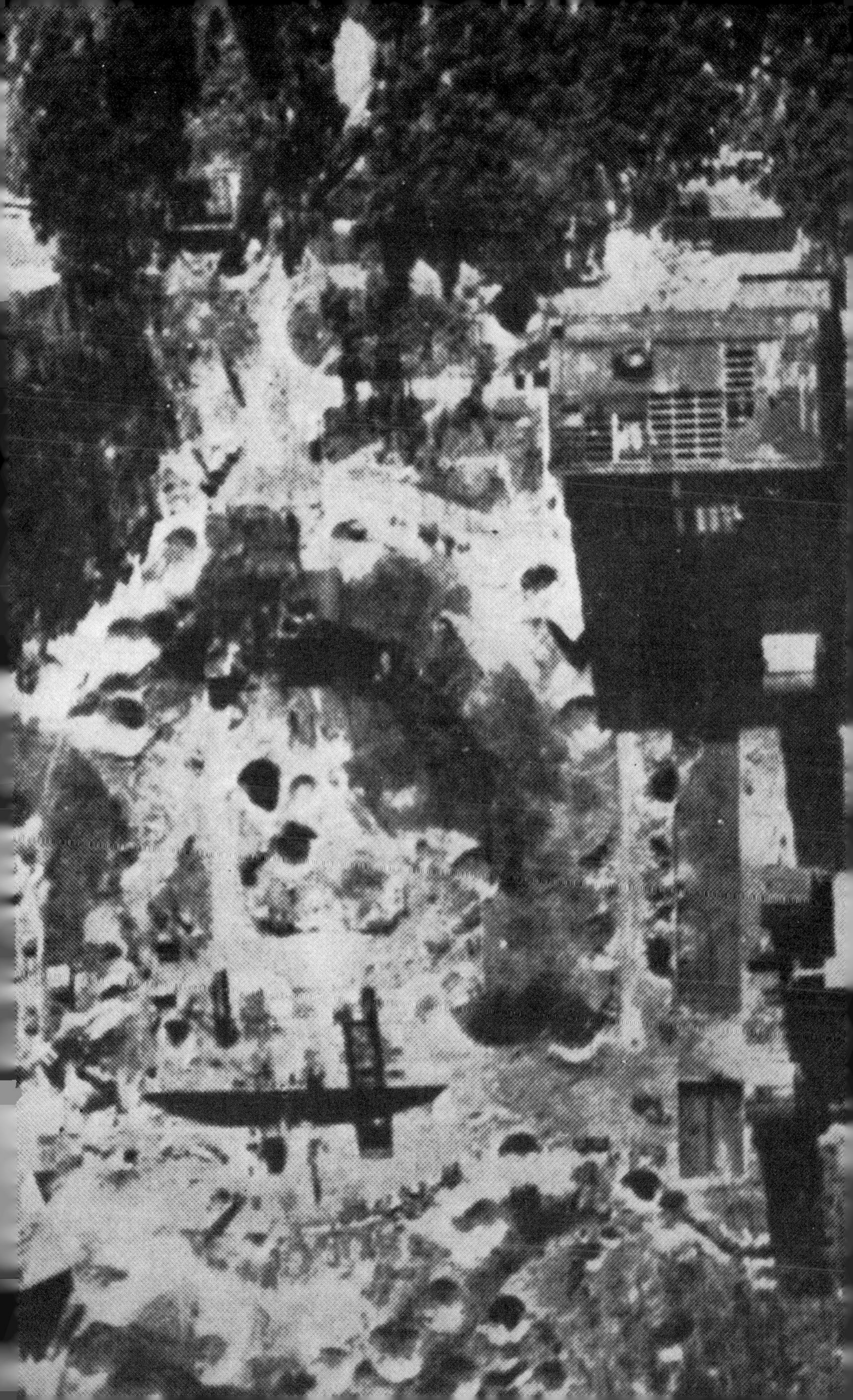

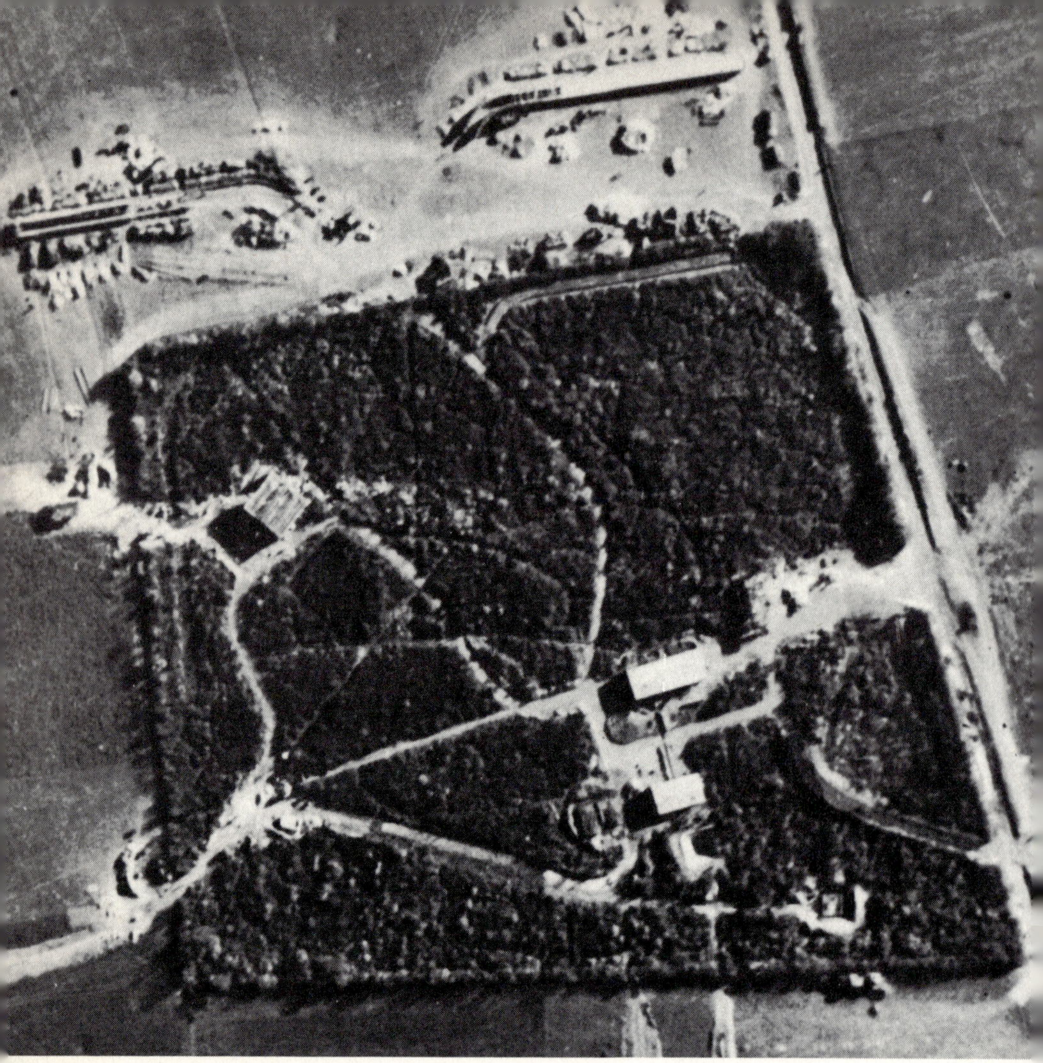

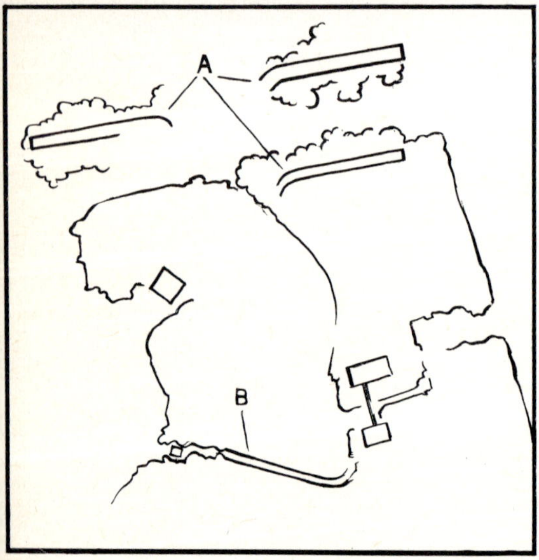

Above: Bois Carré flying-bomb site. Three ski-shaped buildings are at A while a launching ramp is under construction at B. *CC. Top right:* John Merifield's print of the tip of Peenemünde airfield, taken on November 28th, 1943, from which Constance Babington-Smith first discovered a V-1 (arrowed) on a firing ramp. *IWM. Bottom right:* The driving force behind RAF camera development in the Second World War – Gp Capt Victor 'Daddy' Laws.

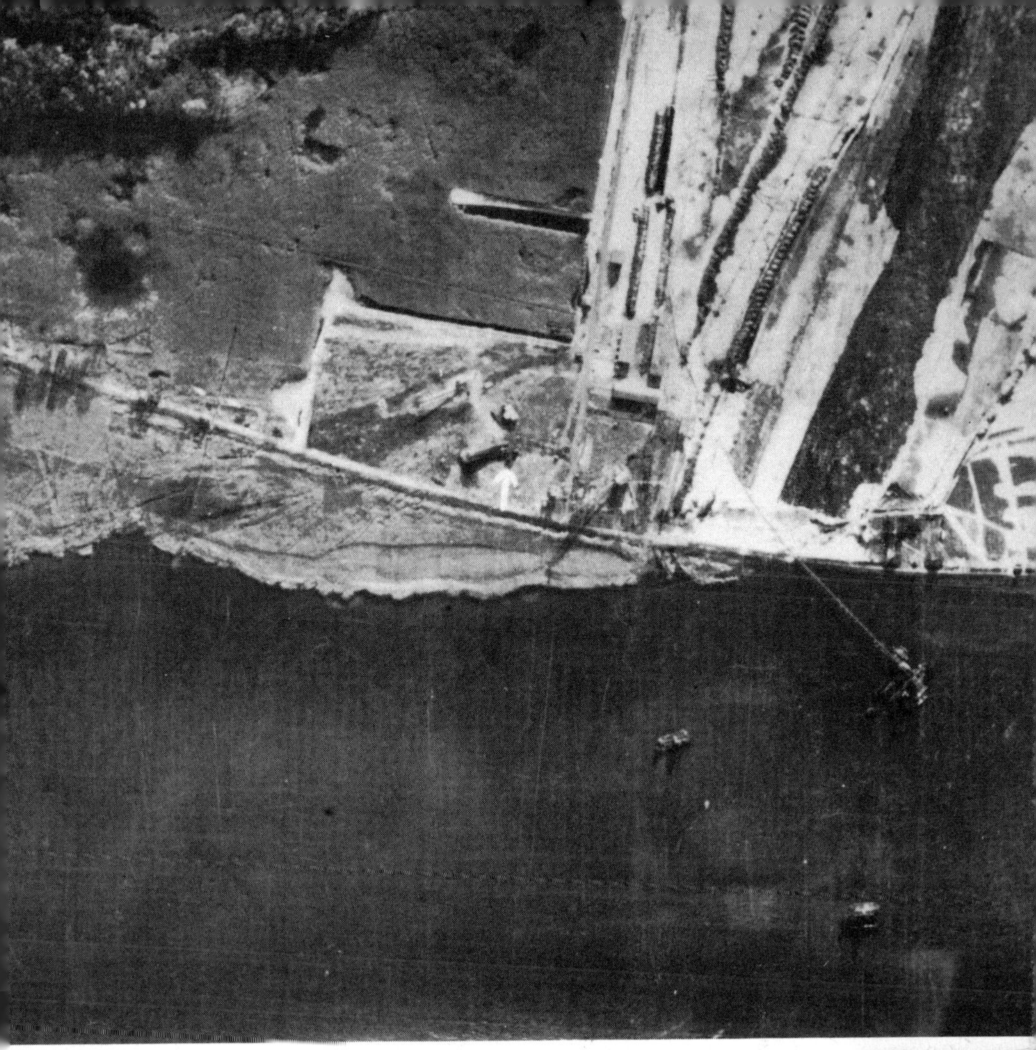

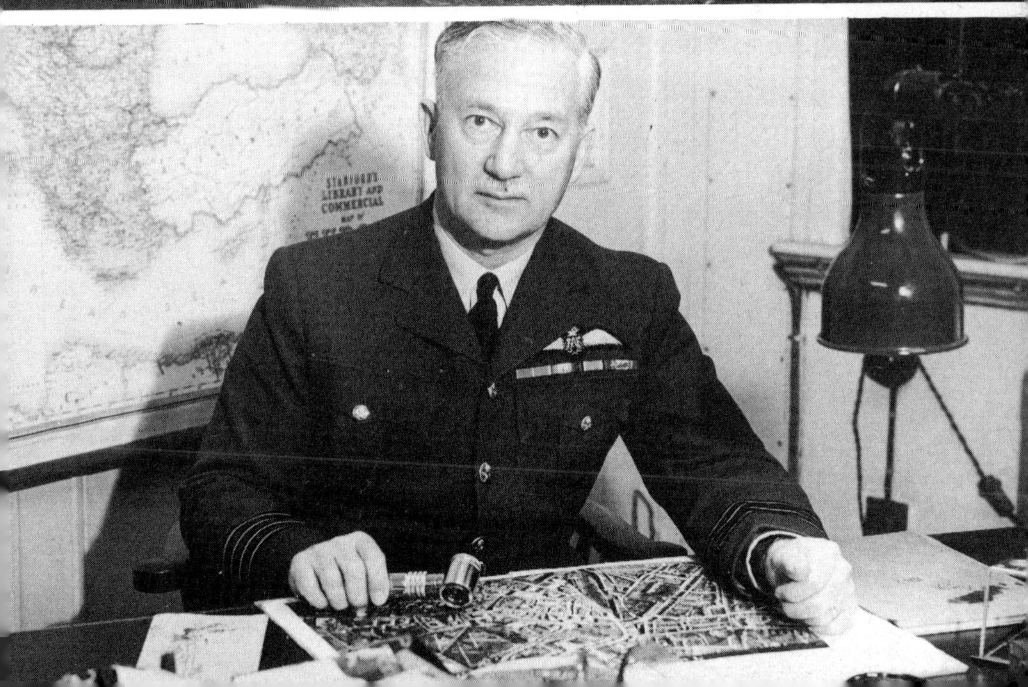
STANFORD'S
LIBRARY AND
COMMERCIAL

Some low level camera fits. *Below:* Shows a pair of F 24 8in cameras fitted into the 90 gallon slipper-type drop-tank of a Spitfire. *Bottom left:* Shows a single F 52 14in camera in the nose of a Mosquito. With this forward-facing camera, a Mosquito crew could fly straight towards the target to be photographed. *Bottom right:* A typical print exposed in this fashion shows the Wizernes V-2 bunker after a visit by Bomber Command with Tallboy bombs. *CC*

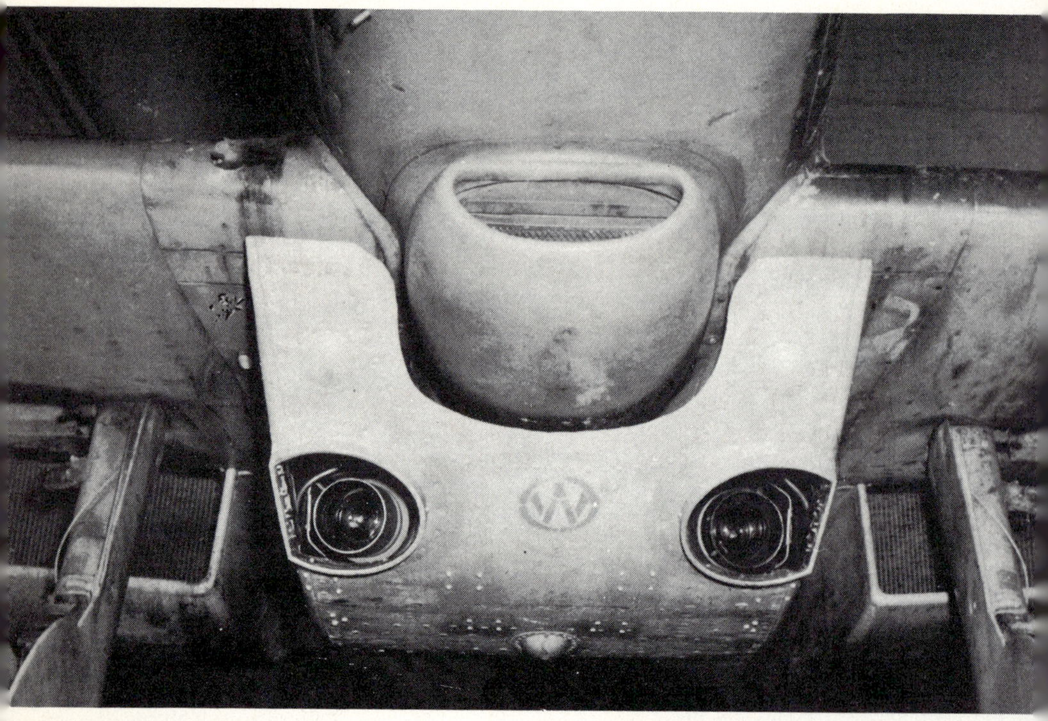

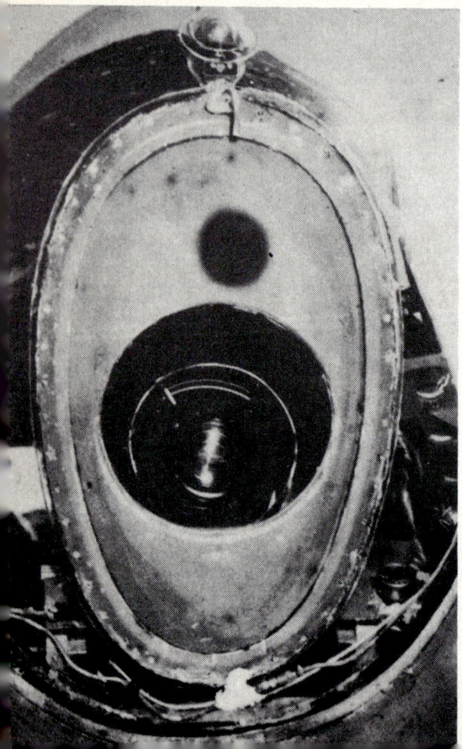

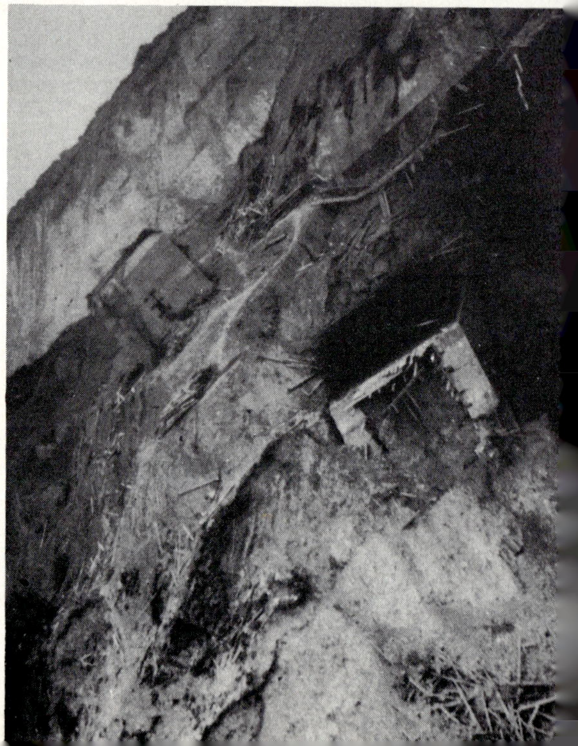

foray against Allied shipping, the Prime Minister wrote to the CAS on May 1st asking, "Will a PRU be sent over *Tirpitz* today? This might reveal tugs in position round her. It is most important to get information." Top level concern such as this accounted for the fact that 74 PRU sorties were flown from Leuchars and Wick between January 19th and May 23rd, 1942 to photograph the *Tirpitz*, for the loss of three Spitfires and one Mosquito. The *Scheer* and *Lutzow* were discovered in Narvik during May, apparently in preparation for a German naval assault on the Allied convoys to Russia.

Grand Admiral Raeder had indeed planned to justify his fleet's existence in Norway by an ambitious plan called *Rösselsprung* (Knight's Move). This involved a coordinated strike by all available surface warships divided into two Groups; as soon as a convoy had been sighted by the Luftwaffe, the Narvik Group would sail at once for the Alten Fiord near the North Cape, while the Trondheim Group would move up to Narvik. Both Groups would then rendevous 100 miles north of the North Cape and fall on the convoy well to the east of Bear Island.

Range was crucial to the PRU if they were to give warning of such an operation. Over the years, as more and more fuel was crammed into PR Spitfires, so Raeder responded by moving his major units further and further away from the British Isles. Trondheim was the furthest limit for a Spitfire PR IV, so anything beyond that had to be given to the Mosquitoes. However only ten Mosquito PR Is were built, including the prototype, and periodic losses left Wg Cdr Ring short of long-range reconnaissance resources. Two Mk II fighters were drafted in as a temporary measure, to be converted into 'PR Mk IIs', and in April the first two Mosquito PR IVs arrived with their 50 gallon drop tanks and a safe range of 2,350 miles, or Narvik and back. Fg Off Higson made the first PRU trip to Narvik on May 15th.

However, when Raeder set *Rösselsprung* into motion on July 2nd after the Luftwaffe reported sighting the ill-fated convoy PQ 17, even the Mosquito PR IV was found to have its limitations. On July 3rd, the Admiralty heard that the *Tirpitz* and the *Hipper* had left Trondheim, which was verified by PR three days later. The PRU revealed that the *Scheer* and the *Lutzow* had left the Vest Fiord anchorage near Narvik on July 4th, and although it was "tolerably certain" that they had made for the Alten Fiord, no-one knew where the Trondheim Group had gone. If they too had gone further north than Narvik, even the Mosquito PR IV could not find them and return safely, so it was arranged that the PRU could refuel in the Soviet Union before setting out on the homeward leg. On July 8th, Fg Off Bayley and Flt Sgt Little took off from Leuchars at 0706 hrs on the first of many such lengthy sorties. By then the PQ 17 had been shattered and the *Tirpitz*, *Hipper*, and *Scheer*, which had sallied forth to track the convoy down, had been recalled.[1] Bayley and Little found them steaming back towards Narvik, after which they refuelled at Vaenga airfield, 17 miles from Murmansk, and then returned directly to Leuchars, landing finally at 2250 hrs.

[1] The *Lutzow* had run aground leaving harbour.

The trauma of the PQ 17 taught one vitally important lesson at least – the decision to scatter the convoy was made because British air reconnaissance could not pinpoint the position of the German warships at a vital moment in time. Britain was too far removed from the scene of conflict to coordinate and maintain a timely watch and response to such a German threat. A mixed air detachment of Catalinas, Hampden torpedo bombers, and PR Spitfires was therefore dispatched to Russia in an attempt to give adequate protection to the next Russian convoy to sail.

On 1st September, three PR Spitfires under the command of Flt Lt E. A. Fairhurst flew from Sumburgh to Vaenga to join the ground party, which had left the Clyde a fortnight earlier. Situated 170 miles inside the Arctic Circle, Vaenga airfield was a new experience for the men of the PRU. The airfield had been constructed in a silver birch plantation, each aircraft being hidden in a wooden clearing from which it would emerge to take off on a central treeless strip that acted as a runway. Each 'hide' or building was separated from its neighbour by up to half a mile so that no one bomb could do much collective damage. The main officers' mess was a large, gaunt, two-storey, red-brick affair, half barrack-block, half country house, that was affectionately known as the 'Kremlin'. At times the whole airfield basked in a picturesque glow as the sun shone through the silver birch trees; on other occasions, when the autumn rains turned the tracks into quagmires and heavy trucks sank up to their axles, many people wished they were back in Oxfordshire.

Churchill had written to Stalin at the beginning of September to say that he hoped the PRU presence would deter the Germans from sending a naval force against convoy PQ 18 as they would be denied the vital element of surprise. The Germans agreed, and as soon as the Luftwaffe patrols sighted PQ 18, they bombed Vaenga on September 9th. When the dust had settled, one Spitfire was found to be riddled with holes and temporarily of no further use.

One of the two surviving PR aircraft took off on the detachment's first operational mission two days later and photographed the *Scheer*, the *Hipper*, the cruiser *Koln*, and four destroyers in the Alten Fiord. The Admiralty assumed that the *Tirpitz* would move north from Narvik to join them, especially when a PRU Mosquito reported on September 14th that the battleship had left her Vest Fiord berth, but repeated cover of the northern fiords by the Vaenga Spitfires, sometimes from as low as 4,000 feet because of the cloud, failed to locate her. On September 19th, Sgt Hardman brought another PR Spitfire over from Scotland and the hunt for the *Tirpitz* was intensified, but another nine days work over the North Cape brought no success.

The Admiralty need not have worried, for Hitler had refused to allow his capital ships to sail against the PQ 18 in case they were needed to repel the invasion of Norway that the Führer believed was coming. The *Tirpitz* had merely sailed for four days of sea exercises in the Vest Fiord and she returned to Narvik on September 18th. Having no knowledge of this, Leuchars and Vaenga scoured the sea-lanes to see whether the battleship was lying in wait for the return convoy from Murmansk, QP 14. Scottish-based Mosquitos searched southern Norway, but when Sqn Ldr M. J. B. Young DFC[1] refuelled at Vaenga after a lengthy sortie from Leuchars he had nothing to report. Then, five days later, Flt Lt John Merifield finally discovered the *Tirpitz* back in her usual berth. He photographed her steaming down the Ofot Fiord towards Narvik on September 28th, unescorted and apparently with no intention of putting to sea.

The detachment stayed at Vaenga until the third week in October, photographing the coast of Norway to the east of 24°E, while the Mosquitos covered the littoral to the west of 24°E, in preparation for Operation Jupiter. After a detachment involving nineteen sorties and one death – Plt Off Walker failed to return on September 27th. Aircraft and equipment were handed over to the Russians, and the party sailed for home on October 23rd, the same day that the *Tirpitz* moved down to Trondheim and back into range of aircraft from the UK.

PR Mosquitos also extended the PRU watch over continental Europe. On March 3rd, 1942, John Merifield had coaxed a PR I as far east as Königsberg on the Baltic,[2] and the advent of the Mosquito PR IV brought the whole of industrial Germany and the Sudetenland within range of Benson. More and more factories came under the stereoscope at Medmenham, varying from the famous Skoda armaments works at Pilsen to others of equal importance to the German war effort but whose existence hitherto had not been appreciated.

In March 1942 the aerial cameras turned over the hydrogenation plant at Rodleben and the synthetic oil refineries of Bohlen/Rotha for the first time. In July it was the turn of the chemical plants of I. G. Farben, Ludwigshafen, and the Leuna Ammonia and Fertiliser Works to come under scrutiny, and on August 19th, Plt Off Barraclough covered the ball-bearing centre of Schweinfurt for the first time in two years. On October 6th, Plt Off McKay brought back pictures of the major refineries of Upper Silesia, including two at Blechhammer and one at Deschowitz, the existence of which came as a complete surprise to all concerned.

Sqn Ldr Hamshaw-Thomas was then in charge of Third Phase industry interpretation, and one thing that particularly interested him as he looked at the prints of Leuna was the large synthetic oil plant next to the chemical works. Oil refineries were regarded by many as a classic 'panacea' target for Bomber Command, for it was argued that if High Wycombe ignored everything else and concentrated on Hitler's oil refineries, the German war machine would be forced to grind to a halt. From 1941 onwards, Medmenham watched for

[1] When Mike Young was promoted to take over the Mosquito Flight, he took his Mosquito down to Berchtesgarten to deposit an empty champagne bottle, a relic from the party the night before, on to Hitler's mountain retreat. Empty bottles dropped from height make a great deal of noise.

[2] John Merifield was one of the most talented Mosquito pilots in the RAF. His gentle touch and deft use of the trim wheel enabled him to coax that little bit more air mileage out of the Mosquito than anyone else. In his log book, this small unassuming man was assessed as 'Exceptional' both as a pilot-navigator and as an aerial photographer.

drilling programmes to extend existing oil-fields and the construction of pipelines so that estimates could be made of Germany's total oil resources.

The Leuna plant was interesting because it was such a large synthetic oil refinery. Isolated from the great oil fields of the world, Germany had to rely on the hydrogenation of coal to supply much of her oil, and Hamshaw-Thomas set himself the task of producing an accurate system for estimating synthetic plant capacity from aerial photographs. He measured every installation at Leuna, had detailed plans of the installation drawn up, and passed these on to experts who then assessed the probable output.

At the beginning of 1942 German technical journals started advertising for oil engineers to work at a new refinery at Brüx in the Sudetenland. Conventional intelligence sources 'guesstimated' that the plant could produce some 240,000 tons of synthetic oil per year, but there was no indication of the exact position or size of the refinery.

When a PRU aircraft went over to fill in the missing details it was found not only that the plant was far from completed but also that its size would be much greater than imagined, covering a site of some 1½ square miles. Hamshaw-Thomas' analytical process estimated that the refinery would be initially capable of producing a mammoth 750,000 tons of oil per annum and that production was likely to start in six months.

Eleven months later the refinery was photographed again. Yet again there was a surprise in store, for the construction work over the previous year had only been a start and extensions were under way in 1943 to increase output to a colossal 1,250,000 tons per annum, a capability far in excess of any other synthetic refinery in existence. The PR watch was intensified from then on as successive stages in the plant were brought into operation, and by the beginning of 1944 the plant was producing approximately 700,000 tons.

Because of their close consultation with experts, the PIs of the Industry Section became experts themselves and they were therefore able to detect one highly vulnerable area at Brüx. The only power supply available to the whole plant was a group of gas generators concentrated in an area 200 feet square. Bomber Command struck at this pin-point target on May 12th, 1944, and subsequent damage assessment showed that enough damage had been caused to put the refinery out of action for two months. Benson monitored repair work from then on and full production was never achieved for more than a few weeks before the bombers were called in again. Later attacks increased in size and were directed against the high pressure equipment that was harder to replace. By 1945, Brüx was being put out of action for periods of three months or more.

Target information like this was sifted and fed into dossiers in 1942, either for use at the time or in case it might herald e start of some development that would reach fruition in the future. One instance of the latter occurred after a sortie on May 15th, 1942. Flt Lt Steventon had been sent to photograph Swinemünde and he left his cameras on as he crossed a Pomeranian island in the Baltic 70 miles from Stettin. At the north end of the island on a peninsula was an airfiield, so the prints were passed to the Aircraft Section where a PI noticed that construction work was taking place on the aerodrome. The information was filed away for future reference – one never knew, it might be of importance at a later date. The name of the island was Usedom; the airfield, Peenemünde.

The first United States Army Air Force (USAAF) Recce Group arrived at Mount Farm, Benson's satellite airfield, in 1942 to work alongside the PRU. It was generally thought that the Americans were the first to use the aerial camera in war eighty years earlier when General McLellan was supposed to have sent a photographer up in a balloon to help raise the Confederate siege at Richmond, Virginia; however neither McLellan nor the photographer mention the incident in their papers and further research tends to imply that balloons were only used for visual reconnaissance in the American Civil War. The US Signal Corps' Air Service did gain valuable experience in aerial photography when General John J. Pershing used Curtiss Jennys with cameras attached during his punitive expedition to Mexico in 1916, but it was due to the dedication of a man named James Bagley that the Air Service was able to enter the First World War with a camera equal to that possessed by their allies.

The years after 1918 were as lean for American military aviation as they were for the RAF, but on top of that no one in the emaciated Air Service "gave a tin nickel for the advancement of aerial photography"[1]. No one, that is, apart from Brigadier General 'Billy' Mitchell. Mitchell had been impressed with the potentialities of aerial photography ever since he had conducted experiments with cameras attached to kites in 1904, but with funds in short supply for his beloved Air Service he realised that he would have to 'sell' the aerial camera to the nation. Nine Corps' photo sections were established throughout the U. S., and over the inter-war years a variety of aircraft[2] carried out photography over the vast continent of the United States on behalf of State and local authorities. Anything was undertaken if it would attract favourable comment in the Press or Congress, be it a mosaic map of Washington for the Shriners' national convention or a general survey of the Tennessee River Basin for the TVA power and water conservation programme.

Twenty years of mapping meant that the USAAF entered the Second World War with some very efficient survey and tactical cameras but with very little appreciation of the potential of, or the problems associated with, aerial photo-intelligence gathering. Apart from one clandestine sortie by a DH-4 over Mexico just after the First World War to check on reported border violations, the USAAF had no experience of evading defences to gain information

[1] 'Overview' by George Goddard, then a young man but soon to become one of the leading experts in the application of aerial cameras in the United States.

[2] The first American aircraft designed to carry cameras was the Fairchild C-8. This high wing monoplane appeared around 1930 with cockpit visibility like a greenhouse and camera openings in the floor and fuselage. Sherman Fairchild was also the main contractor for aerial cameras to the Air Service in the inter-war years.

and therefore saw no need to build specialised reconnaissance aircraft. In fact a meeting chaired by General Henry H. Arnold in 1939 turned down a request from George Goddard for the development of a special high speed, high flying PR aircraft designed to fly long distances, (even the far-sighted Goddard was not willing to dispense with defensive armament). Spared the critical defensive position of the British after 1939, the Americans made no effort to develop a photo-intelligence gathering force as distinct from an aerial mapping agency in support of their army, with the result that at the beginning of 1942 they found themselves, in the words of an instructor at the newly formed Army Air Forces Intelligence School at Harrisburg, Pennsylvania, "completely dependent for intelligence on the RAF Air Ministry and the editors of 'Time', 'Life' and 'Fortune'!!"

Converted B-17s were nominated as the standard USAAF camera-carrying aircraft early in 1942, but when a pair of these aeroplanes was sent out to the US Eighth Air Force in the summer it soon became apparent that they stood no chance unescorted against Luftwaffe fighters. Work therefore began at Fort Worth, Texas, to convert the Lockheed P-38 Lightning into the main American PR aircraft of the war. First came the F-4 variant, with its heavy armour and four machine guns removed from the nose to make way for a forward-facing camera and a tri-metrogon fan of three cameras installed to take simultaneous pictures from horizon to horizon. By the end of the war, some 13 million sq miles of territory had been photographed using these metrogon mapping lenses.

After the F-4 came the more powerful F-5 with its bulbous nose accommodating up to five cameras, usually a tri-met fit and a long focal-length pair for high altitude work. Of all the USAAF pilots to fly this fine aircraft, Lieut Col Karl 'Pop' Polifka was probably the most outstanding. After leaving flying training this heavy-set, fearless man with Slavic features surmounted by blond hair passed through the photographic school at Lowry Field and soon won a reputation for flying and photographic aptitude second to none. After taking pictures from the assigned altitude of 28,000 or 29,000 feet he would hurtle down to low level to dice the main ground features so that nothing would be missed because of camouflage.

It is interesting to compare the attitude of the best USAAF pilots with that of their British counterparts. Another highly decorated American recce pilot, Leon Gray, who flew 146 missions over Europe, only came to love PR when, in the words of Elliott Roosevelt[1] "he found that it really wasn't very sissified and discovered that we had a higher rate loss than any other outfit in World War II". It was a great accolade for the war memoirs but it meant that a lot of pilots went dicing when they should have been taking their photographs back to base; USAAF losses only started to decrease when their pilots learnt that there was more to PR than enthusiasm and bravado.

In August 1942 the Americans launched their first daylight bomber raids over

[1] Son of the President and CO of the 3rd US Recce Group.

Europe with the PRU following to record the action. Bomber Command too was not averse to making the odd daylight foray against a precision target. On April 17th, 1942, twelve Lancasters of 5 Group had made a daring raid on the engine assembly shop at the MAN Diesel Works at Augsburg. Seven days later, Victor Ricketts flew over Bavaria to photograph the damaged building. On October 17th, 94 Lancasters set out on an even more ambitious foray against the great Schneider Armaments factory at Le Creusot. The following day Tony Hill, now a Squadron Leader, diced the works to assess the damage, but in spite of a round trip of 1,719 miles he brought back no pictures because an exposed film had been put into the camera by mistake. Gordon Hughes went over on October 19th but he diced the undamaged side of the factory. So Tony Hill went in again. He was mad to do it – the factory had been diced on two successive days already and Gordon Hughes had only escaped from the attentions of the waiting flak because he had flown along the side where they were not expecting him. But, as at Bruneval, there was no stopping Tony Hill. Off he went and sure enough he was shot out of the sky. He broke his back in the crash and had to be dragged from the burning wreckage by the French Resistance. A special aircraft was laid on to fly him home, but as he was being carried out to it he died. Tony Hill had tried once too often to prove to himself that he had enough press-on spirit even though he had proved it to others long ago. One of nature's gentlemen was dead.

The PRU was working well for Bomber Command by the autumn of 1942. After a spectacular raid on the Gestapo HQ at Oslo on September 25th, Flt Lts Sinclair and Van Damm brought back some marvellously clear prints on September 26th and 28th respectively to show the extent of the damage. However High Wycombe was still not satisfied. There were many people there who thought that as a PR Spitfire could outpace the Luftwaffe, the PRU should be able to bring back prints as and when required. The influence of such obstacles as poor weather was greatly under-estimated. In the first six months of 1942 for instance, 1 PRU could only complete 45 damage assessment missions compared with 62 that were either fruitless or abandoned. The weather was so bad at times that a wag at Leuchars was moved to write, "Never have so many gone so far for so little." But from the lofty standpoint of High Wycombe, where everyone believed that the work of Bomber Command should take priority over everything else, such practicalities were ignored. The PRU had photographed the results of the Oslo raid within three days; why could they not do this on every occasion? The answer had to be that 1 PRU was not according enough priority to the needs of Bomber Command and therefore, in October, Sir Arthur Harris wrote to VCAS,[1] Air Vice Marshal C. E. H. Medhurst, to say that in his opinion he would not obtain the results necessary to enable him to direct his bombing policy adequately until changes were made. The C-in-C concluded by reminding VCAS of the agreement made in July 1941 that the question of control of 1 PRU might be reviewed if Bomber Command was not satisfied with results obtained over a

[1] Vice Chief of Air Staff.

prolonged period. There was no mention of the frozen limbs, the hours of strain and solitude, not to mention lives, expended in the service of Bomber Command up to then.

Although the Air Staff was not willing to take the retrograde step of splitting up the PRU again, they had been considering changes for some time. By the summer of 1942, 1 PRU had grown into an empire of eight Flights divided between Benson, Mount Farm, Wick, Leuchars, St Eval, and Gibraltar,[1] not to mention a Maintenance Unit at Benson to modify all aircraft to PR standards and a training unit to convert the crews. By May, 1 PRU was flying an average of ten sorties a day, compared with four the previous year, and Spencer Ring had 73[2] aircraft under his command, or the equivalent of four fighter squadrons.

On October 19th, 1 PRU was divided into five operational squadrons. The two Mosquito Flights were combined to form 540 Sqn; the six Spitfire Flights became 541, 542, and 543 Sqns; and the hotch-potch remaining, containing the Gibraltar Flight and the Night Photography Flight, was christened 544 Sqn. Sir Arthur Harris' request for his own PRU was unacceptable as it cut across the Air Staff's policy of centralised control, and after further discussion the matter was declared sub judice. However, one Flight on each of 541, 542, and 543 Sqns was earmarked primarily for bomb damage assessment photography over a specific geographical area of responsibility, in the hope that this would go some way towards placating High Wycombe.

To the men of 1 PRU the changes meant little. Squadron loyalty never replaced loyalty to 'the PRU', that indivisible organisation so lovingly built up by Cotton, Tuttle, and Ring, and the new squadrons tended to be regarded, as the flights before them, as purely administrative divisions of the corporate whole. Officially 1 PRU disbanded on October 18th, 1942, but the new squadrons and their personnel still considered themselves part of 'the PRU' until the end of the war.

To cater for the expansion of PRUs in 1942, both at home and abroad, the whole aircrew training programme had to be reorganised. Up to the autumn of 1941, pilot training had altered little since the days when Cotton pointed a new man towards a PR Spitfire and told him to get on with it. This rather basic approach generally worked with experienced aircrew, for the average GR pilot only needed an average of ten hours to convert himself on to type and role, but as the number of inexperienced pilots reaching Benson increased, the 'teach yourself' formula was seen to have its limitations. Two training flights were therefore established, and in January 1942 one of these was moved to Detling where a revised programme of thirty hours flying and a number of lectures was introduced. In February 1942, PR pilots began to be posted in direct from the Advanced Flying Training Schools, and so a PR conversion course was introduced at No 3 School of GR at Squires Gate, fol-

[1]Now a permanent fixture on the Rock.

[2] 12 Mosquitos, 53 Spitfires, 2 Wellingtons, 4 Ansons, 1 Maryland, and a Tiger Moth.

lowed by a month at Detling before pupils moved to the advanced training unit at Benson.

As the overseas PRUs expanded – in March 1942, 2 PRU received four Spitfire PR IVs with a promise of Mosquitos to follow – it was decided to relieve Benson of the burden of training PR crews completely. On May 18th, 1942 a special PR Operational Training Unit – No 8 OTU – was inaugurated at Fraserburgh, taking over the work of the conversion flights at Squires Gate and Detling, to provide crews for all PR units in existence and those about to be formed.

It had been decided in London in July 1941 that the Middle East would have priority for the first PR Mosquitos off the Hatfield assembly line, and two Mosquito PR Is had been dispatched from Benson for Egypt on September 2nd, 1941 for tropical trials and to fill the urgent need for long-range reconnaissance PR aircraft. They never reached Heliopolis; Hugh Pughe-Lloyd was also desperately short of reconnaissance aircraft as his Maryland resources began to dwindle, and he commandeered the pair when they landed in Malta.[1] They were destroyed during a particularly heavy blitz on the island and no more Mosquitos were forthcoming for the Mediterranean until the end of 1942.

As an interim measure, Spitfire PR IVs were sent out to Malta and Egypt in March 1942. MacPhail continued to use his Hurricane IIs for a time but the PR Spitfires were far superior in range and ceiling. On July 10th, Fg Off Gubb in a Spitfire was bounced by two Me 109s on his way back to Derna; he gave them two long bursts with both cameras, veered away sharply, gave the Luftwaffe an errand boy's salute, and sped off at full power. By August, 2 PRU had eighteen PR Spitfires at its disposal and operational Hurricane missions virtually ceased.

Back home, 1 PRU virtually monopolised PR because it had pioneered high level photography at a time when strategic reconnaissance was of paramount importance to Britain. As there were no land battles being fought in the vicinity, a tactical PR squadron like 140 Sqn had a very secondary role to play. The situation was very different in the Middle East. For a start 2 PRU was a relative newcomer to the area and enjoyed no greater status as an intelligence provider than 1437 Flt which had replaced 39 Sqn at the AHQ Western Desert. Not only did 2 PRU share long range duties with the Marylands, and later Baltimores, of 1437 Flt, but strategic PR was not the be-all and end-all that it was in the UK. With Rommel threatening Egypt with uncomfortable regularity, 208 Sqn engaged on tactical work with cameras and the flight of 60 SAAF Survey Sqn carrying out mapping duties for the Eighth Army were just as crucial to the survival of British power in the Middle East.

Whenever the Eighth Army needed extra cover, and if 2 PRU was not fully committed to reconnaissance duties elsewhere, MacPhail would send a detachment from Heliopolis – the second XI – to supplement 1437 Flt. The main difference between the two units, apart from the fact that the latter did a

[1] One had been damaged on landing, injuring the observer.

lot more visual reconnaissance, was that MacPhail's Spitfires could bring back far larger and clearer pictures of pinpoints than was possible with the locally improvised F 24 camera fits on the Marylands. Between them they provided all long-range cover for the RAF and Eighth Army in the Western Desert, operating from one 'far flung hole' or another depending on whether it was the Allies' or Axis' turn to be on the defensive. In fact people often asked the CO of 1437 Flt, Sqn Ldr Sidney Ault, whether they were attacking or defending as his unit was the only one 'in the know'.

Desert conditions really showed that there was more to PR than the taking and interpretation of photographs. For the prints to be of any use the information gleaned from them had to be disseminated quickly to all concerned for, as in Fleet Street, there was nothing as worthless as yesterday's news. A desert PI, Bill Kerr, recounted his problems in trying to pass interpretation reports from a forward landing ground occupied by 2 PRU to the Wellingtons back in the Delta who needed the information to plan their nightly raids on Benghazi:

"Each evening I sent a signal to various units in the Delta, such as the Naval HQ Alexandria and the Wellingtons. But when the intelligence officer came up to see us he said that our signals did not reach him until long after the Wellingtons had taken off and so, even if they did find the harbour in the dark, they were bombing ships which may not have been there since he had briefed them on a signal referring to shipping present on the previous day. Of course the photographs we sent him took even longer to reach the poor fellow. I promised to try to speed things up but I never succeeded. I was entirely dependent on a number of factors absolutely outside my control. There is no way of hurrying up the processing of photographs although I did get wet prints, but I never got even them until five o'clock by which time the briefing (of the bomber crews) was already on. I used my privilege of sending 'Most Immediate' signals if I thought that the shipping was particularly important, but even that was no use. I tried the telephone but at that time there were no boosters on the line to Egypt and it proved quite impossible to get a single message down the wires. Poor communications added to the failure of Middle East HQ to keep us informed of intelligence matters, and my own unwillingness to make a nuisance of myself combined to make aerial reconnaissance less useful and bombing less effective than they might have been."

There was only a thin dividing line between the tactical cover provided by 208 Sqn, with its eight Hurricanes fitted with oblique cameras to provide close support photography for the Eighth Army, and the strategic work undertaken by the forward detachment of 2 PRU. When a PR Spitfire flew on a strategic mission to cover the Axis dispositions at Tobruk, it would also record any tactical movement along the coast road that might make suitable targets for the Beaufighter attack. This overlapping of duties tended to lead to duplication, and with the increasing number of air operations coinciding with the Battle of Egypt it was decided to coordinate the efforts of all PR units in the desert. Accordingly in July 1942 285 Reconnaissance Wing was formed to control all visual and photographic reconnaissance activities, including photo-interpretation, in the Western Desert.

The new Wing comprised the 2 PRU detachment, 60 SAAF Survey Flight, 1437 Strategic Reconnaissance Flight, and two Tac R squadrons, of which 208 Sqn had a photographic capability. The value of this coordinated approach was soon demonstrated at the Battle of Alamein. While 208 Sqn photographed the forward areas from 5,000 feet looking for movements, observing for the artillery, and locating targets for straffing, 60 SAAF Flight surveyed and mapped the territory behind enemy lines with their Baltimores. Up above, 1437 Flight watched the whole battlefield and its supply lines, assisted by 2 PRU over heavily defended targets or when large-scale pinpoints were required. All this photographic effort was transcribed onto a complete mosaic of the battle-area by the Cairo CIU detachment working alongside the Eighth Army. Just as strategic PR evolved at Heston, so battlefield PR came of age in the desert; it was at Alamein that most of the techniques to be employed so successfully in Europe in later years were first defined and demonstrated.

Hugh Pughe-Lloyd was down to his last couple of Marylands when the first two PR Spitfires arrived in Malta in March 1942. It was a time when the Luftwaffe was attempting to neutralise this troublesome island in the "heaviest and most sustained bombardment in the history of aerial warfare", and Pughe-Lloyd immediately tasked his two PR Spitfire pilots with monitoring the build-up of Kesselring's bomber forces in Sicily. Even though Luqa was being subjected to almost continual air attack, each Spitfire pilot still managed to average one sortie every two days for eight months to provide an accurate assessment of the numbers, types, and dispositions of Axis aircraft on Sicily. It was a remarkable achievement.

On April 21st, when the blitz of Malta was at its height, a new spectre arose to haunt Pughe-Lloyd. One of the prints exposed that day revealed a rectangular area, marked out by a plough and measuring some 1500 × 400 yards in size, close to the large bomber base at Gerbini. The site was levelled three days later and it seemed that another bomber satellite was under construction. But when two more flattened areas were discovered a pessimistic PI concluded that they could be glider strips for an airborne invasion of Malta. Past cover of the plain to the south-west of Catania was examined, and, sure enough, other embryo landing strips were found, all close to the main railway line from the Messina ferry along which glider components and troops might pass. Complete cover of other flat areas in southern Sicily was therefore ordered and every existing strip was watched on alternate days. By May 10th, many appeared complete with their erected huts and buried underground cables, but, despite a watch through the summer, no gliders ever appeared. The Germans staked all on Alamein, and once Rommel was in retreat the Axis were in no position to invade Malta.

The Luftwaffe made its last sustained effort against the island in October, when some 600 aircraft were photographed in Sicily, but the glider fields remained dormant throughout. They were only put to use as dispersal airfields for Gerbini and Catania when the Allies returned the compliment and started bombing Sicily.

Although more PR Spitfires reached the island during the summer of 1942, there were not enough trained pilots to form a separate PRU, so 69 Sqn was divided into two flights – A Flight with Baltimores for GR work, and B Flight with Spitfires to become Malta's specialised PR flight.

The Baltimores and the PR Spitfires were as much concerned with the protection of Allied shipping as they were with the severing of Rommel's supply lines, and every Allied attempt to run a convoy to Malta from Gibraltar or Alexandria was accompanied by a period of intense reconnaissance activity. The need for PR over every Axis naval and air base from Navarino to Cagliari had been emphasised by the fate of convoy MW 9 from Alexandria in February 1942. It had been shattered by Luftwaffe bombers from Crete, but, even if it had survived, the vessels would almost certainly have come to grief at the hands of the cruiser force in Messina. In June, a convoy had to return to Alexandria because the RAF failed to locate the Italian Fleet after it had sailed from Taranto. The Royal Navy had to know the dispositions of the enemy in future.

While the famous convoy of August 1942 was sailing through the western Mediterranean from Gibraltar, Taranto and Palermo alone were photographed nine times in four days. As a consequence of all this increased reconnaissance activity over Axis bases, a powerful force of three 8 in and three 6 in cruisers was spotted steaming westwards in the Tyhrrenian Sea to intercept the largest and most crucial of all Malta convoys. The cruiser force was almost within striking range when it was induced to turn back by a plain language signal from Malta indicating that an aerial attack on the warships was imminent. The signal was a bluff and it saved the day, but only because 69 Sqn had seen the threat while there was still time. An Italian Admiral was interviewed after the surrender in 1943 and asked why his navy had made such a poor showing in the Mediterranean. "No one can play chess blindfolded," he replied. "We never knew where the Allied Navy was. But the Allies knew the exact position of every unit of our fleet at all times." They had 69 Sqn to thank for that.

Despite the clamour around the Mediterranean for PR Spitfires, there was one man who never needed one. In December 1941, Adrian Warburton had been detached from Luqa to 2 PRU for a well deserved rest, with an added brief to test the Baltimore while in Egypt because it was shortly to replace the Maryland in Malta. During his stay at Heliopolis he 'borrowed' a Beaufighter, stripped it of all armament and armour plate, and fitted vertical cameras into the fuselage. Off he flew down the Cairo canals, photographing the barges from ground level and pulling up just before he hit them. Then he flew down the Cairo-Suez road to photograph a car coming towards him but he was thwarted because the petrified driver turned his vehicle into a ditch. After a quick foray into the desert to photograph an old arab on a camel he returned to Heliopolis.

Warby dismissed the Baltimore with a disdainful, "No bloody good. But this Beau," he continued, "is the fastest aircraft in the Mediterranean." He took his Beaufighter back to Luqa, where Pughe-Lloyd had been trying in vain to get some PR cover of Sicily to check on the Luftwaffe build-up there. The following day, Beaufighter and Warburton landed with all the ports and airfields of Sicily superimposed on film taken from the suicidal height of 6,000 feet or less. The next day he did the same for every airfield in Tripolitania. Sometimes he photographed targets in Sicily and North Africa on the same day, always coming back unscathed even when he had been shot up in error by Malta's Hurricanes. "You should speak to them," he told the CO of the fighter squadron involved. "Their shooting is terrible."

When 69 Sqn re-equipped with Baltimores, Warby stayed faithful to his personal Beaufighter, and to his photographers Haddon and Shirley. It was said that he refused to fly the Baltimore because he disliked flying with regular aircrew, and despite the lowly rank of his photographers Warburton ensured that they got DFMs. He only once flew a Baltimore and that was because he had to photograph a shipping strike off the Greek coast and needed an aeroplane with W/T. Warburton called a meeting to ask for volunteers to fly with him, but there was little response from the trained Baltimore crews to fly with a man whose experience on type was virtually nil. In the end he said, "All I want is a W/Op," so Flt Sgt Cliffe, a New Zealander, volunteered. After landing the Flt Sgt said that he had particularly admired Warby's cool instructions over the intercom – "Keep an eye on that 110 just coming up on the starboard side . . . don't worry about the 109 on the port side – I'm watching him – and the 110 coming up under our nose, he's no problem." Cliffe declared that from now on he would fly anywhere with Warburton in a Baltimore, or any other aircraft for that matter.

Warburton's exploits were legend and he became a household name in Malta because of his dash and panache. Crowds rushed to greet him as he walked through the streets of Valletta, or as he drove in his old car, sometimes in pyjamas and slippers. People would congregate round the airfield waiting for his familiar Beaufighter to land, and one day on his way back from Sicily he put on a grandstand show for his audience by deliberately getting into a dog-fight with a German fighter, and in full view of the island manoeuvring him into the sea.

Not only was he a marvellous pilot but he was a magnificent aerial photographer. The story goes that the first time he carried a 36 in lens camera he photographed the whole sweeping arc of the port of Messina on a single print. At a time when Malta was suffering daily bombardment, there was nowhere in southern Italy and North Africa that was denied to Warburton and his Beaufighter. He was Hugh Pughe-Lloyd's greatest single asset and not without reason was he called the "King of the Mediterranean".

The only other possible threat remaining to Allied interests in Africa which could not be covered properly from either Egypt, Malta, or Gibraltar, was Vichy French territory in West Africa, and, in particular, the battleship *Richelieu* at Dakar. Air HQ West Africa had been formed in September 1941 with two flying boat squadrons, one Hudson GR squadron (200 Sqn), and one Hurricane squadron (128 Sqn), to mount anti-submarine patrols and to protect Freetown, Takoradi, and the West African air routes. As many Frenchmen in the area had shown themselves to be anti-British and anti-de Gaulle, all three British services became concerned about the future intentions of their neighbours and it was decided to form a small reconnaissance force to monitor French possessions. Fortunately the SASO of Air HQ West Africa, Gp Capt Carter, had been the first CO of the CIU at Medmenham, and at a time when no-one else in West Africa had much idea or experience of PR developments back home he proposed that a PR and PI organisation be established to work alongside the PRU detachment at Gibraltar.

There were no PR aircraft to spare from the UK, and, as the Air Ministry was loathe to add to the maintenance problems of West Africa by introducing a new type like the Maryland, Carter had to make do with what was available. In December 1941 he asked for two Hudson IIIs, suitably modified, to be sent to 200 Sqn, but there was no sign of them by the time four PIs arrived in the New Year. West Africa therefore borrowed a Maryland from Gibraltar and this was sent on its first mission on January 9th to photograph Dakar harbour and peninsula. It was not until March that a couple of Hudsons, each with a split-pair of 14 in cameras and a long-range tank, arrived to replace the Maryland which had crashed on landing at the beginning of the month after returning from Senegal. Two Hurricanes were modified locally to carry long-range tanks and F 24 8 in cameras to supplement the Hudsons.

Most of the PR work was undertaken from Jeswang airfield in Gambia, though one Hudson was sent down to Sierra Leone to extend the area of operations. Latitude 30°N separated Gibraltar's and West Africa's areas of responsibility, below which 200 and 128 Sqn had three main tasks. Firstly there was the watch on the French warships at Dakar. Large supply dumps were photographed there in March, and by April the PIs had enough prints at their disposal to issue a report on the intricacies of the harbour defences. The naval watch was extended that month to include the island of Fernando Po in case the Spanish authorities were extending facilities to Axis shipping and submarines.

Secondly there were the Vichy airfields. French fighters in North Africa had often tried to intercept aircraft from Malta and Gibraltar and there was always the fear that Vichy Marylands might bomb British West Africa. A regular watch was therefore kept on all neighbouring French airfields – on one occasion a Hudson flew on an eight hour trip to cover the landing grounds of French Guinea – but most of them were seen to be very inactive.

Finally there were the patrols over the desert trails from the north in case Axis troops attempted to cross the Sahara to interfere with the Allied air ferry route from Takoradi to Egypt. The importance of this vital supply line, stretching 3,697 miles from the Gold Coast through the Sudan to Egypt, may be judged from the fact that by October 1943 some 5,000 aircraft had been erected and dispatched along it to reinforce the Allied air forces in Africa.

A small but effective PR organisation had been welded together in West

Africa by the summer of 1942, and in July an appeal went up to the Air Ministry for two PR Spitfires so that a separate PRU could be established. After further requests two PR Spitfires were allocated to West Africa from those in transit at Takoradi, arriving at Freetown in October. A special PRU was then set up at Yundum in Gambia,[1] comprising the two Spitfires, two Hurricanes, and one Hudson, with a brief to watch certain strategically important French positions, especially Casablanca, to see how they reacted to the Allied landings in North Africa.

Every other reconnaissance unit in the Mediterranean was working frantically during October to provide planning data for the 'Torch' landings. While West Africa photographed French airfields and defences, plotted Vichy shipping, and produced mapping material, 69 Sqn covered the North African coast as far west as Oran where Gibraltar took over responsibility for PR around the Mahgreb. Their efforts were supplemented by periodic excursions from Benson. On October 2nd, Plt Off McKay flew his PR Mosquito down to Malta. During the outbound leg his observer photographed Venice, Trieste, Pola, and Fiume for the first time in the war, not to mention the ship-yards at Monte Falcone near Rome and Littorio aerodrome. The next day McKay took off from Malta for North Africa but had to turn back because of persistent low cloud, though they managed to photograph Palermo as a consolation. On October 4th the Mosquito succeeded in covering Tunis, Bizerte, Bône, and Philippeville before McKay returned to Benson via Gibraltar on the following day. He and his observer had taken nearly 1,000 photographs in 4,000 miles but there was to be no respite – on October 6th they were to be over Prague and Upper Silesia.

All the photographic effort from Benson, Malta, Gibraltar, and West Africa on behalf of 'Torch' produced seven tons of prints for the planners and 46 different models of the invasion beaches – eventually Medmenham ran out of floor space to store them all. When the landings finally took place on November 8th, the aerial cameras continued to turn with increasing frequency. A new PRU – 4 PRU[2] had been set up at Gibraltar just prior to 'Torch', and its six Spitfires flew repeatedly over Algiers, Oran, and Casablanca. A Mosquito detachment from 540 Sqn was sent out to watch the French Fleet in Toulon while Malta's Spitfires ranged over the South of France, photographing Marseilles six times during the landings to see if aid was being supplied to Axis forces in North Africa. Mosquitos photographed Toulon on eleven occasions between November 7th and 26th, and each time the same vessels remained at their positions. Then the Germans announced that the French Fleet had sailed, but it was not until November 28th that Plt Off Hardman confirmed that nearly all the ships that had been there two days previously had been scuttled. Four cruisers were still on fire on the last day of the month, and only two 6 in cruisers and some merchantmen appeared afloat and undamaged.

[1] Sierra Leone, Takoradi, and Nigeria also had their own detached aircraft and small PI sections for local PR work.

[2] Commanded by Sqn Ldr A. H. W. Ball.

Further sorties were flown from Gambia over Dakar for several weeks after this, but the benevolent attitude of the Vichy French in Africa to the Allied landings heralded the end of the West African PRU. In its short life, terminating at the end of December 1942, it had completed 184 PR sorties, but isolation had robbed some of these prints of much of their usefulness. It was never possible to send prints to the UK by air and so the PIs had to rely on the fast mail steamers, with the result that information was often out of date by the time it reached London, as was intelligence sent out to W. Africa by the Air Ministry. Nevertheless, had circumstances been different and had the Vichy French forces resisted the Allies in Africa, the home-grown PRU built up by such men as Gp Capt Carter would have had a very vital role to play.

If the Middle East was poor in PR resources, then the Far East was poverty-stricken. Little or no provision had been made for obtaining strategic photographic reconnaissance before 1941, due largely to the fact that no-one was aware of the developments and lessons being taught by Heston and Benson many thousands of miles away. Whenever any aerial photography had been required before the war, for counter-insurgency operations or for the Survey of India, cameras were simply installed in any suitable aircraft and the resulting prints interpreted locally by Air Intelligence Liaison Officers.

As the Japanese threat grew larger, British planners did see that some strategic cover of surrounding territories like French Indo-China might be necessary in the event of a major thrust towards British possessions, but unfortunately there were few modern aircraft available in the theatre capable of such long-range sorties. In the summer of 1941, a Brewster Buffalo was adapted to carry an F 24 camera, but although successful trials were carried out at 13,000 feet its range was limited to 300 miles. On July 1st, 1941 the Air Ministry decided to allocate six PR Mosquitos to the Far East, but these were unlikely to arrive for at least a year so Far East Command was asked to make do with its available resources. In October two Blenheim IVs of 34 Sqn at Tengah were modified to carry cameras, but as there were no long-range tanks available their value was limited. At a time when information should have been available on Japanese movements and preparations in Siam and Indo-China, there were no PR aircraft in Far East Command capable of providing it.

Shortly after mid-day on December 6th, 1941, a Hudson of 1 (GR) Sqn, operating from northern Malaya at the extreme limits of its range, reported Japanese naval convoys some 80 miles SE of Cape Cambodia. At 0915 hrs two days later, a badly damaged PR Blenheim landed at Kota Bharu with the news that an invasion force was landing at Singora and Patani. From then on the Japanese advanced like a knife through butter, and by December 12th the RAF had been forced to abandon its forward airfields in the north to regroup at Butterworth. From here the solitary Buffalo flew on 'long-range' PR missions, bringing back some very useful information that no one was in a position to put to much use.

Boxing Day saw the remnants of Far East Command striking out from

The vast synthetic oil refinery near Brüx in the Sudetenland, photographed just a few weeks before the first bomber attack was made upon it. This enormous plant can be seen to be in operation and the continuous building of new hydrogenation stalls gives some indication of the tremendous output that the Germans had in mind but which they never attained. *CC*

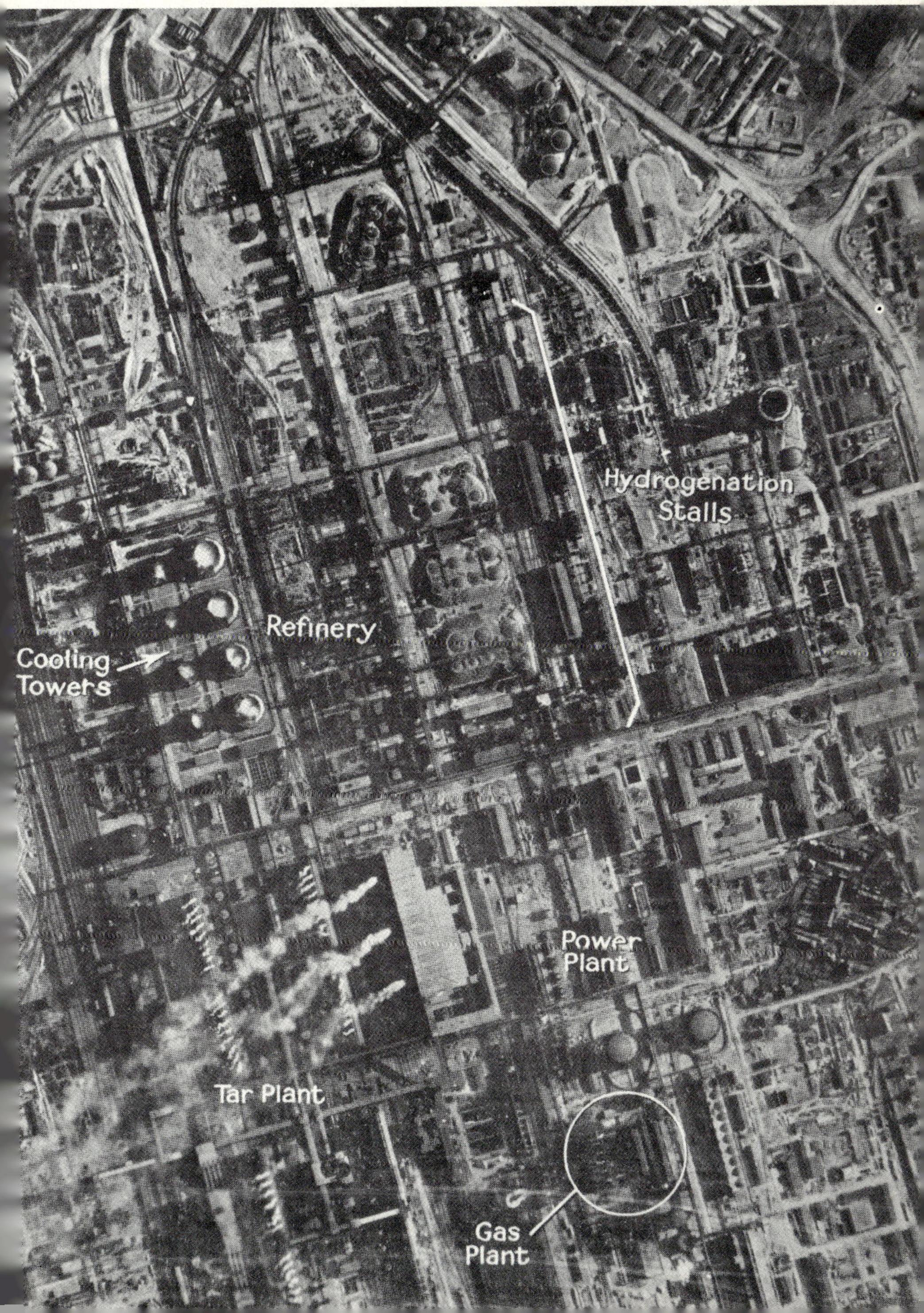

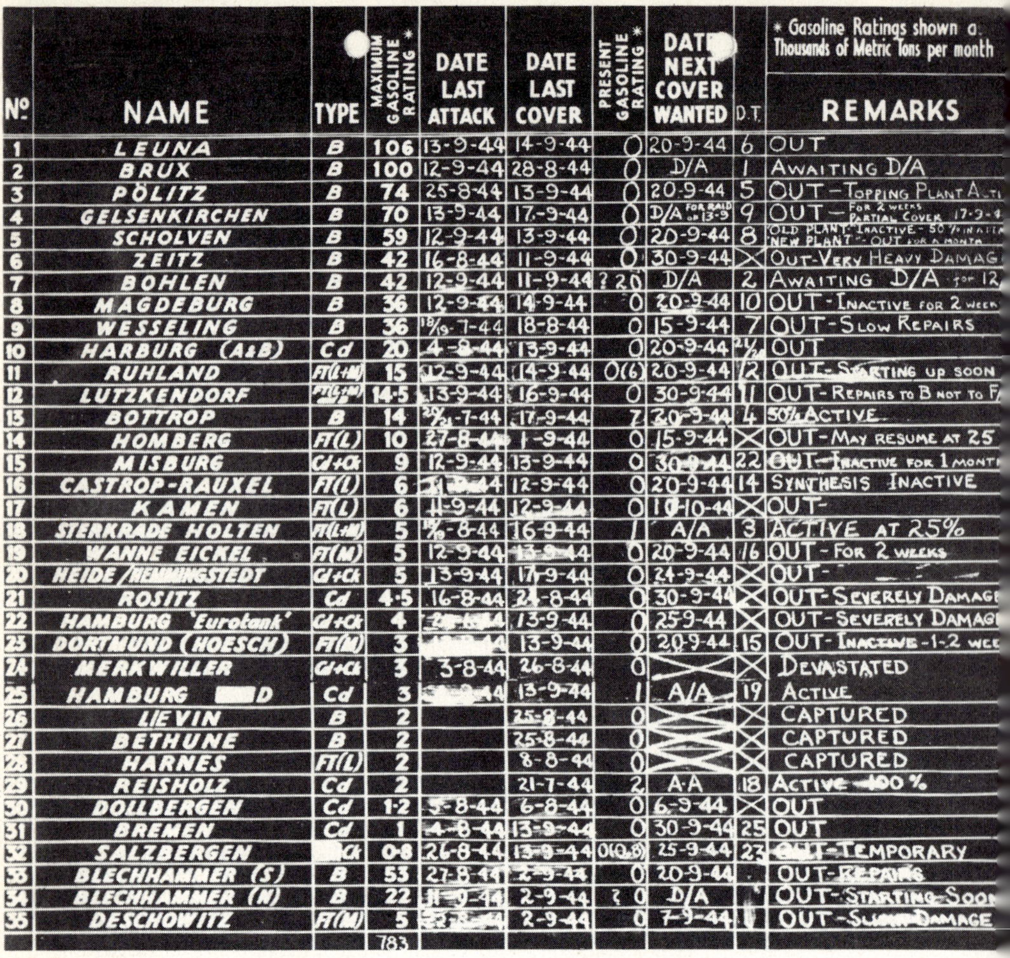

Nº	NAME	TYPE	MAXIMUM GASOLINE RATING *	DATE LAST ATTACK	DATE LAST COVER	PRESENT GASOLINE RATING *	DATE NEXT COVER WANTED	D.T.	* Gasoline Ratings shown as Thousands of Metric Tons per month — REMARKS
1	LEUNA	B	106	13-9-44	14-9-44	0	20-9-44	6	OUT
2	BRUX	B	100	12-9-44	28-8-44	0	D/A	1	AWAITING D/A
3	PÖLITZ	B	74	25-8-44	13-9-44	0	20-9-44	5	OUT – TOPPING PLANT A…
4	GELSENKIRCHEN	B	70	13-9-44	17-9-44	0	D/A FOR RAID OF 13-9	9	OUT – FOR 2 WEEKS PARTIAL COVER 17-9-4…
5	SCHOLVEN	B	59	12-9-44	13-9-44	0	20-9-44	8	OLD PLANT – INACTIVE – 50% … NEW PLANT – OUT FOR A MONTH
6	ZEITZ	B	42	16-8-44	11-9-44	0	30-9-44	X	OUT – VERY HEAVY DAMAG…
7	BOHLEN	B	42	12-9-44	11-9-44	? 20	D/A	2	AWAITING D/A FOR 12…
8	MAGDEBURG	B	36	12-9-44	14-9-44	0	20-9-44	10	OUT – INACTIVE FOR 2 WEEK…
9	WESSELING	B	36	18/19-7-44	18-8-44	0	15-9-44	7	OUT – SLOW REPAIRS
10	HARBURG (A&B)	Cd	20	4-8-44	13-9-44	0	20-9-44	2½	OUT
11	RUHLAND	FT(L+M)	15	12-9-44	14-9-44	0(6)	20-9-44	12	OUT – STARTING UP SOON
12	LUTZKENDORF	FT(L+M)	14·5	13-9-44	16-9-44	0	30-9-44	11	OUT – REPAIRS TO B NOT TO F…
13	BOTTROP	B	14	20/21-7-44	17-9-44	7	20-9-44	4	50% ACTIVE
14	HOMBERG	FT(L)	10	27-8-44	1-9-44	0	15-9-44	X	OUT – MAY RESUME AT 25…
15	MISBURG	Cd+Ck	9	12-9-44	13-9-44	0	30-9-44	22	OUT – INACTIVE FOR 1 MONTH
16	CASTROP-RAUXEL	FT(L)	6	[illegible]	12-9-44	0	20-9-44	14	SYNTHESIS INACTIVE
17	KAMEN	FT(L)	6	11-9-44	12-9-44	0	10-10-44	X	OUT
18	STERKRADE HOLTEN	FT(L+M)	5	[illegible]-8-44	16-9-44	1	A/A	3	ACTIVE AT 25%
19	WANNE EICKEL	FT(M)	5	12-9-44	13-9-44	0	20-9-44	16	OUT – FOR 2 WEEKS
20	HEIDE/HEMMINGSTEDT	Cd+Ck	5	13-9-44	17-9-44	0	24-9-44	X	OUT
21	ROSITZ	Cd	4·5	16-8-44	24-8-44	0	30-9-44	X	OUT – SEVERELY DAMAGE…
22	HAMBURG 'Eurotank'	Cd+Ck	4	[illegible]	13-9-44	0	25-9-44	X	OUT – SEVERELY DAMAGE…
23	DORTMUND (HOESCH)	FT(M)	3	[illegible]	13-9-44	0	20-9-44	15	OUT – INACTIVE – 1-2 WEE…
24	MERKWILLER	Cd+Ck	3	3-8-44	26-8-44	0	X	X	DEVASTATED
25	HAMBURG [illegible] D	Cd	3	[illegible]	13-9-44	1	A/A	19	ACTIVE
26	LIEVIN	B	2		25-8-44	0	X	X	CAPTURED
27	BETHUNE	B	2		25-8-44	0	X	X	CAPTURED
28	HARNES	FT(L)	2		8-8-44	0	X	X	CAPTURED
29	REISHOLZ	Cd	2		21-7-44	2	A-A	18	ACTIVE 100%
30	DOLLBERGEN	Cd	1·2	5-8-44	6-8-44	0	6-9-44	X	OUT
31	BREMEN	Cd	1	4-8-44	13-9-44	0	30-9-44	25	OUT
32	SALZBERGEN	[illegible]Ck	0·8	26-8-44	13-9-44	0(0.8)	25-9-44	23	OUT – TEMPORARY
33	BLECHHAMMER (S)	B	53	27-8-44	2-9-44	0	20-9-44		OUT – REPAIRS
34	BLECHHAMMER (N)	B	22	11-9-44	2-9-44	? 0	D/A		OUT – STARTING SOON
35	DESCHOWITZ	FT(M)	5	[illegible]	2-9-44	0	7-9-44		OUT – S[illegible] DAMAGE
			783						

Above: The famous 'Oil Scoreboard' at Medmenham, showing the serviceability state of the 35 main synthetic oil refineries within range of the aerial camera.

During and after the bombing onslaught on the communications systems of France in preparation for D-Day. *Top right:* Shows the Aulnoye marshalling yards after two attacks in March and April 1944 – each of the 32 tracks has been cut in several places and there are signs of scattered damage to sheds and rolling stock. However this damage was minor compared with that inflicted by the concentrated Bomber Command raid on April 27/28th. *Bottom right:* During the raid the site was completely obliterated. The road at the top of the picture is in use again but it has become a series of curves caused by vehicles and people trying to get to the scene of desolation. *IWM*

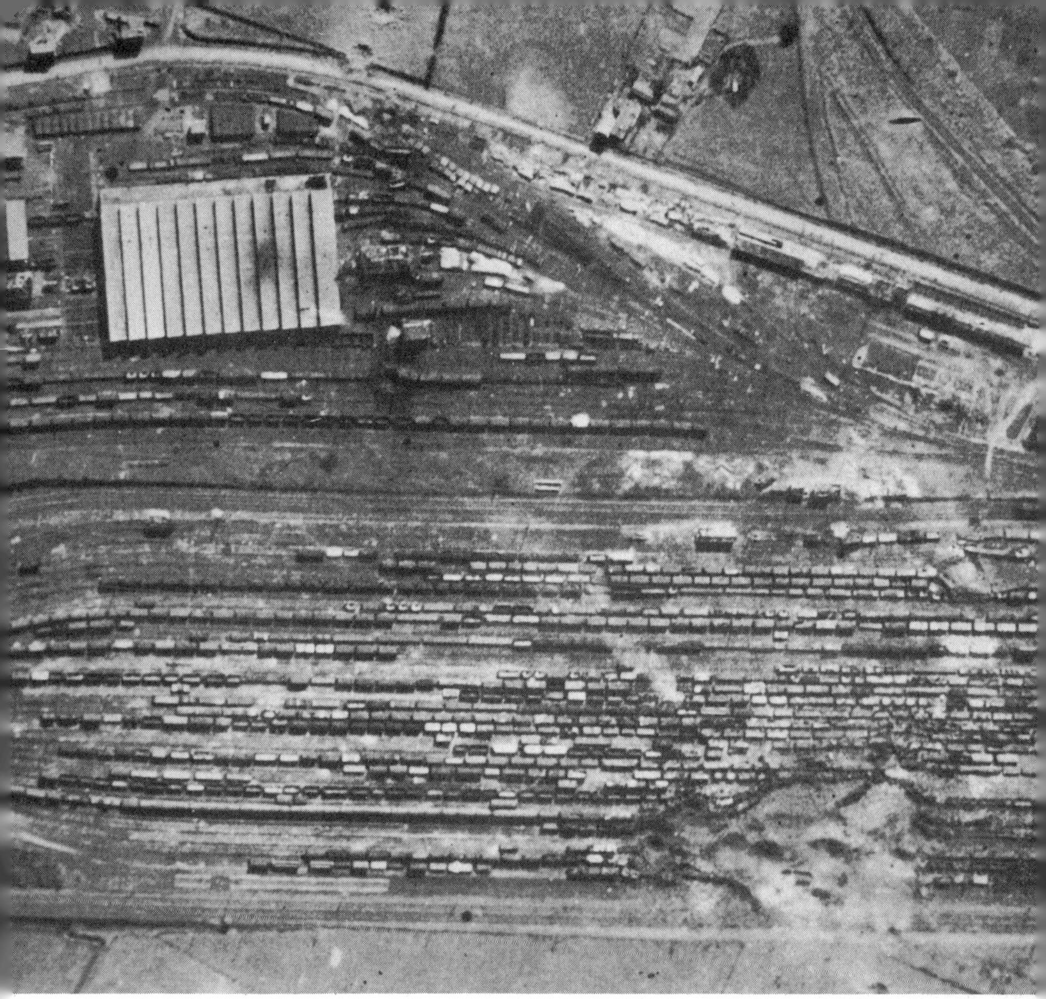

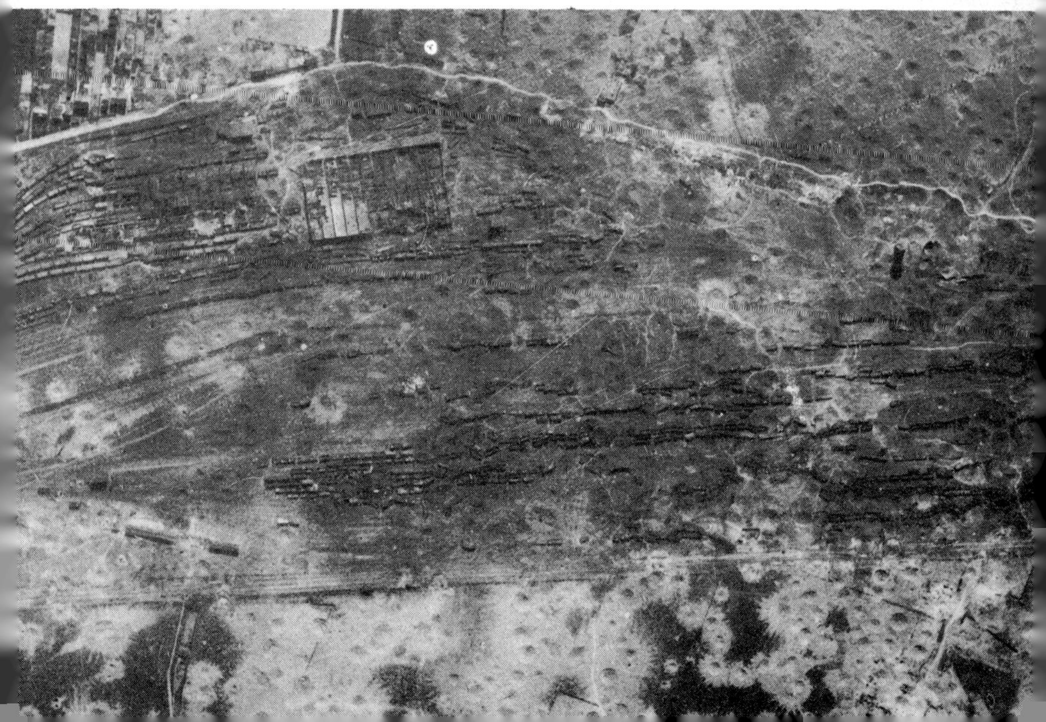

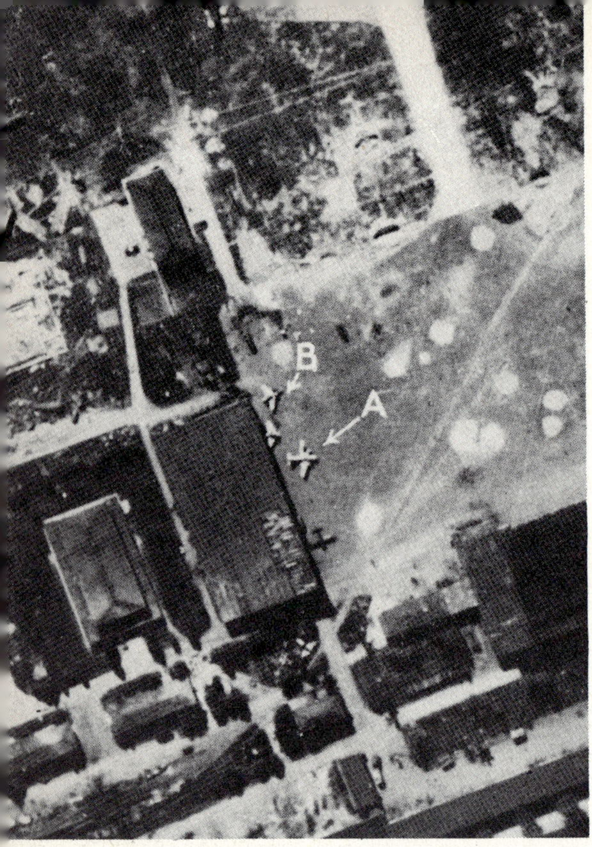

Left: PR provided much useful information on the development of new types of German aircraft, especially the first jet fighters. The contrast between the Me 163 (A) and Me 262 (B) is well illustrated on this print of Lechfeld. *CC.* Last of two distinguished lines of PR aircraft – *Below:* Shows a Spitfire PR 19 lashed down after a storm at Blankenseer/Lubeck in 1946. *Nicoll. Top right:* Shows a Mosquito PR 34 with its swollen bomb-bay fuel tank and 200 gallon wing tanks. *IWM. Bottom right:* The end of the *Tirpitz* as photographed by Sqn Ldr F. L. Dodd and Plt Off E. Hill from their 544 Sqn Mosquito over the Tromso Fiord on March 22nd 1945. Much of the capsized hull is covered with snow but tracks have been cleared to permit access. No major repair work is visible although salvage vessels are evident alongside. *IWM*

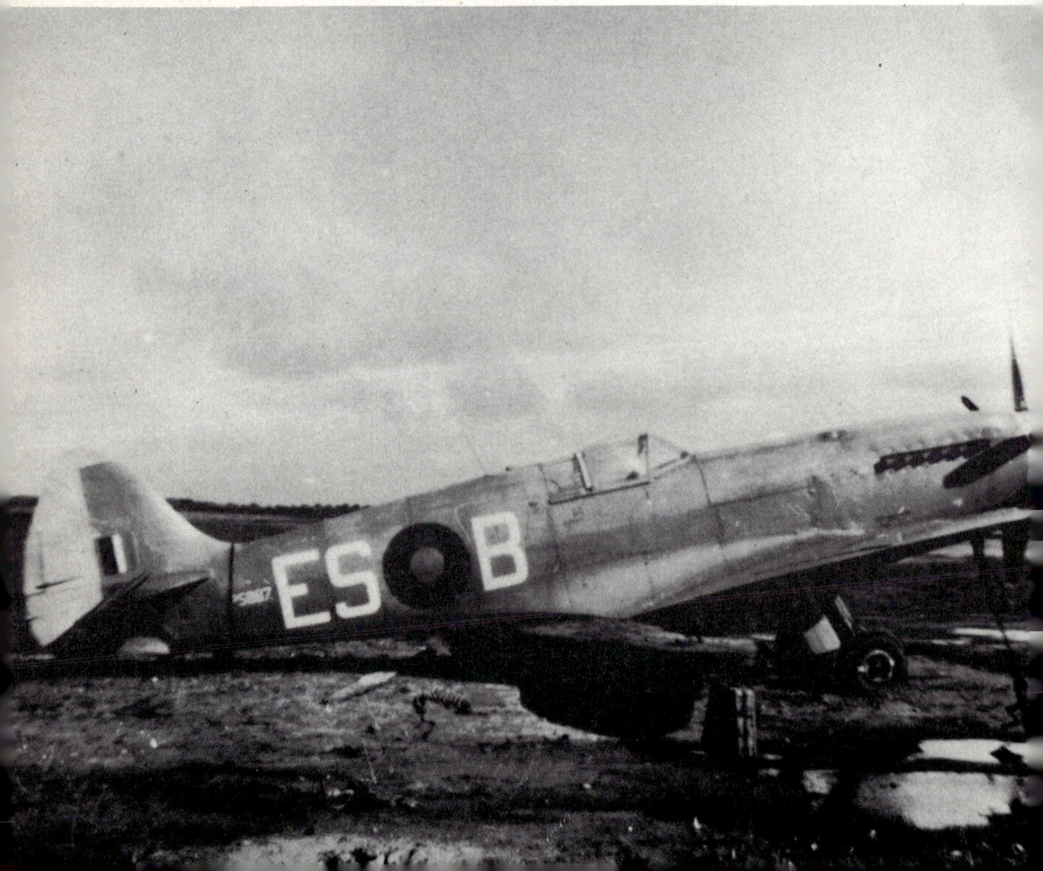

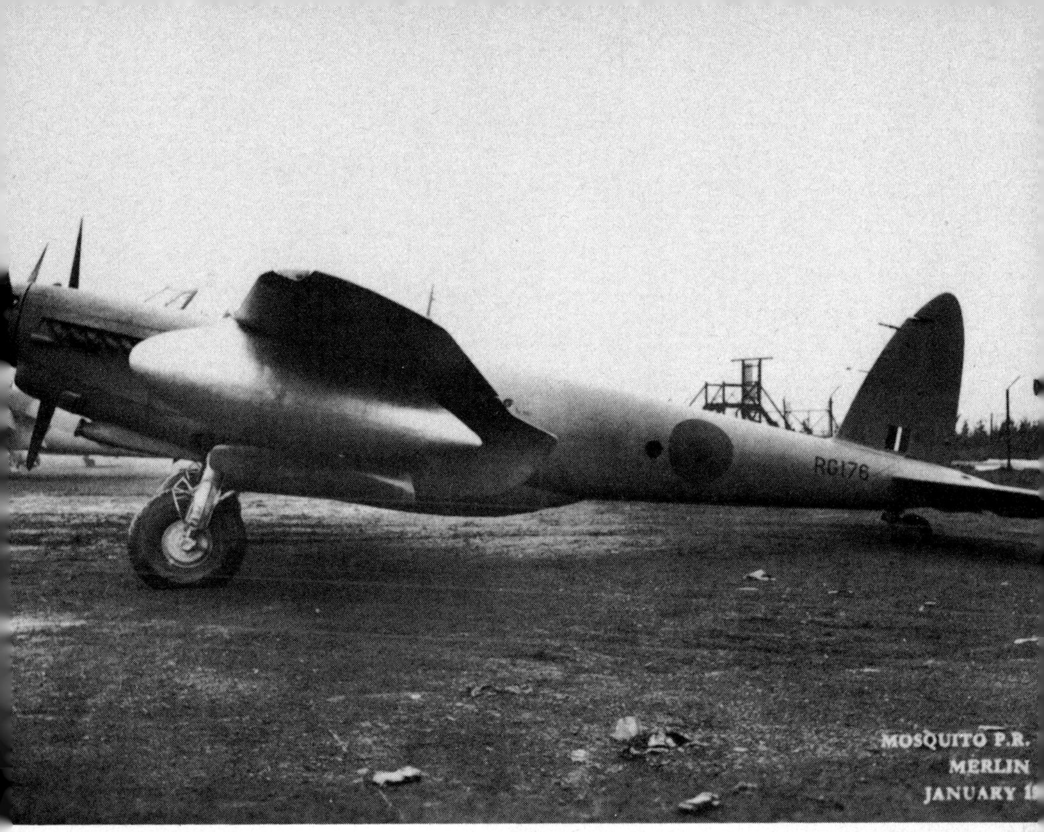

MOSQUITO P.R.
MERLIN
JANUARY 1

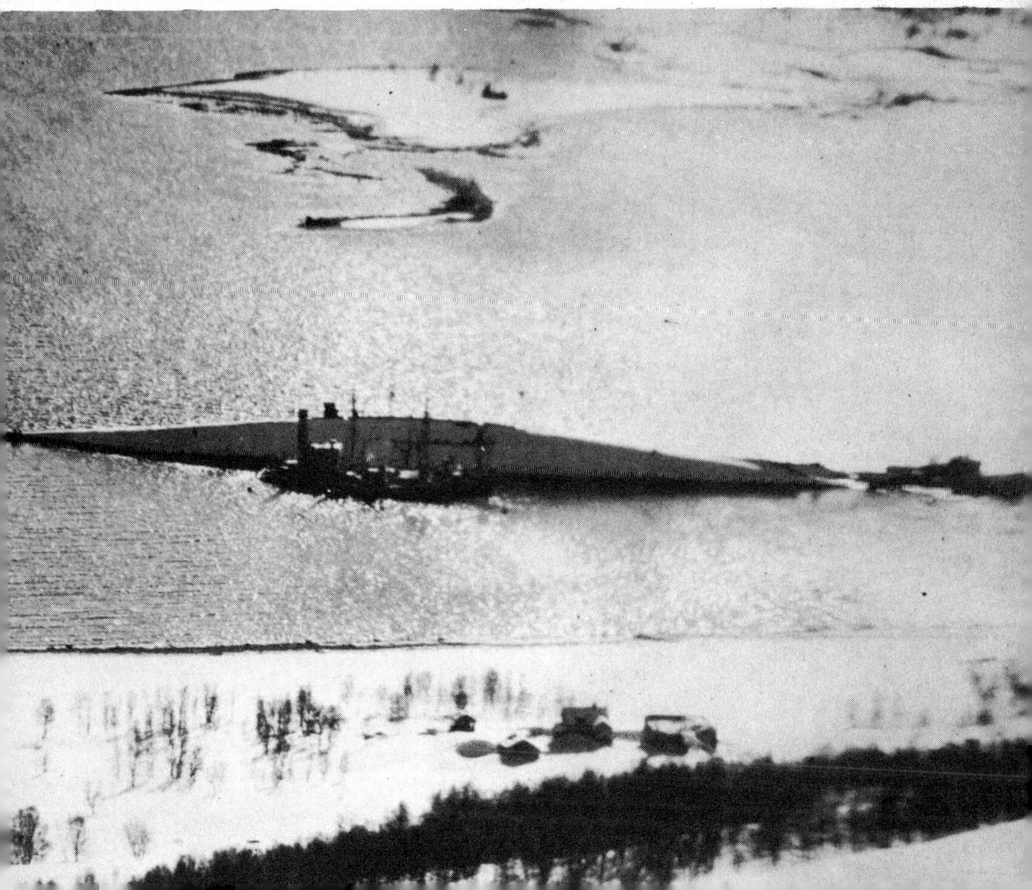

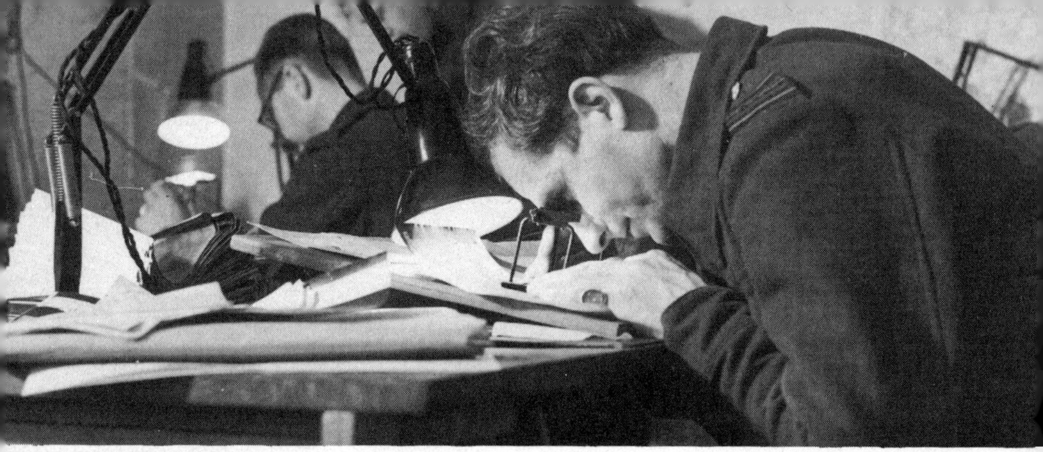

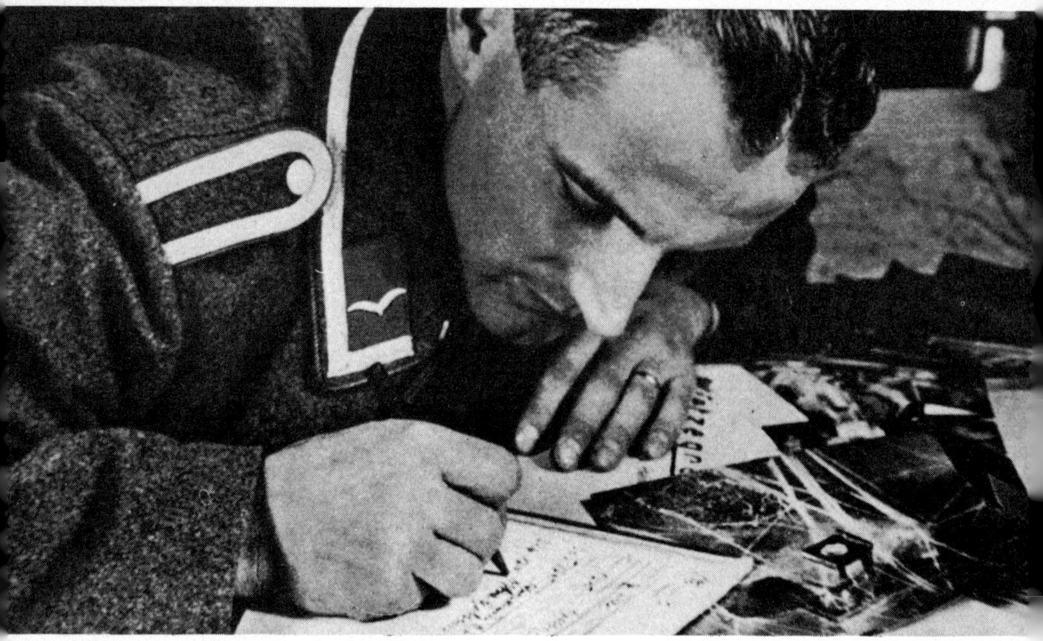

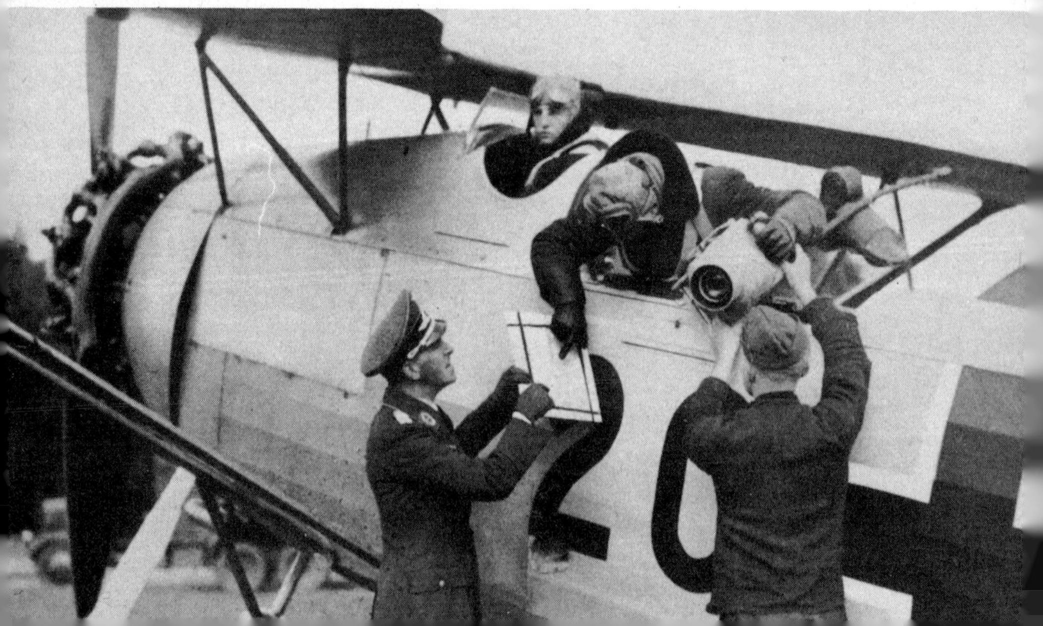
20

Photo-interpreters on different sides. *Top left:* Shows Sqn Ldr Michael Spender, brother of the poet Stephen Spender, examining prints of German troop movements through a stereoscope. *Middle left:* Shows a Luftwaffe Unteroffizier PI recording his findings from an aerial print. *Schliephake. Bottom left:* The crew of an He 46C of Aufkl. Gr. (H)/112 receive their pre-flight briefing, circa 1938. *Schliephake. Below:* An Hs 126 on tactical reconnaissance duties with the observer operating a hand-held camera from the rear cockpit. *Schliephake. Bottom:* A promise that was never fulfilled – the He 119. *Schliephake*

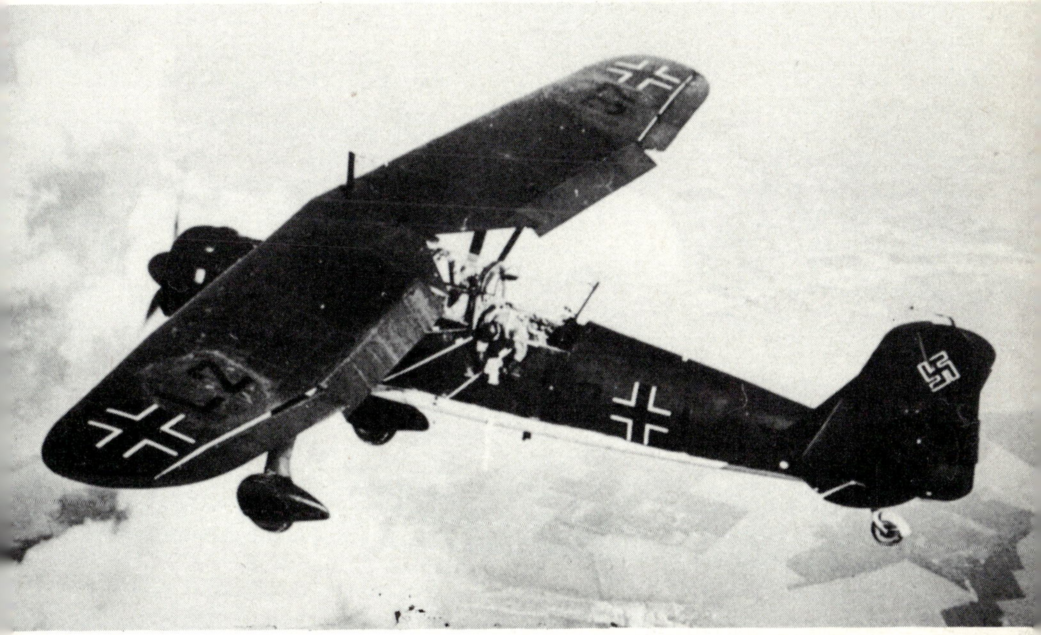

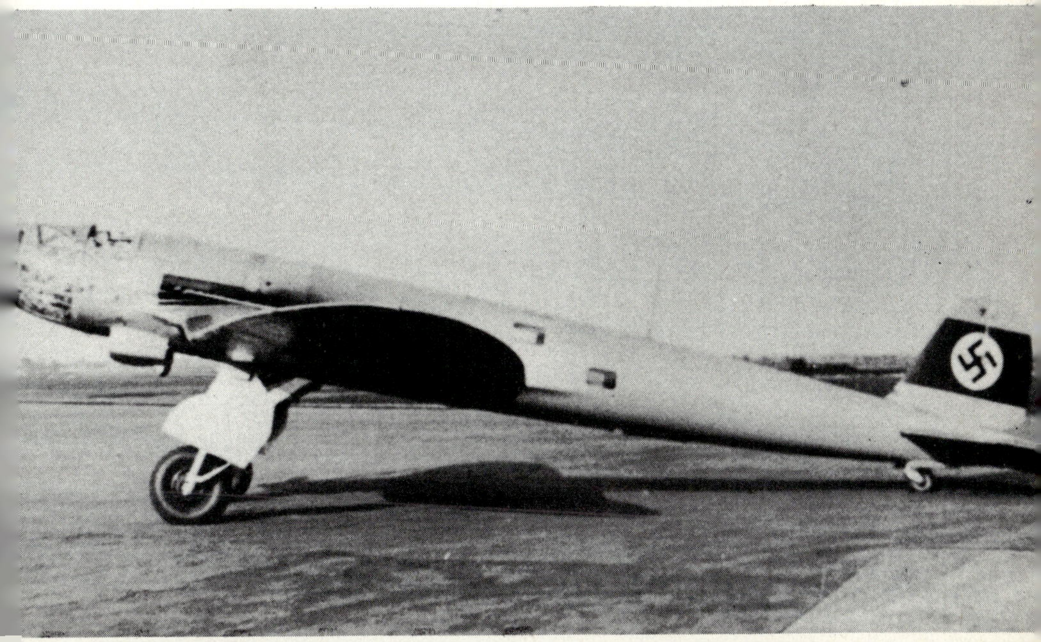

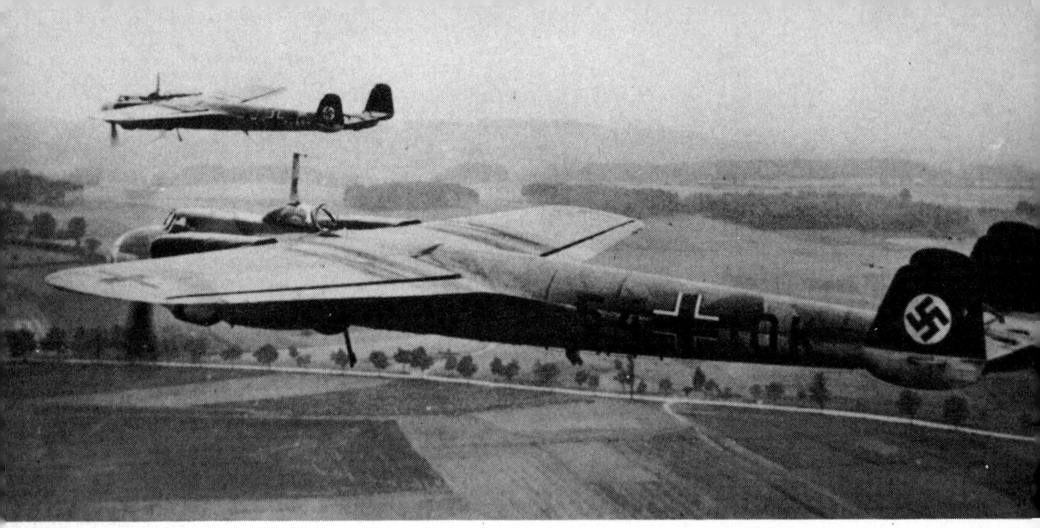

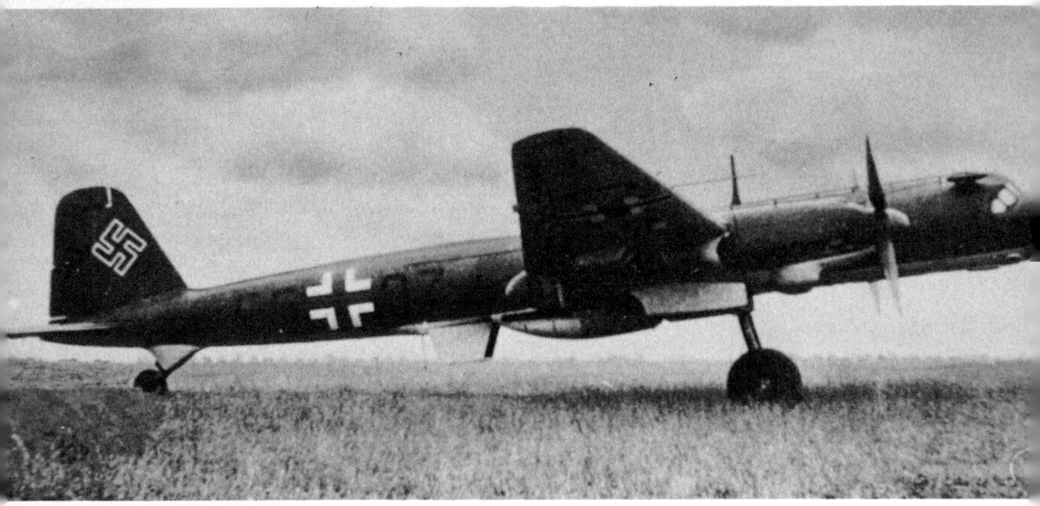

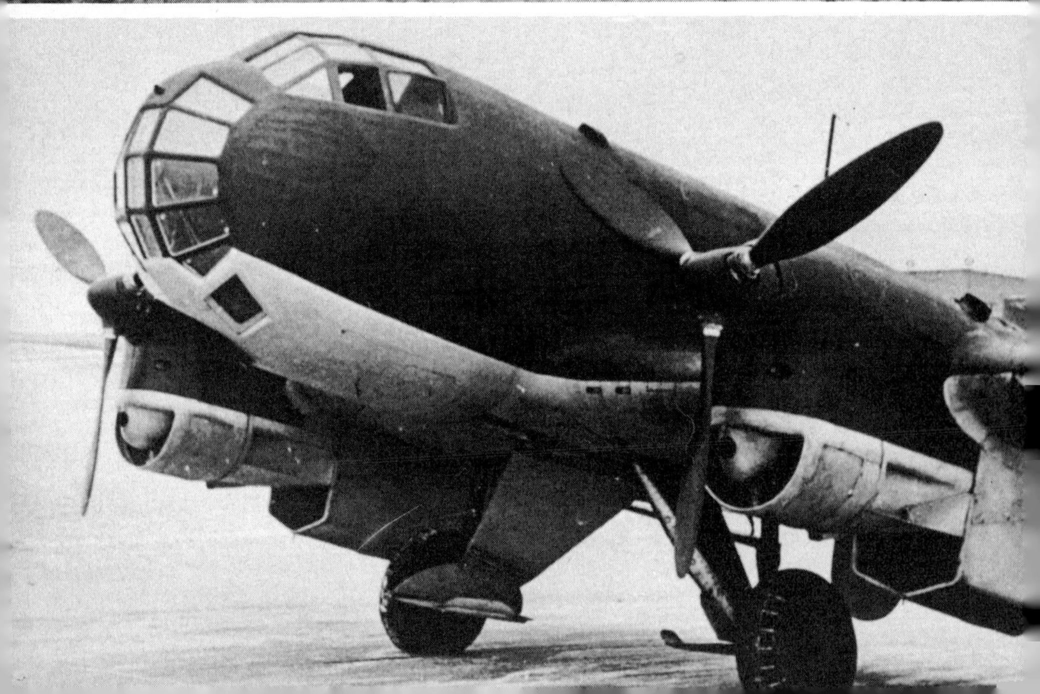

Top left: The standard Luftwaffe long-range reconnaissance aircraft of 1939 – the Do 17. *Schliephake. Middle left:* One of the seven pre-production models of the Hs 130 E-O high level PR aircraft, modified for the Aufkl. Gr. Ob.d.L. in May 1943. Like many other Luftwaffe aircraft, it suffered from technical troubles and never saw operational service. *Schliephake. Bottom left:* A more successful high level Luftwaffe PR aircraft – the Ju 86 P-1. Nevertheless only a small number of these aircraft were adapted to the reconnaissance role, to be operated by 4./Aufkl, Gr. Ob.d.L. over the British Isles during 1941. *Schliephake Below:* The first operational PR jet in the world – an Arado 234B single-seat reconnaissance bomber in Allied markings. *IWM. Bottom:* The DFS 228 reconnaissance vehicle on the back of a Do 217K. This ingenious PR aircraft was carried or towed up to 33,000ft before being released to rocket climb up to 75,000 ft. It would remain at altitude for 45 minutes during which time photographs would be taken by two Zeiss infra-red cameras housed in the wooden fuselage. After the rocket fuel was exhausted, the pilot, lying in a prone position throughout, would start the 650 mile glide for home. The war ended before prototype trials were completed, but design work had already started on a supersonic DFS 346 which it was hoped would reach a speed of Mach 1.9 at 66,000 ft. *Price*

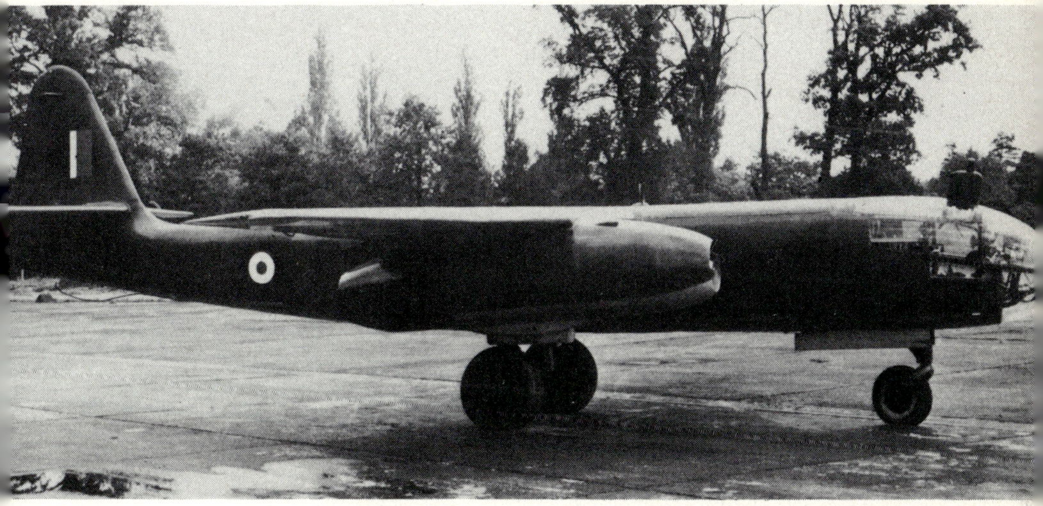

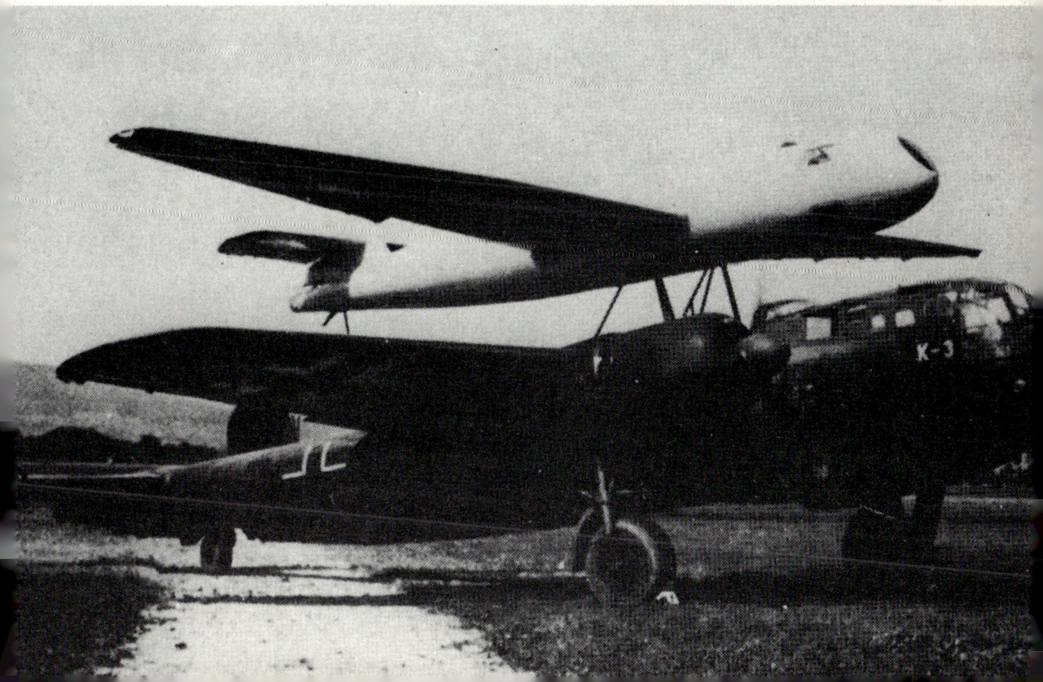

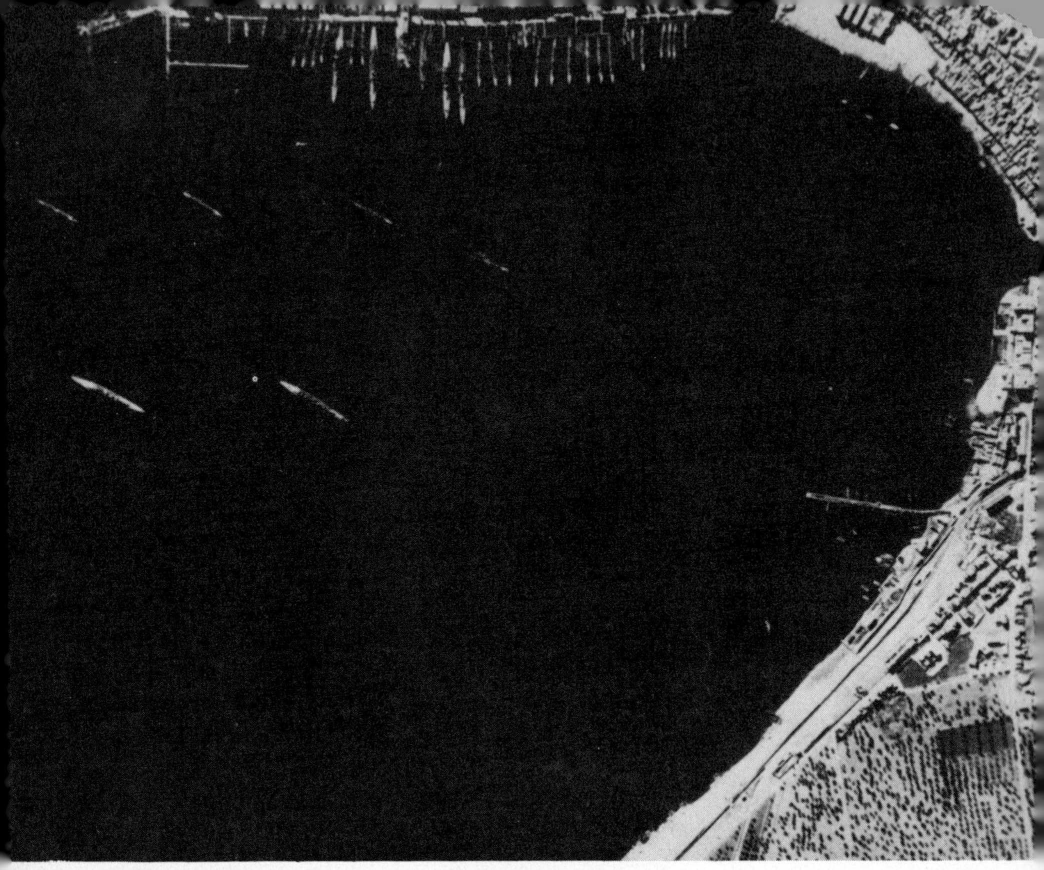

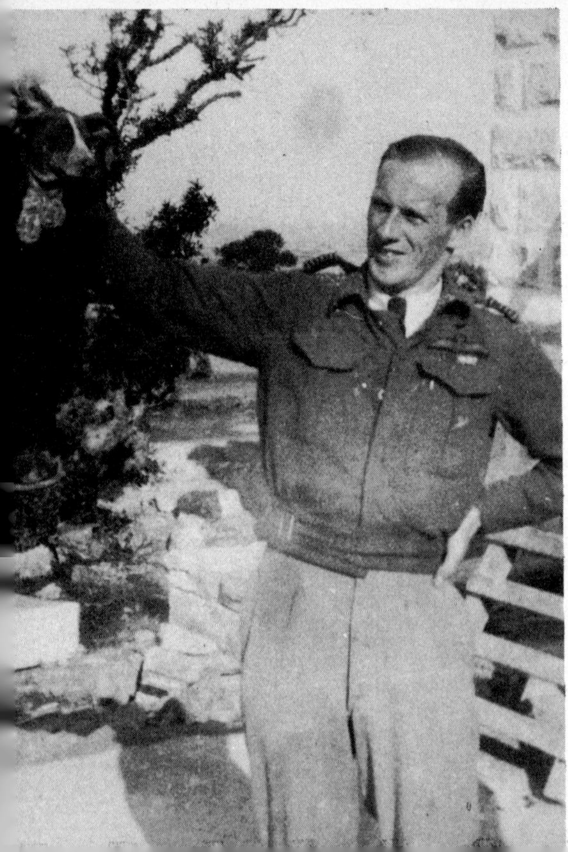

Above: Taranto harbour as seen from a Maryland of 431 Flt just before the Fleet Air Arm attack in November 1940. *IWM. Left:* The most daring PR pilot of them all – Wg Cdr Adrian Warburton, DSO and bar, DFC and two bars, American DFC, with a friend outside the 683 Sqn HQ at Luqa, Malta, in 1943. *Rutter. Top right:* A typical Warburton low-level print, taken from a Spitfire PR IV when he accompanied a raid on a chemical works at Palermo. *Mowlam. Middle right:* A reconnaissance Maryland churns up a desert air-strip. *Bottom right:* The Axis landing ground at Sidi Barrani as photographed by 2 PRU. *Kerr*

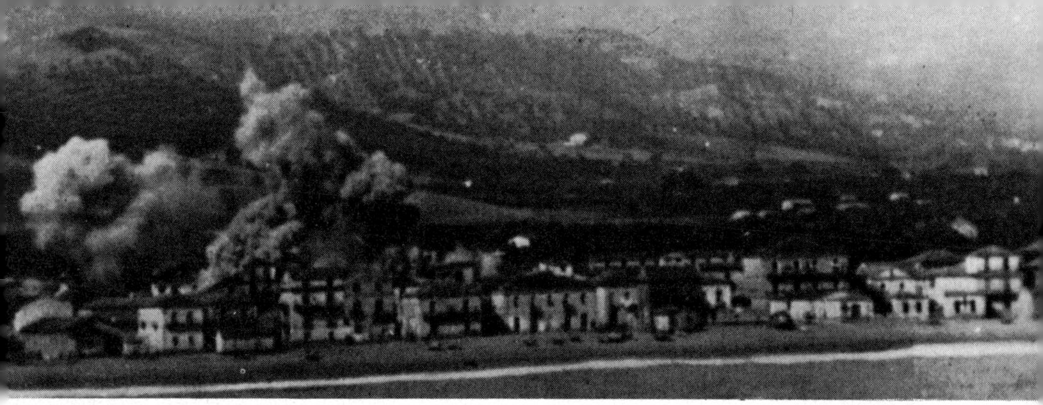

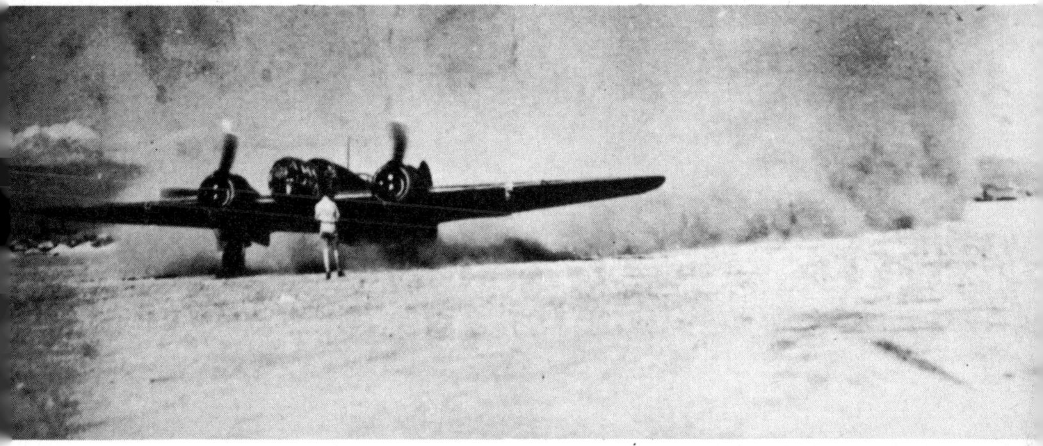

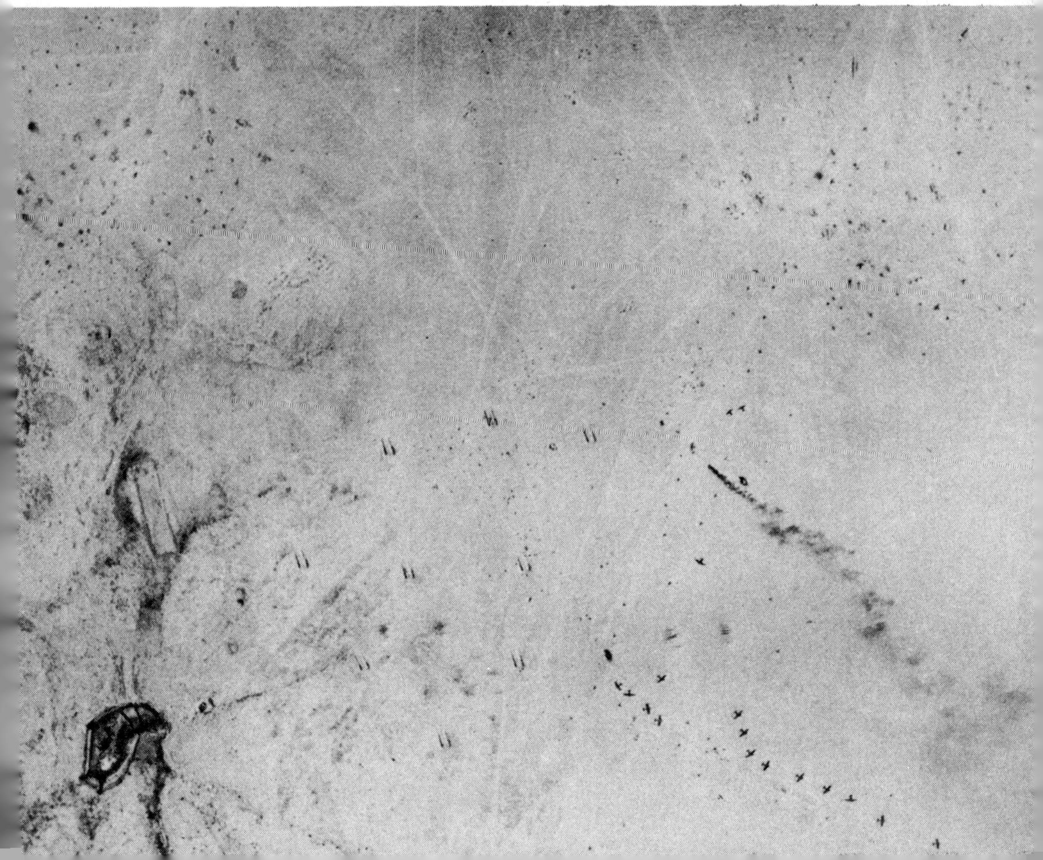

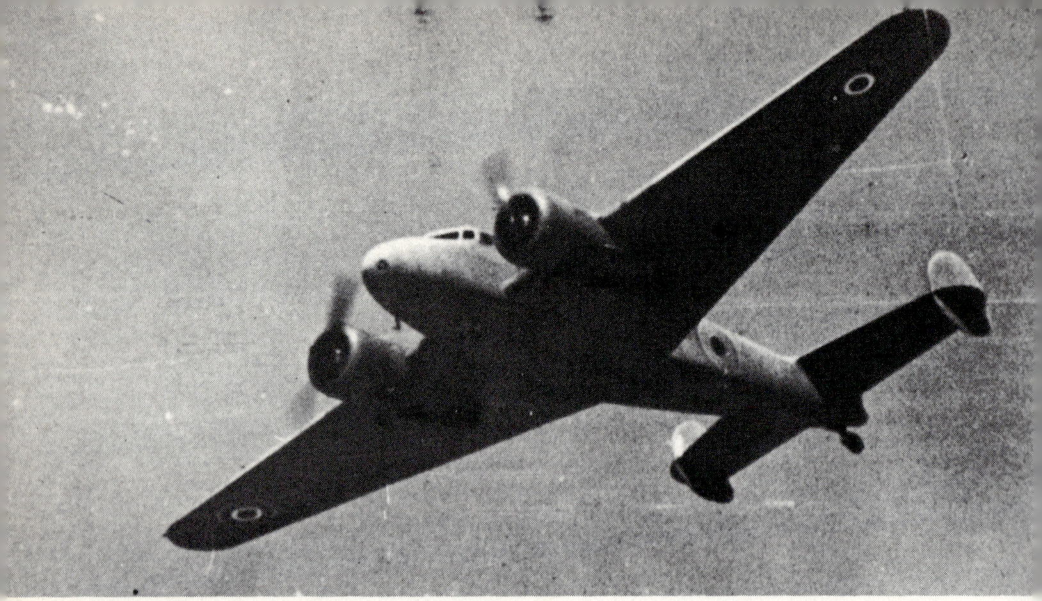

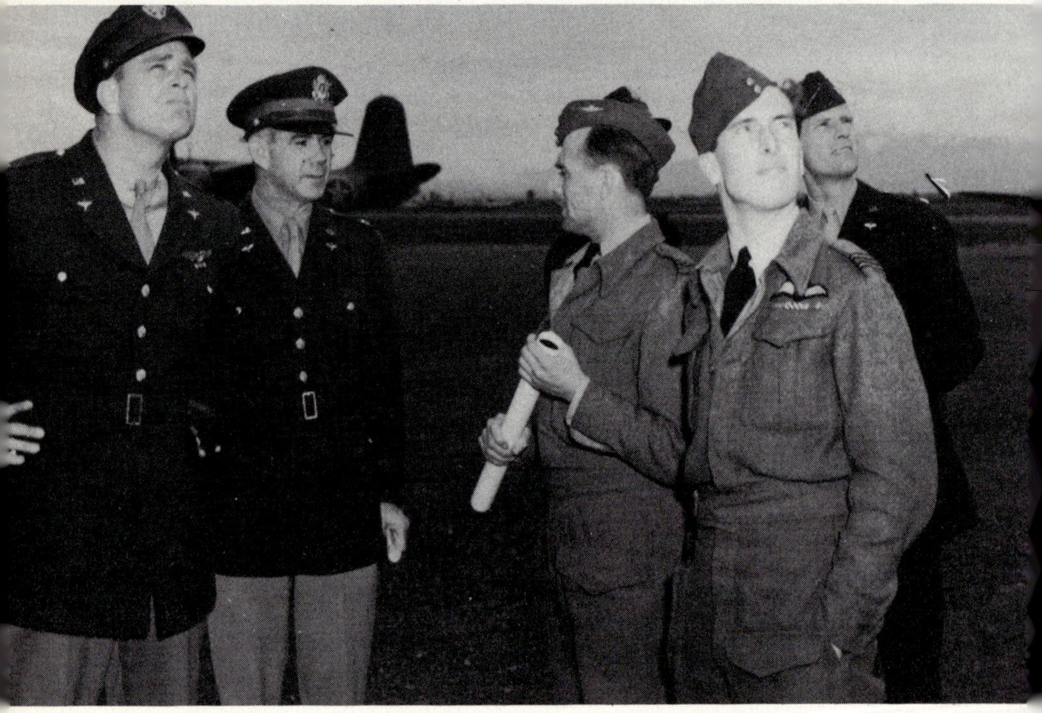

Top: The faithful Lockheed Electra, 'Cloudy Joe'. It was finally written off on August 25th, 1944 while returning to Lakatamia in Cyprus. *Kerr. Above:* Meeting of allies at Maison Blanche, Algiers, in 1943. Elliott Roosevelt is on the far left with hands on hips while the nonchalent RAF officer at right foreground with hands in pockets is 'Freddie' Ball. *Eggleston* Damage assessment prints taken during and after the 'Operation Bowler' raid on Venice harbour on March 21st, 1945. *Top right:* Shows a warehouse full of landmines erupting as the 680 Sqn Spitfire passed overhead. *Bottom right:* Shows the damage after the smoke had cleared. *CC*

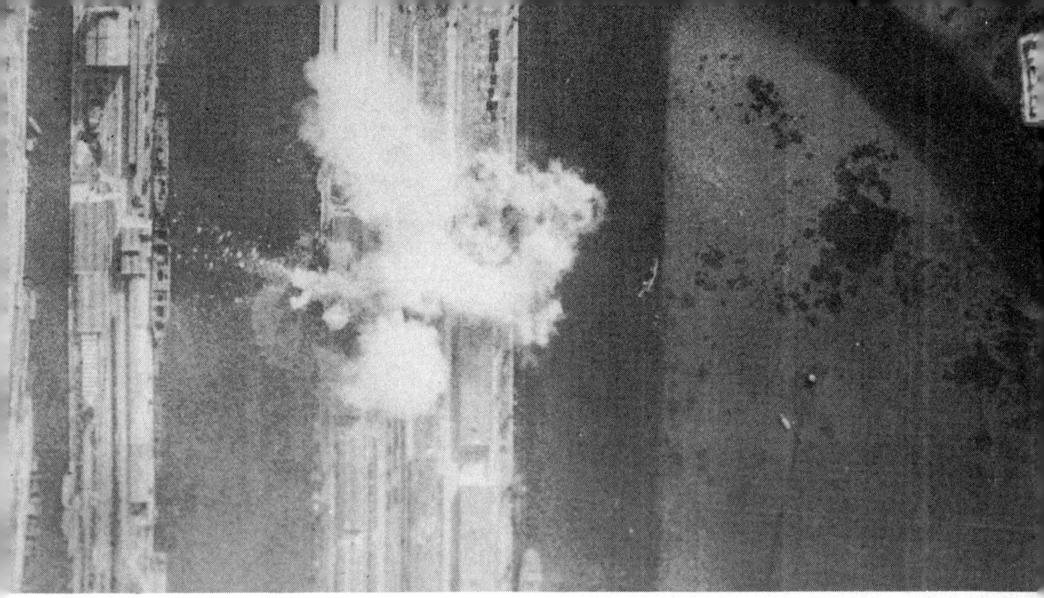

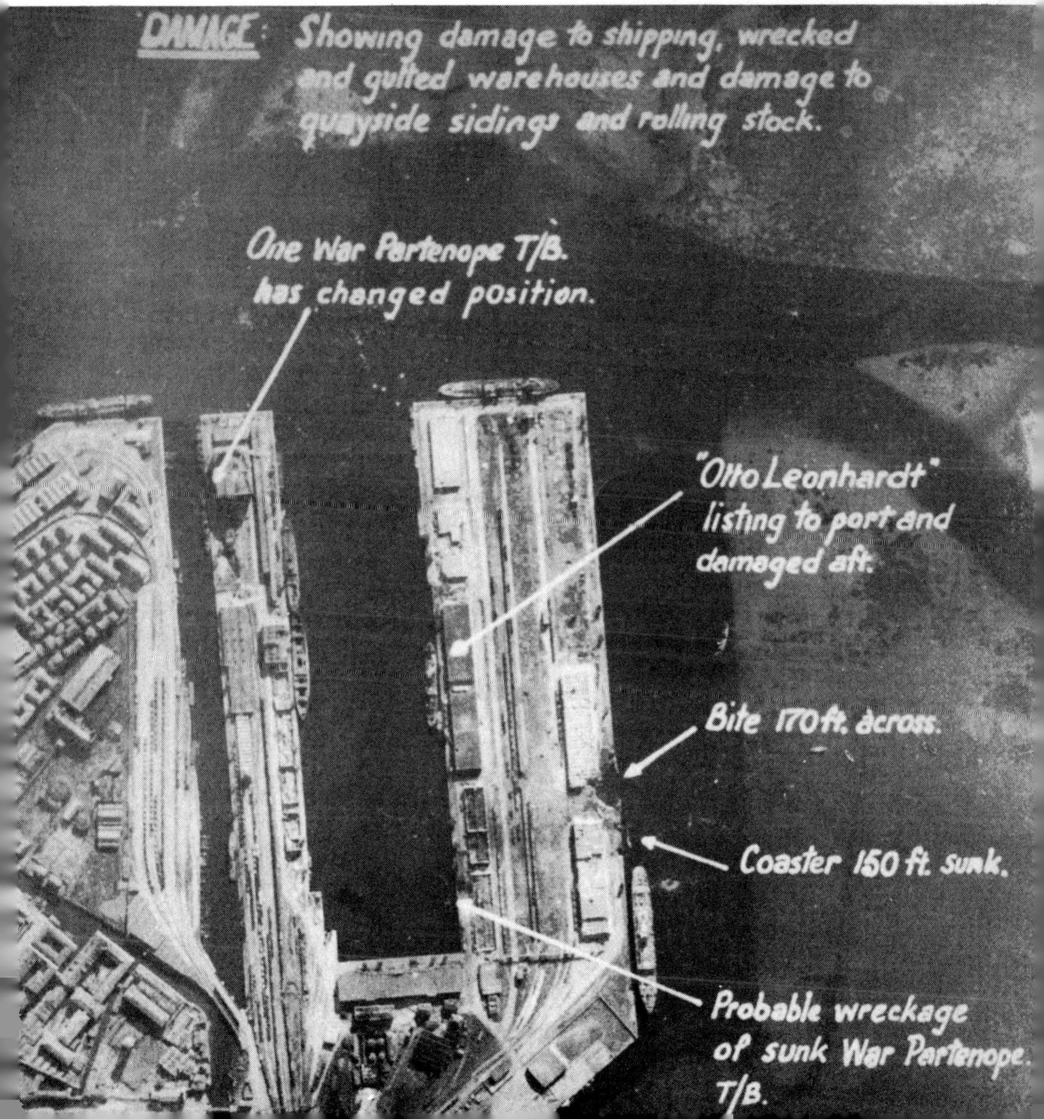
DAMAGE: Showing damage to shipping, wrecked and gutted warehouses and damage to quayside sidings and rolling stock.
One War Partenope T/B. has changed position.
"Otto Leonhardt" listing to port and damaged aft.
Bite 170 ft. across.
Coaster 150 ft. sunk.
Probable wreckage of sunk War Partenope. T/B.

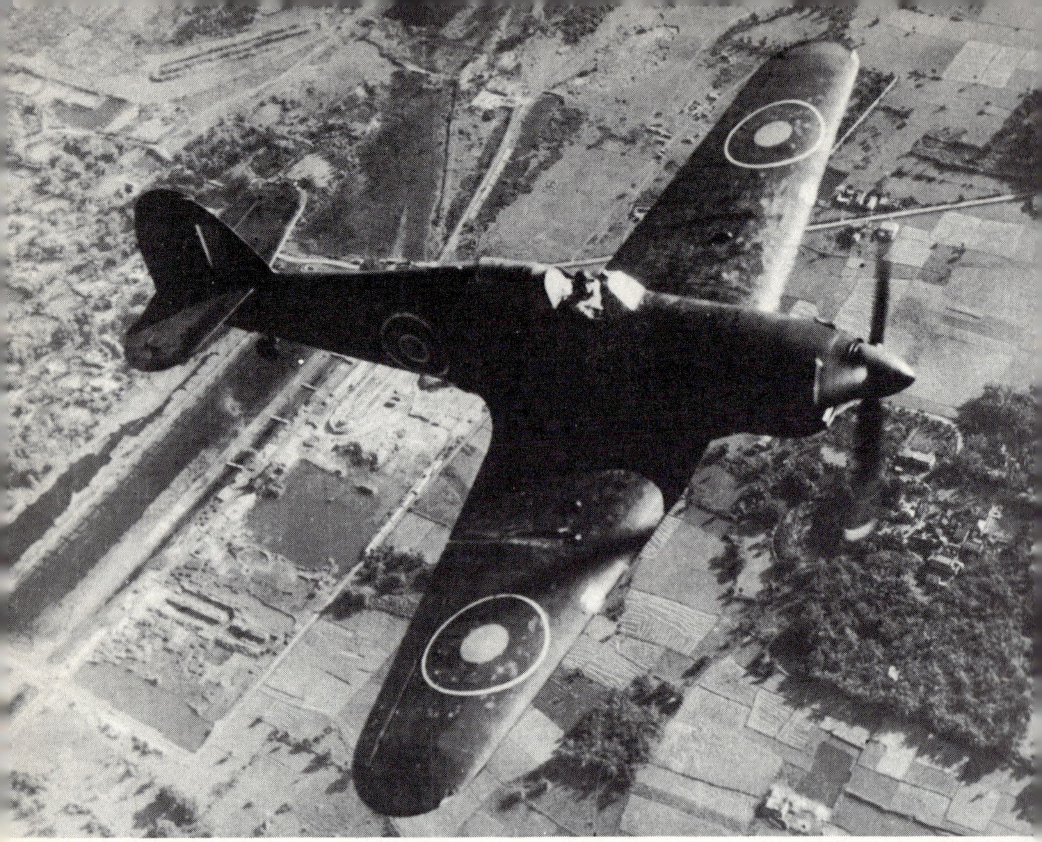

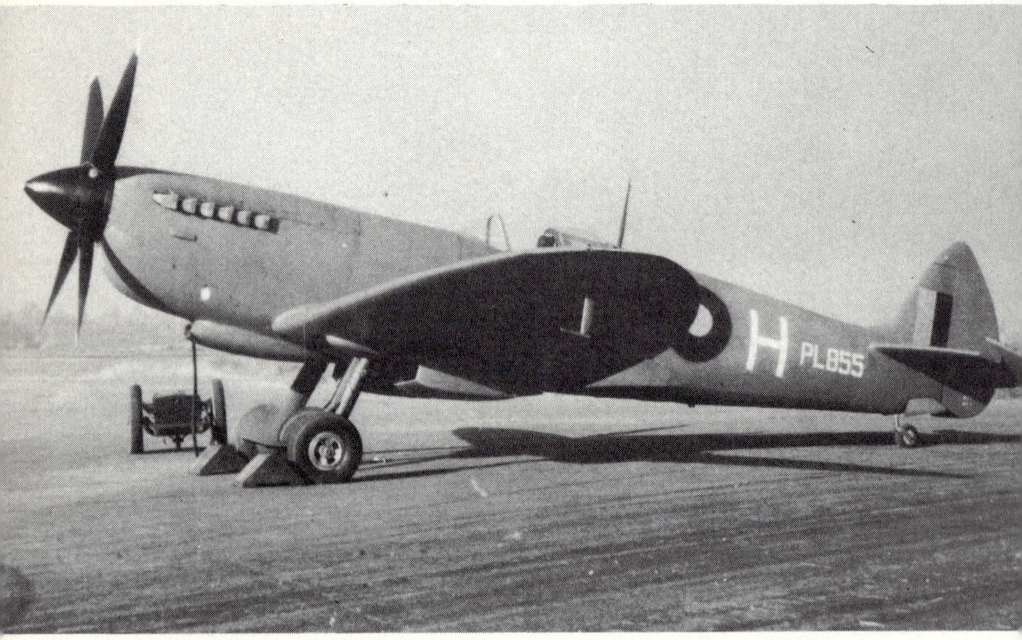

Top: A PR Hurricane over Bengal. *Proctor Above:* Spitfire PR XI polished up for a visit by the King of Nepal. *Proctor. Top right:* Camera servicing in the Photo Section at Dum Dum. *Theobald. Bottom right:* "Don't forget your cameras . . ." F 8s cameras standing guard over their flying platform. *Proctor*

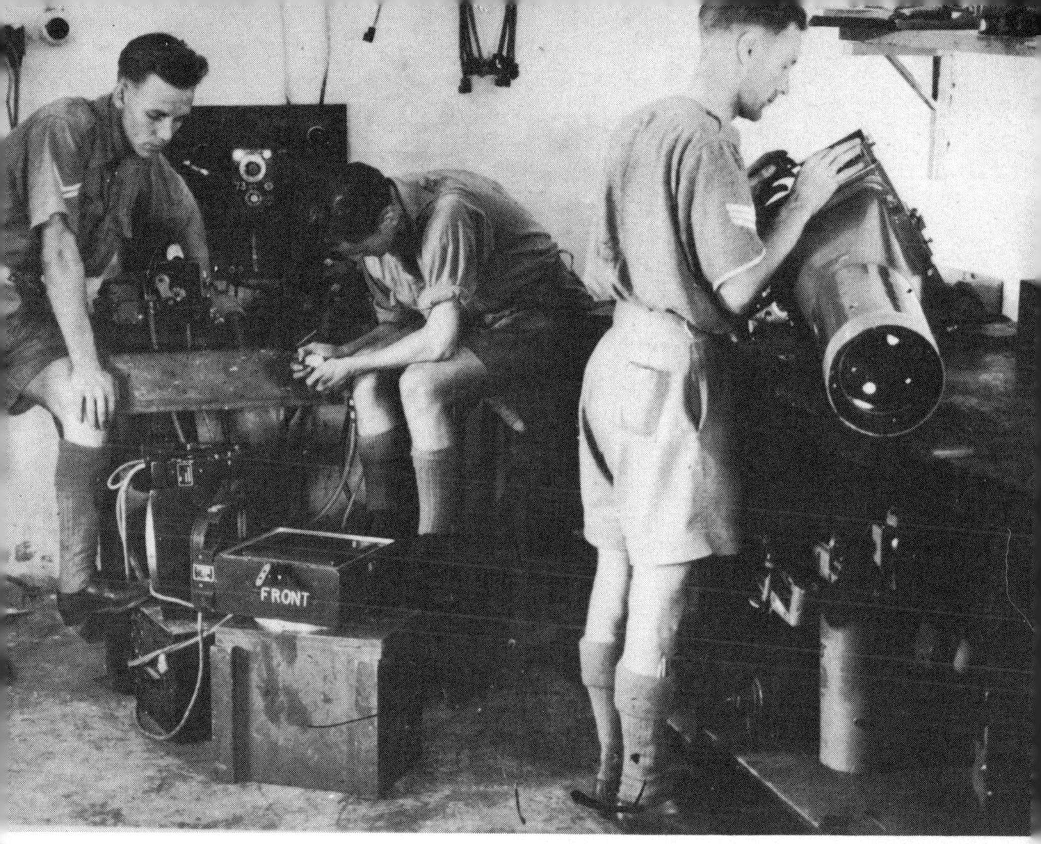
FRONT

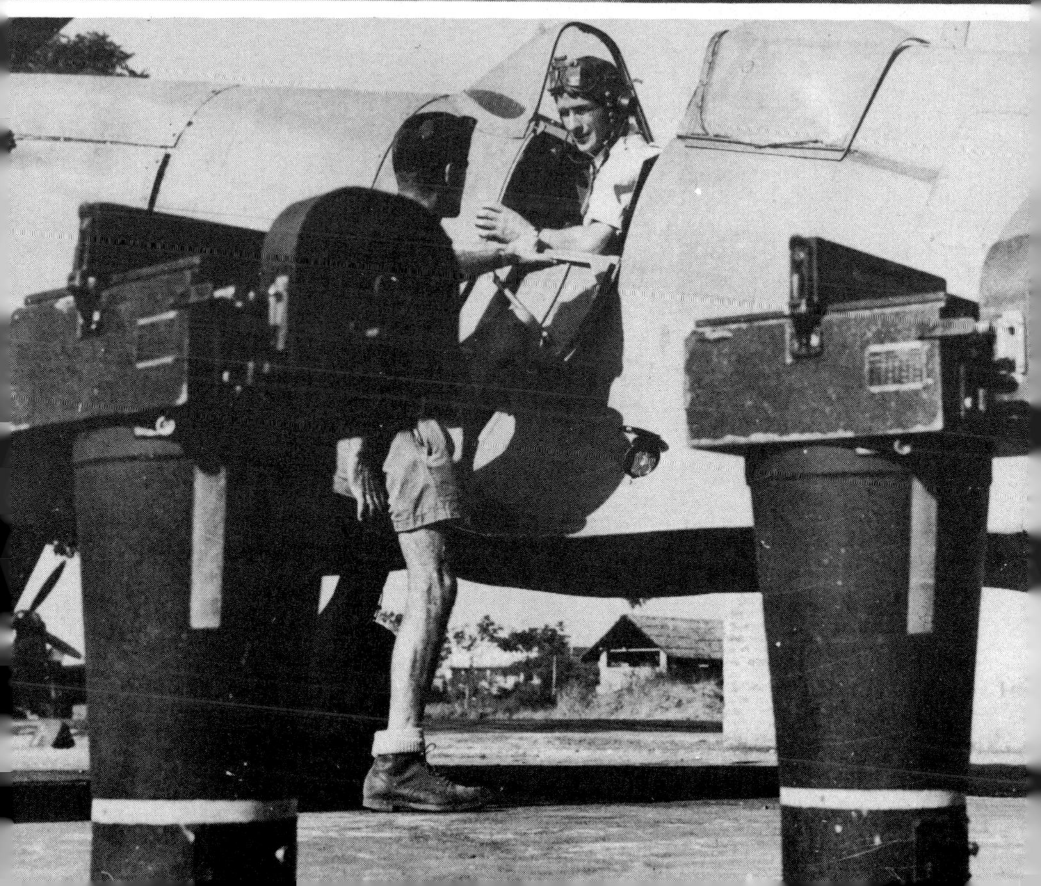

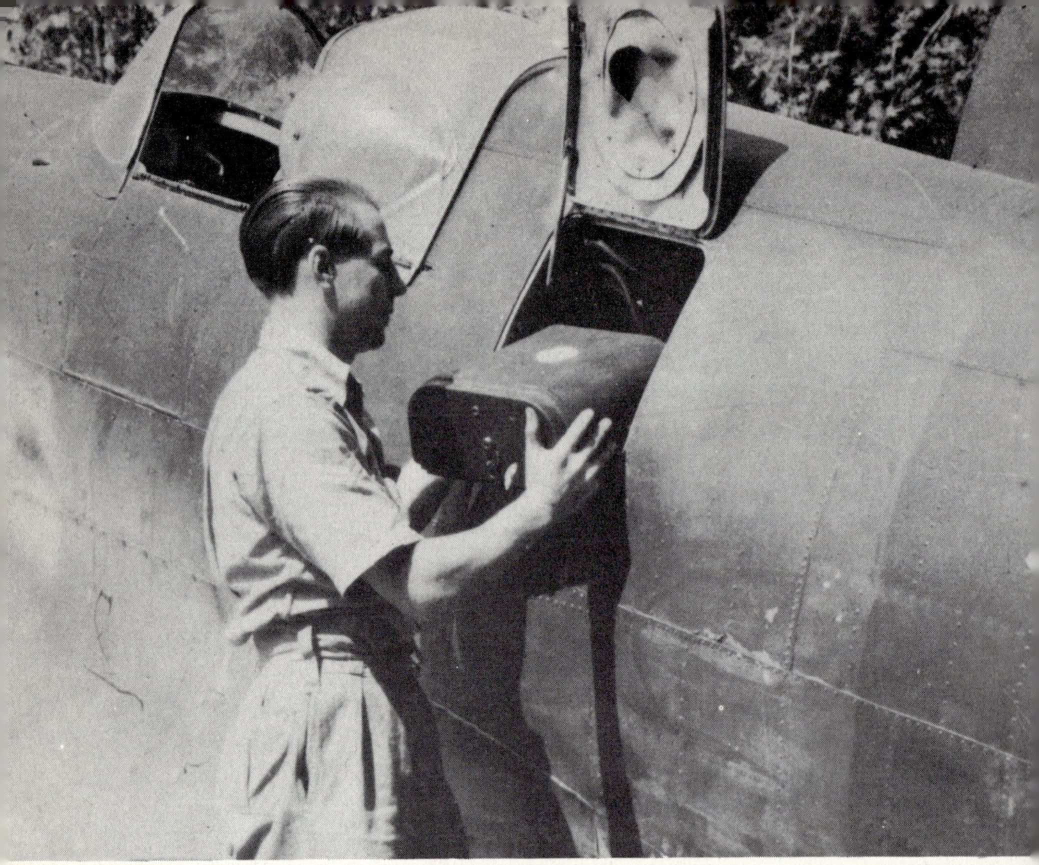

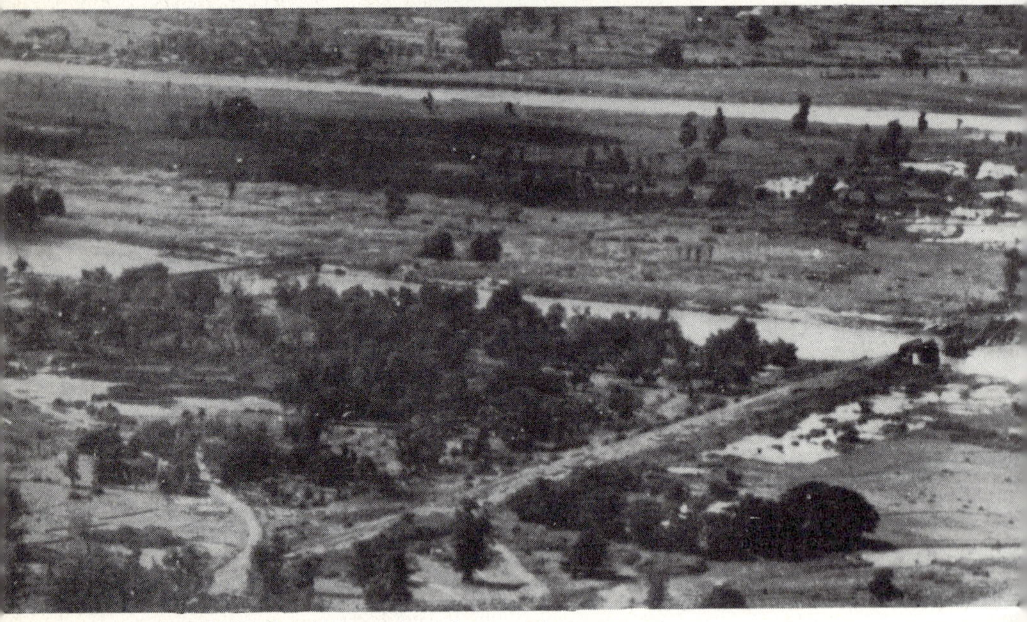

Top: Unloading the magazines after a sortie. *Theobald. Above:* The results of a low-level strike on the Burma-Siam railway. *Proctor*

Singapore like Canute against the tide, with the little Buffalo flying northwards time and time again to bring back pictures, each set more discouraging than the last. Over two years had elapsed since Cotton's first trials with a PR Spitfire, yet there were still no trained PIs in Singapore – it was only when the Buffalo and Blenheim prints started to come in that the Air Ministry decided to form a Far East Interpretation Unit at Seletar. The first PIs sailed from England in February 1942; it was too little too late – on February 15th Singapore surrendered.

If the lessons had not been learned in time to save Singapore, at least they were appreciated in India. The PIs who had set sail for Singapore were diverted to India to help in the creation of a CIU alongside the Air HQ India in March 1942. The main drawback was that India was no better endowed with PR aircraft than the Far East had been, and the next few months saw the birth of a 'gash' PRU out of the hotch-potch of aircrew and aeroplanes that drifted back with the retreat from Burma.

One such pilot was Flt Lt Freddie Proctor. He had volunteered, along with another pilot, to take a couple of PR Hurricanes from the Middle East to Singapore early in 1942. They could not make it in time so they stopped in Rangoon to cover Singapore after its collapse for the AOC Burma. Both PR Hurricanes managed some 25 sorties over occupied territory before they were written off; their pilots were then caught up in the exodus back to Calcutta, where they met two more PR pilots who had been sent out to replace Proctor and friend, whom the Air Ministry thought had been captured in Singapore.

So it came about that four aircraftless PR pilots were stranded in Calcutta waiting for some aeroplanes to fly and a leader to follow. Both problems were soon solved with the arrival in India of Flt Lt A. C. 'Fatty' Pearson. Alec Pearson was a Kenyan who, despite a knowledge of the right people and a Cranwell education, had left the RAF in the Thirties, only to rejoin again when war was declared. He flew for MacPhail for a time on 2 PRU and was then chosen to go out to India to organise a new PRU. The story goes that he boarded the aircraft in Egypt as a Flt Lt and climbed out in India as a Sqn Ldr, having decided en route that his substantive rank did not accord him enough status for the job in hand, and that if the Air Ministry did not have the sense to promote him he would have to do it himself.

In the absence of any suitable long-range aircraft in India, Pearson commandeered five B 25C Mitchells from Ceylon where they had been left after being 'appropriated' by the RAF from the Dutch air force in the East Indies. Cameras replaced the guns, some ex-Blenheim crews were put under Pearson's command, and the sum total was christened 5 PRU by the Air HQ India.

When the first PR Spitfires arrived in the Middle East in March 1942, the Air HQ India, ever grateful for any aircraft that might come their way, asked the AOC Middle East if he could send his outmoded PR Hurricanes down to Bengal. A month later the first two PR Hurricanes touched down at Dum Dum, Calcutta; each Hurricane still sported its Middle East roundels – red roundels on a dark blue background – and as these could easily be confused with the rising sun a yellow ring was hastily added.

By May, 5 PRU had become large enough to divide into two mobile flights, one of five B 25s and one of three Hurricanes. On May 13th the whole unit moved to Pandaveswar, but aircraft returning from an operational sortie always landed at Dum Dum first so that the magazines could be unloaded and taken for processing and First Phase interpretation at Barrackpore. This redeployment was not the only change – the unit name was amended to 3 PRU to follow consecutively after those in the UK and Middle East, and on May 16th Bill Wise, now a Wg Cdr, was posted out to India to take it over.

The first 3 PRU sortie left Pandaveswar on June 2nd for Toungoo, Lampang, and Chiengma in Burma. It was not an auspicious beginning – the B 25 had to turn back with engine trouble when 70 miles from the Indian coast. The first successful missions were flown by a Hurricane and a B 25 on June 6th. To compensate for its lack of range the Hurricane Flight had to operate from Argatala near the front line. Even so their time over the target was often limited – one Hurricane did four runs over Magure, the standard task area of the time, and then had insufficient fuel to make it back to Dum Dum to unload its magazines. The pilot crash-landed at Kancharpara but the films were recovered undamaged from the wreck.

As the weeks went by, 3 PRU began to photograph more and more of Burma. Additional Hurricanes from the Middle East moved in to operate from forward airfields such as Chittagong and Akyab so that Mandalay, Schwebo, and Maymyo could be photographed. The faithful old B 25s, with their cold and miserable cockpits, flogged along at 16,000 feet to cover the docks at Rangoon or the Andaman Islands anchorages to see if the Japanese Navy was contemplating any raids into the Indian Ocean. Unfortunately the Mitchells were limited in ceiling, and by the end of July they had all been temporarily put out of action by Japanese fighters or AA fire. This left only the Hurricanes, which meant that at a time when India was desperately short of intelligence on Japanese preparations, apart from information brought back by flying boats, India Command was limited to PR on enemy activities within a 200 mile radius of Chittagong. The situation had deteriorated still further by September, and it was feared that the Japanese could launch an attack against Ceylon or NE India without the British being any the wiser until it was too late. The AOC-in-C India Command was moved to make a personal appeal to the VCAS for "even two PR aircraft with an adequate supply of spares, which would be worth their weight in gold". Another plea was sent to the Middle East for a couple of PR Spitfires, now in reasonable supply at Heliopolis, because India's Hurricanes "were insufficient for the operations planned after the end of the monsoon period". The AOC-in-C Middle East was asked to send four PR Spitfires to Dum Dum in September followed by two more the following month; he split the difference and the first two Spitfires were delivered to 3 PRU in October.

CHAPTER EIGHT

Reorganisation and Marking Time

An Independent Air Force formed with all the resources a nation has at its disposal for its aerial forces, made up of a mass of battleplanes and an aliquot part of reconnaissance planes, acting decisively and exclusively on the offensive, will soon wrest command of the air from an enemy air force constituted, organised, and performing in a different way. General Guilio Douhet – 1921.

By the end of 1942, the improved efficiency of the Luftwaffe aerial defence system, brought about largely by the growing chain of early-warning radars and the new FW 190A and Me 109G fighters, had eroded much of the superiority previously enjoyed by the Spitfire PR IV. PRU losses rose, compounded by the increasing number of 'first tour' pilots reaching the squadrons, and the call went out from Benson for an improved PR version of the Spitfire. A PR variant of the Spitfire IX fighter, designated the PR XI, was put forward as the answer, but it would not be ready until September 1943 because each PR aircraft took a third more man-hours to build than its fighter counterpart because of its special wings. In the meantime Benson cleaned up and fitted cameras to some Mk IX fighters and the first of these PR IXs was flown by 541 Sqn on November 30th, 1942.

Many people considered the delay in receiving the PR XI to be unacceptable, however, and at the beginning of 1943 the Deputy Director of Photography at the Air Ministry suggested that all PR squadrons be equipped with PR Mosquitos instead. This solution would prevent encroachment on fighter production and it would enable the PR squadrons to receive an aircraft more than capable of holding its own against the Luftwaffe earlier than they had expected. VCAS agreed that 90% of all PR work could be done by the Mosquito, and he therefore recommended that only enough Spitfire PR XIs be built to cope with the remaining 10% of tasks for which the Mosquito was either unsuitable or uneconomical.

The record of the PR Mosquito strongly endorsed this argument. Both Mosquito PR IVs and PR VIIIs were arriving at Benson early in 1943; the latter was a PR IV with two-stage supercharged Merlin 61s, and although it could only reach 38,000 feet its performance was not inconsiderable. When Wg Cdr Mike Young, then CO of 540 Sqn, became the first Mosquito pilot to photograph Berlin, on March 8th, he left an Me 109G and an Fw 190 A comfortably behind by opening up to 410 mph at 26,000 feet.

An even more powerful variant arrived at Benson on May 29th in the shape of the Mosquito PR IX. Its ceiling was no higher than that of the PR VIII, but extra tankage allowed a range of 2,450 miles and its Merlin 72s gave a performance second to none. In the winter of 1943, a PR IX of 544 Sqn proved this by taking on the fighters of 11 Group in a trial. The Mosquito approached the Thames estuary at 34,000 feet from just west of the Scheldt, aiming for Southampton. The controllers of 11 Group employed their standard procedure for intercepting high altitude aircraft and they vectored a fighter section of Spitfire VIIs to a position just below the contrail layer and directly under the intruder. The fighters then entered a battle climb to intercept. Up above in the Mosquito, both pilot and navigator watched the Spitfires as they began to trail 7,000 feet below. There would have been plenty of time to take avoiding action but it was not necessary – the Spitfires of 124 Sqn just could not close up on the Mosquito and they eventually gave up the unequal struggle and went home in disgust. A few days later, a crew from 544 Sqn proved the point in anger when their Mosquito PR IX left no fewer than nine Fw 190s behind over Europe.

Despite the attraction of replacing Spitfires with Mosquitos, the C-in-C Coastal Command, Air Marshal Slessor, echoed the views of the PRU in March 1943 when he argued most strongly against it. In his opinion the PR Spitfire enjoyed three advantages over its twin-engined counterpart:

"(i) The quicker rate of climb of the Spitfire gives shorter warning of approach to the enemy RDF systems, thus reducing the risk of interception on short range tasks.

(ii) The greater manoeuvrability and smaller size of the Spitfire makes evasion of enemy fighters at high altitude easier, and decreases its vulnerability to AA fire at low altitudes.

(iii) The small size and comparative quietness of the Spitfire increases the chances of passing undetected through the enemy RDF network, sound location, and visual reporting system."

The Spitfire, continued the C-in-C, was a much more economical aircraft over short ranges than the Mosquito, and there would always be a need for a single-engined PR aircraft for low-level work. If anything the production of Spitfire XIs should be increased rather than reduced because there were nothing like enough Mosquitos in the UK to cope with the growing number of reconnaissance commitments. He concluded by proposing that two squadrons of PR Spitfires and two of PR Mosquitos should be the order of the day.

The VCAS was so impressed by these arguments that he ordered production of the Spitfire PR XI to be given still greater priority, even at the expense of the fighter force. It was a wise move – although the range of the PR Mosquito exceeded that of the Spitfire PR XI by 800 miles, the performance of the latter was eventually found to be superior. With its top speed of 422 mph at 27,500 feet, the Spitfire PR XI needed to fear nothing with wings, especially as it had a ceiling of 44,000 feet. The last characteristic was particularly useful over Berlin, where Luftwaffe interceptors were being encountered up to 42,000 feet. Out of the 72 sorties flown by Spitfire PR XIs of 541 Sqn in November 1943, 30 were made above 36,000 feet. High altitude flying had its drawbacks though, one of which was canopy icing. Icing on the outside of the perspex became pronounced during skidding turns to the right when vapour trails from the air compressor cooling duct on the starboard side of the engine were swept onto the cockpit hood. Canopy icing, however, was soon dispersed in level flight. Internal icing was more of a problem. Long journeys at high altitude necessitated low RPM for fuel economy, but this often meant that the engine was running sufficiently coolly to allow one radiator to be cut out by a thermostat. As this thermostat was fitted to the starboard radiator, which was the source of warm air for the cabin heating, the result could be pretty chilling. An unknown genius and patron saint of freezing pilots had the thermostat transferred to the port radiator so that it would cut out first.

The superiority of the Spitfire PR XI soon relegated the Spitfire PR IV to the advanced training role, and the Air Staff accepted the Coastal Command proposal that the PRU should be equipped with equal numbers of Spitfires and Mosquitos. The establishment was altered in October to comprise two Spitfire squadrons – 541 and 542 – and two Mosquito squadrons – 540 and 544 – with 20 aircraft apiece.[1] The limitations of each type were compensated for by the strengths of the other, and the PRUs of the RAF ended up with a pair of thoroughbreds that could take on all comers.

A number of camera improvements were also incorporated into the new types entering service. Camera bays were now specially designed compartments with mud flaps and oil traps to prevent fouling of the lenses and camera flats,[2] rather than spaces in the structure into which a camera could be squeezed. Camera heating, fed by hot air from the cooling system, worked much more efficiently in the separate compartment.

The most important advance, as far as the PIs were concerned, was the capability to carry a split-pair of cameras with telephoto lenses. The F 52 had been introduced in January 1942, and this scaled-up version of the F 24 not only had provision for a 500 exposure magazine (double that of the F8 Mk II), but it could also carry lenses up to 36 in in focal length, producing a scale of 1:8000 at 24,000 feet or clear enough to show the black crosses on the wings of the *Prinz Eugen's* seaplane. It was only possible to fit one of these lenses into the confined fuselages of the aircraft of the time, but with the Spitfire PR XI and the Mosquito IX onwards split-pair fits became practicable. The amount of large scale cover from each sortie using these cameras, with their contact prints of 7 in × 8½ in and 500 exposure magazines, or the equivalent of 1,000 rolls of amateur film, increased tremendously, thereby reducing the number of missions or runs necessary to complete a task. The introduction of the split-pair of telephoto lenses, though not very dramatic, ranked as one of the most important technical achievements in PR during the war.

Camera fits varied depending on the nature of the sortie – for low-level work, for example, a forward-facing F 24 with an 8 in lens would be fitted into

[1] 543 Sqn was disbanded on October 18th as it was now surplus to requirements; A Flight was divided between 541 and 542 Sqns, and B Flight became No 309 Ferry Training and Aircraft Dispatch Unit to train all pilots destined to fly their aircraft to overseas PRUs.

[2] Optically flat glass panels in the outer skin of the aircraft.

each wing. However the standard Spitfire fit was a pair of F 52s with 36 in lenses, mounted in tandem to allow for a 60% overlap, and an 8 in or 14 in oblique camera. These were operated by a small Type 35 control box fitted above the instrument panel, and once a pilot had calculated his TI from the height and speed, he had only to switch on the individual cameras and 500 exposures would be made at regular intervals.

The larger Mosquito, on the other hand, could carry five cameras, usually separated into a split-pair of 36 in cameras in the bomb-bay, another pair of F 24 14 in cameras behind the pilot, and an oblique F 24 8 in or 14 in also in the bomb-bay. The latter was operated by the pilot but the rest were 'lined up' by the observer through the bomb-sight in the nose.

1943 saw the continuation of the game of hide and seek with the German Navy. 540 Sqn's first mission on October 21st, 1942 had been to photograph the *Tirpitz* and *Scheer* in Trondheim, and from then onwards the PR Mosquitos operated from Scotland over thousands of miles of coastline from Narvik to Gdynia in the search for warships. By the end of January 1943 the *Tirpitz* was alone in the Lo Fiord at Trondheim; the *Koln* had moved down from the Alten Fiord to Kiel by February 19th, while the *Scheer* was seen to have sailed south for a refit to Wilhelmshaven on January 25th, to be photographed there in company with the *Hipper* on February 20th. For the first time since the Channel Dash, a large proportion of the German Fleet was again within striking distance of Bomber Command. Four night raids by the RAF and one in daylight by the USAAF on Wilhelmshaven were not a great success; PR on February 27th showed no serious damage to either the *Hipper* or *Scheer*. By March 29th, neither vessel was to be seen on prints of the port.

The *Scharnhorst* had been spotted on sea trials near Gdynia in December, and, although she was photographed by Flt Sgt J. D. Mair on January 25th in company with the *Prinz Eugen* on a westerly course through the Skaggerak, she was found back in Gdynia sixteen days later. PR over the Baltic on March 8th showed her to be no longer there, and a routine trip by Flt Lt Lenton to Trondheim five days later showed the *Tirpitz*'s berth to be empty also. The reconnaissance picture had altered completely in six weeks; – whereas every major German vessel had been accounted for by the PRU on February 11th, by the end of March most of them had disappeared from view.

The *Tirpitz*, *Lutzow*, and *Scharnhorst* had in fact moved up towards the Alten Fiord but the Royal Navy had no confirmation of this. A 540 Sqn sortie to Narvik on March 27th revealed nothing, so a request was made to the Russians for cover of the North Cape. After several attempts the Soviet Air Force succeeded in photographing the *Scharnhorst* and three cruisers in the Alten Fiord at the end of April, where they were joined early in May by the *Tirpitz*. The Admiralty wisely decided to suspend all Russian convoys during the summer months.

Meanwhile the search went on for the rest of the German Navy. The *Scheer* was found by Plt Off W. J. White on April 22nd at Swinemünde along with the *Graf Zeppelin*, but when the port was visited on May 5th, the pocket-battleship had disappeared again. On May 3rd the *Nurnberg* was spotted moving south from Norway en route for Kiel and by June 21st she had joined the *Emden* and *Prinz Eugen* in Swinemünde. But by now the *Graf Zeppelin* had vanished. This solitary German aircraft carrier had been watched regularly over the years, especially after January 1943 when construction work on her appeared to have speeded up. She seemed to be nearing completion in the summer, and an immediate search of the eastern Baltic was ordered when she disappeared, only to be called off when she was found alongside the western bank of the Oder near Stettin by Gordon Hughes on June 26th. Although the *Graf Zeppelin* was photographed refuelling on one occasion she was never commissioned; Doenitz, now C-in-C of the German Navy, recommended that work on the aircraft carrier be discontinued. By the end of August the *Scheer* had arrived in Swinemünde but the *Nurnberg* and *Emden* had left.

All these movements, and the threat posed by the force in the Alten Fiord, led the Royal Navy to consider new ways of neutralising German warships when they were beyond bomber range. During the spring and summer of 1943 the British perfected a midget submarine for use in the restrictive fiords of Norway, and an operation employing these potent craft against the Alten Fiord force was proposed for the end of September. Complete details of the ships to be attacked and their defences was essential, and on September 3rd three PR Spitfires of 543 Sqn took off from Sumburgh for another detachment at Vaenga.

All three aircraft landed safely at about 1300 hrs, though Fg Off Kenwright, who had lost his way en-route, was so short of fuel that his engine stopped while he taxied in. The 'Operation Source' detachment, commanded by Sqn Ldr F. A. Robinson DFC, was detailed to photograph "all enemy activity, all defences, the beach contours and gradients, the surrounding topography and all enemy patrol vessels and other naval units" in the twin anchorages of the Alten Fiord, known as the Kaa and Lang Fiords. A total of 31 sorties were flown by the three pilots of 543 Sqn before October 23rd when the photo light got too poor, of which 25 were successful. The majority of the photography involved oblique cover using 14 in lenses from approximately 21,000 feet; after landing the prints were processed in an MFPS darkroom before being flown to Medmenham in a Catalina flying boat.

The photographs illustrated the dramatic sequence of events over several weeks. On September 7th, only the *Lutzow* and the tanker *Altmark* were visible in the fiords; the *Tirpitz*, *Scharnhorst*, and five destroyers were in the process of bombarding the settlement and meteorological station on Spitzbergen, from which they returned three days later, the *Tirpitz* and the *Scharnhorst* anchoring in the Kaa Fiord and the *Lutzow* in the Lang.

Eight successful sorties were flown over the following days to provide last minute data for the midget submarine raid, due to take place in the early hours of September 22nd. A final run had been authorised for the 21st but bad weather prevented any photography. This was unfortunate, for the scene below the clouds had altered considerably; the *Lutzow* had already sailed for new waters, and the captain of the *Scharnhorst*, disgusted with the showing that his gun crews had put up on the Spitzbergen raid, had decided to leave the Kaa Fiord for high and low level gunnery practice. Thus, although three out of the six X-craft submarines managed to evade the boom defences, they could attack only the *Tirpitz*. The naval commander in charge of the operation recorded that the information on the fiord defences revealed by PR was 'invaluable' to the limited success achieved. The battleship was temporarily crippled but the *Scharnhorst* survived; her captain learned of the raid as he returned to the head of the Kaa Fiord on 22nd and he was ordered to seek sanctuary in the Lang Fiord where the battle-cruiser was photographed the following day.

It was hard to tell from the prints how much damage had been caused to the *Tirpitz*, but by September 28th the oil slick surrounding her stretched out into the Alten Fiord. Two vessels came alongside to supply power on 29th and it soon became evident that the battleship would be out of action for the rest of the year. As the Arctic darkness closed over the *Tirpitz* and *Scharnhorst*, now left alone in their respective berths, the detachment packed up and handed their equipment and aircraft over to the Russians once more. Sqn Ldr Robinson received the "Order of the Patriotic War, 1st Class" from a grateful ally, and the exiles returned home on 1st November only to find that their Squadron had ceased to exist.

The *Lutzow* was found off Tappeluftnes on September 23rd, and five days later she left northern Norway for good. Reports filtered in that she was heading for the Baltic but nothing definite was discovered until Flt Lt Lenton covered the Baltic on October 7th. Reggie Lenton was one of the few men to be awarded the Military Cross while serving in the RAF. During his time on Beaufighters in the Mediterranean he had force-landed in German occupied Crete, where he joined up with the partisans and fought with them in the hills. After a few hair-raising months he managed to steal a fishing boat and sail himself to Egypt, where he was awarded the MC. On his return to the UK he joined 540 Sqn, and now on October 7th, 1943 he was photographing the German ports of the Baltic. In a very productive 5 hours and 35 minutes, he and his observer, Plt Off Haney, managed to plot the positions of the *Lutzow, Scheer, Prinz Eugen, Nurnberg, Leipzig, Emden, Gneisenau,* and *Schlesien*.

There they all stayed until the end of the year. The Russians took over responsibility for watching the Alten Fiord and 540 Sqn covered the remaining anchorages, but there was nothing dramatic to report. Russian convoys were resumed again in November and the Admiralty hoped that the two planned for December would lure the *Scharnhorst* out of hiding. The bait was swallowed, and shortly after a routine Russian reconnaissance on Christmas Eve the great battle-cruiser left the Lang Fiord with three destroyers in attendance to attack the second convoy. In the early hours of Boxing Day she was engaged by a British force led by the *Duke of York* and sunk in the twilight of the same day. The PRU had lost one of its longest serving and most regular customers.

While A Flight of 540 Sqn was preoccupied with the German Navy and far off northerly coastlines, B Flt down at Benson was primarily concerned with long-range work over central and southern Europe. Czechoslovakia, Austria, and Italy were all in a day's work, and the Squadron began to use forward refuelling bases to extend their range as more and more Axis territory fell into Allied hands around the Mediterranean. On August 20th, Plt Off W. J. White photographed construction work on the German-Polish border – after being airborne for 8½ hours he refuelled at Algiers and returned to Benson the next day. Hungary and Roumania came within range of the 'all-seeing eye' once Sicily became available to the PRU.

Detachments to the Mediterranean were great fun, with the CO, Wg Cdr the Lord Malcolm Douglas-Hamilton, leading the evening sing-songs on his 'squeeze-box' and Fg Off Alex Paus fleecing the 'Yarpies' at crap with his own dice. But the real reason for venturing south was to cover southern Germany and northern Italy on the way out, central Europe and Jugoslavia from Tunis or Malta, and the south of France on the way back via Gibraltar. Fg Off Hugo and his observer, Fg Off Rose, undertook one of these lengthy missions between September 17th and 21st. They left Benson at 1050 hrs and flew over 10/10th cloud from the English coast down to Basle. They then followed the Danube to Linz and Vienna, "with apologies to Strauss, but the Danube is not blue (at least not from height). Our photographic runs over Vienna were brightened by the formation of heavy vapour trails, but since there are many 'bowed heads' in Europe today, we sought to fly unnoticed."

The Mosquito turned south from the Austrian capital, across the Adriatic to coast in at Foggia at 1420 hrs. "The country below appeared barren, sandy and mountainous, and under the prevailing wartime circumstances going on 'way down', à tout à fait unfriendly." They left the mainland just south of Salerno, photographed the landing craft on the beaches, and then flew on to Sicily to land at Bo Rizzo just south of Trapani.

After a night with the small RAF community – "how's the Old Country getting on – beer's pretty weak I hear" – it was off to Malta for minor repairs. At first photo-light on the 19th, Hugo and Rose took off again, climbing NE past Catania and over the Bay of Taranto and Brindisi to Jugoslavia. Belgrade was photographed at 1215 hrs, followed by some small targets of interest nestling in the mountains to the south. The cameras were left on over Albania and then it was back to Malta to land at 1445 hrs. That evening "the chatter was gay, the liquid was Bitter" followed by an early take-off the next morning for Tunis. They crossed Pantelleria, turned over Tunis, and followed the coast round to Oran before heading for Gibraltar. "Gibraltar reminds me of another Croydon as the airfield is crammed with transit aircraft continually taking off and landing . . . At night we drank sherry (cheap and good) and sat on the Mess veranda looking across the frontier at the lights of La Linea." Next day it was back to Benson where it was pouring with rain.

The poor old Spitfire pilots rarely saw this side of life; for them it was the long round of intelligence gathering over western Europe and following the increasing number of bomber raids flown by the RAF and the US Eighth Air Force. With the introduction of the Pathfinder force, and navigation and bombing aids like Oboe and H2S to point the way, Bomber Command embarked on the Battle of the Ruhr. The Ruhr was the acid test for any bomber force, protected as it was by industrial haze and man-made defences, and on March 7th and 8th 1943 Bomber Command staked the reputation of its new bombing techniques on Essen, hitherto immune from large-scale damage. It was not so this time; the prints reaching Medmenham from three daylight PR missions showed that 'destruction was exceptionally severe and widespread' throughout the whole town. The best news of all was that the central aiming point – the town centre – had been virtually destroyed. 160 acres had been 'laid waste' and the CIU estimated that three-quarters of the buildings in another 450 acres had been demolished or gutted by fire. Krupps finally experienced the effects that their armaments had on others, for the pictures showed that thirteen main buildings in the Konzern and 53 of its separate shops had been destroyed or damaged in some way.

A raid on Barmen-Wuppertal two months later devastated over 90% of the town's built-up area; it was estimated from the Spitfire photographs that 34,000 'housing units' had been made uninhabitable and that 118,000 people were now homeless. The main railway station, two power stations, two gasworks, and a water works were seriously affected, as well as five out of the six most important factories and 108 other industrial concerns. The most heartening thing of all for High Wycombe was that most of this damage occurred within one mile of the aiming point.

Bomber Command went on to prove that range was no barrier to their newfound effectiveness – the evidence of the night cameras suggested that 256 out of the 304 crews who claimed to have reached Stettin on April 20th had dropped their bombs within three miles of the aiming point, and daylight PR showed that nearly all damage was concentrated around the town centre where 100 acres of closely integrated industrial establishments had been destroyed.

Thus, by November 3rd, 1943, Sir Arthur Harris was able to approach Churchill with a list of nineteen German towns which he claimed had been 'virtually destroyed', another nineteen towns described as 'seriously damaged', and a further nine that were 'damaged'. All these claims, explained the C-in-C, were based upon 'vertical' photographic reconnaissance. "We claim," he said, "only what can be seen in the photographs. What actually occurs is much more than can be seen in any photograph."

Harris made shrewd use of aerial photography in his campaign to win support for his bombing strategy. He would show distinguished visitors his three volumes of 'Blue Books', containing photographs of every German city with the extent of the latest damage painted over in blue, or guide them to peer into his stereopticon where the results of his nightly raids would stand out in vivid detail. The days when damage assessment photography had been dismissed by High Wycombe as "of little account" were past; Bomber Command had learned the unflattering lessons taught by PR in the early years of the war with the result that it could now bask in the photographic confirmation of its successes.

The most interesting PR work in support of the bomber squadrons concerned the precision raids of 1943, the most famous of which was against the Ruhr dams. Benson was first asked on January 25th, 1943 for cover of the Moehne Dam and its reservoir, followed on February 13th by another request for large-scale cover of the dam so that its dimensions could be accurately assessed and a crew-briefing model made from them. Weather thwarted both tasks until February 19th when Flt Lt R. C. Cussons successfully photographed the area.

Details of the water levels[1] and defences around the Moehne had been evaluated by April 5th, and the dam was photographed periodically after that to see if anything had changed. The PRU took great pains to cover other targets on the same flights so as not to arouse German suspicions; when Plt Off Burniat took off in his Spitfire on April 4th for example, he photographed Liege, the Soest area and the dam, a strip from Neheim to Arnsburg and back, then north to Borkum before turning south for Essen, Duisburg, and Rotterdam.

On April 5th the tasking was extended to include the Sorpe and Eder dams as well, and they were photographed along with the Moehne by Fg Off F. G. Fray on May 15th. The same pilots tended to concentrate on the dams and they became so familiar with the landscape that they were able to report back accurately on the size of the flooding and changes in the countryside after the raid on May 16th.[2]

Towards noon on the crucial day a Mosquito landed at Scampton with the final pictures of the dams fresh from processing. That evening the CO of 542 Sqn, Sqn Ldr Salwey DFC, was warned of the time of attack and told that immediate post-strike cover would be required; eight hours after the last Lancaster set course for home, Fg Off Fray was over the Sauerland in his Spitfire PR IX. His prints of the Moehne, with its breach some 180 feet – 200 feet wide, must have been the most publicised of the war, and he went on to photograph the damage to the Sorpe and the torrent of muddy water flowing down the Eder Valley. 542 Sqn mounted three sorties to the area on May 17th, by which time a million tons of water from the now practically empty Moehne reservoir had travelled 25 miles down the valley, but Bomber Command had to wait until the following day for Fg Off D. G. Scott to photograph the damage to the Eder dam for the first time. By now its waters had submerged the Unterneustadt industrial suburb of Kassel forty miles away, and the floods had reached as far as Kerdecke in the Ruhr. Within fifty miles of the Moehne and the Eder the story on the prints was the same – roads, railways, and canals washed away or damaged, factories flooded and collapsed, airfields, power-stations, water-works, and homes under water. Chaos reigned, albeit temporarily.

In July 1942 the CAS, Sir Charles Portal, decided to try to rationalise photo-reconnaissance in the RAF by creating an independent Group to be respon-

[1] The water level was assessed accurately to within one foot.

[2] As a point of interest, the first bouncing bomb to be tested successfully was dropped by Shorty Longbottom, then a test pilot at Vickers, on April 29th.

sible for all PR in the United Kingdom. The proposal floundered because of opposition from the Chief of Naval Staff, who insisted on retaining responsibility for all reconnaissance work north of 54°N, and the Chief of the Imperial General Staff, who wanted 140 Sqn to remain within Army Cooperation Command.

The idea was shelved, but in time Portal's belief that a centralised PR Group would lead to a much more efficient utilisation of resources was shown to be correct. 140 Sqn soon found itself unable to cope with the growing demand for prints in preparation for the invasion of Europe, and, despite the loan of four Spitfires and a Mosquito from Benson, General Paget had to make a personal appeal to Portal for more PR aircraft. "Requests such as yours," replied the CAS sardonically, "seem to me to support the view which I have long held that we can combine maximum efficiency and flexibility with economy only by pooling our resources and forming a Reconnaissance Group. My proposal received no support from you nor from CNS . . . I am considering raising the matter again."

The CAS was not alone in his opinion. Dr Merton of the Ministry of Supply wrote to the VCAS in 1943 complaining that "a lack of coordination in the PR organisation prevented obtaining the best results"; his minute concluded by recommending that a separate HQ be established to control both the PRU and the CIU.

As the year progressed, opposition to such an idea declined. The depleted German Navy no longer justified the Admiralty's monopoly of part of the PRU, and on June 1st, 1943 Army Cooperation Command was replaced by the 2nd Tactical Air Force (2 TAF). This included 34 PR Wing (16 and 140 PR Sqns) and two tactical PR squadrons (4 PR Sqn within 35 Reconnaissance Wing and 400 (RCAF) Sqn within 39 Reconnaissance Wing) to work alongside the Allied land forces once they invaded Europe. In the meantime these reconnaissance units worked for the D-Day planners and the Army was happy to let the RAF reorganise the rest of its PR squadrons as it thought best. On June 26th 1943, therefore, 106 PR Wing was brought into being at Benson.

The new Wing, which was given to Air Cdre John Boothman AFC,[1] controlled Benson and its squadrons, No 309 Ferry Training and Air Dispatch Unit, and 8 OTU, now at Dyce. VCAS was not willing to go so far as to include the CIU in the new organisation, but he hoped that Benson and Medmenham would continue to work closely together under the watchful eye of the Air Ministry. Henceforward 106 PR Wing at Benson and the US 7th Photo Group at Mount Farm would be responsible for all strategic PR within the European theatre, apart from that flown by 34 PR Wing which would be

[1] Boothman's personal aircraft at Benson was the Speed Spitfire. This aircraft, the 48th production model of the Mk I, had been modified in 1939 for an attempt on the World Landplane Speed Record, and after a short period of development flying this streamlined Spitfire was handed to Heston for conversion to the PR role. Its performance was not very satisfactory so it became the personal aircraft of successive COs of the PRU. Boothman flew it quite often as befitted an ex-Schneider trophy winner, and he brought back prints taken over the Normandy beaches on D-Day. The Speed Spitfire was reputedly scrapped at Benson in 1946.

controlled by the Supreme HQ Allied Expeditionary Forces (SHAEF).

The Air Ministry did not take the final step of amalgamating 106 Wing and the newly titled Allied CIU (ACIU) into 106 PR Group until May 15th, 1944. One could criticise the delay in reaching a conclusion that had seemed logical to devout PR men from Cotton onwards, but PR was always a difficult animal to control because it served so many different Service and government agencies, and their needs and views had to be considered and reconciled before drastic changes could be made. The PRU had always been a pioneer outfit, and as befitted an organisation in the forefront of aviation techniques it was always one step ahead of the RAF establishment, which in turn was continually trying to perfect a system of control for an organisation it did not quite understand.

No format could please everyone and the new 106 Group, which now received its taskings from the recently-established Joint Photographic Reconnaissance Committee (JPRC), was no exception. The JPRC had been set up in May 1944, with representatives from all three Services and the USAAF, to examine all PR requests dispassionately and to allocate priorities to the AOC 106 Group for implementation. The Group stayed in Coastal Command, but for administrative purposes only, an arrangement which irked their C-in-C. He pointed out that the existence of an operational Group within a Command, which had no authority to direct that Group, was unsatisfactory. Either the PR Group should be given its full independence, stated the C-in-C, or the Command to which it was given – and it need not be Coastal Command if there was another formation more suitable – should be allowed to have more responsibility over it.

VCAS pondered over the matter for some time, and then replied that 106 PR Group had such a specialised role that it did not fit into any Command, but it would "suffer least" if it stayed within the established framework of Coastal Command. Here was the crux of the matter. There would never be an optimum solution to the question of control as long as 106 PR Group was too small or too important to be left to its own devices, so the criterion would have to be not what was best, but which arrangement would cause least dissatisfaction among the many agencies concerned with PR. It was a negative approach but not necessarily a bad one. The control system that evolved during the Second World War was based on political and operational expediency, and the growth of the PRU was so rapid that little more could have been done without offending an even greater number of people.

However the debate over who was to control the very effective PR organisation that had developed within the RAF was nothing compared with the German problem of trying to restructure a massive system that was no longer suitable for the work it was being asked to do. The Luftwaffe was finding it increasingly difficult to provide enough PR by 1942, mainly because the Germans were saddled with a number of tactical air forces in a strategically defensive campaign. On the interpretation side, for example, although the Stabia Gens was renamed the Hauptbildabteilung (Habia) in 1942, no attempt was made to turn it into a Luftwaffe equivalent of the

CIU. Most interpretation continued to be carried out at Fliegerkorps or Staffel level, with the result that German intelligence lacked the assistance of a coordinated Third Phase organisation. There was no organisation like A Section at Medmenham to correlate and beome expert in all PR of interest to the German Navy; there was no day to day coordination of information obtained by Aufkl. Gr/113 over British ports with that brought back for the Fliegerkorps Atlantik, or with that provided by Aufkl. Gr/122 over Alexandria. The RAF overseas CIUs worked closely with Medmenham to build up a clear picture of the war situation in a particular field; the decentralised Luftwaffe photo-sections, on the other hand, worked in isolation. Since every Fliegerkorps thought its own photographic empire was working very efficiently there was no incentive to change. Such moves as there were to improve cooperation, like the creation of the Stabsbildabteilung-Luftwaffe Kommando Ost at Smolensk to sift through all prints taken over the Russian front, were only made in response to the needs of the army on the ground. If only the Luftwaffe had been allowed to develop its own independent strategy its PR system might well have progressed along British lines, but while it continued to play second fiddle to the land war its reconnaissance resources remained geared to the Army rather than to other intelligence requirements such as naval or economic warfare. Consequently the Third Phase potential of the centralised Habia was never appreciated, and it became nothing more than a vast library of training and reference material.

The standard of German photo-interpretation also deteriorated as the war progressed. In January 1943 all fit personnel were combed-out to serve in the Luftwaffe's Infantry Division, removing experienced brains as well as muscle. Harsh punishments began to be introduced for serious misinterpretations – one Unteroffizier who incorrectly identified some Russian tanks as motor vehicles found himself in prison for six months. Far from improving standards such draconian measures only made PIs more cautious and noncommittal in their reports.

Another problem was the excessive decentralisation of the PR Staffeln themselves, geared as they were to separate Luftflotten and Armies. France was a case in point. Luftflotte 3 controlled the airspace from the Low Countries to the Franco-Spanish border, while Aufkl. Gr/123 was nominally responsible for all reconnaissance activities within that area. This Gruppe comprised eight Fernaufklärungsstaffeln based between the Netherlands and Brittany, but for shipping reconnaissance Fliegerfuehrer Atlantik had his own independent Fernaufklärungsgruppe 5 at Mont de Marsan, and when the Luftwaffe High Command (OKL) needed special cover of Allied invasion plans they had to send a special detachment of Rowehl's Aufkl. Gr. Ob.d.L. to France.[1]

It is worth examing why the Luftwaffe continued to persevere with a decentralised framework at a time when they should have been co-ordinating their reconnaissance resources to counter the growing Allied offensive threat. The

[1] In January 1943 the CIU estimated that the Ob.d.L. had two detachments in Norway, two in France, one in the Central Mediterranean, another in Denmark, and five on the Russian Front.

main obstacle to change was the lack of effective leadership from the top, compounded by the fact that no-one was allowed to admit that there was a problem because everyone from Hitler downwards had to adhere to the official belief that the Reich was still on the offensive. It is true that an Air Photography Department was set up in the Air Inspectorate of Reconnaissance in 1942 to coordinate photo-intelligence throughout the Luftwaffe, but it was staffed largely by staff officers with neither the technical appreciation nor the power to implement sweeping changes or initiate dramatic technological advances. Although a 75 cm variant of the Rheinbildner was produced in greater numbers to cope with higher altitude operations, the Air Photography Department failed to initiate any major new camera research after 1942,[1] and it soon stagnated into a registry for requests and demands.

Even if there had been a separate Inspectorate of PR instead of just a minor Department it is doubtful if any drastic improvements would have come about. The stylised Inspectorate structure waited on Goering who vacillated and prevaricated to such an extent that there was no constant directing force at the top of the Luftwaffe. Within an inflexible hierarchy like this, the scope for rational re-appraisal based on military rather than political considerations was virtually non-existent.

So the Luftwaffe carried on with an increasingly unsuitable PR organisation and aircraft that were now incapable of flying over a growing number of areas without suffering severe losses. Machines such as the Ju 88 were still holding their own over the Russian Front, but the converted medium bomber had had its day as a PR aircraft in airspace where the Luftwaffe did not enjoy massive air superiority. Improvements were made to the old faithful Ju 86 – several Ju 86P-2s were stripped of their armament and pressurised before being delivered to Kastélli in Crete in May 1942. They could cruise-climb up to 45,000 feet, and for several months these Ju 86s operated with impunity over Egypt until a specially cleaned-up Spitfire V fighter was sent up after one of them on August 24th. The interception took place at 37,000 feet just north of Cairo, and after a long chase the starboard engine of the Ju 86 was shot away at 42,000 feet and the aircraft crashed into the sea. The Luftwaffe responded in a very negative way and hastily fitted 'respect armament': lacking superior speed and manoeuvrability the only thing the modified Ju 86P had in its favour was ceiling, and even this was reduced once its all up weight was increased. By August 1943 the remnants of the only Fernaufklärungsstaffel in the eastern Mediterranean were withdrawn from Crete to the safer skies of Greece.

The solution to the problem of bringing back the prints should have been obvious. The Luftwaffe had captured a fairly intact PR Spitfire in 1941 and they fully appreciated what the PRU was achieving with a relatively limited

[1] In fact the Germans were very patronising towards Allied cameras. A writer in the February 1942 edition of the magazine 'Luftwissen' expressed a sense of regret at the backwardness of non-German aerial cameras and he concluded that Germany was supreme in the fields of optics and instrument manufacture for historical and racial reasons.

number of these aircraft despite the concentrated defences of the Reich. Why then did it take the Luftwaffe so long to produce an equivalent of the Aufklärungsspitfire? The answers are many and various. For a start, few would admit that there was a need for such an aircraft. Despite their losses the PR Staffeln of the Luftwaffe still managed to expose an average of 40,000 metres of film per month in 1943, and it would have been hard to convince the High Command that the Aufklärungsgruppen lacked the means to bring back the prints. The fact that only a small proportion of this monthly film total had been taken over important targets in the British Isles was not readily appreciated.

Neither was there anyone with Cotton's stature or foresight in the right place at the right time. The General der Aufklärungsflieger was summed up very unflatteringly after the war:

"Although he was possessed of considerable energy, and in some cases clear vision . . . he had neither the technical ability nor the level of intelligence required of a general officer in his position. His genius for top heavy organisation, together with his preoccupation with the publication of multi-coloured diagrams and his lack of comprehension of technical matters certainly proved detrimental to the efficiency of the organisation which he commanded."

The Luftwaffe also lacked the advantage of having powerful agencies at their elbow complaining bitterly about their inadequacies and demanding change. Cotton's achievements owed much to the pressures applied on the Air Staff by the Royal Navy, in the persons of Churchill and the Chief of Naval Staff, to abandon the Blenheim IV concept and give more support to Heston. In Germany the Navy could exert no influence over Goering, and as the Army was happy with the tactical support it received there was no-one else in a sufficiently strong position to bring unpalatable truths to the notice of the Luftwaffe hierarchy.

Then, at a more mundane level, the Luftwaffe was frustrated by the fact that it did not possess a suitable camera for use in small aircraft[1] The Rheinbildner, designed for survey work in support of the army, was a great heavy instrument, and the only aircraft that could accommodate two of them with 75cm lenses was the Ju 86. The Do 17, Ju 88, and Me 110 could only carry one each, and even this fit was beyond the capability of early versions of the Me 109 and Fw 190. Add to this the pronouncement by the Test Centre at Rechlin that long focal length cameras could never be fitted into the Me 109 (shades of Cotton and Farnborough) and one can see why little was done. It was only at the insistence of the operational Staffeln that cameras were eventually fitted into the Me 109. Even then a lot of shibboleths about gunners, armour, and defensive armament would have to be abandoned before a small cleaned-up PR aircraft could enter service with the Luftwaffe in any numbers. In the meantime it was much easier to ascribe the failure to bring back prints from England to the cowardice or incompetence of the crews involved rather than

[1] A British expert wrote in 1944 that, "a first glance at the German cameras suggests that they would only be really successfully installed, operated, and maintained by a cross between an acrobat and a college professor."

to the unsuitability of their aircraft.

So the Luftwaffe continued to tinker and experiment with totally unsuitable machines in a vain attempt to turn sows' ears into silk purses. The Ju 88 was fitted with extra fuel tanks to become the Ju 88H, its speed was boosted to produce the Ju 88T and it was even stretched into the Ju 188. In emulation of the PR Mosquito, cameras were fitted into the Me 110, the Me 210, and the Me 410, but with little success. By the end of the 1943 Aufkl. Gr/123 had to resort to night photography to stand any chance of bringing back damage assessment prints after bombing raids on Britain. The Me 410s of 1(F)/121[1] at Paris/Buc clung to the raiding bomber formations for protection; it did them little good and they lost seven crews in four months compared with a total casualty rate of twelve for the four Benson squadrons during the last six months of 1943.

It is only fair to point out that German PR pilots had a lot more to contend with than their British counterparts. For a start they were up against RAF Fighter Command, an organisation blessed with higher morale, better equipment, and a much smaller area to defend than the over-stretched aerial defence system of the Reich. Whereas a PRU man felt confident in the knowledge that he was flying the best high-level reconnaissance aircraft in the world and that his chances against being intercepted were 100:1, the Luftwaffe crews of Gr/123 had been taking such a hammering for months that they were at a severe psychological disadvantage before they took off. Even when a high-level PR Me 109H was given to 3(F)/121 at Bernay they were unable to make much use of it. A pilot recorded that he had to return before he could take any photographs because of British fighter activity and yet he was far above the normal Spitfire operating heights at 40,000 feet. Unlike the PRU, a lot of Luftwaffe hearts were not in their work, and for this reason above all others the Germans were rarely able to photograph targets in daylight further than 25 miles inland from the south coast of England even though their British equivalents were operating up to 800 miles inside the Reich.

Thus, at a time when the Allies were preparing for D-Day, the Luftwaffe was incapable of bringing back anything like enough intelligence on the scale of the operation or its likely landing point. Perhaps the most damning indictment of German PR was the admission by Aufkl. Gr/123 that the only way that they could suggest of getting some daylight pictures was to use a captured Thunderbolt in Allied markings.

The main agency concerned with the development of revolutionary new PR aircraft was still Theodore Rowehl's Aufkl. Gr. Ob.d.L. However Rowehl was now a Colonel and the Aufklärungsgruppe formed only part of his Versuchsverband Ob.d.L. (Commander-in-Chief's Experimental Formation).

[1] Part of the reconnaissance resources controlled by the Aufkl. Gr/123 HQ at Buc included detachments of Gruppen 121 and 122. Staffeln moved around as required – the dispositions of Aufkl. Gr/122 for example in January 1943, although its HQ was in Italy, were as follows:

1(F)/122 – Central Mediterranean	4(F)/122 – Russian Front
2(F)/122 – Central Mediterranean	5(F)/122 – Russian Front
3(F)/122 – Amsterdam/Schipol	

Consequently Rowehl could devote only part of his time to the development of PR aircraft because his organisation was concerned with the testing of a wide range of air force weaponry. Nevertheless the Aufkl. Gr. of the Ob.d.L. did experiment with some sophisticated PR prototypes, such as the Ar 240 which was delivered for operational evaluation in the late summer of 1941. This highly advanced aircraft was a pressurised twin-engined Kampfzerstörer (heavy fighter), capable of a top speed of 384 mph, a range of 1,242 miles with an auxiliary tank, and a service ceiling of 34,450 feet. Rowehl had the fixed forward-firing armament removed and a pair of Rb 50/30 cameras installed, and Colonel Knemeyer flew several unarmed high level sorties over Britain without once being intercepted. The PR Ar 240 appeared to have a bright reconnaissance future, so it was modified and improved still further. Eight self-sealing fuel tanks totalling 500 gallons were installed and a 132 gallon drop tank was fitted below the fuselage, together with an Rb 50/30 vertical camera in the tail of each engine nacelle, bringing the total all-up-weight to 20,843 lbs. Despite a certain reduction in performance Arado had virtually finished jigging up for production when an edict from Erhard Milch in December 1942 called a halt to the entire programme because of the aircraft's inherent lack of aerodynamic stability. A few pre-production models of the PR Ar 240 saw service with Aufkl. Gr./10 over southern Russia and with 1. Staffel of the Aufkl. Gr. Ob.d.L. but that was all.

Rowehl continued to experiment enthusiastically but it was generally with heavy bombers like the He 177 Greif rather than with proven high performance machines. The Luftwaffe always had to complicate the issue by pinning their hopes on some revolutionary machine or other, a good example being the rocket-powered DFS 228 manned glider designed to be launched from the back of a Do 217 at 33,000 feet, after which it was supposed to rocket up to 75,000 feet over enemy territory before gliding back to friendly airspace with its cameras turning. After five years of trial and effort, the DFS had built a pre-production batch of ten by the time the war ended. The DFS 228 was an ingenious concept, but it was too far ahead of its time. By aiming for the wonder machines of tomorrow in preference to the quite adequate aircraft of the day, the Luftwaffe soldiered on with yesterday's aircraft for far too long.

In the end, though, the OKL finally backed a winner. On June 15th, 1943 Flugkapitän Selle lifted a neat shoulder-wing monoplane off the runway at Rheine near Munster and the Arado 234 was born. Here at last was a high-speed aircraft designed for reconnaissance. Weight had been kept scrupulously to a minimum, even to the extent of fitting a jettisonable undercarriage,[1] so that a range of 1,340 miles could be achieved. Although its operational ceiling was only 32,810 feet, the twin Junkers Jumo DO4A turbojets were capable of a top speed of 461 mph at 19,685 feet.

Two prototypes reached 1. Staffel of the Ob.d.L. at Juvincourt near Rheims in July 1944, and each aircraft soon accumulated over a score of successful and interception free PR hours over Allied positions. On August 27th

[1] This system had obvious complications when it came to landing and a conventional retractable undercarriage was soon fitted, reducing the range somewhat.

the Staffel retreated to Chievres, then to Volkel in Holland, finally reaching Rheine on September 5th, where they were joined by 3. Staffel. There were eleven Ar 234s at Rheine by the end of the month watching the Allied advance through Europe, together with those of the recently formed Sonderkommando[1] Gölz, which operated with great success around 29,000 feet over British east coast harbours and airfields between the Thames Estuary and Yarmouth to see if there were any signs of a proposed Allied invasion of the Netherlands.

Two more special detachments – the Sd. Kdo Hecht and the Sd. Kdo Sperling – were formed in November 1944 with Ar 234s, and by the end of January the new aircraft had acquitted itself so admirably that the Luftwaffe decided to entrust it to regular units. The three Sonderkommandos were therefore disbanded and replaced by 1(F)/33 in Denmark, 1(F)/100 (who also operated PR Me 262s),[2] and 1(F)/123 both in Germany.

Following complaints from the German Army in March 1945 that the aerial reconnaissance reports it was receiving in northern Italy were totally inadequate, the Sd. Kdo Sommer was set up with three Ar 234s at Udine near Trieste. The unit enjoyed such immunity from interception over the skies of Ancona and Leghorn, and assisted the German defensive capability so drastically, that the Sonderkommando would have been bolstered to full Staffel strength had the war continued.

Unfortunately for the Luftwaffe, the Ar 234 and the PR version of the Me 262 arrived too late to play any decisive part in a conflict that was already lost. Had such aircraft been available a year earlier to monitor the Allied D-Day preparations as Heston had watched over Sealion in 1940, the invasion force might well have been flung back from Normandy and the war considerably extended. By the time they did arrive on the reconnaissance scene these aircraft could only bring back confirmation of the massive superiority built-up by the Allies. The last Luftwaffe mission over the British Isles was made on April 10th, 1945 by an Ar 234 to northern Scotland from Stavanger/Sola; it was ironic that the Luftwaffe PR force could operate once more with impunity over the UK while the rest of the air force was on its knees, and it provided another example of what the Luftwaffe might have achieved given some inspired leadership from the top.

From the birth of the Luftwaffe onwards, the Germans remained convinced of the value of the aerial camera. They started off well, with 20% of their airborne forces committed to reconnaissance duties in 1939, but their error was to persevere with the strategy and techniques of 1939 long after they had ceased to be relevant. The story of PR in Luftwaffe, like that of the Luftwaffe itself, was one of a vast and very efficient organisation that grew too big too quickly, and as a consequence was unable to exploit its considerable potential because it failed to recognise and adapt to a changing war situation until it was too late.

[1] "Special detachment".

[2] Only two units had any PR Me 262s by the end of the war.

CHAPTER NINE

The Invasion Years

It is time to state that no Commander will now undertake an operation unless he has been completely equipped with air intelligence, not only with photographs and mosaics but also with models of the beaches he is to land on. VCAS – January 1943.

The photographs one brings back are submitted to stereoscopic analysis, as organisms are examined under a microscope; the interpreters of these photographs work exactly like bacteriologists. They seek on the vulnerable body of France traces of the virus which devours her. One can die from the effects of these enemy strongholds and depots and convoys which, under the lens, appear like tiny bacilli.

And then those hours of poignant meditation as one flies over France – so near and yet so far. One feels separated from her as though by centuries. All one's tender memories and associations, indeed one's very raison d'être, are to be found there, stretched out, as it were, 35,000 feet below, in the clear glint of the sun; and yet, more inaccessible than the treasures of the Pharoahs. Antoine de Saint-Exupéry.

The first move in the Allied plan to re-conquer Europe was to cross from North Africa over the island stepping-stones of the Central Mediterranean and into the 'Festung Europa' through southern Italy. In preparation for this, a North African CIU was formed on February 23rd, 1943 to coordinate all requests and taskings for the Mediterranean PRUs, which had recently been converted into PR squadrons. 2 PRU and 4 PRU[1] were replaced by 680 and 682 Sqns respectively, while B Flt of 69 Sqn on Malta became 683 Sqn. A North African PR Wing was set up in March to coordinate the forces most concerned with the crossing to Italy, comprising the North African CIU, the US 3rd Photo Group, and 682 Sqn, under the command of Elliott Roosevelt.

Henceforward the demarcation lines between the various RAF PR squadrons around the Mediterranean were to be clearly defined. The North African PR Wing covered the area to the West of 12°E including Tunisia, Sardinia, and Corsica; 683 Sqn was made responsible for the area to the East of 12°E including Pantellaria, Sicily, and Italy with the dividing line through Tripoli and Corfu; 680 Sqn looked after the Eastern Mediterranean and Greece with the exception of Corfu. Northern Italian ports such as Genoa and Spezia had to wait until supplies of aviation fuel on Malta had increased enough to allow

[1] 4 PRU moved from Gibraltar to Maison Blanche near Algiers after the successful completion of 'Torch'.

Mosquitos from Benson to 'turn-round' at Luqa.

Sardinia was originally intended to be the first stepping stone to Italy, and the US 3rd Photo Gp carried out some intensive survey work over the Sardinian coastline in January 1943 with two PR Mosquitos borrowed from the 544 Sqn detachment at Gibraltar. However Sardinia was soon abandoned in favour of Sicily, but despite repeated appeals from 544 Sqn for the return of their aircraft the US 3rd Photo Gp held on to them throughout the winter. Elliott Roosevelt let it be known that he would willingly exchange his Lockheed Lightnings for PR Mosquitos.

The North African PR Wing was then given the task of surveying the entire Sicilian coastline, assisted by Mosquitos in transit from Benson to Malta. Catania was the first choice as a landing area, but the large scale F 52 prints provided by the Benson Mosquitos soon showed it to be unsuitable because of the formidable defence-works along that stretch of coast.

To the planners of the invasion of Sicily, codenamed 'Husky', the value of these periodic Mosquito visits from Benson was considerable. Their F 52 cameras were not their only advantage – 683 Sqn fitted F 52s into some of their Spitfire PR IVs, but despite fifty flights to Sicily in February and March, 683 Sqn still asked for a Mosquito of their own to complete the survey work. The PR Mosquito was much less vulnerable to interception than the Spitfire PR IV, but requests from the Mediterranean Air Command for PR Mosquitos were always sympathetically refused on the grounds of lack of resources. It needed a blast from General Montgomery to effect a change in priorities. His Eighth Army in the desert relied heavily on survey photography by 60 SAAF Sqn to produce maps for the assault on the Axis Mareth Line. Day after day elderly Marylands and unsuitable Baltimores took off to try to photograph such crucial points as El Agheila, and time and again they were driven off by the Luftwaffe defences. Frustrated at the delay in receiving his assault maps, Montgomery sent for the CO of 60 SAAF Sqn, Owen Davies, and on discovering his problem asked what sort of aircraft he needed to ensure success. "Mosquitos," replied Davies succinctly. Two days later he received the news that the RAF had refused to release any Mosquitos to Egypt, so Davies proposed that a Flying Fortress be used in the hope that its concentrated fire power would fend off the opposition until photography was completed. However Montgomery's personal request to Eisenhower for the loan of a few B-17s was curtly refused, so 60 SAAF Sqn persevered as before, with the same negative results, until Montgomery finally erupted and dictated a signal to Churchill saying that unless his survey squadron was equipped with Mosquitos immediately he would be unable to attack the Mareth Line. Within 24 hours a signal came back saying that two Mosquito Mk IIs were on their way.

A camera was hastily fitted beneath the seat of each aircraft, and on February 4th both Mosquitos began work at Castel Benito. News of their arrival spread throughout the PR world and 683 Sqn soon asked for the loan of one aircraft to complete its 'Husky' cover. With a vision of a rampant Montgomery firmly in his mind, Owen Davies had to reply that his precious

Mosquitos were too heavily employed over the Mareth Line and Tunisia to be spared. Nevertheless 683 Sqn's problems were partially alleviated once the Air Ministry started sending out Spitfire PR IXs to the Mediterranean in March.

Between North Africa and Sicily lay a number of Italian islands, the most important of which was Pantelleria with its batteries and command posts embedded into solid rock. These would have to be neutralised, but to avoid the wasteful and time-consuming process of area bombardment it was necessary to plot the position of every emplacement so that pin-point attacks could be mounted. From the prints obtained by 682 Sqn, two models of Pantelleria were made at Medmenham, and an elaborate method was devised by the North African PIs, together with a team of geologists headed by Professor Zuckermann, to select the optimum bomb load for each target. By careful study of bomb craters on the prints, the geologists were able to calculate which type of bomb was most effective against the differing protective rock structures, and this information, together with an estimate of the number of probable direct hits from each bomb load, gave the planners a good idea of how many bombs of a certain type were necessary to neutralise a particular strong-point.

During May the Allied bomber forces averaged 19 sorties per day over Pantelleria, with such effect that the garrison was forced to surrender on June 11th. For the first time in history a heavily defended fortress had fallen to air power alone, mainly because the camera had sharpened up the blunt instrument of aerial bombardment.

With the successful completion of the Tunisian campaign on May 14th, 1943, the two Mosquitos of 60 SAAF Sqn were released by the Eighth Army to assist in the planning of 'Husky'. They were sorely needed because 683 Sqn had still to maintain its regular watch over the Italian Navy, and, after further appeals by Generals Arnold and Eisenhower, four Mosquito PR IXs were loaned to Malta at the end of June for a six-week detachment. Daily their telephoto lenses surveyed the terrain of Sicily while the PR Spitfires swept in below to take low-level obliques over the landing beaches. A courier service was introduced between Luqa and Algiers so that First and Second Phase cover from Malta could be in the hands of the 'Husky' planners in North Africa as soon as possible. By July 9th, when the invasion started, all HQ ships were in possession of the latest pictures of the beachheads, and the Allied staffs enjoyed complete knowledge of all Axis defensive dispositions and reserves. General Patton considered the pre-assault PR as "essential to the success of the operation", and after the landings Montgomery signalled that "the success of the campaign was largely due to the magnificent air photography with which I was provided".

The military centre of gravity in the Mediterranean was now moving rapidly from North Africa in general and 680 Sqn in particular. At the end of the Tunisian campaign 680 Sqn had recalled its forward detachment from the desert and the two halves rejoined at Landing Ground 219, a sandy strip just south of the Cairo-Suez railway 5½ miles NE of Heliopolis. By now the squadron had taken on a distinctly international flavour. The CO, Wg Cdr Roger Whelan DFC, was a Canadian, and he found himself in charge of Britons, South Africans, New Zealanders, Australians, and an American called Westinghouse who damaged so many aircraft on landing when he first arrived that he became universally known as 'Stoop' (short for 'Stoopid'), a nickname that stuck long after he became one of the most daring and competent PR pilots on the Squadron. It was indicative of the Squadron's prowess that it took five months after its inception for an aircraft to return with even one bullet hole in it.

Perhaps their most spectacular exploit of this period was the long-mooted cover of Salonica. This northern region of Greece had been an unknown quantity because it lay beyond Spitfire range from Egypt, but it came within reach once the Squadron moved up to Tocra in Libya in the wake of the Eighth Army. Roger Whelan decided to take the sortie himself because of the risks involved, but on his first attempt he had to turn back through lack of fuel after evading both bad weather and Luftwaffe interception – he just managed to stay aloft long enough to force land on the metalled road that ran along the coast of Cyrenaica.

The second time he went he was again overdue and every Squadron aircraft went up to scour the Mediterranean for him, only to give up when night fell. That evening 680 Sqn received a signal saying that their CO had blacked out over Athens, recovered consciousness off the coast of Turkey, and decided to land at Nicosia. In the end it was third time lucky for Whelan and he brought back a fine set of prints of the hitherto mysterious port at the top of the Aegean.

Despite this watch on the ports and airfields of the Eastern Mediterranean, especially during the Sicilian landings, and the odd clandestine mission here and there – three pilots force-landed in Turkey during 1943 – 680 Sqn found itself increasingly on the periphery of the war. Life still had its lighter moments – when one pilot diced the Peloponnese he found no troop movements but he was able to report that the "natives are friendly especially the one in the red silk dress" and he had the low-level obliques to prove it. Nevertheless by the autumn of 1943 the most important PR work around the Mediterranean was to be found in Italy, and there was little left for 680 Sqn apart from clearing up operations in the desert and some long-range mapping work.

By the end of August, 60 SAAF Sqn and the US Combat Mapping Squadrons had transposed virtually the whole of the Italian peninsula on to small scale vertical photographs, while 682 and 683 Sqns attempted to provide larger pictures of all important airfields, harbours, lines of communication, and landing beaches within range. For some time before this the Allied bomber forces had been preparing the way for the invasion by softening up ports and transportation bottle-necks in southern Italy, culminating on July 19th with the first air raid on Rome. Apart from some military targets on the outskirts of the city, the main target in the raid was the great Lorenzo marshalling yard, surrounded by a wealth of historical buildings which on no account had to be destroyed by a bomber force reputedly fighting for the survival of civilised society. So the planning had to be meticulous. The results of three successive PR flights were combined to form a target mosaic of the city so that four points – the Vatican and three famous churches – could be clearly annotated 'MUST ON NO ACCOUNT BE DAMAGED'. The bomber crews were scrupulously briefed and every man was given a copy of the mosaic; even so the damage assessment prints were awaited with some trepidation. The boss of 682 Sqn, Sqn Ldr J. Morgan, decided to fly this precision sortie himself. He left two aircraft on standby at La Marsa in case he did not return, but he brought back an excellent set of prints to show that every military target had been attacked successfully and that the only damage in the city was sustained around the Lorenzo marshalling yards.

Once the Allies invaded Italy on September 3rd even La Marsa and Malta got left behind. A detachment of 682 Sqn moved across the Mediterranean to Foggia where they took over Malta's reconnaissance commitments in southern Italy. The 682 Sqn presence in Italy acted as the long-range component of 285 Reconnaissance Wing, formed originally to coordinate reconnaissance in the western desert, and now tasked with supplying aerial intelligence for the Eighth Army in Italy.

683 Sqn remained on Malta for a time watching the eastern Adriatic, Albania, and Jugoslavia, under the command of Adrian Warburton, now a Wing Commander with a DSO. He had converted on to a PR Spitfire when the Luftwaffe finally destroyed his beloved Beaufighter on the ground, but despite his elevated status he continued to operate as before. As the Allies were entering Tunis in May 1943 he was shot down over the sea and just managed to glide into Bône. After landing safely he was kept under lock and key for two days under suspicion of being a German spy, but he managed to contact the local Governor – a French admiral – who got rid of his embarrassing guest by flying Warby to Gibraltar in his personal plane. On the Rock he 'borrowed' a Spitfire and flew back to Bizerte – almost over the very spot where he had been shot down he destroyed one Ju 88 and damaged another before arriving 'back from the dead' on Malta after being missing for four days.

The Americans loved Warburton from the first moment they met him. When Elliott Roosevelt's Lightnings landed at Malta to help with the mapping of Sicily they were greeted by the amazing sight of a Wing Commander dressed in old grey flannels and a battledress tunic, topped by a forage cap haphazardly shoved onto a mop of fair hair. His dash and bravado appealed to the USAAF. One day he had to crash-land one of their Lightnings just after taking-off from La Marsa – he leapt clear of the burning wreckage, jumped into another Lightning, and was airborne again within twenty minutes, leaving an astonished American audience behind him. When he began to follow the big USAAF daylight bombing raids he was soon awarded the American DFC to add to his DSO and bar, and DFC and two bars.

There is a classic story of the time Warburton returned to Luqa after being shot out of the sky by the American Fleet during the Sicilian landings. As he stepped out of what remained of his Spitfire, passing over the foot diameter hole in the wing and the tattered aileron hanging limply down, he walked up to a mechanic staring in wonder at the pepperpot of a fuselage and said laconically as he took off his helmet, "My R/T is u/s."

683 Sqn was his first and only command, and it marked the climax of his brilliant and meteoric career. Warby was an inspiring leader and a marvellous pilot, completely self-confident in his ability to escape from any adversity. He was no respecter of persons – when he felt that his squadron was being denied the facilities it needed he would go to the Air Ministry in London, insult every senior officer in sight, and then fly back to the safety of Pughe-Lloyd's wing before the offended personages in Whitehall could discover who he was. But he had compassion for others – when he found that a fitter had removed a rear-view mirror from a Spitfire to put it on his aircraft, Warburton quietly said to the man, "Return it: some other poor blighter will need that more than I do." He was supreme and he knew it, but unlike Alistair Taylor, who achieved his greatness by strict adherence to the PRU conventions, Warby mocked the opposition by flying at them in a suicidal manner rather than by out-thinking them. His 'kill' total over the Mediterranean stood at eleven by the middle of 1943: he defied every rule in the PR book, but then there was never a book written that applied to men like him.

On October 1st, 1943 Warby was posted from 683 Sqn to La Marsa to take command of a new Wing created specially for him. 336 PR Wing was established to coordinate the efforts of 680, 682, 683, and 60 SAAF Sqns,[1] and it needed someone with his experience and reputation to weld the various PR squadrons together. Warby's rapport with the Americans also boded well for future cooperation with the USAAF 3rd and 5th Photo Groups.[2] However, when 683 Sqn moved across to La Marsa in November to work alongside the Wing HQ, there was no familiar gangling blond figure to greet them. Warby had been shipped back to England after a serious motor accident in Tunis and Gordon Hughes was sent out to take his place. Both he and 683 Sqn were given little time to appreciate North Africa, for once the Allied armies passed Naples, 336 Wing moved en-masse to San Severo in southern Italy.

San Severo was soon to become the Benson of Italy. This sleepy township, supposedly founded by refugees from Troy and lying on the old Roman route across the plain to the seaport of Sepontium, found itself transformed overnight. Schools, inns, palazzi, the opera house, and even the prison were converted into laboratories, workshops, cookhouses, and messes to accommodate the host of pilots, mechanics, photo-interpreters, wireless operators, clerks, dispatch-riders, and police that had descended upon it.

"It was not the first time that the town had housed the main intelligence provider, and a British one at that, of an invading army," wrote a PI, Alan

[1] With effect from January 1st, 1944, 682 and 683 Sqns were established for ten Spitfires each, 680 Sqn was to re-equip with six Mosquitos, and 60 SAAF Sqn was divided into two Flights of seven Mosquitos each.

[2] Both RAF and USAAF PR units were controlled by the Mediterranean Allied PR Command.

Worthington, in the *Manchester Guardian* after the war. "Seven hundred years before, Michael Scott, the 'wondrous wizard' from whom Sir Walter Scott, in his gayer moments, used to claim descent, had rested there awhile as astrologer to Frederick II of Hohenstaufen. His requirements of space for working out the information must have been considerably less than those of the latest arrivals. No doubt an upper room with a view of the heavens served his purpose, since he, too, made his findings from up above. Certainly he did not need to take over all secular buildings of any size and to level a large area of ground on the outskirts. Moreover, his equipment was probably limited to the famous grimoire with a few alembics and, perhaps, a stuffed crocodile for subsidiary researches – nothing to compare with the aircraft, cameras, and automatic processing machines which were now coming in."

From here the Spitfires and Mosquitos ranged over everything and anything of strategic interest between Munich and Ploesti – Gordon Hughes reached the furthest north-west when he visited Ulm on June 25th, 1944, while Roumania marked the limit in the east.

By February 1944 all bomber raids mounted from Italy were coordinated with operations from the UK. The great Roumanian oil centre of Ploesti had been bombed the previous August using target material and models supplied by Medmenham, and PR on August 3rd and 19th revealed a certain amount of damage that was still being repaired on October 25th. The next cover of Ploesti was provided by 60 SAAF Sqn on January 10th, 1944, and they found that during the last two months of 1943 a complete decoy town, containing every feature of Ploesti right down to dummy refineries, had been erected to confuse the bomber crews.

Nearer San Severo there were the German lines of communication and dispositions in northern Italy to photograph, and battle area coverage in support of the Fifth and Eighth Armies to provide in case any new defence lines were being constructed. First the Gustav Line and then the Gothic Line came under close and regular scrutiny under the watchful eye of an Army PI known affectionately as "the Major".

682 Sqn's line book was a classic, full of Plt Off Prune[1] -type statements like "my navigation is so accurate that the RDF people call up to find out where they are!" Sqn Ldr Morgan started the habit of writing post-flight reports in verse:

I just had reached Pescara Town
When that occurred which brought a frown
Upon my brow.
Some flak came up behind, but thickly,
So I banked round and left as quickly
As I knew how!

From that point on I lost the ground

[1] A fictional cartoon character created in the interests of operational efficiency to illustrate how *not* to do things.

But pressed right on, on course so sound
And 'snapped' on ETA!
And though this sounds a shocking line
Thro' 9/10 cloud I could define,
The shape of Spezia's Bay.

Two runs were done to prove my case,
Then seeing fighters twelve in chase,
Heart leapt to mouth;
And when they turned in my direction
I did not wait for close inspection
But headed South.

During the flight from there to 'home'
'Shot' four ports and the odd 'drome
With usual skill.
"Shall I go on?" "Oh, please say 'Yes'"
"What? No" "Oh well, perhaps I guess
You've had your fill.

Taskings arrived by signal at San Severo every day to be divided among the squadrons, depending on the range involved, the type of cover required, and the availability of crews and aircraft. An anonymous poet recounted a typical division:

Ten little PR trips came through on the line
Give that one to 60 SAAF that leaves nine.
Nine little PR trips, this one's off quite late
Peter T's just the boy, that leaves eight.
Eight little PR trips, one off at eleven
Let Groupy go in treble eight, that leaves seven.
Seven little PR trips, this one's got no strips[1]
Let the new boy take it, that leaves six.
Six little PR trips, its good to be alive;
683 got that one, that leaves five.
Five little PR trips lined up on the board;
Johnny's off to Munich, that leaves four.
Four little PR trips, one's an SIB,[2]
Flight Commander does this, that leaves three.
Three little PR trips, this one's hard to do;
Tommy's got a mapping job, that leaves two.
Two little PR trips, both quite fun,

[1] New arrivals covered easy targets like the Jugoslav islands until they became proficient – strip photography needed someone who could fly a precise and accurate track over the ground on the first run, so such work was usually given to an experienced man.

[2] Special Intelligence Briefing.

Richy gets the BDA[1], that leaves one.
One little PR trip, is this where I come?
No, the Wing Co goes a-dicing, that leaves none.
No little PR job, round Ops room I pace,
The Major gives a shout of joy, "Here do this bloody trace."

In the beginning 336 PR Wg met little effective Luftwaffe opposition. On the contrary they had more to fear from trigger-happy American fighter pilots on their return journey to San Severo. Weather was more of a hindrance than the Germans, especially as it seemed to be so unpredictable. Allied Met men were soon dubbed 'Duff Gen Merchants' by 680 Sqn, and one frustrated pilot from 682 Sqn was moved to remark acidly that "reference to Old Moore's Almanack might give a more positive clue" to the weather.

Back in England, Adrian Warburton tired of kicking his heels after his motor accident and, despite being grounded for medical reasons, he 'borrowed' a Lightning from his American friends at Mount Farm and set off on April 12th, 1944 on a trip across the Alps to see his old friends at San Severo. He never made it – he was last seen by a USAAF pilot over Lake Constance and his fate after that remains a mystery to this day.

Tedder, when he was AOC-in-C Middle East, is reported to have described Warburton as "the most valuable pilot in the whole RAF". He died on his way back from the alien skies of England to the only home he knew, as if, like a delicate flower, he needed the warmth and companionship that only the Mediterranean could offer in order to survive and blossom. He would have relished life at San Severo, the repository of the PRU spirit of wonderful informality that was slowly being crushed under the weight of expansion and efficient organisation at Benson. It was perhaps fitting that he should disappear into oblivion, like Alistair Taylor before him, rather than be seen to end his days in the manner of lesser mortals.

Planning for the return to France had begun back in 1940 when the Royal Navy started interviewing Royal Mail captains and anyone else with an expert knowledge of the French coastline. Touring maps, personal sketches, and picture postcards were all accumulated and filed away for future reference.

In May 1942 a special Army Photographic Interpretation Section was set up alongside GHQ Home Forces to examine all photographs taken within 30 miles of the European coastline from Den Helder to the Spanish frontier. The task facing these PIs was immense; although 140 Sqn was given the special task of photographing all coastal defences between Calais and Cherbourg and the beach gradients around the Brest peninsula, most information had to be sifted from the thousands of routine PRU prints exposed for other reasons over the area.

During 1942 all maps were re-drawn because the Army's charts were based

[1] Bomb Damage Assessment.

on a sixty year old French survey that was not only of dubious accuracy but also lacked any information on current German defence-works. At the start of 1943 the planners were ready to start selecting the best invasion area, and distant and close obliques were used to produce coastal mosaics onto which were superimposed all pertinent topographical and military details. By the autumn of 1943 there was hardly a pill-box or a reel of barbed wire on the French Channel coast that the PIs had not plotted.

Three 'softer' or less defended areas stood out from these annotated mosaics: the coastal stretch between the Somme and Le Havre, the Calvados bay between Le Havre and Cherbourg, and the north coast of Brittany. Of these, the most favourable seemed to be the coast of Calvados. The aerial cameras turned with increasing frequency from now on, but to prevent arousing German suspicions weekly records of sorties were kept to make sure that the 'Overlord' coast did not receive a disproportionate amount of reconnaissance attention. Nevertheless, all Squadron and Flight Commanders of PR Squadrons were grounded a fortnight before D-Day in case they were shot down and made to disclose the position of the proposed landing area before the invasion took place.

By the spring of 1944 both 106 Wg and the 2 TAF PR squadrons were heavily committed to D-Day preparations. Low level photography was particularly important, and the latest armed PR G-type, the Spitfire PR XIII[1], was often to be seen photographing the French coast obliquely from three to four miles off-shore so that landing craft coxswains would have an idea of what they would see on D-Day, followed by runs 1500 yards from the beaches so that platoon commanders could have pictures of their landing points, and finally over the beaches themselves so that infantry commanders would be able to orientate themselves on the day.

The performance of the PR XIII was so superior to that of its low-level predecessors – the PR IG and the PR VII[2] – that camera modifications had to be incorporated so that large-scale low-level negatives would not be blurred. Benson therefore elaborated on an American idea of using a moving film strip to compensate for the movement of the aircraft. An F 52 with 'image movement compensation' (IMC) became known as the F 63, and by fitting two F 63s with 5 in or 8 in lenses into an aircraft, and by wiring these two cameras so that there was a very short TI between exposures, it was possible to achieve the desired 60% unblurred overlap on missions below 6,000 feet.

Medmenham's Third Phase expertise had been called in at an early stage to assist the Army Photographic Interpretation Section, and one of their first contributions was to study and locate all German coastal batteries. Between October 1942 and D-Day they identified 90% of the batteries in existence, the remaining 10% being largely mobile flak batteries. Another exacting and important task was the detection and identification of underwater obstacles off

[1] The PR XIII was built around the Mk V fighter fuselage but it was powered by the Merlin 32 engine. The standard photographic fit was one F 24 5 in and two F 24 24 in cameras.

[2] The PR VII was the armed derivative of the PR IV.

the beaches. Some landing craft at Dieppe had encountered steel stakes driven into the sand below the water line, and the Royal Navy was convinced that the off-shore waters of Normandy would be similarly infested with such unfriendly devices. On May 12th, 1943 a pilot photographed a row of curved rails off shore at Quineville, but nothing similar was discovered elsewhere that year despite a thorough and intensive search.[1] Ten months later a PR Spitfire brought back the first prints of underwater obstacles being laid in bulk off the Normandy beaches. The shallows were watched even more closely after that, but it was only by a stroke of good fortune and some erratic bomb-aiming that the Allies discovered what was being attached to the obstacles. During an air attack on a coastal battery a stray bomb fell into the sea some 700 yards off shore, producing 14 small explosions on the strike photograph taken at the time, and by plotting these it was possible to say that they occurred within the depth of the obstacle belt. During April and May, American PR Lightnings flew over the shallows at zero feet, photographing the various types of obstacles to see how they were erected and how many mines had been attached to them.

During March 1944 an abnormal amount of tree-felling was noticed in Normandy, and Medmenham soon discovered that the Germans were intending to obstruct all possible glider landing grounds with a network of mines suspended between poles. Fortunately few of these "anti-air landing devices" were erected by D-Day.

The positions of all obstacles, be they natural or man-made, were added to the large-scale models being prepared at Medmenham. 32 models of northern France, each measuring 5 feet x 3 feet, were made for a start, showing all topography, communications, and built-up areas to a scale of 1:12,500, followed by two very detailed models of 1:900 scale to illustrate the special airborne landing sites. Finally there were 63 models of different sections of the landing areas. Made from synthetic rubber, these 16 ft square masterpieces showed every detail from low water level to a point 12 miles inland at a scale of 1:5000, and a further 186 plaster copies were made for distribution to the planning staffs. These models, together with the seven million prints of NW France that Medmenham turned out every month, helped to ensure the success of the Normandy invasion before the first soldier even got his feet wet.

Behind the coastal wall, 106 Wg and the 2 TAF squadrons intensified their watch on Luftwaffe airfields so that the opposing air strength could be assessed and neutralised before D-Day. The next task was the photography of 91 separate areas in Normandy to select the best sites for forward Allied airfields once the invasion force was established: this involved flying with special survey cameras at 9,000 feet, an unenviable altitude in airspace where Me 109s were prevalent, but the Mosquitos of 34 PR Wg completed the task by April without loss.

Finally the Germans had to be kept in the dark over what was about to befall them. No amount of pre-invasion planning would suffice if the German

[1] Quineville was only a testing ground.

Army was to be found behind the Normandy dunes as the invaders stepped ashore, so the German photographic and electronic eyes and ears had either to be confused or put out. Dummy barges were massed in Dover, and after 106 Wg had photographed them to see if aerial prints revealed any features that distinguished them from the real thing, a Luftwaffe PR aircraft was allowed free rein over the harbour on June 5th. His prints of dummy barges and gliders and a harbour teeming with troops helped to delude von Rundstedt into believing that the invasion armada was bound for Calais.

The ACIU also estimated that there was one German radar station for every 4½ miles of coastline from the Franco-Belgian border to Cap Frehel in Brittany, and every one of these had to be put out of action if the vital element of surprise was to be maintained. By April 1st, 1944, Medmenham had compiled a 300 page report listing every early warning station with details of layout, descriptions from large-scale photographs, and notes on the most vulnerable points for attack. This report was constantly up-dated as June approached, for mobile *Freyas* and *Würzburgs* could be moved quickly and set up at a new site in a matter of hours. To assist PR location, therefore, three special ground direction-finders, nick-named 'Ping-pong', were ranged along the south coast of England to fix the position of any new transmitting station by triangulation.

On May 22nd, rocket-firing Typhoons and Spitfires began 'Operation Rhubarb', or the systematic destruction of every German radar station along 450 miles of coastline. It was a mammoth task to silence them all, and the onslaught had to be maintained for three weeks with a PR aircraft going in at low level after every raid to see whether or not another attack had to be initiated. The German Signal Intelligence Centre at Urville-Hague, near Cherbourg, which was responsible for coordinating all German radar activities in NW Europe, was shattered by a 95 bomber raid on June 3rd. Three days later the aerial cameras and 'Ping-pong' were able to report that only 5 out of 98 located stations were functioning in any way and none of these was capable of detecting the vast aerial and naval armada that was moving towards Normandy. With neither the PR capability to monitor Allied preparations in Britain, nor the electronic ears to hear when the force was coming, the Germans had to wait blindly for the blow to fall.

The smooth running of the landings themselves and the speed with which the Allies established their foothold in NW Europe owed much to the meticulous aerial photography, interpretation, and planning that had gone on for two years beforehand. Air Chief Marshal Sir Trafford Leigh-Mallory, then AOC-in-C Allied Expeditionary Forces, paid tribute to the accuracy and vital importance of PR in his Dispatch on the operation. The Festung Europa had been breached, not so much because of the weakness of its concrete walls as because the Germans had neglected to put an adequate roof over the top.

CHAPTER TEN

The V-Weapon Search

If the Germans had succeeded in perfecting and using these new weapons six months earlier than they did, the invasion of Europe would have proved exceedingly difficult and perhaps impossible . . . Eisenhower

The defeat of Germany would not be brought about by the Normandy invasion alone. D-Day was only a flesh wound and demise would never come about until the vast German military and economic machine was dismembered and its vital transport arteries severed. To this end the Allied bomber forces embarked in 1942 on the progressive destruction and dislocation of the German military, industrial, and economic infrastructure, culminating in the winter of 1943 with the Battle of Berlin. Although each raid was invariably followed a few hours later by a tiny blue speck in the sky sporting a bevy of cameras, daylight prints of ground damage were only possible on two occasions between mid-November 1943 and mid-February 1944 because of persistent cloud cover.

Priorities shifted at the beginning of 1944 away from the disruption of German production and morale, and towards the dislocation of the communications systems of western Europe in preparation for the re-entry into Europe. In March 1944 the great marshalling yards of Trappes, Le Mans, Amiens, Laon, Aulnoye, Coutrai, and Vaires came in for photographic and destructive attention. Eighty of the most important railway centres of France were photographed, bombed, and photographed once more when repairs neared completion, in an attempt to paralyse the whole railway system emanating from the Rhine to prevent reinforcements reaching the Front. Precision bombing played a major part in such raids – on April 18th Leonard Cheshire demonstrated his skill as a low level marker in his Mosquito when he led 617 Sqn and 5 Group in an attack on the Juvisy marshalling yards, eleven miles south of Paris. Cheshire marked the aiming point visually, 617 Sqn turned his flares into a conflagration, and 200 bombers from 5 Group added wave after wave of high explosive into the flames. The following morning a PR Spitfire recorded the scorched and jagged jigsaw of mutilated rails, twisted skywards by a thousand precise and overlapping craters. The Juvisy yard was not to be fully repaired until 1947.

By June 3rd such raids had proved so effective that the 8th Abteilung was forced to record that "the Reichsbahn authorities are seriously considering whether it is not useless to attempt further repair work." The same softening up process was also applied to the main fighter airfields and naval bases of

France – some very spectacular prints were taken of the damage inflicted on a large proportion of the German light naval Channel forces following a heavy raid on Boulogne and Le Havre.

Once the Normandy invasion forces were well entrenched, Allied bomber forces were directed once more towards the major cities and crucial war industries of the Reich. Oil refineries were particularly important and the oil offensive began in June with raids on Gelsenkirchen, Sterkrade, Wesseling, and Scholven. PR showed good results at Gelsenkirchen, and nine buildings at the Sterkrade plant were damaged. Wesseling was seen to be severely devastated after an attack on July 18th, and from then on the campaign against synthetic oil plants, benzol plants, refineries, and oil storage depots intensified.[1] The bad old days had long since gone when Bomber Command could not hit a five mile square in the dark – with Pathfinders, Gee, Oboe, and H2S to guide them, virtually every raid was of value. 106 Group would then go in, guaranteeing to provide an assessment of the damage within 24 hours as long as the weather was fit for photography.

In the ten months after July 1944, Bomber Command reduced the total German oil refinery production from 697,000 tons per month to 33,000 tons per month. Each plant from Brüx downwards was watched regularly, and one of the Medmenham showpieces for VIPs was the 'oil scoreboard' which showed the latest damage state of the top 35 plants in the German synthetic oil league.

The German aircraft industry also suffered from the repeated attentions of Bomber Command. The aircraft section (L Section) at Medmenham began concentrating on Luftwaffe aircraft types in 1941, and PIs soon learned to classify microscopic specks on runways or dispersals by minutiae such as wing shape, dihedral, position and number of engines, tail unit design, etc. Shadows, for instance, were useful for highlighting twin boom aircraft. In the end the aircraft PIs became so skilled with their optical instruments that they could measure the span, length, and even root chord of wings with great accuracy.

One of L Section's first 'finds' was a prototype Fw 190 among a row of Fw 189s at Bremen in 1941. The Erprobungsstelle at Rechlin was a particularly fruitful source of new discoveries once it came within range, being the Luftwaffe equivalent of the British Aeroplane and Armament Experimental Establishment (A & AEE) at Boscombe Down. It was at Rechlin that the first He 280 was spotted on the runway, a discovery that was only overshadowed by the PI's amazement at the host of Wellingtons, Blenheims, and Spitfires standing on the dispersal awaiting evaluation by the Luftwaffe.

An He 280 had in fact been noticed on cover following the Bomber Command raid on the Heinkel works at Rostock/Marienehe in April 1942, but no-one realised it at the time. Among the debris and wreckage that had been cleared out of the damaged hangars and workshops was a whispy shape

[1] Oil fields were ignored because wells were often too small or too scattered to be worth consideration.

almost hidden in the shade. There was no disguising the fact that its two small engine pods were too close to the fuselage to be propeller driven; here was a partially constructed version of Ernst Heinkel's claimant to the title of being the world's first practical jet fighter.

Other bits of aircraft were also scattered around Marienehe including what appeared to be the result of a collision between two He 111s at an intersection. This was dismissed by the aerodynamicists as a nasty accident, but the PIs, after contemplating the phenomenon at their leisure, declared otherwise. It turned out to be the Heinkel Zwilling, or a pair of He 111s joined like Siamese twins by their wing tips to form a twin boomed five engined tug. The discovery of the He 111Z convinced the PIs of L Section that one had to be stone-cold sober to interpret photographs.

The upshot of the surprise appearance of the Fw 190 on the European scene was that aircraft and aircraft engine factories achieved greater status as targets for PR and Bomber Command. Every one of the 58 aircraft and engine factories built during the expansion of the German aviation industry between 1933 and 1942 was located and graded in order of importance by the CIU. Luck played some part in this; the position of the Flugmotorenwerke Ostmark, the largest aero-engine factory in the world, was only discovered by watching construction activity to the south of Vienna. Then the bombers went in. Marienburg, once Medmenham had declared it to be the main Fw 190 assembly plant, was destroyed in the space of twelve minutes during a precision raid. The Me 109 factories of Wiener Neustadt and Regensburg /Prufening suffered a similar fate, and the climax came in February 1944 when 15 German aircraft factories were bombed in one week.

In an attempt to break out from the vicious circle of PR, bomb, PR, repair, PR, and bomb again, the Reich Minister for Armament and War Production, Albert Speer, ordered the dispersal of 32 of his aircraft factories. Their various departments were spread over 729 separate locations, some above ground in garages, workshops, or anywhere where there were benches and tools, and others, usually the larger sections, underground. By 1945 a total of 12,912,000 sq feet of underground floor space[1] had been taken over by the German aircraft industry, mainly through the conversion of mines, caves, tunnels, and wine cellars.

As they could not hope to find all the component workshops, the ACIU concentrated on airfields, in the knowledge that final assembly of aircraft often took place in adjacent wooded or camouflaged spaces. Airfields were not always conspicuous – autobahns were sometimes used as runways – but the new breed of jet aircraft entering service with the Luftwaffe often left telltale scorch marks that stood out on photographs, and once the runways were found it was sometimes possible to work backwards to the main production line. Following an agent's report of a new spur railway line running off the Weimar-Halle railway line into the Thuringian hills, a special PR mission was sent to investigate. The spur line led to a heavily wooded hill at Kahla, the top

[1] Compared with 52,900,000 sq feet for the total German aircraft industry in 1942.

of which had been cleared and levelled, and by looking around the PIs discovered that excavations had been started into the side of the hill. A further sortie by Fg Off K. Durbridge of 542 Sqn on March 19th, 1945 showed the hill-side factory to be in production. A lift had been built from the factory entrance up to the top of the hill, and on it, as the PR Spitfire passed over, were two Me 262s en-route for the airfield at the top.

Other strategically important industries followed suit and went underground after 1943, so much so that a special section had to be set up at Medmenham in October 1944 to look for them. It was virtually impossible to tell when a beer storage cellar had been converted to other uses, but the massive new Bunkerwerken now under construction were easier to discover. Fortunately the Germans followed a standard pattern of construction in hewing these underground factories out of the earth, and once the hill-side aircraft factory at Langenstein and the underground V-weapons assembly plant at Neidersachswerfen near Nordhausen had been followed through their evolutionary stages, similar earthworks were soon spotted. Hill-sides with roads leading into them stood out clearly, but there were also many minor workshops that exhibited no unusual signs of surface activity. Out of the 227 underground establishments set up at Speer's command, only 60 were discovered before the war ended.

It was against targets like these, and others like oil refineries and armaments factories that could not be dispersed because of their size, that the Allied bomber forces were sent again and again. "By the autumn of 1944", wrote Webster and Frankland,[1] "Bomber Command had developed a paralysing power of attack which, in all but the most exceptional circumstances, could accurately be brought to bear by day and by night against targets large and small and near and far." Yet the glowing damage assessment reports leaving Medmenham only told part of the story. By 1945 the Ruhr was producing more than ever before. "Give me six hundred tanks a month," Hitler said to Speer, "and we will abolish every enemy in the world." At the end of 1943 Germany was producing 1000 tanks every month, an output that had grown to 1,800 by November 1944. As the Allied armies closed in towards the Rhine the armaments factories of the Reich were producing three times as much armour as the year before, the Luftwaffe's reserve of fighter-bombers had been tripled, and the output of night-fighters had increased by a factor of eight. Despite all that L Section could do, German aircraft production reached an all time peak of 3,750 machines a month by the summer of 1944.

It was only when the bombing emphasis changed from industries to communications that the effectiveness of the German war machine was finally neutralised. The introduction of the Tallboy bomb heralded the destruction of previously impregnable transportation bottlenecks such as tunnels and viaducts. The Dortmund-Ems canal was spectacularly breached on September 23rd, 1944, and photographs taken over Glane showed that 21 barges were

[1] 'The Strategic Air Offensive Against Germany' – Vol 3.

stranded in a 6½ mile section that was now drained dry. Railways, roads, and canals were all attacked with increasing ferocity during the last six months of the war until they became so clogged with craters, burnt-out locomotives, and shattered bridges that the Germans were unable to move more than a fraction of the 30,000 tons of finished goods that the Ruhr was producing every day. "The Ruhr strangled finally . . . on its own production," declared one of Speer's deputies, "it did not cave in under blast."

Strategic bombing and photographic reconnaissance had grown up together, the latter pointing out the deficiencies of the former and acting as a monitor of its efforts. Unfortunately the relationship had swung from one extreme to the other over the years, from the time when Bomber Command had attached little credence to the work of the aerial camera to a state of almost total dependence and reliance on its findings. Too many people were deluded into thinking that the aerial camera was an oracle, and that the importance and value of its prints was proportional to the number exposed over a particular area, just as targets photographed infrequently were dismissed as of limited importance. The results of bombing raids could be over-estimated, and were for the most part from 1943 onwards; likewise the speed with which the Germans could recover from these attacks or in other ways minimise their effects was underestimated. It was only when the Allies finally occupied Germany, and compared their intelligence assessments with what actually happened, that they started to appreciate that the aerial photograph was only as reliable as the pre-conceived prejudices and notions of those who employed and interpreted it would allow.

As the Allies struck at the Reich from all sides, so German propaganda agencies referred increasingly to Vergeltengswaffen (revenge weapons) that would shortly turn the tide of war back in Hitler's favour. British Intelligence was given the task of discovering whether there was a foundation to these stories or if they were merely morale-boosters for the German people. There were in fact three German revenge weapons in 1943 that had progressed beyond the stage of being a malignant gleam in Hitler's eye. Firstly there was the Fieseler 103 flying bomb, developed on behalf of the Luftwaffe and soon to be known as the V-1. Then there was the A-4 liquid fuelled rocket, financed by the Army to carry a warhead and from which was to evolve the V-2. Finally there was the dubious brain-child of an armaments engineer called Coenders, to be designated the V-3, which envisaged pouring a continual stream of shells on to London from a series of 'high pressure pumps' embedded in northern France.

The trouble was that all these schemes were beyond the comprehension of British Intelligence at the time. It is hard to look back today from a vantage point where missions to the moon have become almost commonplace, and appreciate that few in Britain in 1943 had ever heard of jet engines let alone liquid-fuelled rockets. The experts were not much help as Dr R V Jones discovered:

"Four situations can arise with any technical development:

(i) neither side makes it work; this presents no intelligence problem;

(ii) both sides succeed; this is the normal intelligence problem, for it soon becomes a matter of general knowledge and intelligence is reasonably well briefed as to what to seek;
(iii) our experts succeed, the Germans fail; this is an intelligence worry, for proving the negative case is one of the most difficult of intelligence exercises;
(iv) our experts fail, or do not try; the Germans succeed. This is the most interesting intelligence case, but it is difficult to overcome the prejudice that as *we* have not done something, it is impossible or foolish."[1]

The search for V-weapons was not helped by the fact that, as far as British projectile technologists were concerned, all three German schemes fell into the last category.

There were three sources of information available to scientific detectives like Dr Jones – the detailed interrogation of Axis POWs, reports from Allied agents or sympathisers, and the interpretation of aerial photographs. The most revealing of these was to be aerial photography, not because it was always superior to ground intelligence, but because it translated conventional reports into pictures, which were often the only way of convincing the sceptics who mattered that something was afoot. It must never be forgotten that the PRU remained heavily dependent on ground intelligence throughout the V-weapons investigation to tell them where to point their cameras.

To the PRU and the CIU fell the honour of identifying the German secret weapons, discovering their launching sites, and providing enough information in time to allow effective counter measures to be taken before any great damage was done. Medmenham did not discover everything there was to find, but it is amazing that the PIs did not miss more than they did considering the technical sophistication of the problem facing them, the fact that they were looking for one weapon when three existed (not counting red herrings like jet aircraft and anti-aircraft missile development), the confliction of technical advice available to them, and the over-riding drawback that for a long time no-one was really sure that there was anything for them to find. That so much information on V-weapons was derived from aerial photography before the end of the war stands as a tribute to the skill of the aircrews, PIs, and Intelligence staffs involved in the quest for some of the smallest needles in the European haystack.

The first indication of any German experimentation with rocketry was contained in the Oslo Report. This very informative document had been received with scepticism in 1939, but as more and more of its revelations were proved to be correct, so Dr Jones gave increasing credence to the information that a rocket glider was being tested at a large experimental station called Peenemünde on the Baltic island of Usedom. Although the Oslo Report was received on November 4th, 1939, no PR aircraft was specifically tasked to cover Peenemünde until April 22nd, 1943 – it was a time delay that British Intelligence could have done without.

[1] 'The Mare's Nest' – David Irving.

The experimental station and airfield had in fact appeared on film on May 15th, 1942 when Flt Lt D. W. Steventon left his cameras on in transit from Kiel to Swinemünde, but the PIs could determine little from the small-scale prints apart from "heavy constructional work" and some mysterious elliptical emplacements at the northern end of the airfield. It was a pity that no-one at Medmenham had access to the Oslo Report, for only a day earlier a young Pomeranian engineer named von Braun had watched the successful completion of the first hot test on his prototype A-4 rocket. The following morning, as Steventon flew unconcernedly onwards in the clear spring sky, the rocket was still erect at its gantry in the centre of Test Stand VII in the elliptical enclosure. There was more to be seen at Peenemünde than "heavy constructional work".

The Germans did not waste the following months while the matter rested on the shelves of the Medmenham print library. On October 3rd the fourth A-4 prototype was launched successfully on its inaugural flight of 118 miles, while three months later Gerhard Feisler launched his first flying bomb over Peenemünde from beneath an Fw Kondor bomber. The odd PR aircraft continued to photograph the station on an 'opportunity basis', but no signs of these activities were ever noticed.

It was not until the beginning of 1943 that the British received any more information to confirm the Oslo Report that Peenemünde was an experimental rocket establishment. One agent referred to "large rocket" trials at a site near Swinemünde, and another spoke of a projectile that could carry 10 tons of explosives over 70 miles being tested at Peenemünde. The mounting evidence became so impressive that the Chiefs of Staff recommended on April 15th that a senior investigator be appointed to co-ordinate all scientific and intelligence investigations in an effort to assess the seriousness of the German 'secret weapon' threat. That same day the Prime Minister handed this important task to Mr Duncan Sandys.

At his instigation the Air Ministry instructed the CO of Medmenham, Gp Capt Stewart, to accord the highest priority to the search for secret weapons. The erudite and ubiquitous Wg Cdr Hamshaw-Thomas[1] was put in charge of the investigation, and he had all past prints of Peenemünde and any other likely establishments taken down from their shelves and re-examined. In addition every photograph exposed over Europe within a 130 mile radius of London since January 1st, 1943 was put under the stereoscope again, and where there were any gaps in the cover, the PRU was ordered to fill them.

This was all very well as far as it went, but there was no getting away from the great obstacle that no one at Medmenham had any clear idea of what they were looking for. When the CIU had first heard of the investigation in February 1943, their Army Interpretation Section had been asked by the War Office to "keep a close watch for any suspicious erections of rails or scaffolding" that might form part of a "long-range projection capable of firing on

[1] Now in charge of all Third Phase Sections.

this country from the French coast". An Air Ministry directive mentioned a "rocket launched from a tube, possibly in a disused mine" and it was for such features that Hamshaw-Thomas's team searched. But this theory of rockets fired from tubes or rails only illustrated the infant state of the science of projectile technology in Britain. British pre-war rocket trials had centred around solid fuel vehicles, so it was assumed that the Germans would use a propulsive agent like cordite. For such a vehicle to carry any appreciable bomb load to London, British experts calculated that the Germans must be building a solid fuel rocket weighting approximately 70 tons. This in turn led to the conclusion that any firing site would be conspicuous because it would need a firing ramp at least 100 yards in length to support the cumbersome projectile until it reached firing speed, and would have to be surrounded by massive lifting gantries and an adjacent railway supply line. Basically the British were talking about an outsize firework rocket, and if Medmenham did not actually go so far as to look for a giant milk bottle, that is essentially the sort of concept on which they were briefed to work.

On April 24th, 1943, Flt Lt André Kenny,[1] in charge of the search for experimental work around Peenemünde, examined some enlarged prints of the area taken during the previous year. In company with both a projectile and an explosives expert he noted that land reclamation was in progress at the northern tip of the Peenemünde peninsula, but although they could account for most of the machinery in the area there was one piece of equipment that defied analysis. Kenny suggested that it might be pump machinery associated with the reclamation, an assessment readily endorsed by his colleagues. This deduction showed how much British Intelligence had yet to learn – four months after the launching of the first V-1 prototype, there was no one at Medmenham with the technical knowledge to differentiate between a 'sludge pump' and a launching ramp for a German flying bomb.

Nevertheless there was plenty at Peenemünde to warrant further investigation, especially the elliptical earthwork with its traverser cranes, mysterious pits, and concrete pill-boxes. No one was willing to say officially what the purpose of this 670 yd earthwork was, but Kenny was convinced that it was a rocket launching pad. On April 22nd the first full scale PR cover of Peenemünde was authorised, and a detailed report was produced on the two large factories to the south-east, the "elliptical earthwork" at the northern end of the island, the equally impressive earthworks to the south-west, and the power station on the western shore. One paragraph of Kenny's report, referring to a building alongside the elliptical earthwork was especially interesting:

"A large cloud of white smoke or steam can be seen drifting in a north-westerly direction from the area. On photograph 5010, an object about twenty-five feet long can be seen projecting in a north-westerly direction from the seaward end of the building. When photograph 5011 was taken four seconds later this object had disappeared, and a small puff of white smoke or steam was issuing from the seaward end of the building."

[1] I/C D Industrial Section at Medmenham.

While Plt Off White was holding his Mosquito steady so that his observer could expose photograph 5010, the 21st model of the A-4 rocket was being tested on the elliptical Test Stand VII below him. As he turned for home he would never know that he had missed the most successful Peenemünde launching to date by a couple of hours. If Kenny had been looking for a liquid fuelled rocket he might have realised that the "white smoke or steam" was probably condensation from the transfer of liquid oxygen into the A-4's fuel tanks. As it was the two vast factories were classified as "possible nitration houses" concerned with the production of explosives; the V-1 firing ramps remained "sludge pumps"; and the vital liquid oxygen factory was merely referred to as "a large building 220 feet by 140 feet". Even the significance of the power station went unappreciated – Kenny reported that it "shows no sign of activity at the time of photography, apart from the stores of fuel present in the coal yard. Not one of the six chimneys of the boiler house is smoking." Kenny should have gone by that which he could see rather than that which he could not – the fuel stocks showed that the power station was not idle, and the lack of smoke was due to the electrostatic dust and smoke removers that had been fitted into the chimneys to confuse just such a photo-interpretation report. With this report in his hands, Mr Sandys concluded that the experimental station was not yet in full productive use, but he remained convinced that explosives and projectiles were being tested there. He therefore instructed that Peenemünde be kept under fortnightly photographic surveillance, a watch that was extended in June to encompass suspicious stations at Griefswalder Oie, Bornholm, Rügen, Holzkirchen near Munich, and Lettstädter Höhe.

The Mosquitos of 540 Sqn photographed Peenemünde seven times during the first half of 1943. A sortie by Gordon Hughes on May 14th also coincided with the launching of an A-4 rocket, but this time Kenny noted "that the general level of activity on the whole site is high". There were a large number of vehicles on the roads and railways, and on a truck leading into a tall building by the elliptical earthwork was a "cylindrical object thirty-eight feet by eight feet". On checking back to the sortie of April 22nd, Kenny noticed a similar object on another wagon, but as the CIU was not willing to commit itself on white blurred shapes only 1½ mm long they were classified as "objects".

Another mission on June 2nd added little new information. However the next sortie ten days later revealed "a thick vertical column about forty feet high and four feet thick" but it was 470 feet away from the elliptical earthwork which Kenny believed was the launching site. No wonder that, while everyone at the CIU was looking for massive ramps, they should overlook this object on the foreshore, which in fact was a standard A-4 rocket on its fins.

It fell to Flt Sgt E. P. H. Peek on June 23rd to bring back the most illuminating prints of Peenemünde that month. On the wonderfully clear pictures he brought back to Leuchars were two rockets lying horizontally on their trailers inside the elliptical earthwork. British Intelligence had a clear picture of a German rocket at last, but they still had no idea that it was liquid fuelled.

Suspicious activities elsewhere were noted by 542 Sqn at Wissant, Marquisse, Noires, Bernes Wambringue, and Bruneval, but pride of place went to a site in the Bois d'Eperlecques, one mile from Watten, in the Artois district of France. The Todt organisation had started work here the previous December on the first of eight launching bunkers designed to house V-2 missiles when they were in mass production. The CIU reported "a large rail and canal-served clearing in the wood, possibly a gravel pit" at Watten on May 17th 17th, but by July construction activity had increased to such an extent that a model was made of the area. New railway lines carried men and supplies to the "heavy constructions" taking place, and soon the great pit had been completely enclosed awaiting the beginning of concrete pouring. It was decided that both Peenemünde and Watten were sufficiently advanced to receive visits from Bomber Command.

Only two PRU missions were mounted to Peenemünde during July so as not to arouse German suspicions, but after the second by Gordon Hughes on July 26th, the CIU found that not only had the anti-aircraft defences been considerably strengthened but also six smoke generators and a complete decoy site covering 20 acres had been erected to confuse any attacking force. Although 40 aircraft were lost in the Bomber Command raid on Peenemünde on August 17th, the Pathfinders were convinced that they had found the target successfully and the 457 night photographs indicated that "nearly all the aircraft bombed within three miles, and the majority within one mile of the aiming point".

The Master Bomber, however, was a cautious man who would not commit himself until he had seen the daylight photographs. At 1000 hrs the following morning Fg Off J. R. Chubb switched on his cameras and, from his prone position in the Mosquito nose, guided Gordon Hughes on his run over Usedom. Detailed analysis revealed that 50 out of the 80 buildings on the experimental station had been rendered useless, including von Braun's administrative and design offices in Block Four. Ten days later the USAAF dropped 370 tons of bombs on Watten to such good effect that the civil engineer, Sir Malcolm MacAlpine, declared after looking at the post-strike prints that "it would be easier for the Germans to begin again elsewhere". Reichsminister Speer agreed, and he ordered that work commence on a new rocket bunker at Wizernes, while at Peenemünde research activity was deemed by Medmenham to have been put back by at least several months. British Intelligence had won itself a precious breathing space.

But what were they to do with it? Monthly cover continued to flow from the cameras of 540 Sqn, but its value was diminished by the cunning of the Peenemünde CO, General Dornberger. He left the old burnt timbers across the roof of the surreptitiously repaired Block Four to give the impression that the building had been abandoned, and he had as many craters as possible left unfilled along the streets and railway lines. This subterfuge proved so successful that the British Chiefs of Staff turned down a request from the USAAF at the end of August to carry out another raid on Peenemünde because it did not seem necessary.

Many scientists, including the learned and very influential Lord Cherwell, were sceptical of the threat posed by the "rockets" on Peek's photographs. Not only did they seem too small to encompass a solid fuel projectile plus warhead, but also Cherwell could not believe that the Germans would have painted such a valuable weapon white and left it on display for all to see if it had been the real thing. So the time gained by the bombing of Peenemünde and Watten was used to try to make the various pieces of PR evidence fit in with tales of rockets and small pilotless aircraft. Flt Off Constance Babington-Smith, herself involved in the V-weapons search, described the PI's problem: "Both in London and at Medmenham it was a time of frustrating confusion in the secret weapon investigation, which by now had been given the code-name *Bodyline* – a time of groping in the dark, of trying to lay foundations on swamps. It was as though the parts of two or three jigsaw puzzles had been jumbled together, and it was sorely tempting to try to find only *one* answer – only *one* weapon. It seemed a triumph when two or three bits of puzzle fitted together and could be identified as 'Rocket'; and it was all too easy to ignore the bits which did not fit in with these:"[1]

The truth of the matter was that the mass of visible activity at Peenemünde was concerned with the V-2 rocket, while the bulk of launching sites that were shortly to come to light were for the V-1 flying bomb. The problem was complicated further by work on several V-2 bunkers between Calais and the Somme, and burrowing in the limestone hill at Mimoyecques near Calais to house the V-3 'high pressure pump'. But the Cabinet did not appreciate the differences, and from now on they pushed the future V-2 into the background to concentrate on the growing number of V-1 firing sites appearing in France.

Towards the end of October 1943 a French agent reported the pin-point locations of six "secret weapon launching sites" near Abbeville. As these had not been visible on the last full-scale cover of northern France in July, Mr Sandys asked once more for PR over the whole of western Europe within 150 miles of London. The same day, October 28th, Fg Off Hosking managed to photograph one of the pin-points at Bois Carré, a wood ten miles NE of Abbeville, but cloud obscured the remaining five, and Medmenham had to spend a frustrating few days waiting for November 3rd when 541 Sqn filled the gaps.[2]

All six locations showed the same similarities – a concrete ramp 30 feet long by 12 feet wide with its central axis bearing on London, together with numerous support buildings including at least one shaped like a giant ski laid on its side. The ski buildings were too narrow to accommodate a Peenemünde rocket, so it was assumed that the Bois Carré-type sites were intended for some pilotless aircraft or glider bomb. All previous cover of Peenemünde was examined again in the light of these new assumptions, and there, on Peek's photographs, sitting in a small enclosure some way behind the hangars on the airfield, was a strange little object with a wing-span of 20 feet. As the print

[1] Somewhat surprisingly, the only man in Britain involved in liquid fuelled rocket research – Isaac Lubbock – was not drawn into the V-weapons inquiry until September 1943.

[2] 541 Sqn took over responsibility for PR in this part of France from 542 Sqn in November 1943.

scale was too small to show any more detail than this it was designated 'Peenemünde 20'.

The missing link to connect 'Peenemünde 20' with the 72 ski sites then known to be in existence was not provided until November 28th. This month had seen the start of Bomber Command's concentrated onslaught known as the Battle of Berlin, and on November 28th, Sqn Ldr John Merifield strapped into his Mosquito with his observer, Fg Off Whalley, to try to pierce the wall of cloud that had prevented any damage assessment photography over the German capital for nearly a fortnight. Berlin was still covered by 10/10 ths cloud so Whalley plotted a course to take in their secondary targets around the Baltic. First they went north to photograph the ports of Greifswald, Stralsund, Anklam, Stettin, and Swinemünde, and as they still had some unexposed film left Merifield turned towards Usedom. The airfield of Peenemünde was covered first, followed by a couple of runs over Zempin, a radar station eight miles to the south-east, which was suspected of being a monitoring station for Peenemünde launchings. The personnel of Zempin, indignant at being spied upon for the first time, alerted the air defences, and the Mosquito was driven off by the anti-aircraft battery at Karlshagen. Six hours and five minutes after take-off, Merifield and Whalley landed back at base.

Merifield was unhappy with his photographs of Zempin – they were not up to his usual high standard. Although there was nothing on them to interest the radar interpretation people unduly, they were clear enough to show three long ramps gently inclined at about 10° and pointing out to sea. There were no 'ski' buildings at Zempin, but these ramps were identical to the concrete platforms seen at every Bois Carré site in France. Whatever was undergoing trials here was obviously going to be used in France.

Even as the Intelligence officers were trying to imagine what sort of projectile could be dispatched from these shallow ramps – "no gear was visibly capable of handling forty-five ton rockets" – the Aircraft Section at Medmenham was filling in the last pieces of this particular jig-saw. On the first print of Merifield's run over Peenemünde airfield, Constance Babington-Smith found two identical ramps on the north-east edge of the island, and at the foot of one was a 'Peenemünde 20' which could clearly be seen to have no cockpit. The CIU had found the flying bomb at last; the clouds that had thwarted Merifield over Berlin had had a silver lining after all.

The hunt for more Bois Carré sites – now codenamed 'Crossbow' – was intensified, especially after some pessimist had come to the sobering conclusion that if each ski building held 20 flying bombs, and if there were approximately 100 firing sites to be found in France, London could expect to receive 2,000 tons of high explosives within the space of 24 hours. The answer had to be a pre-emptive strike, and from December 5th until the end of the year the medium bombers of 2 TAF and the US VIIIth Air Force deposited 3,216 tons of bombs on the 52 most advanced Bois Carré sites. Every PR Spitfire squadron was called in to assist with the pre- and post-strike photography – 541 Sqn alone visited the area between Cap Gris Nez and the Cherbourg peninsula 88 times during December with each sortie averaging just under two hours. By the beginning of 1944 every Bois Carré site apparently nearing completion had been destroyed, and the Germans, recognising the conspicuity of their ski site layout, decided to abandon the rest.

Bombs continued to fall on the remaining sites throughout January, but by February the PIs had become suspicious of the air of abandonment surrounding every flattened firing zone. On closer examination they found that 28 of the 73 damaged sites had undergone surreptitious repair with craters and other debris left close to ostensibly dismantled buildings which were in reality virtually intact. But the British had been doubly deluded. The Germans had in fact abandoned their ski sites, but, by pretending to repair some of their installations, they bluffed the British into expending a considerable proportion of their valuable bomb capacity upon empty countryside. By June 12th, 23,196 tons of bombs had been dropped on northern France to little purpose, and the Germans could congratulate themselves not only on keeping such destructive power away from the Reich but also on diverting Allied attentions away from important V-weapons developments that were taking shape elsewhere.

On April 27th, 1944 an Army PI, Capt Robert Rowell, was examining some fresh cover of the Cherbourg peninsula when something caught his eye near the village of Belhamelin. There, between two farm buildings, was a flying bomb launching ramp. It was the first indication that the Germans had devised a modified and simpler form of V-1 launching site, devoid of conspicuous appendages like ski-shaped storage buildings, and requiring only a non-magnetic square building to align the flying bomb's gyros before launching. All that the V-1 regiments now had to do was to locate their ramp in a wood or farmyard, fit pre-fabricated rails on to it, and they were in business. Within a few days PR had located twelve of these modified Belhamelin sites, and the Air Ministry ordered that the whole of northern France be covered yet again. At the same time as the Bois Carré ploy was exposed, all launching troops were withdrawn from the battered ski decoys and redeployed among the numerous well-hidden modified sites strung out between the Cherbourg Peninsula and the Pas de Calais.

The Chiefs of Staff were in a quandary. The flying bomb threat, which they believed had been eradicated by the bombing onslaught at the start of the year, had now reappeared within a bare month of the Normandy landings. Twenty of the 'modified' ramps had been discovered by May 13th, but most of these were sited so close to dwellings that another bombing onslaught was out of the question, even if there had been any surplus bombing capacity so close to D-Day. Apart from an attack on a suspected V-1 supply base at Beauvoir, which achieved little because the Germans stored most of their flying bombs underground, there was little that the 'Crossbow' staffs could do apart from keep a close photographic watch on each site. Whenever the PIs thought that the ramps were about to go into action, which meant when the prefabricated rail sections and square building arrived, the CIU was to send a signal to the Air Ministry using the codeword 'Diver'.

The seven days between June 4th and 10th were frustrating for Medmenham, for bad weather and the priority demands of D-Day prevented any photography over the 'rocket coast'. When 'Crossbow' PR was resumed on June 11th, the total number of 'modified' sites stood at 66, but the most important feature was the amount of activity around six of the ramps and the fact that rails had been laid on four of them. That evening a 'Diver' signal was sent from the Comms Centre at Medmenham, to be received by the Air Ministry about the same time as an agent's report stating that 33 railway wagons full of 'rockets' had passed through Belgium on their way to northern France two days earlier. Hereafter the tragedy became a farce – it only takes one weak link in a chain, one badly briefed or unconcerned man in the right place at the wrong time, and all the months of watching, the hours of flying, the miles of films, and the sheaves of interpretation reports can be as nothing. The 'Diver' signal and the agent's report were filed away at the Air Ministry, despite the 'Immediate' precedence of the former. No one bothered to show them to Air Marshal Hill, the man responsible for co-ordinating Britain's defences against the flying bomb – the first that he, and many others in senior positions, heard of the warnings was after the first V-1 landed on England in the early hours of June 13th.

The 2,000th flying bomb left its launching ramp on the night of June 29th, but by this time the troops in Normandy had become so well established that over 40% of the Allied bomber forces based in the UK could be spared to concentrate on the Belhamelin sites. PR had located 133 modified sites by September, for few of them escaped detection once the Argus ram-jets of the V-1 had scorched their mark on the countryside,[1] and the bombing campaign proved so successful that the Germans were never in a position to utilise more than one-third of their flying bomb capacity at any one time.

Bombers were also sent against the V-1 storage centres and factories of Germany that were suspected of manufacturing flying bombs and their fuel.[2] The former proved more resilient than the latter for most of the storage depots were underground. Vertical cameras were not really suited to looking inside quarries so it was back to dicing. Forward facing oblique cameras were fitted into some Mosquitos to allow pilots to fly directly towards their targets, but, because such profiles were so vulnerable to flak, 106 Group refused to countenance them unless they were absolutely necessary. Three Mustang IIIs with their South African pilots were loaned to 541 Sqn to assist in this work, and on August 15th, Capt Williams SAAF and Lt Godden SAAF took some wonderful low-level obliques of the heavily defended mushroom caves cum V-weapons depot at Saint-Leu-d'Esserent. These caves had been enlarged, reinforced with concrete, and fitted with steel doors, but the prints brought back by the two Mustang pilots were so precise that Bomber Command could see exactly where to place their bombs so that they could block the entrance by dislodging a landslide of overhanging earth.

[1] Only eight Belhamelin sites were never found by PR because they were so well camouflaged.

[2] The Fieseler works at Kassel, the Zeppelin factory at Friedrichshafen, Henschel's Rax Works at Wiener-Neustadt, and the Argus factory at Berlin.

By September the remaining Pas de Calais sites had been over-run by the Allied advance and the flying bomb barrage petered out. To the PR squadrons of 106 Gp, 325th US Photo Gp, and 2 TAF must go the credit for flying over 3,000 sorties in search of the V-1, which Medmenham turned into 1,200,000 prints and a mountain of reports. Unfortunately all this effort on behalf of the V-1 was ordered in the mistaken belief that it was the only secret weapon worth bothering about; it was only on September 8th, when the first of von Braun's rockets fell on London, that British Intelligence realised that in keeping one step ahead of the V-1, they had fallen completely behind the V-2.

Dr Jones had warned in December 1943 that the discovery of the V-1 in no way invalidated the evidence of the Peenemünde rockets, but as one revenge weapon at a time was enough for most people, his words were ignored. PR did keep watch on the V-2 bunker systems taking shape at Wizernes, Siracourt, Lottinghem, Sottevast, and Martinvast, and the 'high pressure pump' at Mimoyecques, but the CIU still had no clear indication of their use. However Siracourt, Lottinghem, Sottevast, and the shattered Watten were all aligned on London, Martinvast on Bristol, and Wizernes was positioned within half a degree of the Great Circle bearing on New York. This was cause enough to send in the bombers. During the summer and autumn of 1944 all these sites were devastated by high explosive, including Mimoyecques which received its fair share of Tallboy bombs on July 6th. "The installations," bemoaned a dismayed German engineer, "were not designed to withstand bombs such as these."

With the eradication of these bunker sites, together with the failure of PR to detect any Peenemünde type installations (e.g. elliptical firing areas) outside the Baltic, British Intelligence concluded that all was well. But once again no-one learnt from the past – Bois Carré should have taught that the ever resolute Germans were always ready to adapt their technology to the changing circumstances.

In March 1944 a report reached London saying that secret weapons were being tested at Blizna in Poland. Too far from Benson, it was only 600 miles from San Severo, and on April 15th a Mosquito from 60 SAAF Sqn set off for south-east Poland. The prints revealed a 'modified' flying bomb catapult in position, but more importantly, when Blizna was covered again three weeks later, a Peenemünde type rocket had been conveniently left on view. By June 3rd the flying bomb catapult had disappeared, but there were signs of increasing activity in the form of camouflaged trains and huge road trailers, known as 'Meillerwagen', standing around. The rocket was now identified as having four fins, but the disturbing thing was that it was obviously being tested at Blizna without any of the elliptical earthworks and attendant paraphenalia associated with Peenemünde.

In August Dr Jones received his first intimation that the rockets were fired vertically. This, together with the discovery of gas-vanes in the wreckage of a V-2 that had crashed in Sweden, confirmed that the V-2 could make a standing start from any hard surface. Adrenalin flowed again, and every print of Peenemünde dating back to June 1943 was re-examined. Objects previously dismissed as "thick vertical columns, about forty feet high and four feet thick" were now confirmed as vertical rockets standing on their four fins. It was all so simple; for 18 months the CIU had searched high and low for giant ramps, 'projectors', and 'giant mortars', when all the time the thing could be launched from any bit of concrete or metalled road. On the fan-shaped foreshore to the north of Peenemünde lay a stretch of asphalt like a parade ground, and on ten different occasions Mosquitos had photographed 17 rockets standing there for all to see. The elliptical earthworks had only been for prototype launchings; it had been Dornberger's dream to produce a finished object that could be launched from "a bit of planking on a forest track, or the overgrown track itself". This was what worried British Intelligence; alongside the vertical rockets were clusters of transporter lorries and Meillerwagen trailers just waiting to whisk mass-produced V-2s to any of a thousand clearings in NW Europe.

The first V-2 fell on Chiswick at 0643 hrs on September 8th, 1944. Benson had scoured northern France with renewed vigour during the previous month, but with no bunkers or ski sites to guide them they found nothing. The only hope was to try to photograph a great V-2 road trailer and crew in the process of setting up in business, but it was a faint chance. PR aircraft could only go in with any certainty after ground reports and radar plotting had identified an operational site, as on December 29th when 13 rockets were photographed under the leafless trees of the Haagsche Bosch park near the Hague.

As the V-2 menace increased during the New Year, a very intensive search was made by the PR squadrons of 106 Gp and 2 TAF for sites in Holland, but they never succeeded in locating an ominous cone pointing skywards. It was only on February 26th, after seven months of fruitless activity and a quarter of a million prints, that Sqn Ldr J. E. S. White of 544 Sqn finally saw a V-2 in its vertical launching position on a road leading past the Duindigt racecourse. It was ironic that, after so much searching, three crews from 544 Sqn should independently photograph this site within five minutes of each other.

As the war drew to a close and the V-weapons threat receded, the Prime Minister wrote to Sir Archibald Sinclair:[1]

"You have no grounds to claim that the Royal Air Force frustrated the attacks by the V-weapons. The RAF took their part, but in my opinion their effort ranks definitely below that of the anti-aircraft artillery, and still further below the achievements of the Army, in cleaning out all the establishments in the Pas de Calais which so soon would have opened a new devastating attack upon us in spite of all the Air Force could do.

As to V-2, nothing has been done or can be done by the RAF. I thought it a pity to mar the glories of the Battle of Britain, by trying to claim overweening credit in this business of the V-weapons. It only leads to scoffing by very large bodies of people."

[1] Secretary of State for Air.

This was a cruel and unfair indictment. Leaving aside the rest of the RAF, the PR squadrons and the ACIU between them provided virtually all of the 'best evidence' available on the A-4 rockets and their bunkers, the V-1s and their Bois Carré and Belhamelin sites, and what little information there was on the 'high pressure pump' at Mimoyecques. Time and again the PR pilots flew wherever they were sent to bring back sufficient information to keep Britain just one step ahead of all German developments apart from the V-2. It must never be forgotten that had the British been carrying out similar experiments in the Hebrides, Cumberland, or even north Devon, it is doubtful whether the Luftwaffe would ever have got through to photograph any of them.

The whole episode of the Vergeltungswaffen, lasting nearly three years, was the story of a lot of hard brain work by a large number of people, together with a great deal of luck. But just as the winds favour the best navigator, so the PRU and the ACIU deserved their share of fortune because of the efficiency of their organisations. The failure to predict the V-2 bombardment was the only serious omission throughout the whole business, and the blame for not following up or according enough credibility to the information that the aerial cameras brought back must lie outside the RAF.

CHAPTER ELEVEN

The Watch on the Rhine

Elevatis Nihil Celatur, 'To those high up, nothing is concealed'[1]

D-Day marked the parting of the PR ways in western Europe. Ever since the defeat of France in 1940, land forces in Britain had been in no position to confront their German opposite numbers, with the result that whatever confrontations took place usually involved naval or air forces. Thus for four years the PRU provided information for a war that was largely being fought on a strategic plane; it was only after 1944 that the British Army in Europe found itself once more in the market for every bit of tactical PR that the RAF could provide.

In order that 106 Gp could continue to serve old-established customers like the Royal Navy and Bomber Command, several tactical PR units had been created in July 1943 to serve the Allied armies once they were back in France. 34 PR Wg – 16 and 140 PR Sqns – was set up as the long-range eyes of the 21st Army Group and 2 TAF, while short range tactical cover for the two armies in the British Sector – the 2nd British and 1st Canadian Armies – was to be the responsibility of 4 and 400(RCAF) PR Sqns respectively.[2]

34 PR Wing came into being on July 1st, 1943 at Hartford Bridge. It was not an easy birth; 140 Sqn, veterans of many a dice over northern France, tended to regard themselves as vastly superior in expertise to 16 Sqn, who in turn did not relish the transition from their former Tac R role to high level PR. Neither squadron had much time for the Ops room, and it took a great deal of patient work by Gp Capt Roch Lousada to build up a spirit of unity and co-operation within his Wing.

During the last six months of 1943 the four tactical PR squadrons re-equipped with aircraft supplied by the Aircraft Preparation Section at Benson: 4, 16, and 400 (RCAF) Sqns received Spitfire PR XIs, while 140 Sqn got Mosquito PR XVIs. By February 1944 the four Squadrons were ready to take over all PR work within the Allied Expeditionary Air Force area of responsibility, and from now on they would only call on Benson for assistance

[1] Proposed motto for 681 Sqn underneath a Bengal tiger with an aerial camera in its paws. The badge was lost in transit to the College of Heralds and so was never approved.

[2] These squadrons formed part of 35 and 39 Reconnaissance Wings respectively, which also contained a pair of FR (Fighter Reconnaissance) squadrons each. These FR squadrons carried cameras at times to provide confirmation of their visual sightings, but I shall concentrate here on the pure PR elements. The PR squadrons provided much larger and clearer prints than their FR counterparts.

whenever they were unable to complete a task from their own resources. Generally the Squadrons were responsible for providing large-scale cover for the day to day planning of ground operations, with 4 and 400 (RCAF) Sqns fulfilling tasks within 150 miles of the front line and 34 PR Wing photographing everything of interest beyond this for their Army Group and 2 TAF.

34, 35, and 39 Recce Wings continued to operate from England during the first weeks of 'Overlord' – watching the growth of Mulberries was a standard 34 Wg 'milk-run' – but at the end of July 35 and 39 Wgs moved across to France to work alongside their respective Army HQs. Both had settled in by the beginning of August in time to support the Falaise advance.

34 PR Wg, now commanded by the ex-CO of the old Bomber Command PRU, Gp Capt Pat Ogilvie DSO, DFC, had three main tasks to fulfil.[1] The first involved regular cover of the principal railway lines of northern France. Between 2,000 and 3,000 miles of track were surveyed daily so that train movements could be analysed and estimates of German reinforcements made. Mosquitos were best for this precise work because the observer in the nose could guide his 'airframe driver' to keep the thin strip of railway line continually underneath the camera lens. SHAEF gave this task such a high priority that it had to be diced if the weather was bad. Few were happy with this because stations and some trains bristled with AA guns following the Allied bomber onslaught on the French railway system. When Ogilvie lost three aircraft in four sorties between Somain and Montdidier after operating at embankment height, SHAEF was prevailed upon to do without its daily PR cover when medium level missions were unfeasible.

The other two commitments involved daily trips to assess bomb damage to the main marshalling yards of France, and the provision of the latest information on the Luftwaffe's order of battle.

On September 9th 34 Wg followed the others and crossed over to France, but by the end of the month the Mosquitos of 140 Sqn were finding it increasingly difficult to go about their business, mainly because of the new breed of jet fighters entering Luftwaffe service. Consequently the Squadron was divided into two flights – A Flight converted to the night PR role, leaving B Flight to concentrate on daylight survey work. The bulk of the daylight long range intelligence gathering burden was therefore taken up by the PR Spitfires of 16 Sqn.

It is worth digressing slightly here to follow the development of night photography after the demise of 3 PRU at Oakington in 1942. When 3 PRU moved down to Benson to join 1 PRU, their night PR Wellingtons were sent to the A & AEE at Boscombe Down where trials continued to improve night cameras, flares, and operating techniques. Boscombe Down considered the PR Spitfire to be quite unsuitable for the night role because they believed that such missions necessitated a minimum crew of a pilot, an observer with W/T, and a bomb aimer/camera operator. On this basis the Mosquito was also unsatisfactory, so when Benson was given a 24 hour capability to enable the

[1] Pat Ogilvie failed to return from a weather check over the North Sea in December 1944.

PRU to watch important targets like Brest at night, the Air Ministry decided to add a flight of Albemarles to 1 PRU. Tests soon showed, however, that once the Albemarle was burdened down with cameras and flash bombs its range and performance became totally inadequate. So it had to be Wellingtons or nothing.

As far as Bomber Command was concerned it should be nothing. Any Wellingtons for 1 PRU would have to be diverted from the bomber offensive, together with some good crews, for only the most skilled crews could be employed on night photography, but the Air Staff was insistent and VCAS was instructed to transfer two Wellington IVs from Bomber Command to Benson. They were given to 544 Sqn which, after a period of installation, trials, and familiarisation, carried out its first night PR mission on December 12th, 1942.

The following February Sir Henry Tizard visited Benson, where he expressed the view that night photography was much safer and more effective than daylight operations. There were not many among his listeners, especially those from 544 Sqn, who agreed with him. They had found that the 'Wimpey' was both too large and too slow for operations under 12,000 feet (then the limiting height for night PR), and that it was very vulnerable to night-fighter attack when illuminated by the exploding flares.[1] Night sorties were also very demanding on manpower.

For these reasons Benson proposed that unarmed bomber Mosquitos be used instead. The bomber was preferable to the PR variant because the latter would have to have all its camera installations and long-range belly tankage removed to accommodate night flares, whereas the standard bomber needed only to have a night camera fitted to be ready for operations. The Air Ministry agreed that a more effective night photographic platform ought to be provided before D-Day when 24 hour cover of German deployments would be essential, but as all Mosquito bomber production was already spoken for Benson would have to convert its own aircraft to the night role.

The best night camera of the time was the American K-19 with its 13½ in lenses. "The night camera I had developed, the K-19," wrote George W. Goddard, "was strictly to expose the enemy's moving of men and supplies by land or by sea under cover of darkness and thus it was a reconnaissance weapon in the true sense of the word." It must have been good for the RAF to use it because the director of photographic research and development at the Air Ministry, Gp Capt Victor C. Laws, set out from the start of the Anglo-American alliance to prove that his equipment was the best. 'Daddy' Laws, "short in stature, very proper in manner", had learnt his PR as a Flt Sgt with Moore-Brabazon in 1915, and he was in awe of no-one else's photographic equipment. But the K-19 was good, and when used with the American M 46 flash bomb, which actuated the shutter mechanism by means of a photo-

[1] These were still pretty lethal, and experimental research was divided between the development of a safe illuminant and the provision of an armoured container to protect those currently in use.

electric cell in the camera, night PR became feasible up to a height of 24,000 feet.

As a general rule the minimum scale for interpretation at night should be double that for daylight. Thus, although the K-19 could work at 24,000 feet, its scale of 1;25,000 at that height was much too small, and so the night Mosquitos of 140 Sqn usually had to operate at lower levels. It made little difference as it happened – by March 1945 the Squadron had carried out 627 night missions below 10,000 feet without loss.

December 1944 saw the onset of the Battle of the Bulge. At a time when the Allied PR formations could range over Europe at will wheedling out minutiae like a 20 feet flying bomb, the Germans amassed some twenty divisions in the Ardennes over a period of months without anyone seeming to be the wiser. "Where in hell has this sonovabitch gotten all his strength?" exclaimed a surprised General Bradley on December 16th as his forces were driven back under the onslaught – it was a question that should have been answered weeks before, and, because it was not, a lot of questions had to be answered afterwards.

This audacious counter-thrust was launched after two weeks of low cloud ceilings and winter fogs, but nevertheless the two USAAF PR Groups in that area did manage to fly 174 sorties during the first half of December. They brought back pictures of massing troops, and tanks and bridging equipment being moved forward; why then did these prints, and the mass of confirmatory conventional intelligence, receive such scant attention? Sir Basil Liddell-Hart provided some of the answers:

"The Intelligence head of the First Army was not on very good terms with the Operational head, nor with the Intelligence head of the Army Group, and was also regarded as an alarmist inclined to cry 'Wolf'. Moreover, even he failed to draw clear deductions from the facts he had gathered, while the imminently threatened 8th Corps formulated the perilously mistaken conclusion that the change-round of divisions on its front was merely the enemy's way of giving the new ones front line experience prior to use elsewhere."

The Battle of the Bulge proved once more that Intelligence is only as useful as the men who employ it. There was plenty of PR information available to the Americans before the Battle of the Bulge to suggest that something sinister was afoot, but there was no CIU in Europe to co-ordinate the warning signals coming in from the various PR Groups and Intelligence agents along the whole front. To use a simile, the Intelligence staffs before the Battle were like a group of men with candles in a darkened room. Each illuminated candle was comparable to an important print, and each man who held it created a small area of light, though he still could not see the whole room. If all the men pooled the fruits of their labours they would see the room in its entirety; if they failed to co-operate and retired to their own corners to drool over their little bits of light, then no-one would see the overall situation in perspective. "Interpretations which aren't co-ordinated," said Douglas Kendall in January 1945, "are sometimes no more use than undeveloped films."

This lack of co-ordination can easily happen in a fluid tactical environment, but the offence was compounded because the Allies had been on the offensive for so long that they never imagined that the Germans might try to take the initiative once again. It was a sad reflection on the blinkered thinking of the time that when an American Intelligence officer reported that the German Army appeared to be massing for an assault on the Ardennes, he was immediately sent on sick leave to Paris because he was thought to be suffering from overwork.

As the war moved inexorably towards its close, so the tactical PR squadrons moved further and further into Europe. "The operation for seizing the town of Wurselen," wrote one regimental Intelligence Officer, "was conducted entirely with aerial photos. All preliminary planning, initial reconnaissance, and the regimental commander's final plans were based on the photos. His attack order was issued with an overlay made from them. The photos also were used for planning by supporting artillery, tanks and tank-destroyer units. All artillery targets pinpointed by the infantry were entered on the artillery photographs. The photos were the basis for all intelligence overlays sent to lower units. The interrogators of prisoners of war used aerial photographs to orientate the prisoners. The cannon company used aerial photos to select likely locations for advance gun positions; the anti-tank company, to select positions for night defence; and the service company, to select possible supply routes and bivouac sites."

At the end of February 1945, after a SHAEF request for their own strategic PR element along the lines of 106 Gp, ten Mosquitos and ten Spitfires were sent out from Benson to Coulommiers to form 104 PR Wg. There was little for them to do before Germany surrendered. Tactical taskings also became fewer and fewer because the armies were advancing so rapidly in March that many targets had been captured before they could be photographed. Thus the PR crews found themselves on odd jobs such as shipping reconnaissance, anti-submarine patrols off the Dutch coast, and ferrying maps and photographs from Brussels to the 2nd Army HQ at Hannover. The German Navy surrendered on May 3rd and 34 Wg was sent to photograph a convoy of 200 German ships trying to evacuate troops from Denmark to Norway. Four days later a 16 Sqn Spitfire took off to cover the Danish coast and Friesian Islands to make sure that the German forces were obeying the surrender order – it was to be the last tactical PR mission of the war.

Down south in Italy tactical battlefield photography was provided by PR Spitfires, in the shape of a Flight from either 682 or 683 Sqns working alongside the FR squadrons of Gp Capt Millington's 285 Recce Wing. The blue Spitfires moved from forward airstrip to forward airstrip as the armies advanced past Rome, an arrangement which Gordon Hughes disliked, not because he lost control of some of his aircraft but because he believed that high level Spitfires were unsuited to tactical work. The Army agreed. One day 285 Wg lost a PR Spitfire, and by the time the RAF got to the wreckage they found that the cameras had already been removed. It was later found that the Army had cut a hole in the floor of a Piper Cub and fitted a Spitfire camera into it. Hughes did not mind – a Piper Cub with a 36in lens at 800 feet stood a much better chance of detecting a tank in a ravine than a high flying Spitfire.

Nevertheless the Spitfires attached to 285 Wg provided much valuable information for the Allied armies as they moved towards the Gothic Line. During July 1944 alone they carried out 110 missions and brought back 54,261 negatives,which were converted into 551,338 prints by the MFPS trailers that dutifully followed through the mud and across the mountain roads as the detachment moved up Italy.

Once the Gothic Line had been breached on August 25th, both 285 and 336 Wings concentrated on photographing targets for interdiction sorties against Axis lines of supply. Roads and railways became so clogged that eventually the Germans had to resort to transportation by sea. Vessels photographed in Trieste one evening were found to be in Venice the following morning, having sailed under cover of darkness. Venice had to be bombed to cut off this line of supply and March 21st was chosen for 'Operation Bowler' – anyone who missed the port and bombed the free city would be 'bowler-hatted' – because it was expected that the large supply ship *Otto Leonhardt* would be alongside the quay that day. The neutralisation of the flak batteries and the accuracy of the raid itself were due almost entirely to the information provided by the pre-strike prints. As a pilot of 680 Sqn flew his Spitfire over at 20,000 feet with the fourth bomber wave he not only saw the *Otto Leonhardt* burning but he felt the shock wave as a warehouse full of land mines exploded.

There were other 'one-off' missions, like the low level dice over the Piazzo Loreto in Milan to see whether Mussolini had indeed been strung up from a lamp-post, but 336 Wg was still mainly concerned with strategic targets beyond northern Italy. Southern Germany was visited regularly and it was here that the Me 262 first made its presence felt. This new Luftwaffe jet fighter had first appeared on film in February 1944 following a sortie to Lechfeld aerodrome near Augsburg, but it was not until five months later that a PR pilot got a close look at the latest opposition. On the afternoon of July 25th Flt Lt A. E. Wall and Fg Off A. S. Lobban of 544 Sqn set off from Benson in their Mosquito for southern Germany. Suddenly, over Munich, an Me 262 appeared out of nowhere; Wall pulled into a tight turn and the jet overshot. Six times the Me 262 pilot swept in for the kill and each time he had to overshoot because the Mosquito out-turned him at the last moment. Twenty minutes later a very relieved Mosquito crew escaped into cloud over the Tyrol and made an emergency landing at Fermo on the shores of the Adriatic.

The aircraft of San Severo came up against the new threat for the first time on August 15th, 1944 when Captain S. 'Pie' Pienaar of 60 SAAF Sqn was intercepted in his Mosquito at 30,000 feet en route to Gunzburg and Leipheim. He jettisoned his drop tanks, turned to starboard, and put the Mosquito into a spin as the jet made its first pass. Pienaar then found that his throttle had jammed open, and his airspeed indicator was passing through 420 kts by the time he recovered at 19,000 feet. On levelling out he discovered that his flaps, ailerons, and elevators on the port side had been shot away, but 'Pie' still managed to steep turn his way out of trouble twelve times during the next 40 minutes. The German finally gave up when they were 90 miles away from where the battle had started, and Capt Pienaar and his observer, Lieut Archie Lockhart-Ross, limped home to immediate DFCs.

Southern Germany was a bad place for PR during August. The Luftwaffe seemed to have selected PR aircraft as the best sparring partners against which to evaluate and devise tactics for their new jets, and four Benson aircraft were 'bounced' that month of which one was shot down. The best way to evade the jets was to wait until they were committed to their run in and then stand the PR aircraft on its wing tip and haul it round at maximum 'g'. But to evade them one had first to see them. Mosquitos were not too badly placed, and around Munich two pairs of eyes stuck out on stalks, but the solitary Spitfire pilot soon developed a complaint known as 'PR neck'.[1] By September 106 Gp casualties were double those of the previous June, and over half of these occurred around known Me 262 haunts.[2] For the first time since the introduction of the Fw 190, the strategic PR squadrons of the RAF had met an opponent worth worrying about; "the long boast that the PR Spitfire could outclimb and outrun anything," wrote the 683 Sqn Operations Record Book, "was radically altered."

Fortunately there were new aircraft in the pipeline. The maximum ceiling of the Spitfire PR XI could not be exploited because the aircraft lacked a pressure-cabin. Aeromedical tests had proved that aircrews suffered considerable discomfort, with a resulting loss of efficiency, without pressurisation above 38,000 feet, yet it was becoming increasingly necessary to operate at these very high altitudes to evade trouble-makers such as the Me 163 and Me 262. The C-in-C Coastal Command therefore recommended that all his PR Spitfires be fitted with pressure cabins, and that a proportion of these should have Griffon engines to provide greater height and speed, and thereby greater security, over the sensitive area of southern Germany.

The first pressurised PR Spitfire was the PR X – basically a PR XI with a pressure-cabin – which was unpopular with pilots because they had difficulty seeing out of the dirty yellow hood. However, only sixteen of these were produced – by the end of the year the Griffon-powered PR 19s were appearing in appreciable numbers.

The PR 19 was the last in a distinguished line of photographic Spitfires. Built around the Mk XIV airframe with PR bowser wings and a Griffon 66 engine, the PR 19 was capable of 446 mph at 20,000 feet and a ceiling of 42,000 feet. Its normal safe range was 1,160 miles, but this was extended to 1,550 miles by the addition of a 170 gallon overload drop-tank. Some 225 models came off the assembly line, of which all but the first 25 were pressurised, and the PR 19 was to remain in RAF PR service until 1954.

Pressurised Mosquitos also appeared in 1944. The first pressurised model was the PR XVI, but the crews disliked the new cabin because "the look-out

[1] This was partially balanced by the fact that the Spitfire was less conspicuous than the Mosquito.

[2] Nevertheless losses still only accounted for 2.95% of the total flying effort.

above was bad, around limited, and below nonexistent." The perspex canopy also suffered from hoar frosting – this could be cleared on the Mk IX by opening the side windows, but this was not possible in a pressurised cockpit. To add insult to injury, crews found the PR XVI's ceiling to be only 36,000 feet, and as this was only 1,000 feet above that of the Mk IX, a pressurised cockpit did not seem to be worth all the trouble.

Next came the Mosquito PR 32 with its specially lightened and extended wing tips which raised the ceiling by 5,000 feet, but the ultimate PR refinement from de Havilland's drawing board was the Mosquito PR 34. Back in 1943 Wg Cdr the Lord Douglas-Hamilton had pointed out that some of the missions his crews were being given were really beyond his squadron's capability. He cited Gleiwitz in Poland, 800 miles away, as an example of the extreme limits to which the Mosquitos were being asked to fly. Extra large drop-tanks were the answer, and the PR 34 gave Benson everything it wished for and more. The bomb-bay was expanded to take more fuel and a 200 gallon drop-tank was placed under each wing. Needless to say the wings had to be specially strengthened; when these drops were fitted experimentally to a PR XVI, the dihedral sagged by 49 minutes of arc. The PR 34 could carry a total of 1,256 gallons of fuel, compared with 860 gallons on the PR XVI, which could be translated into a phenomenal 3,340 miles. With a top speed of 425 mph and a ceiling of 43,000 feet as well, the PR Mosquito crews were very impressed.

Spitfire PR 19s were reaching their squadrons by October 1944, but the latest Mosquitos took some time to arrive, especially overseas. As late as December 1944, 60 SAAF and 680 Sqn sorties from Italy to "sensitive areas" had to be escorted by up to six P-38 or P-51 fighters; the South Africans were set upon so often that they dubbed themselves "No 60 SAAF PR and Decoy Squadron".

The jet menace declined once the Allies entered Germany. Heavy bomber raids on the Luftwaffe's jet factories kept the numbers of aircraft leaving the assembly lines within reasonable bounds, but there was still the odd encounter worthy of mention. On March 16th, 1945, Plt Off R. M. Hays of 544 Sqn set off for Germany in his Mosquito PR XVI. At 30,000 feet over Leipzig he saw two Me 163s climbing rapidly towards him. Within three minutes they were at 30,000 feet and starting their runs in for simultaneous beam attacks on the Mosquito. Hays did a half roll and dived vertically, but as he pulled out at 12,000 feet with 480 mph on the clock he found that not only were the jets still on his tail but also their number had increased to three. Hays did a steep dicing turn and fled down to tree-top height, whereupon the Luftwaffe gave up the chase and flew off. He feathered his starboard engine, which had been struck by cannon fire and was producing nothing but smoke, and made for the Allied lines at 2,000 feet. The crippled Mosquito was intercepted 30 minutes later by an Me 109, so Hays had to dive for the hedgerows again to shake it off. Forty-five minutes later the Mosquito was staggering along a valley near Kassel when a flak battery opened up hitting the aircraft and injuring the observer. An hour later Hays sighted Lille and approached to land, unaware that his tyres had been punctured by gun fire. As he touched down the undercarriage collapsed, severely damaging everything that was left apart from the crew. Hays escaped from the wreckage and was awarded an immediate DFC.

Luckily such interference was the exception, not the rule. In fact small arms fire and flak batteries were much more troublesome, especially at low altitudes. On April 30th, 1945 the pilot of a 680 Sqn Mosquito was shot and killed by ground fire, whereupon his observer took over and flew back to base at 2,500 feet. After 2½ hours he sighted the airfield, but could not reach the throttles as he was strapped in, so he landed at something over 200 kts. Two great bounces later the aircraft finally landed as the undercarriage collapsed; the impromptu pilot was also awarded an immediate DFC.

As the Allies gained sway over more and more of the skies, as well as the ground beneath, such incidents tended to decrease, but Hays' experience showed how vulnerable the Spitfire and Mosquito had become. They had done sterling service and had flown where they pleased for virtually the whole of the war, but by 1945 they were incapable of maintaining that inherent superiority over everything that flew which was the great trademark of the PRU. Jet technology had come of age, and if the war in Europe had continued for much longer, or if the Germans had produced jets in any appreciable numbers, the PR squadrons would have had to have been equipped with jet aircraft themselves to keep their usual one step ahead.

106 Gp saw out the Second World War in much the same manner as the PDU saw it in; D-Day and V-weapons would come and go, but the routine of watching the German Navy seemed to go on forever. By the end of 1943 several old faithfuls had disappeared from photographic view – the *Scharnhorst* had been sunk and the *Gneisenau* dismantled – but there was still much to watch as every vessel except *Tirpitz* congregated in the eastern Baltic. Throughout 1942 the German U-boat production rate was estimated at five per week, varying from 1,000/1,200 ton types at Bremen to small vessels of 250/300 tons at Hamburg. Construction work continued apace through 1943, but by February 1944 the whole situation seemed to have altered. Whereas 271 submarines were counted under construction in June 1943, eight months later the number had declined to 168 and no new hulls were appearing. Either U-boat warfare was being abandoned or something new was about to emerge.

On April 19th, 1944, a Mosquito PR IX of 540 Sqn flown by Flt Lt A. Graham with Plt Off T. Osborn as his observer lazily crossed the skies over Danzig. From their prints a PI noticed a patch of debris in the water close to a newly launched U-boat in the Schichau basin. It had obviously just descended from slipway 5, yet cover of Danzig on March 8th had shown that slipway to be empty. It had therefore taken no more than six weeks to build a submarine from laying down to launching, a feat possible only with prefabricated sections.

This discovery was confirmed by the sight of a partially completed vessel on another slipway with its stern section nearby waiting to be attached to the hull. The U-boat photographed by Graham and Osborn was the first Type XXI – the U 3501. Laid down on March 20th, it had been built in record time to be Doenitz's birthday present to the Füehrer on April 20th; fortunately the PRU was there to witness the celebrations.

By the end of June 1944, twenty-one of these 251 feet craft had been discovered, along with eleven of a smaller 110 feet prefabricated type first seen at Hamburg and Bremen in May. The average assembly and fitting out time was reckoned to be three months, and had D-Day not gone successfully these prefabricated craft, produced at a rate more than sufficient to balance operational losses, would have posed a serious threat to the Allied shipping lanes by the end of 1944. Heavy bomber raids based on PR evidence frustrated German attempts to build prefabricated submarines in any numbers before their construction yards were captured or cut off by the advancing Allied armies.

At the beginning of March 1944 the *Tirpitz* was reported to have left the Alten Fiord in the company of five destroyers. Plans were made to launch a Fleet Air Arm attack and a third PR detachment was sent to Vaenga to provide pre-strike information. Three Spitfire PR IVs[1] left the Shetlands on March 7th – the earliest time for adequate photo-light in northern Norway – together with 542 Sqn personnel under the command of Sqn Ldr D. R. M. Furniss. The *Tirpitz* was found on the second mission out of Vaenga six days later, in the same Kaa Fiord berth she had occupied the previous autumn; the prints were flown back to Britain in a Catalina and the CIU report was in Admiralty hands within 30½ hours of the Spitfire touching down.

This sortie provided all the necessary planning information, so the detachment watched the battleship only obliquely from afar during the next few weeks in order not to arouse German suspicions. The climax of their work came on April 2nd when the Kaa Fiord was photographed seven times in final preparation for the attack which was to be made the following day by aircraft from *Victorious* and *Furious*. Bad weather prevented damage assessment until April 7th, but even then it was impossible to say more than that the great vessel had been damaged because the *Tirpitz's* port side lay in the deep shadow of the fiord wall. As the weather also prevented any further air attacks, the PR detachment returned home on June 12th.

1944 also saw the end of several long PR associations with the Celtic fringe. The demands of Overlord and Europe were more pressing than the limited threat posed by the German Navy, and in April the 544 Sqn detachment at Leuchars was recalled to Benson. The St Eval Flight followed suit on July 20th, and a month later the improving situation in southern Europe permitted the return of the Gibraltar aircraft.

Despite the efforts of a detachment of 28 Lancasters and one PR Mosquito to finish off the *Tirpitz* in September, the great vessel still remained seaworthy, and the following month it was suspected that she might move south

[1] The Soviets were not to be allowed a look at the more advanced PR XI.

to try to escape from the advancing Russian armies. A 540 Sqn detachment was sent to Dyce with a watching brief, and on October 18th Fg Off H. S. Powell DFC located her surrounded by booms four miles west of Tromso. At last the pride of the German Navy was back within range of UK-based heavy bombers; three times the Lancasters went in, and on November 12th a 12,000lb bomb delivered the telling blow. Flt Lt A. R. Cussons was in position with his PR Mosquito within 100 minutes of the raid, and from 17,000 feet he photographed the battleship lying on its back with no superstructure in sight.

On March 22nd, 1945 Sqn Ldr F. L. Dodd DSO and Plt Off E. Hill DFM left Benson for a last look at the *Tirpitz*. They refuelled at Sumburgh and then flew to Tromso where they took some magnificent obliques of the partially submerged ship from zero feet. After being airborne for 10½ hours and flying over 3,000 miles they landed back at Benson. The longest PR sortie of the war was also a final salute to the now rusting hulk that had occupied PRU attentions for over three years.

With the demise of the *Tirpitz* there was little left to worry the Royal Navy. The light cruiser *Koln* was photographed with two large holes in her side after a USAAF raid on March 30th, 1945; the *Scheer* met its end in Kiel at the hands of Bomber Command on April 9th; the *Lutzow* was similarly dispatched after being discovered by PR in the Kaiserfahrt Canal near Swinemünde.

On May 3rd the *Prinz Eugen* and the *Nurnberg* were seen in Copenhagen, while the *Hipper* was on fire to the north of Kiel. The last remnants of the German Navy surrendered that day, and 106 Gp spent the next few days plotting the position of nearly 150 vessels to make sure that they were obeying the surrender order.

The RAF had continuously watched over the German Navy, like hawks over a pack of wolves, for nearly six years. First the SIS, then the PDU, PRU, and five squadrons scattered from the north of Scotland to Gibraltar had come into being primarily to keep one step ahead of, or as often happened, as close as possible behind, German naval strategy. The German Navy was the raison d'être of high level PR in the RAF; it was appropriate that the warships which brought the PDU into the world at Heston at the start of the war should preoccupy 106 Gp at Benson at the end.

The war had ended in Europe but in the Far East the RAF still had a "lone furrow to plough". 3 PRU at Dum Dum had expanded during 1942, and in line with the general reorganisation of PR throughout the RAF it was rechristened 681 Sqn in January 1943. Squadron resources were divided to meet as many commitments as possible; heavily defended areas in Burma, China, Assam, and the Andaman Islands were given to the Spitfire PR IVs; long range but lightly protected targets could safely be left to the B-25s; short-range tactical sorties were generally given to the Hurricanes.

Flying PR Spitfires in the Far East was no sinecure. The Japanese in Burma might not be able to mount the same degree of opposition as the Luftwaffe, but there were other daunting obstacles to overcome, not counting cholera and dysentery. First there were the winds. Aircrews fresh from the Middle East were used to flying East to West, or out against the wind so that they could assess its strength and homeward with the wind behind them. From Dum Dum it was West to East, or out with the wind, giving a pilot little chance to assess its velocity. If he misjudged his time for photography over 'hot-spots' like Rangoon, he could easily be caught out as he flogged back into wind towards Bengal at less than 200 kts ground-speed and with ever decreasing fuel reserves.

Then there were the great unstable air masses that built up during the afternoons. Photo-light in the tropics lasts from 1000 hrs to 1500 hrs, and if a pilot wanted to get back before the tropical air mass built up it meant a very early start. So most pilots set out at dawn intending to reach their targets, often 600 miles away, by 1000 hrs so that they could be back over India before the clouds covered the ground underneath completely. If they were late or unlucky it meant flying over 10/10ths cloud until they were reasonably sure that they were past the 12,000 feet high Arakan mountains, and then down through the murk to find and follow the coastline for 200 miles back to Calcutta.

It was this violent tropical air that was the great destroyer of PR aircraft, not the Japanese Zeros that could rarely get high enough to intercept the PR Spitfire. By the middle of the afternoon, cloud columns of unstable air could stretch up to 50,000 feet and anyone attempting to fly through them risked being hurled about by the turbulent airstream. Freddie Proctor, returning at 13,000 feet from a sortie to the Andamans, suddenly felt his aircraft rise like a lift and he could only watch helplessly as his altimeter revolved like an instrument possessed up to 20,000 feet. He came out of cloud upside down and finally recovered at 3,000 feet over the sea. Others were even more lucky. One pilot was sucked into cloud over Bengal, remembered nothing after his aircraft disintegrated around him, and recovered consciousness strapped to his seat in a paddy field with his parachute still packed.

Up to the beginning of 1943, PR in the Far East had been primarily concerned with supporting the defence of India, but by the summer Allied forces were beginning to request cover to help plan the long advance back to Singapore. This meant extending the scope of PR operations beyond Burma to Malaya and Sumatra, and although four specially modified PR Liberators of 160 GR Sqn[1] coped with the long distances involved from Ceylon, they were cumbersome beasts and vulnerable to Japanese fighter opposition.

It came as a complete surprise to everyone when two Mosquito PR IIs landed at Dum Dum on August 9th, 1943. Mosquito PR IVs began to arrive a month later, and the first one went on an operational sortie in the hands of Flt Lt McCulloch to Rangoon and Mague on October 21st. There were five PR Mosquitos at Dum Dum by November which, together with the four remain-

[1] Aircraft of 225 Gp at Bangalore were also used for PR on missions beyond the range of 681 Sqn. Ceylon and Bangalore had their own First and Second Phase Sections, but all interpretation was co-ordinated by the CIU at Delhi.

ing Mitchells, became the nucleus of the newly formed 684 Sqn.

The Mosquito introduced a new dimension into PR in the Far East, as it had done in every other theatre of war. Areas such as the Andamans, barely within Spitfire range, and Siam, which was far beyond it, now came under regular scrutiny by the PIs at Delhi. On December 15th, 1943 Sqn Ldr B. Jones covered Bangkok for the first time since the evacuation of Burma, and from now on the B-25s could be safely retired to communications duties and taking crews on leave.

On November 16th the RAF in India and the 10th USAAF were amalgamated into Air Command South East Asia. Eastern Air Command, including 171 PR Wing, which now controlled the destinies of 681 and 684 Sqns, was given responsibility for Bengal and Assam. The following February reorganisation went a step further with the incorporation of 171 PR Wg and the 8th US Photo Gp into the Photographic Reconnaissance Force (PRF), with Bill Wise as its Commander.

January 1944 saw the beginning of the survey of Burma in preparation for its reoccupation. The Mosquitos of 684 Sqn inevitably flew the longest and most productive sorties, especially once the tropicalised PR XVIs arrived. In May, Flt Lt K. J. Newman flew to the Nicobar Islands to prove that the Mosquito had enough fuel to cover the distance and still have time for photography. After Car Nicobar (1,903 mls return) and Bangkok (2,000 mls) came sorties to cover Singapore and its railway (2,028 mls), survey work around Mergui (2,084 mls), the Koh Si Cangs Islands (2,1´3 mls), and Nawcawry (2,256 mls).

681 Sqn also provided a great deal of equally important though shorter-range cover during these months, including two outstanding trips in March, the first to photograph every airfield en-route to Rangoon and the other to survey all the roads between Imphal and Tamu for the 14th Army. By May 30th, 1944, the two PR squadrons had photographed some 232,100 sq mls of enemy territory.

There were also special missions in preparation for Wingate's second Chindit campaign. Jungle clearings known as 'Piccadilly' and 'Broadway' had to be photographed in preparation for glider landings. Last minute cover showed 'Piccadilly' to be blocked by rows of teak logs hidden in the long buffalo grass, but as 'Broadway' appeared clear Wingate decided to risk everything and land all his gliders there.

The PRF also assisted in a secret operation designed to evacuate Chindit casualties from northern Burma. Unfortunately the evacuation coincided with the monsoon period and the torrential rains played havoc with PR activities; monthly numbers of PRF sorties could be numbered in hundreds apart from May to July when the monsoon was at its height – 684 Sqn was restricted to nine flights in July, and several of these were weather checks. The monsoon made it impossible to land an ambulance aircraft on the flooded landing strips behind Japanese lines, so the PRF was asked to provide prints to help select a suitable landing area for a seaplane.

In April 1944 the PRF had moved up to Alipore in preparation for the

Allied advance into Burma. Its primary role during the offensive was defined as the detailed coverage of enemy airfields and communications, possible bombing objectives and areas for mine laying, targets required by the Intelligence services, and aerial surveys for map production. Work in support of the advancing armies was no problem, but Air Command SE Asia was still handicapped by the lack of any long-range aircraft capable of operating 1,500 mls away. It was suggested that aircraft carriers be used, with the result that the Admiralty converted six portly Hellcats to the PR role and sent them with the 21st Aircraft Carrier Sqn to the Far East, where they earned their keep by photographing 30,000 sq mls of the Malayan coastline.

As Ceylon was the nearest RAF base to the Dutch East Indies and Indo-China, three PR Mosquitos were detached to operate alongside 160 GR Sqn at China Bay, from whence they began the first ever large-scale survey of northern Sumatra. With its capacity of 860 galls the PR XVI could just about manage 30 minutes photography over Sumatra before starting back on the long 1,000 ml flog to Ceylon. Navigation was strictly of the 'watch and compass' variety, although crews occasionally enjoyed the luxury of a doubtful W/T bearing from Madras.

There were twelve Mosquitos on the strength of 684 Sqn at Alipore in January 1945, and, by using forward refuelling airfields like Cox's Bazaar and Akyab, the PR XVIs began to fly further and further to the south and east. The legendary Burma-Siam railway was a regular target – Mk XVIs with an F 24 forward-facing oblique camera in each wing tank and another in the nose would dice the railway line to photograph the results of bombing attacks on bridges and railway cuttings. Just in case flak batteries were about a PR Mosquito would do a short run, break off into the surrounding hills, and then carry on PR further down the track.

On January 21st, 1945, 684 Sqn photographed the Mekong river for the first time, while on March 22nd Flt Lt Jack Irvine broke the distance record for the PR XVI in any theatre of war when he flew 2,493 mls to cover the Bangkok-Singapore railway down to the Malayan border. But this record did not last long once the PR 34s started to arrive in June. On August 20th Flt Lt J. R. Manners and WO F. A. Burley flew 2,620 mls from the 684 Sqn forward detachment on the Cocos Islands to Penang Island and Taiping in just over nine hours.

By March 1945 684 Sqn had finished three-quarters of all the basic survey work required for the advance towards Malaya. Underneath, the PR Spitfires of 681 Sqn darted from pin-point to to translate the features on the new maps into large-scale reality. Between them 684 and 68´ Sqn mapped 57% of the total area of Burma, an area three times the size of England.

While aircraft from Alipore fulfilled strategic tasks such as providing damage assessment following the bomber raids on Rangoon, a forward detachment from 681 Sqn moved up in support as the 14th Army advanced into Burma. The rush was on after Imphal to reach Rangoon before the monsoon, and the tactical element of 681 Sqn moved from Kalemyo to Monywa, and then to Meiktila in March. By the time Rangoon fell the Japanese had been driven back 800 mls, all of it under the watchful eye of the aerial camera.

On June 16th Sqn Ldr Clif Andrews RNZAF and Flt Lt Jack Irvine left Alipore to photograph Mount Everest. "We made a wide circuit and had a splendid view of the southern slopes of the South Peak, Lhotse and the saddle between Lhotse and Everest," reported Andrews. "I was so dazzled with this scene of beauty that I think I just kept on circling." The cameras turned over the peak for twenty minutes and then the Mosquito flew over the summit in a farewell salute with only 30 ft to spare.

Andrews also entered Singapore a day ahead of the Allied forces of occupation. He had been sent from the Cocos Islands on August 31st to photograph Singapore in preparation for the Allied arrival, but over the island one of his constant speed drive units failed. Fearing that he would not have enough power to climb over the mountains of Sumatra, Andrews decided to land at Kallang. He and his observer stepped out of the Mosquito with some trepidation for, although the Japanese had surrendered a fortnight earlier, there was no telling what the reaction of the forces on Singapore would be. Their fears were groundless – they were met with much bowing and scraping, the local radio broadcast news of their force-landing for the benefit of 684 Sqn, and Andrews was introduced to the Senior RAF officer at Changi Jail who arranged for an Engineer officer, a fitter, and a rigger to repair the faulty engine. The Japanese even refuelled the Mosquito with their best 100 octane fuel before Andrews, not a little relieved, took off for the Cocos Islands.

The surrender caught everyone unawares. Instead of extending their watch over Bangkok and Mergui the 681 Sqn detachment at Meiktila concentrated on making sure that Japanese forces in the field were laying down their arms. One of the most rewarding sorties of the war was flown ten days after the surrender when a PR Spitfire brought back prints of the waving and cheering inmates at a POW camp at Kanchanaburi in Thailand. But no-one wanted to stay in the sweltering jungle any longer than necessary and soon the detachment moved to more convivial surroundings. Everything of value went with them, but this did not include the six PR Hurricanes that had served, first the Middle East PRU, and then the Far East so well. They were left in a straight line at Meiktila to be stripped by the local populace and then absorbed by the same encroaching jungle whose secrets they had worked so diligently to pierce.

From the high point of RAF PR in 1945 it is worth looking back for a moment at some of the achievements of the Second World War. In that time the strategic and tactical PR squadrons of the RAF had earned a professional competence and stature that was second to none. They had taken on and surpassed the defensive might of the Luftwaffe and the Regia Aeronautica, proved to the Japanese that none of their possessions within range were immune to the attentions of the aerial camera, and demonstrated admirably to the USAAF that dedication and perseverance were worth far more than inexhaustible supplies of men and equipment.

The credit for all this must go to many men of differing ranks and persuasions; to the Air Ministry staffs for a start, who avoided the trap into which every other air force fell of treating PR as a servant rather than as an equal of the more glamourous bomber and fighter organisations. To them, knowledge came before power, and, by keeping the intelligence gatherers away from the power wielders, the Air Ministry ensured that 106 Gp was strong enough to fight for the best aircraft and equipment available.

Then there were the men on the ground who made everything in the air possible – the Intelligence Officers, the engineers, the PIs, and those hard worked but often forgotten men, the camera servicing personnel. We have only to look at the amount of fuss that an amateur photographer makes over lighting, viewpoint, and exposure to realise how much depended on the men who maintained and installed the aerial cameras that were expected to operate time and time again in a temperature of – 30°C while rushing through the air at 350 mph and being shaken by two 1700 h.p. engines running flat out. It is to the eternal credit of the ground camera sections that their aerial charges only failed to work on 5% of all PR sorties from the UK.

Finally there were the aircrews themselves – the heirs and successors of Cotton, Longbottom, and Niven. Their exploits are too numerous to mention individually, but it is interesting to note that the same names kept reappearing again and again throughout the war. The spirit of Heston and Benson was kept alive because the disciples of Cotton and Tuttle influenced PR throughout the war, rising in rank or moving around the world, but as likely as not eventually coming back to look after aeroplanes with cameras attached to them. PR in the RAF was a great family tree, and from the trunk at Benson came the guidance, expertise, and spirit that was to be found in every branch.

Between 1941 and 1943 the various detachments of 1 PRU averaged some 200–300 sorties a month. This rose to 460 by 1944, and in the August of that year 106 Gp flew a record 799 missions. During the first week of August PR aircraft covered 1302 different targets all over Europe on behalf of the Air Ministry, Bomber and Coastal Commands, the Navy, SHAEF, the 8th USSAF, and the War Office. There was no target on earth over which aircraft from Benson could not have operated with relative immunity given the range. The PR squadrons of the RAF had reached a zenith of superiority that was unchallenged; from then onwards they could only go downhill.

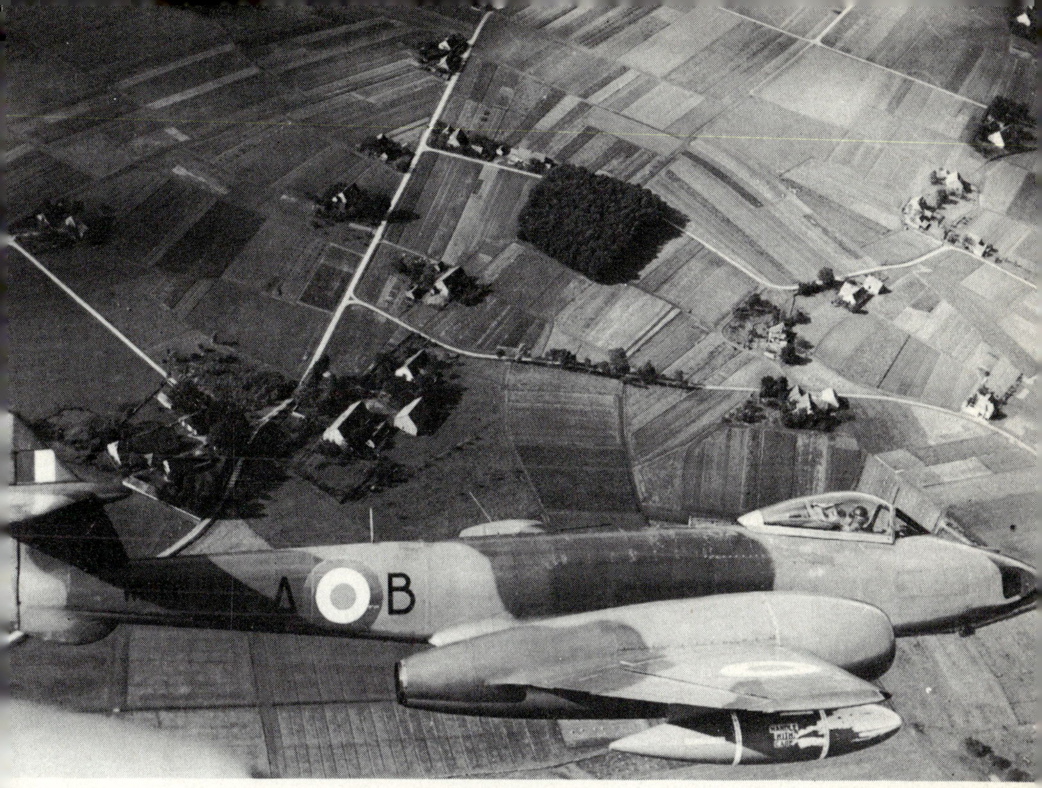

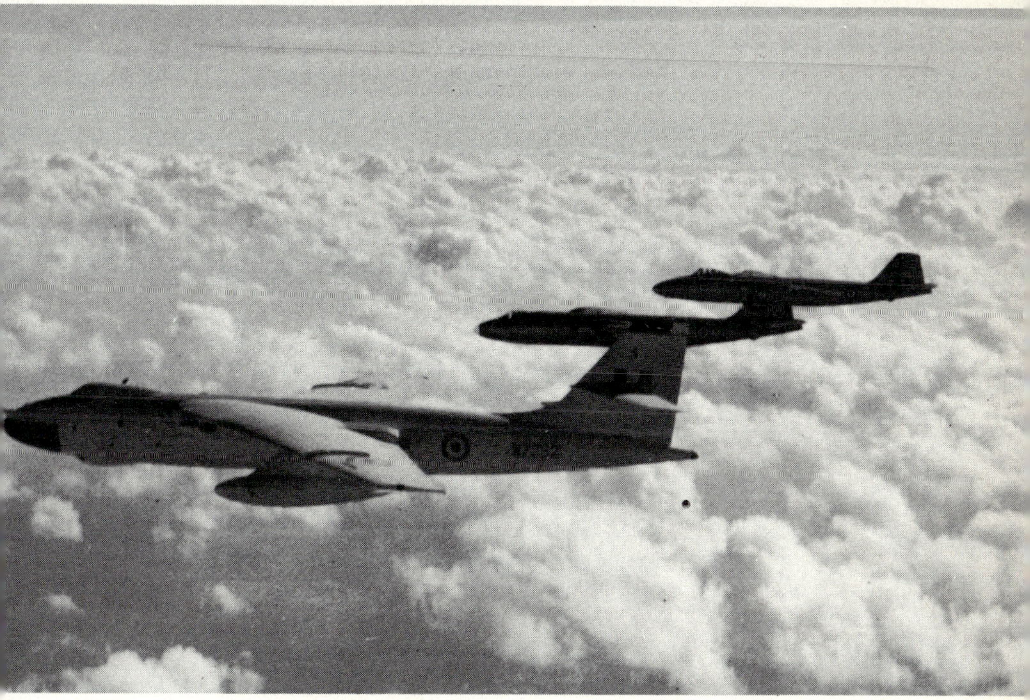

Top: Meteor PR 10 taking part in Exercise Royal Flush (an annual NATO PR competition) from Gutersloh, Germany, in September 1954. *Flight. Above:* Representatives from the UK Recce Force in the early Sixties – a Valiant B(PR)1 of 543 Sqn in company with a Canberra PR and Canberra PR9 of 58 Sqn. *CC*

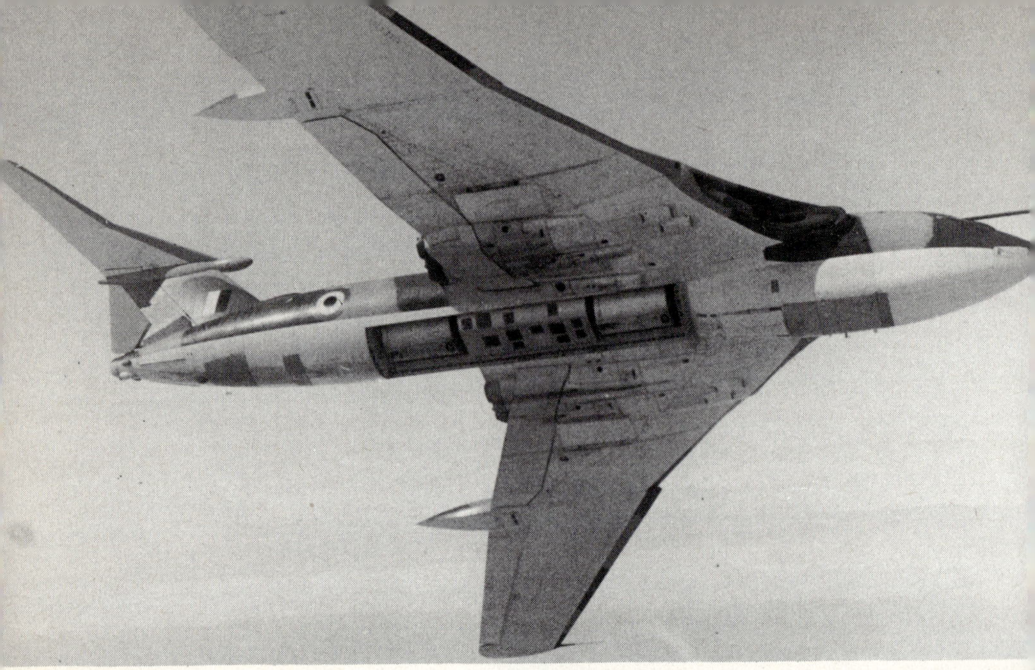

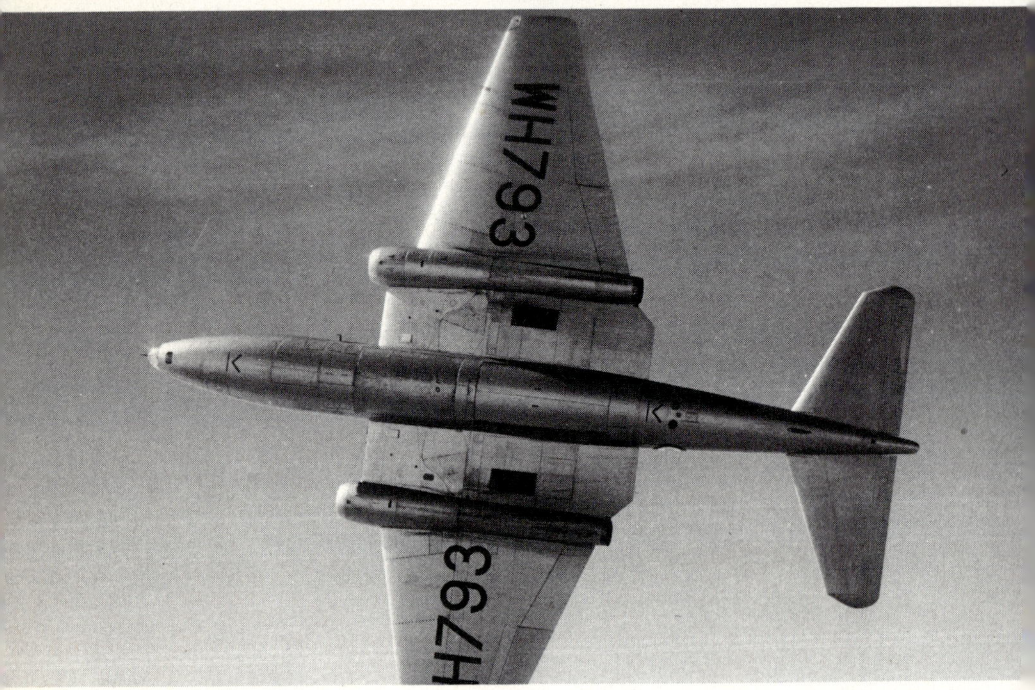

Last of the RAF's strategic PR aircraft. *Top:* A Victor B2SR of 543 Sqn with bomb-doors open to display the camera crate. *CC. Above:* This picture shows the underside of the prototype Canberra PR9, vividly illustrating the increased chord at the centre-section of the wings to provide aerodynamic lift at high altitude. *British Aircraft Corporation. Top right:* Gary Powers holding a model of the U-2 before he testified to a Congressional Committee in Washington after his release from Russian captivity. *Keystone. Bottom right:* The MRBM site at San Cristobal, Cuba, at the height of the Cuban missile crisis in October 1962. The launch area is nearing completion with two prepared launch positions in evidence. Two missile erectors, missile trailers and signs of intense activity are apparent. *Keystone*

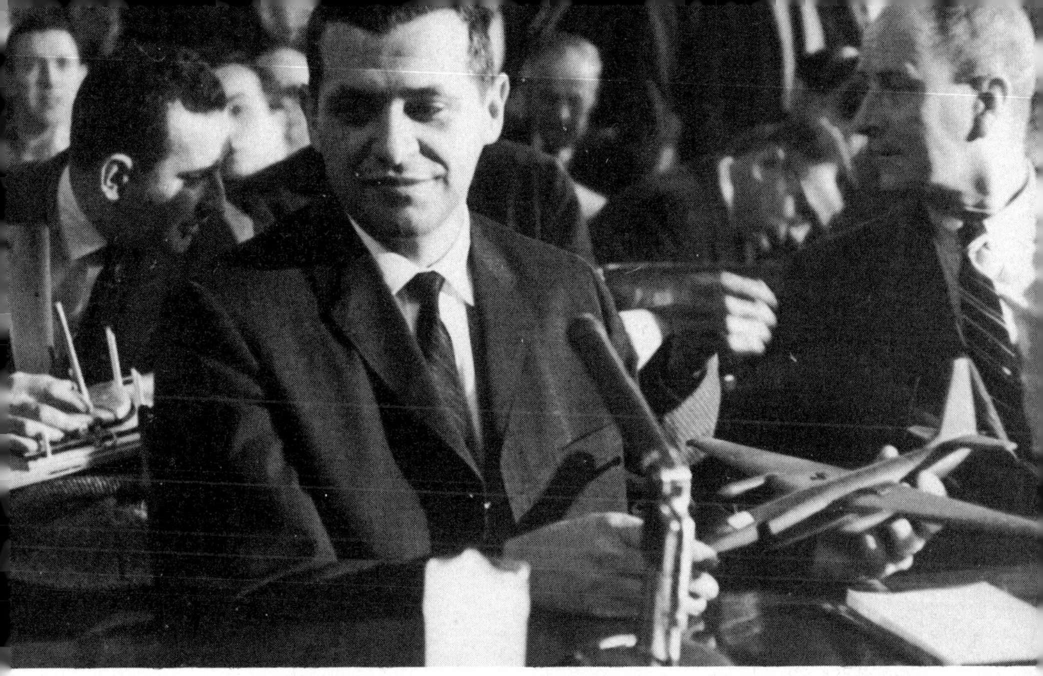

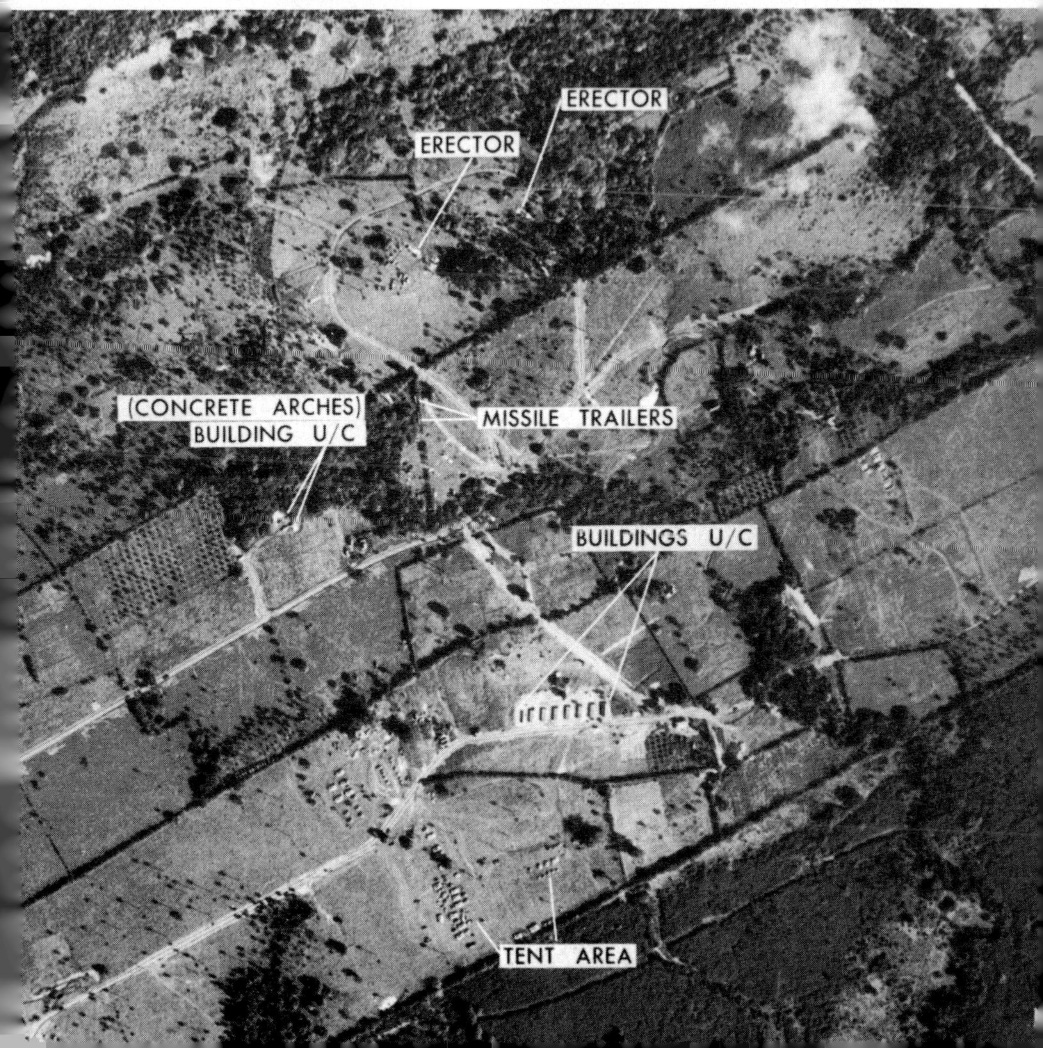
ERECTOR
ERECTOR
(CONCRETE ARCHES)
BUILDING U/C
MISSILE TRAILERS
BUILDINGS U/C
TENT AREA

Below: U-2s in a less provocative guise – NASA aircraft operating out of Moffat Field, California, on duties associated with the US Earth Resources Programme. *Lockheed*
Bottom: The most sophisticated PR aircraft in the world today – Lockheed's SR-71 – photographed in 1972 during a record flight covering 15,000 mls in 10½ hours. This mission, equivalent to flying from London to San Francisco and back, was flown at altitudes in excess of 80,000 ft. By way of comparison, a Canberra PR3 won the speed section of a race from Heathrow to Christchurch, New Zealand, in 1953, covering 12,270 mls in 23 hrs 51 mins. *Lockheed*

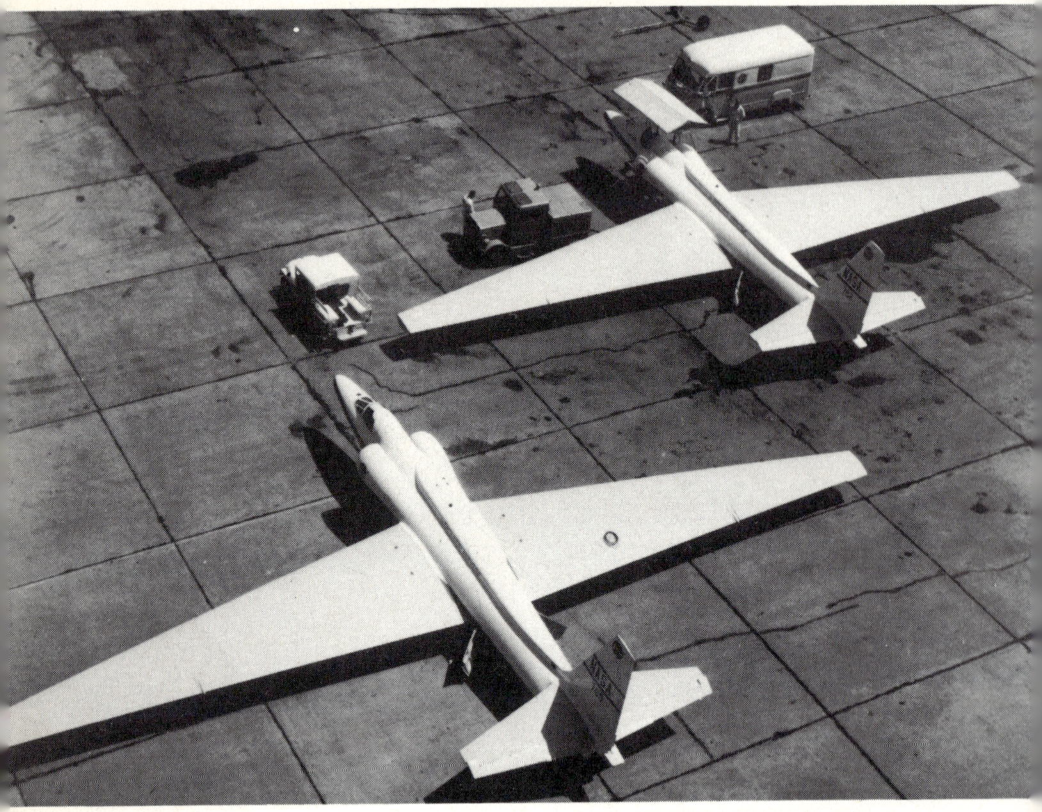

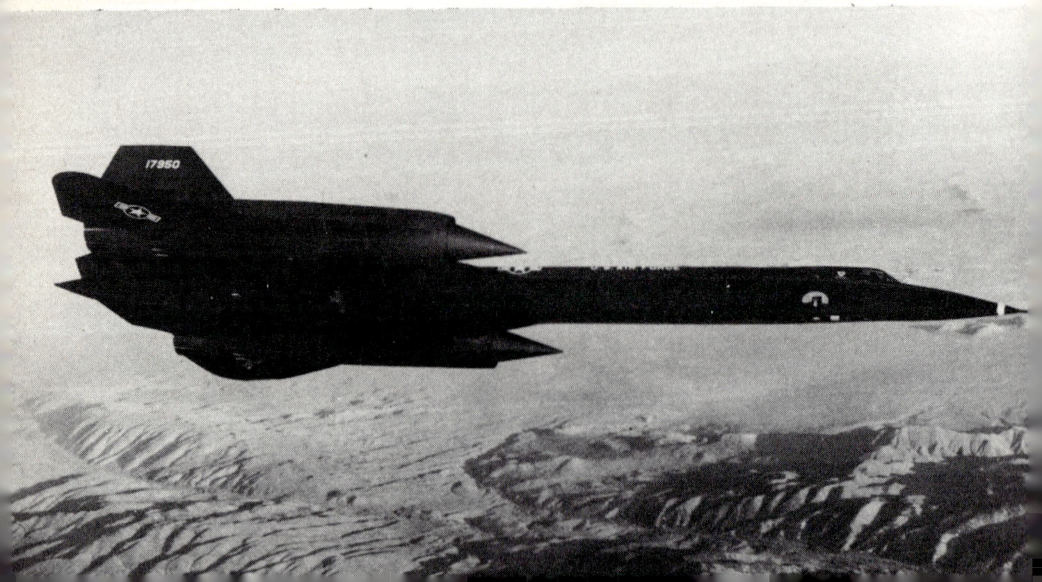

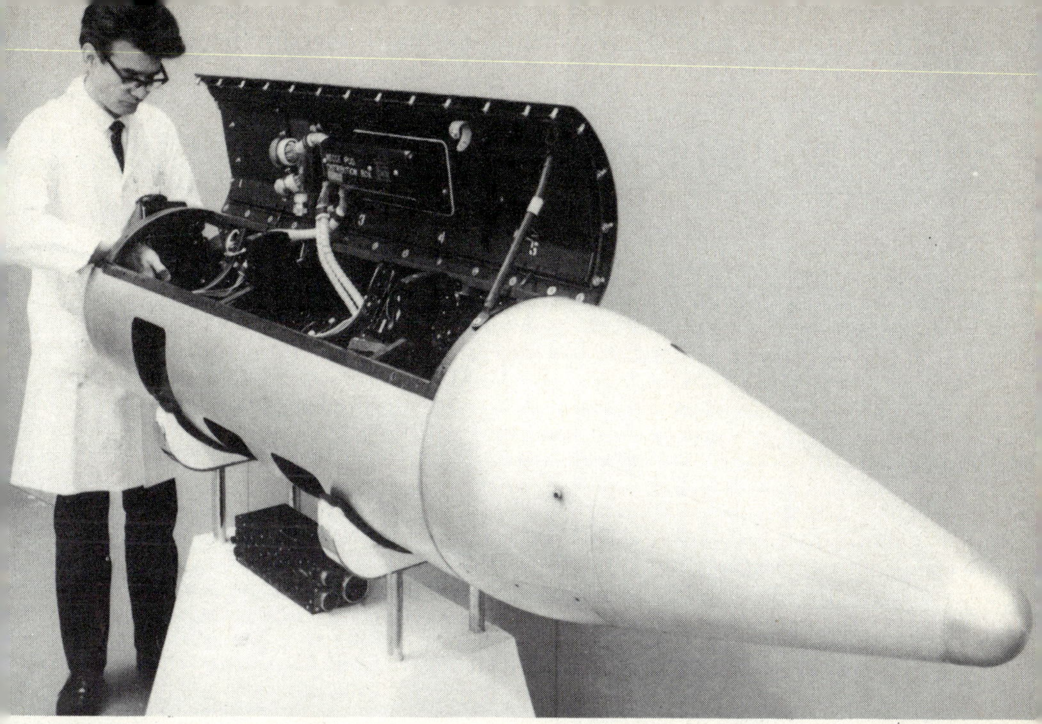

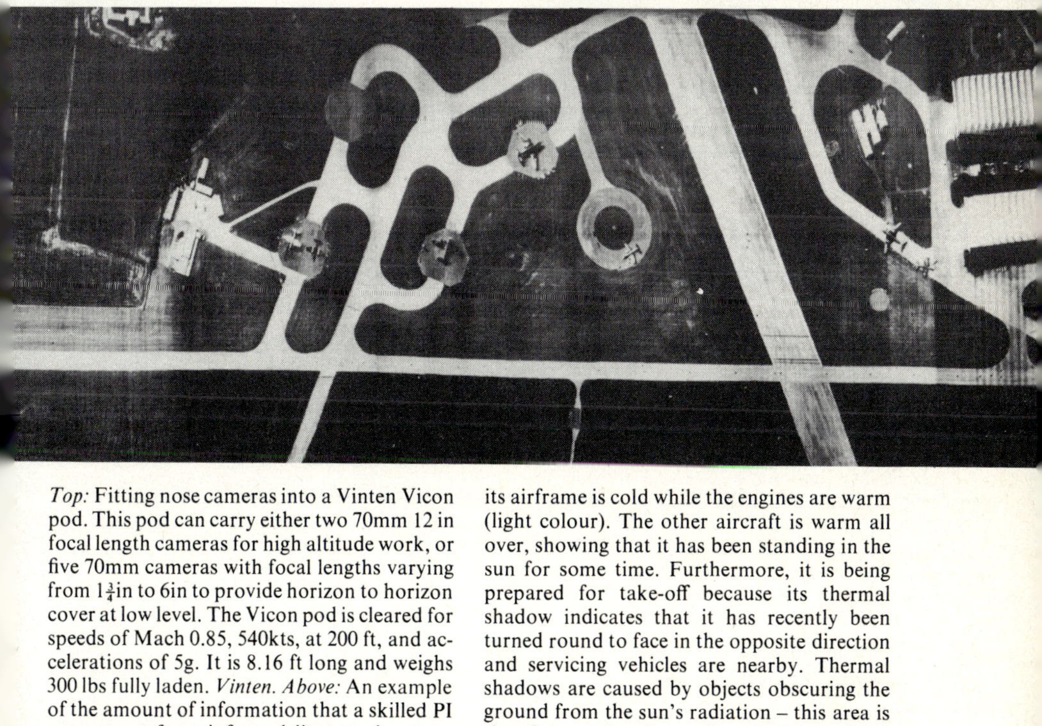

Top: Fitting nose cameras into a Vinten Vicon pod. This pod can carry either two 70mm 12 in focal length cameras for high altitude work, or five 70mm cameras with focal lengths varying from $1\frac{3}{4}$in to 6in to provide horizon to horizon cover at low level. The Vicon pod is cleared for speeds of Mach 0.85, 540kts, at 200 ft, and accelerations of 5g. It is 8.16 ft long and weighs 300 lbs fully laden. *Vinten. Above:* An example of the amount of information that a skilled PI can extract from infra-red linescan imagery. The photograph shows a pair of identical Canberras on their dispersal but the PI can tell that the darker of the two has just landed because its airframe is cold while the engines are warm (light colour). The other aircraft is warm all over, showing that it has been standing in the sun for some time. Furthermore, it is being prepared for take-off because its thermal shadow indicates that it has recently been turned round to face in the opposite direction and servicing vehicles are nearby. Thermal shadows are caused by objects obscuring the ground from the sun's radiation – this area is therefore cooler than other similar surfaces and the thermal silhouette of the object is left on the ground for some time after the object has departed. *CC*

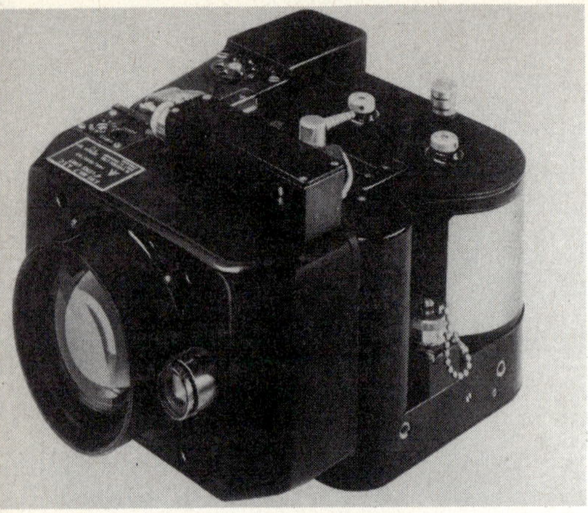

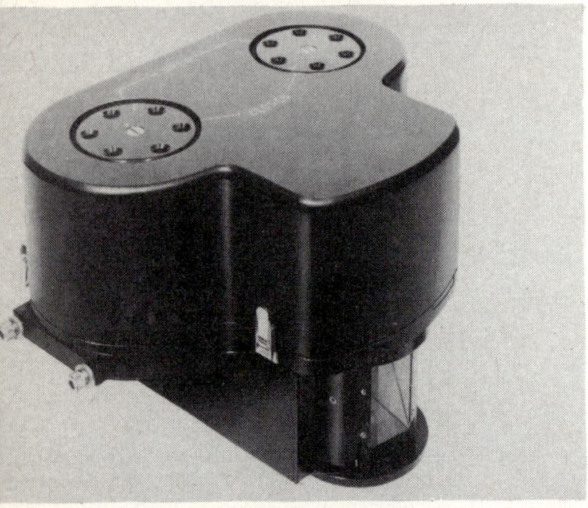

Some of the latest aerial cameras. Top left: Shows the F 95 low-level high speed camera – the Mk 7 variant in the picture can be fitted with Leitz or Zeiss high resolution lenses varying from 3 in to 12 in in focal length, and 100 ft or 200 ft magazines of 70mm film. The F 95 incorporates an Image Motion Compensation mechanism to ensure sharp photography even at 200 ft while travelling at Mach 1. Although the F 95 was first introduced into RAF service in 1950, it is still regarded by many as the best low-level camera in NATO. *Vinten. Middle left:* The Vinten Type 750 Panoramic camera. This revolutionary device enables a series of wide angled (180°) photographs to be recorded on one continuous length of film with much better picture-edge resolution than was previously possible from conventional very-wide-angle cameras. The main feature of the Type 750 is its rotating optical unit, comprising two mirrors, the central f 2.8 lens with aperture mechanism, and focal plane shutter, all of which are fixed to rotate anti-clockwise around a common axis. During the exposure cycle this optical unit revolves through 180° to provide a clear panoramic picture. By effectively combining a fan of cameras into one, Vinten have produced an instrument that can transform any aircraft into a very effective photographic platform, an advance that is particularly important at a time when strike aircraft need to be able to confirm the effectiveness of their missions promptly and easily. *Vinten*

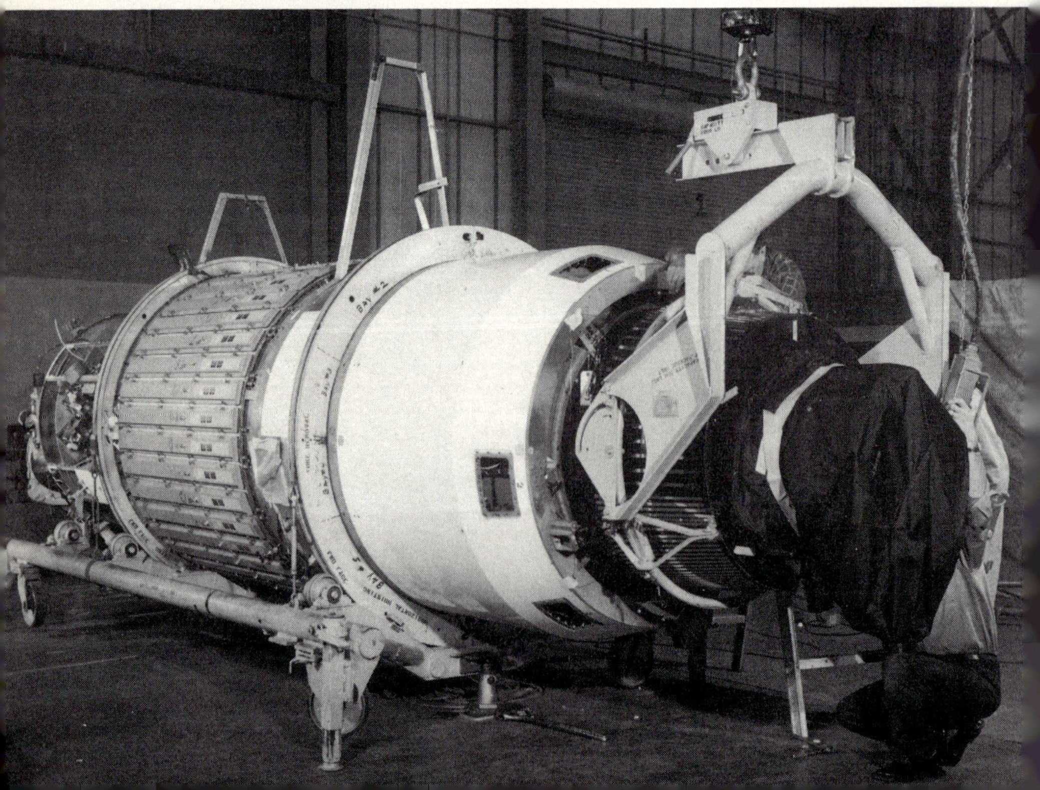

Bottom left: The beginnings of a new reconnaissance system – the camera payload for the first SAMOS photographic satellite being prepared in the missile assembly building at Vandenberg AFB, California, in 1960. *USAF*

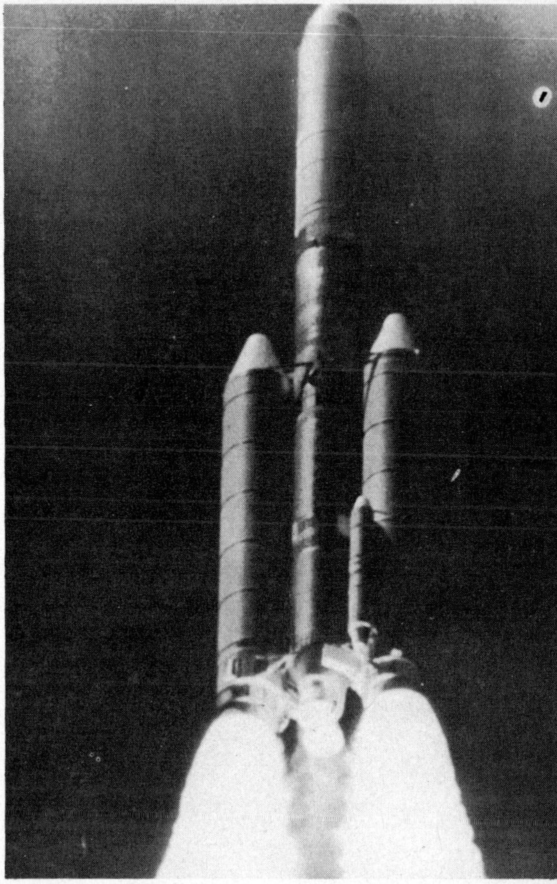

Right: A Titan IIID launching one of Lockheed's 'Big Bird' reconnaissance satellites into orbit from Vandenberg AFB in 1972. *USAF* *Below:* An unusual view of a pair of Teledyne Ryan Model 154 RPVs prior to air launch from under the wings of their DC-130A director aircraft. *USAF*

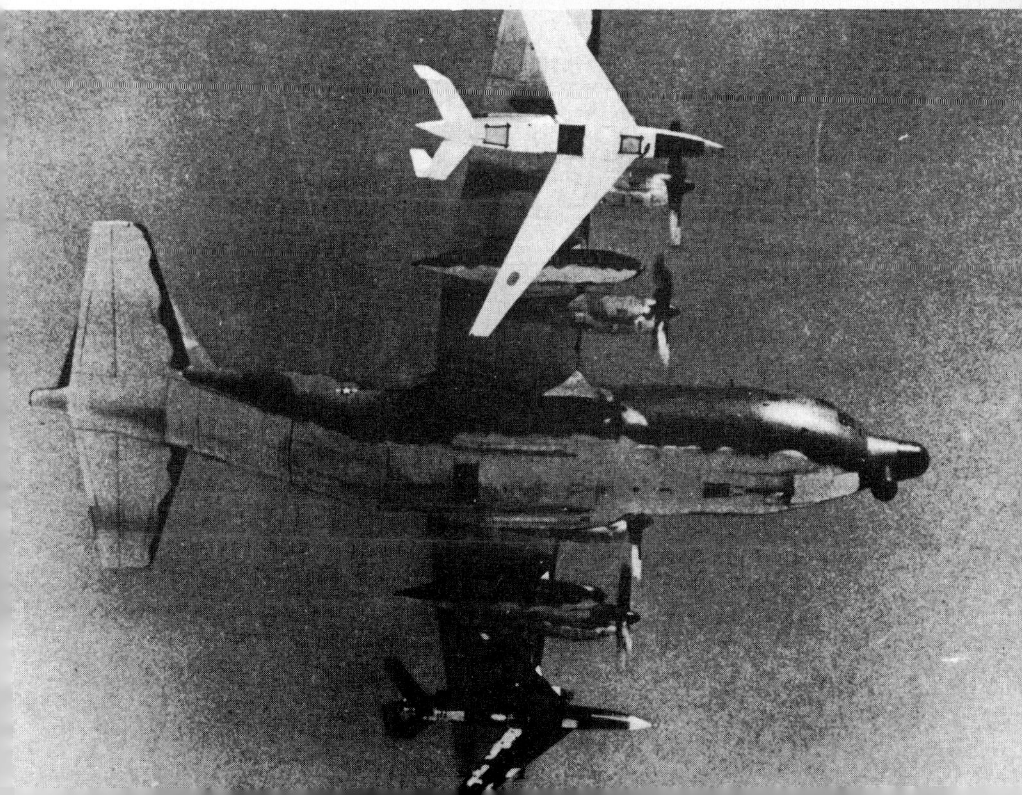

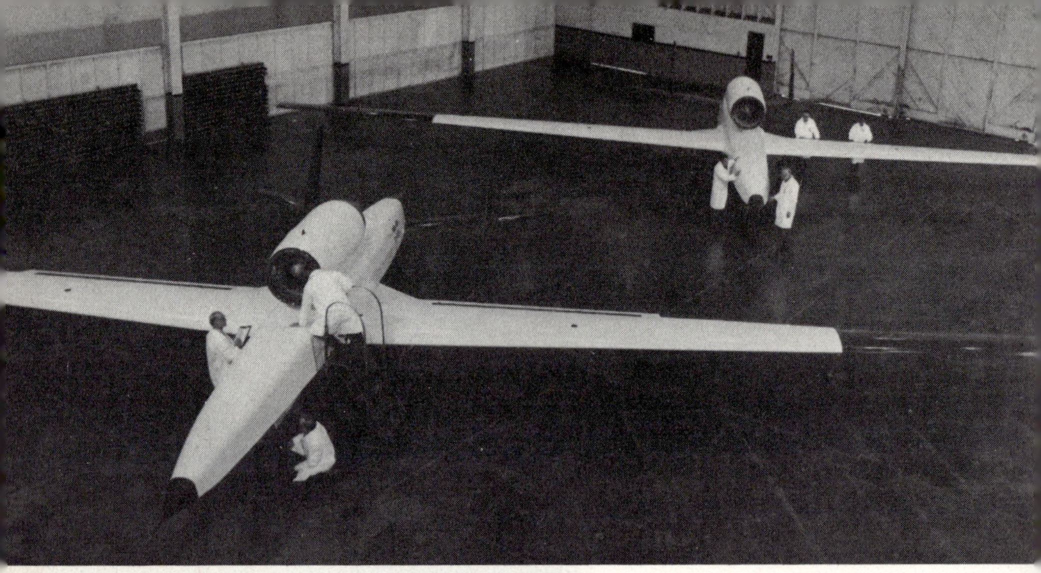

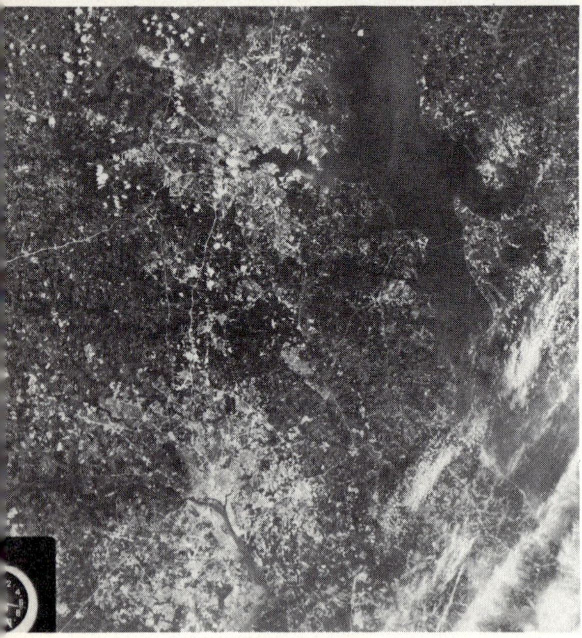

Top: Teledyne Ryan's submission for the USAF Compass Cope programme – a pair of prototype YQM-98A RPVs before their roll out at San Diego on January 4th 1974. The YQM-98A is designed to carry 700 lb of reconnaissance equipment for up to 30 hours over mixed altitude profiles from 50,000′ to 70,000′ at speeds of Mach 0.6 to 0.9. Its narrow wings have a span of 81.2′ and an aspect ratio of 19 for maximum lift. To reduce the chances of detection, the bottom of the fuselage is flattened and the sides gently bank inwards to minimise radar signature; the fuselage is shaped to reduce the likelihood of any incident radar energy directed from a low-level interceptor or ground radar returning to the radiating source, and the Garrett AiResearch ATF-3 turbofan engine is placed on top of the fuselage to lessen the radar signature when viewed from below and to shield the hot exhaust gases from infra-red seekers. The YQM-98A is the first Ryan drone to incorporate a retractable undercarriage for conventional take-offs and landings, thereby dispensing with air launches and parachute recoveries. This RPV can be dismounted and transported to its operating theatre in a C-5A transport aircraft. Financial considerations permitting, the USAF will probably buy 40 production RPVs like the YQM-98A at a cost of about 1.5 million each excluding mission payload. *Left:* Birds-eye view from a very high flying bird – a vertical view of the Washington D.C. and Baltimore area as seen by the Skylab 3 Earth Resources Package in October 1973. The detail achieved by the five-inch Earth terrain camera from space is very impressive. The Chesapeake Bay is on the right (East) while the Potomac River flows through Washington at the lower left. Roads are particularly conspicuous, especially Interstate 95 between Baltimore and the capital, and Interstate 70N leading West from Baltimore. Clearly identifiable features in the Washington area include the Capitol building, the Mall area, the Robert F. Kennedy Stadium (white circle), the 5 bridges across the Potomac and Andrews Air Force base. *Keystone*

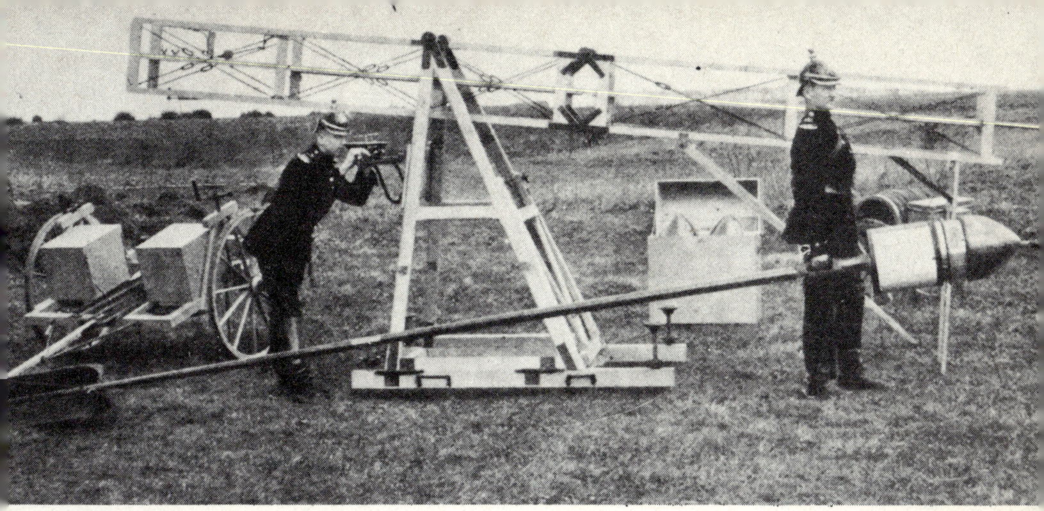

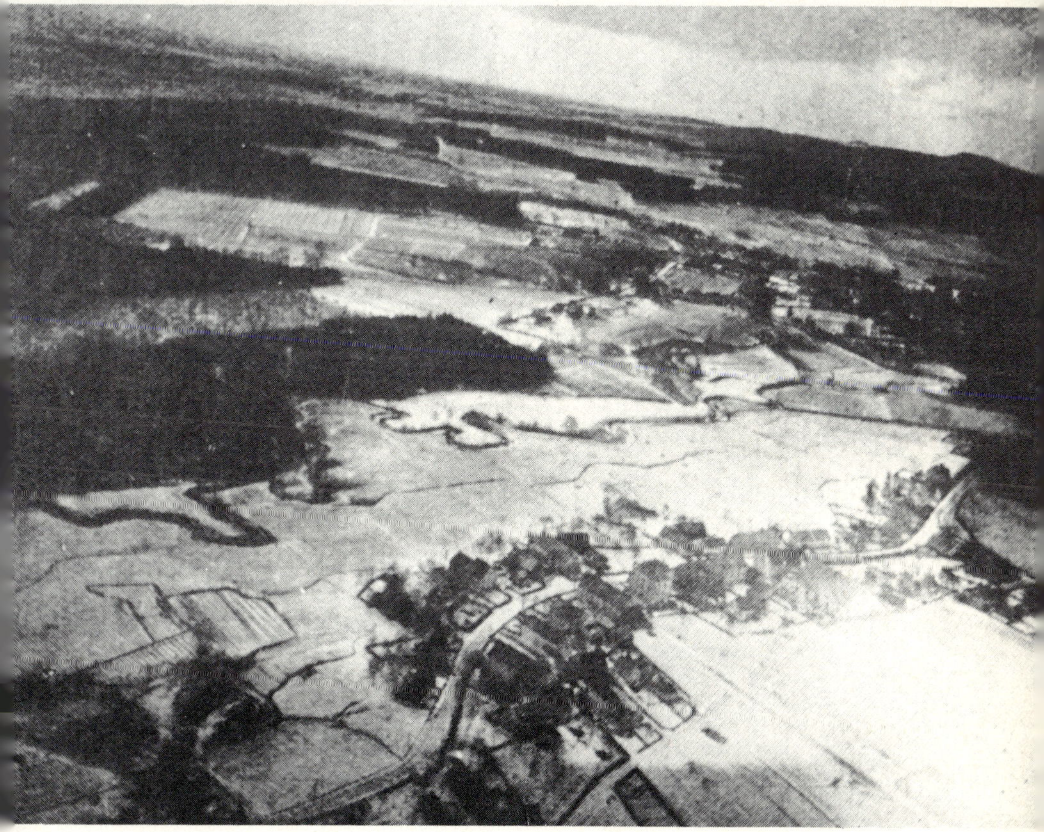

Top: The world's first operational rocket camera. This apparatus was designed by Alfred Maul and these pictures, taken in 1912, illustrate its employment in the field by the German Army. The complete rocket measured 19ft 9in long, weighed 84 lb, and was divided into two main parts – the nose cone, containing a camera with a pneumatic electrical contact on top, a gyroscope and a parachute, and a shaft with wooden feathers at the end. The rocket took 8 seconds to reach its zenith of approximately 2,600 ft. As the rocket started to fall, the fine-lensed camera, held stable by the gyroscope, would make an exposure. The parachute would then be released and cone and shaft would descend to earth. *Above:* The photograph shows the snow-covered village of Stenz as photographed by Maul's camera rocket. *Illustrated London News*

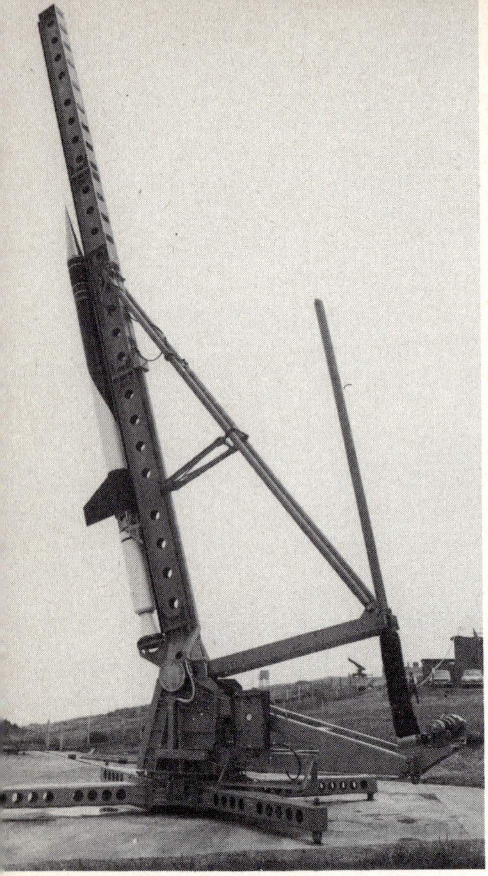

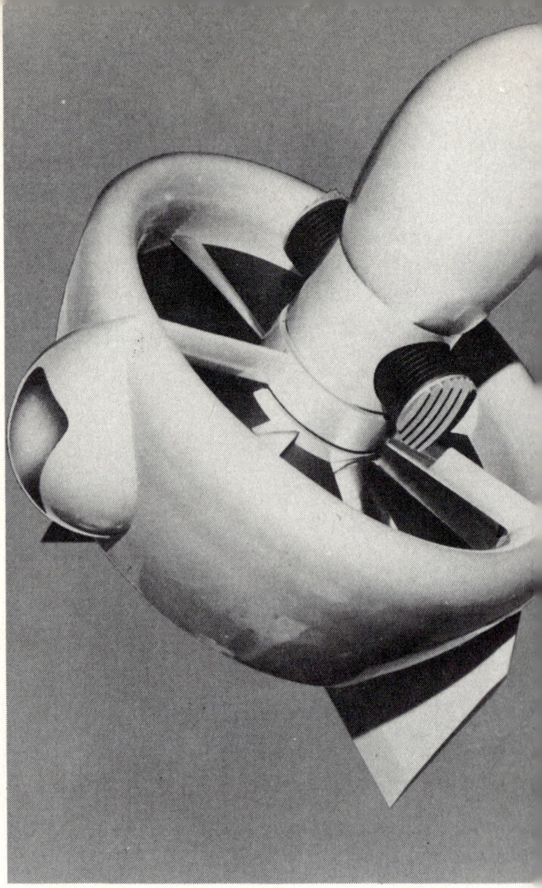

Above: BAC Skylark photographic rocket and transportable launcher. *British Aircraft Corp*
Above right: The Shorts Skyspy. This PR flying saucer derives its lift and propulsion by vectoring the thrust from a low-pressure ducted fan and it can be controlled and recovered very accurately from the ground. These features, together with its low infra-red signature and small radar echoing area, make it highly suitable for use over high risk battlefield zones. Studies are in progress to produce a turbine-engined Skyspy to carry bigger and more sophisticated payloads over greater distances. *Shorts*

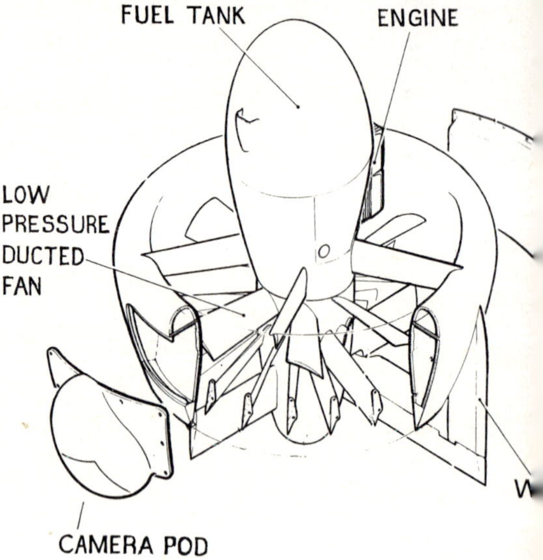

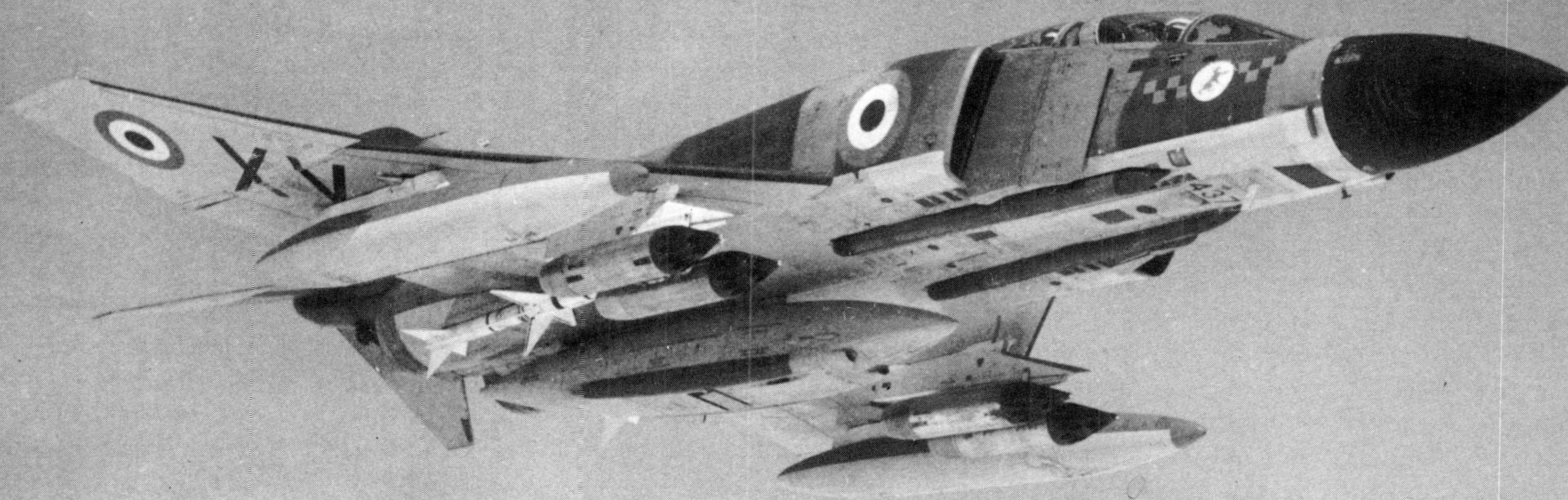

The RAF Phantom FGR 2 showing its underbelly reconnaissance pod. Part of the space in one of the 370 gallon wing tanks is also taken up by night flash equipment, a vital necessity for the Phantom FGR2 as night work accounts for one-quarter of the total reconnaissance effort of 2 ATAF in Germany.

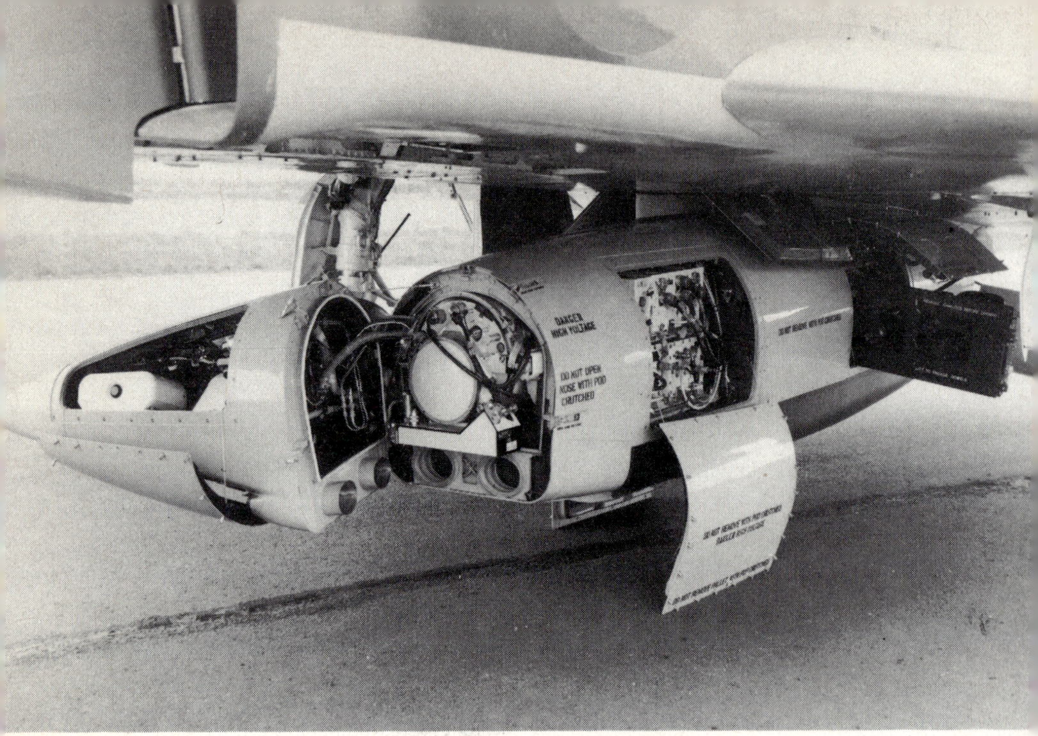

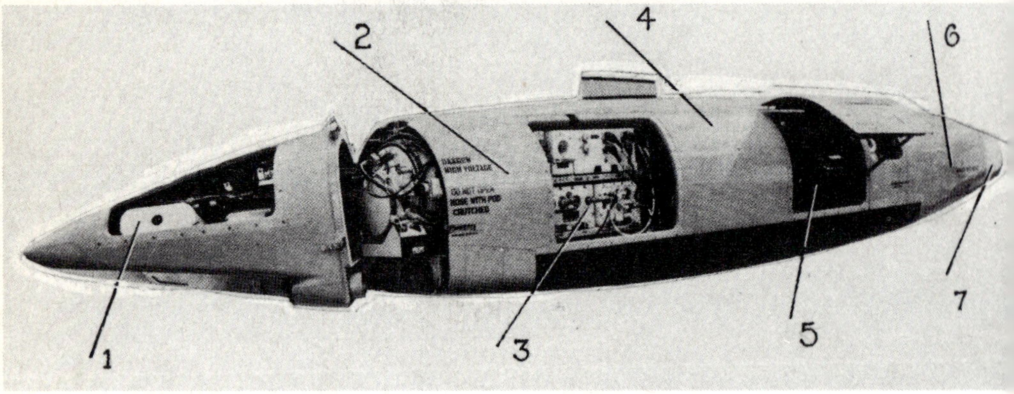

Close-up of the EMI reconnaissance pod. It is 23 ft 9 in long and partitioned into bays to accommodate the following equipment: Air cameras at 1 and 5 – these bays house five day or four night low-level cameras, positioned to provide horizon to horizon cover. (2) Sideways-Looking Reconnaissance Radar (SLRR). This high definition Q-band radar is beamed sideways and downwards by aerials on either side of the pod which are fed from the radar transmitter receiver. The radar returns are then taken to a recorder (*6*), consisting of two cathode ray tubes, from whence they are focused optically into a straight line and a film drawn across them at a rate proportional to the ground speed of the aircraft. According to the CO of 2 Sqn in Germany, "The SLRR will pick up half a mile of baked-bean cans just about as easily as it will half a mile of tanks." (*4*) Texas Instruments' Infra-Red Linescan (IRLS). This sensor is sensitive enough to pick out three personnel asleep in a tent. (*3*) Radar Modulator Data Converter. This records, and marks in code on the film strip, the position, speed and heading of the aircraft when any of the cameras or sensors are working. (*7*) Power supplies. The seven film magazines can be removed in under a minute for processing and the complete pod can be fitted to an aircraft in an hour. These EMI pods are reputed to cost £1 million each. *Hawker Siddeley Aviation Ltd*

CHAPTER TWELVE

Tomorrow, and Tomorrow, and Tomorrow

The key to the deterrent power of our armed forces is our ability to obtain early warning of an enemy's intentions through reconnaissance, and to strike at his offensive forces from a distance in case of need. British Defence Review – 1965.

Qui desiderat pacem, praeparet bellum – He who desires peace prepares for war. Vegetius.

The early post-war years were a time of contraction and change all round for the RAF. In August 1946 106 Gp was replaced by the Central Photographic Establishment (C Ph E), which controlled the operations and technical development of the PRU and the CIU[1] and acted as the fount of knowledge for PR units overseas.

542 and 544 Sqns were disbanded at the end of 1945, leaving 540 Sqn equipped with Mosquitos, and 541 Sqn, which was divided into A Flt with Spitfires and B Flt with Lancasters for mapping work. B Flt provided the nucleus of the reformed 82 Sqn which then moved out to the Gold Coast and Kenya to survey East and West Africa until 1952. In the Mediterranean theatre 682 Sqn was disbanded in August 1945, followed by 683 Sqn a month later. 680 Sqn soldiered on for some time, surveying countries from Italy to Persia, before being renumbered 13 Sqn in August 1946. In the Far East, 681 Sqn operated for a time from Hong Kong and the Dutch East Indies before flying its last operational mission on July 15th, 1946; 684 Sqn became part of the 'Gremlin Task Force' to help root out Japanese forces that had not or would not surrender, but it too bowed before the wind of change to become 81 Sqn in September 1946 at Seletar.

In America, wartime losses had convinced Elliott Roosevelt and other influential people of the need to build specialised PR aircraft, the first of which was the twin-boomed Hughes XF-11. However old habits died hard. As late as 1952 the eminent American aviation authority, Alexander de Seversky, wrote that, "Strategic reconnaissance over enemy territory must be made by battleplanes, since reconnaissance means combat". Consequently for the first post-war decade the strategic PR requirements of the newly formed USAF were provided by converted armed bombers in the shape of the RB-36 and RB-47E.

Unfortunately the arrival of these new aircraft disguised the fact that much American reconnaissance experience had evaporated as PIs returned to civilian life and air-crews moved on to other specialisations. The shortage of

[1] The CIU moved from Medmenham to Nuneham Park in April 1946.

trained manpower was particularly noticeable at the outbreak of the Korean War, and the resulting disorganisation in the early days of the conflict was noted by Colonel James T. Stewart in 'Airpower in Korea':

"Many of the agencies which used recce facilities, both within the Air Force and without, had forgotten the arduously learned lessons of the past in the capabilities and limitations of aerial recce. Everyone expected prints the same day the sorties were flown. Users were reluctant to accept the interpreters' word for anything which they themselves could not identify on a photograph. Consequently there was great demand for extremely large-scale photographs, or dicing shots . . . Not only did this unnecessarily endanger the pilots and their aircraft, but it was a time-consuming demand upon undermanned squadrons already struggling to meet the requirements of normal coverage.

"A further difficulty arose from decentralised control. In the early days of inadequate facilities each operating agency attempted to create its own reconnaissance agency and use it for its own ends. The result was that there were gaps and overlaps in photographic cover. A Bomber Command RB-29 and a Fifth Air Force RF-80 would fly over the same communist airfield in the same day, while another airfield 20 miles away was not covered at all. Or a Marine camera-equipped F 7F and a Fifth Air Force RF-80 might fly near collision tracks over the same area, as they did when both were photographing the Wonsan landing operation." It was only when all reconnaissance requirements were coordinated by HQ Far East Air Forces that commanders in the Korean theatre started to regain their reconnaissance perspective.

The early Fifties were the nuclear years – a time when atomic weapons held sway over men's minds and when the spectre of a pre-emptive strike against American cities by a seemingly ruthless Soviet expansionist government appeared very real. Washington decided that it could no longer afford not to know what advances the Soviets were making in missile and nuclear weapon development, and so President Eisenhower, who had appreciated the value of PR ever since the 'Torch' invasion of Africa, proposed to Premier Bulganin of the USSR at the Geneva Summit of 1955 that the super powers open their skies to each other's reconnaissance aircraft to "ease the fears of war in the anxious hearts of people everywhere".

In preparation for this 'Open Skies' policy, the Eisenhower administration had authorised the production of the U-2 reconnaissance aircraft in December 1954. The idea for what amounted to the first pure PR aircraft in history came not from the USAF but from Richard Bissell, a first-class espionage agent who at the time was deputy director of the Plans Division in the Central Intelligence Agency (CIA). The CIA, in its role as the world's policeman against communism, attached great importance to the task of monitoring Soviet military developments, and Bissell proposed that the CIA should extend its means of gathering information to include very long-range, high altitude aircraft. His plan was approved and Bissell approached the creator of the P 38 Lightning, now Lockheed's chief designer, Clarence 'Kelly' Johnson, who came up with the U-2 (Utility Two). Every design feature of this revolutionary aircraft was geared to maximum altitude – structural weight was kept to a minimum, only the thinnest metal was used,[1] and even the stabilising 'pogo' wheels under the wing tips were jettisoned after take-off. High aspect ratio sailplane-type wings were fitted to provide maximum lift at rarefied altitudes, and what was aerodynamically a PR glider was propelled by a special Pratt and Witney J 57C jet engine with a thrust of 11,000 lbs.

The U-2 took shape in a top secret hangar known as the 'Experimental Department' or 'Skunk Works' behind Lockheed's Burbank factory in California. Shotgun carrying security guards patrolled the perimeter, while inside 200 specially selected men virtually hand-built each aircraft at a cost of a million dollars each. A veil of mystery surrounded the project – queries about it were answered by a Lockheed statement that the U-2 was "a private venture to obtain information on the question of electrical and engine systems at extreme altitudes, one of its main purposes being to gather fuel flow and fuel metering data for use in developing the F 104A Starfighter." It was barely credible; even allowing for the fact that the F 104 would be able to zoom climb to reach 91,000 feet for a brief period, 53 test-beds seemed very extravagant. So another statement was issued claiming that the U-2 was designed for high level meteorological research for the benefit of future jet airliner operations. As the U-2 could cruise at 65,000 feet, a wag was moved to remark "high weather we've been having lately."

The first U-2 took to the air in August 1955 from Watertown Strip, Nevada. Anyone who has seen a U-2 take off can never fail to be impressed – painted black and devoid of national markings, the U-2 climbs like a lift even from small runways, not against a background of noise and bluster like a shiny aluminium interceptor, but almost silently like a giant bat. It soon disappears from view, climbing remorselessly upwards into the stratosphere. The U-2A could reach 65,000 feet in 1956, no mean height considering that the official world altitude record of the time was 65,876 feet[2], and the more powerful U-2B was capable of well over 70,000 feet. By shutting down the engine in flight and gliding for long distances, the U-2B pilot could stretch his 1,112 US gallons fuel capacity into a range of 4,000 mls.

By 1956 the CIA possessed ten U-2As, all flown by civilians or USAF pilots who had temporarily resigned their commissions, and all ostensibly engaged on meteorological flights for NASA. A similar number was ordered by the USAF for the 4028th and 4080th Strategic Reconnaissance Sqns of Strategic Air Command (SAC), based at Laughlin AFB, Del Rio, Texas and Ramey AFB, Puerto Rico respectively. By this time Eisenhower's plea for open skies had been rejected by Marshal Bulganin in a speech to the Supreme Soviet on August 4th, 1955 when he declared that, "aerial photography cannot give the expected results, because both countries stretch over vast territories in which, if one desired, one could conceal anything." The U-2s were sent over the USSR nevertheless; two U-2 squadrons were established at Incirlik AFB at

[1] A man's fist could almost punch a hole in the fuselage.

[2] Set by Wg Cdr W. F. Gibb, in a Canberra in August, 1935.

Adana in Turkey, and in 1957 another U-2 'Weather Observation Squadron' was formed at Atsugi in Japan.

From their lonely pressurised cockpits the U-2 pilots could see very little of the ground below, not that they could have distinguished much from 70,000 feet. So they concentrated on flying accurately to be over a certain spot at a given time, leaving their electronic sensing equipment and new breed of aerial cameras to discover what was going on below. The U-2 cameras were superb. Gone were the war-time days when men designed aircraft and cameras separately and then tried to fit them together; the Americans fully utilised the blue-prints and expertise which had been brought over by German scientists who had fled from the optical plants of Zeiss and Schott when the Russians occupied Jena in 1945. The Perkin-Elmer camera for the U-2 was designed by a team headed by Dr Edwin Land, the inventor of the Polaroid camera, and its capabilities were described fully by Dr Istomin Gleb Alekseyevich at the trial of Gary Powers in 1960:

"In the course of the flight the air camera was used for seven strip photography, consecutively through seven glass-encased windows in the skin of the plane. The lens cover was from 160 to 200 kilometres (100-125 mls) in width. The camera was loaded with two films about 2000 metres long (6000 feet) . . . The supply of film in the camera made it possible to receive about 4000 paired aerial pictures in the course of the flight, along a route of about 3500 kilometres (approximately 2700 mls).

"The camera lens with a sufficiently long focus made it possible to obtain from the high altitudes at which the plane was flying relatively large scale photographs suitable for the purposes of aerial reconnaissance. The image scale of the pictures obtained over the territory of the USSR on May 1, 1960 was 220-230 metres in one centimetre . . . (Approximately 1 in to 1,830 feet)." We do not know the focal length of the U-2 camera, but even if it was only 48 in it has been estimated that it should have been capable of a ground resolution of 1½ feet. Prints have been published that were clear enough to pick out a golf-ball on a putting green from 55,000 feet.

For several years the U-2s and their cameras operated over the USSR with impunity. "From these flights," testified Secretary of Defence Thomas S. Gates before the Senate in 1960, "we got information on airfields, aircraft, missiles, missile testing and training, special weapons storage, submarine production, atomic production and aircraft deployment . . . all types of vital information. These results were considered in formulating our military programmes." But once the USSR launched Sputnik, then the USA really got worried about the missile threat. Pentagon fears of a 'Missile gap' in favour of the Soviet Union led to an intensification of the U-2 flights over the USSR, so that Washington could plan an adequate deterrent to whatever numbers of Intercontinental Ballistic Missiles (ICBMs) Moscow was deploying. On April 9th, 1960 a set of U-2 prints revealed excavation work that possibly marked the site of the first Soviet ICBM installation. Consequently a U-2 was dispatched from the 2nd Weather Observation Wing at Incirlik on 27th April for Peshawar in Pakistan in preparation for the first full overflight of the Soviet

Union. The flight path from Peshawar lay NNW to eastern Afghanistan before starting the 2,900 mile journey over the USSR from Stalinabad to the missile testing site of Tyura Tam east of the Aral Sea, then up to Chelyabinsk and Sverdlovsk before turning west to Murmansk and finally to Bodo in Norway. The risks involved in such a lengthy trip were felt to be worthwhile considering the importance of the mission, and in more ways than one it was to be the most eventful U-2 mission of all time – at 1100 hrs on May 1st, 1960 Gary Powers was shot down just south of Sverdlovsk.

The Soviets claimed to have hit the U-2 with a surface-to-air missile (SAM) at 68,000 feet, and Powers testified after his release that while he was turning to port at 68,000 feet he heard a loud bang followed by a brilliant orange light. The Soviets seemed to have scored a near miss with a SAM and the U-2 entered an inverted spin from which Powers was forced to bale out at 15,000 feet. Whatever the accuracy of the missile the Powers' Incident heralded the end of U-2 flights over the Soviet Union, not only for political reasons but also because the Americans realised that any target worth photographing would henceforward be heavily defended by SAMs. Unfortunately for the RAF, the appearance of a Soviet SAM capable of destroying an aircraft just below 70,000 feet coincided with the introduction of their most sophisticated strategic PR aircraft, the Canberra PR 9.

By now the C Ph E had been disbanded as an economy measure and control of the PRU and CIU[1] had been transferred to Bomber Command. The PRU[2] had also moved to Wyton in Huntingdonshire, and from 1953 onwards local villagers started to notice black Canberras operating out of the airfield under conditions of great secrecy. The Canberra PR 3, successor to the Mosquito PR 34,[3] was similar to the Canberra B 2 bomber except that its fuselage was lengthened by 14 in to accomodate a fan of six F 52 36 in cameras and an F 49 survey camera, and extra tankage was fitted to increase the fuel capacity to 1917 gallons.

The Canberra PR 3 was followed by the PR 7, a version of the B 6 bomber with more powerful Avons and a fuel capacity of 2,817 gallons. The PR 7 reached the newly reformed 542 Sqn in 1954, and it subsequently re-equipped 13 Sqn in Cyprus, 17, 31, and 80 Sqns in Germany, 81 Sqn in Singapore, and 58 and 82 Sqns at Wyton. However, a still higher ceiling was necessary if the PR Canberra was to remain inviolate from sophisticated defence systems, and so the PR 9 was designed with up-rated Avons and a new long-span wing with its chord increased at the centre section. This improved PR Canberra, which entered service in 1960, had a ceiling well in excess of 60,000 feet – it was quite amusing to hear the crew of 9 PR 9, encased in their pressure suits, shouting ironic encouragement to a Javelin fighter as it wallowed like a bag of

[1] Now called the Joint Air Photographic Intelligence Centre (JAPIC).

[2] The UK PRU then consisted of 58, 82, and 540 Sqns.

[3] 541 Sqn in Germany had also received a jet replacement for the Spitfire PR 19 – the Meteor PR 10 with its nose and fuselage cameras, a speed of 575mph at 10,000 feet and a range of 1,400 mls.

nails 12,000 feet below them trying vainly to get into position for a practice intercept.

The Canberra had the potential to be exploited still further – General Dynamics built it under licence for the USAF, extended its wing-span to 122 feet, and created the RB 57F with a reported range of 4,000 mls and a ceiling in excess of 100,000 feet. It has often been said in America that if the USAF had appreciated the performance of the PR Canberra early enough, the U-2 would never have been built. But the British refused to consider improving the PR 9 still further – overawed by the threat of the SAM and convinced that the strategic manned aircraft had had its day, the Air Ministry turned its back on a specialised replacement for the Canberra PR 9.

The fifties saw a steady decline in the status of PR in the RAF. Not only did Bomber Command control the PRU at Wyton, but also control of the JAPIC[1] was handed back to ACAS(I) at the Air Ministry once again. Nothing demonstrated the fragmentation of PR more forcefully than Suez. It was all too easy to believe that, because the RAF possessed the best PR aircraft of the day, the acquisition of prints was a foregone conclusion. So a detachment of PR Canberras was sent out from Wyton to Cyprus and everyone waited for the prints to roll in. The trouble was that that was just what happened. Every crew let their cameras rip, bringing back mountains of prints that took days to process. No joint services committee was set up on Cyprus to decide which targets should have priority, no one decided which magazines should be developed first, and no extra processing or interpretation staff were sent out to cope with the massive influx of photographic material. Suez proved to the RAF once again that sheer numbers of aircraft were not enough, and that efficient PR meant getting extracted intelligence from the right photographs to the right people in time, not a mass of prints.

In response to Suez, and to meet the need to evolve new reconnaissance techniques to cope with the jet age, the RAF decided once more to combine all its UK strategic reconnaissance forces into one Group. Thus the Central Reconnaissance Establishment (CRE) came into being at Brampton on April 1st, 1957, to control JARIC and the successor to the PRU, the UK Reconnaissance Force, whose PR element following disbandment of 82, 540, and 542 Sqns comprised 58 Sqn and 543 Sqn, the latter having reformed in 1955 with Valiant B(PR)1s.

Valiants were particularly useful because of the number of cameras they could carry. In preparation for their possible involvement in the 'Open Skies' project, the RAF had developed the F 96 high altitude camera to replace the F 52. The British differed from the Americans in their approach to focal length. George Goddard is supposed to have coined the phrase "there is no substitute for focal length" and his disciples in the USA went on to produce 100 in and 240 in lenses in preparation for the day when PR aircraft would operate at

[1] This was soon renamed the Joint Air Reconnaissance Intelligence Centre (JARIC) to reflect the growing belief that the aerial camera was about to give way to more sophisticated electronic sensory equipment.

100,000 feet. However, the greater the focal length the smaller the area of coverage, and the British fought shy of sacrificing area cover for scale, especially as they could not afford to design an aircraft around a 240 in lens. So, to obtain the best of both worlds, the RAF installed fans of cameras to provide horizon-to-horizon cover, an expedient which reached an extreme in the Valiant B(PR)1 which carried a camera crate in the bomb-bay capable of holding a fan of eight F 96s with 48 in lenses and four F 49 survey cameras.[1]

Despite its camera capacity, the introduction of the Valiant B(PR)1, and its successor with 543 Sqn, the Victor B 2 SR, marked the end of the Cotton era in the RAF. V-bombers were designed to penetrate Soviet airspace for only as long as it took to deposit their bomb load, not to loiter over Moscow for an hour taking photographs. They were the product of a declining military budget, and like the Blenheim IVs twenty years earlier they were supposed to be able to revert to their bombing role very quickly. This begged the obvious question that fortunately never needed an answer – in wartime, would the Valiant B(PR)1s be primarily used to take photographs or to drop bombs? While they were controlled by Bomber Command, PR men felt that there could only be one answer.

Having mentioned Soviet efforts to develop an ICBM strategic capability, it is only fair to record that the Soviet Air Force had also built-up a very efficient aerial reconnaissance force during the immediate post-war years. The first recorded Russian pioneer of aerial photography was Kovanka, the commander of an aerostat crew, who took pictures of the Kronstadt and Petersburg fortresses from a free balloon in 1886. A year later, Batut experimented with cameras attached to kites, a line of research that was taken up by a government official, Thiele, who perfected a 'panoramagraph' for mapping remote areas by tying seven kites with cameras together.

The best photographic aircraft in the Tsarist Air Force during the First War was the four-engined Sikorsky Ilia Mourometz – two reconnaissance officers would fly in these 'Flying Ships' to photograph the lie of the land up to 150 miles behind enemy lines, and it was said that 7000 prints were taken in this fashion over German positions by October 1917.

The inter-war years saw the evolution of a Red Air Force that was very much concerned with assisting the Army and security forces on the ground. By 1928 it possessed more than twice as many aircraft as the US Army Air Service, but, although some 40% of its number was assigned to reconnaissance and light bombing duties, most of the former work was visual in nature and the Commander of the Soviet Air Force declared in 1930 that one of the principle shortcomings of his squadrons was their lack of proficiency in aerial photography.

Specialisation in PR was hindered by the multi-purpose nature of Soviet aircraft in the Thirties, and no attempt was made to form any long-range re-

[1] Probably the longest focal length ever used operationally by the RAF was the 60 in lens attached to an F 52 camera which was jammed in between the bulkhead and open door of a Valetta and used over the Berlin corridor during the Blockade.

connaissance divisions to watch over German territory. In fact, although the Soviets made good use of PR in the Finnish war to provide data for their infantry and artillery units, less than 5% of Soviet air regiment strength was earmarked for reconnaissance duties in 1941.

Like every other air force, excluding the Luftwaffe, the Soviet Air Force entered the Second World War completely unprepared to exploit the potential of the aerial camera. It soon learned its lesson. Devoid of any efficient wireless monitoring service in 1941, the Soviet air commanders needed aerial reconnaissance to provide the latest information on Axis dispositions, and they took three practical steps to acquire it. Firstly, the number of reconnaissance training schools for observers was increased; secondly, three crack reconnaissance regiments were formed with the best crews; finally, a long-range element of approximately thirty aircraft was attached to each Red Army group. Army air staffs decided on the targets for PR sorties and the resulting prints were usually channelled via the air army to the Red Army group.

At Stalingrad in 1942, Soviet PIs plotted the dispositions of German defences and the location of Luftwaffe airfields from aerial prints. Such achievements increased in number as the Luftwaffe was worn out of the sky, but despite their enthusiasm the Soviets were burdened by inadequate cameras, poor communications, and lack of technical expertise. No specialised PR aircraft were produced – modified Yak and La fighters were employed on short-range duties, while the bulk of the long-range cover was provided by Petlyakov's versatile PE-2 bomber and Ilyushin's DB-3. Nevertheless, PR was used to good effect in planning the relief of Stalingrad in January 1944, and later that year a Soviet Army commander wrote:

"Photo-reconnaissance is our mainstay, for without it we are virtually blind. Ground observation cannot furnish a commanding officer with all the information he needs; only when I have before me aerial photomosaics showing me not only the front line but also the depth of the terrain ahead, can I properly make tactical decisions."

After the defeat of Germany, the USSR came into possession of a host of aircraft factories (complete with jet aircraft such as the Me 262 and Ar 234), as well as Peenemünde and the optical centre of Jena. The Soviet Air Force blooded its first generation of jet fighters over Korea, and by the early Fifties it was able to start long-range aerial intelligence gathering operations. First came the modified strategic bombers – the turbo-prop Tu 20 Bear E and Myasishchev's Bison – followed by the Soviet equivalent of the high-flying U-2, the Yak 25 Mandrake. In 1960 the Japanese Self Defence Agency reported that Soviet PR aircraft were making bi-weekly flights down the coast to Tokyo Bay but Japanese F-86D interceptors were never able to reach the heights at which they were operating. Currently there is nothing to catch the reconnaissance version of the MiG 25 as it hurtled about its business over the skies of Israel.

However the Powers' Incident taught both the Soviet Air Force and the USAF that the future of strategic PR lay not so much in higher flying aircraft, which were both politically provocative and very dependent on the physical endurance of the men who flew them, as in spying satellites. Rocket photography was first mooted in 1888 by a Frenchman, Amédée Denise, but the first successful rocket camera was patented by a Saxon engineer, Alfred Maul, in 1903. His camera was fitted into the nose of a gunpowder rocket, 19ft 9in tall, and the exposure was timed to take 8 seconds after launching when the projectile would be at a height of about 2,600 feet. The rocket and its camera would then descend on a parachute.

In 1946 the US Army launched a number of captured V-2 missiles from the White Sands Proving Ground, New Mexico, and in one of them was a De Vry 35mm motion picture camera. It made a continuous record of the ascent up to 65 mls, and at 25,000 feet on the way down the camera was ejected. No doubt the Soviets carried out similar experiments with their V-2 trophies. Their Sputnik did not carry a camera, but in 1959 an American Atlas missile carried a camera up to an altitude of 700 mls to bring back the first pictures of the rotund earth. However, rockets were of limited value to the Intelligence agencies – their fields of vision were limited and their cameras only had time for a few exposures before the missiles started on their descent. What was needed was an orbital PR platform capable of travelling around the earth at a constant speed and for a considerable period of time.

In March 1955 the USAF, at the behest of the CIA, issued a requirement for Weapon System 117L, part of which included the development of a PR satellite system known as Samos. Based around the Agena satellite vehicle, and powered by an Atlas launcher, the first Samos – Satellite and Missile Observation System – was launched unsuccessfully from Vandenburg AFB, California, on October 11th, 1960. Samos II was more successful, and it was placed into a polar orbit on January 31st 1961. It was a propitious launching – within seven days Secretary of Defense McNamara was telling reporters that there was no missile gap, because examination of the Samos II prints had put the total number of deployed Soviet ICBMs at 14. One satellite had proved itself to be worth far more than a host of provocative U-2 flights.

Following the launching of Samos III on September 9th, 1961, a curtain of secrecy was drawn over the whole proceedings, so subsequent developments must remain a matter of conjecture. It is clear, however, that the Samos programme was part of a very sophisticated space watching system designed to spy on Soviet missile silos and other military deployments. Before discussing Samos in detail it is necessary to understand the flight characteristics of satellites. Space vehicles are likely to enter elliptical orbits, with the point on the orbit at which the satellite passes nearest the Earth being known as the 'perigee', and the point furthest from the Earth the 'apogee'. Kepler's Third Law, to which all planetary orbits conform, states that the square of the revolution period is proportional to the cube of the major axis of the orbit. In other words, a satellite in an elliptical orbit increases in speed as it passes through the perigee and slows down as it approaches the apogee. This variation in velocity can be used to good effect by placing the perigee of the orbit over the area to be photographed and the apogee over friendly territory – the satellite can then make a fast low run over the enemy, giving best photographic resolution and the least time for counter-measures, followed by a 'dwelling' at apogee to permit long transmission time for data to be relayed to ground stations.

Equally important is the track produced over the Earth's surface. There are three types of orbit that interest the PR staffs. Firstly there is the polar orbit, whereby the vehicle can be positioned to pass directly over the North and South poles in each revolution. However, as the Earth rotates beneath this fixed orbit, each successive pass over other latitudes will be displaced westwards. A polar orbit has the advantage of allowing a reconnaissance satellite to make a complete revolution of the Earth every sidereal day.[1]

Secondly there are the general orbits which are employed if one wants to confine an orbit to certain regions of the world. A satellite's movements within fixed limits of latitude are dependent upon the inclination of the orbit to the Equator. Thus, if one wished to watch only the Tropics, one would launch a vehicle with its orbit inclined at 23½° to the Equator; the path over the ground would still be displaced westwards with each revolution but the satellite would always stay within 23½° of either side of the Equator.

Finally there is the geostationary orbit, in which the satellite is placed in a circular orbit at such a height and speed that it revolves with the Earth, thereby remaining stationary with respect to the area immediately below it. Unfortunately pure geostationary orbits are practicable only over the Equator; when a trouble spot is not exactly on 0° latitude, then a satellite has to be placed in an inclined circular orbit whereafter it will traverse a 'figure of eight' pattern around a given ground region.

With perigees of about 100 mls and inclinations of 80° – 90°, Samos satellites in the early Sixties were able to watch the whole of China and virtually all of the USSR. When the space vehicle came within range of one of the seven ground relay stations positioned around the globe to take advantage of the apogees, the processed film would be scanned by a laser beam device, the image translated into an electronic signal, and this would be transmitted to earth and thence to the Samos command centre at Sunnyvale, California.

Despite their sophistication, the early Samos vehicles were restricted in the weight of cameras they could carry and they were therefore classified as 'area surveillance' satellites designed to provide low resolution cover[2] of large areas. As more powerful Thor boosters came into service, so the instrument load in the Agena could be increased, until by 1967 a typical Samos probably contained a longer lensed camera, a larger film supply, an infra-red optical system for night work, and an improved data transmission system. 'Close-look' satellites now started to appear, designed to examine any targets that merited closer inspection. The 'close-look' Samos craft were heavier than their 'area cover' brethren, due largely to the longer focal length and wider aperture of their lenses. They also moved in a lower orbit, with an average

[1] 23 hours 56 minutes.

[2] They could photograph an object 30 in in diameter from 100 mls.

perigee of 80 mls,[1] to improve ground resolution, and they remained airborne for approximately two weeks photographing missile sites, nuclear submarine yards, and the movement of army divisions in its short lifetime. Close-look satellites carried five or six film capsules, and when each was exposed it was ejected for recovery by special HC 130s operating out of Hawaii which 'snatch' the capsule out of the sky by means of trapeze-like snares that loop over the descending parachute.

The Soviet Union entered what it termed the optics race on April 4th, 1962 with the successful launching of Cosmos 4 from Tyuratam. The Cosmos designation covers all types of Soviet satellites, but Dr Charles Sheldon of the Research Division of the US Library of Congress estimated in 1967 that reconnaissance vehicles were "the single largest element in the Soviet programme". Out of the first 234 Cosmos launchings, it was calculated that 100 were for military reconnaissance.

Until the summer of 1968, a Cosmos spy satellite stayed in orbit for up to eight days, employing cameras which their designers claimed could photograph objects 16 in in diameter from an altitude of 100 mls. When its mission was completed, the whole satellite would descend to earth on a parachute in much the same way as a manned vehicle. From Cosmos 228 onwards, Soviet reconnaissance satellites began to stay up longer and consequently the number of launchings was reduced. Today they remain in orbit for about a fortnight, after which their film capsules are ejected and 'snatched' from the sky in the American fashion, the Soviets having tired of wasting valuable intelligence time scouring mountains and dredging lakes for their precious pictures.

During the Sixties the United States made 526 satellite launchings of which 323 were sponsored by the armed forces. Most of these were of the Samos variety, and from the middle of 1963 onwards the US launched an average of one reconnaissance vehicle a month. Several area cover satellites might circle the USSR at any one time, some in polar orbit to encompass the earth, and others in a geostationary orbit over areas of specific interest. Both the USA and the USSR keep reconnaissance satellites on standby on their firing platforms for use in times of acute political tension – American vehicles were prominent over the Arab-Israeli war of 1967, and a Cosmos is always launched whenever the Chinese make belligerent noises around the eastern Soviet borders.

Satellites with cameras have several great advantages over manned PR aircraft. For a start they are less controversial. It is now all but universally recognised that a state's control over its airspace ceases at an altitude where the atmosphere becomes so rarefied that it can no longer provide an acceptable amount of aerodynamic lift, i.e. 50–60 mls above the earth's surface. This is very convenient for the satellite operators because the altitude where lift becomes insignificant is also the start of the zone where frictional resistance to the basically centrifugal motion of a vehicle in orbit becomes of little account.

Secondly, for the foreseeable future reconnaissance satellites are invulner-

[1] Satellites in any lower orbit than this will be greatly affected by atmospheric drag and will therefore 'decay' quickly.

able. There are rumours that the USSR is experimenting with 'orbital intercept tests' but it is unlikely that such a concept will be practicable for many years. Thirdly, satellites are generally much more effective than aircraft. It is true that scientists had to overcome many problems associated with the stabilisation and orientation of spacecraft, the design of light cameras with long lenses, and the transmission of data back to earth, but the age-old PR banes of vibration and predictability of position are much reduced in space. In addition, satellites can cover far more territory than an aircraft, and, of equal importance, they can photograph it all in the same day so that Intelligence staffs can see the overall picture. The lack of U-2 evidence that the Soviets were deploying ICBMs was not conclusive proof that none existed – now, with high resolution cameras, infra-red and multi-spectral equipment for looking through camouflage, and sideways-looking radars for penetrating cloud cover, it is virtually impossible for one side to construct and deploy any revolutionary breed of weapons without being detected by the other, especially as it takes nearly a year to install a Soviet SS-9 ICBM.

To see just how much the US government relies on its watching satellites, it is worth following the sequence of events after the discovery of new Soviet missile silos in 1971:

November 18th – December 11th, 1970 – area surveillance satellite shows that some unfinished SS-9 silos are being dismantled and that holes of a different size are being dug.

January 21st, 1971 – close-look satellite sent to inquire further – film capsule returned on February 9th.

March 4th – Intelligence officers testify before the Senate Armed Services Committee and reveal that a new type of Soviet missile silo has been discovered.

March 24th – April 12th – another area surveillance satellite sent up to search for more sites.

April 23rd – Secretary of Defense Melvin Laird reports that approximately 40 new silos have been discovered at more than six different sites. Three days later Laird discloses that work has been resumed on the construction of an anti-ballistic missile (ABM) system around Moscow.

May 13th – capsule recovered from close-look satellite launched on April 22nd. Five days later, Pentagon reveals that 60 new missile silos have now been found, of which one-third are for SS-9s and the rest for SS-11s. As the inner diameter of the differing silos varied by only four feet, it is a considerable feat of detection.

"I wouldn't want to be quoted on this," said President Lyndon Johnson to a group of reporters in March 1967, "but we've spent 35 to 40 billion dollars on the space programme. And if nothing else had come out of it except the knowledge we've gained from space photography, it would be worth ten times what the programme cost."

At first glance, Samos and Cosmos would appear to have brought peace to an uneasy world by largely eliminating fear of the unknown. As the world becomes an open book, with light being shed into dark corners, it would seem to be a safer and less suspicious place in which to live. But there are still some drawbacks to be overcome. Many nations of the world are still 'closed societies' and they are unlikely to welcome embarrassing disclosures about their activities. Washington is now faced with the problem of what to do with all its satellite information – it is much harder to turn the Nelsonian blind eye to some aspects of international politics when everyone knows that you know what is going on.

Then again, reconnaissance satellites can never reveal the intentions of another country, and consequently they can never eliminate the uncertainties involved in Intelligence 'guesstimations'. Military men will always plan for the worst eventuality, but it is to be hoped that the reconnaissance satellite will act as a restraining influence in the arms race by verifying agreements like the Strategic Arms Limitation Talks.

It is in the tactical environment that the manned PR aircraft scores over the satellite. Time is usually at a premium in scenarios such as Vietnam, as it would be if the divisions of the Warsaw Pact marched on the Rhine, and space vehicles are very demanding of time. Additionally, satellites are far too costly to be used to look for guerilla bands or supply convoys.

Fidel Castro's Cuba was just one area that continued to be reconnoitred by manned aircraft after 1960. At first the island was covered by CIA aircraft, but after reports of a Soviet missile build-up the task was given to the U-2s of the 4028th Strategic Reconnaissance Sqn, and on August 29th, 1962 they discovered that SAM sites were being erected. Surface-to-air missiles were acceptable because they were purely defensive in character, but American Intelligence was worried in case offensive surface-to-surface missiles were also being shipped into the Caribbean. It happened that the prints of August 29th were handed to a PI who had recently returned from a spell at the U-2 base of Incirlik, and he noticed that the SAMs around the town of San Cristobal, 100 mls SW of Havana, were positioned in the same way as those that protected ICBM sites in the Soviet Union. The PI therefore asked for more detailed cover of the area; a pair of U-2s was sent over Cuba on October 14th and their prints, interpreted for President Kennedy by the foremost PI in America, Arthur C. Lundahl, confirmed for the first time that Soviet-built Intermediate-Range Ballistic Missiles (IRBMs) were being erected at San Cristobal.

Further U-2 flights were mounted, supported by RF-101 Voodoos and RF-8A Crusaders which had been hurriedly equipped with special low-level cameras that had been gathering dust for many years. President Kennedy demanded the immediate withdrawal of the missiles and on October 22nd he imposed a naval blockade around the island. For nearly a week the world and the PIs watched and waited, and tension reached a climax on October 27th when Major Rudolf Anderson Jr was shot down by a SAM as he descended below 30,000 feet in his U-2 to try to get below cloud. The following day Premier Krushchev announced that the missile sites were to be dismantled, a development that the aerial cameras were to verify over the next few weeks.

Some American PIs became very expert in the specialisation of 'crateology' as they watched the missiles being packed for shipment back to Europe.

"War over Cuba," wrote John A. McCone, then Director of the CIA, "was avoided because every weapons system was correctly identified in time to give the President and his policy advisors time to think, to make a rational estimate of the situation and to devise means of dealing with it with a maximum chance of success and a minimum risk of global war."[1] Of equal importance was the fact that aerial photography had now become a tool of the politicians as well as of the military. As DeWitt S. Copp put it, "no other proof could have been more irrefutable, and no other proof would have been acceptable to many among ourselves, our allies, and, of course, those unsympathetic to us. The UN could not debate away the iron reality of aerial photographs, nor could the world."[2]

Although the Powers' Incident had marked the transition from high flying aircraft to even higher flying satellites, Cuba reminded everyone that altitude was not the be all and end all of PR. It was the low flying Voodoos of the USAF, not their U-2s, which brought back the indisputable prints to convince US opinion that the nation should risk a Third World War. With Vietnam and the return to conventional warfare just around the corner, the aerial camera was about to go down to tree-top height at the same time as to the frontiers of space.

While it took the USAF some time to appreciate the usefulness of a low level reconnaissance aircraft for ferreting out cleverly concealed Viet Cong positions in a tangled jungle, the RAF, beset by counter-insurgency operations in Palestine and Malaya, had ushered in the era of low-level high speed tactical PR with the Vinten F 95 camera in 1950. Fitted into Hunters and Swift F 5s, this relatively simple instrument had a large aperture lens of up to 12 inches focal length, 70 mm film, a high cycling rate of up to eight frames per second, and a minimum shutter speed of 1/2,000th second. The British espoused the cause of low-level photography sooner than most because of their early withdrawal from the concept of high-level strategic manned-flight. For reasons of economy and because of their faith in the omnipotence of the missile, the RAF cancelled its high-level successor to the V-bombers, the Avro 730, and decided to concentrate after 1957 on aircraft that could penetrate enemy radar defences at very low altitudes. Consequently they also cancelled the replacement for the Meteor PR 10, the unarmed Swift PR 6, and decided to put the whole of their strategic shirt on the TSR 2.

Many PR men were bitterly opposed to accepting an aircraft designed primarily for other roles. Tactical and Strike were acceptable, but they did not want the R for Reconnaissance tacked on to the end. In the end the TSR 2 never arrived, and the RAF finally settled for the McDonnell Phantom. America originally offered the RF 4C variant, their reconnaissance successor to the RF 101C Voodoo. The slimline nose of the RF 4C had been extended to

[1] Stewart Alsop – 'The Center'.

[2] 'Overview'.

accommodate a Hycon KS 72 or KS 87 forward-facing oblique camera and a Fairchild KA-56A low altitude and KA 55A high-level panoramic camera, all of which were placed on special mountings, developed at great cost, to dampen vibrations. This battery of marvellous cameras could operate in all weathers, by day or by night, and from ground level to Mach 2.4 at 48,000 feet. In addition the RF 4C carried infra-red and electronic sensors, sideways and forward looking radars, and the capability to process films in flight and eject them to field commanders on the ground.

However the RAF wanted operational flexibility and so it ordered its own modified Phantom, to be employed either as a tactical fighter bomber or as a reconnaissance aircraft when fitted with a specially developed camera pod underneath. This RAF Phantom FGR 2 is a good example of how modern reconnaissance aircraft can provide a round-the-clock all weather surveillance capability. The Phantom pod can carry either four F 95s and one F 135[1] cameras for daylight work, or four F 135s and electronic equipment for night operations. The fan of five cameras can be operated simultaneously to give horizon-to-horizon cover, and for special tasks an F 126[2] or an oblique F 95 camera may be added. But the other contents of the EMI pod best indicate how far PR has progressed since 1945. As well as sideways looking reconnaissance radar (SLRR), designed for the TSR 2 to detect minutiae such as trains and vehicles at night, the pod also contains a heat-seeking infra-red linescan (IRLS) apparatus. Infra-red photography has been used since before the Second World War and employs a phenomenon first appreciated by William Herschel in the early nineteenth century. Every object responds in an individual way to the electro-magnetic energy spectrum, (that band which covers long radio waves, shorter infra-red rays, the still shorter waves in the visible spectrum, and the very high frequency X-rays and cosmic rays) and infra-red film records the relative temperatures of surface features rather than visible light as in normal photographs. Coloured infra-red prints are known as 'false-colour' photography because natural green shows as red. Newly turned earth covering mines registers as a dark patch on the lighter red of its surroundings because it is cooler than the untouched surface warmed by the sun, while dying foliage or the pigments in green paint also have a different hue, thereby making camouflage detection much easier. In South-east Asia, infra-red photography clearly detected vehicles hidden under dense foliage along the Ho Chi Minh trail by sensing their engine and exhaust heat. IRLS is particularly useful for penetrating haze because of its lack of sensitivity to blue, the predominant colour reflected by haze.

It is worth following a tactical PR sortie flown by a Phantom FGR 2 of 2 Sqn in 1974 to compare modern aerial reconnaissance techniques with those of thirty years ago. 2 Sqn is based in Germany where it is assigned to the Second Allied Tactical Air Forces (2 ATAF), and its primary role is to provide reconnaissance information should Warsaw Pact forces ever advance

[1] A low altitude camera with Automatic Exposure Control (AEC) to provide a 'minimum light seeking' capability to ignore scattered clouds and 'expose for the shadows'.

[2] The latest high altitude camera.

into Western Germany. From past experience, a Warsaw Pact advance would involve leap-frogging by smallish groups of armour hoping to cover 60 miles a day – 2 Sqn is expected to buy time for NATO by discovering which 60 miles have been covered and which 60 miles are likely to be the next. As the USSR clearly demonstrated that it was well trained in deploying forces by night during the 1968 invasion of Czechoslovakia, the EMI pod is particularly vital to detect such manoeuvrings through darkness and in all weathers.

Once the targets have been allocated, the Phantom crew of two can start planning their sortie. After fixing his desired track, turning points, and two-minute time marks on a map, the navigator plots his target to within a 100 metre square and then looks around for a suitable Initial Point (IP), usually between 60 and 90 seconds flying time from the target, from which the run-in will be started.

Down at 250 feet, hopefully below the height at which an enemy might be able to hit it with an SA-3 Goa missile, the Phantom hurtles along at 420 kts at the start of a training sortie due west of Koblenz. The radar altimeter and inertial navigation system keep the pilot at height and on course as he sweeps across the Mosel and Rhine towards the Tacan beacon north of Wiesbaden. He then turns north-east across the Taunus before descending into the Lahn valley and towards the first IP at Lollar railway station just north of Giessen. At the start of the 74 second run-in, the navigator selects two oblique cameras on the camera panel just behind the pilot's right ear so that the films are turning as the target passes by seconds later. Simultaneously the crew scan the railway line visually for any interesting information and then they are off towards the River Weser and the Eder dam.

Turning north just before Herford, the Phantom clears a range of hills and immediately the pilot identifies the canal bridge ahead which is the next IP. He pulls 3g to position the aircraft over the bridge, the details of which are noted visually, and the oblique cameras go on again in time to photograph a radar site 90 seconds later. Fifty minutes after the mission started, the Phantom turns back for its base at Laarbruch.

After landing the reconnaissance pod is 'downloaded' from the Phantom, or the magazines simply removed, and the films from the cameras, SLR, and IRLS are sent for processing in the Moveable Air Reconnaissance Exploitation Laboratories. MAREL is a labyrinth of 12 transportable interconnecting processing and interpretation buildings which the inhabitants of the wartime MFPSs would hardly recognise. The films are taken to the first building in the MAREL complex where their priority is assessed and the subsequent work flow controlled. Then they pass to the processing cabins before moving on for 'intelligence exploitation' by the PIs. Each interpretation workpoint has a film viewing table backed up by computer calculators for photogrammetrical mathematical analysis. PIs can feed all seven films out of the pod across their viewing tables at the same time if they wish by means of motorised spools. In this way they can quickly select which frames they want to examine first, and these negatives are then passed for printing and enlarging before being returned for detailed interpretation.

Reconnaissance pods fitted to multi-role aircraft are here to stay in the RAF. They are being added to the Harrier in the field and the Jaguar will carry them when it takes over the reconnaissance role of the Phantom FGR 2. Pods are a great boon to air forces trying to fill a variety of roles with a limited number of aircraft types, especially now that miniaturisation has made it possible to fit IRLS and cameras into a pod only 8 feet in length. The latest Vinten Vicon pod can carry a panoramic fan of five cameras, and it can be fitted or removed from its fuselage or underwing mountings in approximately four minutes.

However the pod-carrying aircraft has one great disadvantage, apart from the fact that external appendages increase the drag factor and pose problems of vibration and camera heating, over aircraft such as the Phantom RF 4C, Mirage IIIRD, and Viggen SF 37 that carry their cameras internally. Given that an air force has only a limited number of aircraft for strike and reconnaissance duties, when will they carry bombs and when will they be fitted with pods? Supposing that both roles are of equal importance, will the troops on the ground have to forgo their aerial support or their aerial reconnaissance? And, in this age of increasing specialisation, can a crew be trained to maximum proficiency in both strike and reconnaissance duties, bearing in mind that the Second World War taught us that both were very separate and specialised arts? The quest for solutions to problems like these was not helped by the disbandment of the main reconnaissance authority, CRE, in October 1970. Reconnaissance in the RAF has been decentralised again, and it is now left to the various Groups to decide on the control and employment of their PR components. Increasingly they are discovering that it would be totally unrealistic in a rapidly changing European war situation to expect squadrons with multi-role aircraft to take off pods, fit on bombs and rockets, take them off again to fit pods, and so on. We are now finding that certain units, like No 2 Phantom Sqn, despite their theoretical multi-role capability, are now specialised PR squadrons in all but name.

On June 15th, 1971, a Titan IIID with its two strap-on boosters lifted off the first of a new breed of American reconnaissance satellites known as Big Bird. This modified Agena measured 50 feet long by 10 feet in diameter, and its all-up-weight of 25,000 lbs was sufficient to carry the instruments necessary for both area surveillance and close-look duties. Big Bird is believed to carry a Perkins-Elmer camera of at least 8 feet focal length, capable of a ground resolution approaching the atmospheric limit of 6 in from 100 miles, as well as infra-red cameras, sideways looking radar capable of 'seeing' through three layers of foliage, and an unfurlable antenna 20 feet in diameter for relaying information back to earth. Big Bird can cover every part of the globe in twelve hours, and with its half dozen film capsules and the ability to raise its orbit to stave off decay it can remain aloft for up to two months. Owing to its traditional superiority in booster technology, the USSR can shortly be expected to launch its own variant of Big Bird. Big Bird, rather than Big Brother, now watches over us all.

The future of observation satellites is as endless as science fiction. A new generation of US space-watching vehicles, code-numbered 1010, is now under development, and it is expected to enter service in 1976. Type 1010 will almost certainly incorporate a zoom-type telephoto lens to provide simultaneous television pictures to ships or ground stations below. Space television for military purposes has been a long time in coming because of its inferior definition, but once it arrives it will greatly increase the 'real-time' reconnaissance potential of the system and will allow ground observers to zoom in to anything that takes their interest.

After 1010 may well come manned observation satellites. The USAF manned Orbiting Laboratory (MOL) was to have had a major reconnaissance capability before it was cancelled, but watchers from space will surely come if only to save time by having a human brain on the spot. Part of MOL's work may well be taken up by NASA's Skylab which was first launched in May 1973.

At the next level below the orbiting reconnaissance umbrella comes the successor to the U-2, the Lockheed SR-71. The CIA contracted for this aircraft in 1958, under the guise of the A-11 prototype long-range fighter, but when it was finally unveiled to the public as the SR-71 in 1964 it was described by President Johnson as, "a long-range advanced strategic reconnaissance plane, capable of worldwide reconnaissance for military operations." Built almost entirely of titanium to withstand the heat of '*cruising*' at Mach 3.5[1] the SR-71 is slightly over 107 feet long and 55 feet wide with two Pratt and Witney J-58 engines mounted away from the pencil-shaped fuselage on double delta wings. Pre-flight briefing and preparation for the pilot and a Reconnaissance Systems Officer (RSO) begins on the day before take-off and includes a full medical check; then, clad in their 'silver tuxedo' pressure suits, the crew strap in for a round trip involving nearly 3,000 miles at 80,000 feet during which they will photograph 60,000 sq mls of territory every hour.

The SR-71 are a dying breed nevertheless. They have a poor accident record, for when things go wrong at Mach 3.5 then one really is in trouble, and at least four were lost before 1968. Those that still remain are with the 9th Strategic Reconnaissance Wing at Beale AFB in the Sacramento Valley of California, from whence they continue to photograph Communist China from 100,000 feet. As rapprochement is in the air between Washington and Peking, and as China develops as a major military power, such flights are unlikely to be feasible for long. SR-71s and U-2s will probably continue to be used over international hot-spots like the Middle East until the end of the decade.

If the U-2 is coming to the end of its useful life, what of the strategic PR aircraft of the RAF? The Victor B2 SRs of 543 Sqn are now to be modified to the tanker role, leaving two squadrons of Canberra PR 9s – 39 Sqn at Wyton and 13 Sqn in Malta – to carry the long-range PR burden. 13 Sqn is particularly

[1] Mach 3 is 3,100 feet per second compared with the 3,000 feet per second velocity of a .30–06 rifle bullet.

important to the defence of southern Europe, but the PR Canberra cannot soldier on forever. Will the RAF be capable of anything other than short-range tactical PR after 1980? Before answering this, one must first determine whether the RAF needs to stay in the strategic PR business at all. Many would argue not. Over the years the British have put their money into the provision of very sophisticated photo-interpretation equipment and facilities, centred around JARIC at Brampton, because it was felt to be wasteful to try to duplicate much of the strategic PR effort being put in by the USAF. After all it is very unlikely that Britain will ever enter another major war outside NATO, and as the USA is part of NATO they could be relied upon to provide most of the necessary strategic pictures. However, events over recent years have tended to cast doubts on the wisdom of this division of responsibilities. Although Britain has declined as a major world power, it still maintains an independent nuclear capability and a wish to have an effective voice in the councils of the world, yet neither of these aims can remain credible if the British Government is dependent for its facts on whatever intelligence data Washington chooses to disseminate. A strategic PR capability is not just an expensive luxury for use in times of war – it is a tool of modern diplomacy and a vital necessity if the British Government wishes to retain an informed and effective say in international affairs.

Then there is the emergence of the European Economic Community as a third power bloc in the world. If Western Europe is ever to speak with one independent voice, it must be seen to be uninfluenced by either Washington or Moscow, and it should therefore have a strategic reconnaissance organisation of its own. The impetus for this may well come as the USA draws away from overseas military commitments, leaving a resurgent Europe to shoulder more of its own defence. Both France and Britain have the expertise to develop a European space reconnaissance system, and the French Defence Minister, M. Michel Debré, announced in 1972 that France would have a requirement for a military reconnaissance satellite in twelve years time to coincide with the modernisation of her strategic forces. Such a vehicle is likely to be boosted by the LS 433 rocket now under development by Aérospatiale and Thomson – CSF.

What of the tactical skies underneath once the Phantom, Jaguar, and Harrier have gone out of RAF service? The British have already developed a tactical PR rocket, the BAC Skylark, which carries an F 24 survey camera, two Hasselblad 500 70mm cameras (one with infra-red and the other with colour film), and a telephoto Hasselblad for detailed cover. They are switched on 163 secs after launch at a height of 124 miles, and they operate automatically every 2.5 secs after that up to the apogee of 150 miles. Tests have shown that the Skylark can be operated far more cheaply than a satellite, and it can photograph an area approximately equal to the United Kingdom in one flight. At present Skylark is only being used to survey the earth's resources, but it could easily be employed in a military role in time of war.

In an age when Western governments are spending a decreasing proportion of their Gross National Product on defence, and when aircraft are becoming far more costly and complicated, the RAF is likely to turn increasingly to Remotely Piloted Vehicles (RPVs) to meet its needs. The Germans first developed a remote controlled camera aircraft at Rechlin in 1939, but as usual it was left to the Americans to put the idea into service. In 1960 the Ryan Aeronautical Company, later taken over by Teledyne Inc, proposed that the USAF buy a reconnaissance version of its BQM-34A target drone. The Powers' Incident and the resultant Eisenhower decree that no more manned flights be made over the USSR stimulated support for a remote controlled aircraft, but in the autumn of 1960 all funding for reconnaissance drones was transferred to the development of the Lockheed SR-71. It took the death of Major Anderson over Cuba in 1962 to resurrect the RPV drone project, and, under the auspices of the Big Safari multi-million dollar intelligence gathering programme, Ryan produced the Model 147 Firebee reconnaissance drone in less than ninety days. Over a thousand of these jet-propelled PR drones were produced, to be launched from and directed by specially modified DC-130 transports, and so many were used over Vietnam that the area became known as the 'Tonkin Gulf Test Range'.

The low altitude version of the 147 Firebee has a speed of between 420 and 560 kts and a range of 650 nautical miles. On a typical mission the vehicle makes low level runs at 1,500 feet to operate its Fairchild F415Y 3 in lensed camera before climbing up to height and then diving down for another run. The camera can make a total of 2,000 exposures before the Firebee finally climbs up above 50,000 feet and glides home when its fuel is exhausted. A television camera and data link transmitter can also be carried together with the Fairchild camera, and video information can be transmitted to a receiving station up to 150 miles away. The vehicle's speed and manoeuvres are controlled by a pre-set programmer or by the remote operator from the TV display.

After several years of successful penetrations of Chinese airspace by photographic RPVs, the USAF commissioned Ryan to build a smaller number of high altitude, highly surviveable reconnaissance drones to be known as Model 154 Fireflies. The Firefly bears a passing resemblance to the U-2, but despite its wingspan of 49 feet it is designed to provide a minimal radar return to ground stations. The intake and exhaust of its General Electric J 97 turbo-jet are mounted on top of the fuselage to mask them from hostile heat-seeking devices, and the smooth curves of the Firefly prevent corner reflections for the benefit of tracking devices below. In fact it has been calculated that a ground radar scanner would have to be in the unlikely position of watching the skies directly above it to detect the Firefly 154.

The 154 drone carries an Itek KA-80A 24 in panoramic camera, and when fully loaded with 6,500 feet of film it can take 1,500 exposures, each measuring 45 in long by 4.5 in wide. The Firefly is believed to carry its own inertial navigation and Doppler sensor system, the accuracy of which is sufficient to guide the vehicle back after a lengthy mission to within 200 miles of the controlling aircraft, from whence it will be directed to a recovery zone for a parachute landing.

The USAF hopes soon to have a high altitude reconnaissance RPV in service capable of remaining airborne for up to 24 hours, and there is no reason why the RAF should not look to vehicles such as this for its strategic salvation. BAC already build the supersonic Firebee II target drone under licence from Teledyne Ryan, and this vehicle can more than hold its own in mock combat with an F-4 Phantom by virtue of its manoeuvrability. Britain is also cooperating with Canada in the development of the AN/USD 501 PR drone, an RPV powered by a Williams single stage turbo-jet which will operate over the battlefield at heights between 1,000 and 4,000 feet. In addition, Shorts of Belfast have brought out their own 'Skyspy', a flying saucer 3 feet in diameter which can hover invisibly over a battlefield for three hours at 10,000 feet while sending back television pictures of the ground beneath.

What of the future? The visual camera will continue to be the primary instrument of PR because of its greatly superior definition, and the only restrictions on its employment will be those imposed by the limitations of the airframe that carries it. We can expect to see bigger and better satellites and more unmanned PR vehicles in the coming years, but the main developments in aerial photography will probably centre around extending all-weather round-the-clock capabilities and the extraction of more information from films in less time than before.

Sensor development will concentrate on the further exploitation of the various portions of the electro-magnetic energy spectrum. Laser linescan is one possibility. This system beams a continuous gas laser to the ground by a scanning mirror which receives back the reflected signal to be converted into an electronic impulse by a photo-electric mechanism. This signal modulates a light beam which then 'paints' a continuous strip image on to a moving film. Low light television is another promising field and Marconi have already obtained good results in 'bright starlight' conditions using an ultra-sensitive Image Isocon tube. Thermovision (coloured television) could be used to enhance poor quality infra-red linescan imagery to give a complete activity picture, while multi-spectral and spatial discrimination image enhancement will make camouflage disappear leaving other details in relief. We may even see the practical exploitation of Wave Front photography before the end of the century, thereby producing prints which show a three-dimensional picture of the ground over which the sensor platform is flying.

In the tactical situation it will be increasingly important to get information from the air to the commander on the ground as quickly as possible. All linescan and radar systems lend themselves to in-flight transmission because their image information is largely in electronic form, but it should not be too difficult to process an optical film in flight and then convert it into an electronic signal for immediate transmission to a surface station.

Down on earth, PIs will work increasingly from transparencies instead of prints because the former can accommodate a contrast range ten times that of a paper print. Machines will become the hand-maidens of every self-respecting PI Section as the amount of information coming in becomes too great and too complicated for humans to handle unassisted – image-enhancement and automatic data reading equipment will be necessary, as will computers to store masses of Third Phase data and to make legible the output of aerial sensors that reduce imagery to a pattern of laser light colours.

It is now just over a century since man first exposed a photograph from an aerial platform, and yet we are rapidly approaching the time when men may be excluded from the air altogether. Soon aircrew officers will sit on the ground remotely controlling their various PR platforms while intelligence officers wait for their computers to read out every piece of garnered information right down to the car registration numbers in the Kremlin car park. In response to promptings the computers will also be able to provide comparative photo cover, up-dated defence overlays, and new order of battle displays for transmission over a world-wide data network.

Nevertheless, no matter how sophisticated and all-embracing PR becomes, the lessons of the Second World War still hold good despite the advent of satellites and electronic sensory devices, for reconnaissance systems are only as good as the men who employ them. The camera cannot lie but neither can it tell the whole truth, and men will always be needed to determine target priorities, allocate resources, and separate the crucial intelligence wheat from a mass of irrelevant or not so important chaff. As Dr Kissinger said after the 1973 Arab-Israeli war, "Facts are easier to come by than intentions.'

In addition, the old canon that knowledge comes before power will have an increasing rather than decreasing relevance as future world wars promise to be of very limited duration. At a time when NATO forces in Western Europe are outnumbered 3:1 by the Warsaw Pact, every weapon in any future conflict must count; as a consequence, the RAF must be in possession of a vast amount of up to date intelligence *before* any strike aircraft leave the ground so that their power is not dissipated against inconsequential targets. The strong arm is of little use without the keen eye – it is a maxim that several generations of PR pilots have striven to teach us and it is one that future military strategists will neglect at their peril.

Index

Index